A RELIGIOUS HISTORY OF THE AMERICAN PEOPLE
has received widespread reviews and critical acclaim seldom accorded any book in this century. Here are just a few samples:

"No previous religious history of America has achieved [such] fine balance of scope and proportion. . . . It is so massive, thorough and comprehensive that it is a fitting conclusion to an honorable tradition. Historians, present and future, will have to come to grips with it, but from its perspective it will be difficult to improve upon."

—*Church History*

". . . this monumental history of American religion [is] a labor of love which was ten years in the making and will undoubtedly have the field to itself for the indefinite future. There is really nothing like it on the market. It's a model of historical scholarship and also makes for delightful reading. Enthusiastically recommended."—*Commonweal*

"The work is massive in scope. . . . The fact that [it] took a full decade to write is no surprise. It is a monumental feat of scholarship which places religious history in the larger framework of world history."

—John Barkham, Saturday Review Syndicate

"Sydney E. Ahlstrom's huge but readable *A Religious History of the American People* has already become a standard."

—*Time*

"[Ahlstrom's work] is the fruition or fulfillment of the accepted religious history, the longest, most detailed, most polished of the works in its tradition."—*The New York Times*

". . . a first, full-scale, comprehensive history of religion in American society. The craftmanship of his research, teaching and writing skill stand forth on a distinctive plateau. Ahlstrom has succeeded to an eminent degree in giving a panoramic view of the full religious dimension in American life. . . . This volume is a must for any basic library on American life. It has not been attempted before and will remain not only a 'first' but unique in its creative and stimulating approach to a fascinating subject."—*Religious Education*

"It will instruct every scholar in American studies, for, however much you may know about some part of the histories of religion in America, no one is apt to have done what Ahlstrom has done, which is to learn about virtually every aspect of American religious history. . . . It would be difficult to write a better book. Ahlstrom's style is controlled and lucid, often graceful and never sloppy. . . . In all, this book is more of an encompassing experience than merely an account of various facts."—*American Jewish Historical Quarterly*

". . . a truly first-rate work of history. . . . Ahlstrom has worked a great wonder in producing a history of religion in America which is not only comprehensive enough and sufficiently non-academic in tone to be accessible to the general reader, but also so adept in its use of sources and so scrupulously objective in its treatment of the personalities and events as to quash the most scholarly cavil . . . one of the most distinguished [works] of its kind to appear for several decades."—*Virginia Kirkus Service*

". . . a historical synthesis that should stand for some years to come as the finest achievement of the historical mind both to comprehend and to communicate in a telling way the story of American religion. . . . The author has integrated [a compendium of materials] within the matrices of his informed, often brilliant insights . . . an intellectual delight that one does not so much read as savor. This reviewer recommends the book unreservedly."—*America*

"In scope, sources of information, clarity and achievement of purpose, and judiciousness of judgment, this book sets standards those in the future must use as their criteria for model scholarship."—*Christianity Today*

SYDNEY E. AHLSTROM

A
RELIGIOUS
HISTORY
OF THE
AMERICAN
PEOPLE

VOLUME 2

IMAGE BOOKS

A DIVISION OF DOUBLEDAY & COMPANY, INC.

GARDEN CITY, NEW YORK

1975

Image Books edition 1975 by special arrangement
with Yale University Press
Image Books edition published November 1975

ISBN: 0-385-11165-7
Library of Congress Catalog Card Number 75–22362
Preface Copyright © 1975 by Sydney E. Ahlstrom
Text Copyright © 1972 by Yale University
All Rights Reserved
Printed in the United States of America

9 8 7 6 5 4 3 2

FOR
MY MOTHER

CONTENTS

VOLUME 2

CHAPTERS TO BE FOUND IN VOLUME 1

ILLUSTRATIONS

by Michael Graham

Page 75: The old African Methodist Episcopal Zion Church in Tuskegee, Alabama, in which Booker T. Washington convened the first classes of the Tuskegee Normal and Industrial Institute on 4 July 1881.

Page 187: Trinity Church (Episcopal), Boston, Massachusetts, designed in 1872 by Henry Hobson Richardson and completed in 1877, though significant alterations and additions were made in later years.

Page 355: The Greek Orthodox Church of the Annunciation, Milwaukee, Wisconsin, designed by Frank Lloyd Wright and consecrated in 1961.

Page 463: Composition, after a photograph by Edward Weston, *North Wall*, Point Lobos, 1946.

THE ROMANTIC MOOD

"I have at the distance of half a mile, through a green lane, a forest," wrote Thomas Gray to his friend Horace Walpole in 1736, about six years before he began his famous "Elegy Written in a Country Church-yard." "The vulgar call it a common," he went on, but it is

> all my own, at least, as good as so, for I spy no human thing in it but myself. It is a little chaos of mountains and precipices; mountains, it is true, that do not ascend much above the clouds, nor are the declivities quite so amazing as Dover Cliff; but just such hills as people who love their necks as well as I do may venture to climb, and crags that give the eye as much pleasure as if they were more dangerous. Both vale and hill are covered with most venerable beeches, and other very reverend vegetables, that, like most other ancient people, are always dreaming out their old stories to the winds. At the foot of one of these squats ME (*il penseroso*), and there I grow to the trunk for a whole morning. The timorous hare and sportive squirrel gambol around me like Adam in Paradise before he had an Eve, but I think he did not use to read Virgil, as I commonly do.

More than a century and a half later Edmund Gosse would refer to this celebrated passage as "the first expression . . . of the modern feeling of the picturesque."[1] Given Gray's still

---

[1] Edmund W. Gosse, *Gray,* English Men of Letters series (London, 1892), p. 16. We have already seen Jonathan Edwards's "new sense of glory" in this context, however (see chap. 19, n. 3).

obvious classical enthusiasms, one can hardly call it a bold announcement of a new spiritual epoch; yet it does mark an unmistakable shift of spiritual temper. More forcefully than Gray, moreover, other English writers would give substance to the change. James Thomson's *Seasons,* Edward Young's *Night Thoughts,* and Richardson's novels seem almost to have made a heavier impact on the Continent than at home. And behind all of these loomed the titanic achievements of Shakespeare and Milton, whose reputations rose to new heights among the early romantics.

Of the several great alternations of mind and feeling which have convulsed Christendom since the age of the Reformation, none had larger consequences than the many-sided movement which, despite denials and confusion, is persistently named "romanticism." The concept has never been satisfactorily clarified, yet it points reliably and steadily to a broad phenomenon in Western culture, a pervasive mood which manifested itself in almost every realm of activity—literary, philosophical, political, artistic, and religious. And American religious history was involved in this variegated impulse at many points and in very divergent ways. The crisis, in fact, was especially severe for Americans because the most disturbing elements of the new sensibility were seldom indigenous; and they created very painful conflicts for peoples and churches with heavy commitments to Puritanism and the Enlightenment. The young nation was not only confronted by a whole galaxy of bold ideas and revolutionary attitudes, but at the same time it had to adjust itself to receiving influence from new quarters, for after 1815 the intellectual life of the European continent, especially of Germany, began to play an entirely new role in the United States. Scottish and English thinkers continued to perform an immense mediatorial function—Walter Scott, Thomas Carlyle, Samuel Taylor Coleridge, William Wordsworth, and Lord Byron were very widely read; but a major fact of modern intellectual history should be remembered: the nineteenth century was separated from the eighteenth not only by the age of Napoleon, but by the Rhine.

Yet "separated" is too strong a word. The Enlightenment had been an international movement, not simply French, however important France may have been in expressing the movement's genius. So with romanticism. Despite the primacy of Germany, its enthusiasms flowed back and forth across national frontiers with surprising ease.

In dealing with the history of romanticism it is probably more valuable to locate the period by the leading proponents of the new post-Enlightenment frame of mind than to add another definition to the world's overflowing store of abstractions. If this course is taken, there is only one person with whom the narrative can begin, and he is also the one whose works provided the most direct inspiration to those who continued the movement. By living and writing in the midst of the Enlightenment's flowering time, he also illustrates the perils of periodization and shows how the polarities and debates of one age fructify the future. In Jean-Jacques Rousseau, in fact, one finds the first major romantic, one might even say the movement's founder, among the *Encyclopédistes* and *philosophes* of the *ancien régime*.

ROMANTIC PRECURSORS

Jean-Jacques Rousseau (1712–78)

What was for Thomas Gray a moment of exhilaration through which the older voices of Milton and Virgil continued to speak became for Rousseau the passionate concern of an agonized lifetime. He is uniquely the source, the self-supplying fountainhead, of a new spiritual tendency in Western thought. A wandering son of Geneva, Rousseau was a music copyist by trade and a discerning writer on music. He is now most often remembered for the social and political theories announced in *The Social Contract* and related treatises, but the writings which contributed most to his fame while he lived and which did most to promote a major shift in later attitudes were those which criticized the artificialities of civilization and dealt with man's relation to nature, with human selfhood, and with the essence of true religion: *La Nouvelle Héloïse* (1761), *Émile* (1762), and his posthumously published *Confessions* and *Rêveries*. What Rousseau protests—through his own sin and spitefulness—is the goodness of man; through the buffeting of history that foils his every purpose he posits the freedom of man, and through the miseries of perpetual homelessness, the peace that comes from communion with Nature and with God. Out of some secret center of himself he came like a missionary to the eighteenth century, denouncing its spurious values and calling it to a larger vision of human possibilities. Yet he also wrote confessions that exposed his finitude and failure.

It was in *Émile*, however, ostensibly a tract on education, that he overturned traditional views of "natural theology" even before they had reached their ultimate rationalistic development in the work of men like William Paley. The "Confession of Faith of the Savoyard Vicar" is not another moralistic homily on natural law or an injunction to duty in the Stoic mode, but a fervent call, a sermon on a text from Rousseau which Friedrich Schiller took as his motto, *"Si c'est la raison qui fait l'homme, c'est le sentiment que le conduit"* (If it is by reason that man is made, it is his feelings that guide him).

Immanuel Kant (1724–1804)

Immanuel Kant, a professor of mathematics and natural philosophy in the University of Königsberg (East Prussia), was among the many who gained a new sense of man's active powers from a reading of *Émile*, and this discovery would begin to play a major role in the history of modern philosophy in 1772 when Kant was "awakened," as he said, from his "dogmatic slumbers" by David Hume's incisive assertion that the principle of causality was neither self-evident nor demonstrable, and by his consequent denial that experience by itself can ever validate or certify any inductive inference. Kant, of course, had never believed that induction could provide sure knowledge. He regarded empiricism as a form of skepticism, and to this degree he qualified his relation to the Enlightenment, especially as it unfolded itself in France. Kant was a rationalist; his "slumbers" were those of a man who trusts in the truly legislative and creative power of pure reason, believing that reason could discover truth out of its own resources. Now fully awake, he set out to determine for himself the nature and limits of human knowledge.

Kant accomplished his task in 1781, the year Cornwallis was defeated at Yorktown, with the publication of his famous *Critique of Pure Reason.* As he himself said, this was a "Copernican Revolution" in the realm of philosophy. It reversed the accepted order of human thought, not by making new calculations, observations, and objective discoveries, but by a thorough examination of man's way of dealing with the data. Words so famous should be quoted.

> Hitherto it has been assumed that all of our knowledge must conform to objects. But all attempts to extend our knowledge of objects by establishing something in regard to them *a priori,* by means of concepts, have, on this assumption, ended in failure. We must therefore make trial whether we may not have more success in the task of metaphysics, if we suppose that objects must conform to our knowledge. . . . If intuition must conform to the constitution of the objects, I do not see how we could know anything of the latter *a priori;* but if the object (as object of the senses) must conform to the constitution of our faculty of intuition, I have no difficulty in conceiving such a possibility.[2]

Kant's *Critique,* of course, created a ferment among thinkers, and he extended his influence in successive volumes on ethics, law, value theory, and religion. But underlying the entire Kantian argument are two central doctrines which continue as active elements of subsequent European (and American) religious thought. The first is the revolutionary idea summarized in the quotation above. Kant drew a distinction between the *phenomenal* and the *noumenal,* between the reality which man experiences and the thing-in-itself. He then went on to demonstrate that man's knowledge, strictly speaking, is limited to the phenomenal world, and that the form or structure of such knowledge is conditioned by the nature of mind and the laws of thought. In this sense man does have a priori knowledge of reality, of *phenomena* though not of *noumena.* Kant's philosophy, therefore, enfranchises the mind, conceives of it as creative and active, as having a truly constitutive role in man's cognition of the world. Repudiating the notion of the mind as a mirror, a *tabula rasa,* or a receiver mechanism—a notion which flowed so ineluctably from Lockean premises and which had been so convincingly developed by Condillac in France—he substituted a notion of mind as a lamp which brings something *to* reality.

Yet Kant's franchise to reason was by no means the unlim-

---

[2] Immanuel Kant, *Critique of Pure Reason,* ed. and trans. Norman K. Smith (London: Macmillan & Co., 1933), p. 22. Passage quoted is from the preface to the 2d ed., 1787.

ited one which Leibnitz had provided (Hume had spoiled that possibility for him). He denied that man's knowledge can extend beyond experience: it cannot penetrate to the noumenal mysteries of God, eternity, and freedom, and it cannot prove or disprove propositions about this realm. Kant agrees with Hume that "natural theology" in its standard forms was a useless enterprise, a position that explains Kant's often quoted remark that he had to destroy reason to make room for faith. In his *Critique of Practical Reason* (1788), Kant developed another line of thought that compensated for what he withdrew and opened up an equally fertile area for further philosophical discussion. Here he insisted that man's moral nature and will testify to the existence of a divine reality, moral law, and human freedom. Wilhelm Windelband is surely not exaggerating when he asserts that "the compelling power which Kant's philosophy gained over the minds and hearts of men was due chiefly to the earnestness and greatness of its ethical conception of the world."[3] By the time of Kant's death, however, a group of young thinkers—most notably Fichte, Schelling, and Hegel—were building a new tradition of philosophical idealism. They not only drew on other "romantic" sources of inspiration, but also entertained more ambitious aims for philosophy than Kant's critiques had intended.

SOME EARLY ROMANTIC THEMES

One of the most exciting aspects of this new impulse was its appropriation of Spinoza's pantheistic conceptions. Several men contributed to this revival but most influential perhaps was Johann Gottfried Herder (1744–1803), who sought both to ward off the charge of atheism and to imbue Spinoza's "mechanistic" monism with the dynamic sense of organic process. These bold notions were gradually infused with the emphasis on consciousness which Kant had licensed. Yet Kant's mysterious "thing-in-itself" receded, and reality was increasingly construed in dynamic idealistic terms as an interrelated organic whole. Subjectivity and objectivity were seen as interpenetrated aspects of the whole. With *becoming* the prime category under which nature, reality, reason, and

[3] Wilhelm Windelband, *A History of Philosophy*, trans. James H. Tufts (New York: Macmillan Co., 1926), p. 573.

history were understood, causal explanations tended to yield to teleological considerations.

Yet this recovery and transformation of Spinoza is only one aspect of the romantic flowering. Other streams of thought, scholarship, poetry, and art were also stimulated by a sense of surfeit with the static certainties and artificialties of rococo civilization. The dissatisfaction with formality and decorum which had also been characteristic of the pietistic revolt from the Age of Reason welled up anew, both with and without evangelical motivation. Poets, dramatists, and composers cast aside ancient rules and regulations, while critics applauded their new boldness in self-expression. A new vaunting of the subjective self—the feelings, the intuition, and the passions—was evident. Even "immorality" and freedom from convention became a badge of the new ideas. The ego asserted itself and the demonic was championed. Pascal's old dictum that the heart has its reasons which the mind can never know became a slogan. Nature in its wildness and unrestraint was a wellspring of inspiration. Where the Age of Reason had gloried in its geometrically patterned gardens, the new era reveled in the natural grandeur of mountains and forests. And pervading this entire impulse was an emphasis on spirit that accorded wonderfully with the new idealistic and antimechanistic trend of philosophy. It was a concept that could be blended with traditional Christian thinking about the Holy Spirit but it was also connected with all the animating forces of man and nature. Because Europeans generally were responding to similar circumstances, the good tidings were proclaimed almost simultaneously in several countries. English readers heard the new message on nature, man, and God primarily in the works of Wordsworth, Coleridge, and—somewhat later—Emerson.

A New Emphasis on History

The discovery and enthronement of history was another major accomplishment of the age. The Enlightenment, of course, produced great historical writing. In Britain alone the classics of Gibbon, Robertson, and Hume attest to that. And Ernst Cassirer devotes an exciting chapter of his great study of the Enlightenment to its "conquest of the historical world." But the overall conception of history also underwent something of a romantic transformation that owed much to both Herder and Kant. The idealist philosophers tended to conceive nature itself in historical evolutionary terms. In the most obvious sense, this brought with it a marvelous stimulus to the historical imagination as well as the rebirth of historical scholarship. And for more than a century, this stimulus had a prodigious effect on nearly every academic discipline. Most controversial of all, a new age of biblical study was inaugurated with Herder's *Spirit of Hebrew Poetry* (2 vols., 1782–83). Knowledge and belief were "historicized." In the system to which Georg Wilhelm Friedrich Hegel dedicated his life (1770–1831), theology, philosophy, and logic itself were turned to the task of elaborating a dialectical view of all reality, natural, human, and divine. For this reason Hegel can be regarded as the philosopher *par excellence* of the romantic spirit.

Historicism had immense moral, legal, religious, and aesthetic implications. Not only could nations and institutions be "historicized" but also every presumed certainty, every belief and assumption, every law, every standard of judgment, every source of authority, and every sacred text. Each had its history. It might even be contended that all such things were historical without remainder. History could disrupt, destroy, and dismay. Yet its vision of the future could inspire and ennoble.

The new interest in history also aroused an intense interest in the past, nourishing the primal romantic instinct that "distance lends enchantment to the view." The remote, the bizarre, and the ancient acquired a new fascination even as historical research provided increasing gratification to the aroused curiosity. The ages which the Enlightenment had found so "dark" were now seen to be filled with grandeur, heroism, and beauty. For the eighteenth century, "Gothic" had been almost synonymous with barbarity, and the medieval stained glass of old cathedrals had sometimes been replaced to admit the clear light of day. The nineteenth century turned with enthusiasm to a Romanesque and Gothic revival, followed by a Greek and even an Egyptian revival. The new scholarship combined with pantheistic enthusiasm to discover profound expressions of truth in the religions of the pagan East—especially those of India. And when this created acute religious problems, it became the task of an historical approach to religion and theology to solve them. History, in short, became queen of the *Geisteswissenschaften* (sciences of the spirit); and because of its emphasis on the social context of human events, history stimulated the kind of studies which we now call sociology. Further, the belief that all reality is in a state of becoming set the stage for an evolutionary way of regarding all nature.

Here then in brief and unsystematic compass is the revolution of romantic idealism as it flowered first and most riotously in Germany, in part perhaps as a nationalistic reaction against an Age of Reason over which France had proudly presided. Magnificently summing up its meaning were the overpowering personality and works of Johann Wolfgang von Goethe (1749–1832). The gargantuan scope of his genius made him a virtual *homo universalis,* perhaps the last such: a revolutionary theorist in evolutionary biology, personification of historicism, novelist, dramatist and poet of classic stature, and philosophical thinker whose personal development through successive stages almost defines the periodization of German intellectual history during his lifetime. Born in Frankfurt, educated at Leipzig and Strasbourg, Goethe became famous in 1774 with the publication of *The Sorrows of Young Werther,* an epistolary novel of romantic despair which took Europe by storm. A year later he was invited to the court of Saxe-Weimar where, in various capacities, he spent the rest of his life. His final work, *Faust, Part Two,* made it clear that Weimar had become a shrine of deep religious significance: a dynamic and mystical pantheism, owing much to the thought of Spinoza, Herder, and Schelling, found its prophet in Goethe. What Rousseau's Savoyard vicar had suggested gains full expression in a view which understands Nature as instinct with the divine. Reason strives upward through its material forms to the organism in which it achieves consciousness. Man's spiritual life becomes a culminating reality.

A New Theology

For Christian thought, the comprehensive genius of the epoch and the "father of modern theology" was Friedrich Schleiermacher (1768–1834). When he suddenly achieved notice in 1799 with the anonymous publication of *Speeches on Religion to Its Cultured Despisers,* Schleiermacher was a little-known chaplain to a Berlin hospital. The son of an army chaplain, he received his education and seminary training in the schools of a small pietistic sect. At the University of Halle he became engrossed in the study of Kant, and later, in Berlin, he was associated with a brilliant circle of philosophical and literary personalities, leaders in the German romantic movement. In this environment he came to his central conviction that religion is a deeply experiential reality, a sense of the Infinite, an element of man's spiritual life without which aesthetic, philosophic, and ethical concerns were but empty husks. After leaving Berlin to proceed with his great translation of Plato and to lecture at Halle, he returned to Berlin in 1807 where he became a remarkably successful preacher at Trinity Church. In 1810 he was appointed professor of theology in the new University of Berlin.

During the years which followed, Schleiermacher's thought deepened as he elaborated and applied his famous contention that the essence of all religion is a feeling of absolute dependence upon God, and that the religious consciousness is a primary object of theological inquiry. After some important work in historical criticism of the New Testament, Schleiermacher produced in 1822 his magnum opus, *The Christian Faith.* Reiterating his basic motif that living experience—an immediate awareness of God and of man's dependence on him—is the heart of religion and the source of all religious beliefs and institutions, he goes on in this work to distinguish Christian experience from the common element in all religion, on the basis that the person of Jesus Christ defines Christian dependence and awakens the awareness of sin and grace. On this central christological affirmation he reinterpreted Christian doctrine and elaborated his understanding of the Church as a community of such awareness. Thus at one stroke, Schleiermacher removed Christianity from the traditional arena of apologetics by establishing it as an experience which is *sui generis* and which can be understood only through itself. At the same time he transformed theology into an "empirical science" with its own data and its own mode of treating the data, though it must also be said that he simultaneously opened it to the objection that religious faith is only the psychological projection of one's own inner hopes and desires. It is difficult to overstate the crucial place which he occupies in the development of modern Christian thought, or to gainsay the assertion of his admiring colleague Augustus Neander, who is himself remembered as "the father of modern church history": "From [Schleiermacher] a new period in the history of the Church will one day take its origin."

Only one qualification need be added: Schleiermacher inescapably stands with Hegel. The two together express the central dialectic of romantic religion.

THE RISE OF ROMANTICISM IN FRANCE

The *Sturm und Drang* of intellectual, literary, and religious transition which actually brought the "romantic movement" into existence was not exclusively a German experience. France could claim the patriarch of the spiritual revival, Rousseau. And it was the destiny of France to culminate the revolutionary process that Cromwell and George Washington had anticipated, and which is *the* great background event of all romanticism. But only after the violent changes wrought by the French Revolution, the Napoleonic wars, and the Restoration did France undergo a spiritual renaissance similar to that in Germany. By then it had felt the effects of Madame de Staël's remarkable book *Germany* (1810), which remains one of the most contagious affirmations of the new spirit that has ever been written. The impact of her "gospel" would soon be strengthened by the work of her sometime lover, Benjamin Constant, whose semiautobiographical work *Adolphe* (1816) is an account of personal despair and torment reminiscent of Rousseau's *Confessions* and Goethe's *Werther*. Constant also wrote a five-volume work on religion in which he proposes that the religious sentiment is imperishable, even though it undergoes many successive transformations.

Among the Roman Catholic émigrés and others who had suffered at home during the Revolution, there was another group—one which made romantic enthusiasms and neomedievalism captive to the church. While Napoleon was at the height of his power, François René de Chateaubriand (1768–1848) published *The Genius of Christendom,* in which he developed a new apologetic based on the aesthetic and emotional satisfactions of traditional religion and chanted a magnificent poem to the splendors of the Christian tradition. Chateaubriand also gave brilliant expression to almost every other theme that romantic writers would exploit; but it was left for Louis Gabriel de Bonald (1754–1840) and Joseph de Maistre (1754–1821) to develop the full political significance of the Catholic revival. In the realm of political theory they sought to rally a return to the church around a loyalty to conservative institutions, particularly to the papacy. History and tradition, they insisted, not reason and science, were the keys to peace and social order. Felicité de Lamennais (1782–1854) was at first similarly motivated. Though repudiated by the pope, he attempted to achieve a rapprochement between the church and democratic institutions, assisted in his campaigns by two other romantic thinkers, Jean Baptiste Lacordaire (1802–61), and Charles René de Montalembert (1810–70), whose enthusiasm for the monastic ideal of the Middle Ages was especially remarkable. During Napoleon's last years and the early years of the Restoration, the romantics led a widespread return to the Roman church. Their hopes for a liberal (i.e. constitutional monarchy were soon shattered, however, and the papal condemnation of Lamennais took the heart out of their ecclesiastical hopes and sharpened the antagonism between Catholicism and democratic aspiration in France.

In many cases only the historicism, the fascination with the Middle Ages, a fervent opposition to materialism, and an immense, often very nationalistic faith in progress were all that remained at midcentury. The historian Jules Michelet and the great man of letters Victor Hugo reveal aspects of this tendency in their long careers. The best instance of the routinization of the romantic spirit, however, is the "official" *spiritualisme* sponsored by Victor Cousin (1792–1867) who appeared on the somewhat jaded philosophical scene in 1815 as a lecturer at the École Normale. After various vicissitudes, he returned from exile with great éclat in 1828, fired by the new philosophical influences he had absorbed in Germany. Until his death under the Second Empire, Cousin was a dominant force in French philosophical education, suppressing the materialism of the *philosophes* and inspiring a great movement of historical research. Cousin's "Eclectic Philosophy" actually never strayed far from the safe and sound principles of his first love, the Scottish common-sense philosophy; yet, perhaps because of this very moderation, it had a provocative impact on the early Transcendentalists in America.

ROMANTICISM IN GREAT BRITAIN

Not long after Thomas Gray wrote the letter with which this chapter begins, Edward Young ruffled classical waters with his *Conjectures on Original Composition* (1759). In this vigorous critical work, twice translated in Germany, Young bade writers leave behind the "soft fetters of easy imitation" and "soar in the regions of liberty." Further, he used and evoked that great shift from mechanical to organic metaphor that became a hallmark of the transition from classic to romantic literature, and which in due course (to borrow M. H. Abrams's phrase) would transform critical literature from a wilderness of mirrors into a jungle of vegetation.

> An *Original* [said Young] may be said to be of a vegetable nature; it rises spontaneously from the vital root of genius; it *grows*, it is not *made; Imitations* are often a sort of *manufacture*, wrought up by those *mechanics, art* and *labor*, out of pre-existent materials not their own.[4]

Young had many followers, for discontent with the standards of Alexander Pope and the ideals of the Augustan Age was widespread. One of the more influential was Edmund Burke, who as early as 1756 had rejected neoclassic ideals in his essay *On the Sublime and the Beautiful*. But Burke was to be remembered far better for his success in turning the romantic revolt against the eighteenth century into an argument for conservative traditionalism. He applied the organic metaphor to the whole culture—to society, religion, and above all, to politics. Certain types of reform, such as conciliatory action toward Ireland, India, or the American colonies, he defended as a kind of preservative pruning; but radical change of any sort was to him the equivalent of a blow at the roots. Burke's *Reflections on the French Revolution* (1790) was immediately recognized as a classic statement of the organic theory of the state and nation. As a critique of anticlericalism and revolutionary upheaval, his message became the broad, tolerant, typically British parallel to the impassioned Roman Catholic affirmations of Maistre and Bonald in France.

Samuel Taylor Coleridge (1772–1834)

In his religious outlook, Burke was in many respects a child of his century. Although he defended the established ec-

---

[4] Quoted in M. H. Abrams, *The Mirror and the Lamp: Romantic Theory and the Critical Tradition* (New York: Oxford University Press, 1953), p. 199.

clesiastical system, he never reaped the full theological harvest of his basic presuppositions, and the significance of the *Reflections*, therefore, is not nearly so important a religious event as the publication in 1798 of the *Lyrical Ballads* by William Wordsworth (1770–1850) and Samuel Taylor Coleridge. Wordsworth's introduction, in particular, was a virtual manifesto. While its immediate preoccupation is literary, and its major assertions stem from his conception of poetry as an expression of feeling opposed not so much to prose as to science, there are vast implications in Wordsworth's definition of a poet as one who "rejoices more than other men in the spirit of life that is in him." Perhaps he and his fellow spirits felt threatened by science or jostled by the commercial world with its "getting and spending," but they nevertheless were advancing a theological cause. Wordsworth lapsed rather soon into a conservative and uncreative orthodoxy which contrasts almost inexplicably with his early fervor, but Coleridge carried out the revolution they had proclaimed together, and during his later "theological phase," he developed its full import for Christianity.

Not without reason did John Stuart Mill designate Coleridge and Jeremy Bentham as the master spirits of nineteenth-century Britain. What made Coleridge a major figure in British intellectual and religious life was not simply that he symbolized a point of view at the far pole from Bentham's utilitarianism, but that he was a powerful interpreter and champion of the spiritual life. His understanding of religion and theology, moreover, grew out of his own peculiarly vivid and painful spiritual journey. Coleridge was the British Schleiermacher, but not simply because he made the most of a brief sojourn in Germany. After his early enthusiasm for German literature deepened into a full appreciation of the idealistic philosophical tradition, the speculative and metaphysical side of his thinking was much enhanced. Plato, Kant, and above all, Schelling informed his ideas, and he began to identify himself with the "Platonizing divines" who had flourshed in England before Locke's day. Convinced that "this dead English Church especially, must be brought to life again," he made Christian thinkers alive to the divine Reason. Coleridge called attention to the spiritual center of man's being and related it to the spiritual center of the universe. "The first range of hills that encircles the scanty vale of human life is the horizon for most of its inhabitants," he said; but he was one of those few who, "sounding the rivers of the vale . . . have learned that the sources must be far higher and far inward . . . [and] detected elements which neither the vale itself nor the surrounding mountains contained or could supply."[5] Though less systematically than Schleiermacher, he also related his speculations to Christian doctrine.

Coleridge's best remembered work, especially in America, was his *Aids to Reflection* (1825) which fended off the encroachment of science and materialism by making a sharp distinction between reason and the understanding. The understanding was merely sensuous, variable in every man, and restricted to a mundane concern for things and animal needs. A person living on its plane is a prisoner. But in Reason he detected the divinity of man. Reason was universal, the image of God in all men, providing insight into the harmony of man's essential nature with the attributes of God. Even the mysteries of the Christian faith were not closed to Reason, and Coleridge was able to justify an extensive apologetic for Christian doctrine which, though liberal, remained in contact with traditional Anglicanism. By espousing his version of Kant's doctrine of the practical reason, Coleridge could also attack the hedonistic ethic of the *philosophes* and inspire men with a passionate moral concern. In this spirit he developed optimistic views of a National Church, broad in membership and led by a "clerisy" constituted by the clergy and intellectuals of all denominations.

Thomas Carlyle (1795–1881)

The secular corollary to Coleridge was the Scottish thunderer and sage of Ecclefechan, Thomas Carlyle. Although he shared none of Coleridge's interest in traditional doctrines and ridiculed the opium eater's philosophy as "plaintive snuffle" and "transcendental moonshine," he could still refer to Coleridge as "a sublime man, who, alone in those dark days [of Carlyle's youth], had saved his crown of spiritual manhood; escaping from the black materialisms and revolu-

[5] The quoted phrases are from Coleridge's *Biographia Literaria*, chap. 12, where he discusses the concept of the "transcendental" and in due course gives a name to New England's romantic movement.

tionary deluges, with God, freedom, immortality still his; a king of men . . . a kind of *Magus*, girt in mystery and enigma." But Carlyle more than Coleridge received his inspiration directly from Germany, and Goethe was "the Great Heart" who raised him out of the Slough of Despond. The spirit of Schiller, Goethe, Kant, and Fichte convinced him that English philosophy after Locke had ceased to be a philosophy of mind and had become merely a genetic history of what is in the mind, with "no word in it of the secret of our Freedom, of our mysterious relations to Time and Space, to God and the Universe."[6] With all these men Carlyle cherished an antipathy toward the church which rose at times to disdain; but from them (especially from Kant and Fichte) he gained that immense concern for duty and the moral will which gave such Olympian grandeur and prophetic force to his critique of the age. As a thinker, he was even less systematic than Coleridge; but his forceful language made his message contagious, and his scholarly historical and biographical works opened broad pathways into the land of his inspiration.

In America, for reasons not entirely clear, Carlyle's reputation was greatest of all. Frothingham was not exaggerating when he recalled in 1876 that "thirty-five years ago Carlyle was the high priest of the new philosophy . . . the dregs of his ink-bottle were welcomed as the precious sediment of the fountain of inspiration."[7] Needless to say, there were many other voices from across the Atlantic that conveyed the new spiritual stirrings to the land of the transplanted Puritans. Most difficult to measure is the quiet and steady influence of Wordsworth. Many aspects of the impulse have necessarily been slighted in this chapter—movements as diverse as the immensely popular blending of historical interest and romantic sentiment in Walter Scott's novels and narrative poems, the great poetic outpourings of Keats, Shelley, Byron, and Burns, and the massive historical and philological scholarship of the Continental biblical critics. Yet something of the spirit, breadth, and power of the total impulse has at least been suggested, and still other dimensions of the "romantic revolu-

[6] John H. Muirhead, *The Platonic Tradition in Anglo-Saxon Philosophy* (New York: Macmillan Co., 1931), p. 130.

[7] Octavius Brooks Frothingham, *Transcendentalism in New England: A History*, pp. 93–94.

tion" will become apparent in our consideration of America's diverse responses.[8]

[8] American romantic movements are the concern of chaps. 37 and 38, which follow; but see also chaps. 31 and 33 (of Volume 1) on Lutheran and Roman Catholic developments respectively. Some aspects of Southern romanticism are treated in chap. 40. Liberalism, in large degree an outgrowth of romantic thought, is considered in chap. 46.

37

ROMANTIC RELIGION IN NEW ENGLAND

Just after the turn of the nineteenth century, Samuel Miller, a Presbyterian minister in New York who was soon to become professor of church history at Princeton Seminary, published his *Brief Retrospect of the Eighteenth Century* (1803). In this wide-ranging two-volume survey he remarks that "it would be improper to pass in silence the celebrated *Immanuel Kant*, Professor at Koeningsberg [sic], in Prussia"; but having heard that "the acutest understanding cannot tolerably comprehend [this profound and extensive system] by less than a twelve-month's study," he satisfies himself with a short secondhand report. Miller also took note of the new literary tendencies evinced by Edward Young, Oliver Goldsmith, Thomas Gray, and the "romantic" forgeries of James Macpherson and Thomas Chatterton. To Goethe he devoted two sentences; to Schiller, one sentence plus a footnote of warning that "such characters [as Schiller and Kotzebue created] ought never to have been exhibited at all," since they "undermine" the virtue of those by whom they are contemplated. Yet even Miller's mild interest in the newer trends of thought was then unusual in America. During these turn of century years the battles of rationalistic infidelity and revivalistic orthodoxy were a more immediate concern.

In Europe, on the other hand, these years witnessed one of the most amazing outpourings of innovative genius in history: Schleiermacher's *On Religion*, Freidrich Schlegel's *Lucinda*, Beethoven's *Eroica*, Chateaubriand's *Genius of Christianity*, Schiller's *Wallenstein* and Coleridge's translation of it, Novalis's *Hymns to the Night*, Wordsworth and Coleridge's *Lyrical Ballads*, Maistre's *Considerations on France*, Hegel's essay on Fichte and Schelling, and a dozen other epoch-making works. But the United States remained a land of romantic silence. One might say that the most promising "romantic" event of the period was the birth of Ralph Waldo Emerson in 1803, though the father of this promising infant viewed Europe's cultural flowering with no more enthusiasm than Miller.

In due course America would awaken from its dogmatic slumbers. The first new nation was becoming aware of its powers and determined to express its genius. Before long writers with less restricted tastes and bolder conceptions of the national spirit were making themselves heard. This meant that democratic individualism was abroad in the land; and individualists, because they think first of themselves, put neoclassical rationalism on borrowed time.

Washington Irving (1783–1859) is frequently credited with being the first to respond creatively. During an extended stay in Europe after 1815, he wrote *The Sketch Book of Geoffrey Crayon, Gent.* (1819), which included essays on "Westminster Abbey" and "The Mutability of Literature," and tales like "Rip Van Winkle" and "The Legend of Sleepy Hollow." Irving was the first American to gain an international reputation as a man of letters, and during the course of his life he turned his talent to all of the less speculative interests of the romantic movement: primitive lore, ancient legend, medieval life, Roman Catholic culture, and non-Western religion, including both Moorish culture and the life of Mohammed.

Yet anomalously or not, it was only in the land of the Puritans that American romanticism gained expression across nearly the full range of its possibilities. The historical explanation of this remarkable development involves no more than an extension of earlier narratives. Economic and social circumstances continued to encourage New England's literary and intellectual life in both the orthodox and liberal communities, as did a remarkably literate public, and the existence of support for libraries, colleges, seminaries and periodicals. And behind all of this was a learned tradition and a heritage of religious passion. New England's romantics belong first of all to the genus of religious enthusiasts, of which Puritanism was another, earlier species. The Edwardsean New Lights were an intermediate factor no less important for the Transcendentalists than was German pietism for Schleiermacher. Emerson stands in the tradition of Thomas Shepard and Jonathan Edwards as an awakener of the sleeping spirit.[1] In the field of religious scholarship and thought the orthodox showed slightly more creative energy; among the Unitarians, meanwhile, the lifting of old Puritan inhibitions about literature and art, as well as a larger measure of doctrinal freedom, provided many advantages. Since the romantic gospel was in one sense a specific prescription for the spiritual paralysis brought on by a diet of common-sense rationalism, the "corpse-cold Unitarianism of Boston and Harvard College" (Emerson's epithet) was soon experiencing a Transcendental awakening.

THE EMERGENCE OF TRANSCENDENTALISM

The religious revolution carried out in antebellum New England is associated inescapably with Transcendentalism, but it rose with equal spontaneity outside of the Unitarian circles usually designated by that name. It was in fact but a distinctive American phase of a great alternation of mood and mind that affected most of Western Christendom. All the spiritual dissatisfaction created by the Enlightenment motivated its quest. All the social and economic forces that underlay the political revolutions in America and France conditioned its form. In a sense, therefore, its origins are unfathomable and its causes are beyond explanation. In a new and culturally underdeveloped country, and especially in a region where the Puritan tradition was, if anything, overdeveloped, the need for outside influence was great.

If fresh impulses had not come in from abroad, American religion and especially the later forms of Puritanism would have stewed much longer in their own juices. For this reason one can ascribe more than symbolic significance to the decision of four gifted New Englanders to pursue advanced

---

[1] The term "transcendentalist" is of uncertain origin and ambiguous in meaning. Kant gave currency to the term, but the early Transcendentalists were not rigorously Kantian. The term, whether used in ridicule or as finally accepted, indicated their concern for the higher use of Reason and its objects: the Good, the True, the Beautiful, the Divine.

studies at Göttingen University.[2] Every one of these students returned to America as at least a temporary apostle for those aspects of German intellectual life that had impressed him most. In their train came two accomplished German scholars to the Harvard faculty. In the meantime many men, both orthodox and Unitarian, were improving their linguistic equipment in growing recognition of German scholarship, while still others, in mounting numbers, followed the pattern of study in Germany. But the real source of excitement was the printed word: reviews and articles in the journals, first and always the great English romantics—Scott, Wordsworth, Coleridge, and Carlyle—but also the works of German and French writers, many of them in translation. In this realm the contributions of James Marsh were extremely important, especially his edition of Coleridge's *Aids to Reflection* (1829), accompanied by an extremely thoughtful introduction, and his translation of Herder's *Spirit of Hebrew Poetry* (1833). Though intended primarily to strengthen the orthodox cause, Marsh's works served almost immediately to arouse the enthusiasm of the more restive elements in the Unitarian and later the Congregational ministry. During the 1830s this restiveness, strengthened by a convergence of many other influences, led to a continuous series of earnest discussions of recent literature and speculative thought in the *Christian Examiner*, the *North American Review*, and other journals.

The *annus mirabilis* was 1836. Not only did it bring forth an unusually stimulating crop of articles and translations, but it witnessed the appearance of Emerson's classic *Nature*. Though published anonymously and dismissed by some as the work of a Swedenborgian publicist, it was clearly a pivotal utterance. When implications of this essay were more clearly understood, Emerson became the acknowledged leader of what Convers Francis was to call the "German School" of American Unitarianism. In September of that year the Transcendental Club met for the first time at the parsonage of the most active of the insurgents, George Ripley (1802–80) of the Purchase Street Church in Boston. Also

[2] These were George Ticknor, Joseph Green Cogswell, Edward Everett, and (the next year) George Bancroft. Professor Levi Hedge sent to Bancroft his brilliant thirteen-year-old son, Frederic Henry, for precollegiate training—an equally momentous decision.

present were Bronson Alcott (1799–1888), Orestes Brownson (1803–76), James Freeman Clarke (1810–88), Ralph Waldo Emerson (1803–82), Convers Francis (1795–1863), and Frederic Henry Hedge (1805–90). All but Alcott were Unitarian ministers, as were seventeen of the twenty-six persons (including five women) who entered the club during its three or four years of activity. The publications of the club members would alone provide an outline for a literary history of the period, but it was a group which by its concentration of talent, zeal, variegated eccentricities, and intense libertarian convictions would have made history in one way or another in any age or clime. Together with the men and women whom they won to their banner, they constituted the Transcendental movement in New England. Simply because they were so active and so diverse it is impossible to trace here the complicated course of their interwoven careers. Happily the stature of Emerson and Parker as leaders of the movement's two major tendencies allows a simplified bifocal approach.

Ralph Waldo Emerson

Matthew Arnold once stated that Emerson had written the most important English prose of the nineteenth century. The philosopher John Dewey declared him to be the only American thinker worthy of being ranked with Plato. Yet the career of the Seer of Concord creates grave difficulties for every biographer and historian: an early life showing few signs of genius, a short middle period of brilliance during which the renowned intellect never quite disengaged itself from its parochial milieu, and an unnaturally long maturity—Emerson was already a "grand old man" by the time he was forty.

He was born in the parsonage of Boston's First Church; his father, the dignified and cultivated William Emerson, died eight years later, leaving Mrs. Emerson with six children under ten. At Harvard he received a formal classical education under safe Unitarian auspices, accomplished little that presaged extraordinary greatness, and graduated in 1821 in about the middle of his class. Most significant for him were the disciplined rhetorical training of Professor Edward Tyrell Channing (Brother of the minister and a man to whom many New England writers were indebted) and the splendid lectures of his idol, Edward Everett, just returned from study and travel in Germany. Emerson kept school for a time, attended the Harvard Divinity School, and in 1829 was ordained as junior colleague of Henry Ware, Jr., at the Second Church in Boston. When Ware accepted a professorship at Harvard, Emerson became the church's pastor—but not for long. In 1832 misgivings about administering the Lord's Supper and a disinclination for public prayer led him to offer his resignation.

Emerson did not renounce the ministry at once, however, but supplied for a time in various churches when he was not otherwise occupied. In 1833 he began his lifelong career as a public lecturer with a series in Boston on natural history. By 1836, the year of *Nature* and the Transcendental Club, Emerson had arrived at his mature position, one which in future years he would perhaps modify, but would never significantly alter. That his views had revolutionary religious implications was only hinted in his plea for an indigenous American literature before the Harvard Phi Beta Kappa chapter in the following year. But in 1838, in his now famous address to the graduating class of the Harvard Divinity School, he cast aside the veil, revealed his accumulated distaste for the prevailing tradition, and announced the Emersonian alternative. Woven into the poetic phraseology of this manifesto were ideas on religion and the "sentiment of virtue" like nothing previously heard in America.

Opening with an evocative yet idea-laden hymn to nature, Emerson moves immediately into an exposition of his most fundamental metaphysical views. The phraseology is deceptive, but the heart of his "sublime creed" is made explicit: "the world is not the product of manifold power, but of one will, of one mind; and that one mind is everywhere active, in each ray of the star, in each wavelet of the pool; and whatever opposes that will is everywhere balked and baffled, because things are made so and not otherwise. . . . All things proceed out of the same spirit, and all things conspire with it. . . . The preception of this law of laws awakens in the mind a sentiment which we call the religious sentiment, and which makes our highest happiness. . . . By it the universe is made safe and habitable." Only against the background of this almost Spinozan monism can one discern the stark force of Emerson's harsh contribution to the controversy over miracles that was stirring the Unitarian churches: "The word Miracle, as pronounced by Christian churches, gives a false impression; it is Monster. It is not one with the blowing clover and the falling rain."

Nor was this all, for he called not for mere assent, but for a change of heart, a consent to Being reminiscent of Jonathan Edwards. "There is no doctrine of the Reason which will bear to be taught by the Understanding."

It cannot be received at second hand. Truly speaking it is not instruction but provocation, that I can receive from another soul. What he announces, I must find true in me, or reject; and on his word, or as his second, be he who he may, I can accept nothing. On the contrary, the absence of this primary faith is the presence of degradation.

With his primary faith thus stated, Emerson launched into an indictment of the New England tradition that shocked most of his contemporaries:

Historical Christianity has fallen into the error that corrupts all attempts to communicate religion. It has dwelt, it dwells, with noxious exaggeration about the *person* of Jesus. Men have come to speak of revelation as somewhat long ago given and done, as if God were dead. The church seems to totter to its fall almost all life extinct. The prayers and even the dogmas of our church, are like the zodiac of Denderah, and the astronomical monuments of the Hindoos, wholly insulated from anything now extant in the life and business of the people. Historical Christianity destroys the power of preaching, by withdrawing it from the moral nature of man, where the sublime is, where are the resources of astonishment and power. . . . In how many churches, by how many prophets, tell me, is man made sensible that he is an infinite Soul; that the earth and the heavens are passing into his mind; that he is drinking forever the soul of God? Where now sounds the persuasion, that by its very melody imparadises my heart, and so affirms its own origin in heaven? . . . I look for the hour when that supreme Beauty which ravished the souls of those Eastern men, and chiefly to those Hebrews, and through their lips spoke oracles to all time, shall speak in the West also. The Hebrew and Greek Scriptures contain immortal sentences, that have been bread of life to millions. But they have no epical integrity; are fragmentary;

are not shown in their order to the intellect. I look for the new Teacher that shall follow so far those shining laws that he shall see them come full circle; shall see their rounding complete grace; shall see the world to be the mirror of the soul; shall see the identity of the law of gravitation with the purity of the heart; and shall show that the Ought, that Duty, is one thing with Science, with Beauty, and with Joy.[3]

With the Divinity School Address, Emerson became America's first "death-of-God" theologian, and it goes without saying that his efforts were not received with enthusiasm by the pillars of church and society. In a later day the address would be regarded as a Unitarian manifesto, ranking with Channing's Baltimore Sermon. At the time, however, the Harvard authorities and the more official custodians of "the Unitarian mind" looked upon it as an affront and a scandal. Nor were they slow to say so; but before considering the Second Unitarian Controversy, which erupted almost immediately, it is useful to consider more carefully the message which had been elaborated so unostentatiously in *Nature* and brought to such precise focus in the address, and which was to be explicated and applied in a long series of lectures, essays, and poems throughout the next forty years of Emerson's quiet but busy life. Such an interruption of the narrative might even be justified by the fact that Emerson himself withdrew from the conflict, retired to Concord, and left the ecclesiastical battle in the hands of more belligerent spirits while he became Transcendentalism's sage and seer until his death in 1882. Because every American lives with at least faded memories of words that were pressed upon him by uninspired (or perchance inspired) teachers in various school rooms, and because some of Emerson's themes have been woven into the fabric of American idealism, his version of the Transcendental evangel remains important. It is also surprisingly relevant.

The essential greatness of Emerson as a religious thinker stems from his acute sense of the modern spiritual situation, its fears, assurances, and hopes. He absorbed the full impact of the romantic movement, and in his capacious and medita-

---

[3] The address is given in *Theology in America,* ed. Sydney E. Ahlstrom, pp. 293–316. See also the introduction. In the above summary quotation only large omissions are indicated.

tive soul blended its special enthusiasms with what he called "the total New England." Yet his vision went far beyond his region. Like almost every American of his age, he was thrilled by the newness of this nation's history and ecstatic about its unique potentialities. "One cannot look on the freedom of this country, in connection with its youth," he said, "without a presentiment that here shall laws and institutions exist in some proportion to the majesty of Nature." The revolutionary quality in his unrestrained optimism was the radicalism of antitraditional individualism. Emerson was bitterly opposed to tradition as much and almost savagely critical of all existing ones. America, he said, "has no past: all has an onward and prospective look." The past was not a building to be renovated for present living, but a quarry to be pillaged, as he himself pillaged the Western and later the Eastern intellectual traditions, transforming every element he appropriated into an instrument of his boundless hope.

Emerson was no more concerned with history than with tradition. The historicism of the age made no impact upon him. At no other point, in fact, are his relations with Plato and the Neoplatonic tradition more prominent than in his refusal to think historically or to rehearse ancient debates. His essay "On History" (1841) made this tendency explicit; in *Representative Men* (1850) his subjects become timeless symbols, ideal types rather than actors in human history. It was this disposition that drew him, as it had drawn Coleridge, to the "transcendental genius" of the seventeenth-century Cambridge Platonists, yet he ultimately rejected them because of what he could only regard as their bondage to Christianity. Religiously speaking, this rejection of history and heritage makes Emerson a new kind of romantic pagan, one who throws from the temple not only the money changers, but the priests as well, and with them their beliefs, creeds, and rituals.

Even Emerson's more positive doctrines are lifted out of their venerable contexts. Taking seriously his own call for an original relationship to the universe, he made his form of individualism a solvent for old dilemmas. His radicalism stems from the absolute way in which he defined and defended personal autonomy—his own, and that of anyone else who would fully realize himself as a human being. "Nothing is at last sacred," he would say, "but the integrity of your own mind." "Man's dazzling potentiality," in the words of F. O.

Matthiesson, was the base of Emerson's credo, and both Thoreau and Whitman elaborated its implications in authentic ways.

Emerson made self-reliance the cardinal virtue. Yet because he understood the self as a microcosm of the All, the various aspects of his thought attain full expression only within the pantheistic view of man, nature, and God which frames his entire message. Naturally idealistic, he drew much from the Platonic tradition; yet he rejects its emphasis on permanent forms and seals his bond with the romantic's tendency to combine post-Kantian idealism with an enthusiasm for Spinoza and the mystic spiritualism of Emanuel Swedenborg. He also commits himself wholly to the organic metaphor: the identity of mind and nature was his first postulate, but he conceived of reality as a dynamic, creative process; growth was its primary feature.

These several tendencies led him to discover a community of spirit with the higher philosophy of India. Brahma and karma and other concepts of Oriental religion entered his thinking. The *idea* of a thing was more important to him than its materiality, yet he regarded no fact as profane—the Each was taken up in the All, the system of Nature was identical with the Oversoul. This is the rationale behind the remark that Emerson saw sermons "not just on stones but in bean rows at Walden Pond and mud puddles on Boston Common." In this sense, one can say that his "self-reliance" was a kind of God-reliance. This persistent monism in Emerson's thought serves in turn to account for the most serious limitation of his thought, his nearly total unconcern for evil, pain, and death. Sin, despite his New England background, could mean little more to him than narrowness of view or blindness to Nature. The revival of religion which Emerson desired, in other words, would come only when men repented of their membership in the Party of Memory, forswore the sins of looking backward, joined the Party of Hope, and realized their participation in the Oversoul with confidence and optimism. There was a strongly implied corollary, moreover, that Americans were specially "elected" to be thus converted, and that in their response they would fulfill their country's destiny.

The Emersonian message was not a mere softening of traditional doctrines, but a dramatic and drastic demand for a complete recasting of religious life and thought. "Like all puritans, Emerson was an extremist." Some have argued that his was a benign and etherealized form of democratic individualism. Others have pointed to Emerson's parochialism, his puritanic suspicion of the theater, his perennial sermonic tone, his tendency to take the edge off of every sharp romantic insight, his insistence on reducing philosophic discussion to a popular, even a pedestrian, level. Still others have made of him chiefly a "literary" rather than a speculative figure. There is a great deal of truth in all of these observations. Yet they do not fully account for his obvious importance or explain why he is, with William James, peculiarly America's own philosopher. They fail to recognize that Emerson is in fact the theologian of something we may almost term "the American religion." Most important for our present purpose, none of these deprecations explains why such strident opposition should have arisen against him and those who came to share his outlook.

The opposition sprang into action almost as soon as what we now call American Transcendentalism began to make itself seen and heard. In the fall of 1836 Andrews Norton had taken strong exception to George Ripley's approval of new and more liberal views of biblical interpretation, particularly as these theories tended to minimize miracles as proof of scriptural authority. He grew more irate as champions of the "Newness" gave substance to Moses Stuart's old charge that Unitarianism was a halfway house on the road to infidelity. This tempest had by no means subsided when Emerson blew it up again with his demand at the Divinity School that ministers replace their "faith in Christ" with a "faith in man like Christ's." Again Norton was soon into the fray with an abusive public letter. A month after the address, Emerson's old colleague at Second Church, Henry Ware, Jr., now a professor at Harvard, asserted "The Personality of the Deity" in a pubic sermon. The Unitarian press took up the issue. In the following year Norton delivered and published his *Discourse on the Latest Form of Infidelity;* and this, in turn involved him in a new public debate with Ripley into which leaped another who took the pseudonym Levi Blodgett. His real name was Theodore Parker (1810–60), and he was the largely self-educated son of a Lexington farmer. From the Harvard Divinity School he had come to be minister of the church in nearby West Roxbury. Around him swirled the second phase of the Second Unitarian Controversy.

Theodore Parker

Parker stepped into the fierce light of public controversy in the same year that Ripley resigned from the ministry. Invited to deliver the sermon at the ordination of Charles Shackford in the Hawes Place Church of South Boston on 19 May 1841, he chose as his subject, "The Transient and Permanent in Christianity." When his discourse was published, a clamor arose among the Boston clergy, including the more conservative Unitarians whom until this time Andrews Norton had tried in vain to mobilize. Christians of nearly every sort were scandalized by Parker's acceptance of German critical studies of the "historical Jesus," including those of the notorious Friedrich Strauss, and above all by Parker's insistence that Christianity did not depend on the actual existence of Christ at all. Theism, as he came to understand it, was "permanent," not historically rooted or "transient." With considerable goading from the orthodox, accusations and rejoinders again filled the Unitarian press. And the controversy grew in intensity rather than waned, because Parker did not retire to obscurity, leave the ministry, or even relinquish the name of Unitarian and Christian. In 1841–42 he gave public lectures in Boston which appeared in book form as *A Discourse on Matters Pertaining to Religion* (1842), followed in 1843 with his heavily annotated translation of DeWette's *Introduction to the Old Testament*, on which he had labored since divinity school days at Harvard. In 1844 he twisted the dagger in Unitarianism's wounded side by using his turn as "the great and Thursday Lecturer" at First Church to offer another succinct exposition of his views on Jesus. This audacity led to virtual ostracism by the Boston Association of Unitarian Ministers.

Parker advanced the battle the next year by accepting the invitation of a group of Unitarian laymen to preach regularly in the Melodeon Theater, an assignment which was soon regularized by their formation of the Twenty-Eighth Congregational Society. For six years after 1852, when the "Twenty-Eighth" moved into the spacious Music Hall, Parker exposed the full range of his ideas to the largest regular audience in Boston. His thought as now exhibited in a vast corpus of treatises, lectures, sermons, and occasional essays was always sharply phrased and activistic in the extreme. Yet he never achieved a reconciliation of the Transcendental fervor, the Enlightened absolutism, the positivistic interest in fact, and the humanitarian reformism that warred for supremacy in his soul.

At least as early as 1852 a decisive break between "Christian" and "theistic" Unitarians had occurred; and as Norton had long insisted, the critical issue was that of biblical authority. In 1853 the executive committee of the American Unitarian Association, "in a denominational capacity" so far as that was possible, separated itself from the errors of Transcendentalism and declared its faith in "the Divine origin, the Divine authority, [and] the Divine sanctions of the religion of Jesus Christ." Many of the younger men, lamenting this statement as the next thing to a creed, rallied to the more radical wing. Many of them, it must be added, were further attracted by Parker's stand on the slavery question, where his continuous decisive statements ranked him with Garrison and Phillips as a major force in arousing the New England conscience. The profound degree to which the Unitarian community was riven appeared in 1859, when Parker lay on his deathbed in Florence, Italy, and the assembled alumni of the Harvard Divinity School voted down a motion to convey their sympathy.

The Civil War temporarily quieted these harsh dissensions, but after the war they broke out again, and from 1865 to 1872 the Parkerites were excluded from the newly formed National Unitarian Conference. After 1867 many of them were active in the Free Religious Association, but gradually their position won recognition as legitimately Unitarian, even though they had by then adopted evolutionary doctrines and Social Darwinism—tendencies which actually made them more "humanistic" than "theistic" in Parker's old sense. By 1885 the theological faculty at Harvard was of their persuasion, and at the century's end Emerson's Divinity School Address and Parker's South Boston Sermon had been fully accepted into the official canon of Unitarian scriptures. Emerson's essays and poems, meantime, had become stock items of American literature as it was studied in the country's schoolrooms and parlors. There can be little doubt that both Emerson and Parker would have objected to being absorbed by the "genteel tradition"; yet the very existence of that mild and inclusive tradition testifies to the pervasiveness of the Transcendental influence in America.

Though always a minority in antebellum New England, Transcendentalists inspired many brilliant persons not mentioned here.[4] Several Transcendental Club members became involved in the celebrated communitarian project at Brook Farm, and some of these, in turn, becoming disenchanted, moved off in wildly various directions. George Ripley, a central figure in the early years, became a New York journalist; his wife entered the Roman Catholic church. Orestes Brownson had gone through a long series of conversions before his Transcendental phase; and in 1844, after several years as a radical social critic, he became a Roman Catholic, as did another brief sojourner at Brook Farm, Isaac Hecker. Bronson Alcott, more famous as the father of Louisa May and other "little women," was the movement's least practical, most contemplative member. Yet his mystical Platonism notwithstanding, Alcott made educational history with an experimental school for children in Boston. In him the "Newness" became most "transcendental." In James Freeman Clarke and Frederic Henry Hedge one best sees the Transcendentalist as a loyal and conservative Unitarian minister. Both men were also scholars of real significance who did much to establish the historical standpoint. Clarke's *Ten Great Religions,* like *The Religion of Asia* by Samuel Johnson, a more radical Transcendentalist, documents the new interest in Oriental thought and other world religions which Emerson, Thoreau, and Parker jointly inspired. Clarke further represented an important medium of transfer for the incoming German influence. As a professor first of church history and later of German at Harvard, Hedge was even more noteworthy as a transmitter of German literature, scholarship, and speculative thought. Appropriately, it is his translation of Luther's "A Mighty Fortress Is Our God" that Americans have usually sung. And Hedge's Dudleian Lecture of 1850 marks the transition from Enlightenment rationalism to romantic idealism in natural theology at Harvard. After the Civil War, he and Clarke were leaders in the effort to maintain Unitarianism as

4 Among those not named or discussed in this chapter are Elizabeth Peabody, the educational reformer; Sampson Reed, the Swedenborgian; William H. Furness, biblical scholar and minister in Philadelphia; and George Bancroft, the historian.

an explicitly Christian denomination. Together they represent the many ways in which Transcendentalism was a movement of church reform.

In a class by herself was Margaret Fuller (1810–50), a protégé of Elizabeth Peabody and the only woman to play a major intellectual role in the Transcendental movement. Her education was begun by her father and extended chiefly by herself, but she came to embody more aspects of the romantic spirit than any of her associates. A mystic by disposition, she was already wrestling with Spinoza and the debates of the German romantic idealists in 1832. A translator of Goethe's conversations and his defender against Puritanic critics, she was also a leading literary critic and the chief editor of the *Dial*, the movement's major periodical. She was a warm admirer of Mazzini and while in Italy served as a nurse in the Roman republican uprising of 1848. Her unique place in American intellectual history is made especially secure by her book, *Woman in the Nineteenth Century* (1845), which was the first thorough and mature treatise on feminism and sexual equality by an American. She married the Marquis Angelo Ossoli, a follower of Mazzini; but along with her husband and infant son, Margaret Fuller was lost in a shipwreck off the Long Island coast in 1850.

New England was not the only locus of Transcendental activity. Both James Freeman Clarke and William Henry Channing (a nephew of the minister) tried to establish outposts in the West, in Louisville and Cincinnati. Two other movements of idealistic thinking—the so-called Hegelian movements of Ohio and Missouri—also received considerable stimulus from one or another of the New Englanders, but they owed more to their German lineage, their pride in the post-Kantian tradition, and the active German intellectual life in Cincinnati and Saint Louis. Both groups showed great freedom in their use of Hegelian ideas and applied idealistic thought to a wide range of American problems—in education, science, law, religion, literature, social analysis, and politics. As befitted such westering intellectuals, most of them were, by American evangelical standards, fairly radical. The Ohio movement flourished earlier, with Moncure Conway, August Willich, and John B. Stallo as its leading thinkers. The more publicized Saint Louis group had its flowering after the Civil War, with Henry C. Brokmeyer, Denton T. Snider and

William T. Harris as its leading lights and the *Journal of
Speculative Philosophy* to disseminate its ideas.[5]

ROMANTIC INFLUENCES ON NEW ENGLAND ORTHODOXY

In 1894, when John White Chadwick published his fine
historical study, *Old and New Unitarian Belief,* he could
report that the hostilities of the Unitarian Controversy had
waned; new trends in historical and philosophical thought
had brought the old antagonists onto common ground; Harvard and Andover were contemplating merger. He felt an
especially close sympathy with the Progressive Orthodoxy of
the Congregationalists and the Boston University Theology of
the Methodists. This phenomenon itself will be taken up in a
later chapter, but the origins of the rapprochement must be
considered here. The heralds of this new spirit in Congregationalism were men like Moses Stuart, the professor of biblical studies at Andover Seminary, and his student James
Marsh of the University of Vermont who introduced to their
American contemporaries some of the most important scholarly and speculative achievements of the time.[6] But the man
who absorbed these impulses and by his unusual powers as a
writer and preacher made himself virtually the "American
Schleiermacher" was Horace Bushnell (1802–76).

Born near Litchfield, Connecticut, Bushnell "owned the
covenant" at the age of nineteen in the little stone church of
New Preston, where his family had moved in 1805. After
receiving his baccalaureate from Yale (1827), he turned fit-
fully to teaching, commerce, and law, until a conversion experience of sorts led him to the Yale Divinity School. Here he
occupied the liberal ground which Nathaniel William Taylor
and the New Haven Theology had won; but he later
confessed that it was Coleridge's *Aids to Reflection* and

[5] Thinkers as interesting as these deserve lengthier exposition,
but see Loyd D. Easton, *Hegel's First American Followers: The
Ohio Hegelians* (Athens, Ohio: Ohio University Press, 1966);
and Henry A. Pochmann, *German Culture in America,* pp. 257–
93, 639–58.

[6] Marsh's work has already been alluded to. Stuart translated
an essay of Schleiermacher's on the Trinity, and even more importantly promoted much interest in German biblical scholarship
during a long teaching career. See pp. 394–96.

Schleiermacher on the Trinity that transformed his entire view of Christianity.[7] A further influence was the challenge presented by the North Church in Hartford where he served from 1833 to his retirement, ministering to an urban, socially aspiring congregation. Faced after his ordination by a controversy-torn parish, Bushnell tried to develop a theology of comprehension. He reshaped the New England Theology and the old Congregational understanding of the church so as to satisfy and yet awaken those "who believed in reform, self-improvement, and gentility, who were nervous and nostalgic about the faith of their fathers, who were affronted by Calvinistic accusations and bored by theology."[8] His congregation, like many others, was committed to American democratic optimism, repulsed by revivalism, concerned about the religious nurture of its children, and attracted to the social amenities and liturgical graces of Episcopalianism. Recognizing these eroded foundations, he entered upon his ministerial task.

Bushnell was a preacher more than a theologian; and his thought is practical and apologetic in purpose; he set out to fit the Christian message to the dominant presuppositions of his time by modifying those aspects of belief or practice which scandalized many educated Americans. His first and most famous work, *Christian Nurture* (1847), dealt with the problem of Original Sin, provided an escape from revivalism, and became the foundation stone for new approaches to religious education. Accepting the view of Hopkins and Taylor that "sin is in the sinning," he denied that children were lost in sin until visited by the Spirit in conversion; a person need never know a time when he had not been a Christian. Bushnell's intensely organic view of family, church, and nation led him to view nurture as the means of evoking the goodness of human nature. Conversion was ideally a gradual lifelong process of growth and deepening awareness. Such views opened Bushnell to the charge that he made Christianity a matter of natu-

[7] Bushnell was influenced chiefly by genuine mediators between traditional Christian doctrine and the new romantic emphases. Hence Coleridge, Schleiermacher, and possibly F. D. Maurice counted for more than either Emerson or Parker. The Unitarian who meant most to him was the conservative Transcendentalist Cyrus Augustus Bartol of Boston's West Church.

[8] Barbara Cross, *Horace Bushnell*, p. 157.

ral development, but his actual teaching on grace and Atonement blunts the accusation.

A vital theological complement to these views was his *God in Christ* (1849), which consisted of a revolutionary "Dissertation on Language" and three theological addresses delivered at Harvard, Andover, and Yale. *Christ in Theology* (1851) was a point-by-point defense of the former, and hence an assertion of his own orthodoxy. His starting point in both books was the insistence that verbal communication is essentially evocative, symbolic, and social in nature.

> The crux of Bushnell's theory was not, as in the case of Emerson, the metaphysical status of language. . . . Bushnell's aim was to differentiate the logical and the poetic modes of language, to define the function of each, and to demonstrate the priority of poetic method. . . . Bushnell would replace a scientific, logical, mechanistic, or abstractive ideal of language with an aesthetic, symbolic, organic, literary one. . . . Rational speech is not the rule of language but a special case, and it goes wrong when it tries to be anything more.[9]

In effect, he made a literal appeal to scriptural and creedal statements impossible. Having thus robbed language of the precision which dogmaticians and heresy hunters had assumed it to possess, Bushnell went on to explain the doctrine of the Trinity in modalistic terms. He regarded Father, Son, and Holy Spirit as merely three different modes through which the ineffable One revealed himself to man. Bushnell called this an "instrumental Trinity," but its similarity to the Patripassian heresy of the Church's early centuries indicates his difficulty in asserting the real humanity of Christ. An uproar of criticism drove Bushnell to reconsider his views, and brought him in later years to stronger sympathy for the Athanasian doctrine of the Trinity.

Even more offensive to his New England contemporaries was his revival of the moral influence theory of Atonement, first enunciated by Abelard and advocated by the Socinians and Unitarians. This view asserts that the sinner beholding in

[9] Charles N. Feidelson, Jr., *Symbolism and American Literature* (Chicago: University of Chicago Press, 1953), pp. 151–52.

Christ the forbearance and forgiveness of God ceases his disobedience and distrust.

> My doctrine [said Bushnell] is summarily this; that, excluding all thoughts of a penal quality in the life and death of Christ, or of any divine abhorrence to sin, exhibited by sufferings laid upon his person; also, dismissing, as an assumption too high for us, the opinion that the death of Christ is designed for some governmental effect on the moral empire of God in other worlds,—excluding points like these, and regarding everything done by him as done for expression before us, and thus for effect in us, he does produce an impression in our minds of the essential sanctity of God's law and character, which it was needful to produce, and without which any proclamation of pardon would be dangerous, any attempt to subdue and reconcile us to God, ineffectual.[10]

In orthodox circles these works of Bushnell aroused a furor hardly less violent than Parker had created in the Unitarian community. Old Bennet Tyler turned from his assaults on Nathaniel William Taylor to decry this new source of error, while Bushnell's ministerial brethren in Hartford became increasingly reluctant to exchange pulpits with him. Finally in 1852, to forestall a prosecution for heresy which seemed imminent, Bushnell's church withdrew from the consociation. On this subject, however, as on the subject of the Trinity, his later views show a movement toward traditional doctrine, in this case, toward an acceptance of Saint Anselm's insistence that God was affected ("satisfied") by Christ's atoning sacrifice.

In *Nature and the Supernatural* (1858), Bushnell set forth his defense of religion and the Christian faith in comprehensive terms, unfolding a total view of the cosmos. Although he guards himself from pantheism, protects the special historical significance of Christ (still with small stress on his humanity), and recognizes the reality of miracles and spiritual gifts in New Testament times and his own, in this work Bushnell exhibits his most radical innovation: his very untraditional use of the word "supernatural." For him this category in-

---

[10] Quoted in Williston Walker, *History of the Congregational Churches in the United States*, ACHS, vol. 3 (New York, 1894), p. 367.

cludes all that has life, every aspect of reality which is not caught up in the mechanical chain of physical cause and effect. In such a view, nature and supernature are consubstantial and interfused; man by definition participates in supernatural life, while (conversely) God is asserted to be immanent in nature. Taken together, nature and the supernatural constitute "the one system of God."

Much more could be said of Horace Bushnell, for his creative mind illuminated and enlivened many complex topics, almost always by the application of his basic views on the organic, corporate, or social nature of language, the Church, and man's everyday life in the family or the nation. The unity and coherence of his thought is one of the factors that contributed most to the steady expansion of his influence, which was large—larger perhaps than that of any liberal theologian in American religious history. On the "new" geology and Darwinian views of evolution as on women's rights and slavery he was conservative, and he aided the nativist cause. Yet his adoption of romantic notions of process and development facilitated an accommodation of evolutionary thought and opened into the Social Gospel of Washington Gladden. On two broad social issues, moreover, he was a pioneer. His essay "City Planning" (1864), as well as his active efforts in Hartford, make him "one of the most incisive proponents of the city that a national tradition may possess."[11] In his essay "Work and Play" and on many other occasions he also did much to alter older Puritan attitudes on leisure and recreation. Almost immediately his theory of language began to make its mark on liberal theologians; but he also won a conservative following, notably in the person of Edwards Amasa Park, the influential theologian at Andover Seminary. Park adopted Bushnell's paradoxical view of the "theology of the intellect and that of the feelings" with such vigor that he disrupted the cordial relations that had prevailed between Andover and the ultra-orthodox Presbyterians at Princeton Seminary. Bushnell's *Christian Nurture*, in due course, became a foundation stone of the religious education movement. His broad antisectarianism, his emphasis on religious experience, his flexible view of dogma, and his eloquent optimism all made him truly "the father of American religious liberalism." Through him the romantic movement made

11 Robert Wheeler, in an unpublished volume on the arts, leisure, and the city in later nineteenth-century America.

its entrance into theological seminaries and pulpits just as, in a more indirect though perhaps more pervasive way, Emerson brought it into the nation's schoolrooms and parlors.

THE BROADER REACH OF NEW ENGLAND ROMANTICISM

The foregoing section closed with references to the pervasive presence of Bushnell's and Emerson's thought in the churches, classrooms, and parlors of America—and one could say even more of their contribution to America's ways of understanding itself and expressing its ideals. But it would be grossly improper to speak of these two without considering the enormous influence of another group of New England writers, some of whom are seen as constituting the American Renaissance (Hawthorne, Melville, Thoreau, and Emily Dickinson, for example), others of whom are often demeaned as the "parlor poets" (Longfellow, Lowell, Whittier, Bryant, and Homes), and still others who are remembered as the country's "classic historians" (Bancroft, Ticknor, Prescott, Motley, Palfrey, and Parkman). To consider these writers in proportion to their religious influence would require several chapters, for nearly all of them were very widely read. Persons they created in their fictions—Evangeline, Captain Ahab, Hester Prynne—became part of American history. Millions of people memorized their verse and cherished their wisdom. But one must simply give thanks for the historians and critics of American literature who have dealt with their works intensively.

These writers spoke to the central religious questions in diverse ways and for diverse audiences. Longfellow and Whittier seem almost deliberately to have assumed roles as lay preachers to the American people. And if Holmes's bidding, "Build thee more stately mansions, O my soul," lacked depth, Hawthorne, Melville, and Dickinson brought reminders of tragedy, terror, and human perversity. Even the most superficial of them broadened the American's awareness of his heritage and heightened his appreciation of both nature and Western culture. All of them wove romantic themes and insights into the fabric of the American's religion and self-understanding.

38

CATHOLIC MOVEMENTS IN AMERICAN
PROTESTANTISM

The set of attitudes and convictions that give the romantic individual his characteristic identity in Western history was pervaded by religious concern. In this sense the Transcendentalists were true to their tradition. But the forms into which this concern was poured were almost infinitely diverse. Tridentine Catholicism, orthodox Protestantism, and rationalistic Free-masonry all felt its transforming influence. In Germany two roommates, both active in the early "romantic school," went their separate ways: Friedrich Schlegel to Metternich's Vienna as a Roman Catholic apologist for a restored empire, Friedrich Schleiermacher to the new University of Berlin as the liberal theologian of the Prussian Union. And in America, too, this variety was exhibited, Emerson moving to Self-Reliance, Brownson to Church-Reliance. That a return to historic traditionalism is a vital aspect of romanticism has already been illustrated in connections with the crisis in Lutheranism and the series of conversions to Roman Catholicism that included Brownson's. Two other American movements that exhibit this Catholic interest warrant particular attention, however: one of them is linked to an ancient university in England and the other to a new German seminary in Pennsylvania.

THE MERCERSBURG MOVEMENT

The most creative manifestation of the Catholic tendency in American Protestantism was the movement of theology and church reform which flowered for two or three decades after 1840 in the German Reformed church. This body had grown slowly but steadily since its separation from Dutch Reformed jurisdiction in 1793. At that time it had consisted of twenty-two ministers, 178 congregations, and about fifteen thousand members, all organized into one synod. In 1819 this synod divided itself into eight classes (a classis is the equivalent of a presbytery), and in 1824 the Ohio classis organized itself into an independent synod. By the time a seminary was founded the next year, the denomination was perhaps twice as large as 1793.[1] Its greatest strength remained in Pennsylvania though it was slowly spreading westward. Serious losses had been sustained due to the secession and continued proselytizing of two Methodistic groups (the United Brethren and the Evangelical Association) and to a schismatic "Free Synod," numbering about a hundred churches at the peak of its strength, which broke away in 1822 but returned in 1837. Further disruptions had occurred in 1823, when John Winebrenner, an extreme revivalist and antipedobaptist, withdrew to found the Church of God, a group that closely resembled the earlier Church of the Brethren. In each of these four instances the schismatics had protested against various types of church formalism in the name of revivalistic experientialism.

Since 1820 thoughtful leaders of the synod had been considering founding a seminary, and in 1825 a feeble school was opened in conjunction with Dickinson College, a Presbyterian institution at Carlisle, Pennsylvania. This school languished, however, and a move to York in 1829 did little to revive it. Stability was finally achieved through the receipt of large gifts of money and books from Germany, and in 1836 the seminary moved to Mercersburg, where it combined with Marshall College (founded as an academy in 1831). There among the lovely mountains of Franklin County, in the struggling educational center of a very small denomination, appeared one of the most imrpessive constellations of religious thinkers in American history.

The man chosen to guide the infant seminary during its

[1] Statistics for 1825, are very incomplete: but the "mother synod" included eighty-seven pastors and reported 23,291 communicants at that time (Joseph Henry Dubbs, *A History of the Reformed Church, German, in the United States,* ACHS, vol. 8 [New York, 1895], p. 336).

first precarious years was Lewis Mayer, a self-educated, somewhat rationalistically inclined pastor. But the first really eminent figure was Friedrich Augustus Rauch (1806–41), a German-born graduate of Heidelberg and student of Carl Daub, who first distinguished himself as a teacher in the academy and then served as president of Marshall College from 1836 until his untimely death. His *Psychology, or a View of the Human Soul, Including Anthropology* (1840) was meant to be the first of a series in which he planned to bring the results of conservative Hegelian thought to the attention of the American people. Its influence on a wide range of American thinkers was considerable.

Shortly before death ended Rauch's promising career, the synod in a most unusual course of action elected as his colleague John Williamson Nevin (1803–86), a Scotch-Irish Presbyterian, graduate of Union College and Princeton Seminary, sometime instructor at Princeton, and since 1828 professor of biblical literature at Western Theological Seminary (Presbyterian) near Pittsburgh. Although Nevin was known to be strongly attracted to the German Reformed church and its confessional standards, not even he could have foreseen the future that awaited him after accepting the call to Mercersburg in 1840. Before long, however, he was working out the implications of his decision. In 1841–42 he published a series of essays entitled *The History and Genius of the Heidelberg Catechism,* depicting that document as "the crown and glory of the whole Protestant Reformation." These essays mark the beginning of an American movement to recover the spirit and content of Reformation theology.

What this meant for the rampant New Measures of the revivalists who were making large inroads on German Reformed congregations as on other groups Nevin soon made clear with a forthright attack, *The Anxious Bench* (1843). A far more profound work, *The Mystical Presence; or a Vindication of the Reformed or Calvinistic Doctrine of the Holy Eucharist* (1846) further penetrated Reformation theology, charging that the sacramental practice of nearly all the "Calvinistic" churches of America had fallen from the views that reigned among the Reformed churches during the sixteenth century. Even in the Westminster formularies he found standards by which to weigh American practices and find them wanting. Singling out "modern Puritanism" as the chief villain, Nevin leveled serious criticisms at Jonathan Edwards and Timothy Dwight, and by no means spared American Episcopalians or even Professor Hodge and the Presbyterians in his indictment of spiritualistic, subjective, and memorial views of the Lord's Supper. In this controversy he provoked from Hodge the unexpected and damaging statement that on the Lord's Supper Calvin was virtually a "crypto-Lutheran," who had introduced "foreign elements" into Reformed sacramental theory in an effort to stand on better terms with the Lutherans. These compromises, said Hodge, had been expunged in the course of time as out of harmony with the true spirit of the Reformed churches.[2]

By this time Nevin was not alone on the Mercersburg faculty. Phillip Schaff (1819–93) had left a promising career at the University of Berlin to replace Rauch in 1843. Schaff was an historian and theologian who like Nevin drew much inspiration from Schleiermacher and from Augustus Neander. But his intellectual heritage was much richer than this. During his years in Germany he had been profoundly impressed by other movements of historical revival and churchly renewal. He had been confirmed after a conversion experience under Lutheran pietistic auspices, and he had felt the full impact of Hegelianizing church history and biblical study at Tübingen University, the more evangelical influence of Professor Tholuck at Halle, and the strict orthodoxy of Hengstenberg at Berlin. Gifted and amiable, Schaff was in a unique position to make an important mark on American scholarship and theology. In Nevin, moreover, he found an extraordinarily compatible colleague.

The Mercersburg professors articulated two fundamental convictions: (1) the person of Christ is the ultimate fact of Christianity, which makes Christology and the Incarnation the essential starting point of Christian theology; (2) the historical development of the Church reveals by its richness and diversity how the Christian faith fulfills and culminates every human or historical tendency, blessings which are lost when and if the Church becomes static and unresponsive to its history. Schaff drew out some of the implications of these atti-

[2] See James H. Nichols, ed., *The Mercersburg Theology*, pp. 245–59. The Heidelberg Catechism which Nevin championed was written by Zacharias Ursinus and Casper Olevianus and published for the Church of the Palatinate in 1563. Reflecting both Lutheran and Reformed influences, it has had a strong mediating effect in the Reformed tradition.

tudes in his inaugural address, *The Principle of Protestantism, as Related to the Present State of the Church.* Stressing the developmental principle, he shocked his audience by discussing the Reformation itself as a flowering of the best in medieval Catholicism. As expanded by Schaff and translated and published with an aggressive introduction by Nevin (1845), this work became one of the central manifestos of the Mercersburg Movement. Beside it, however, must be placed Schaff's very important work of 1846, *What Is Church History? A Vindication of the Idea of Historical Development.* Here he described the main schools of church history since the sixteenth century (orthodox-dogmatic, pietistic, and rationalistic) and placed himself with the new "historical school" that looked to Herder as its prophet, seeking not to impose present-day values on past events, but stressing the themes that unite past and present. The work is a milestone in the history of American historical theory.

These works on the nature and general tendency of church history set the keynote for the many scholarly articles and reviews that made the *Mercersburg Review,* at least during the years of Nevin's editorship (1849–53), one of the great theological journals of pre-Civil War America. In its pages one can trace the way in which their scholarship roved over the whole history of the Church, to greatest effect probably when they drew lessons from the early centuries and patristic writings, stressing subjects that Protestants had ignored, giving vitality to the doctrine of the Church as the body of Christ, and emphasizing its objective and visible character.

Because it was so forcefully advocated, the Mercersburg Movement provoked violent controversy from the very outset, but antagonisms were heightened during these years because immigration and other domestic anxieties were provoking America's endemic anti-Catholicism into overt acts of violence. In this atmosphere the charge of "Romanizing tendencies" was much more inflammatory than it otherwise might have been, and it was pressed with vigor by those who had been taught to regard Protestantism as purely a revolt from ecclesiastical authoritarianism and corruption. Other, complementary sources of unrest were the resurgent revivalism of the period and the practice of the mainstream denominations to carry out their programs through the great voluntary associations. The Mercersburg Theology tended to create difficulties for both simple anti-Catholicism and uncritical non-denominationalism. In an "era of strong feelings" ecclesiastical conflict was inevitable.

Dr. Joseph Berg, the influential pastor of the First Reformed Church of Philadelphia, threw down the gauntlet immediately after Schaff's inaugural address, calling the new professor before the synod for heresy. Schaff was exonerated —in large part because none of his assailants knew what the German Reformed standards were. In 1851 Berg left the denomination for the Dutch Reformed church and later became a professor at its seminary in New Brunswick, New Jersey. During the 1860s the promulgation of a new liturgy led to another round of bitter controversy, with Dr. J. H. A. Bomberger (1817–90), Berg's successor in the Philadelphia church, leading the anti-Mercersburg forces.

In his early days Bomberger had been something of an adherent of the Mercersburg view, but in Philadelphia he gradually exchanged these sympathies for a theological outlook that undergirded his active participation in the many interdenominational campaigns of the day. To gain institutional strength for his cause, he helped to found Ursinus College in Collegeville, Pennsylvania, and in 1870 he became its first president. As a professor of theology there, Bomberger was able to bring a more Reformation-oriented theology to the "Ursinus Movement" in the Reformed church and to avoid an open schism. In 1878 the General Synod formed a "peace commission" which gradually worked out the necessary liturgical and doctrinal compromises. The denomination continued to expand westward, and in 1907 the Ursinus School of Theology merged with the seminary which the Western Synod had founded in conjunction with Heidelberg College at Tiffin, Ohio, in 1850.

Continuous conflict within the denomination partly explains why Nevin shifted his responsibilities to the college after 1851—and why Schaff resigned from the seminary in 1863. During their years of collaboration, nevertheless, these two men put their mark unmistakably on the German Reformed church, and the attitudes they championed probably achieved widest acceptance in 1863, when the tercentenary of the Heidelberg Catechism was celebrated with a great convention in Philadelphia. Nevin and Schaff were largely responsible for the renewed interest in history shown even by their critics, for the awakening of sacramental concern in the church, for the return of their church to liturgical patterns of worship—unique among American Reformed bodies—and for a lively theological tradition carried into the twentieth century by a long succession of able thinkers.

Despite its profundity and intellectual force, the influence of the Mercersburg Theology was small. It ran counter to too many ingrained American attitudes. Yet it did reveal with startling clarity that the basically Puritan forms of church life which had become so pervasive in America could be subjected to searching criticism by men who still honored Calvin and treasured the Reformation's confessional heritage. And in a limited but important way, it did radiate beyond its proper denominational setting. American Lutherans were stimulated in their own process of theological and liturgical recovery not only by the scholarship of Nevin and Schaff, but by the Mercersburg insistence that American Protestantism would be impoverished and static until the great Reformed-Lutheran dialetic became an experienced theological reality. An Episcopal theologian like William Porcher DuBose of Sewanee was led to deepen his thinking about the Church. Bushnell was jogged by Rauch's *Psychology*. "Modern Puritans" and Presbyterians were forced to sharpen their historical instruments and reconsider the direction of their drift. And, of course, Schaff through his monumental labors as a church historian became an international figure, important also as an interpreter of America to the Germans and of Germany to the Americans.[3] Finally, the Mercersburg men—

[3] A church-historical work should not neglect to mention the immense contribution of Philip Schaff in this area. His *Apostolic Christianity* (1851) was followed by three more books delineating the history of the Church to 1073, and later by two volumes on the German and Swiss Reformations respectively. (In the later eight-volume set the two volumes on the Middle Ages were contributed by his son, David Schley Schaff.) Schaff edited the series of *Nicene and Post-Nicene Fathers* (28 vols., 1886–1905) and the first edition of *The Schaff-Herzog Encyclopedia of Religious Knowledge* (3 vols., 1884). He was instrumental in founding the American Society of Church History, and he arranged for the writing and publishing of the American Church History series (13 vols., 1893–97). He was also active in the field of exegesis (an American edition of Lange's *Bibelwerk*, 25 vols.), of hymnology (*Christ in Song*, 1868), of symbolics (the monumental and indispensable *Creeds of Christendom*, 3 vols., 1897), and biblical translation (playing a leading role in the preparation of the revised version of 1881–85). Schaff's *America* (1854) is a major inter-

especially the ex-Presbyterian Nevin, who for a while tee-
tered on the verge of Roman Catholicism—exposed a latent
dissatisfaction with Puritanic evangelicalism that was fairly
widespread. And because this yearning for more catholic
forms of church life had always led many to Anglicanism, it
was only natural that the Protestant Episcopal church itself
would become a major locus of these strenuous controversies.

THE CATHOLIC MOVEMENT IN THE PROTESTANT EPISCOPAL CHURCH

Simultaneously with the coming of Nevin and Schaff to
Mercersburg, the Episcopal church was also being agitated
by the "Church Question." In this case, too, the chief provocation came from theological stirrings abroad. The entire
Anglican communion, to be sure, had been in a state of unsettlement on the Catholic-Protestant issue for three full centuries, but special problems within the established Church of
England now precipitated a genuine crisis.

English Precursors

The Oxford Movement began, according to Cardinal Newman, with John Keble's sermon on the "National Apostasy"
on 14 July 1833, at a time when the church and state issue
was much agitated. Close on the heels of the Reform Bill of
1832, which had greatly extended the franchise, Parliament
had passed a bill to suppress ten redundant Anglican bishop-
rics in Ireland. Keble's sermon was a ringing call for an autonomous church, holy and catholic and worthy of its independence, a divine society sprung from heaven, not a
plaything of politicians or a casual appurtenance of the people. When very soon thereafter he and a small group of colleagues in Oriel College set out to end the national apostasy,
they stirred up the greatest storm the English church had experienced in almost two centuries.

---

pretation of the United States, as is his memorable essay on the
Civil War (1865). Besides this, he was extremely active in the
Sunday school movement, the Sabbath Committee, and the Evan-
gelical Alliance. After leaving Mercersburg he taught at Andover
Seminary for a time, but from 1870 until his death he taught at
Union Theological Seminary in New York.

Among the leaders of this group of determined reformers were the brilliant Richard Hurrell Froude (1803–36), John Henry Newman (1801–90), whose keen intellect made him the dominant figure in the movement until he became a Roman Catholic in 1845, and Edward Bouverie Pusey (1800–82), professor of Hebrew, who was destined to be the main stabilizing force in the loyally Anglican phase of the movement. They decided on an aggressive strategy of rallying all loyal churchmen, especially those with High Church sympathies, by a series of outspoken yet scholarly *Tracts for the Times*. In the very first tract, which appeared in September 1833, Newman put the matter squarely: *Choose* your side, since side you shortly must, with one or other party, even though you do nothing." What his readers were asked to choose was a "Catholic" view of the Church, its ministry, and its sacraments. His movement was not primarily ritualistic or liturgical, but theological. Its chief emphasis was upon the objective, visible Church and its means of grace as the very ship of salvation; and upon the importance of historic episcopate to a valid ministry. Inseparably connected with these concerns was an insistence upon a return to the faith of the ecumenical councils of the "undivided church" and of the early Fathers. Because the movement was by no means simply intellectual, they also called all men to a renewed sense of Christian discipline, worship, and holiness—here again with an emphasis on the older Catholic literature and practice rather than that which Puritanism had informed.

The Oxford reformers were heard. Ninety tracts running to six volumes appeared between 1833 and 1841. And men did choose sides, even within the movement. Some followed Keble with his desire for an uncontroversial restoration of Caroline ways; others followed Pusey's concept of the Church of England as a catholic *via media* between Protestantism and Romanism; and a third, more restless party, moved away from the very idea of an autonomous Church of England toward submission to the pope. When Newman turned down this last road and followed it to the end, "the nightmare which had oppressed Oxford for fifteen years" (his own phrase) came to an end. But an immense struggle within the Church of England had only begun. And by this time, too, the noise of battle was heard elsewhere, perhaps most influentially in an "ecclesiological" movement of another sort which had been launched in Oxford's great sister university.

The Cambridge Movement stemmed from the Ecclesiological (later the Camden) Society organized at Cambridge University in 1837 to promote the appreciation of Gothic church architecture and other "ecclesiastical antiquities," both by the study of actual English churches and by documentary research. Its leaders were clergymen and fellows of various colleges, most of whom sympathized with the Tractarians. John Mason Neale (1818–66), now most often remembered for his translations of medieval and ancient hymns, was a founder and leading spirit. Between 1841 and 1870 the society's journal, *The Ecclesiologist*, became an enormously influential arbiter of the "laws" of restoring, building, decorating, and furnishing churches. And in due course its fiercely dogmatic confidence in the inerrancy of the medieval church emerged as a powerful force throughout the Church of England. As the society came increasingly to take up the cause of the Ritualist movement, it also worked a large effect on liturgical practice, championing medieval ways and divorcing the Church from the modern world. Because its demands were more superficial and aesthetic, its influence probably exceeded that of the Tractarians.

Romanticism and the Catholic Spirit

Viewed in perspective, the Oxford and Cambridge movements exhibit important differences; yet because they are complementary the Catholic movement as a whole becomes more obviously a manifestation of the same romantic currents which were moving Brownson, Bushnell, and Nevin during the same years. The frequency with which romantic feeling awakened a nostalgia for Catholic tradition is a commonplace, illustrated over and over again at high intellectual levels as well as in changing popular tastes. In America one notes the Spanish and Catholic interests of Ticknor, Irving, Longfellow, Prescott, and Parkman. In England these signs were also evident. The rediscovery of monasticism documented in Samuel Roffey Maitland's great work *The Dark Ages* (1844) is an English parallel to the work of Count Montalembert in France, revealing how both nostalgia and intense historical interest underlay the entire movement. Nor was it to end with medievalism and Gothic revival. In John Henry Newman most notably, the principle of development became both an argument for the Roman church as the proper bearer of catholicity and a means of understanding the history of dogma. Newman's historical studies of medieval English saints, moreover, were an immediate prelude to his final decision to submit to Rome.

Another "romantic" tendency, separable from the Catholic movement but often related to it, was a revival of philosophic idealism which brought with it a recrudescence of mysticism and Platonic thought as well as an interest in metaphysics, a pursuit which British empiricism had tended so long to suppress. The future of the English church during the early nineteenth century was, according to one English historian, "largely being moulded, not at Lambeth and Bishopthorpe, but at Rydal Mount and Highgate, by men [Wordsworth and Coleridge] who little dreamed that they were doing anything of the kind."

The Rise of Parties in American Episcopalianism

The predicaments of Anglicanism in England and in America during the early nineteenth century were different in the extreme. In England the national church had retained all its prerogatives, vested interests, encumbrances, and temptations. In the United States, the Episcopal was one voluntary church among others. The Revolution had left it "a church in ruins," but by 1792 the structures necessary for self-preservation were reconstituted: a united episcopate, a prayer book, and a federal system of government. Yet Episcopal historians agree that vitality was lacking during the early nineteenth century. The bishops made almost no visitations; the clergy were few in number, lax in their duties, and uninspired in their preaching. Rationalism, indifference, and suspicion were rife. Deprived of their glebe lands, the country parishes of Virginia languished in desuetude. Bishop James Madison busied himself almost exclusively with the affairs of William and Mary College, of which he had been elected president in 1790. At the state convention of 1812 only thirteen priests appeared; and the following year, when the fervent Evangelical Richard C. Moore (1762–1841) was elected bishop to succeed Madison, there were only seven. Chief Justice Marshall thought that the church was on the road to extinction. In the Middle Colonies the desolation was even greater, for here the Loyalist exodus had been largest and the odium of Toryism strongest. Bishop Samuel Provoost

of New York had simply retired from his ecclesiastical vocation.

The most hopeful signs of life were visible where Anglicanism had never been taken for granted or publicly supported, as in New England—and particularly in Connecticut
where the High Church (almost Nonjuring) tradition of the
SPG and of Bishop Samuel Seabury still prevailed. In New
England the Episcopal church also benefited from the dissatisfactions that arose among members of the "orthodox" Congregational churches, due in some cases to a distaste for the
prevailing revivalism, in others to dislike for the doctrinal
and disciplinary rigor of reawakened Puritanism. In eastern
Massachusetts, where orthodoxy yielded to Unitarianism, the
antipathy for Anglican Loyalism gave way to desires for
social prestige, aesthetic satisfactions, and a church that
resisted Transcendental radicalism.

The Evangelicals

The year 1811 is often designated as the turning point in
American Episcopalian fortunes, because it marks the resurgence of both the Evangelical and High Church parties, neither of which at that time could look to more than a few
parish ministers for vigorous leadership. In that year Alexander Viets Griswold (1776–1843) was consecrated bishop
of the "Eastern District" comprising all of New England except Connecticut, an area with only sixteen priests and
twenty-two feeble parishes. Griswold experienced a religious
crisis at the time of his consecration and became thenceforth
a dynamic preacher of experiential Christianity and a ceaseless visitor of his vast diocese. By the time of his death he
had ordained well over a hundred priests and watched his
original jurisdiction develop into five dioceses with a hundred
parishes. In the meantime, Bishop Moore had similarly resus-
citated the church in Virginia. In the more sparsely settled
regions beyond the Appalachians, Bishop Philander Chase
(1775–1852) went his storm way, founding Kenyon College
in Ohio, Jubilee College in Illinois, laying Episcopal foundations in such remote places as Michigan and New Orleans,
and arousing concern for domestic missions.

As the years went by, these militant Evangelicals were
joined by other strong bishops, notably William Meade of
Virginia and Charles P. McIlvaine, who became Chase's

successor in Ohio after having virtually turned West Point into a conventicle during his term as chaplain. Evangelicals were never able to gain a decisive majority in the House of Bishops in the antebellum period; but after 1840, when nativism added to the growing fear of the Tractarian movement, they were spokesmen for the church's most swiftly growing parishes, strong supporters of Episcopal home missions, and prominent figures in many interdenominational voluntary associations.

In matters of doctrine they met the other denominations on their own ground. Sin, justification by faith, and the experience of regeneration held an important place in their teaching, as did a strong sense of scriptural authority and a disinclination for arguments from tradition. In matters of parish practice, they were less decorous than the High Church leaders. Extemporaneous prayer, special night meetings for devotional exercise, and occasional revivalism were permitted, sometimes even encouraged. The sacraments were not accorded great significance or efficacy. Holy Communion was administered quarterly and understood in the subjective manner of the "modern Puritanism" so roundly condemned by John W. Nevin. The Real Presence was not asserted, the word "altar" was avoided (as it is in the prayer book), and the *Agnus Dei* was not sung. Evangelicals also opposed the doctrine of baptismal regeneration. Deeply suspicious of Romish tendencies, their church buildings, like their public worship, displayed an almost puritanic austerity: the pulpit dominated the "Lord's Table," crosses and candles were rare, and even Gothic architecture was suspect until the romantic revival made it popular. On questions of church order, however, fears of sacredotalism and "priestcraft" did not exclude genuine gratitude for the heritage of the threefold ministry of deacons, priests, and bishops. Amid the perils of sectarianism and popery, they treasured the prayer book and the orderly worship it provided.

The High Churchmen

The High Church party could also look back to 1811 as memorable. In that year John Henry Hobart(1775–1830) became a bishop of New York, an office which enabled him to become perhaps the greatest religious leader the American Episcopal church ever produced. Hobart's background provides a cross-section of the British religious heritage in America. Of Puritan stock, his grandfather had become an Anglican after moving to Philadelphia. He himself was baptized, confirmed, ordained, and consecrated there at the hands of Bishop William White. Hobart was educated in the Calvinistic atmosphere of Princeton, where he imbibed an evangelical outlook which he never lost, while at the same time he sharpened his arguments for episcopacy. After parish experience in Hempstead, Long Island, and Trinity Church in New York City, he was made assistant bishop of New York in 1811 and bishop in 1816. For fourteen extraordinarily busy years he devoted himself to reconstituting his diocese, eschewing bigotry and arrogance in advancing the High Church cause. His preaching was accounted by many as unduly enthusiastic, even Methodistic. Yet Hobart demanded that his fellow Episcopalians claim their special heritage with resolution and confidence. To further this purpose he vigorously advocated a seminary, and later became a mainstay of the General Theological Seminary founded in 1817 and opened in New York City in 1819, where, as professor of pastoral theology and pulpit eloquence, he had great influence on a whole generation of students. In 1821 he also founded a college at Geneva, New York, which in 1860 changed its name to Hobart College. Episcopal tract, Sunday school, prayer book, and Bible societies owed much to his sponsorship and support, as did the *Churchman,* a journal which under the editorship of Samuel Seabury, Jr., became a semiofficial voice of the High Church party.

The centrality of Hobart's work in New York cannot be minimized; but the High Church movement was strongly fortified at many other important points. Theodore Dehon in South Carolina (consecrated 1823) were both of similar mind; and during the next decade their party was to be augmented by aggressive bishops in New York, New Jersey, and Pennsylvania. As a result, the High Church party, both North and South, became a strong factor in the church.

The Impact of the Tractarian Controversy

The Tractarians at first created almost no stir in the land of the Puritans. They seemed dry, academic, and devoted to the malaise of a foreign situation. Even John Keble's collection of devotional poetry, *The Christian Year,* though first published in 1827, did not appear in America until Bishop Doane's edition of 1834. Newman's *Essay on Justification by Faith* (1838) broke the calm. Then in the following year when publication of the *Tracts* was announced, a tart exchange ensued. The *Churchman* favored this publishing venture; the *Gambier Observer* and other Evangelical journals opposed it. Needless to say, the younger Seabury's rather naïve hope "that no controversy may be awakened by [the project]" was far from gratified. Bishops Doane of New Jersey, Onderdonk of New York, and John Henry Hopkins of Vermont all praised the purpose of the Oxford reformers. After the appearance of Tract Ninety, however, Hopkins published *Letters on the Novelties Which Disturb Our Peace* (1842). Bishop Eastburn of Massachusetts went farther, denouncing the *Tracts* as "work of Satan" concocted by advocates of the Dark Ages and "followers of the Scarlet Woman." Bishop McIlvaine published a major treatise in the same general vein.

During this conflict the General Seminary in New York became a decisive force. Built up under the watchful eyes of Bishops Hobart and Onderdonk, it had become the church's strongest seminary—and after 1839 it was considered, as one convert to Rome remembered, "a little Oxford on this side of the Atlantic . . . in a little suburban appendix to New York City, known as Chelsea." Here the *Lyra Apostolica* of Frederick Faber (who went over to Rome in 1845), the works of Newman, Keble, Pusey, and the rest inspired a new concern for the Church, its ministry, and its sacraments. Along with this concern, of course, came a growing sympathy for the Roman Catholic church and even for the Council of Trent, with the result that there was soon a considerable (but disproportionately publicized) number of converts from among the seminary students. In 1843 Bishop Onderdonk ordained Arthur Carey, who frankly confessed his Tridentine tendency. This act sent a shudder through the church. The next year a committee of bishops visited the institution, interrogated the faculty, and finally acquitted it. But shortly after his vindication, a secret society for the propagation of "Romish views" was uncovered, and two students were expelled, one of whom later became a Roman Catholic bishop. In the America of the 1830s and 1840s, the seminary faculty was obviously only one among many sources of Catholic tendency; but General Seminary was then, and continued to be, the leading American center of both the older High Church and the newer Tractarian attitudes.[4]

The typically post-Tractarian Catholic tendency was more explicitly institutionalized by four students of the seminary who enlisted for service on the frontier under Jackson Kemper, missionary bishop for the Northwest. Led by James Lloyd Breck, they founded Nashotah House in Wisconsin in 1841 as a semimonastic center for study, worship, and evangelism. Breck later moved on to Minnesota, where in 1857 he founded Seabury Divinity School in Faribault. On these foundations and others of similar nature arose a tradition of churchmanship to which the name "Anglo-Catholic" may be applied. This later movement bore little relation to the creative features of Cardinal Newman's thought, however, and it came to be increasingly recognizable for its emulation of nineteenth-century Roman Catholic practice, especially in the externals of architecture and worship. In America as in England a small Anglican monastic movement was initiated.

Catholic-Protestant Conflict

Works that drove so deeply into the heart of Evangelicalism as Newman's *Essay on Justification* and *Tract Ninety* (which sought to harmonize the Thirty-nine Articles with the decrees of Trent) inevitably drove men to more than a war of words. The Episcopal church did not simply grow quietly in two directions. Until the 1870s, moreover, the idea of comprehending these two deep-seated tendencies within a single church did not begin to win acceptance. Controversy quickly transformed the General Convention into a proving ground of party strength. Events of a formal nature, however, were neither momentous nor numerous. Official declarations of the General Convention of the House of Bishops were necessarily compromises, and they usually only reiterated a loyalty to the Bible, the prayer book, and the traditions of the Anglican communion. But a bitter party conflict did occasionally become public.

The most sensational developments had to do with the trials of the three most important leaders of the early Catholic movement, the Onderdonk brothers and Bishop Doane.

[4] The extent of Tractarian influence cannot be determined. Of the 1,976 men who were ordained between 1822 and 1855 at least 29 entered the Roman Catholic church. Some of them are discussed briefly on p. 658 in Volume 1.

Bishop Benjamin Tredwell Onderdonk of New York and his brother, Bishop Henry Ustick Onderdonk of Pennsylvania, were suspended from office in 1844, on charges of unchastity and unbecoming behavior in the former case, drunkenness and drug addiction in the latter. In 1852 Bishop George Washington Doane of New Jersey was much harassed, though never convicted, for questionable financial dealings in connection with the two schools he had attempted to found and foster. In all three cases the voting closely followed party lines, though the formal issues were hardly theological. Only slightly less sensational was the submission to Rome in 1852 of the bishop of North Carolina, Levi Silliman Ives, who had earlier encountered much criticism for his attempts to found a monastic community in his diocese.

As might be expected, the controversies provoked by the Oxford Movement were not resolved. Even in the Catholic party there was dissension, and a notable figure in the Nashotah tradition insinuated that the chief hindrance to the progress of Catholic principles in the Protestant Episcopal church came not from the Evangelicals but from the High Church party. It is true that this party showed little or no awareness of the special need for charity and moderation in a country where anti-Romanism was almost a birthright. At the same time, and possibly for the same reason, it had small evangelistic success despite its undeniable zeal.

THE MEMORIAL MOVEMENT

The closest these opposing forces came to a resolution of their contrarieties was probably in the person of the professed "Evangelical Catholic," William Augustus Muhlenberg (1796–1877) and the Memorial Movement which he sponsored. A great-grandson of the Lutheran patriarch, Henry M. Muhlenberg, he was baptized as a Lutheran but grew up in a thoroughly Anglicized Philadelphia family at a time when the Lutheran church was almost completely unresponsive to the religious needs of English-speaking people, especially in places where there were Episcopal churches. Young Muhlenberg was prepared for confirmation by the future missionary bishop, Jackson Kemper, and confirmed by Bishop William White of Philadelphia. After his ordination he served for a time in White's Philadelphia parish and in

Lancaster, Pennsylvania; then in 1826 he accepted the charge of Saint George's in Flushing, Long Island. Two years later he became occupied exclusively with the Flushing Institute, a Christian preparatory school for boys, where during his eighteen years of dedicated work he became an American parallel to the famous Dr. Thomas Arnold of Rugby. Muhlenberg thus made a very large contribution in an area which would become an important adjunct institution of the Episcopal church—the private preparatory school. His interest in deepening the liturgical and devotional life of the school, moreover, led him to an "Evangelical Catholic" outlook of considerable breadth. He thus became at the same time—ironically—a founder of the ritualist movement.

Although Tractarianism appealed to him for a time, Newman's essay *The Development of Christian Doctrine* (1845) deflected him in another direction. Later he described his final decision:

> I was far out on the bridge, so to speak, that crosses the gulf between us and Rome. I had passed through the mists of vulgar Protestant prejudices, when I saw before me "The Mystery of Abomination." I flew back, not to rest on the pier of High Churchism, from which this bridge of Puseyism springs, but on the solid rock of Evangelical truth, as republished by the Reformers.[5]

As it developed along these new lines, Muhlenberg's thought shows an interesting similarity to that of the Mercersburg reformers and their Lutheran parallels. But he was still, as he said, "in the Penumbra of Puseyism" when in 1846 he became rector of the new Church of the Holy Communion in New York City. Here in a Gothic structure designed by Richard Upjohn, complete with canopied altar, he introduced the weekly Eucharist, daily morning and evening prayer, antiphonal chanting, lighted candles, regular pews and kneelers in place of private box pews, and voluntary offerings instead of pew rents.[6] His church conducted a very successful apos-

[5] Anne Ayres, *The Life and Work of William Augustus Muhlenberg* (New York, 1880), p. 173.

[6] Pew rents, which involved a kind of property right, were passing out of use in this period. Abolishing them was also part of James Freeman Clarke's reform when he founded the Church of the Disciples in Boston (1841). Gothic church architecture was

tolate among the poor, aided by the sisterhood of the Holy Communion, A deaconess society founded in this parish. Muhlenberg himself also led in the founding of Saint Luke's Hospital. In 1851 his short-lived journal, *The Evangelical Catholic*, began to explicate the full meaning of his reforms.

In 1853 his famous "Memorial" to the House of Bishops inaugurated a movement to make the Protestant Episcopal church on the one hand something more than a "church . . . only for the rich," and on the other, an instrument of Christian unity in America. This document raised the question whether the church

> with only her present canonical means and appliances, her fixed and invariable modes of public worship, and her traditional customs and usages, is competent to the work of preaching and dispensing the Gospel to all sorts and conditions of men, and so adequate to do the work of the Lord in this land and in this age.

The Memorialists suggested the extension of orders to sincere men, Episcopalians or not, who for all their zeal to fulfill the Great Commission, "could not bring themselves to conform in all particulars to our prescriptions and customs, but yet [are] sound in the faith, and who, having the gifts of preachers and pastors, would be able ministers of the New Testament."[7] This would not only accomplish great good, but it would be an important step in cementing a central bond of unity among Protestant Christians. The church as a whole failed to accept the larger purpose of the Memorial, and its immediate result was little more than slightly larger liberties

---

then coming into vogue, stimulated by Augustus W. Pugin in England (who became a Roman Catholic in 1834) and the English-born American Episcopal Bishop John Henry Hopkins's *Essay on Gothic Architecture* (1836). Richard Upjohn furthered the cause with his designs for Trinity Church in New York City. A New York Ecclesiological Society, imitating the English one, was founded in 1846. With the founding of the American Institute of Architects in 1857, the age of dogmatic commitment to "correct" Gothic "principles" began to yield to more improvisational attitudes; yet the Gothic revival contributed powerfully to the rising concern for environmental factors and professional design in church architecture (see Phoebe B. Stanton, *The Gothic Revival and American Church Architecture 1840–1856*).

[7] Ayers, *Life of Muhlenberg*, pp. 263–67.

in the use of the prayer book; but some continuity could probably be traced between these efforts and the several major ecumenical proposals to be advanced by Episcopalians in the next century.

Muhlenberg exemplified the most productive forces in his church during the pre-Civil War years, especially those factors and appeals which account for the remarkable expansion of Episcopalianism in America's urban centers, where it grew by 46 percent in the decade before the war alone. He illustrates as well the process by which much of the Oxford Movement's advocacy gradually made a decisive mark on the faith and practices of the church, even upon those who were professedly evangelical. And finally, he serves as a reminder of the impact of romanticism. There were, to be sure, several other Episcopalians, like Caleb Sprague Henry (1804–84) of New York, who are remembered more explicitly as Christian Transcendentalists and as champions of Coleridge. Yet Muhlenberg adopted much of their spirit, including the proposal to make Anglicanism a means of uniting divided Christendom through a principle of comprehension.

The inner diversity of Episcopal life, however, must not obscure the fact that dissension and party rivalry were characteristic features of the church's history down to the 1870s when a minor schism in the church actually took place. The Reformed Episcopal Church was organized in 1873 in New York, after a secession led by George David Cummins, the assistant bishop of Kentucky. He was a strenuous Evangelical who desired more explicit checks on ritualism than the General Convention would enact. Because the convention of 1874 did take action against "Catholic" extremes, and also because the policy of allowing widely divergent views within the church began to gain increasing acceptance, the new church benefited from very few defections and grew very slowly, having but 8,700 members in 1954, and 7,085 in 1966.

In the mid-twentieth century the Protestant Episcopal church was still embroiled in questions of churchmanship. During this entire long period, however, there were many prominent Episcopalians, both lay and clerical, who adhered to neither of the two main parties that arose out of the Tractarian controversy. They were the moderates, the incipient Broad Churchmen. Pacific in spirit and socially concerned, they looked to Bishop William White of Philadelphia as a founding hero. Such men often embraced the new currents of Transcendental thought and the newer trends in historical biblical criticism. Tending toward theological liberalism, and after the Civil War drawing much sustenance from English Christian Socialists such as Maurice and Kingsley, this group would play a leading role in the American Social Gospel movement.

VI

Slavery and Expiation

In the late 'fifties the people of Illinois were being prepared for the new era by a series of scenes and incidents which nothing but the term "mystical" will fittingly describe.

Things came about not so much by preconceived method as by an impelling impulse. The appearance of *Uncle Tom's Cabin* was not a reason, but an illumination; the founding of the Republican party was not an act of political wirepulling, but an inspiration; the great religious revivals and the appearance of two comets were not regarded as coincidences, but accepted as signs of divine preparation and warning.

The settlers were hard at work with axe and plough; yet, in spite of material preoccupation, all felt the unnameable influence of unfolding destiny. The social cycle, which began with the Declaration of Independence, was drawing to a close, and during Buchanan's administration the collective consciousness of men—that wonderful prescience of the national soul—became aware of impending innovation and upheaval.

Francis Grierson, *The Valley of Shadows* (1909)

That Western Christendom turned Africa into a hunting ground for slaves rather than a field for philanthropic and missionary endeavor is one of the world's great tragedies. That the New World became the chief arena for the European exploitation of slave labor is an extension of the same tragedy. That the United States—the first new nation, the elect nation, the nation with the soul of a church, the great model of modern democracy—moved into the nineteenth century with one of the largest and cruelest of slave systems in its midst with full constitutional protection is surely one of the world's greatest ironies.

Because European racial stereotypes were well formed and New World slavery widely institutionalized by the time England's colonies were founded, it is not surprising that the irony of Christian slave-keeping was rarely perceived during the seventeenth century. With the revolutionary generation's failure to put slavery on the road to extinction except in the North, where it did not exist in the full sense, the irony deepened. That the antislavery movement did not become an outspoken and powerful movement until the 1830s is thus one of the facts most in need of explanation.

The rise of abolitionism marks the beginning of the nation's central experience, its first truly fundamental moral encounter. Not surprisingly, this encounter led by steady steps to the country's *Volkskrieg*, the war that ended the old federal Union and brought forth on this continent in 1865 a new nation not really dedicated to the proposition that all men are created equal, but nevertheless one that could be led to put the right words in the Constitution. The antislavery movement did survive the war, moreover, and it did press on for Reconstruction; but given the wartime destruction of the South and the seemingly endemic racism of the human race, not even the finest evangelical leadership—and General Howard at the head of the Freedman's Bureau was that—possessed the requisite attitudes and will. So the southern churches, like American society from the beginning, made discrimination and segregation the basic pattern.

Yet one thing was new: the black churches replaced the invisible institution of slavery days and became a major means of preserving and giving voice to America's largest underclass. To this whole encounter from the rise of the humanitarian crusades through the ordeal of war and the failures of Reconstruction, all of the chapters in Part VI are related. In this sense they culminate all that had gone before and lead into the fundamentally new religious situation that came to prevail in the Gilded Age.

39

THE HIGH TIDE OF HUMANITARIAN REFORM

Nothing in America was safe from the reformer's burning gaze during the first half of the nineteenth century. Everything from diet and dress to the social structure itself—even the family and motherhood—were up for critical review, while panaceas and nostrums ranged from graham crackers and bloomers to free love and socialism. Crackpots and dreamers, sober philosophers and millennial prophets had their moment if not their day. In 1840 the Chardon Street Chapel of Boston was host to a convention of nothing less than the "Friends of Universal Reform," whose chairman was Bronson Alcott. By this time the great American epoch of political theory and constitution making was becoming legend. The victory at New Oreans had been won in 1815, and out of the new nation's exuberant self-assurance came a great surge of nationalism that made itself heard and felt over the cracker barrels in crossroads stores as well as in European halls of state. Men as sharply at odds as John Quincy Adams and Andrew Jackson heralded the new era. The old Federalist party yielded to National Republicanism. The Age of the Common Man was at hand. The future beckoned. It was, as Lewis Mumford said, America's "Golden Day." Why should not social reform and utopianism have their inning?

America did hear a new and authentic message in those antebellum years. The historical roots of humanitarian reform lay, first of all, in the Puritan's basic confidence that the world could be constrained and re-formed in accordance with God's revealed will. Revivalism intensified the nation's sense of millennial expectancy, and a doctrine of "disinterested benevolence" of Edwardsean lineage informed the Second

Awakening's manifold activities, giving rise to the evangelical vision of a great Christian republic stretching westward beyond the Appalachians as a beacon and example for the whole world.

Enlightened rationalism, so inescapably associated with the nation's Founding Fathers, was another source of the prevailing optimism and the idea of progress which accompanied it. Because the War for Independence had conferred something like dogmatic status upon this sort of moral idealism, patriotic doctrines about man and history became stock components of Protestant preaching. Among the Unitarians philanthropic concerns were even more emphatically the order of the day. A "perfectibilitarian" like Channing praised the "devotion to progress" arising among his contemporaries and could count a score of reformers among his spiritual children. Transcendentalism, too, was in Channing's lineage. When Octavius Brooks Frothingham spoke of his own conversion to the new spiritual philosophy of Concord, he literally defined the movement in moral-reformist terms. "Not only was religion brought face to face with ethics, but it was identified with ethics."[1] Transcendental votaries in succeeding years would give fervent support to a dozen reform causes. Evangelicals, in the meantime, by no means yielded up perfectionism to Unitarians and Transcendentalists: for a century this doctrine had been a distinctive feature of Wesleyan preaching, and during the great revival of the 1830s it spread far beyond Methodism. After 1835 Finney and his following took up the same demand for holiness, calling for socially relevant Christian commitment as the proper sequel to conversion.

Timothy Smith's sweeping statement is essentially accurate:

> The Calvinist idea of foreordination, rejected as far as it concerned individuals, was now transferred to a grander object—the manifest destiny of a Christianized America. Men in all walks of life believed that the sovereign Holy Spirit was endowing the nation with resources sufficient to convert and civilize the globe, to purge human society of all its evils, and to usher in Christ's reign on earth. Religious doctrines which Paine, in his book *The Age of*

[1] Octavius Brooks Frothingham, *Recollections and Impressions, 1822–1890* (New York, 1891), p. 50.

Reason, had discarded as the tattered vestment of an outworn aristocracy, became the wedding garb of a democratized church, bent on preparing men and institutions for a kind of proletarian marriage supper of the Lamb.[2]

In the impetus which this gave to temperance, antislavery, and other moral crusades, the evangelical foundations for the social gospel of a later day were laid. Even when sectional tensions led many groups and individuals to avoid divisive issues, the seeds of social Christianity were being sown.

PROBLEMS OF INDUSTRIALIZATION AND URBANIZATION

A distinctively new arena for early social reformism was provided by the poor and unfortunate, especially as they came to be clustered in the nation's cities. Urban poverty was a result of the steady growth of American industrialism after 1785 and, more markedly, after the War of 1812. Newly invented machines were rendering obsolete the old patriarchal economy in which each family supplied its own needs by handicraft and homespun, while the growth of the transportation system made possible steadily expanding markets. Between 1810 and 1860 American consumption of iron quintupled. As the overwhelmingly agricultural cast of American society began slowly to change, it changed most rapidly in New England, where farming had always been a struggle and where water power and the concentration of capital encouraged the rapid rise of factories. The result was a new kind of city, in which low wages, exhausting hours, and crowded living conditions became everyday facts of life. Before the "ten-hour campaign" swept the country in 1835, most laborers worked fourteen hours a day for an average of six dollars a week, while control of the factories and corporations gravitated to a small class of financiers. Women and children under twelve years of age worked the same long hours in the factories, and frequently whole families could be found in a single employ, though even this rarely secured enough income to maintain a decent level of existence. In 1829, the Boston Prison Discipline Society estimated that

2 Timothy L. Smith, *Revivalism and Social Reform in Mid-Nineteenth-Century America,* p. 7.

seventy-five thousand delinquent debtors, many of them owing only petty sums, were being held on this charge in unsanitary, crowded jails. Needless to say, the situation presented a compelling challenge to the country's idealists.

Caring for the poor and unfortunate had immemorially been the task of the church, but in America institutionalized responses to such needs had been few and weak. The pioneer hero of active church concern is the Boston Unitarian minister Joseph Tuckerman (1778–1840), described by his chief biographer (a Roman Catholic) as a veritable American Saint Vincent de Paul. A Harvard graduate and close friend of William Ellery Channing, Tuckerman moved in 1826 from his rural parish of Chelsea to become the first "minister-at-large" to serve Boston under the sponsorship of the Benevolent Fraternity of Churches, a Unitarian organization formed for the purpose of bringing a Christian ministry and charitable aid to the city's poor. During a decade of intense activity, Tuckerman became an effective social welfare worker, a crusader for his cause, and an influential theorist. Strong in his conviction that Christianity was a social principle and not merely a private pact with God, he became the first in a long and distinguished line of American apostles of the "Social Gospel." Not for half a century would his work be taken up in earnest by the American churches, but the concern was continual and rising.

The most remarkable living symbol of the era's rising concern for the underpaid and overworked working classes was that dynamic pilgrim and agitator, Orestes Brownson. Beginning his religious pilgrimage in Stockbridge, Vermont, and proceeding through the series of theological phases described in an earlier chapter, Brownson absorbed the socialistic sentiments of Robert Dale Owen, helped to form the Workingman's party in New York City, and by 1836, having come under the influence of Channing and then of Emerson, was ministering in Boston to his own Society for Christian Union and Progress. Perhaps no American before the Civil War testified more strenuously to the significant relationship between religion and social problems. Upon entering the Roman Catholic church in 1844, however, he began a long second career in which the problems of theology and Catholic apologetics became his primary concern.

THE REFORM CAMPAIGNS

The dominant tendency of early nineteenth-century reformism was not toward the creation of a new society by total revolution (except insofar as American democracy and Jacksonianism were "revolutions") nor primarily toward founding islands of communitarian perfection (though these were founded by the dozen). Following patterns set in England and in this country during the Second Great Awakening, most reformers dedicated themselves to specific campaigns. This did not prevent a given reformer from carrying several portfolios, and some men, like Lyman Beecher and Theodore Parker, put no limits on their interests. Though the diversified humanitarian movement was not nearly so closely linked to churches and church organizations as, say, the temperance crusade, church leaders of one sort or another frequently provided the initial impulse, ministers and dedicated laymen were often active agitators, and nearly all the campaigns were pervaded by appeals to "Christian principles." If the collective conscience of evangelical America is left out, the movement as a whole is incomprehensible.

Education

The most pervasive of all the crusades was that in behalf of education. Not always did it create the excitement of the more dramatic cases; but its results, if often prosaic, were far-reaching. Its vision of a better day rested on the conviction that the extension of knowledge would dissipate human misery. In this principle converged the Enlightenment ideals of Jefferson, founder of the University of Virginia, and the rationale of Harvard's Puritan founders. Idealists refused to be complacent in the fact that already America's high rate of literacy was probably unequaled anywhere in the world. More and better education was the cry. Some wanted it more Christian, others wanted it more secular; but the demand was sustained, and the hopes that rode upon it were high. The Reverend Samuel R. Hall of Concord, Vermont, founded and conducted a normal school, produced texts for most of the secondary curriculum, and worked steadily for better school laws. Graduates of Princeton and Yale flowed westward and southward in a steady stream, founding academies, colleges, seminaries, and universities, and staffing their faculties. This half-century was the great age of the church college, an age in fact when these church-related institutions virtually constituted American higher education.[3] Some state universities were in existence, to be sure, and more were being founded; but in view of the country's dominant Protestant ethos, and the fact that the clergy was still the leading intellectual class, these universities were rarely secular in spirit. A rather different approach was that of Josiah Holbrook, the enterprising founder of an "Agricultural Seminary" at Derby, Connecticut, who became an itinerant lecturer on scientific subjects in 1826. His mission expanded into an association of adults for mutual education which, as the American Lyceum, was imitated by many similar programs, all of which used the lecture platform to appease the appetite of a nation hungry for enlightenment.

Amid all this diversified interest, Horace Mann (1796–1859) stands out clearly as the age's most effective educational crusader as well as its outstanding philosopher of education. Like so many of his fellow reformers, Mann's family background included a strict orthodox upbringing. He grew up in the parish of Nathanael Emmons at Franklin, Massachusetts, but far from becoming a New Divinity man, he moved steadily during the course of his life toward a liberal form of Unitarianism. Dr. Channing's fervent exclamation when Mann took up his ultimate career as secretary of the Massachusetts Board of Education in 1837 reflected their common ideal: "If we can but turn the wonderful energy of this people into right channels, what a new heaven and earth might be realized among us!" Posterity was his client. His great *Annual Reports* (1837–48), no less than his creation of a public school system that became a model for many parts of the world, reflected this optimism and conveyed it to orthodox and liberal alike as a fundamental element of the American dream. Mann thus received, transmuted, and pressed on an unquestioning faith (too unquestioning perhaps) in the wonder-working power of the schoolroom.

[3] Of all the colleges and universities founded before 1860, 182, or only about 20 percent, survive. Of these 9 were founded before 1780, 25 before 1799, and 49 before 1820. About 90 percent of the pre-Civil War college presidents were clergymen.

Dogmatic Puritanism was banished from Mann's mind, and the public education system he envisioned naturally made no place for it. When his famous *Seventh Annual Report* made this position explicit, it aroused orthodox wrath and endangered his project. But the determination to remake the world survived, as did the conviction that education, however nonsectarian, must instill the historic Protestant virtues. No humanitarian crusader reveals more clearly than Mann how the reform impulse sprang from and reflected back the evangelical conscience—including both its idealism and its cultural narrowness. In this respect Mann's great contemporary William H. McGuffley (1800–73) forged an even closer bond between Protestant virtues, national ideals, and literary values. Before the century's end over 120 million copies of his graded *Eclectic Readers* had helped to shape the American mind. Not far behind McGuffey's *Readers* in influence were the enormously popular works of instruction written by two New England ministers: Samuel G. Goodrich (1793–1860), known to several generations for his hundred or more "Peter Parley" books; and the prolific Jacob Abbott, whose literary creations "Rollo" and "Marco Paul" instructed American children in almost everything they could or ought to be curious about. The basic outlook and presuppositions of these dedicated men pervaded the nation's schools until well into the twentieth century, when a greater awareness of the country's pluralism required adjustments which are still in the process of being made.

Women's Rights

Rivaling education in its basic significance for the spirit and structure of American society was the crusade to gain fuller rights for women and to give them a larger role in the country's life. Unlike educational reform, however, this campaign encountered considerable resistance. The opposition can be traced in part to the Reformation's critique of monasticism and its concomitant exaltation of the family. Woman's place was in the home. Protestant churches also tended toward a strict interpretation of Saint Paul's demand that women be silent (I Cor. 14:34), and women lost their opportunity to be heard in the churches—except among the Quakers. During the eighteenth century and the early years of the Republic, the general legal status of women noticeably declined, in part, it has been suggested, as the price of their becoming "ladies." In the nineteenth century the time had come for feminist reform.

Margaret Fuller's *Woman in the Nineteenth Century* (1845) was the first full philosophic and historical statement of feminism by an American; but important steps had been taken long before that. One breakthrough resulted from the revivals, especially in the West, where Saint Paul's stricture was ignored, notably by Charles G. Finney's new measures. Another line of advance led through the many evangelical voluntary associations growing out of the Second Awakening. In these efforts the support of local women's groups came gradually to be almost essential. Various professions offered limited opportunities which a growing number of determined women grasped. In 1850 Oberlin, the country's first coeducational college, even granted a theological degree to a woman, Antoinette Brown, who after many difficulties was ordained three years later. A few daring pioneers broke into the medical profession.

But the chief avenue of advance was in education, where women served increasingly as teachers and headmistresses. Two women, each a feminist crusader in her own way, gained special renown for their lasting contributions in this field. Emma Willard (1787–1870), aided by her husband, spent a lifetime as lecturer, poet, teacher, textbook writer, and headmistress. Though "Rocked in the Cradle of the Deep" is her best-known production, she is more worthily remembered for the great "Female Seminary" in Troy, New York, which she founded in 1821. Mary Lyon (1797–1849) led a very similar life, culminating it with the founding of Mount Holyoke College for women in 1836–37. Like Mrs. Willard's seminary, it answered an immense need for the advanced schooling of girls and the training of future teachers. With greater intensity than at most such schools, the activities and ethos at Mount Holyoke were focused on the hope that every student would be brought to a personal knowledge of Jesus Christ. Emily Dickinson became one of the school's most celebrated failures in this regard.

Other significant contributions to the education of women were made by Matthew Vassar, a devout Baptist brewery owner who in 1861 provided an endowment of almost unprecedented size for the first true liberal arts college for women in America. Another subtle but effective feminist, who also did much to advance the work of women's education, was Sarah Hale, a sometime novelist, pious and practical, who for nearly a half-century held a position of unique influence as editor first of the *Ladies' Magazine* and then of Louis A. Godey's immensely successful *Lady's Book.*

The greatest, or at least the most ostentatious, point of feminist advance in the antebellum period was the result of women's involvement in the temperance movement, and then with greater force in the antislavery crusade. Not only did their presence gain attention in causes so notorious, but the antislavery movement itself became deeply involved in the struggle for women's rights. William Lloyd Garrison's insistence on this principle, when combined with other radical demands, led in 1840 to a schism in the abolitionist movement. Such activities did not prevent the organization of a separate feminist movement, however; and in 1848 the inevitable campaign was launched at a Woman's Rights Convention held in the home of Elizabeth Cady Stanton of Seneca Falls, New York. Though its progress before the war was not sensational, more liberal laws were passed in many states and women moved into far more prominent positions in American public life.

Prisons and Hospitals

The Reverend Louis Dwight became the leader of still another humanitarian cause when his work as an agent for the American Bible Society opened his eyes to the shocking conditions in the prisons he visited. Returning to Boston, Dwight became the chief inspiration and in due course the secretary of the Boston Prison Discipline Society. Through his influence the Auburn System (so called because of its initiation at Auburn, New York, in 1824) of cell blocks and group labor began to replace the Pennsylvania System of solitary confinement and solitary labor, in time providing the United States with prisons that were models for the whole world to observe. Alexis de Tocqueville, touring America in 1831, was impressed by the success of the Reverend E. M. P. Wells, the director of Boston's house of correction for children, in making his prison both educational and reformatory.

The most widely influential champaign for the proper hospitalization and care of the mentally ill was that of the indefatigable Dorothea Dix (1802–87), a remarkable spinster

schoolmistress. Channing moderated her strict Puritan upbringing and aroused in her (as in so many others) a moral
passion. With the aid of other reformers, she provoked the
Massachusetts legislature in 1843 to improve and expand the
Worcester hospital for the insane. Among her supporters in
these efforts were Samuel Gridley Howe, already famous for
his work in educating the blind, and Horace Mann. It was
now left for Dr. Samuel B. Woodward (1787–1850) to make
Worcester world-famous for humane treatment and for its
successful cures. Miss Dix's vigorous ministry of compassion
also contributed directly to increased national concern for the
founding or improvement of mental hospitals.

The Peace Crusade

Most idealistic of all the reform campaigns was that which
took its inspiration from the ancient dream of the prophet
Micah—that men would beat their swords into ploughshares
and their spears into pruning hooks. As in so many other
crusades, the Society of Friends was at the root of the movement, articulating the doctrine of Christian pacifism. But it
was not only among Quakers such as Penn, Woolman, and
Benezet that the movement found its pioneers. The optimism
of the Enlightenment influenced Benjamin Rush, Benjamin
Franklin, and many others who saw little glory or value in
war despite their involvement in the American Revolution. In
William Ellery Channing the same streams of Christian moralism and rationalistic optimism ran together, as they did
even more effectively in *A Solemn Review of the Custom of
War,* written by the Reverend Noah Worcester in 1814.

The Massachusetts Peace Society was organized in Channing's own home in 1815, with Worcester as editor of its
journal. Within a few years it had a number of local and state
branches. But what stirred this organization into more than
fitful activity was the organizing ability of two wealthy laymen, William Ladd of New Hampshire, a convert of Channing and Worcester, and David Low Dodge, who had independently organized a society in New York City. Through
their joint efforts the American Peace Society was formed in
1828 along familiar lines. For a decade and more the society
stimulated discussion of the evils of war and the possibilities
of a "Congress of Nations" to avert it.

Soon, however, the Peace Society began to have battles of

its own due to the pugnacious pacifists that it had won to its banner—notably William Lloyd Garrison, through whose influence it became involved in both the antislavery crusade and the struggle for women's rights. A further drift to radical nonresistance, pacifism, and anarchism took place with the accession of three communitarians: John Humphrey Noyes, Adin Ballou, and Bronson Alcott. In 1838 these forces routed the old leadership of the society and formed a new organization, the New England Nonresistance Society.

In 1846 still another organization, international in scope, was founded by Elihu Burritt, "the learned blacksmith" of Natick, Massachusetts. This League of Universal Brotherhood aroused considerable popular strength due to Burritt's tireless zeal in lecturing, writing, and organizing. By making a personal pacifist pledge a chief element of its program, it won a large and dedicated following. Yet both the motives and the effects of the peace movement were ambiguous. Before and during the Mexican War, for example, many prominent figures—James Russell Lowell and Charles Sumner, for example—voiced loud demands for peace, but such actions cannot be explained as simple devotion to pacifism. Sectional controversy was becoming the master fact of the times, and the peace movement's chief historical significance may well be its divisive role in the antislavery movement. In that irony, moreover, the tragic element of America's "golden day" stands revealed.

No one ever stated the hopes of the age with greater confidence and fervor than did that father of many reformers and crusaders, Lyman Beecher, in his sermon of 22 December 1827:

> The history of the world is the history of human nature in ruins. . . . It is equally manifest that this unhappy condition of our race has not been the result of physical necessity, but of moral causes. The earth is as capable of sustaining a happy as a miserable population. . . . A voice from heaven announces the approach of help from above. "He that sitteth upon the throne saith, Behold I make all things new." [Rev. 21:5] The renovation here announced is a moral renovation which shall change the character and condition of men. . . . It shall bring down the mountains, and exalt the valleys; it shall send liberty and equality to all the dwellings of men. Nor shall it stop at the fireside, or

exhaust its blessings in temporal mercies; it shall enter the hidden man of the heart, and there destroy the power which has blasted human hopes, and baffled human efforts. . . .

I shall submit to your consideration . . . that our nation has been raised up by Providence to exert an efficient instrumentality in this work of moral renovation. . . . The origin and history of our nation are indicative of some great design to be accomplished by it. . . . Who can doubt that the spark which our forefathers struck will yet enlighten this entire continent? But when the light of such a hemisphere shall go up to heaven, it will throw its beams beyond the waves; . . . it will awaken desire, and hope, and effort, and produce revolutions and overturnings, until the world is free. . . .

Floods have been poured upon the rising flame, but they can no more extinguish it than they can extinguish the fires of Aetna. Still it burns, and still the mountain heaves and murmurs; and soon it will explode, with voices, and thunderings, and great earthquakes. And then will the trumpet of jubilee sound, and earth's debased millions will leap from the dust, and shake off their chains, and cry, "Hosanna to the Son of David."[4]

The apocalyptic tone and the catastrophic images, as it happened, would receive their partial validation in an unsuspected way. The Civil War would blot the clean white page which the reformers had reserved for future glories. The country faced a problem that humanitarian campaigns and vest-packet utopias could not solve. The greatest moral crusade remained. The problem, of course, was slavery. When Horace Mann was appointed in 1848 to the seat of the late John Quincy Adams in Congress, he soon decided that a national role in educational reform was no longer open to him. Other business, ominous and utterly inescapable, was at hand. A whole nation gradually came to the same realization.

[4] "The Memory of Our Fathers," in Beecher's *Works*, 4 vols. (Boston, 1852), 1:315–17, 324–28.

40

SLAVERY, DISUNION, AND THE CHURCHES

On 22 September 1862, with General Lee's army in at least temporary retreat, Abraham Lincoln announced to his cabinet that, in accordance with a solemn vow made before God on the eve of the battle of Antietam, he would issue an emancipation proclamation. Only twenty-eight years earlier, in October 1835, William Lloyd Garrison, the abolitionist leader, had been dragged through the streets of Boston with a rope around his body—in Massachusetts, the first of the independent colonies to outlaw slavery. Seventeen years before Garrison was hog-tied, the General Assembly of the undivided Presbyterian church had unanimously adopted a manifesto that declared the institution of slavery "utterly inconsistent with the law of God."[1] In 1861 the formal *Address* of the newly constituted Presbyterian Church of the C.S.A. declared in equally positive terms that "We have no right, as a Church, to enjoin [slavery] as a duty, or to condemn it as a sin." Such was the jagged course of events—paradoxical, ironic, tragic—that brought the American people through the most traumatic experience of its history. Between the beginning and the end a titanic drama was played out on a continental stage. Out of the culminating test of arms emerged a new nation, purged and scarred, deprived of innocence, and

[1] This resolution of the General Assembly is often quoted out of context. It was in fact a full-scale compromise that conceded "hasty emancipation to be a greater curse" than slavery. Moreover, the same judicatory in the same 1818 meeting also voted to uphold the Lexington Presbytery (Kentucky) in its deposition of the Reverend George Bourne from the ministry for his antislavery views. But this only heightens the irony (see Andrew E. Murray, *Presbyterians and the Negro*, pp. 20–28).

facing a task of "reconstruction" which after a whole century's passage would still be uncompleted. This ordeal is the crucial experience of the nation—and, not less, of its churches. We do well, therefore, to explain this *crux*, this Cross.

There is a reason why. The Civil War has become enmeshed in the national self-consciousness not simply because of its enormous cost in carnage and death, but because it exposed a fundamental moral commitment which the nation has never been able to discharge. It tested whether Daniel Webster's vision of "liberty and union, now and forever, one and inseparable" was an oratorical ploy or a meaningful hope. In this sense the great sectional cataclysm was a "moral" war. It was not "moral" because one side was good and the other evil, nor because purity of motive was more pronounced on one side than on the other. It was a moral war because it sprang from a moral impasse on issues which Americans in the mid-nineteenth century could no longer avoid or escape. Had there been no slavery, there would have been no war. Had there been no moral condemnation of slavery, there would have been no war. Yet slavery had become a massive American institution, and the South, given its racial predicament, could not entertain emancipation: the peculiar institution was worth disunion. By 1860, on the other hand, the nation's always uneasy conscience had been aroused, and in the North it had been shaped into a crusade which could not accept either indefinitely continued compromise or peaceable secession. So war came. Its origins go back at least to Europe's almost simultaneous discovery of the African Gold Coast and the New World. Its aftermath still constitutes the country's chief moral challenge. Nowhere in Christendom was Negro slavery more heavily institutionalized, nowhere was the disparity between ideals and actuality so stark, nowhere were the churches more deeply implicated. Few subjects, if any, are so fundamental to American religious history.

The year 1619 has fateful significance, for it marked the institution of representative government, the introduction of tobacco culture, and the beginning of black servitude in white America. Slavery soon became an accepted fact of life in Virginia, as it had long since been in New Spain, and as in a few decades it would become in the other colonies, including those of the North.[2] Puritan and Yankee shipowners found equally strong economic grounds for cutting themselves in on the profits of the slave trade, a business far more inhumane than slaveholding. The complicity of the whole nation—in attitude and act—has been general from the beginnings to the present.

Yet very early there were also protests and denunciations. Perhaps the earliest in British America was a petition published in Pennsylvania in 1688 by Francis Daniel Pastorius. In 1700 Judge Samuel Sewall of Boston published his *Selling of Joseph*. The Quakers made similar testimonies during these years though their relapse in New Jersey and elsewhere led to the publication of John Woolman's *Considerations on the Keeping of Negroes* in 1754. More outspoken and effective, however, was the Quaker Anthony Benezet, who in 1776 led the Society of Friends to expel its slaveholding members. And in 1775 a group of Philadelphia Quakers organized the country's and possibly the world's first antislavery society. During the next two decades similar organizations were formed in many states, including Maryland (1790), Virginia (1791), and Delaware (1794). John Wesley took over Benezet's view, and the Christmas Conference of 1784, from which American Methodism dates its formal origins, instituted measures to exclude slaveowners or dealers from membership. Later, where slavery took institutional root, the discipline was progressively relaxed in a pattern visible also among the Baptists, who have a similar history of forceful statements in the revolutionary period, followed by a steady accommodation of Southern practice. In New England the antislavery standard was also raised in the 1770s, most significantly by two strict Edwardsean divines, Jonathan Edwards, Jr., in New Haven, and Samuel Hopkins in Newport.

For the revolutionary generation antislavery questions were subordinate to other concerns, and the federal Constitution came to terms with the institution. Widespread moral uneasiness was exhibited, however, in the Constitution's pro-

2 Slave labor was used to some extent in every colony. In 1775 the total slave population in the seven Northern colonies exceeded forty thousand. In East Jersey slaves made up 12 percent of the population, in Rhode Island, 6 percent (see Arthur Zilversmit, *The First Emancipation: The Abolition of Slavery in the North*, pp. 4–7).

visions to end the slave trade, in the prohibition of slavery in the Northwest Ordinance of 1787, and in the fact that nearly every northern state had by this time abolished or provided for the gradual abolition of slavery. As the country matured, the questioning, lamentation, and protest continued, nurtured by Christian conviction and patriotic idealism. Objections were clearly spoken even in the South, where the institution was firmly entrenched. Between 1808 and 1831, in fact, Southerners were more important than Northerners in the antislavery movement.

In the midst of this state of affairs, the American Colonization Society was organized in 1817 with the support of many distinguished political leaders, Southerners John Marshall, James Monroe, and Henry Clay among them. Its purpose was to raise funds to remunerate slave owners and send free Negroes back to Africa. A paper was published and a farflung organization established. The response was wide; at one time over two hundred local auxiliaries were in existence with ministers and churches playing a prominent role. Yet however well-intentioned, the movement was a failure. It actually diverted criticism of slavery, accepted fully the notion of Negro inferiority, and became chiefly a means of ridding the country of free blacks. Even in its practical workings failure stood out everywhere: the rate of manumission was almost unaffected (only two hundred slaves were freed and transported in the first decade; possibly four thousand by 1860), while Liberia became anything but a radiating center of Christianity in Africa. The society in fact did little more than sow moral confusion; in Dwight L. Dumond's words, "it was a rationalization for the lazy intellect, a sedative for the guilty conscience, a refuge for the politician and the professional man."[3] Yet some of the greatest antislavery leaders in the country were associated with it: Benjamin Lundy, Lewis Tappan, Gerrit Smith, James G. Birney, Theodore D. Weld, Elizur Wright, and many others. The society served as an awakening force and as a transitional organization.

But in the 1830s there occurred a remarkable change, almost a revolution, in the nation's attitude toward the slavery in its midst. The transition which took place in this decade can only be compared to the transformation in American

[3] Dwight L. Dumond, *The Anti-Slavery Origins of the Civil War in the United States,* p. 17.

race relations during the 1960s. Inert pronouncements like that of the Presbyterians in 1818 or those of the many Southern antislavery organizations became acutely relevant. Slumbering acceptances awoke as existential realities; silence, indecision, or mere lip service became increasingly rare, both North and South.

THE NORTHERN REVOLUTION

In the North, where slavery was nonexistent, the experience of William Lloyd Garrison (1805–79) is representative. After a childhood filled with much hardship, followed by uncertain years as a printer's apprentice and editor, Garrison was running a little Baptist temperance journal when in 1829 he was converted to the antislavery cause by Benjamin Lundy (1789–1839). A New Jersey Quaker and the greatest of the precursors, Lundy had organized the Union Humane Society in 1815; and in 1821, as antislavery assumed preeminence among his varied reform interests, he founded the *Genius of Universal Emancipation.* Before the year was out Garrison was helping to edit Lundy's *Genius,* and he was soon jailed for libel. Upon his release he went back to Boston to found the *Public Liberator and Journal of the Times;* and in the first issue (1 January 1831) he took the stand that was to make him famous—and infamous:

> I *will be* as harsh as truth, and as uncompromising as justice. On this subject [of slavery] I do not wish to think, or speak, or write, with moderation. . . . I am in earnest—I will not equivocate—I will not excuse—I will not retreat a single inch—AND I *WILL* BE HEARD.

Never a colonizationist and no longer a gradualist urging emancipation sometime "between now and never," Garrison demanded abolition immediately. Yet he drastically reduced the useful effect of his zeal by his absolutism, his astounding lack of charity, his incapacity to understand the thought or predicament of others, his unyielding demand for women's rights within the movement, his fierce anticlericalism and increasingly radical religious views, his almost anarchistic pacifism, his repudiation of political action, and (after 1843) his demand for *Northern* secession on grounds that the Constitution was a diabolical compact. The extent of his influence on abolitionism will probably always be disputed; but there is little doubt that he did far more than any other man to heighten Southern opposition to emancipation. Yet Garrison was not alone; to the end he had a hard core of followers, some even more radical then he. In a strange way, moreover, his conversion coincides with a great resurgence of conscientious abolitionism in the North.

In 1831 the wealthy merchant Arthur Tappan formed a New York committee and began to move toward a national antislavery organization. A year later, Garrison and a small group of Bostonians organized the New England Antislavery Society on a platform of immediatism. Then in 1833 came the British Slavery Abolition Act, and on its heels the American Antislavery Society was organized in Philadelphia. Despite public opprobrium and fierce opposition, this group wielded an enormous influence in the crucial thirties, planning conferences and lectures, distributing tons of literature, and knitting together the many new reform groups that were springing up across the nation.

Gradually merging with this impulse was a movement linked to the revival activity of Charles Finney in the Old Northwest. In 1834 Theodore Dwight Weld, one of Finney's converts, brought the antislavery gospel to Lane Theological Seminary in Cincinnati, where after a long series of debates the students issued a ringing indictment of the Colonization Society. When their radicalism precipitated disciplinary measures by the seminary trustees, one vocal group of dissidents migrated to Oberlin. This college was then little more than a "bivouac in the wilderness," but under the leadership of Asa Mahan and later Finney himself, and with financial aid from the Tappans of New York, it soon became a center of both abolitionism and Finneyite revivalism.[4]

[4] The linking of conversion and Christian commitment to a socially relevant cause is the clue to antislavery careers such as Weld's or Elijah Lovejoy's. John Gregg Fee (1816–1901) on coming to Lane Seminary long after the abolitionist exodus discovered this nexus for himself. Yielding to the entreaties of his most serious student friends, he says, "I saw that to embrace the principle [of abolition] and wear the name was to cut myself off from relatives and former friends. . . ." Yet one day, on his knees in a nearby woods, Fee consecrated himself with these words: "Lord, if needs be, make me an Abolitionist." He said that he rose from

Just before the Lane debates James G. Birney (1792–1857), a former slaveholder and colonizationist, had moved to Kentucky, where he was converted to abolitionism by Weld. In 1835 Birney organized a short-lived antislavery society in Kentucky; but when mob action threatened, he moved to Cincinnati to publish a crusading journal. Various associates of Weld and Birney carried the work on into Indiana and Illinois. Then in 1837 the murder of Elijah Lovejoy in Alton, Illinois, sent an electrifying tremor all across the North. "A shock as of any earthquake," John Quincy Adams called it. Because Lovejoy died defending his fourth printing press, three others having been destroyed since his forced departure from Saint Louis, the event had the additional effect of demonstrating the ultimate incompatibility of slavery and freedom in the same country. The events in Alton brought Edward Beecher, then president of Illinois College, to a decision for abolitionism. From Beecher issued not only a dramatic narrative of the Alton riots, but in 1845 a series of articles on "organic sin" which gave evangelical abolitionism some of its major ethical and theological insights. Far away in Boston William Ellery Channing was also aroused; and at the Faneuil Hall protest meeting which he organized Wendell Phillips began his sensational career as a radical orator.

In this manner the antislavery axis of the Tappans, Garrison, Weld, Lovejoy, and Birney (who became secretary of the American Antislavery Society in 1837) transformed a despised and presecuted protest movement into a nationally organized crusade that by 1840 was far beyond the reach of catcalls and rotten eggs. In New England, New York, and the Northwest antislavery and evangelicalism had struck a close and powerful alliance that would soon wield great political influence. Among the factors contributing to this result was an equally profound transformation in the South.

---

prayer that day "with the consciousness that I had died to the world and accepted Christ in all the fullness of his character as I then understood him." He went on to a life dedicated first to antislavery and then to the freedman, as the founding spirit of Berea College in Kentucky (see Fee's *Autobiography* [Chicago, 1891], p. 14; and the MS. biography of Fee by Robert Loesch [1966], Yale Divinity School Library, New Haven, Conn.). Gilbert H. Barnes in *The Anti-Slavery Impulse, 1830–1844* presents these matters better than any other study, but he does not cover the crucial period for the churches—from 1844 to 1861.

THE SOUTHERN REVOLUTION

The decade of the 1830s brought a no less decisive change in the slave states than in the North. Perhaps the most important indigenous stimulus to the increasingly vigorous rallying of support for slavery in the South was the outbreak in August 1831 of the Virginia slave revolt led by Nat Turner, a black preacher and visionary. The report of at least fifty-seven white people dead spread a wave of fear and anger through the region and focused Southern attention on the new abolitionist movement—especially on the vituperative language of Garrison. During the winter of 1831–32, to be sure, the Virginia legislature did debate the slavery question, but the chief support for abolition came from the future West Virginia region, while open discussion of this sort soon disappeared altogether. More important than arguments were the measures taken to prevent the dissemination of antislavery literature. Advocates of emancipation were threatened or mobbed, and by 1837 not one of the many antislavery societies that had existed early in the century remained. Even the Colonization Society became suspect; and some of the country's most prophetic voices on the slavery issue had to move north.

The South was rapidly closing ranks. An elaborate "scriptural argument" had long since soothed Christian and Jewish consciences on slavery itself, but now a new kind of Southern nationalism began to take shape, and central to it was a romantic idealization of the "cavalier" tradition. Arguments that slavery was a "positive good" were rare up to this time, but after 1831 they gained more spokesmen and countless new believers. Professor Thomas R. Dew of William and Mary published the first systematic defense of slavery and the structure of Southern society in his review of the Virginia debates (1832). In this area, as in so many others, John C. Calhoun (1782–1850) became the region's leading defender. Before the Senate in 1837 he insisted that "Abolition and Union cannot coexist," then moved to "higher ground" with the declaration that, given the "two races," slavery was a "positive good." In the 1850s the published treatises of Calhoun, Edmund Ruffin, Henry Hughes, and George Fitzhugh would provide elaborate sociological defenses of Southern institutions, often coupling them with thoroughgoing critiques of industrial "wage slavery" in the North. Nor were these theoretical statements without some basis in fact. Eli Whitney's cotton gin, the development of upland cotton, the rising market for cotton, the westward extension of the plantation system, and the growing profitableness of slavery all served to undergird Southern confidence in its way of life.

THE IMPENDING CRISIS

This critical period was fraught with other vital developments. First and foremost was the acceleration of thought in the Western nations toward a larger understanding of human equality and freedom, a trend which erupted in the sporadic European revolutions of 1830. Legislative progress in England included the great Reform Bill of 1832, followed in 1833 by an emancipation act. By 1848, revolutionary repercussions were more severe and widespread, and one result was the abolition of slavery in the French Empire. The time for sweeping American outrage at the injustices of industrialism was not yet ripe, but in the emerging idealism there was almost no place left for serfdom, and even less for slavery. In this sense, Garrison's activity was only one unusually strenuous manifestation of a growing international tendency. It is impossible to imagine how this current of idealism could have been ignored or resisted anywhere in the Atlantic community. Indeed, the strangely retarded response of Americans, even of Northern Americans, is the situation most in need of explanation.

A second factor, peculiar to the American South, was a set of circumstances that prevented the free discussion of slavery and the elaboration of means to eliminate it gradually and peacefully. The basic factor was not the economic value of slavery (which was debatable in any case) but that the slaves constituted a huge nonwhite population numbering 700,000 in 1790 and at least 3.5 million in 1860. Slavery was, to be sure, a labor system, but more fundamentally it was considered an essential means of social control over a race which at that time was regarded by almost everyone (including most abolitionists) as an inferior branch of the human species. In the South the black-white population ratio made this "race problem" preeminent. In the resultant social order Western ideals of equality and freedom simply could not be accepted.[5] We are thus driven again to the moral issue. An increasing number of Americans could not condone slavery or rest at peace while it existed; other Americans could not contemplate life without it. Honorable, ethical, God-fearing people as well as self-seeking, egotistic opportunists and status seekers were on both sides. Social, economic, political, and psychological forces intensified feelings, sharpened disputes, clouded the fundamental issues, and consolidated existing fears and antipathies—but the moment of truth had to come.

In 1840 the American Antislavery Society broke in two. Women's rights was the ostensible issue, though Garrison's insistence on nonpolitical moral suasion was the primary cause. Yet the breach was hardly disastrous, inasmuch as the antislavery movement was thoroughly politicized by 1840. Politicians and statesmen (some of them bunglers, some not) assumed new importance. By this time the Nullification Crisis of 1832–33 was past history and John Quincy Adams was midstream in his battle against the gag rule on slavery; Joshua Giddings from Ohio's Western Reserve had joined him. Weld, who had gone to Washington and set up "one of the most effective lobbies that the country had yet known," saw the facts clearly:

> Nothing short of miracles, constant miracles, and such as the world has never seen can keep at bay the two great antagonistic forces. . . . They must drive against each other, till *one* of them goes to the bottom. *Events*, the master of men, have for years been silently but without a moment's

[5] Slavery in all of its ramifying effects gave the entire social and moral order of the South its characteristic shape and spirit. The plantation economy, as U. B. Phillips insisted, was a "way of life." Eugene D. Genovese has further advanced our understanding of this way of life, emphasizing especially the way in which the dependence of the region's leaders made them violently intolerant of anyone and anything threatening to expose the full nature of their relationship to their slaves. Genovese also observes that it is not "the moral attack on slavery . . . in the world of the nineteenth century" that needs explanation, but its absence (see *The Political Economy of Slavery* [New York: Vintage Books, 1967], pp. 10, 33; and his foreword to Ulrich B. Phillips, *American Negro Slavery* [Baton Rouge: Louisiana State University Press, 1966], p. xix).

pause, settling the basis of two great parties, the nucleus of one slavery, of the other freedom.[6]

After 1840 events would continue to exert their polarizing pressure—but they would not be silent. Indeed, "irrepressible conflict" was an actuality long before William H. Seward uttered the words in 1858. Was not even Weld speaking of unavoidable war?

The annexation of Texas (1845), the Mexican War, legislation for the vast territory won from Mexico, fugitive slave laws, the Kansas-Nebraska Act, "Bleeding Kansas," the assault on Senator Sumner, the Dred Scott decision, the Lincoln-Douglas debates—such were the provocations. In this new context the nation's political life was inescapably transformed. The Liberty party had been founded in 1840 with Birney as its presidential nominee. No match for the Log Cabin and Hard Cider campaign, he garnered only 7,100 votes. But in the 1843 state elections, the party won 43,000 votes. Birney ran again in 1844 and had the enormous satisfaction of seeing 15,812 abolitionist votes in New York swing the state—and the nation—to Polk. Four years later the Liberty party passed its flickering torch to the Free Soil party. Thereafter political antislavery bided its time as the old party structure began to collapse. In the outrage over the Fugitive Slave Law and "Bleeding Kansas" the new "Republican" party was founded, gathered in the growing "antislavocracy" vote, and in the election of 1856 electrified the nation by carrying every Northern state but three. The Whig, Know-Nothing, and even the Northern Democratic organizations were being reoriented to other stars. In 1860 it would be Lincoln—and then secession.

ECCLESIASTICAL INVOLVEMENT

The essential history of the years from 1840 to 1860 was not all written in Washington. Paralleling the political process was a momentous series of events in the religious and moral spheres that made church history intrinsic to both Northern and Southern developments. More than ever the vision of the United States as a beacon to the world was mov-

[6] Theodore D. Weld to James G. Birney, 22 January 1842; quoted in Dumond, *Anti-Slavery Origins*, pp. 91–92.

ing men and women to action. The many voluntary associations for evangelism and moral reform became inseparable from the humanitarian crusades, including the most powerful of these, the crusade against slavery. The great fulcrum for moving the Northern conscience on these matters was the Second Awakening's blending of "modern Puritan" evangelicalism and patriotic idealism. The churches were slow in joining the antislavery cause, but they did most of the pioneering; and as the movement gained momentum the countless auxiliary organizations of mainstream Protestantism became radiating centers of concern and agitation. The national antislavery societies, now moribund and faction-ridden, were superseded by ecclesiastical organizations in which an antislavery "social gospel" was forging ahead, winning new leaders, trampling on compromisers, and bringing schism or conflict when the occasion demanded.

One of the profoundest contributions to this process did not appear until 1852, when the wife of a Congregational professor of Old Testament—and an able lay theologian herself—confronted the divided nation with *Uncle Tom's Cabin,* considered by one of its harshest and least comprehending critics as "perhaps the most influential novel ever published . . . a verbal earthquake, an ink-and-paper tidal wave."[7] Harriet Beecher Stowe was sure that God wrote the book— and in a way this was so, for no author was ever burdened with a more driving sense of Christian moral fervor. But there is much more in the book than ethical passion. Her picture of slavery, though artificial, was not overdrawn but on the verge of idealization; Simon Legree's New England origins gave a national scope to her argument, and though "Uncle Tom" was to become a twentieth-century term of abuse, her conception of the Negro's capacities was in advance of nearly all Southerners and most Northerners, including the abolitionists. She was by no means the first to enlist fiction for the antislavery cause. But no other storyteller matched her intuitions of the essential issue or knew so well how to touch the country's conscience.

[7] J. C. Furnas, *Goodbye to Uncle Tom* (New York: William Sloane Associates, 1956), pp. 4, 7. In assailing the Uncle Tom image of the Negro, Furnas was ahead of most critics, but in seeing Harriet Beecher Stowe as an unusually virulent propagator of the image, he was wrong. Her view of the "political economy of slavery" was in advance of its times.

"Bleeding Kansas" also had its Christian history, for the churches in the East were active in defining the issue so as to lead men westward to save the Great Plains from slavery. Henry Ward Beecher raised money from his pulpit to provide rifles ("Beecher's Bibles") for the cause. Out of Kansas, too, came that Connecticut-born wanderer and Bible-reading son of the Puritans, John Brown (1800–59). Part prophet, part adventurer, he made himself the symbol of the irrepressible conflict; and even with his body moldering in the grave, the memory of his exploit at Harpers Ferry became a living component of Northern esprit during the war.

The same combination of moral certainty and evangelical fervor runs through the great hymns of the movement. As early as 1844 James Russell Lowell's explicit linking of biblical images and antislavery gave an apocalyptic meaning to "The Present Crisis":

> Once to ev'ry man and nation
> Comes the moment to decide,
> In the strife of truth with falsehood,
> For the good or evil side;
> Some great cause, God's new Messiah,
> Off'ring each the bloom or blight,
> And the choice goes by for ever
> 'Twixt that darkness and that light.
>
> Though the cause of evil prosper,
> Yet 'tis truth alone is strong
> Though her portion be the scaffold,
> And upon the throne be wrong,
> Yet that scaffold sways the future,
> And, behind the dim unknown,
> Standeth God within the shadow
> Keeping watch above his own.

Two decades later, when the issue had been joined, Julia Ward Howe added her contribution to the Union's legacy. Beneath the throbbing rhythms of a "battle hymn" later generations have often missed the terrible import of her lines. Her eyes had seen the glory. A Day of Judgment was at hand.

But what of the South? How does one deal with the anomaly of its equally fervent religiosity, its equally strident moralism? Since the postrevolutionary revivals had made equally great—possibly greater—advances below the Mason-Dixon line, the impact of evangelicalism in this region requires comment, even though research on the subject has been remarkably sparse. But above all we must note the immense disparity between avowedly Christian views on slavery in the North and in the South and recognize the degree to which culture conditions religion and ethics, especially when a racial factor is present. Northern righteousness (and self-righteousness) could flourish without serious racial hindrance; in the South it could not. In the North it was possible to examine, even to exaggerate the evil, as Weld did in his *American Slavery as It Is* (1839). In the South it was almost impossible and, in any event, illegal by 1839.

As to the social impact of evangelicalism or of the perfectionist demands stemming from Wesley's or Finney's kind of revival preaching, the most obvious differences spring from the Southern tendency to channel such demands against the weaker provinces of Satan's kingdom, or, in other words, to keep the work of the "evangelical united front" at the tasks which chiefly preoccupied it before 1830. They avoided what Edward Beecher saw as the enveloping "organic sin." Yet this is not the whole fact, for slavery was not ignored. Richard Furman's biblical argument was adopted by the South Carolina Baptist Association in 1822, and by 1841, when John England, the Roman Catholic bishop of Charleston, published his defense, this line of thought had sunk deep into the Southern consciousness and underlay all others. Theologians and laity alike learned to recite the standard biblical texts on Negro inferiority, patriarchal and Mosaic acceptance of servitude, and Saint Paul's counsels of obedience to masters.

Some controversy did break out on the question of the unity of mankind—with the more extreme racists adopting the theory of separate origins of the black race. In general this view was denied, however, and an obligation to Christianize the slaves was acknowledged. In fact, the evangelization of the slaves was prosecuted with increased vigor as the abolitionist attack continued. Revivalism also contributed its emotionalism and anti-intellectual mood to the politics of the era, and in doing so it probably contributed to the expression of extremist views, just as it had in the North. In a political sense this no doubt eased the way of the fire-eaters in their efforts to crush out the more reasonable moderates and commit the slave states to secession and independence, and insofar as this made war seem likely, millennial fervor probably made Southerners as well as Northerners willing to commit the issue to arms and the terrible judgment of God. But the full dimension of the churches' involvement in the era's sectionalism can best be appreciated when considered in a denominational context.

The Presbyterians

The Presbyterian church did not explicitly divide on the great sectional issue until after secession. But the Old School-New School division of 1837 can probably be regarded as the first great ecclesiastical South-North separation. When Calhoun lamented before the Senate in 1850 that "already three great evangelical churches have been torn asunder" by the slavery issue, he was thinking of the Presbyterian church as well as the Baptist and Methodist. The Old School's most solid strength lay in that third of its membership from the deep South, while the New School claimed most of the Presbyterians who were leading the "evangelical united front" in the North. Many of them, to be sure, were still fairly conservative on the slavery issue in 1837, but their susceptibilities were well known, and Lovejoy's murder later in that very year led many of them to cross the Rubicon.

By suppressing official discussion of the slavery issue, the Old School avoided schism until the secession crisis of 1860, though a few congregations were lost during the 1840s to an antislavery offshoot of the New School. In 1845 pressure from midwestern synods brought an end to the enforced silence by forcing a statement from the General Assembly—but this pronouncement acknowledged slavery as biblical, and bade slaveholders treat slaves as immortal human beings. The official position adopted in 1849 was that slavery was a civil institution which should be dealt with by legislatures rather than churches. Countless individuals and groups attacked this official stand—and for a time the seminary at New Albany, Indiana, was their center—but to the very last they were an outmaneuvered minority. In 1859 even the New Albany Seminary was brought under control of the General Assembly, which merged it with the new seminary endowed by Cyrus McCormick in Chicago. When in May 1861 the Old School General Assembly in the mildest of terms expressed its loyalty to the Union, schism followed.

Southern commissioners met separately in Augusta, Georgia, in December, and declaring slavery to be the cause of disunion; they published a forthright defense of that institution and organized a new Old School denomination.

The New School was at first only slightly less conservative on slavery than the church which had expelled it. And because its leadership wished to demonstrate its true Presbyterianism at every opportunity in order to make the injustice of the expulsion more obvious, the Congregationalists, many of whom were ardent in the antislavery cause, tended to lose interest in Plan-of-Union arrangements and to reassert their own denominational tradition. Yet the New School's great numerical strength in areas where abolitionism was strongest, together with its very small Southern constituency, guaranteed that (unlike the Old School) it would at least hold the ground claimed by the General Assembly's deliverance of 1818. This much it did in 1846 and 1849, and it was goaded to go even farther when antislavery men, chiefly in Ohio and nearby states, began leading churches out of both the New and the Old School, forming the short-lived Presbyterian Free Church Synod (1847–67). This church, which at its height had about sixty-four ministers and congregations, explicitly denied membership to slaveholders, though of course its disciplinary measures had little exercise in states where slavery was forbidden by law.

In 1850 the New School General Assembly took the first steps toward a similar position by repudiating the view that slavery was a divinely sanctioned institution. In 1853 steps toward enforcement were taken, and tension increased until 1857, when the Southern presbyteries, with about fifteen thousand members, withdrew to form a separate church. After the war it merged with the Old School Church, South, and this united body has continued as the Presbyterian Church of the United States. In 1958, when it refused reunion with the northern church, the votes in its presbyteries correlated markedly with black-and-white population ratios in the respective districts.

The Methodists

The Methodist Episcopal church was indebted to John Wesley for two closely related characteristics that made a unified weathering of the antislavery controversy very unlikely. It was organized in an exceedingly strict and inflexible way, so that disagreements had to be formally resolved or generally agreed to be unimportant. Methodism, moreover, was not theologically oriented (as was Presbyterianism), and hence it placed far greater emphasis on visible matters of discipline. Due in large part to these factors it had modified Wesley's original regulations on slavery as it sought to extend its membership in the South. By 1843 there were 1,200 Methodist ministers and preachers owning about 1,500 slaves, and 25,000 members with about 208,000 more. The church's unity depended therefore on the strict enforcement of silence or neutrality on the slavery question, and for a half-century this proved to be possible.

At the General Conference of 1836, however, the evils of slavery were formally conceded, though "modern abolitionism" was also condemned in very forceful terms. This ambivalent act only incited the increasing number of Methodist abolitionists, but at the General Conference of 1840 they were again successfully throttled. Before long antislavery Methodists began to secede, organizing the Wesleyan Methodist Church in Michigan (1841) and the Methodist Wesleyan Connection in New York (1842–43). At the same time many other Methodists participating in unsanctioned meetings and conferences raised an outcry over the slaveholding of Bishop James O. Andrew of Georgia and began to clamor for a division of the church. Everyone knew that the General Conference meeting at New York in 1844 would produce a dramatic confrontation of the opposing forces, though perhaps few could have guessed that this would be the last convention of a united Methodist Episcopal church for almost a century.

At the momentous gathering of 1844 the delegates were for almost a fortnight locked in profound debate over two distinct but inseparable issues. First and fundamental was the slavery question: how decisive a stand would be taken upon it, and how directly would the stand be carried out in terms of Methodist discipline? Closely related was the problem of interpreting the church's constitution adopted in 1808: how "democratic" was the church? Were the bishops creatures of the General Conference, responsible to it, and deposable by it? Should bishops retain the immense powers of appointment and control of agendas of annual conferences that they had traditionally exercised? Bishop Andrew's case and the ensuing debates joined the two issues. The Southern delegates were unanimously committed to a strong episcopacy. And when the conference did vote on sectional lines, 111 to 69, that Bishop Andrew "desist from the exercise of his functions," they made clear in a unanimous representation that they would take even his resignation as a sign that division of the church was necessary. The Northern delegates were equally adamant, for they knew that failure to discipline the bishop would result in Northern schism. Given the total situation, it seemed impossible to avert division or even a postponement of the controversy until 1848.

At this point the Southern delegation proposed that an amicable plan of separation be drafted, so that the two churches could at least remain in fellowship with each other. When this proposal won support, a nine-man commission was appointed to work out details of the plan. Three days later the commission presented its detailed proposals, which were to be effected if the annual conferences in the slaveholding states (including Texas) approved. Two general conferences were to replace the present one, state boundary lines would be mutually respected in church extension, clergy could choose their affiliation, the publishing concern and other properties would be equitably divided. After brief debate came a nearly unanimous vote, the negatives chiefly motivated by fears that the plan was unconstitutional. Bishop Leonidas Hamline seemed to express the prevailing sentiment: "God forbid that they should go as an arm torn out of the body, leaving a point of junction all gory and ghastly! Let them go as brethren beloved in the Lord, and let us hear their voice, responsive, claim us for brethren." On this strangely conciliatory basis the conference was adjourned.

Immediately afterward the Southern delegation reconvened to prepare an address to their fourteen annual conferences, asking them to send delegates to a convention in Louisville on 1 May 1845, if they so desired. When they all complied, the Methodist Episcopal Church, South, was brought into existence. Since the South had dominated the episcopacy and gained acceptance for slavery in the discipline, almost no constitutional changes were necessary. The church went about its way in the old manner, continuing its work with alacrity. In 1846 it reported 459,569 members (124,961 of them "colored") and 1,519 traveling preachers.

In 1848 it duly elected a fraternal delegate to the Northern General Conference.

In the North, however, the spirit of brotherly separation quickly evaporated. Charges of unconstitutionality were hurled, abolitionists (now deprived of an easy bone to chew) were furious, officials of the publishing concern was outraged by the violence done to their empire, and many delegates began to have second thoughts. In the 1848 General Conference, therefore, the South's delegate was rebuffed and the Plan of Separation voted, though with heavy opposition, to be "null and void." Though this act was entirely ineffectual, it was rightly interpreted as extremely ungracious. But some grounds for complaint existed. The boundary settlement took no cognizance of some "Northern" conferences which extended into "slave" states, but had not been given time to vote before the Southern church had organized itself. Consequently a "gory and ghastly" border warfare had, by 1848, already begun. Since the legal actions requisite to dividing the publishing concern had not been carried out, the Southern church took legal action, and in 1851 and 1854 was awarded a *pro rata* division. Not until 1872 did the Northern church redress the actions of 1848 by sending a fraternal delegate southward. In the meantime it identified itself increasingly with Northern sentiment on slavery, war, and reconstruction.

The Baptists

The experience of the Baptists in the schisms brought on by sectional strife differed from that of the other denominations primarily because its polity was so distinctly congregational that the chief national agency was in theory no more than a cooperative agency of the churches, a "General Convention . . . for Foreign Missions." Founded in 1814 to support missionaries who had unexpectedly been converted to Baptist views while enroute to Burma, the convention met triennially, after 1832 in conjunction with the new Home Missionary Society and others. During the 1830s it successfully avoided the slavery issue. In 1839–40 the Foreign Missions Board formally declared its neutrality, and in 1843 it was supported in this by the convention's vote. In 1841 Southern delegates and Northern moderates, being still in a majority, had been able to oust Elon Galusha, a vice-president on the board, replacing him with Richard Fuller, a South Carolina minister; and three years later both the General Convention and the Home Board convened and adjourned with the same coalition in control. Francis Wayland, the moderate president of Brown University, was elected president of the convention. In this series of events, Baptist history parallels that of the Methodists, and it continued to do so.

By 1844 abolitionism had gained in both numbers and stridency in the North, while the South became equally demanding of respect for its situation. In state conventions both North and South popular pressures steadily mounted, and before the year was out both mission boards were faced with decisions deliberately thrust upon them by the South. In October the Home Board declined to appoint as a missionary the nominee of the Georgia Baptist Convention, James E. Reeves, who was stated to be a slaveholder. Two months later the Foreign Board took the same ground when petitioned to state its policy by the Alabama Baptist Convention.

The Southern response to these two decisions might have been predicted. Long dissatisfied with the Home Board's neglect of the South and Southwest, leading Southern Baptists welcomed the slavery issue as an occasion for instituting a more distinctly connectional polity. The Virginia Baptist Foreign Mission Society took the lead, addressing a call to "all our brethren, North and South, East and West, who are aggrieved by the recent decision of the Board in Boston." A consultative convention set for 8 May 1845 at Augusta, Georgia, was to decide on the type of organization to be formed. On that date 293 delegates from nine states convened, and after only a few days' deliberation, the Southern Baptist Convention had a constitution and a "provisional government." Dr. W. B. Johnson of South Carolina was president of the organization he had done so much to found and shape. After 27 December 1845 the convention had a charter under the laws of Georgia. The first regular triennial session held at Richmond in 1846 ratified these labors and with great enthusiasm began an ambitious project of consolidation and extension.

The Southern Convention was a new departure for American Baptists. It was frankly denominational in spirit and scope, designed by men who did not hesitate to speak of the Baptist "Church" (in the singular). It could undertake multiple tasks and organize appropriate boards as it saw fit. In this very important sense it objectified what had long been latent in the Southern Baptist tradition—what its historians have referred to as a "centralizing eccelesiology." But one cannot discount the long-term basis for hierarchical and authoritarian modes of social organization which were engendered both by slavery and by the major intellectual defenses of it. The same tendency is evidenced by Southern Methodists in their struggles over ecclesiastical polity, and to a lesser degree, by the strict views on polity of the Presbyterian Old School.

The Southern Convention also bore the marks of the "society" type of organization which had preceded it: in basic essentials it was, like a hundred or so earlier Baptist societies both large and small, a fund-raising agency: its membership consisted of those "who contributed funds, or are delegated by religious bodies [usually churches] contributing funds." Its main innovative feature was its power to carry out such "benevolent objects" as it determined to be necessary, though missions were its primary interest at the outset. Theologically, therefore, it was very different from a Presbyterian synod, the Episcopal House of Bishops, or a Roman Catholic provincial council. That it gradually took on the functions of all of these and came in some ways to wield an authority that equaled any of theirs is a major anomaly. Even during the remaining antebellum years these constitutional innovations became a divisive factor, and after the war they would be so again. The slavery issue was now excluded from convention activities, however, and a period of growth and activity ensued. During its first fifteen years, the Southern Convention's membership grew from 351,951 to 649,518.

The old General Convention, meanwhile, was refashioned under President Wayland's leadership according to contrasting principles which reflected the extreme congregationalism which the Great Awakening had intensified and which the influential New Hampshire Confession of 1833 clearly expressed. This "American Baptist Missionary Union" was composed of individual memberships only, with provisions to exclude proslavery members.

Undivided Churches

No church in either its local or its collective manifestation could long escape the disruptive impact of the moral issue which the abolitionists belatedly thrust into American life. In the Presbyterian and Methodist churches, for example, events marched forward with a steady inexorable step that trampled individual and corporate loyalties. Schisms in two highly structured churches of the socially dominant Protestant mainstream, with large constituencies in both regions, anticipated the national rift. The Baptists were in a somewhat different category. Though they also had a nationally dispersed membership, the division of 1845 had occurred within a coordinating agency of a denomination in which state and local loyalties had always been paramount.

The Disciples of Christ very closely resembled the Baptists. But these ultracongregational followers of Barton Stone and the Campbells had not yet even developed the sense of cohesion which leads to the founding of national missionary societies. Indeed, "Stonites" and "Campbellites" only began to blend their traditions in 1832. There was thus very little that the slavery issue could really divide except local congregations. Moreover, the border-state mentality which prevailed in the chief areas of Disciple strength greatly reduced the divisive impact of abolitionism, and even of the war itself. As the Disciples expanded northward and southward, characteristic attitudes did take shape and schisms with social and sectional overtones would occur, but not until the postwar era.

American Judaism can be similarly classified, since its basically congregational polity made institutional division almost out of the question. During these years of controversy the Reform was growing very swiftly, both North and South, with largely German Jewish leadership. Perhaps because it was so enthusiastically bent on identifying with American life, its views on slavery tended to vary from place to place according to the prevailing views. When Rabbi David Einhorn took an antislavery stand in Baltimore he was forced to resign. Isaac M. Wise and the institutions over which he presided at Cincinnati remained neutral. Efforts by individual Jews to gain public prominence were rare, although Judah F. Benjamin's dedicated service in the legal, state, and treasury departments of the Confederacy are an outstanding exception.

Another group of churches escaped division chiefly because they did not have a constituency in both regions. The Congregationalists were the most prominent in this group, but Unitarians, Universalists, and many other small groups were in a similar situation. In the North these churches contributed powerfully to the antislavery movement, and with the passing years they became increasingly unified in their witness. The Texas question and Mexican War, however, sharpened the cleavages in the Congregational antislavery movement; and in 1846 a group of radicals—mostly New School Congregationalists—met in Albany to protest against the compromised position of the evangelical voluntary associations. They organized the American Missionary Association on evangelical *and* abolitionist principles, and began rapidly to expand its work, especially in the West and Upper South, but also in the British West Indies and among fugitive slaves. After 1865 they became the major educational agency at work in the South. Still other churches were undivided because for ethnic or doctrinal reasons they were withdrawn or isolated from the country's problems. The Mennonites are one good example, the Mormons another.

The Lutheran, Episcopal, and Roman Catholic churches constitute a final category. These three large churches for all practical purposes remained undivided until secession created two sovereign nations, despite the fact that each of them had relatively large constituencies in both regions, and each contributed vigorous polemicists to both sides in the slavery controversy. Their separate histories are dissimilar, but certain resemblances remain: in each case a combination of ecclesiastical, theological, and social factors prevented a head-on collision within the church. For example, Lutheran synods, like Episcopal and Roman Catholic dioceses, tended to be organized on a territorial basis, so that extreme views often did not meet at this level. For Lutherans, moreover, a truly "national" echelon was virtually nonexistent, since the General Synod, which often took a strong antislavery stand, had little more than advisory or coordinating functions. Hence each territorial or ethnic synod came to terms with the issue much as did other segments of the population. The single significant exception was the Franckean Synod which in 1837 organized itself in western New York as a separation from the Hartwick Synod. Antislavery figured prominently in its rationale, along with temperance, Sabbatarianism, Finneyite "new measures," and dissatisfaction with the Lutheran confessions. The Lutheran synods organized by new immigrant groups were for the most part in free territory, and they tended to oppose slavery, though they naturally preferred not to commit the church on what they regarded as secular political issues.

The general conventions of the Protestant Episcopal church did, of course, provide an opportunity for controversy; but the church was at no point threatened by schism or even seriously torn by the slavery issue. Even its own historians have found the church's extraordinary passivity difficult to understand, but the explanation probably lies in the fact that Episcopalians were generally conservative and for good reason rather well satisfied with the status quo. The church, moreover, was already very deeply aroused by issues stemming from the Oxford Movement. Separate dioceses could and did adapt themselves to local conditions.

The official position of the Roman Catholic church in the antebellum period was that slavery as a principle of social organization was not in itself sinful, though in 1839 Pope Gregory XVI had reiterated the church's condemnation of the slave trade. Bishop Francis P. Kenrick sought to interpret the church's teaching in his *Theologia Moralis* (3 vols., 1840–43) and from 1851 until his death in 1863, as archbishop of Baltimore he occupied the most influential post in the American hierarchy. But his teaching shows a persistent failure to clarify the differences between the actual American form of slavery and that which the church had condoned. He has been justly accused of equivocation. "Kenrick seemed to have been satisfied to let conditions remain in *status quo*," writes a careful student of his ethics.[8] American Catholics as individuals expressed the full range of opinion on slavery; but the church took no official position. The successive Pastoral Letters of the assembled bishops between 1840 and 1852 remained silent on the nation's moral dilemma. Only in 1840 was there an ambiguous, indirect allusion to the nation's political parties—an admission that the hierarchy was divided. When the war came, the church maintained this stance, while bishops and archbishops North and South kept contact with Rome and with each other so far as circumstances would allow.

[8] Joseph D. Brokhage, *Francis Patrick Kenrick's Opinion on Slavery*, pp. 239, 242.

RETROSPECT ON THE ROAD TO WAR

Democratic government and involuntary servitude began their uneasy coexistence in America soon after 1619. Moral doubts about the peculiar institution arose almost as soon. Yet slavery extended its hold until the social order of an entire region was shaped by its dependence upon the bondage of a black race in its midst. The early witness of the churches and the access of egalitarianism in the years of the Revolution deepened the anomaly of slavery in the land of the free. After 1800 broadening democratic processes and evangelical resurgence intensified the sectional aspect of the conflict, until in the 1830s an acceleration of activity rapidly drove the nation toward its moment of truth. As intellectual communication and mutual confidence deteriorated, political rivalry deepened. Controversy became endemic and irrepressible. The federal Union itself came to be regarded in the South not as a beneficent source of strength but as a threat. Those who counseled compromise and moderation lost their adherents in both sections as the impasse became increasingly stark. In this hardening of attitudes the churches were a powerful factor. They provided the traditional recourse and appeal to the Absolute. They gave moral grandeur to the antislavery cause and divine justification for slavery. In the North the churches did much to hold the party of Lincoln on its antislavery course despite the efforts of local politicians, especially in the cities, to stress lesser, more immediate issues. The drastic step of secession followed immediately the Republican victory in the presidential election of 1860. On 4 February 1861, delegates of six states of the Deep South convened at Montgomery, Alabama, to organize the Confederate States of America. Not long after Lincoln's inauguration, on 12 April 1861, with the firing on Fort Sumter in Charleston harbor, the terrible war began.

41

THE CHURCHES AMID CIVIL WAR AND
RECONSTRUCTION

To Leonidas Polk, the Episcopal bishop of Louisiana, the justice of slavery, a state's right to secede, and the necessity of Southern nationhood were as certain as the multiplication table. Having already declared his church in Louisiana to have "an independent diocesan existence," and having signed the call to organize a separate Protestant Episcopal Church of the South, he laid aside his episcopal duties when the guns of Sumter sounded and entered the Confederate army as a major-general. "I believe most solemnly," he confessed in June 1861 to his dear friend, Bishop Stephen Elliott of Georgia, "that it is for constitutional liberty, which seems to have fled to us for refuge, for our hearth-stones, and our altars that we strike. I hope I shall be supported in the work and have grace to do my duty."[1] Far away in Newport, meanwhile, Thomas March Clark, the Episcopal bishop of Rhode Island, addressed a farewell service for the state militia as they left for the war. "Your country has called for your service and you are ready," he declared. "It is a holy and righteous cause in which you enlist. . . . God is with us; . . . the Lord of hosts is on our side." He closed with a prayer bidding divine protection for the soldiers "now going forth to aid in saving our land from the ravages of sedition, conspiracy, and rebellion."[2]

[1] William N. Polk, *Leonidas Polk: Bishop and General,* 2 vols. (New York, 1893), 1: 325.
[2] Quoted in Chester F. Dunham, *The Attitude of the Northern Clergy toward the South, 1860–1865,* p. 112. Quotations from denominational spokesmen which follow are from this valuable work unless otherwise indicated.

In this manner did God go to battle in America, sustaining hearts, inspiring hopes, and justifying anger. And so through the long dark years he led on. The words that came to Julia Ward Howe on a sleepless night in the autumn of 1861 before the fighting had really begun became, as it happened, the crusader's hymn of the Union, but the literal content of her verses would not have prevented the Confederacy from adopting it:

> I have seen him in the watch-fires of a hundred circling
>   camps;
> They have builded him an altar in the evening dews and
>   damps;
> I have read his righteous sentence by the dim and flaring
>   lamps;
>   His day is marching on.
>
> I have read a fiery gospel, writ in burnished rows of steel,
> "As ye deal with my contemners, so with you my grace shall
>   deal";
> Let the Hero, born of woman, crush the serpent with his
>   heel,
>   Since God is marching on.[3]

Southerners were equally certain that God willed their defense of liberty, hearth, and altar; and they shared the hymn's sense of ultimate apocalyptic urgency. Nor did four years of war dim their conviction that they were fighting God's war, though defeats and exhaustion gave them less and less occasion to proclaim their faith in God's justice-dealing power.

In April 1865 at a Thanksgiving service after the fall of Richmond, the Reverend Phillips Brooks, the future Episcopal bishop of Massachusetts, lifted his voice in prayer:

> We thank Thee, O God, for the power of Thy right arm, which has broken for us a way, and set the banners of our Union in the central city of treason and rebellion. We thank Thee for the triumph of right over wrong. We thank Thee for the loyal soldiers planted in the streets of wickedness. We thank Thee for the wisdom and bravery and devotion which Thou has anointed for Thy work and crowned

[3] Julia Ward Howe, *Reminiscences, 1819–1899* (Boston, 1899), pp. 269–76, stanzas 2 and 3 in original draft.

with glorious victory. . . . Thou has led us, O God, by
wondrous ways. . . . And now, O God, we pray Thee to
complete Thy work.[4]

After a few weeks no more prayers for military victory would
be needed.

Volume after volume could be filled with the same bloodthirsty condemnations, the same prayers for aid from the Almighty, the same self-righteous benedictions. The statements
above are chosen from Episcopal spokesmen not because that
church was more extreme, but because it praised itself and
won the suspicion of others for its neutrality on the great
issue of the day. In other communions the language was even
more self-righteous. The Southern Presbyterian church, for
example, formally resolved in 1864 that "we hesitate not to
affirm that it is the peculiar mission of the Southern Church
to conserve the institution of slavery, and to make it a blessing both to master and slave."[5] This church's Pastoral Letter
of 1865, written after slavery was overthrown and the Confederacy done, spoke out on this "question of social morality"
more vehemently than ever:

> When we solemnly declare to you, brethren, that the
> dogma which asserts the inherent sinfulness of this relation
> [slavery] is unscriptural and fanatical . . . that it is one
> of the most pernicious heresies of modern times, that its
> countenance by the church is a just cause of separation
> from it (I Timothy 6:1–5), we have surely said enough to
> warn you from this insidious error as from a fatal shore.[6]

In the North, the *Methodist Magazine* in 1864 took the contrary view:

> We must take the moral, the sacred, the holy right of our
> struggle up before the throne of God. We must accustom

[4] A. V. G. Allen, *Life and Letters of Phillips Brooks*, 1: 531.
[5] Quoted in Paul H. Buck, *The Road to Reunion*, p. 60. This
from a church that had justified its separation from the Northern
church on grounds that otherwise "politics would be obtruded
on our church courts"!
[6] Thomas C. Johnson, *History of the Southern Presbyterian
Church* (New York, 1894), p. 426.

ourselves to dwell before the divine throne, clothed in the smoke of our battles. . . . We have a right to plead and to expect that God will let his angels encamp about our army; then he will make our cause his own—nay, it is his already.[7]

Although the extremity of feeling and conviction expressed in these quotations was a continuous feature of the entire sectional crisis, yet for violence of statement and ultimacy of appeal, the clergy and the religious press seem to have led the multitude. "We have been accustomed to observe, for years past," wrote an Illinois Baptist editor as he reflected on the exchanged periodicals that came to his desk, "[that] the most violent and radical pro-slavery men in that quarter [the South] were ministers." Chester Dunham's research on the Northern clergy makes it clear that these extreme views were reciprocated. Both in the North and in the South, moreover, the ministers had the largest and most regular audience, not only at Sunday and weekday meetings, but through a vast network of periodicals. By 1865 the official Methodist papers alone were reaching four hundred thousand subscribers. Even more important was the fact that in an age of great evangelical fervor, the clergy were the official custodians of the popular conscience. When the cannons roared in Charleston harbor, therefore, two divinely authorized crusades were set in motion, each of them absolutizing a given social and political order. The pulpits resounded with a vehemence and absence of restraint never equaled in American history.

Recognizing the churches' large role in dividing the nation, we may return to Calhoun's famous last words with advantages that he lacked. Was not the snapping of ecclesiastical cords to which he referred in 1850 more than a useful illustration for his oration? Were not these church divisions demonstrations that the nation's conscience was already in twain? William Warren Sweet, the church historian, posits an even deeper involvement. "There are good arguments," he says, "to suport the claim that the split in the churches was not only the first break between the sections, but the chief cause of the final break."[8] In 1864 Professor R. L. Stanton of the

---

[7] Quoted in Dunham, *The Attitude of the Northern Clergy*, p. 205, passim.

[8] William W. Sweet, *The Story of Religion in America*, p. 312. Henry Clay on the eve of his death in 1852 also thought this

Presbyterian theological school at Danville, Kentucky, gave substantial support to the same theory in his book *The Church and the Rebellion*. The South's rebellious defiance of lawful authority, he said, was born "in the Church of God." He also implicated Northern "doughface" preachers who by defending "southern rights" encouraged the growth of secessionism. And his conclusions are supported by recent research. "As its greatest social institution," writes Professor Silver,

> the church in the South constituted the major resource of the Confederacy in the building and maintenance of civilian morale. As no other group, Southern clergymen were responsible for a state of mind which made secession possible, and as no other group they sustained the people in their long, costly and futile War for Southern Independence.[9]

The main facts must be kept in mind. Churchmen played leading roles in the moral revolutions that swept the North and the South in opposite directions between 1830 and 1860. Between 1846 and 1860, churchmen gradually converted the antislavery movement into a massive juggernaut, and dedicated the South to preserving a biblically supported social order. To these opposing causes, moreover, they transmitted the overcharged intensity of revivalism, carrying it even to the troops when war finally came. Nor were the preachers repentant. "We are charged with having brought about the present contest," declared the Northern Methodist Granville Moody in 1861. "I believe it is true that we did bring it about, and I glory in it, for it is a wreath of glory around our brow."[10]

---

was the case: "I tell you, this sundering of the religious ties which have bound our people together I consider the greatest source of danger to our country" (in an interview reported in the *Presbyterian Herald*, published at Louisville; quoted in Dunham, *The Attitude of the Northern Clergy*, p. 2.

[9] James W. Silver, *Confederate Morale and Church Propaganda*, p. 101 (the book's final paragraph).

[10] My own reading of sermons and tracts suggests that Moody's statement was typical rather than extreme, and that in 1861 it could have been uttered in either section of the country.

THE CHURCHES DURING THE WAR

Once disunion was a reality, the sovereign ecclesiastical fact was the division of the churches. Those with international connections of one sort or another remained in some kind of indirect communion with each other, but even they functioned as churches in separate nations and professed their patriotism in unquestionable terms. The Episcopal Church, C.S.A., brought much obloquy upon itself by formally changing the Book of Common Prayer; but all churches, in effect, did as much. At a meeting in 1862, the General Synod of the Lutheran church—bereft of its Southern synods—appointed a special committee to apprise President Lincoln of its wholehearted support, characterizing the "rebellion" as most wicked, unjustifiable, unnatural, inhuman, oppressive, and "destructive in its results to the highest interests of morality and religion."[11] The Southern Presbyterians who had with equal vigor insisted on the neutrality of the church on all "political" issues, including slavery, shifted their ground. In 1862 they expressed their deep conviction "that this struggle is not alone for civil rights and property and home, but also for religion, for the church, for the gospel, for existence itself."[12] Monotonously the same positions were formally taken or practically demonstrated in virtually every church.[13] Even the Roman Catholic church provided powerful champions of both causes, though every bishop of its eleven small Southern dioceses was born outside the South.[14]

[11] Henry E. Jacobs, *A History of the Evangelical Lutheran Church in the United States*, ACHS, vol. 4 (New York, 1893), p. 452.

[12] Johnson, *Southern Presbyterian Church*, p. 427. After the war the Southern Presbyterian church most categorically disavowed this wartime stand and reasserted the doctrine of the "nonsecular character of the church" and that its relation to any and all governments was *de facto*, not *de jure*.

[13] The Missouri Synod Lutheran church may be the only exception among major denominations, in part because its headquarters were in a border state, but also because it was theologically opposed to pronouncements on sociopolitical issues.

[14] Three Roman Catholic bishops of the C.S.A. were born in the North, three in Ireland, and four in France, including

Not only did the churches attest their loyalty to their respective governments and armies through sermon and prayer, but they actively participated in the war effort by bringing a Christian ministry to the soldiers and by organizing noncombatant support among their constituencies. Of all these wartime activities, the chaplaincy was the most time-honored. The United States War Department authorized one ordained and denominationally certified chaplain per regiment, giving each the grade of private; and in 1862 it authorized their assignment to hospital duty as well. The Confederacy made similar arrangements. To this challenge the denominations responded with alacrity, the Northern Methodist church alone providing nearly five hundred chaplains, the Southern Methodist and Episcopal churches about two hundred and one hundred respectively. Other churches, North and South, showed proportionate concern. In light of the disruptions wrought by the war the number of chaplains who volunteered was remarkably high, though the men in service always felt that they were hopelessly few to do the work at hand.

Chaplains performed heroic duties in many circumstances, in battle and behind the lines, and won countless tributes for their services to the sick, the wounded, and the dying. As in no other American war, they also carried on their preaching ministries with astounding success, as their great revivals won many converts even among the highest ranking officers. In these revivals as well as in their pastoral work and many other tasks, the chaplains were often joined by clergy of the locality. The diary of a Southern Methodist chaplain, John B. McFerrin, gives a vivid picture of this ministry:

The Federals occupied Chattanooga, and for weeks the two armies were in full view of each other. All along the foot of Missionary Ridge we preached almost every night to crowded assemblies, and many precious souls were brought to God. After the battle of Missionary Ridge the

Archbishop Odin of New Orleans (see Benjamin J. Blied, *Catholics and the Civil War*). After the war nativistic Radical Republicans made much of the fact that the pope was the only sovereign power to have recognized the Confederate government. In fact, this recognition consisted of no more than the pope's addressing Jefferson Davis in a letter of 1863 as "Your Excellency."

Confederate army retreated and went into winter quarters at Dalton, Ga. During these many months the chaplains and missionaries were at work—preaching, visiting the sick, and distributing Bibles, tracts, and religious newspapers. There was preaching in Dalton every night but four, for four months; and in the camps all around the city, preaching and prayer meetings occurred every night. The soldiers erected stands, improvised seats, and even built log churches, where they worshiped God in spirit and in truth. The result was that thousands were happily converted and were prepared for the future that awaited them. Officers and men alike were brought under religious influence. In all my life, perhaps, I never witnessed more displays of God's power in the awakening and conversion of sinners than in these protracted meetings during the winter and spring of 1863–64.[15]

So continuous were these manifestations of piety that William Wallace Bennett could devote an entire book to "the Great Revival" in the Southern armies. Most remarkable of all was the "revival on the Rapidan" which deeply affected the army making its mournful way from the bloody struggle at Gettysburg in July 1863. Underlying these great evangelistic successes, of course, was the unusually homogeneous religious tradition of the South.

The voluminous reports of the Christian Commission amply show that the Union armies were also responsive to the revival spirit. A missionary's report from General Sherman's army as it paused on the long road to Atlanta provides an authentic picture of the war's religious side:

When we found that the army [of General Sherman] was to be at rest over the Sabbath, appointments were made in different brigades for two or three services to each preaching Delegate. I had an appointment in the Baptist church in the morning, and at General Howard's headquarters, in the woods, in the afternoon. . . . It was too late now to look for help. I took off my ministerial coat, and for one hour with the mercury at ninety degrees, worked with might and main. When I had swept out the straw,

15 Quoted in Gross Alexander, *History of the Methodist Episcopal Church, South,* ACHS, vol. 11 (New York, 1894), p. 72.

cleared the rubbish from the pulpit, thrown the bunks out the window, pitched the old seats down from the loft, arranged them in order on the floor, and dusted the whole house over twice, it was time for service. . . .

In the afternoon I rode over to the Fourth Corps, four miles away. General Howard had notified the regiments around of the service. Two of his division commanders were present, and Brigadier-General Harker, whose promotion was so recent that the star had not yet supplanted the eagle on his shoulder. This was the last Sabbath service which this manly, modest, gallant officer attended. Five weeks later, in the charge at Kenesaw Mountain, he was shot dead. That Sabbath in the woods I shall never forget;—the earnest attention of all to the theme,—"The safety of those who do their duty, trusting in God,"—and the hearty responses of the Christian men, and the full chorus in the closing hymn, "When I can read my title clear." But the most effective sermon of the day was by the General commanding the corps, given upon the piazza of his head-quarters, surrounded by his staff, his division commanders and other general officers. Nothing could be more natural than the turn of the conversation upon religious topics. The General spoke of the saviour, his love for Him and his peace in His service, as freely and simply as he could have spoken in his own family circle. He related instances of Christian trust and devotion and triumph. Speaking of the high calling of chaplains, and the importance that they should always be with their regiments at the front, he told us of his visit to Newton's division hospital the night after the battle of Resaca, where he found a fair-faced boy who could not live till morning. He knelt down on his blanket and asked if there was anything he wanted done for him. "Yes," said the boy, "I want somebody to tell me how to find the Saviour." "I never felt my ignorance so much before," said the General. "Here was a mind ready now to hear and act on the truth. What if I should give him wrong directions? How I wished I had a minister's training." And then he told us what directions he gave, and of the prayer, and of the boy's smile and peace,—appealing now to me and then to his generals, if it was not right and beautiful; and so, under the pressure unconsciously applied by their superior officer, with lips all unused to such confession, they acknowledged the power and grace of God.[16]

Estimates of conversions among the military during the war vary wildly between one and two hundred thousand; but even if certain, such information would only tell part of the story, for the "religious interest" reached untold numbers of men who could never become a chaplain's statistic. In the last analysis the vast tomes compiled by the religious emissaries to either the Blue or the Gray—so replete with stories of impromptu worship services, of mass meetings by torchlight, and of individual conversions of the living and the dying—could be interleaved one with another without distorting the overall picture. One can hardly deny the assertion of J. William Jones, a chaplain all the war long in Lee's Army of Northern Virginia, that "any history of that army which omits an account of the wonderful influence of religion upon it—which fails to tell how the courage, discipline and morale of the whole was influenced by the humble piety and evangelical zeal of many of its officers and men—would be incomplete and unsatisfactory."[17] One could only wish to apply it more generally. A fervently pious nation was at war, and amid the carnage and slaughter, amid the heroism and weariness, men on both sides hungered for inspiration and peace with God. Dedicated men and women on both sides responded to their hunger with wide-ranging ministries. On both sides the soldier's sense of duty was deepened, his morale improved, his loyalty intensified. More cynical commanders and more despairing men might have been less sure that the Almighty was with them and that victory must surely come. They might have felt a stronger impulse to compromise. Perhaps piety lengthened the war. Certainly it

16 Lemuel Moss, *Annals of the United States Christian Commission* (Philadelphia, 1868), pp. 498–500. The General Howard whom Moss mentions is O. O. Howard, later head of the Freedman's Bureau. Howard University is named for him. On the Confederate side during these same weeks, the biography of General Polk contains very moving accounts of his private baptismal services for Generals Hood and Joseph E. Johnston (Polk, *Leonidas Polk*, 2: 329–30).

17 J. William Jones, *Christ in the Camp; or, Religion in Lee's Army* (Richmond, Va., 1888), pp. 5, 6. A densely printed book of 624 pages.

deepened the tragedy and made the entire experience a more enduring scar on the national memory.

ORGANIZED PHILANTHROPY IN THE NORTH

In the North a vast special ministry to the armies was organized through the Christian Commission which was formed early in the war in a manner similar to dozens of other evangelical voluntary associations. It was pervaded by a piety that owed much to the great "businessman's revival" of 1857–58. Local groups began forming soldier's aid societies as soon as hostilities began; but the task of coordinating these diverse impulses was begun by Vincent Colyer, a New York artist who had rushed to Washington after the first battle of Bull Run out of interest in a religious mission to soldiers. He soon prevailed upon the YMCA to call a convention to put such work on a solid footing, and at this meeting in November 1861 the Christian Commission was established, with George H. Stuart (1816–90) as permanent chairman. Stuart was a deeply religious Philadelphia banker who devoted his whole life to evangelical missionary agencies. During the war his talents at arousing the interests of others made the commission a major religious force in the Union armies.[18] It raised money and enlisted volunteer workers to aid the military chaplains, and in many other ways performed spiritual and charitable tasks. The provision of reading materials was one major concern, because the soldiers' hunger for the printed word was insatiable. Vast numbers of Bibles, tracts, and books were given away, and portable lending libraries circulated.

The printed certificate earned by every "delegate" of the Christian Commission made very clear, however, that other kinds of service were also performed:

His work will be that of distributing stores where needed, in hospitals and camps; circulating good reading matter among soldiers and sailors; visiting the sick and wounded, to instruct, comfort, and cheer them, and aid them in correspondence with their friends at home; aiding Surgeons on

[18] See George H. Stuart, *The Life of George H. Stuart*, ed. Robert Ellis Thompson (Philadelphia, 1890). The role of America's intensely evangelical businessmen as public servants and philanthropists has not begun to receive the study it deserves.

the battlefield and elsewhere, in the care and conveyance of the wounded to hospitals; helping Chaplains in their ministrations and influence for the good of the men under their care; and addressing soldiers and sailors, individually and collectively, in explanation of the work of the Commission and its delegates, and for their personal instruction and benefit, temporal and eternal.[19]

The Christian Commission also made a special effort to arrange speedy communications between soldiers and their families and to provide soldiers with special "luxuries" of the sort that families would want to send. For its total work it raised nearly $3 million in cash and marshaled many more millions' worth of supplies and services. Over five thousand volunteers were enrolled in its work. To countless men and women it provided the experience of a lifetime.[20]

More directly relevant to the Northern war effort was the Sanitary Commission, an equally large and somewhat more revolutionary service organization intended chiefly to augment the work of the army's medical bureau. This organization came into being during the summer of 1861 largely through the efforts of Henry W. Bellows (1814–82), the enormously energetic minister of All Souls Church (Unitarian) in New York City, who continued to lead the agency throughout the war, with Frederick Law Olmstead as general secretary. In the sequence of events leading to its formation this organization resembled the Christian Commission. First, several newly founded local societies were coordinated. Supporters than accomplished the difficult task of convincing the president and other government officials that their service was needed; and finally, they recruited volunteers and funds.[21] The commission did not seek to take over military functions, however, as its sponsors made clear in their appeal for government authorization:

The general object of the [Sanitary] Commission is through suggestions reported from time to time, to the

[19] Moss, *Annals*, p. 542.

[20] In addition to Moss's *Annals*, see Edward P. Smith, *Incidents of the United States Christian Commission* (Philadelphia, 1869).

[21] These remarkable achievements are described in Charles J. Stillé, *History of the United States Sanitary Commission* (Philadelphia, 1866).

Medical Bureau and the War Department, to bring to bear upon the health, comfort and morale of our troops, the fullest and ripest teachings of sanitary science, in its application to military life, whether deduced from theory or practical observations, from general hygienic principles, or from the experience of the Crimean, the East Indian, or the Italian wars. Its objects are purely advisory.[22]

Through its two hundred agents it sought persistently to expose problems of sanitation, drainage, preventive medicine, faulty diet, rest camp needs, hospital mismanagement, etc. In the Vicksburg campaign it rushed fresh vegetables to Union troops threatened with scurvy, thus directly contributing to the military action. In short, it served as a vast composite Florence Nightingale, and was an essential component of the war effort.

The Western Sanitary Commission, organized in Saint Louis by another dynamic Unitarian minister, William G. Eliot, aided the Sanitary Commission in its work, and the two groups developed methods for cooperating with the Christian Commission in 1862. Taken together, these organizations played a major role in the long struggle to bring humane care to soldiers everywhere in the world. After the war Henry Bellows remained interested in "sanitary reform" until his efforts, together with the campaign of Clara Barton, led to American signing of the Geneva Convention and the organization of the American Red Cross.[23]

A third major concern of organized philanthropy was the increasing number of freed slaves. Freedman's relief societies were organized in most of the major Northern cities, with $150,000 being raised during the first year in New York, Boston, and Philadelphia alone. A particularly strong impetus was given to these efforts after the so-called Draft Riots in New York City during July 1863, when many free Negroes

[22] Linus P. Brockett, *The Philanthropic Results of the War in America* (New York, 1864), p. 39.

[23] In 1863 J. Henri Dunant of Geneva published *Souvenir de Solferino*, a vivid account of the horrors of that Italian "victory" of Napoleon III. He also spurred the movement to adopt an international code of warfare and to establish an agency of mercy. In 1866, the year in which the Red Cross was organized in Switzerland, Henry W. Bellows became president of an American auxiliary committee for these purposes. The American Red Cross, however, was not organized until 1884.

fell before angry mobs. Through the efforts of these early societies, moreover, Congress was persuaded to establish the Freedman's Bureau (3 March 1865) in order to discharge this enormous national responsibility more adequately. It was in the context of postwar reconstruction, however, that these activities attained their greatest significance.

In the meantime many of the older associations, including even those in foreign missions, continued their wide-ranging activities, most of them on increased budgets. The American Bible and Tract Societies and the YMCA responded with special vigor, launching large fund drives and distributing thousands of Bibles, tracts, and edifying books. They even succeeded in reaching Confederate troops, though similar organizations were formed in the South for the same purpose. The Methodist Society was the largest and most active agency for supplying literature to Confederate troops; but the Southern Baptist Convention reported in 1863 that it had distributed five million pages of tracts.

Accompanying this total work of charity was the amazing surge of fund raising which went forward at all levels. Every town and church was involved. Through the ladies' aid societies that were formed everywhere, women assumed a new role in local churches and, as a result, in national life. Innumerable local ministers also became involved as never before in public and secular undertakings. Throughout the land a philanthropic revolution occurred. Early in 1864, in order to stimulate further generosity in connection with the Metropolitan Fair being held in New York in behalf of the Sanitary Commission, Linus P. Brockett published his important little book, *The Philanthropic Results of the War in America.* After describing the manifold philanthropies, local, regional, and national, which the war had stimulated, he presented a statistical table showing contributions that totaled $212 million in the North alone—and more than a year before the end of the war. Quite rightly he contends that "neither in ancient nor modern times has there been so vast an outpouring of a nation's wealth for the care, the comfort, and the physical and moral welfare of those who have fought the nation's battles or been the sufferers from its condition of war."[24] Brockett might have said more, for this outpouring raised the charitable and missionary plans of the churches to a new order of magnitude. It extended the American reformer's conception

[24] Brockett, *Philanthropic Results of the War,* p. 150.

of the possible, and because its effects were enduring, it opened a new philanthropic era in American history. On this same theme one must add that the churches, not only on account of their role in stimulating this philanthropy, but because of their entire involvement in sectional controversy and war work, were permanently altered in their public stance and in their attitudes toward social affairs. Like the nation as a whole, they would never again be the same.

INTERPRETING THE WAR

Palm Sunday, 9 April 1865, was the day of silent guns at Appomattox. Lee surrendered the Army of Northern Virginia while Jefferson Davis and his cabinet fled southward. On 17 April, just before leaving Raleigh, North Carolina, to treat with General Johnston for peace, General Sherman received word by telegraph that Abraham Lincoln had been assassinated on Good Friday. He died on Saturday. America did its best to celebrate the paschal feast on Sunday. By 26 May all Confederate armies had laid down their arms. The "close of the Rebellion" was proclaimed by President Andrew Johnson on 20 August 1866; and this was recognized as the official date by act of Congress on 2 March 1867. The Constitution of the United States, as interpreted before God's throne in the court of war, was again the law of the whole land. But what, in fact, had happened? A million casualties; six hundred thousand dead. For what had they died—if anything? And what—if anything—did it all mean?

The answers were no more easily given then than they are now, though intense feelings were registered and numberless statements made. In the South there was relief and dejection and smoldering rage. In the North—as Lincoln's funeral train made its way to Springfield—the exultation that might have burst forth yielded to relief and dejection and smoldering rage. The grief of the two sections differed greatly: that of the South was far more deeply etched, while that of the North was modified by victory and relatively large grounds for hope.

Father Abram Ryan, sometime free-lance chaplain to Confederate troops, whose spirit, as someone said, shall "keep watch over the Stars and Bars until the morning of the Resurrection," put his pen to paper a few days after Lee's surrender.

Furl that Banner! furl it sadly!
Once ten thousands hailed it gladly,
And ten thousands wildly, madly,
     Swore it should forever wave;
Swore that foeman's sword should never
Hearts like theirs entwined dissever,
Till that flag should float forever
     O'er their freedom or their grave!

Furl that Banner, softly, slowly!
Treat it gently—it is holy—
     For it droops above the dead.
Touch it not—unfold it never,
Let it droop there, furled forever,
     For its people's hopes are dead!

Ideologically many Southerners never transcended this kind of nostalgic resignation. They might work to restore their personal situation, but their hearts were with the Lost Cause, filled with memories of military valor and a half-mythic past. "Our people have failed to perceive the deeper movements under-running the times," said Sidney Lanier, their greatest poet. "They lie wholly off, out of the stream of thought, and whirl the poor dead leaves of recollection round and round, in a piteous eddy that has all the wear and tear of motion, without any of the rewards of progress."[25] The major religious corollary of this memory-laden view would be a firm attachment to the evangelicalism of antebellum days and a refusal to admit the relevance of issues raised by modern thought. Its ecclesiastical results will be the subject of the two succeeding chapters.[26]

In the North Walt Whitman spoke to a nation's grief for the Captain whose lips were "pale and still":

When lilacs last in the dooryard bloom'd,
And the great star early droop'd in the western sky in the
     night,
I mourn'd, and yet shall mourn with ever-returning spring.

Ever-returning spring, trinity sure to me you bring,

[25] Quoted in Buck, *Road to Reunion*, pp. 31–32.
[26] The cult of the Lost Cause not only encouraged retention of "the old-time religion," but led to the near transfiguration of Robert E. Lee—and other similar phenomena.

Lilac blooming perennial and drooping star in the west,
And thought of him I love.

. . . .

In the dooryard fronting an old farm-house near the
    white-wash'd palings,
Stands the lilac-bush tall-growing with heart shaped leaves of
    rich green,
With many a pointed blossom rising delicate, with the
    perfume strong I love,
With every leaf a miracle—and from this bush in the
    dooryard,
With delicate-color'd blossoms and heart-shaped leaves of
    rich green,
A sprig with its flower I break.

. . . .

Coffin that passes through lanes and streets,
Through day and night with the great cloud darkening the
    land,
With the pomp of the inloop'd flags with the cities draped in
    black,
With the show of the States themselves as of crape-veil'd
    women standing,
With processions long and winding and the flambeaus of the
    night,
With the countless torches lit, with the silent sea of faces and
    the unbared heads,
With the waiting depot, the arriving coffin, and the sombre
    faces,
With dirges through the night, with the thousand voices
    rising strong and solemn,
With all the mournful voices of the dirges pour'd around the
    coffin,
The dim-lit churches and the shuddering organs—where
    amid these you journey,
With the tolling tolling bells' perpetual clang,
Here, coffin that slowly passes,
I give you my sprig of lilac[27]

As men looked through their grief and sought the meaning
of the war, the old theological presuppositions of the "crusades" usually sufficed for most. Even for the learned, the cat-

[27] These, of course, are but a few isolated passages drawn from
a much longer poem.

egories of judgment and punishment were often sufficient, though they were invoked with more assurance in the victorious North.

One of the most articulate theologians of Southern Presbyterianism was Robert Lewis Dabney (1820–98). A professor before the war, he had served as adjutant under Stonewall Jackson, and remained for nearly two decades in Virginia and Texas as a major spokesman for his denomination and his region. In lectures, sermons, published works, and in the deliberations of his church he expounded his convictions. The war, according to Dabney, had been "caused deliberately" by abolitionists who "with calculated malice" goaded the South to violence in order to revolutionize the government and "gratify their spite." "I do not forgive," he declared of the Northern Presbyterians. "What! forgive those people, who had invaded our country, burned our cities, destroyed our homes, slain our young men, and spread desolation and ruin over our land! No, I do not forgive them." He yearned for a "retributive Providence" that would demolish the North and abolish the Union.[28]

Henry Ward Beecher was moderate compared to Dabney. He counseled compassion for the generality of Southerners. Yet he minced no words in his indictment:

I charge the whole guilt of this war upon the ambitious, educated, plotting political leaders of the South. . . . A day will come when God will reveal judgment and arraign these mighty miscreants, . . . and every maimed and wounded sufferer, and every bereaved heart in all the wide regions of this land, will rise up and come before the Lord to lay upon these chief culprits of modern history their awful witness. . . . And then these guiltiest and most remorseless traitors, these high and cultured men with might and wisdom . . . shall be whirled aloft and plunged downward forever and ever in an endless retribution.[29]

While Beecher painted his graphic picture of the Last Judg-

[28] From *A Defence of Virginia* (1867) quoted by William A. Clebsch, "Christian Interpretations of the Civil War," *Church History* 30 (1961): 4.

[29] From an address delivered in Charleston on 14 February 1865, when the Stars and Stripes were restored to Fort Sumter. Presiding over the ceremony was General Robert J. Anderson, who as a major had surrendered the fort in 1861.

ment with primary attention to Southern leaders, a more widely held view regarded the whole region as the proper victim of God's wrath. Theodore Thornton Munger, the distinguished pastor-theologian of New Haven, did not allow his liberal doctrines of progress to soften his conviction that divine retribution had already been accomplished. Indeed, they served to harden him to the plight of the South. In his essay on "Providence and the War," written two whole decades after Appomattox, Munger explained the "divine logic" by which the South had been punished "for its sins," with the North as the "sacrificing instrument."[30] Not only had a death-blow been dealt to a diabolical slave state so that America could realize its destiny, but justice had also been done in more detailed ways. That the war's carnage was felt chiefly in the South was the main fact, but within this lay a justification for Sherman's long march and Sheridan's devastation of the Shenandoah Valley. Munger even saw God's cunning in the failings of General McClellan, since his vacillations precluded a sudden Northern victory and made sure that the whole South would suffer the brunt of a long war.[31]

In the last analysis Dabney and Munger did little more than deck out the gut reactions of popular extremism in the trappings of theology. Other men, fortunately, revealed profounder theological grounds for understanding America's ordeal. Less confident in their knowledge of God's purposes, more aware of the ambiguity of historical events, less assured of their own or their region's moral purity, these men searched for a way of seeing the entire tragedy—its triumphs and its defeats—as primarily meaningful for the American people and nation as a single corporate whole. To them fire eaters and abolitionists alike were unacceptably self-righteous.[32] With greater or lesser confidence in their vision of America's destiny, they sought to bring all Americans first to

[30] Munger professed a great indebtedness in these matters to Elisha Mulford, whose book *The Nation* (1870) he regarded as a supreme American contribution to political science. "The War," said Mulford, "was not primarily between freedom and slavery. It was the war of a nation and the Confederacy. Confederation, in its attack upon the nation, is in league with hell" (p. 340). Mulford's was an eloquent adaptation of the idea of the state which was developed in the German historical school.

[31] See Clebsch, "Christian Interpretations of the Civil War."

[32] William Lloyd Garrison was an exception. He by no means believed in the purity of the North.

penitence and reformation, and only then to reconciliation. Of the considerable number of thinkers who contributed to this view, three are outstanding. One was a Northerner and, oddly enough, Munger's hero, Horace Bushnell. The second was a German immigrant who spent his prewar years just above the Mason-Dixon line at Mercersburg, Pennsylvania, Philip Schaff. The third was born of Virginia parentage in Kentucky and grew to manhood in the proslavery climate of southern Indiana and Illinois, Abraham Lincoln.

Bushnell's great contribution stemmed from the two central concerns of his life. First, he stressed the organically *social* nature of human existence and hence the necessity of understanding the war as a single experience of one corporate being. It was a *Volkskrieg* in which the *nation* was purging itself and realizing its unity. Then out of his long meditations on the nature and meaning of expiation and vicarious sacrifice, especially as instanced in the Crucifixion, he sought to understand the suffering and sacrifice of war. In one case as in the other, the expiation of corporate sin and guilt opened the way for atonement (at-one-ment). Bushnell wrote his treatise *The Vicarious Sacrifice* as the nation bled on the battlefield; he delivered it to the publisher while the people were mourning Lincoln's death. He dared to think that the war could be good in some way akin to the way in which Good Friday was good.[33]

Philip Schaff had published a brilliant interpretation of America in 1854–55, but a visit to Germany after the war occasioned a long address explaining the significance of America's great tragedy. He, too, understood the war as a judgment on the centuries-long complicity of an entire nation in the sin of slavery. Like Bushnell, too, Schaff saw the possibility of a new and redeemed sense of nationhood rising out of the death and carnage. Reflecting his Hegelian heritage, however, he interpreted the war in a larger sense as having readied America for its great role in the cause of human freedom. Schaff felt grateful to have participated in an experience of world-historical significance.[34]

By a general consensus the Gettysburg Address and the

[33] See especially Bushnell's "Our Obligations to the Dead," delivered at Yale at a gathering to honor those who had fallen (*Building Eras in Religion* [New York, 1881], pp. 319–56).

[34] *Der Bürgerkrieg und das Christliche Leben in Nord-Amerika* (Berlin, 1865). A translation was published in the *Christian Intelligencer* 37, nos. 9–20 (1866).

Second Inaugural are Lincoln's supreme statements on the meaning of the war. In the latter especially he expounded the duty, destiny, and present woe of the "almost chosen people" from whom he would so soon be separated. We can apprehend even in these few words the astounding profundity of this self-educated child of the frontier, this son of a hard-shell Baptist who never lost hold of the proposition that nations and men are instruments of the Almighty.

Both parties deprecated war; but one of them would *make* war rather than let the nation survive; and the other would *accept* war rather than let it perish. And the war came.

One eighth of the whole population were colored slaves, not distributed generally over the Union, but localized in the Southern part of it. These slaves constituted a peculiar and powerful interest. All knew that this interest was, somehow, the cause of the war. To strengthen, perpetuate, and extend this interest was the object for which the insurgents would rend the Union, even by war; while the government claimed no right to do more than to restrict the territorial enlargement of it. Neither party expected for the war, the magnitude, or the duration, which it has already attained. Neither anticipated that the *cause* of the conflict might cease with, or even before, the conflict itself should cease. Each looked for an easier triumph, and a result less fundamental and astounding. Both read the same Bible, and pray to the same God; and each invokes His aid against the other. It may seem strange that any men should dare to ask a just God's assistance in wringing their bread from the sweat of other men's faces; but let us judge not that we be not judged. The prayers of both could not be answered; that of neither has been answered fully. The Almighty has His own purposes. "Woe unto the world because of offenses! For it must needs be that offenses come; but woe to that man by whom the offense cometh!" If we shall suppose that American Slavery is one of those offenses which, in the providence of God, must needs come, but which, having continued through His appointed time, He now wills to remove, and that He gives to both North and South, this terrible war, as the woe due to those by whom the offense came, shall we discern therein any departure

from those divine attributes which the believers in a Living
God always ascribe to Him? Fondly do we hope—fervently
do we pray—that this mighty scourge of war may speedily
pass away. Yet, if God wills that it continue, until all the
wealth piled by the bond-man's two hundred and fifty
years of unrequited toil shall be sunk, and until every drop
of blood drawn with the lash, shall be paid with another
drawn with the sword, as was said three thousand years
ago, so still it must be said "the judgments of the Lord are
true and righteous altogether."

With malice toward none; with charity for all; with
firmness in the right, as God gives us to see the right, let us
strive on to finish the work we are in; to bind up the nation's wounds; to care for him who shall have borne the
battle, and for his widow, and his ophan—to do all which
may achieve and cherish a just, and a lasting peace, among
ourselves, and with all nations.

In this inspired document do we not see Lincoln's central
convictions on the Union, the nation under God with its
moral purpose; the great testing of its central proposition by
an ordeal of blood; and the way of charity to a new birth?[35]

Whether Lincoln could have led the United States along
the path marked out in his last great utterance no one will
ever know. Certainly he would have run into difficulties of
massive proportions. The vindictive positions of Munger and
Dabney lived on in too many war-embittered hearts to give
charity much of a chance.[36] And the nation's endemic racism
stood squarely athwart the freedman's opportunity for genuine freedom.

Very soon after peace was established, still a third, and
more assimilable interpretation of the war began to appear, a
view which would ultimately predominate. One may call it
the "sentimental view," though not without recognizing its

[35] See William J. Wolf, *The Almost Chosen People: A Study
of the Religion of Abraham Lincoln,* a major contribution.
[36] Washington Gladden, the future Social Gospel leader, was
among the few that counseled moderation even after Lincoln's
assassination. He pointed out that Booth got little or no applause in
the South. But Gladden admitted that his words were very coldly
received, affecting the course of the nation about as much "as the
chirping of the swallows on the telegraph pole affects the motion of
the Twentieth Century Limited" (*Recollections* [Boston: Houghton Mifflin Co., 1909], pp. 147–53).

many positive, even noble aspects. It arose, in part, because the more extreme forms of postwar animosity simply ran counter to the whole spirit of the national memory and the national hope. Lincoln himself had appealed to "our bonds of affection" in his First Inaugural. "The mystic chords of memory, stretching from every battlefield, and patriot grave, to every living heart and hearthstone, all over this broad land, will yet swell the chorus of the Union, when again touched, as surely they will be, by the better angels of our nature." And this in due time they did, though not by accepting the judgment of that "great tribunal, the American people" as Lincoln had hoped in 1861, but over more battlefields and many, many more graves. In growing numbers people tired of sectional invective.

A more responsive chord was struck by the ladies of Columbus, Mississippi, who in 1867 placed flowers over the fallen Blue as well as the Gray. Francis Miles Finch, a Yale graduate and attorney, called attention to their deed with verses which became the folk poem of Memorial Day. Millions of Americans, North and South, decade after decade, learned it by heart—and took it to heart.

> From the silence of sorrowful hours
>   The desolate mourners go,
> Lovingly laden with flowers,
>   Alike for the friend and the foe:—
>   Under the sod and the dew,
>   Waiting the judgment day;
>   Under the one, the Blue
>   Under the other, the Gray.
>
>   . . . .
> So with an equal splendor
>   The morning sun rays fall,
> With a touch impartially tender
>   On the blossoms blooming for all.
>
>   . . . .
> No more shall the war-cry sever,
>   Or the winding rivers be red.
> They banish our anger forever
>   When they laurel the graves of the dead:—
>   Under the sod and the dew
>   Waiting the judgment day;
>   Love and tears for the Blue
>   Tears and love for the Gray.

Memorial Day took its place in the American calendar not as an occasion for waving the bloody shirt but as a day of reconciliation.[37] It joined Independence Day and Thanksgiving as a time when the American's love for his country was blended with the solemnities of religion. In villages and cities it became a day for invocations, benedictions and hymns, Finch's poem, the Gettysburg Address, and patriotic orations —a day for flags and flowers, a "Decoration Day" in the nation's cemeteries. A unique American way of remembering a *civil* war emerged. Sentiment celebrated its conquest of logic as the country traveled the "road to reunion." Battle flags were returned; joint observances were held at great battlefields; and in 1874 Senator L. Q. C. Lamar of Alabama delivered his famous memorial oration in honor of Charles Sumner. In his words the illustrious Senator from Massachusetts speaks from the grave: "My countrymen! know one another, and you will love one another."[38]

Ironically, however, the Centennial Year 1876 witnessed not only a tumultuous national celebration, but the great sellout of Reconstruction, a "victory" of reconciliationism in which the freedman was left to his own tragically inadequate devices. America's moment of truth regarding the issue at the bottom of the crisis was postponed until the centennial years of the Civil War and Reconstruction. Thus collapsed Lincoln's profound hope that the Union of an "almost chosen people"—made "more perfect" in the Constitution and given a new birth in the agonies of war—would assume the moral burden laid upon it by the Almighty.

RECONSTRUCTION AND THE CHURCHES

When the war ended, two weary armies rapidly disbanded, the victors marching home in ordered array to cheering multitudes, the defeated making their way as best they could

[37] The origins of this American holy day are obscure, but on 30 May 1865, with much national publicity, James Redpath led a group of Negro children to put flowers on the Union graves near Charleston. The Grand Army of the Republic (Union veterans) pressed for the day's regular observance. In 1873 New York led the states in making it a legal holiday.

[38] Sumner, one of the most adamant and powerful of the Republican Radicals in the Senate, had died in 1874. Lamar became the first ex-Confederate in a cabinet post.

amid desolation and ruin. With the tasks of peace at hand,
the two sections remained as desperately at odds as before.
Indeed, the chasm between them was wider than ever. For
most Southerners reconstruction could mean only one thing:
to put back the pieces so far as possible in the way they were
in 1860, *status quo antebellum.* "They stacked their arms but
not their principles," said one Northern Presbyterian editor.
As Merton Coulter put it, they hoped to do for their way of
life what all the king's horses and all the king's men could not
do for Humpty Dumpty. Most Northerners, on the other
hand, regarded restoration of the old regime in the South as
precisely the solution to be avoided. They might differ on
theories and strategies, but they agreed that the cause for
which Union soldiers had fought and died should not suffer
eclipse. There would be a "new South" in a new and stronger
Union.

But the war had also created a "new North," and in this
transformed region social and political problems arose with
such speed that Reconstruction soon became a task for the
left hand, then for neither hand, and finally not even for the
lips. At both of the political party conventions of 1876
"Grantism" was repudiated. Two relatively unsmirched candidates were placed before the electorate, though the Demo-
crat, Samuel J. Tilden, was not untainted by associations with
the Tweed Ring in New York, while the Republican (and
former major-general), Rutherford B. Hayes, had freely exploited Ohio's anti-Catholicism in running for governor there.
A disputed election followed, in which Hayes (in any case
not a radical reconstructionist) finally became president after
an involved series of political maneuvers had resulted in the
Compromise of 1877. The result is well known: with Federal
military support withdrawn, the remaining Republican governments in the South collapsed; the "Solid South" emerged
again, effectively keeping the Negro from the polls by legislation, party organization, and the Ku Klux Klan. With "home
rule" accomplished, the South embarked on a course of its
own, becoming reconciled to the North in certain respects,
yet remaining profoundly separate in its own mind and
memory and in its own distinctive religious history.

Between the early ardor and the later relaxation, the
United States passed through one of its most crucial—and fateful—crises, an unprecedented time of testing when the nation was weighed and found wanting. A long, bloody war, to

be sure, was the worst possible preparation for a profound moral encounter; and perhaps the same racial impasse that had made armed conflict inevitable also made a just reconstruction inpossible. For these reasons the "tragic era" is of maximum importance to the moral and religious history of the American people. Yet its treatment by historians has been apologetic and evasive. Like the political historiography on the period, the conventional church-historical accounts need revision. In both cases the prevailing interpretation is seriously discolored by the fact that it was shaped amid a resurgence of crusading Anglo-Saxonism during the turn-of-century decades. Northern Protestant historians with their commitments to temperance, Sabbatarianism, nativism, and immigration restriction were overtaken by the same realization that Kenneth Stampp ascribes to the historical profession generally: their basic views on ethnic and racial issues "were *precisely* the ones that southern white men had been making Negroes for years. And in their extremity, the old middle classes of the North looked with new understanding upon the problems of the beleaguered white men of the South."[39]

On the other hand, there is an equally important church-historical corollary to Stampp's observation, for the churches had provided the major institutional context in which the antislavery impulse could thrive during the war and Reconstruction, and they provided a place for its survival during the succeeding decades, when even old radical journals like the *Nation* and *Harper's Weekly* accepted the Compromise of 1877, and when the "best men" lost interest in the freedman. Yet by the time of the War with Spain this reforming zeal had lost its force. The Social Gospel itself would almost forget the South and the freedman—despite its debt both in method and theory to the antislavery movement, and even though the plight of the blacks would actually reach its nadir in the "Progressive Era."

During the period of Reconstruction (which in one sense began as soon as Union armies made substantial inroads on Confederate territory) the Northern Protestant churches were a mainstay of the Radical program. They regarded themselves, in fact, as the custodians of the moral factor in the entire sectional crisis, and with the coming of peace they remained the chief popular support for the political leaders

[39] Kenneth M. Stampp, *The Era of Reconstruction, 1865–1877* (New York: Random House, Vintage Books, 1965), p. 19.

who wished to prevent a compromise. This involved them inescapably in the Republican strategies which were designed to prevent or delay the rise of a politically potent South. Yet the needs of the freedman and a grim determination to reform the South best explain why the churches made Reconstruction an extension of the antislavery crusade, and why they won powerful bases of support among agrarian as well as industrial constituencies. The most influential of church papers, the *Independent* of New York, put the matter in a way that no doubt satisfied the overwhelming majority of its seventy thousand subscribers: "These venomous [Southern] masters should be put under tutors and governors till the time appointed. A freedman's bureau is less needed than a rebel's bureau."[40]

Resisting this "Radical" program were the Democrats, who had a party to rehabilitate, and a small group of Republican moderates such as Henry Ward Beecher. These men were congenial to President Johnson's program of restoring the Union expeditiously—on the theory that secession had been illegal. Republicans, seeking to hold their party together, tended strongly to the opposite pole; and under the leadership of Thaddeus Stevens and Charles Sumner they advocated a far more complete and detailed reconstruction. Soon thoroughly at odds with the president, and piling up great majorities in the congressional elections of 1866, these Radical Republicans took the federal power into their own hands, overriding presidential vetoes, administrating the "conquered provinces," and controlling the readmission of states to the Union. As the party of principle, they won massive support in the Protestant churches until a combination of flagging fervor, stubborn Southern resistance, new distractions, and the rising spirit of reconciliationism led to widespread abandonment of Radical aims.

During the Reconstruction decade, however, exalted principles were more easily formulated than implemented. The Grand Old Party learned that social structures, immemorial folkways, and the legacy of slavery could not be transformed by governmental fiat or by the general run of civil servants. Yet the almost classic Southern version of Reconstruction's barbaric failures is faulty. Despite devastation and depression, agrarian recovery and industrial advance were achieved.

[40] Vol. 17, no. 871 (August 1865): 4; quoted in Dunham, *The Attitude of the Northern Clergy*, p. 234.

The Bureau of Refugees, Freedmen, and Abandoned Lands, established in 1865 and extended over President Johnson's veto in 1866, never did fulfill the freedman's hope for a place on the "abandoned lands," yet in some states it did ease his transition from one form of bondage to another. In the end the Bureau, like so many other noble plans, became a victim of political interference, weak leadership, and racist presuppositions.

The whole cause of civil rights, nevertheless, was greatly and permanently advanced by the Civil Rights Act of 1866 (also passed over a veto) and three great amendments to the federal Constitution which probably could not have been passed at any later period. The Thirteenth Amendment, which abolished slavery, was passed to the states and ratified in 1865; the Fourteenth, which incorporated the principles of the Civil Rights Act and forbade the abridgment of any citizen's privileges or immunities, was passed in 1866 and ratified in 1868; and the Fifteenth, which guaranteed to all citizens the right to vote, was passed in 1869 and ratified in 1870. As every American knows, the provisions of the latter two amendments, even after a century, were very ineffectively enforced. Yet in the epoch-making court decisions and civil rights struggles since the end of World War II the Reconstruction Amendments played a vital role. In 1968, the Supreme Court cited the Civil Rights Act of 1866 in an openhousing case. Unless one simply accepts the idea that the United States was meant to be a *"Herrenvolk* democracy," the statesmen and private citizens who led the struggle for a real reconstruction deserve something better than *Gone With the Wind*.

That the Reconstruction Radicals were fiercely partisan cannot be denied; but equally undeniable is their consistent concern for civil rights, a concern that had been shaped in the abolitionist movement. The ideals and temperament of that crusade are clearly represented in the character of Thaddeus Stevens (1792–1868). Born in poverty in rural Vermont, reared by a pious Calvinstic Baptist mother, and educated at Dartmouth, Stevens became an eminent Pennsylvania lawyer and iron manufacturer. He had cast his lot with the antislavery cause in 1823, and in 1848 he went to Congress as a "Conscience Whig," an office which he held until his death. As the leader of the Republican Radicals he was, during the early postwar years, the freedman's most un-

deviating champion and the South's most implacable foe; in
addition, he was perhaps the most powerful man in American
politics. In 1850 the Southern Speaker of the House, Howell
Cobb, recognizing a formidable opponent, had described him
in words that remind one of William Lloyd Garrison's opening editorial in the *Liberator*:

> Our enemy has a general now. This man is rich, therefore,
> we cannot buy him. He does not want higher office,
> therefore, we cannot allure him. He is not vicious, there-
> fore, we cannot seduce him. He is in earnest. He means
> what he says. He is bold. He cannot be flattered or fright-
> ened.[41]

It is unrewarding to explain the motives of a man like this in
terms of social status, economic gain, or other concerns. What
Stampp says of Charles Sumner, Stevens's powerful colleague
in the Senate, seems equally true of Stevens himself: "To deny
the reality of his moral fervor and humanitarian idealism is to
deny the reality of the man himself."[42] The same could be
said of many Radical leaders.

So intense was the commitment of most Northern Protestant churches to the congressional Radicals that even their
most questionable effort—to impeach the president in 1868—
won widespread support. The Methodists, meeting in general
conference at the time of the trial before the Senate, set aside
an hour of prayer in order that "corrupt influences" might be
brought to an end. They also believed that even Southern
Methodist church property should be confiscated. It is altogether possible, moreover, that if General Grant had not
proved so ineffective as president, some measure of idealism
and moral integrity might have pervaded reconstruction
activity during the crucial years from 1869 to 1877. As it
happened, corruption, indecision, and scandal became so
widespread that many of the most ardent and most capable
reform leaders were drawn away from the "Southern question."

While churchmen brought support to Reconstructionists in
Washington, they also attempted through ecclesiastical chan-

[41] Quoted in Fawn Brodie, *Thaddeus Stevens: Scourge of the
South* (New York: W. W. Norton & Co., 1966), p. 110.
[42] *The Era of Reconstruction*, p. 102.

nels to aid the newly freed blacks. Hundreds of relief associations for this purpose were organized in the towns and cities of the North, some as early as 1861. To coordinate this work the United States Commission for the Relief of the National Freedman was formed in 1863 by a merger of five of the larger city organizations, followed by the American Freedman's Union Commission, organized in 1866 to embrace a still larger range of such societies. After 1869 much of its activity ceased, as Congress took increasing control of reconstruction and freedman's aid, and because denominational societies were proceeding independently. The Northern Presbyterians organized their freedmen's committee in 1864; the Methodists their much more vigorous Freedman's Aid Society in 1866, and other churches did likewise.

By far the most effective of these church-oriented agencies for the freedman was the American Missionary Association, founded at Albany in 1846 by the merger of several small societies of Congregational origin who shared a missionary commitment to nonwhite peoples and a strong antislavery bent. By 1860 its 112 abolitionistic home missionaries outnumbered its workers abroad, and at the war's end it had 528 missionaries and teachers at work in the South. After the war the AMA also helped to implement joint projects for founding and staffing schools in the South, a philanthropic effort which marshaled millions of dollars and supported thousands of teachers and school administrators for work among the Southern blacks. One of the noblest and least recognized chapters in Reconstruction history was written by these poorly paid educators, most of them women, as they struggled amid penury, ridicule, hostility, and sometimes outright violence to demonstrate their faith in the nation's ideals and in the Negro's natural capacity to enter fully into American life.[43] Shortcomings there were—cultural condescension and curricular inflexibility, to name two—yet at no other point did the old antislavery impulse so clearly reveal the moral quality of its motivation.

Gradually, however, the sheer magnitude of the task, the hostility of Southern whites, and the decline of fervor even

[43] In 1870 the president of Talladega College (Alabama) was shot and killed by a mob. Southern aid and protection could be gained only for trade schools, and this but grudgingly until after World War I.

among leaders of the denominational agencies caused many projects to be abandoned. This trend continued with the steady deterioration of the Freedman's Bureau, the end of official reconstruction in 1877, and the catastrophic rulings of the Supreme Court in 1883 which declared crucial sections of the Civil Rights Act of 1875 unconstitutional. Nevertheless a limited number of institutions, such as Lincoln University in Pennsylvania, Morehouse College and Atlanta University in Georgia, Talladega College in Alabama, Tougaloo University in Mississippi, Hampton Institute in Virginia, and Fisk University in Tennessee, all founded or supported by the churches during these years, managed to survive. Prior to 1900, "practically all of the faculty members of Southern Negro colleges were idealistic educational missionaries who had been educated in Northern colleges."[44] The decision of George Peabody of Massachusetts to create a $3.5 million trust fund for the furtherance of Southern education gave great impetus to the cause, and with the Reverend Barnas Sears, president of Brown University, as its general agent until 1880, this fund accounted for much of the later advance in black education made in the South. In 1882 John F. Slater of Rhode Island created another million-dollar fund for similar purposes.

Support for radicalism and aid to the freedman were not the only efforts at reconstruction undertaken by the churches. Their most direct attempts were strictly ecclesiastical. The three large denominations which had divided over the slavery issue projected plans for displacing the Southern branches of their denominations. Because the Southern "schismatics" had in fact proclaimed slavery as God's will with far more absolutism and unanimity than the Northern churches had shown in their opposition, they were now simply considered disqualified. On 27 July 1865, the *Independent* again voiced the majority view: "The apostate church is buried beneath a flood of divine wrath; its hideous dogmas shrine on its brow like flaming fiends; the whole world stands aghast at its wickedness and ruin. The Northern church beholds its mission." But it was one thing for religious journalists to behold a mission and quite another for Northern churches to carry it out. Although some large churches actually did at one time or another use the opportunities provided by military or radical

[44] John S. Brubacher and Willis Rudy, *Higher Education in Transition* (New York: Harper & Brothers, 1958), p. 75.

reconstruction to "occupy" Southern churches, their successes in winning a new black membership or in forcibly reuniting their denominations were exceedingly modest. Only the Northern Methodists made significant gains among the freedmen, but this new black membership was organized in a separate jurisdiction with its its own hierarchy.

The only successful reunion efforts carried out by the larger denominations were those of the Episcopal and Roman Catholic churches, where a diocesan polity and a record of ambivalent moderation on the central issues allowed the "Southern solution" to be carried out in appropriate territories of the united church. In 1861 the dioceses of the Confederacy, led by Bishops Stephen Elliott of Georgia and Leonidas Polk of Louisiana, had organized a Protestant Episcopal Church, C.S.A. No changes of doctrine, polity, or liturgy were made in the South, except for a few political references in the prayer book and the consecration of a new bishop in Alabama. The Northern church, meanwhile, merely noted the absence of Southern representatives at the 1862 meeting of the General Convention (a meeting which issued a mildly controversial declaration for the Union). When it next met three years later, unity was restored with a minimum of bitterness. In a formal sense the Roman Catholic church could not divide, inasmuch as the Holy See was outside and above the conflict. Yet as a practical matter bishops, clergy, and laity acted as if they were loyal citizens of two different nations. When hostilities ceased, the hierarchy resumed its normal functioning, and in the Plenary Council of 1866 all of the country's dioceses were represented. Neither of these churches, however, sought to press reconstructionist policies on their Southern dioceses.

Southern Baptists, Methodists, Presbyterians, and Lutherans, on the other hand, with one voice proclaimed their loyalty to the Lost Cause, accepted or arranged for the transfer or separated status of Negro "members," and in some cases even won accessions among whites in the loyal border states where slavery had once existed. In the small Protestant Methodist church the Northern conferences coalesced with the Southern. Presbyterians in the North meanwhile followed the wartime example of the Southerners, and in 1869–70 found occasion to end the Old School-New School schism which had riven the church in 1837. Because the South as a whole thus went its religious way, the chief new ecclesiastical development of the era was neither reconquest nor reunion of the alienated regions, but rather the rise of independent Negro churches, Baptist or Methodist. These churches played a significant role during Reconstruction days when the Federal army, the Freedman's Bureau, and the Union Leagues utilized them to strengthen Radical Republican power. But after 1877 they, too, became a part of the "Southern solution" (segregation, subservience, and tenantry), not to emerge as a "radical" social force again until the 1950s, and then with slow and uncertain voice. These churches grew apace during the later nineteenth century, however, and gradually developed a distinctive religious ethos which traditional denominational allegiances could neither submerge nor alter. Through a long and bitter century they became the chief bearers of the Afro-American heritage.

42

THE RISE OF THE BLACK CHURCHES

Enslavement and emancipation in changing proportions, though always with the emphasis on bondage, have pervaded the entire history of the African in America. From the earliest times there were sporadic manumissions and escapes; and heavily qualified emancipation during the revolutionary era led to the rise of a partially free black community in the North. But the Civil War was the great time of transition, though the accidents of military strategy made even that a drawn-out process—beginning with the Federal occupation of the Sea Islands of South Carolina seven months after the fall of Fort Sumter and ending only after the final Confederate surrender in 1865. Then began a remarkable period in American religious history. Out of the shambles of Southern civilization and amid the violence of Reconstruction, the freedmen undertook the tasks of church organization. Black Baptist churches were the first to be organized, and these congregations then began to form wider associations. The two African Methodist churches of the North also moved very early toward their newly freed constituency. The "invisible institution" of antebellum days thus became visible—and not only visible, but the chief institution of the freedman. By the century's end there were 2.7 million church members in a black population of 8.3 million.

This astonishing growth calls for explanations of several sorts, but obviously primary—for chronological reasons if for no other—is a degree of familiarity with the nature of black religious life under slavery. Some consideration of certain aspects of this history has already been given in chapters on the early South, the Great Awakening, the Revolution, the antislavery movement, and the Civil War; but a brief discussion of black religion and the rise of Negro Protestantism (as well as the questions pertaining to that distinction) is reserved for this chapter.[1]

THE CHRISTIANIZATION OF THE AMERICAN NEGRO

On exceedingly rare occasions a slave brought to America was a Moslem or showed signs of Islamic contacts; but almost never had the blacks encountered Christianity except through the Europeans who bought and sold them. Bondage constituted their introduction to Western civilization. Virginia, the major slave colony, could in 1670 safely legislate that "all servants not being christians" who were brought into the colony by sea were to be slaves for life.

It was well established by this time that baptism need not be followed by the manumission of slaves, but colonists remained reluctant to convert or catechize blacks. The notion that Negroes were not included in God's scheme of redemption probably justified the inaction of some, but others no doubt found it easier to justify the enslavement of heathen than of fellow children of God. The Society for the Propagation of the Gospel, from its founding in 1701 throughout the century, constantly admonished its missionaries to work among the slaves, and they in turn admonished the laity. Bishops of London admonished both clergy and laity. The

[1] My efforts can be regarded as no more than preliminary. Only the incitements of the mid-twentieth century awakened historians from their dogmatic slumbers with regard to Afro-American history. Until then efforts to understand the Negro's past had been minuscule, and specialists in religion were proportionately more remiss than the others, considering the importance of the churches in Negro life and the uniqueness of black religion. The American Church History series edited by Philip Schaff during the 1890s omitted histories of the African and Colored Methodist Episcopal churches as well as of the Negro Baptist churches. As late as 1970 no scholar had produced a religious history of the American Negro that even pretended to replace Carter G. Woodson's *History of the Negro Church* (1921), though E. Franklin Frazier shortly before his death had improved the situation with a brief overview adapted from lectures delivered in Paris in 1953, *The Negro Church in America*. Many important monographs have been written by both black and white authors, to be sure; but the amount of work yet to be done is awesome.

Society of Friends continued to testify, as George Fox had done, that "Christ by the grace of God tasted death for every man"; and beginning with John Woolman in the mid-eighteenth century one can trace a continuous Quaker testimony against slavery. But reluctance among the chief slaveholders and opposition from many others (including Quakers) tended strongly to limit the effects of evangelistic zeal; and the early missionary efforts of Anglicans and Quakers usually expired after some modest program of instruction or even a school had begun. "Amid the blare of trumpets rallying Christians to the work of God," writes Winthrop Jordan, "one can easily detect the shuffle of dragging feet."[2] Outside New England, where slaves were few, ministers or catechists were in any case in such short supply that most of the white population was an almost equally needy mission field.

Only with the Great Awakening did a break in the Southern religious situation begin to occur. The preachers of that tumultuous revival upset the established order in many ways. They spread abroad a confidence in the people that made them harbingers not only of the Revolution but of abolitionism. Preaching sin and salvation to the slaves, they broke with the decorous Anglican efforts of the past. They offered no simple catechetical exercises on the Ten Commandments, no homilies of the virtues of obedience to masters and patience in suffering and toil. "The blessed Savior died and shed his blood as much for you as for your master, or any of the white people"—such as the Presbyterian "new light" that Cary Allen brought to the slaves of Virginia. "[He] has opened the door of heaven wide for you and invites you all to enter."[3]

Neither George Whitefield nor the American revival preachers raised direct questions about the institution of slavery, though New Divinity men like Jonathan Edwards, Jr., and Samuel Hopkins even did that. But these preachers did raise for the first time the revolutionary implications of equality before God. Whitefield was even blamed for the 1741 "arsonist-plot" in New York. And Samuel Davies, who would

2 Winthrop D. Jordan, *White over Black: American Attitudes toward the Negro, 1550–1182*, p. 180. See also pp. 244–46 in Volume 1.

3 William Hill, "Reverend Cary Allen," *Presbyterian Quarterly Review* 9: 76–77; quoted by Susan Solomon, "Evangelicalism and Moralism in the Eighteenth-Century South" (seminar paper, Yale University, 1969).

later be president of Princeton, very explicitly defended the slave's equal ability to appropriate the gospel:

> Your Negroes may be ignorant and stupid as to divine Things, not for Want of Capacity, but for Want of Instruction; not through their Perverseness, but through your Negligence. From the many Trials I have made, I have Reason to conclude, that making Allowance for their low and barbarous Education, their imperfect Acquaintance with our Language, their having no Opportunity for intellectual Improvements, and the like, they are generally as capable of Instruction, as the white People.[4]

As the American experience gradually undermined old views on the necessary, God-given stratification of society, such views would gain new significance.

Carter Woodson rightly placed "the Dawn of the New Day" in the Christian history of the American Negro in the later eighteenth and early nineteenth centuries, after the Revolution had lifted most hindrances to freedom of religion.[5] There is a monumental irony in this observation, however, for these very decades between 1790 and 1815 were the time in which the cotton gin, new breeds of cotton, and westward expansion were giving the American slave system those features that made it "the most awful the world has ever known."[6] Descriptions of camp meetings, weeping sinners, great conversions, and rhythmic song must never blot that fact from view. Slavery shaped not only the political economy of the South, but its whole culture. Insofar as absolute power corrupts absolutely, the Southern white was reduced in his humanity by his lordship over the blacks he bought, sold, and raped. Harriet Beecher Stowe illustrates this point in the first ten pages of her great novel, which she first planned to subtitle, "The Man That Was a Thing." The slave, in turn, to make his own life endurable, had to act out the stereotype of childish immaturity by which his masters justified the system

---

[4] Quoted in Jordan, *White over Black*, p. 188.

[5] Woodson, *The History of the Negro Church*, chap. 2.

[6] Nathan Glazer, introduction to Stanley M. Elkins, *Slavery: A Problem in American Institutional and Intellectual Life* (New York: Grosset & Dunlap Universal Library, 1963), p. ix. Elkins overdraws the Sambo image, though his cautious comparative use of the Nazi concentration camp is instructive.

—in the process alienating himself from his blackness. Where the sin was in this unlovely picture—and what the sins were —was not a question on which an itinerant revivalist would have the last word.

During these years, nevertheless, the Baptists and Methodists did begin their active programs of evangelization, being aided in their efforts by mobility, fervent experientialism, and straightforward preaching. Bishop Benjamin T. Tanner of the African Methodist Episcopal church vividly contrasted the evangelistic methods which accounted for the changed religious spirit in the South—for whites and blacks alike:

> While the good Presbyterian parson was writing his discourses, rounding off the sentences, the Methodist itinerant had traveled forty miles with his horse and saddle bags; while the parson was adjusting his spectacles to read his manuscript, the itinerant had given hell and damnation to his unrepentant hearers; while the disciple of Calvin was waiting to have his church completed, the disciple of Wesley took to the woods and made them re-echo with the voice of free grace, believing with Bryant, "The groves were God's first temples."[7]

Under such auspices a considerable number of black preachers were ordained, some of them to very successful ministries. Occasionally it was even possible to organize Negro congregations. That of the Baptists at Silver Bluff, South Carolina, between 1773 and 1775 is credited as the first. Scattered historical evidence indicates that a dozen others had been formed by 1800—most of them Baptist, but a few Methodist or Presbyterian.

After the Revolution considerable activity took place in the free or partially free black communities of the North; and by 1821 two independent African Methodist Episcopal churches had been formed.[8] In virtually all of the slave states, however, there were laws to restrict the slave's freedom of assembly, so that the usual practice was to compose local churches of both white and black members, allotting special seating to the blacks, who often outnumbered white members. In 1790 the Methodist church reported 11,682 "colored" members,

[7] Quoted in Woodson, *The History of the Negro Church*, pp. 97–98.
[8] See pp. 161–62 below.

almost a fifth of the church's total; and the Baptists at that early date are generally believed to have converted many more. Statistics are inconclusive, but diverse reports from scattered parishes support the view that these two groups were far more successful than the Episcopal, Presbyterian, and Lutheran churches.

When the antislavery movement shifted to a new level of intensity, the South took a much more defensive stance than formerly, with the result that after 1830 the benefits of Christianization became a common argument in the justification of slavery. The churches, therefore, were spurred to renewed efforts of evangelism. During the last decades before the war this emphasis on missions to the slaves was especially strong among Southern Methodists, who devoted $1.8 million to the cause between 1844 and 1864, partly due to the influence of Bishop William Capers of South Carolina in promoting this mission.[9] The Baptist and other churches also increased their efforts, but just how effectively the mission was carried out is difficult to say. In ideal circumstances the instruction or religious understanding of slaves probably approached that of the whites, but in areas of dense black population and on large "industrial" plantations, slaves were far less adequately churched—if at all.

If the rise of abolitionism had a positive influence on Negro evangelism, Nat Turner's slave insurrection in Virginia in 1831 had the opposite effect. Turner was a Baptist exhorter with strong visionary tendencies, and since there had also been significant religious overtones in Gabriel Prosser's plot of 1800 and Denmark Vesey's attempt in 1822, fear of further rebellions led to increased resistance to the preaching activity of free Negroes, the separate assembly of black congregations, and the spread of literacy among the slaves.

Given the combination of these factors—the sheer vastness of the task, the prohibitions on public assembly, and restrictions on the extension of literacy among the slaves—only the most incomplete kind of Christianization could be carried out. One ex-slave described the situation when he said that "the colored folks had their own code of religion, not nearly

[9] In the year of Capers's death (1854) $25,000 was spent for this effort. The twenty-five plantation missions served by thirty-two preachers then had ten thousand black members, one thousand white (Gross Alexander, *History of the Methodist Episcopal Church, South*, ACHS, vol. 11 [New York, 1894], p. 117).

so complicated as the white man's."[10] On the other hand, it would be unrealistic to exaggerate the complicatedness of the white man's religion. What developed, in fact, were intermingled streams of folk piety with distinctive Baptist and Methodist elements apparent in the religious life of each race. In many areas, especially in the Deep South where planters were more commonly Methodist or Baptist, ministers were cheered by the encouragement they received and by the large number of converts.

The Methodists had an advantage because their annual camp meetings in August, after the crops were in, were the social event of the year. Provision was often made for both blacks and whites to stay in some country grove for several days of rousing religion. U. B. Phillips gives a typical report from one Georgia preacher in 1807, one that shows incidentally how the greater receptivity of the blacks gratified the preachers.

The first day of the meeting [Tuesday], we had a gentle and comfortable moving of the spirit of the Lord among us; and at night it was without intermission. However, before day the white people retired, and the meeting was continued by the black people. [After describing the mounting fervor on Wednesday and Thursday, he continues.] Friday was the greatest day of all. We had the Lord's Supper at night, . . . and such a solemn time have I seldom seen on the like occasion. Three of the preachers fell helpless within the altar, and one lay a considerable time before he came to himself. From that the work of convictions and conversions spread, and a large number were converted during that night, and there was no intermission until the break of day. . . . On Saturday we had preaching at the rising of the sun; and then with many tears we took leave of each other.[11]

Almost everywhere, but particularly in areas where Baptist or Methodist labors were fairly intensive, a kind of semi-independent religious life developed among the slaves. Black preachers and exhorters would continue the work, and in

[10] Quoted in E. Franklin Frazier, *The Negro in the United States*, p. 343.
[11] Ulrich B. Phillips, *American Negro Slavery* (Baton Rouge: Louisiana State University Press, 1966), pp. 316–17.

areas where slaves were relatively more numerous they often had charge of worship services on Sunday. Where whites were numerically predominant, slaves were usually assigned a segregated place in the church of the area. The so-called invisible institution took shape as the slaves combined their understanding of the Bible and their conceptions of life and the world with their suppressed yearnings for freedom from toil and bondage. This is the substance of Frazier's important observation that revivalistic Protestant Christianity became the chief means by which the African slave—bereft of his native culture, language, and religion—defined and explained his personal and social existence in America.

This religion also provided the only means at hand to preserve such vestiges of his African past as had not been utterly extinguished in the successive stages of the slave system. The spirituals, for example, reflect the way in which Bible stories and the gospel message could be invested with intense meaning. They were songs of faith and hope, not coded protest songs nor celebrations of specific events. In their otherworldliness, in their vision of jubilation and plenty "over Jordan," they expressed the same hope that was sung in the white churches, among the German pietists, and in Wesley's England. They also expressed the reality of work-weariness and bondage, with the slaves' condition giving such songs a kind of authenticity that was lacking in socially prominent white Protestant churches when similar hymns were sung. In addition, the theology of the spirituals shaped the religious experience of the singers. Individuals locked in the most awful corporate sin ever perpetrated by one race upon another came to a conviction of their little sins, then, in the fullness of time, they were "borned again." Whether this climactic event was explained in the predestinarian terms of the Primitive Baptists or the Arminianism of the Methodists (distinctions by no means lost on even the most lowly), a new life in Christ was hopefully begun. An eloquent example of this experience is provided by Mortimer———, who recounts the beginnings of his life as a Christian in slavery days:

One day while in the field plowing I heard a voice. . . . Again the voice called, "Morte! Morte!" With this I stopped, dropped the plow, and started running, but the voice kept on speaking to me saying, "Fear not, my little one, for behold! I come to bring you a message of truth."

Everything got dark, and I was unable to stand any longer. I began to feel sick, and there was a great roaring. I tried to cry and move but was unable to do either. I looked up and saw that I was in a new world. There were plants and animals, and all, even the water where I stooped down to drink, began to cry out, "I am blessed but you are damned! I am blessed but you are damned!" With this I began to pray, and a voice on the inside began to cry, "Mercy! Mercy! Mercy!"

As I prayed an angel came and touched me, and I looked new. . . . I again prayed, and there came a soft voice saying, "My little one, I have loved you with an everlasting love. You are this day made alive and freed from hell. You are a chosen vessel unto the Lord. Be upright before me, and I will guide you unto all truth. My grace is sufficient for you. Go, and I am with you. Preach the gospel, and I will preach with you. You are henceforth the salt of the earth." . . .

About this time my master came down the field. I became very bold and answered him when he called me. He asked me very roughly how I came to plow up the corn, and where the horse and plow were, and why I had got along so slowly. I told him that I had been talking with God Almighty, and that it was God who had plowed up the corn. He looked at me very strangely, and suddenly I fell shouting, and I shouted and began to preach. . . .

When I had finished I felt a great love in my heart that made me feel like stooping and kissing the very ground. My master sat watching and listening to me, and then he began to cry. He turned from me and said in a broken voice, "Morte, I believe you are a preacher. From now on you can preach to the people here on my place in the old shed by the creek. But tomorrow morning, Sunday, I want you to preach to my family and neighbors. So put your best clothes and be in front of the big house early in the morning, about nine o'clock."

The permanence of this conversion is suggested by the narrator's concluding lines, spoken in the 1920s: "Ever since that day I have been preaching the gospel and am not a bit tired.

I can tell anyone about God in the darkest hour of midnight, for it is written on my heart. Amen."[12] How this experience differs from that of Saint Bernadette of Lourdes is not easily stated. Even more interesting here is the obviously great similarity of the master's piety to that of the slave. Religion of this sort and music of this sort did not come out of an African past, but they did enable the slaves to find some kind of personal and social replacement for African modes of life and thought.[13]

THE PASSING OF THE OLD ORDER

When war broke out, white fear of widespread slave revolts naturally increased—and a consequence of that fear was a heightened concern for the slave's religious welfare. The rationale as always included the view, more hoped for than demonstrated, that religion would aid in "securing the quiet and peaceful subordination of these people."[14] And in 1863 the loyalty of four hundred slaves on a North Carolina plantation was attributed to regular religious instruction that included Saint Paul's admonition, "Brethren, let every man wherein he is called abide therein with God." At the same time, a Richmond paper asked quite frankly, "May we not hope and pray that large numbers will be savingly converted

[12] Clifton H. Johnson, ed., *God Struck Me Dead*, pp. 15–18.

[13] The question of African survivals in Afro-American culture has been heatedly debated, and religion is the sphere of life in which the most important continuities have been alleged (see Melville J. Herskovits, *The Myth of the Negro Past* [New York: Harper and Brothers, 1941]). My own inclination is to follow Frazier, Fauset, and others in discounting Herskovit's extreme claims. I find the distinctive characteristics of the American Negro's religion more parsimoniously explained as an adaptation of evangelical Christianity shaped by the special needs and conditions of black people in white America. The best case for continuities with an African past is made with regard to rhythmic and musical expression and the Afro-American's pronunciation and inflection of English. Frazier refers to the question in several books: so does Arthur H. Fauset, *Black Gods of the Metropolis*, pp. 1–8.

[14] A plea published in November 1862 by the South Carolina Conference of the Methodist Church, quoted by Bell I. Wiley, *Southern Negroes, 1861–1865* (New Haven: Yale University Press, 1938), pp. 98–99.

to Christ, thus becoming better earthly servants while they wear with meekness the yoke of their master in heaven?"[15]

These well-worn determinations could not be carried out with regularity, however, simply because the war so utterly disrupted the normal means of religious work. Ministers went off as chaplains or soldiers, or sought other employment for lack of support. Candidates for the ministry were in similar straits, with the result that accessions to the ordained ministry were drastically reduced in all churches. Even the lifting of prewar restrictions on the use of black preachers was of little avail. And when Federal troops were expected, or the force of combat was actually felt, the situation became worse.

To make matters even more critical, the slaves themselves became increasingly aware of the issues at stake in the war, so that they could not be encouraged to minister to each other. Needless to say, there are many accounts (And even more postwar stories) of old Negro preachers whose prayers always included the petition, "Protect our massa far away"; but just as many observers reported the tendency of slaves to pray for President Lincoln's armies, and to sing songs of freedom and the Promised Land with a jubilant hopefulness that suggested not a heavenly but an earthly fulfillment. The number of flights to Union armies when the situation permitted confirms Booker T. Washington's reminiscences:

> As the great day drew nearer, there was more singing in the slave quarters than usual. It was bolder, had more ring, and lasted later into the night. Most of the verses of the plantation songs had some references to freedom. True, they had sung those same verses before but they had been careful to explain that the "freedom" in these songs referred to the next world . . . now they gradually threw off the mask and were not afraid to let it be known that the freedom in their songs meant freedom of the body in this world.[16]

Thus a basic result of the war was the gradual breakdown of the customary partially integrated but paternalistic ecclesi-

15 Ibid., p. 99.
16 Booker T. Washington, *Up from Slavery* (New York: Doubleday, Page & Co., 1901), p. 19.

astical system of the Old South. By 1865 it was in a state of nearly total collapse.

At the start of the Civil War, despite fears and difficulties, somewhere between an eighth and a sixth of the South's slave population of approximately four million may have been affiliated with one or another of the churches in at least a vague way. In terms of formal membership about 225,000 of these were Methodist and 175,000 Baptist. By hearsay and song, however, vital elements of biblical religion had spread much farther—how far, or how deeply, no one will ever know. But when the black population of the South was emancipated from the formal restrictions of slavery, it soon became evident that the freedmen constituted a very special kind of home mission field, one in which the Christian faith was a widely apprehended reality. Both the circumstances of its propagation and the conditions under which it was appropriated and extended gave it a character of its own. The religion of the invisible institution, therefore, required very little modification when it became possible for blacks to organize churches under the new arrangements for life and labor that Southern Redeemers provided.

BLACK CHURCH ORGANIZATION

With the coming of peace the churches one by one went their separate, segregated ways. The Colored Primitive Baptists were organized in 1866. The first entirely Negro state convention of regular Baptists was organized in North Carolina in that same year. Since Baptist polity conduced to the formation, on a local basis, of literally countless black congregations (many entirely new and many by separation), other state conventions soon followed. These in turn gradually achieved various regional consolidations, until, by stages, a national foreign missions convention was organized. Finally, in 1895, the National Baptist Convention was formed at Atlanta, Georgia, though many local churches remained independent.[17] Following the same trend, the Cumberland

---

[17] Twelve years later the NBC was divided in a dispute over the control of property and the administration of the publishing house at Nashville. The larger faction was incorporated in 1915 as the National Baptist Convention of the U.S.A., Inc.; the other kept the old name, without the "Inc." In 1893 the Colored Bap-

Presbyterian Church divided in 1869, about a fifth of its hundred thousand members withdrawing to form a "Colored" church of the same name. Five years later the main body of Southern Presbyterians, after almost a decade of extreme vacillation as to policy, made provisions for Negro members, already gathered in separate congregations, to form an autonomous Colored Presbyterian Church. The mother church continued to raise funds in very modest amounts for the aid of its churches and schools.

The Methodists, meanwhile, had achieved a much firmer organization in four different churches. In 1866 the Southern Methodist church released its Negro membership so that it could form a Colored Methodist Episcopal church in 1870.[18] In 1866 the Northern Methodist church, whose wartime additions of southern Negro membership had been large, also made provision within its structure for a separate Negro conference with its own bishop.[19] The larger part of black Methodism, however, came to be included in two older African Methodist Episcopal churches which had been formed in the North well before sectional controversy had taken possession of the country.

The African Methodist Episcopal Church was formed in Philadelphia after two decades of friction between white and black Methodists in that city. Richard Allen (1760–1831), a manumitted layman, had founded Bethel Church for Negro Methodists in 1793, and was ordained a deacon (the first of his race in American Methodism) two years later. Because

---

tist Association of the South could claim about 1.5 million communicants. The relative size of the two NBC's has remained fairly constant:

	1920	1970
NBC	1,000,000	2,670,000
NBC, Inc.	2,000,000	5,500,000

For a history of the NBC see Owen D. Pelt and Ralph Lee Smith, *The Story of the National Baptists*.

[18] In 1954 for social and legal reasons it changed the term "Colored" to "Christian." According to Frazier, a similar move of middle-class members to eliminate the word "African" from the AME church failed because of lower-class objections (*The Negro Church in America*, p. 78).

[19] In 1939, when the three main branches of predominantly white Methodism were reunited, this Negro conference was constituted as a separate nonterritorial "Central Jurisdiction," which then became a serious source of controversy.

jurisdictional disputes after 1814 only intensified Negro dissatisfaction, the AME Church [Bethel] was organized; and in 1816, at its first General Conference, Allen was elected bishop. Twenty years later it had about seventy-five hundred members, and about three times that in 1860. In the meantime it had founded the first Negro magazine in America (1841) and acquired Wilberforce University in Ohio (1856).

In New York a similar controversy in the John Street Church led its black members to found Zion Church in 1801. Due in part to the undesired interference of Bishop Allen, this group announced itself to be the nucleus of another national church in 1821—the African Methodist Episcopal Church Zion, electing James Varick (ca. 1750–1827) as its first bishop. Because it was seriously plagued by controversy and schism, the AME Zion church numbered only five thousand members on the eve of the war. As Union armies moved into the South, both of the AME churches began missions among the freedmen which they sustained with outstanding success during the years that followed. In 1896 the AME church claimed 452,725 members and the AME Zion 349,788, both of them considerably outdistancing the Colored church of Southern Methodist lineage (129,383) as well as the Northern Methodist church's Negro Conference (246,249).[20]

The foregoing statistics and organizational details may seem wearisome and routine, yet they reveal some frequently overlooked dimensions of Protestant church history. Most important perhaps is the massive participation achieved during four turbulent decades by the independent Negro churches despite poverty and oppression. The fact of 2.7 million church members in a black population of about 8.3 million suggests that the pervasiveness of evangelical religion among the slaves must have been far greater than church records indicate.[21] It becomes apparent that Christianity answered to deeply felt needs of a people for whom emancipation had

[20] The AME Zion church had a more democratic polity, with lay representation in annual conferences and elected rather than episcopally appointed presiding elders. For some reason it became especially strong in North Carolina.

[21] "In the South, at least, practically every American Negro is a church member. . . . A proscribed people must have a social center, and that center for this people is the Negro church" (W. E. B. DuBois, *The Souls of Black Folk*, p. 143).

been a less than glorious boon. The churches were the chief means by which a structured or organized social life came into existence among the Southern freedmen. The little churches of the rural South were a psychological and social necessity—the more so because they institutionalized the only area in which a fair measure of Negro freedom remained. The success of this ecclesiastical effort, moreover, demonstrates the inadequacy of the "Sambo" interpretation of slavery's effect on the race. Given the opportunity, blacks showed immense resourcefulness in church organization. If the result did not meet the classic standards of Western ecclesiology, it was because American racism prevented blacks from "classic" forms of participation in the general society.[22]

THE ROLE OF THE BLACK CHURCHES

From the days of emancipation until the mid-twentieth century, the church was by far the most important black institution after the family. Considering the effects upon family life of centuries of chattel servitude and the ways in which the American caste system has interfered with its "normal" development, one could even make a strong case for the unqualified priority of the church. The church has consistently been the chief agency of social control, though in urban contexts its hold was gradually weakened. The churches also gave the first impetus to economic cooperation among Negroes, published the most influential periodicals, and aided Negro education as actively as any other institution.[23] Finally, the churches were a badly needed refuge in a

---

[22] The large political function of many black churches during Reconstruction is undeniable. Northern Reconstructionists often encouraged their organization, but often with strong evangelical and educational purposes as well. After the end of Reconstruction, as part of the larger pattern of enforced white supremacy, this political activity was suppressed.

[23] Even sixty years after emancipation the Southern states had made only the tiniest contribution to the public education of Negroes. Fourteen of the eighteen Southern states had an aggregate of only thirty Negro high schools in 1910, at which time only half the country's blacks were literate. Institutions founded by Northern white and Southern black churches chiefly to train a ministry provided most of the existing opportunities for primary,

hostile world. There is more pathos than humor in the reply
of a rural Alabama Negro who was asked to identify the people in the adjoining community: "The nationality in there is
Methodist."[24] The church was in a sense a surrogate for nationality, answering to diverse social needs and providing an
arena for the exercise of leadership. Far more than for
whites, the black church served other than strictly religious
needs. After 1877, as Jim Crow laws, intimidation, and political suppression steadily intensified, this function of the
church increased in significance. More than ever it became a
vital means of preserving a sense of racial solidarity.

Virtually every major authority, whether black or white,
seems to agree that despite poverty and poignant limitations,
the local church was for good or ill the primary element of
the American Negro's nineteenth-century heritage.

> The Negro Church [says Frazier in a representative pas-
> sage] has affected the entire intellectual development and
> outlook of Negroes. This has been due both to the influence
> of the Negro church which has permeated every phase of
> social life and to the influence of the Negro preacher whose
> authoritarian personality and anti-intellectualism has cast a
> shadow over the intellectual outlook of Negroes.[25]

Yet the institution about which such sweeping assertions are
made was in its outward aspect a very humble thing. It was
usually a plain, ramshackle structure serving a small neighborhood in the Southern countryside. (Until World War I,
we must recall, nearly 90 percent of the Negroes in the
United States lived in the South, and two-thirds of them were
rural.)[26] Regardless of denomination each of these little

secondary, and higher education. These impoverished schools
labored against almost insuperable odds, yet their students did
become the leaders of the Southern Negro churches (see Richard
Bardolph, *The Negro Vanguard*, pp. 98–111). The AME *Church
Review*, edited by Benjamin T. Tanner until he became a bishop
in 1888, was the leading Negro magazine (see August Meier,
Negro Thought in America, 1880–1915, p. 44).

[24] Quoted and commented on by Frazier, *The Negro Church
in America*, p. 44.

[25] Ibid., pp. 41–42.

[26] From 1790 to 1910 this ratio is remarkably constant. After
1910 the percentage of Negroes outside the South and in cities
everywhere steadily mounts.

congregations—or often a group of them—was being led by a very modestly educated minister. In most cases he had no more than elementary schooling. Yet as a member of the only profession open to a Negro, in charge of the blacks' only free institution, he was a very important man, "the greatest single influence among the colored people of the United States," in the judgment of James Weldon Johnson.[27]

In his early book *The Souls of Black Folk*, W. E. B. DuBois stresses the minister's importance: "The Preacher is the most unique personality developed by the Negro on American soil. A leader, a politician, a 'boss,' an intriguer, an idealist—all of these he is, and ever, too, the center of a group of men, now twenty now a thousand."[28] Yet strangely absent from this list of roles is the central one: the conductor of prayer and praise, above all, the preacher—the man who had to proclaim the gospel and apply the law, and yet do so without ever addressing the primary fact of black existence, white supremacy. Against this background Johnson could characterize the preacher as the one "who instilled the narcotic doctrine epitomized in the Spiritual, 'You May Have All Dis World, But Give Me Jesus.'"

The black clergy was by no means unanimously submissive, however. Henry Turner (1834–1915), a former slave who became the first black chaplain in the Union army, was a member of the South Carolina legislature until blacks were expelled in 1868. As early as 1874 he became an advocate of emigration to Africa, and later, as a bishop of the AME church, he was a leading spokesman for that cause, as was another AME bishop, Jabez P. Campbell. His emigration schemes had little effect, but his attacks on injustice were strong and widely heard. "A man who loves a country that hates him," he declared, "is a human dog and not a man." The Constitution he declared to be "a dirty rag, a cheat [and] a libel." After the Supreme Court's fateful Civil Rights decision of 1883, Turner was so disgusted with the United States that he advised blacks "to return to Africa or get ready for extermination."[29] Francis Grimke, minister of the prestigious Fifteenth Street Presbyterian Church in

27 Quoted by William H. Pipes, *Say Amen, Brother! Old-Time Negro Preaching: A Study in Frustration*, p. 3.

28 DuBois, *The Souls of Black Folk*, p. 190.

29 Edwin S. Redkey, *Black Exodus: Black Nationalist and Back-to-Africa Movements, 1890–1910*, pp. 41–42.

Washington, D.C., continuously protested the nation's abandonment of Reconstruction ideals, and in 1909 he and his brother Archibald were active in arousing black resistance to Booker T. Washington's accommodationist policies. Another minister in the nation's capital, Alexander Crummell, led the struggle for Negro rights in the Episcopal church. Crummell also attacked the larger problem of Negro equality, though, like DuBois, always with a somewhat elitist emphasis on higher education and talented black leadership. In 1897 he and Grimke were among those who formed the forty-member American Negro Academy for the promotion of science, literature, and the arts.

But undeniably, the tendency of the Negro clergy to compromise was pronounced. Although they were by no means agents of the white overlords, as some have suggested, they did show considerable complacency about the status quo, and were very ineffective in the movement to displace Tuskegee Institute as the symbol of the Negro's place in American life. Between 1890 and 1915, the years of his almost sovereign influence, Booker T. Washington had a firm hold on the black clergy's loyalty; and by and large his influence was salutary, for he awakened ministerial concern for this-worldly problems. But Washington, though raised as a Baptist and at home in the Bible, was privately disdainful of the Negro clergy's outlook even as he solicited its support.[30]

The disdain for the preachers attributed to Washington as well as the retrospective criticisms of the churches made by Frazier and Johnson are directed primarily at the prevailing theology, which is seen as retarding the Negro's advancement in American society. To a degree the charge is unjust, given the overwhelming fact of white supremacy and the limited sphere in which the ministers could practice their gifts for leadership. In the realm of belief and piety, moreover, it is essential to recognize that this nineteenth-century heritage of the black church was above all an integral—though segregated—part of the evangelical tradition which underlay nearly all Southern and much Northern Protestantism. When the "invisible institution" that had been shaped in the days of slavery merged after the war with the more traditional forms of the instituted churches, it still bore the marks, as Paul

[30] Samuel R. Spencer, Jr., *Booker T. Washington and the Negro's Place in American Life* (Boston: Little, Brown and Co., 1955), pp. 65–66, 139.

Radin has observed, of "the somewhat barren Christianity that prevailed in the antebellum South."[31]

The anti-intellectual heritage was only another name for endemic revivalism, which as it developed in the Negro church may have involved an evasion of reality; but the basic forms of religious experience and the content and style of rural preaching were very similar whether the church was "colored" or white.[32] Both groups lacked a social gospel, both came to terms with the status quo, both evaded the larger corporate sins, and both failed to do what they could to rectify a cruel social order. The fault in a general sense lies with evangelicalism—not with the black church. In a less negative spirit, one might also observe that the black church showed at least equal concern for intellectual improvement and higher education.

Despite all the obvious similarities that grew out of the common cultural situation of whites and blacks in the rural South, historians have convincingly insisted that there were very significant differences as well. Louis Lomax's statement on this question is representative:

> In classical cultural terms there is no difference between the Negro Baptist Church and the Baptist Church proper.

[31] Foreword to *God Struck Me Dead*, ed. Clifton H. Johnson, p. viii. When the twentieth century precipitated a crisis in the Southern churches, the white churches were as profoundly stricken as the black.

[32] A comparative study of black and white preaching in the rural South or of black and white Pentecostal preaching in the twentieth century, with close attention to content and nuance, seems not to have been made. The peculiarities of Negro preaching do not stand out in the collections of sermons made by May, Pipes, and Johnson. In one case as in the other, the real heart of the sermon—when the Spirit was truly working in the preacher—showed the same ecstatic stress on the joy of being in the Lord, of knowing that the life of sin and death was done and gone, of rejoicing in the still greater bliss to come. Nonverbal aspects of worship may vary, but rhythmic singing and freely responding congregations were not reserved for the blacks alone. In 1968, moreover, when the funeral of Martin Luther King, Jr., was televised, millions of evangelical Protestants living all over America, and especially those in the South, could truly participate in every element of the service—the hymns, the anthems, the sermon, and the prayers—as though they were there in the Ebenezer Baptist Church of Atlanta.

In folk terms, however, there is. Not only do we Baptists have a way of preaching and singing, but there is a meaning to our imagery that is peculiar to us.[33]

The preaching does have a folk idiom of its own—and in many cases it is expressed in a distinct dialect of the English language. There may also be a different rhythmic sense in the music, whether vocal or instrumental, and certainly different gestures and body movements. But it is Lomax's final point, on the "meaning to [the] imagery," that is most basic. The key terms of the faith—salvation, freedom, the Kingdom of God, and others—do carry different connotations in the black experience, and they always have. More generally, a certain mournfulness qualifies joy and jubilation just as it does in the spirituals and in the "blues." Long before Emancipation, moreover, black Christians had found strength and hope through their own special identification of themselves as God's Israel, as a chosen people being led out of bondage.

Christian faith and "black religion" became inseparable elements of piety, belief, and aspiration. It was a composite result that stemmed from the American Negro's extraordinary situation: back of him no heritage but slavery and a rumor of Africa which was in effect but an unknown void. Free but not free in the present. Only vague intimations of America's great future destiny, but in any case no confidence that he could participate in its bounty. In the church and through religion these tragic circumstances were made to cohere.

[33] Louis E. Lomax, *The Negro Revolt*, p. 46. For an early formulation of this concept of the "invisible institution," see George F. Bragg, *History of the Afro-American Group of the Episcopal Church* (Baltimore: Church Advocate Press, 1922), p. 39. On the concept of "black religion" as a distinct element in Negro church life, see Joseph R. Washington, Jr., *Black Religion: The Negro and Christianity in the United States*, though the book as a whole is overly dogmatic.

43

THE SOUTHERN WHITE CHURCHES AFTER THE WAR

The desolation of the South as it pulled itself together for the years of peace and survival has always been a challenge to the descriptive powers of men. Even unsympathetic Northern travelers discovered their literary inadequacies. Almost every reason for tears, uncertainty, and hopelessness was to be found: death, hunger, social dislocation, political disorder, racial fear, violence, conscious hate, and subconscious guilt. Pervading the desolation was a memory of military valor which defeat had not paled; and at a still deeper level, a haunting idealized picture of the prewar way of life. Beneath all was a tragic racial heritage, as old as the region itself. This fact had risen up in the 1830s to take possession of the Southerner's mind and soul, and it never again receded to a point where it could be either complacently accepted or rationally evaluated. This indeed is the "burden of Southern history"—as heavy a burden as any sizable portion of Western Christendom has ever borne.

Empancipation merely changed the forms of the South's dark heritage, not its content; and Reconstruction, for one turbulent decade, exposed the magnitude of the region's problems. Then gradually by dint of great exertion, these problems were covered over again for a long season—with the diverse instrumentalities of white supremacy holding down the lid. In the present chapter we consider the major ecclesiastical and religious accompaniments of these events, and in some cases the prewar developments that led to them. This will involve primarily an account of the Methodists and Baptists who, about evenly between them, accounted for 90 percent of Southern church membership (in several states more nearly 95 percent), almost twice the strength (47 percent) of these two communions in the nation as a whole. Receiving more support than dissent from the region's other denominations (among whom Presbyterians, Disciples, evangelical Episcopalians, and Lutherans predominated), these two vast movements virtually constituted the South in its religious aspect. Guided by a ministry which for the most part moved from the grassroots to leadership without benefit of seminary training, the two churches both reflected and defined the region's moral tone; they gave their blessings to the "peculiar institutions" that replaced slavery, inveighed with more consistent vigor against card playing and dancing than against racism or the unpunished murdering of recalcitrant blacks, and led the general run of people to prize the values and practices of the "old-time religion" rather than to ponder the forces that were reshaping modern civilization. (In 1893 the Southern Presbyterian Assembly made dancing a valid ground for excommunication.) The South, in short, followed the exhortation of a Mississippi Methodist preacher during the last days of the war: "If we cannot gain our *political*, let us establish at least our *mental* independence."[1] It came to pass, therefore, that the Civil War, far from collapsing the South's religious tradition, actually rejuvenated this unique component of Western Christianity and guaranteed its existence for at least another century.

The three great evangelical churches which comprised nearly 95 percent of the Southern church membership—Methodist, Baptist, and Presbyterian—decided to maintain their separate existence in the postwar era, as did the much smaller Lutheran church. Their decision provided the Lost Cause with its own altars. The black chattel which had formerly been permitted a subservient place in these churches was encouraged to organize itself separately, and nine-tenths of the ex-slaves became Baptists or Methodists in independent churches whose history is considered in the preceding chapter. The Episcopal and Roman Catholic churches each reunited at the national level in 1866, at the General Convention of the former, and at the Second Plenary Council of the latter. At the diocesan level, however, these churches adopted the developing practices of segregation, serving their small Negro memberships separately. With no significant ex-

[1] Kenneth K. Bailey, *Southern White Protestantism in the Twentieth Century*, p. 1.

ceptions whites and blacks moved into separate ecclesiastical worlds and, as we shall see, into quite distinct "religious" worlds as well.[2] Not only would they worship apart from each other, but piety itself would take different paths and develop characteristic forms.

In a larger, and still more tragic sense, the Southern white churches, on whom the region's intellectual responsibilities necessarily fell, came to rest on old solutions and practices. Modern religious proposals were associated with abolitionism and other Northern errors. Efforts to grapple with issues raised by scientific and scholarly advances were repressed, while poverty and the absence of independently endowed seminaries and universities precluded the emergence of significant intellectual encounter. One must agree, indeed, with two assertions of Samuel S. Hill's recent analysis: that the churches of Dixie were pervaded by "a peculiar variety of evangelical Protestantism which has not flourished anywhere else in Christendom over a long period," and that "the entire region's maturation" was conditioned by the "prevailing state of religious affairs."[3] It was after the war, moreover, rather than before, that the real distinctiveness of this heritage became manifest.

THE METHODISTS

"If America is ever ruined," declared Joseph Cook, the Boston lecturer and preacher, "the Methodist Church will be to blame. For she is the strongest and most influential Church on the continent of America today."[4] A vast exaggeration if taken literally, Cook's statement is nevertheless relatively close to the truth as applied to the South. By seceding from the most tightly organized church in America at the much publicized General Conference of 1844, the Methodist Episcopal Church, South, became the chief ecclesiastical standard bearer of the Southern cause.[5] Firmly rooted amid the planters of the black belt, famous for its successful evangelism

2 On the distinctiveness of black religion and theology see chaps. 42 and 62.

3 Samuel S. Hill, Jr., *Southern Churches in Crisis*, p. xii.

4 Quoted in Hunter D. Farish, *The Circuit Rider Dismounts*, p. 1.

5 The Baptists soon followed in 1845; New School Presbyterians in 1857; Old School Presbyterians and Lutherans in 1861.

among the slaves, and having rid itself of old Wesleyan condemnations of slavery, it was by far the most acceptable and most powerful church in the South. Because its defenses of the "peculiar institution" were unstinting, and because its support of the Confederacy was as remarkable as the Unionist solidarity of Northern Methodism, the war's end found it prostrate. In the meantime, the Northern Methodist church, Bishop Edward R. Ames leading the way, invaded the South as Union armies cleared the way, occupying churches, proselytizing members, leading off the blacks, and unsuccessfully encouraging other Northern churches to do likewise.

Southern Methodism was roused from its apathy by the so-called Palmyra Manifesto, issued in June 1865 by an informally gathered group of Missouri Methodists. Encouraged by this strenuous call for reorganization, the bishops convened a General Conference in New Orleans in 1866, and in defiance of Northern proposals for reunion, Southern Methodism quite literally sprang to life. It repudiated the political heresies of the Northern church, added four new bishops, provided for the separate organization of its remaining Negro membership, and in 1870 revised its constitution to permit lay delegates to attend its conferences. In the face of postwar moral laxity, it called its membership back to Wesley's concern for sanctification and began to reestablish every aspect of its institutional life. Despite the woes of Reconstruction, the church was blessed "with a perfect blaze of revivals," and in fifteen years it had doubled its membership. Speaking now as a custodian of the Lost Cause, it quickly won back the dominant place in Southern life it had held in antebellum days. In 1866 its membership rolled past the million mark, to reach 1,443,517 by 1906. Missionary efforts of modest size were maintained in China, Japan, Brazil, Mexico, and among the American Indians of Oklahoma and Texas. Only the Southern Baptists showed comparable evangelistic vigor.

Accompanying this rapid expansion of Methodist membership were various limited types of institutional growth. In nearly every state academies and colleges were founded or reorganized—though state universities were often opposed. But the culminating achievement of nineteenth-century higher education in the South was the project for a central university and seminary in Nashville. This was founded in 1873 and endowed by Commodore Vanderbilt with a half-million dollar gift which he increased to a million dollars by 1876. As a result of the unusually broad and enlightened leadership provided by Chancellor Langdon Cabell Garland and Bishop Holland N. McTyeire, Vanderbilt began almost immediately to exert a kind of normative influence on higher education in the South, although a majority of both bishops and members were opposed to its founding and suspicious of its probable influence. Anti-intellectualism remained strong and militant. So precarious was the infant university's reputation in 1878 that the trustees had to cut short Professor Alexander Winchell's visiting lectureship in zoology and "Historical and Dynamic Geology" because the Darwinian tendency of his teaching was too dangerous.[6]

Yet Southern Methodism was leaving many old landmarks behind. In 1876 its bishops accurately declared that "a more homogeneous ecclesiastical community does not exist on the American continent." The nature—and the price—of this homogeneity needs to be noted. With the increasing affluence of its membership, the old bias against fancy dress, fine church edifices, organs, and choirs was passing away. A strong middle- and upper-class constituency was developing, at the same time that the church was losing contact with the urban poor. (Statistics showed that the bigger the city, the smaller the percentage of Methodists.) As will become evident in a later chapter, the extreme demands and activities of the Holiness movement thus soon became an embarrassment, and its more strenuous advocates were either suppressed or forced into secession.[7] As the Winchell case revealed, moreover, the serious intellectual problems posed by modern science and scholarship were being most inadequately dealt with. Finally, active efforts with regard to the two major social issues of the

---

[6] Winchell's book, *The Pre-Adamites*, had appeared that year. At its next meeting, the Tennessee Conference of the Methodist Episcopal Church, South, commended the university trustees for having "the courage to lay its young, but vigorous, hand upon the mane of untamed speculation, and say we will have no more of this science." As the university grew, tensions developed between the Methodist bishops and the Board of Trust; and in 1910 the General Conference initiated a campaign to regain control of the university. This led to a long court battle which in 1914 finally resulted in the school's independence (see Edwin Mims, *History of Vanderbilt University* [Nashville, Tenn.: Vanderbilt University Press, 1946], pp. 100–05, 291–318).

[7] On the Holiness and Pentecostal churches, see chap. 48.

South, the rise of industrialism and the intensification of racial segregation, were being sacrificed to an increasingly legalistic militancy on dancing, tobacco, alcoholic beverages, gambling, card playing, and theater going.

The "social gospel" in the South was largely a Methodist phenomenon, to be sure, but it was for the most part an outgrowth of the New South movement expounded by the Methodist layman Henry W. Grady and the Reverend Atticus G. Haygood (1839–96), president of Emory University and later a bishop. Haygood's Thanksgiving sermon of 1880 "The New South," followed in 1881 by his book *Our Brother in Black,* gave clerical support to Grady's vision. He bade Southerners forget a legendary past, face their responsibilities to the Negro, and bring in a great industrial future. Above all he was thankful that slavery was gone forever, and that whites and blacks were learning (and demonstrating) the advantages of work and thrift.[8] Haygood was a natural choice as agent for the Slater Fund for Negro education, and in this capacity he performed a considerable service. His life reveals the way in which the old forms of Methodist piety were playing out without being supplanted by thoroughgoing theological reconstruction.[9] Declining health and frustrated ambition led Haygood into alcoholic disrepute during his later years.

THE BAPTISTS

The national unity of the Baptists had been sundered by the slavery issue in 1844, and in the following year the Southern Baptist Convention was organized with great enthusiasm at a meeting in Augusta, Georgia. A year later, with a constitution that provided for a degree of centralization without precedent among Baptists, the Southern Baptists Convention began its independent history. Led by aggressive men and infused with the rising fervor of the Southern cause, it enjoyed extraordinary growth. In the next fifteen years its

[8] Booker T. Washington would provide the black corollary to these doctrines with his famous Atlanta Exposition address of 1895. See pp. 166–67, 588–89.

[9] One outstanding exception was John B. Robins, who showed a significant awareness of both social and intellectual issues in his *Christ and Our Country* (1889), a response to Josiah Strong's *Our Country.*

constituency contributed seven times more to the missionary cause than it had given to the General Convention's work in the preceding forty years. Dissatisfaction with the old convention's nearly exclusive concern for Northern home missions had created pressure for a separate Southern organization even in the 1830s, and it was in this area that the new Southern Convention scored its most remarkable successes.

When the secession crisis came, the Southern Convention's response was immediate and unconditional. Baptist soldiers were disproportionately numerous in the armies, while the whole gamut of work carried out in the North by the Christian Commission was undertaken with an equal measure of concern among Baptists in the South. To support its foreign missionaries the appropriate board even worked out a system for running long-staple cotton through the blockade, selling it at very high prices in England, and then conveying the funds by secret commercial channels to Asia and Africa. With the collapse of the Confederacy, however, the Baptists, like the Methodists, were at first overcome by apathy and hopelessness. Men wondered if the convention *could* be revived. By 1866 Reconstruction had intensified Southern desires for autonomy, and a policy of continued separation from the North was decided upon. At the same time, Negro Baptists very rapidly moved off into churches and associations of their own, encouraged to do so both by Southern whites and by federal Reconstruction policies. This encouragement had heavy political overtones, for black congregations were often used to strengthen the Republican party, and as a result, Southern Baptists refused to contribute substantial financial aid and educational assistance for Negroes until after the turn of the century.[10] Nevertheless, beginning in 1866, the convention's history is one of continued growth in domestic membership, foreign missions, and other benevolent enterprises. The election of the remarkable Dr. I. T. Tichenor as general secretary of the Home Mission Society in 1882 was especially important for the attainment of these

[10] Various plans to provide institutes for black ministers were launched in the 1880s, but without success. In 1895, a more ambitious "New Era Plan" but was organized in most states (with the cooperation of the Northern Convention), but by this time the Negro churches were disinclined to white tutelage, and the support of state district supervisors for institute programs was soon discontinued.

ends. By 1890 the convention reported 1,101,714 members. Small foreign mission fields in West Africa, China, Japan, Brazil, and Mexico added about 3,500 more.

Poverty, agrarian backwardness, and terrible educational deficiencies prevented the Baptists, even more severely than the Methodists, from coming to terms with the main intellectual currents of the later nineteenth century. Anti-intellectualism was a corollary of revivalism; opposition to higher education and theological seminaries was powerfully evident almost everywhere. Despite this opposition, Southern Theological Seminary had been founded at Greenville, South Carolina, just before the war (1859). Like all other Southern institutions its financial situation was considerably weakened during the Reconstruction period, but in 1877 it began a second and extremely useful phase of its history after receiving further support and moving to Louisville, Kentucky. Even here, however, divisive elements among Southern Baptists worked havoc with its academic program.

Since early colonial days Baptists had been seriously divided in one way or another, but the emergence of the missionary movement and the founding of the General Missionary Convention in 1814 had raised new divisive forces: a widespread, popularly based opposition to organized evangelism, the practice of founding "unbiblical" societies, and a related concern for education. When Alexander Campbell's advocacy added strength to dissenting views during his Baptist years (1813–30), antimissionism became a powerful new force, usually among the poorest and least educated elements of the constituency, who felt threatened by eastern money-raising organizations and their realtively well-educated emissaries. In backward sections of the South, therefore, the condemnatory exclusivism of this "Hard-Shell" movement gained very effective grassroots leadership, notably that of Daniel Parker (1781–1844). Though born in Virginia, Parker was a product of the Georgia frontier who later worked in Tennessee, Kentucky, southern Illinois, and Texas. With great skill and power he expounded the chief convictions of the "anti-effort Baptists," above all, their extreme predestinarian "antinomianism," their belief that God needed neither "new-fangled" societies nor the corrupting influences of higher learning to advance the gospel in the world. Parker himself also developed certain doctrinal innovations that made him the chief prophet of the "Two Seed" predestinarian Baptist sect.[11]

This type of extremist advocacy led to the organization in state after state of separate congregations and associations of "Primitive" Baptists. They made great headway in Tennessee, Alabama, Georgia, Kentucky, North Carolina, and Virginia, and very significant inroads in western states. By 1846 antimission Baptists numbered at least sixty-eight thousand, or about 10 percent of the country's total Baptist population. Throughout the century their preaching hindered the organized work of Baptists, North and South, and won acceptance for Hard-Shell doctrines among countless persons and churches who never became affiliated with Primitive Baptist associations. Their outspoken witness undoubtedly more than compensated for the Arminian tendencies advanced by the Freewill Baptists, but the "compensations" were sectional, since Freewill Baptists flourished chiefly in the North, predestinarians in the South.[12]

During the postwar half-century Baptists in the South continued to divide on these issues, and the Southern Baptist Convention was torn by still another movement that devel-

11 In 1820 Parker began his attack on Baptist missionary efforts with the publication of a pamphlet, *A Public Address to the Baptist Society*. In 1826 he stated his "Two-Seed-in-the-Spirit" doctrine in another pamphlet. This Two Seed theology was an exaggerated and eccentric form of predestinarianism: two seeds were planted in Eve, one by God (good seed), the other by Satan (bad seed). The election of individuals is determined by their "seed," and neither missionary societies nor anything else can do anything about it.

During his two-year stay in Illinois (1829–31), Parker published the *Church Advocate*, a monthly paper. His lifelong efforts led to the founding of churches in several states—chiefly in the South and in the middle region. In 1890 the "Old Two-Seed-in-the-Spirit Predestinarian Baptist" numbered 12,881; but by 1945 the membership had declined to 201 and the number of churches to sixteen.

12 Primitive Baptists numbered 121,347 in 1890, but Hard-Shell tendencies were far more pervasive than these figures suggest. Freewill Baptists, gathered chiefly in two organizations, numbered 100,000, with their chief strength in the North, especially in northern New England, where there were 16,000 communicants in Maine alone (cf. W. W. Sweet, *Religion on the Frontier: The Baptists, 1783–1830*, p. 66).

oped enormous disruptive power within its churches. This was Landmarkism, a type of "high church" movement which stressed not the "episcopal succession" so dear to High Church Anglicans, but the "Baptist succession." Landmarkers believed that since the time of Christ, baptized (immersed) believers had continued to pass on the true church by immersing others in Baptist congregational contexts in an unbroken succession—a trail of blood—even during the Dark Ages when the Antichrist occupied the papal throne. In Reformation times, according to this theory, Baptists had broken into the open again as a diversified international movement. The local Baptist congregation, therefore, was an apostolic institution with a continuous history.

Baptists had formulated variations on this doctrine for centuries, but in antebellum America, in the Southern Convention, as the nation rushed toward civil war amid a great outpouring of intensely subjective revivalism, James R. Graves (1820–93), editor of the *Tennessee Baptist*, articulated the matter anew in a way that gave rise to a powerful, well-organized movement. At the heart of Graves's argument was a doctrine of the Kingdom which allowed a syllogism to do the work of historical research: the Kingdom has prevailed; the Kingdom must always have included true churches; Baptist churches are the only true churches; therefore, Baptist churches have always existed. After presenting his case in various contexts between 1848 and 1851, Graves finally saw his Cotton Grove Resolution formally adopted at a mass meeting in Bolivar, Tennessee, in 1851—along with an injunction to refuse fellowship with all other churches. In 1854 he published a tract by James M. Pendleton entitled *An Old Landmark Re-Set*, whereupon the movement got its name.[13] Then in 1855 he republished G. H. Orchard's *Concise History of Foreign Baptists* (1838) in which the historical documentation is presented.[14] The stage was set for a great resur-

---

[13] Pendleton's *Church Manual* (1867) and *Christian Doctrines* (1878) also had wide influence on Southern Baptist faith and practice.

[14] G. H. Orchard was a Baptist minister in Steventon, Bedfordshire, England, whose book *A Concise History of Foreign Baptists* appeared in 1838. James Robinson Graves added a bombastic introduction praising church history but insisting that for seventeen hundred years none had been written, because existing histories covered the years from 300 to 1600 only by telling the story of the Antichrist, "the scarlet harlot riding on the beast with seven

gence of Landmarkism as the woes of Reconstruction brought doubt and uncertainty to many Baptist Southerners.

In some respects this resurgence of extreme localism, exclusivism, and opposition to supracongregational agencies strengthened old Hard-Shell tendencies, but it also provoked a fierce controversy over Baptist history that wracked the denomination for half a century. Throughout the 1880s and 1890s attacks on the work of the home and foreign missionary boards continued, accompanied by demands that the convention abandon its character as a society of financial donors to become a genuinely ecclesiastical association of local churches. When the showdown on this latter proposal came in 1905, most of the extreme Landmarkers seceded from the church. In the meantime, they loosed a steady flow of criticism upon all who cast doubt on even the historical facts of the succession theory. This kind of strife reached its peak in the Whitsett controversy.

William H. Whitsett (1841–1911), appointed professor of church history at Southern Seminary in Louisville in 1872 was a German-trained scholar whose careful research into Baptist origins contradicted Landmark theory. Although Graves and his followers were critical, open conflict did not ensue until the 1890s, when Whitsett's appointment to the seminary's presidency coincided with the publication of his findings in *A Question in Baptist History* (1896). Landmarkers now opened fire in earnest, with Thomas T. Eaton, a Louisville pastor and editor of the *Western Recorder*, assuming the role left vacant by Graves's death. The threat to the seminary's support became so great that in 1898 Whitsett resigned.[15] His more discreet successor, E. Y. Mullins, actu-

---

heads and ten horns, . . . drunk with the blood of saints." "It is 'high time' for the history of the Church of Christ to be written," he went on, "the world has quite long enough wondered [sic] after the Beast, and the Church of Christ left in the obscurity of the wilderness" (pp. ix, xi). What Orchard did (with enormous dependence on Mosheim's old ecclesiastical history) was to chart the history of antipedobaptist doctrines as they had been held by a long succession of heretical groups (Novatian, Donatist, Paulican, etc.). He then connected these sects with the Baptist emergence in the Reformation period.

15 Whitsett was in fact the second major casualty. The German-trained biblical scholar and historian of religions, Crawford H. Toy, had resigned from Southern Seminary in 1879, due to the unacceptability of his research. Rigorous historical scholarship was

ally continued to uphold Whitsett's views on Baptist history; and due to his strenuous efforts and intellectual force, the rising tide of Fundamentalism did not submerge the seminary, even though the South became the great stronghold of anti-intellectual and antiscientific religion. Among Baptists in the South, however, the message and spirit which Graves represented had an immense and pervasive influence. A century after the Landmark testimonies began to be widely propagated, both local practices and collective policies of the Southern Baptist Convention still exhibited signs of their influence: the closing of the Lord's Supper to all but Baptists (often even to those of other Baptist congregations), and a general willingness not only to refuse fellowship with other denominations but to deny them the name of Christian.

In the rupture of Southern Baptist interdenominational relations Graves was also very influential. In his *Tennessee Baptist* he mounted a vituperative campaign against the popular rival, Methodism. These diatribes were then circulated as tracts, and finally as a widely read book, *The Great Iron Wheel; or, Republicanism Backward and Christianity Reversed* (1856). Graves ridiculed the Methodist church as an infant pseudochurch no older than its oldest living bishop (seventy-two years in 1856)—and in fact (on Landmark principles) no church at all, but "an Antichristian organization," a miserable granddaughter of "the woman clothed in scarlet who put the saints to death." "If the Methodist E. Societies are churches of Christ, scriptural organizations, Baptists are not. The former or the latter are manifestly in *gross error.*" The editor of Orchard's *History*, needless to say, had little doubt as to which was the case.

Methodists, not surprisingly, replied vigorously to such charges—indeed their Book Concern was accused of burying the South and West with tracts, periodicals, and books. And Graves's chief assailant was none other than "Parson" William G. Brownlow, who was to gain fame a decade later as Tennessee's Reconstruction governor. Brownlow could be as vituperative as any man, and before the year was out he had answered Graves's assault in kind. In *The Great Iron Wheel Examined; or, Its False Spokes Extracted* (1856) he refers to Graves's paper as a "low, dirty, scurrilous sheet," and persists in that general spirit for over three hundred pages, defending

virtually excluded from Southern Baptist seminaries during the next half-century or more.

Methodism from slander and in turn slandering the Baptists: "How do they enter the Church? They come in *backwards,* or, if the reader please, *wrong end foremost!* They *back into the Church,* as a goat retreats from its adversary, which, if not an insult to God, is not in accordance with good breeding." Brownlow also (quite rightly) accused Graves of filching his indictment of Methodism from Fred A. Ross, a New School Presbyterian of Alabama, whom Brownlow designated (erroneously) as a "man of color." In a concluding chapter he expounded his total approval of Southern Methodism's defense of slavery, urging Elder Graves to break his silence on this subject or get back to Ohio's Western Reserve where he had come from. Taken together, the two books reveal many major facets of Southern church life—especially, perhaps, the process by which Southern Baptists were pressed to positions and attitudes that left them in many ways alienated from the mainstream of American evangelicalism of which they had long been so important a part.

Southern Baptists (both within the convention and outside it) moved into the twentieth century, nevertheless, with great vitality and expansive force. Because of this rapid Baptist growth, Methodists by 1906 had to surrender their place as the region's largest Protestant communion. Westward expansion, especially in California, would modify the convention's overall "Southernness," though not its conservatism and zeal. The struggle with liberalism in the North would bring to the Southern Convention some accessions of conservative Baptists from that region. And because Southern Baptists were so numerous and so singlemindedly committed to traditional forms of evangelical piety, doctrine, and personal ethics, they became, despite their separatism, a major force in the great Protestant campaigns for Prohibition and immigration restriction, as well as in the Fundamentalist assaults on evolution.

OTHER DENOMINATIONS

In 1890 the Methodists and Baptists, together numbering between 4.5 and 5 million members (approximately half of them Negro), defined the moral and religious ethos of the region. Next in size was the Disciples denomination, with about two hundred thousand members. In interpreting their own unique Campbellite origins, the Disciples were considerably divided among themselves, however, and in chapter 48 consideration is given to the process by which a group of very conservative "Churches of Christ" gradually separated themselves during the postwar half-century, largely in the South. As a denomination, Disciples of all types tended increasingly to blend into the overall evangelical scene, even when they occasioned ecclesiastical conflict and rivalry.

The Presbyterians in 1890 numbered about 190,000, including the small Cumberland church (strongest in Tennessee) whose piety and church life was more closely related to the South's evangelical mainstream than that of other Presbyterian bodies. The Presbyterian church, nevertheless, exerted a disproportionately large influence in Southern affairs on account of the social prominence of its members, its extreme inner cohesiveness, and its demand for a learned, doctrinally orthodox clergy. The war and reconstruction experience had terminated the New School–Old School rift both organizationally and spiritually, but not until 1882 were even a nominal sort of fraternal relations established with the Northern church. In the meantime almost all of its approximately fourteen thousand Negro members drifted away to other affiliations, just as they did among the Episcopalians and Lutherans. The Cumberland Presbyterian church, on the other hand, organized a separate "colored" church in 1869.

The Southern Presbyterian church, therefore, became the prime embodiment of the white establishment in the New South. Even in 1961 its leading historian reprimands his church for being satisfied if in a typical small Southern city the Presbyterian church can draw its membership from the managerial class, leaving wage earners to the other churches and the newer sects. Because of the intensity with which it insisted on its own peculiar doctrine of the "spirituality of the church," moreover, it formally removed itself from popular social and economic concerns.[16] Its membership was little involved in the great political movements that sought to express and harness agrarian discontent. On the racial issue they stood with "the better class of whites" who, in Professor Woodward's terms, adopted the "conservative" view, favoring white supremacy but not Negro degradation.[17] Yet to-

[16] Ernest Trice Thompson, *The Spirituality of the Church: A Distinctive Doctrine of the Presbyterian Church in the United States,* p. 38.

[17] C. Vann Woodward, *The Strange Career of Jim Crow* (New York: Oxford University Press, 1960), p. 29.

ward the turn of the century, the Presbyterians too followed the drift toward segregation and racism.

In Presbyterian seminaries the Princeton theology of Charles Hodge, as adapted for Southerners by Henry Thornwell, continued to be the accepted norm. Its chief expositor and defender was Robert Lewis Dabney, the totally unreconstructed professor of theology at Union Seminary in Virginia. In 1883 Dabney accepted a professorship in moral philosophy at the University of Texas in Austin, where he also helped to found another Presbyterian seminary. In the meantime he played a vigorous role in the widely publicized heresy trial of James Woodrow (1828–1907). This uncle of future President Woodrow Wilson had come to the Presbyterian seminary in Columbia, South Carolina, as professor of science and religion, a subject area which was itself controversial. Woodrow soon heightened the controversy by indicating a cautious willingness to accept the theory of evolution as a "not unreasonable interpretation of the Bible." A public address in 1884 brought his views into the open, and two years later the General Assembly by a vote of sixty-five to twenty-seven recommended his dismissal. In 1888 the General Assembly acted still more decisively and made this conservative position official by adopting a positive deliverance on Genesis, Adam, and evolution. On the great intellectual dilemma of the age, therefore, Southern Presbyterians showed their solidarity with the dominant faction among the Northern Presbyterians, and with Southern Protestantism generally.

Three very small denominations, the Lutheran, Roman Catholic, and Episcopalian, each in its distinctive way, tended to dissociate themselves from the chief theological tendencies of the Southern Protestants, though their institutional life fully reflected the dominant social presuppositions of the region.[18] Almost all of Southern Lutheranism was involved in a confessional movement that was leading them toward a larger awareness of Lutheran unity. Southern Roman Catholics were spared many of the internal problems of immigration. Except in Louisiana, however, they were a small minority in a hostile environment. For both reasons they

[18] In 1890 Episcopalians, Roman Catholics, and Lutherans each numbered between forty and forty-five thousand members in former slaveholding states. The main Lutheran synod merged with the Northern churches in 1918.

tended to support the "Americanists" in the church. The bishop of Little Rock, Arkansas, Edward Fitzgerald, cast one of the two votes, and the only American vote, against the constitution on papal infallibility at the First Vatican Council in 1870. Socially the Episcopal church was in a situation very similar to that of the Presbyterians. Widespread concern for questions of high or low churchmanship and for the intellectual freedom of their seminaries at Alexandria, Virginia, and Sewanee, Tennessee, saved them from much of the environing obscurantism. In William Porcher DuBose (1836–1918), moreover, the South could boast—though in fact it largely ignored—one of the most profound American theologians of the period. DuBose was almost a living stereotype of "classic" Southern upbringing, yet the combination of evangelical fervor and Anglo-Catholic modernism which he expounded in several major works was remarkably attuned to the scholarly developments and philosophical interests of his age.

SOUTHERN PROTESTANTISM AT THE CENTURY'S END

The war with Spain, inadequate though it was as an expression of the martial spirit that Theodore Roosevelt personified, marks an end to the post-Civil War era. Imperial acquisitions in the Caribbean and the Pacific led to the nationalization of Southern attitudes on race. The freed Negro's situation reached its nadir as other domestic issues came to the fore: industrialism, urban political corruption, the "new" immigration, and Prohibition. In the age of Progressivism Southern and Northern Protestantism again joined hands as the need for an "evangelical united front" became manifest. Yet the situation within the dominant churches of the South remained fundamentally unchanged. Jim Crow was at the peak of his career. "Denomination mattered little, for support for the racist creed ran the gamut from urban Episcopalians to country Baptists."[19] The intellectual revolution of the nineteenth century had made only a small impact on prevailing attitudes, and because religious liberalism and troublesome scholarship had few champions and no appreciable constituency in the South, the Fundamentalist controversy remained for several decades a Northern affair. As late as 1927

[19] David M. Reimers, *White Protestantism and the Negro*, p. 29.

only 4 percent of the Southern Methodist clergy were seminary graduates and only 11 percent had college degrees, while 32 percent had no more than an elementary education. It is most improbable that the Baptist situation was any better. In the Negro churches it was very much worse. With few exceptions, moreover, Fundamentalism reigned unchallenged in the denominational colleges and seminaries throughout the region. Their predominantly rural and small-town constituency made the Southern churches the strongholds of social patterns and ways of thought that were increasingly anachronistic. These churches could and did marshal public opinion on a wide range of social questions and enforce those forms of the Puritan ethic that had begun to assume a characteristically Southern tone in the early colonial period. Yet what Rufus B. Spain says of the Baptists could be applied generally: "Their significance in Southern life consisted not in their power to mold their environment . . . [but] in supporting and perpetuating the standards prevailing in society at large."[20] When joining forces with Northern Protestants, they could be an awesome power in the land. Nationalism and the urgencies of war (whether against Spain or Germany) could divert popular attention, veil the facts, and stave off the impending crisis. Yet a rendezvous with the twentieth century could not be postponed indefinitely.

[20] Rufus B. Spain, *At Ease in Zion: Social History of Southern Baptists*, p. 214. On the characteristic Southern forms of the Puritan ethics, see pp. 237–38, 244–46 (in Volume 1) and 167–68 above.

VII

The Ordeals of Transition

That the rapid changes now going on are bringing up problems that demand the most earnest attention may be seen on every hand. Symptoms of danger, premonitions of violence, are appearing all over the civilized world. Creeds are dying, beliefs are changing; the old forces of conservatism are melting away. Political institutions are failing, as clearly in democratic America as in monarchical Europe. There is a growing unrest and bitterness among the masses, whatever be the form of government, a blind groping for escape from conditions becoming intolerable. To attribute all this to the teachings of demagogues is like attributing the fever to the quickened pulse. It is the new wine beginning to ferment in old bottles. To put into a sailing-ship the powerful engines of a first-class ocean steamer would be to tear her to pieces with their play. So the new powers rapidly changing all the relations of society must shatter social and political organizations not adapted to meet their strain.

Henry George, *Social Problems* (1883)

A strange formlessness marks the half-century which follows the Civil War. The term "postbellum America" lacks the specificity of "antebellum America." One explanation for the difficulty is that evangelicalism was no longer calling the tune —or more accurately, that fewer people were heeding the call. The several ordeals to which the country was subjected during these decades of rapid change partially explain this circumstance. Primary, perhaps, was the great social and economic revolution that brought the urban and industrial situation to an acute stage without a corresponding revolution in government and politics. Compounding these social problems was a drastic shift in immigration patterns that put the old Protestant Establishment, already divided by memories of the Civil War, in a far more threatened position. This led to another recourse to nativism, to a revival of the immigration restriction movement, and to varieties of political reform that were less committed to democratic ideals than to keeping the "best men" in power. The Indian problem was turned over to the churches; the Supreme Court gutted the Civil Rights Act; and the Republicans gave up even their nominal role as protector of the freedman.

Another problem which affected the churches directly was America's belated and hence unusually harsh confrontation with many revolutionary forms of modern thought, most notably historical criticism of the Bible and Darwinian evolutionary theory. In this situation many champions of scholarship and science appeared, and there were newly endowed seminaries as well as wealthy congregations to give them a hearing; yet conflict on a large scale between liberals and conservatives ensued. Churches were seriously divided and various sectarian secessions occurred.

In this controversial context crusades of diverse sorts were organized, in part, it would seem, to heal or hide the disunity of the churches. Temperance and foreign missions easily commanded the largest attention, though Dwight L. Moody's great revival campaigns received much publicity. An increasingly shrill accompaniment to these crusades was the renewed emphasis on America's world mission. Josiah Strong as spokesman for the Evangelical Alliance coupled his strong interest in urban problems and home missions with a call to his country to assume its imperial duty to Anglo-Saxonize mankind. "My plea is not, Save America for America's sake, but, Save America for the world's sake." By 1898 widespread acceptance of such thinking had provided a pious major premise for the logic of a war with Spain, and beyond that for America's entrance into the commercial and political affairs of the world.

44

URBAN GROWTH AND THE PROTESTANT CHURCHES

When Fort Dearborn was incorporated as the village of
Chicago in 1833, it was an ugly frontier outpost of seventeen
houses. By 1900, though still ugly, it was a sprawling western
metropolis of 1,698,575 people—the fifth largest city in the
world. Chicago became the most dramatic symbol of the
major social trend of the post-Civil War era: the rise of the
city.

Within a generation after the Civil War the United States
was transformed from a predominantly agricultural to a
manufacturing nation. By 1890 the factory had outdistanced
the farm as the country's chief producer of wealth, and by
1920 the population's center of gravity had shifted decisively
to the city. Making the transition were dozens of new metropolitan centers besides Chicago. Nor was this only a western
phenomenon; old eastern cities like Boston, Philadelphia, and
New York expanded with startling speed.[1]

This social and economic revolution was accompanied by
the final phase of the great Atlantic migration, which brought
European peoples to these shores in such numbers as to dwarf
all previous immigration. Whereas the pre-Civil War peak
came in 1854 with 427,833 immigrants, nearly twice that
number arrived in 1882; and in 1907 the all-time high of
1,285,349 was reached, a figure that exceeded by several
hundred thousand the total number of immigrants to the thirteen colonies between 1607 and 1776. Between 1860 and
1900 about 14 million people arrived, and between 1900 and

[1] Between 1860 and 1890 Boston grew from 177,840 to
560,892; Philadelphia from 565,529 to 1,293,697; and New York
from 1,080,330 to 3,437,202.

1920 that many more. Since no more than one-third of these went into farming or related activities, the already teeming cities had to make room for the rest. Here they would usually carry out the immemorial tasks of new immigrants at the lowest level of the social and economic order. Living together in congested quarters, yet close to old-country friends and customs, they challenged the absorptive powers of the metropolis and added still another problem to the many that were already plaguing the older social and governmental structures.

America's transformation also brought profound intellectual consternation to many sensitive participants in the process. One social analyst remarked in 1889 that "an almost total revolution has taken place, and is yet in progress, in every branch and in every relation of the world's industrial and commercial system." At about the same time Henry Adams shuddered before the awful power of the dynamo and wondered if his whole generation was not "mortgaged to the railroads." As corporations grew stronger, counterorganizations of farmers and workingmen were formed. Individualism in the old sense became a liability for all but the industrial and banking tycoons.

> As the network of relations affecting men's lives each year became more tangled and more distended, Americans in a basic sense no longer knew who or where they were. The setting had altered beyond their power to understand it, and within an alien context they had lost themselves. In a democratic society who was master and who servant? In a land of opportunity what was success? In a Christian nation what were the rules and who kept them? The apparent leaders were as much adrift as their followers.[2]

The moral dilemmas of industrialism, moreover, were compounded by problems created by science, scholarship, and the philosophic speculations of the age. Pervading all was the fundamental difficulty of evaluating urban civilization itself and weighing its values in the light of the nation's agrarian

[2] David A. Wells, "Recent Economic Changes," in *The Nation Transformed: The Creation of an Industrial Society*, ed. Sigmund Diamond (New York: George Braziller, 1963), p. 41. See also Robert H. Wiebe, *The Search for Order* (New York: Hill and Wang, 1967), pp. 42–43.

past. For the churches shaped by frontier evangelism these questions were especially acute. The post-Civil War decades were indeed "the critical period in American religion."[3]

THE CHURCHES AND THE CITY, PAST AND PRESENT

Commercial and maritime necessities spurred the growth of American cities almost from the beginning; and churches in these "cities in the wilderness" began to experience some characteristic urban problems even in the seventeenth century. The founding in 1699 of the Brattle Street Church in Boston, for example, clearly evidenced the growing self-consciousness of a merchant community. After the passage of a century the problems of urbanization had multiplied to the extent that the minister of this very church, the Reverend Joseph Stevens Buckminster, expressed gratitude on Thanksgiving Day that the country had an inexhaustible supply of unsettled western lands. It seemed to him then that the escape they offered from the city's festering problems was the only sure hope for American democracy. Though a stout Federalist addressing a congregation of stout Federalists, Buckminster shared Thomas Jefferson's agrarian ideal.

In many respects, however, westward expansion only enlarged the economic role of the cities, with the result that complications deepened in the older centers of population. Sixteen years after Buckminster gave thanks for rural America, the Unitarian ministers of Boston had felt obliged to form a "Benevolent Fraternity of Churches" and to call Joseph Tuckerman as "minister-at-large" to direct a program of social work among Boston's poor. Discovering that chapels and preaching were not enough, Tuckerman became one of the country's first Christian social welfare theorists and a forerunner of the Social Gospel. Yet urban growth soon created far larger problems than cooperative social work could solve. Remorselessly the population patterns changed. Buildings deteriorated, factories encroached, old residential areas decayed, tenements arose, peaceful streets became crowded thoroughfares. When the constituency of old "downtown" churches moved out into new residential neigh-

3 Arthur Meier Schlesinger, "The Critical Period in American Religion, 1875–1900," *Proceedings of the Massachusetts Historical Society* 64 (1932–33): 523–47.

borhoods, the church itself often followed, perhaps selling the old building to another congregation composed of in-migrants. Later, this church too would follow "its people" to some more favorable location. The changing ownership of church buildings thus documented the demographic history of the city, while the successive locations and edifices of a single congregation recorded the upward social mobility of its membership.

Such trends, tragically enough, meant that congregations which were involved in this struggle for survival were often in a poor position to undertake a program of evangelism in their own neighborhood. In the old location they became financially incapable of a wider social ministry. If they moved, such social problems became geographically and mor-ally remote; if they stayed, the characteristic forms of Protes-tant church life prevented them from establishing cordial relations with the church's new neighbors unless they were of similar social status. In a church already moving up the social scale, the sermons tended toward greater intellectual sophis-tication, the music had a similarly restricted appeal, and parish programs increasingly answered to middle- and upper-class needs. In such congregations, proper sewing-circle con-versation and the niceties of holding a teacup were effective bars to evangelistic outreach.

Urban change thus had two particularly devastating conse-quences. In the first place, large elements of the new urban population had no contact with any Protestant churches. This was especially true of the English-speaking peoples of Protes-tant background who were moving in ever-increasing numbers from the countryside to scattered locations in the cities. Immigrants were not so prominently handicapped, because their ethnic or linguistic isolation often led them to the churches of their fellow nationals, who more often than not were Roman Catholic, Jewish, Eastern Orthodox, or Lu-theran. The liturgical worship and church life of these de-nominations tended to hold congregations together despite the upward mobility of some members. In the second place, urban growth created a serious cleavage in city population in relation to religious affiliation. The people who could afford churches were well churched; those who could not were unchurched—and hardly cared, or even regarded church people as their economic oppressors. Josiah Strong, the general secretary of the Evangelical Alliance, in two heavily documented books, *Our Country* (1885) and *The New Era* (1893), piled statistic on statistic to demonstrate the dramatic exodus of Protestant churches from the growing sections of American cities.

THE PRINCES OF THE PULPIT

Inanition, flight, and class segregation were by no means the only features of urban Protestantism in the Age of Enterprise. Large and wealthy urban churches offered opportunities not only to architects, artists, and musicians, but they also created the context for a new kind of minister whose merits and importance has often been underestimated. The oratorical style of these men finds little favor in the twentieth century; but all across the nation they did address the age's many moral and intellectual dilemmas with considerable intellectual power. Aiming to be understood by an active, socially prominent laity, they carried out an important task of mediating Christianity to the modern world. It was a time when science seemed to undermine the Christian message and when many people doubted the relevance of the church in an industrial-commercial environment. Faced by a widespread yearning for ethical and ideological anchorage, the great preachers took up the task of defending and interpreting the Christian tradition anew. In what they said there was no universal agreement. Some of these wealthy congregations were led by revivalistic Presbyterians, others by radical Unitarians. But there was a discernible central tendency which can be traced to the influence of the new "progressive" theologians making their impact in several centers of learning. Most prominent among the many preachers who set new patterns in the city churches were Henry Ward Beecher (1813–87) of Plymouth Congregational Church in Brooklyn, and Phillips Brooks (1835–93) of Trinity Episcopal Church in Boston.

Beecher, the fourth son of Lyman, graduated from Lane Seminary in 1837 and for ten years afterward followed the revivalistic tradition of his father in various Indiana churches. Coming to the newly formed Plymouth Church in 1847, by the charm of his personality and the force of his oratory he soon attracted a congregation of great size and wealth. From the first Beecher chose to minimize doctrinal differences, demanding nothing of his members save personal loyalty to Christ. Displeased by criticism of his theology, he led his congregation out of the Congregational denomination in 1882, proclaiming himself a free man with obligations to none. He often addressed himself to topics of the times, including the whole gamut of contemporary social and political issues: slavery, reconstruction, immigration, taxes, women's rights, civil service reform, and municipal corruption. In addition, he sought to expound a meaningful Christian accommodation of evolutionary theories, biblical criticism, and the cultural values of the city as such. He edited two widely read journals, the *Independent* (1861–63) and the *Christian Union* (1870–81), and contributed regularly to both the religious and the secular press as well. His sermons were published weekly in the *Plymouth Pulpit* (after 1859), while successive volumes of sermons and lectures reached a nationwide audience. He also delivered the Lyman Beecher lectures on preaching at Yale for three years straight (1872–74), compiled *The Plymouth Collection of Hymns and Tunes* (1855), and wrote a novel that dealt with changing religious values (*Norwood*, 1687). Neither his advertising testimonials in behalf of Pears's Soap, nor a great scandal arising out of his indiscreet attentions to Mrs. Elizabeth Tilton seriously diminished his public.

The broad churchmanship of Phillips Brooks is another example of ebullient confidence in liberal theology and American culture. "The spirit of man is the candle of the Lord," Brooks never tired of telling the Boston congregation to whom he preached for a quarter of a century (1869–93). To him the whole of mankind was the family of God, and the goodness and nobility of men as children of God was the essential article of his faith. His optimism kept him as untroubled by the inequalities of American life as were his self-satisfied parishioners. He found evidence of God's goodness in the thought that each class had its peculiar blessings and privileges. Like Beecher, his ethic rested more on the social assumptions of an earlier age than on those of the new industrial society. He believed that suffering caused by poverty and injustice was for the most part deserved, but that they were, in any event, only temporary problems which the natural narmony of God's purposes would certainly dispel. Suspicion of heresy notwithstanding, Brooks became the Episcopal bishop of Massachusetts in 1891. He published ten widely read volumes of sermons along with a volume of *Essays and Addresses* and his *Lectures on Preaching* delivered at Yale in 1877.

These two princes of the pulpit were in a class by themselves, envied and emulated the country over. Yet each of them had strong rivals even in his own city: George Angier Gordon at Boston's Old South Church, and T. DeWitt Talmadge at Central Presbyterian in New York. In New Haven, Theodore Munger and Newman Smyth, both nationally eminent, held forth in two historic Congregational churches standing side by side on the city green. Rare was the city, especially in the North, that could not boast one or two of these great downtown churches with their carriage trade constituency and impressive buildings. Because they spoke with thoughtfulness and learning, the ministers of these churches did succeed in keeping a remarkable number of America's great men of business and public affairs active in the work and support of the church. Because of the accommodating nature of their message, on the other hand, they often contributed to the "inner revolution" of the epoch by transforming Christianity into a benign and genteel form of religious humanism. This dilemma is considered in greater depth in chapter 46, which deals with the "golden age" of theological liberalism.

PROTESTANT INNOVATION AND TRADITION IN THE CITY

One major explanation for the uneven effectiveness of urban Protestantism during this period was the fact that the churches, like the various institutions of civil government, were slow to overhaul their basic strategies and organization. The half-century before the Civil War had been the age of the nonsectarian voluntary associations, but rising denominational self-consciousness and other factors began to make serious inroads into these institutions even before the war. The conception of the church itself as a mission society began to win increasing allegiance. These shifts in rationale and method, in turn, led to several decades of disorientation during which cooperative home missionary efforts were reorganized. Only in 1908, with the founding of the Federal (later National) Council of Churches, was the full transition more or less accomplished.[4] In the meantime, the long-established tendency to emphasize the rural frontier's missionary call was not broken. The West, both as myth and as reality, was a more compelling lure than the city, and it continued to be the chief concern of home missions agencies. As Professor Handy has pointed out, the new city problems "were unfamiliar to a Protestantism that had flourished in small-town America, and the missionary movement was slow in regrouping its forces and reorienting its thinking."[5] Even when efforts were begun, the middle-class, frontier-oriented mentality of those in charge put its mark on the tactics employed and sharply circumscribed their effectiveness. Rural people were moving to the city in great numbers, but these arrivals tended to bring with them the patterns of congregational life which they had known in the past. In the absence of denominational or interdenominational planning, like-minded groups simply organized congregations as best they could with little concern for other groups or for the needs of the city. Within each denomination, therefore, there were often a variety of churches for different areas of the city and different types of people, most of them following the predictable patterns of America's small towns and rural areas, except that social stratification often became more pronounced.

An increasingly important aspect of congregational life during these decades, and also an invaluable instrument for reaching new members, was the Sunday school. This movement, like so many others, had British origins, and during the antebellum period it had become a vital element in the work of the Evangelical United Front. As a coordinating agency for many regional associations, the American Sunday School Union had been founded in 1824. Thereafter wide-ranging organizational and publication activities were carried forward. The Sunday school became a familiar American institution, and in many congregations the "Bible class" over-

[4] On the reorganization of Protestant interdenominational cooperation, see pp. 270–73 below.

[5] Robert T. Handy, *We Witness Together: A History of Cooperative Home Missions*, pp. 16–17.

shadowed the regular Sabbath worship. On both the local and the national level the evangelistic possibilities of these educational means were exploited, especially during the urban revivals of 1857–58.

During the post-Civil War years the movement experienced still another forward surge. Not surprisingly, Dwight L. Moody had a hand in it. Moody inspired the wealthy Chicago produce broker and real estate man B. F. Jacobs to reinvigorate the Sunday School Union. Jacobs's talents got results, and at the convention of 1872 he gained the adoption of a uniform lesson plan, whereby the same lesson, graded for different ages, could be studied and taught on each Sunday in all the participating churches. The plan encouraged interdenominational teachers' meetings, the expansion of supporting publications, and the foundation of teachers' institutes all across the country modeled on the Moody Bible Institute of Chicago (1886). Revivals and revivalists would come and go, but the Sunday schools remained as a strong stabilizing force in the churches. In small towns and large cities they attracted dedicated lay leaders of great ability, helping to set the tone and temper of American Protestantism and providing an effective means of reaching the unchurched and unaffiliated—adults as well as children. Although they necessarily mirrored the country's values, the Sunday schools did produce a pious and knowledgeable laity on a scale unequaled anywhere in Christendom.

In addition to these more traditional forms of congregational life, however, there were four very diverse but yet distinctly innovative forms of urban concern that became especially important during the postwar period, though they all had had earlier origins. The best known of these is the Social Gospel movement (see chap. 47). The other three are more clearly related to problems of evangelism.

Least heralded were the slum-oriented efforts of the Salvation Army, its offshoot, the Volunteers of America, and a diverse group of rescue missions, many of which were founded by Holiness and Pentecostal sects. (As parts of a distinctive Christian movement these groups are considered in chap. 48.) Far more extraordinary in their special adaptation to city needs were the Young Men's and Women's Christian Associations. Supported by the philanthropy of wealthy church members and catering to the needs of the many unattached young people who were moving to the city, the YMCA and YWCA entered upon their half-century of greatest vitality and usefulness during the 1870s. Though traceable to eighteenth-century experiments in Germany, the history of the YMCA among English-speaking peoples begins with a society formed in London by George Williams on 6 June 1844. By 1851 there were twenty-four such organizations in Great Britain, and in that year one was formed in Montreal and another in Boston. In 1855 the first YWCA was organized. The next year a New York YMCA was formed, and by 1860 there were some 203 associations with about twenty-five thousand members in all North America. During the Civil War the YMCA gave itself largely to the work of the Christian Commission among the soldiers, but afterward it returned to its ministry in the cities. Emphasizing Christianity in practical work, it had four major departments of endeavor: physical, educational, social, and religious. In the first of these fields the YMCA was a pioneer, fostering athletic recreation and defending the values of "play" in the face of much puritanic criticism. Its religious department, at the same time, was so powerful a force that the YMCA functioned not simply as an ecumenical service agency, but virtually as a church and as a Protestant denomination for the many young men and women who owed their Christian commitment to its Bible classes and religious services. All in all, the "Y" was one of the most remarkably functional church agencies of the period.

The fourth great strategy of Protestant advance in the city —and by far the most publicized—was nondenominational professional revivalism. The old methods pioneered by Whitefield, developed by Methodist camp meetings, and further refined by Finney became the major instrument of the urban churches in reaching out beyond the narrow circles of personal acquaintance to penetrate the anonymous mass of city folk who, in their uprooted loneliness, longed for the old-time religion. Revivals also offered a measure of excitement to break the monotony of urban existence, just as camp meetings had performed that function on the frontier. Indeed, the revivalists provided theatrical entertainment to people who regarded the theater itself as sinful. Its country-born practitioners knew these inner yearnings, and the successful ones were masters at appealing to them. Thus from Keokuk and Peoria to New York and Boston, revivalism constituted the single largest response of evangelical Protestantism to the challenge of the urban frontier.

THE GREAT REVIVALISTS

Dwight Lyman Moody (1837–99), like so many of those to whom he preached, was a village-born lad who despite a meager education had made good in the city. At the age of eighteen, leaving his widowed mother at the homestead in Northfield, Massachusetts, he sought his fortune in the Boston shoe store of his uncle. Between 1854 and 1856 Moody sold shoes, enjoyed Boston, listened to his uncle's pastor, discovered the Bible, and "accepted Christ"; in 1856 he became a church member. His conversion was quiet, simple, and unemotional, yet it eventually reordered his entire life. In September 1856, Moody moved to Chicago.

"Chicago hustled!" says one writer, and so did Moody. His energy and enthusiasm soon won him a reputation as a salesman in the shoe trade, but the business world could neither claim all of his immense gifts nor corrode the memory of his religious experience. Joining the Plymouth Congregational Church, Moody rented four pews which he filled each Sunday morning with whomever he could collect on the streets and in the boardinghouses. Taking charge of an out-of-the-way mission Sunday school in North Market Hall, he gathered a membership of fifteen hundred—mostly urchins and drifters whom he picked up off the streets and out of the gutters and cellars of the Sands district north of the Chicago River. And out of this motley group was formed in 1863 the Illinois Street Church, independent and nondenominational. Moody was equally successful in enlisting the support of wealthy friends such as John V. Farwell, B. F. Jacobs, George Armour, and Cyrus McCormick.

In 1861 he gave up business to devote himself entirely to the Lord's work, first as an independent city missionary, during the Civil War as an agent of the Christian Commission, and after the war as president of the Chicago YMCA, where he had been active since his arrival in the big town. One of Moody's first services to the YMCA was as chairman of its Visitation Committee, a capacity in which he indulged his soul-winning zeal to the fullest, visiting over six hundred families in one year—a "new model circuit rider in the urban wilderness." After twelve years in Chicago, Moody was a civic fixture. He was the "drive wheel" of the Chicago YMCA and a remarkable fund raiser after fires in 1868 and 1871 twice destroyed its building. His church was also influential, and although he had begun to preach, he had as yet done nothing to acquire the fame which was soon to be his.

Then between 1867 and 1872 four decisive events occurred. Through Harry Moorehouse, a Plymouth Brethren preacher from England, Moody discovered the love of God for sinners, a message which had been lacking in all his previous experience. In 1870 he persuaded Ira David Sankey (1840–1908) to join him as a chorister in his evangelistic endeavors. The next year, in New York, Moody had some kind of a reconsecration experience which literally set him on fire with a "passion for souls." Finally, in the spring of 1872, while in England on business for the YMCA, Moody was asked to substitute in a London pulpit. After his sermon four hundred people responded to his closing invitation. It was a sign from heaven: here was his life's work.

The first great campaign of the Moody-Sankey team was in Great Britain, where during 1873–75 they must have reached between three and four million hearers. Then it was America's turn. In Brooklyn the transport company laid down additional trolley tracks to accommodate the crowds seeking passage to the Rink, a five-thousand-seat auditorium. In Philadelphia John Wanamaker fitted out a Pennsylvania Railroad freight warehouse for a two-month campaign. After that they began a famous series of campaigns from New York to Saint Louis, and on to the Pacific coast. With listeners in the millions, converts in the thousands, their hymns on every lip, their names a household word, Moody and Sankey rejuvenated the revival. As Bernard Weisberger has put it, "Moody made clear what he had known all along: the American-born, middle-class urbanite of his day was still a villager under the skin. Using the methods and the money of big business, Moody reconciled the city and the old-time religion to each other."[6]

Dwight Moody's message was a simple and relatively innocuous blend of American optimism and evangelical Arminianism. Holding aloft his Bible, he assured his hearers

[6] Bernard A. Weisberger, *They Gathered at the River: The Story of the Great Revivalists and their Impact upon Religion in America*, p. 206.

that eternal life was theirs for the asking, that they had only to "come forward and t-a-k-e, TAKE!" This done, his follow-up instruction was short and to the point: "Join some church at once." Which church did not matter.

> Moody preached a gospel with but one center, God's saving act in Jesus Christ, and one goal, the conversion and salvation of the sinner. All other ends were secondary. . . . Public morality was to be improved through saving individuals. The church was a voluntary association of the saved.[7]

Nowhere in his message was there much help for the thinker who was seriously disturbed by the moral problems of industrialism or the new intellectual dilemmas of the nineteenth century. His optimism was revealed in his confidence that individual conversions would solve every personal and social problem. Charitable works were not an end in themselves, but a means of reaching individuals with a message of redemption.

Just as significantly the campaigns of Moody and Sankey furthered the mounting tendency to convert the traditional message of Protestant Christianity into something dulcet and sentimental. The United States had embarked upon the most extravagantly sentimental period in its history, and through song and sermon across the land, the professional revival teams wove this sentimentality into the warp and woof of American Protestantism. The same mood suffused the new style of "Christian art." Biblical scenes by the German painter Johann M. F. H. Hofmann acquired enormous vogue, while the religious publishing houses and Sunday school suppliers laid the groundwork for twentieth-century America's unbounded enthusiasm for the pictures of Warner E. Sallman. Thus a new pattern was set for revivalism, and in the process, a prophetic faith was transformed into a sentimental moralism. Perhaps in these subtle (or not so subtle) nuances and emphases lies the chief import of the new revivalism.

[7] Robert S. Michaelson, "The Protestant Ministry in America: 1850 to the Present," in *The Ministry in Historical Perspectives*, ed. H. Richard Niebuhr and Daniel D. Williams, p. 256. Conservatives were often critical of Moody's openness, notably his accepting the young British liberal, Henry Drummond, not only as a friend but as a co-worker.

After Moody's retirement in 1892 no figure of equal stature appeared on the urban revival scene.[8] His mantle in a sense was conferred on J. Wilbur Chapman and Reuben A. Torrey, though these men never achieved his wide appeal or impressive results. But two other men continued his work on a grand scale: Samuel Porter Jones (1847–1906) and Benjamin Fay Mills (1857–1916). Sam Jones was a product of rural Georgia who turned from a bibulous past in 1872, became an itinerant Methodist preacher, and was known before long as the "Moody of the South." His revivals were a significant factor in the urban recovery of the Methodist Episcopal Church, South, especially after E. O. Excell joined him as chorister and gospel song writer. Jones began his attacks on the typical vices and shortcomings of city life, but his emphasis was radically practical. "If I had a creed," he declared, "I would sell it to a museum."[9] Sanctification he equated with a resolve to live by the mores of rural Georgia in the wicked city. No man documented so tellingly the long road away from John Wesley's theology which American Methodism had traveled during its first century of independent life.

Mills was of a different sort altogether. Not only was he an important link between America's revival tradition and the Social Gospel, but he made important innovations in revival techniques. His background was Old School Presbyterian, but he was ordained into the Congregational ministry in Minnesota in 1878. After nine years as a parish minister, he entered the field of professional evangelism. His chief distinction is the development of the highly successful "District

---

[8] Moody suffered a heart ailment in 1892 which curtailed his activities considerably. During the last years of his life he founded numerous institutions to perpetuate his witness: the Northfield Seminary for Young Women (1879), the Mount Hermon School for Young Men (1881), the annual student and Christian workers conference at Northfield, and the Bible Institute for Home and Foreign Missions in Chicago (1886). These were financed not only by Moody's affluent friends, but by the not inconsiderable returns on his and Sankey's hymnbook, which went through numberless editions during its long period of popularity (see James F. Findlay, Jr., *Dwight L. Moody: American Evangelist, 1837–1899*).

[9] William G. McLoughlin, *Modern Revivalism: Charles Grandison Finney to Billy Graham*, p. 300. My indebtedness to this history is great, especially on Moody's successors.

Combination Plan of Evangelism." More than anyone up to his time, Mills marks the full accommodation of revivalism to the arts of business and administration. Nothing was left to chance: finance and organization were carried out in advance, and a city was attacked simultaneously in various precincts and by central meetings. Decisions were recorded on cards which were then distributed to the cooperating churches. All church meetings not connected with the revival were canceled, and, if possible, the entire city was encouraged to declare Wednesday a "midweek Sabbath" by closing all of its businesses. Ample press coverage was sought and usually secured. Then, with all these matters prearranged, Mills would mount his campaign on the city and its sins. One of the anomalies of his success was that his message, and hence the meaning of his conversions, was so generalized that Christian Scientists, Unitarians, and Roman Catholics saw no incongruity in signing his cards. In theology Mills moved steadily toward a Bushnellian liberalism and gradually lost favor among evangelicals. In 1899 he left revivalism for the Unitarian ministry.

By the second decade of the twentieth century, it remained only for cheaper, simpler men with gaudier personalities and fewer scruples to bring the revivalistic movement into disrepute. Mannerisms of the theater and the music hall were combined in Knowles Shaw. The growing tendency to emphasize statistics was characteristic of Rodney "Gipsy" Smith, who not only made news on the number of "decisions" he secured, but indicated to his sponsors that he could produce converts for $4.92 apiece. The most spectacular champions of the sawdust trail, however, were the ex-baseball player, Billy Sunday, and his chorister, Homer A. Rodeheaver (1880–1955)—a team, incidentally, that cut conversion costs to $2.00 a soul when they finally got their system working.

William Ashley Sunday (1863–1935) was, like Moody, a farm boy, "a rube of the rubes," as he himself put it. Born in Iowa into a family ravaged by many tragedies, he gained prominence in 1883 as an outfielder for the Chicago White-Stockings. Three years later, after being converted, he began to amend his life. When Bible study classes at the Chicago YMCA aroused his interest in Christian work, he quit baseball to become an assistant secretary at the YMCA in 1891. Two years later he took a job as organizer on the revival team of J. Wilbur Chapman, who at that time was still something of a class-B attraction, touring only the smaller cities of the nation. In 1895 Chapman retired to a Philadelphia pastorate and recommended Sunday as his successor. Billy's debut in Garner, Iowa, was modest; but by 1900 he was able to hire his own musician and to require towns to erect pineboard tabernacles for his meetings. As he developed his innate abilities for vaudeville, he drew larger crowds, and by 1904 he could demand that expense monies be raised before he arrived. After securing Rodeheaver as a great trombone-playing song leader in 1909, he conducted a revival in Spokane, breaking into the 100,000-population circuit for the first time. From then on the team's average improved; and by 1917, the peak year, the average population of the revivalized cities was 1,750,000. This was the major league indeed. Sunday's box score in New York that year showed a total attendance of 1,433,000 for the ten-week campaign. Converts numbered 98,264.

Sunday's phenomenal success was due in no small part to his talent for dramatization before audiences. Accompanying his contortions, furniture smashing, and partial undressing was an unbroken torrent of words. What the church needed, he shouted, was fighting men of God, not "hog-jowled, weasel-eyed, sponge-columned, mushy-fisted, jelly-spined, pussy-footing, four-flushing, Charlotte-russe Christians." Similar language was turned against the familiar sins of the world: high society, worldly amusements, filthy habits, pliable politicians, liberal preachers, trashy immigrants, and especially the "booze traffic." Every man who was not a teetotaler was a "dirty low-down, whisky-soaked, beer-guzzling, bull-necked, foul-mouthed hypocrite." Not only did he define sin almost solely in terms of individual moralism, but he garbled the distinction between the sin and the sinner in a way that simply fostered the self-righteousness of his middle-class audiences.

The "altar call" was, of course, the climax and goal of the revival service. Professional evangelists had made the decision increasingly easier, so that by Sunday's time any "decent American" could painlessly respond. The burden was easy and the sawdust trail was wide. His invitation on the twelfth day of his New York campaign was typical. "Do you want God's blessing on you, your home, your church, your nation, on New York? If you do, raise your hands." . . . "How many of you men and women will jump to your feet and come down and say, 'Bill, here's my hand for God, for home, for

my native land, to live and conquer for Christ?'" Then Rody
and the choir began their musical accompaniment, and a sea
of humanity surged forward—one out of every ten in that audience of twenty thousand.[10]

The high tide of mass revivalism in the trappings of vaudeville came during the decade preceding America's entry into
World War I. In 1911 there were 650 active evangelists in
the field and 1,200 part-time campaigners. Between 1912 and
1918 they staged at least thirty-five thousand revivals; and
according to one careful estimate, the evangelical churches
spent $20 million a year on "professional tabernacle evangel-
ism" during the peak years from 1914 to 1917. But decline
was inevitable. Already in 1915 Alfred and Kilmer Ackley
had asked Billy Sunday to throw a few crumbs their way,
pleading that the "evangelistic situation for the little fellow
this season is going to be mighty hard."[11] With American
doughboys in Europe, the nation's attention was diverted to
less theatrical concerns for a time. In the war's complex aftermath, America's religious climate changed, and professional
evangelism suffered a temporary relapse which some historians, perhaps hopefully, interpreted to be its demise. Even so,
the movement had etched a deep mark on American evangelical Protestantism.

10 William G. McLoughlin, *Billy Sunday Was His Real Name*,
pp. 261, xvii–xxix; see also Weisberger, *They Gathered at the
River*, pp. 240–49.
11 McLoughlin, *Billy Sunday*, p. 261.

45

PROTESTANTISM AND THE LATER IMMIGRATION

Next to rapid urban expansion, probably no historical development of the later nineteenth century had a heavier impact on the spiritual selfconsciousness of the American people than the demographic revolution produced by immigration. Its relatively greatest impact on the population occurred between 1851 and 1860, but the peak volume of the influx did not come until the years between 1901 and 1910. In its totality, the Atlantic Migration involved a much longer period of time and the movement of over forty-five million foreigners. It was during the post-Civil War half-century, however, that the American people felt the full impact—though not really the full import—of the country's ethnic and religious pluralism. Two brief tables reveal both the varying volume of the influx and the diversity of its origins. These bare statistics inevitably leave many vital facts veiled (for example, the ethnic makeup of the exodus from the composite Austro-Hungarian Empire), but they give unmistakable evidence of the new order of magnitude which immigration assumed in the later nineteenth century.

Total Immigration to the United States, by Decade

1821–1830	143,439
1831–1840	599,125
1841–1850	1,713,251
1851–1860	2,598,214
1861–1870	2,314,824
1871–1880	2,812,191
1881–1890	5,246,613

1891–1900	3,687,564
1901–1910	8,795,386
1911–1920	5,735,811
1921–1930	4,107,209
1931–1940	528,431
1941–1950	1,035,039
1951–1960	2,515,479
1961–1970	3,321,677
WORLD TOTAL	45,154,253

Total Immigration by Country, 1820–1969

Europe:

Austria	3,769,854
Germany	6,906,465
Great Britain	4,777,727
Ireland	4,712,680
Italy	5,149,119
Norway	852,891
Russia	3,346,455
Sweden	1,266,127
Other Europe	4,812,326
TOTAL EUROPE	35,593,649

America:

Canada	3,941,858
Mexico	1,547,771
West Indies	1,033,386
Other America	1,784,847
Total America	7,307,862
Total Asia	1,429,020
Total Countries not Specified	458,781
WORLD TOTAL	44,789,312

Source: Department of Justice, Immigration and Naturalization Service, *Annual Reports.*

THE INNER HISTORY OF IMMIGRATION

No statistical table can reveal the billions of tears that were shed in the course of that massive uprooting; numbers cannot register the pain of severed human ties, nor the cumulative nostalgia, nor the anguish of loneliness in a strange land. Yet the tears and anguish are part of the American heritage, even

though their full significance will never be known. Ever since
John Winthrop and his party saw the English coastline sink
from view in 1630, the entire religious life of America has
been conditioned by two inescapable concomitants of the immigration experience. One of these consists of the tenacious
ties to European culture and church traditions which the immigrant brought with him to this country, which he transmitted to his children, and they to theirs. The other, which
became more drastic as the United States developed its own
distinctive ways, is the confrontation with a new culture and
the desire to appropriate the life and ideals of the country
with whose destiny the immigrant has cast his lot. Between
these two loves, desires, and needs, there could only be
conflict, tension, and gradual resolution. The diary-letters of a
young bride sailing away from Norway with her husband
convey something of the grief that millions of emigrants
could never banish:

April 26 [1862] And now the last glimpse of Norway. It
may be somewhere near Arendal, but it's far in the distance like a blue mist; nothing more. I am heavy-hearted.
A silent prayer for comfort in my deepest sorrow and for
strength and courage.

April 27 (First Sunday after Easter). The captain led
the worship. My heart was still heavy. My thoughts were
with you, my dear ones, and of services at home. I could
see you all in church. You know I was never absent—and
now! O merciful God!

Today my last glimpse of Norway. I shall never see my
beloved homeland. O God of Mercy, my fatherland! Oh forgive me for causing my dear ones this anguish! O God, do
not forsake us! Be our comforter and give us patience and
strengthen our faith.[1]

Later, when settled on a farm in Iowa—her husband away
fighting in the Union army—she tried to convey the meaning
of it all to her parents:

I have often thought that I ought to tell you about life
here in the New World. Everything is so totally different
from what it was in our beloved Norway. You never will

[1] Theodore C. Blegen and Pauline Farseth, eds., *Frontier
Mother: The Letters of Gro Svendsen* (Northfield, Minn.: Nor-
wegian-American Historical Association, 1950), p. 14.

really know what it's like, although you no doubt try to imagine what it might be. Your pictures would be all wrong, just as mine were.[2]

After making the initial adjustments, immigrant parents would shed other tears at the sight—or even the thought—of their children taking bolder steps into the new world, many of them compulsively cutting away every reminder of their "foreign" background, especially when under the pressure of nativistic movements. Pastors and church leaders felt the same tensions, needless to say, but their response was complicated by the impossible task of adjusting current practices to the needs of both those who were in the throes of rapid Americanization and those who had just arrived from Europe. To the degree that the foreign traditions and ways of life contrasted sharply with American habits and typical American religious practices, the problems were intensified. Only much later, when the membership and leadership were in the hands of a real or figurative third generation, would a balanced and noncompulsive attitude toward European and American cultures be possible. Even then, the workings of Hansen's law—that the third generation tries to remember what the second generation tried to forget—would complicate matters.[3]

TYPES OF RELIGIOUS RESPONSE

Few of the world's innumerable churches and religious traditions have avoided America entirely, and at the height of the Great Migration the diversity was so great as to preclude a detailed account in a general history. In this chapter, the Protestant immigrants are considered; discussions of Roman Catholicism, Judaism, and the ancient Eastern churches will appear in later chapters. Rather than undertaking a wearisome chronicle of the immigrant churches in all of their variety, however, one may describe five major types of accommodation to the American religious situation.[4]

[2] Ibid., p. 39.
[3] Marcus L. Hansen, *The Problem of the Third Generation Immigrant* (Rock Island, Ill.: Augustana Historical Society Publications, 1930).
[4] This typology will reveal why no statistical estimate of Protestant affiliations in America can be attempted. Father Gerald

The first category includes those immigrants who were merely nominal members of some state church in Europe, or simply unaffiliated, or anticlerical by conviction (as was fairly often the case with certain ethnic groups, especially if they came from industrial cities). Such people neither founded new churches nor sought out existing ones on arrival, but they made an important contribution to the history of American secret societies during their nineteenth-century heyday. They thus aggravated the old hostility of the churches to such organizations, and they often divided ethnic groups into two factions: the "church people," and those who gratified their needs for ritualism and social contacts in the Masonic order, or in dozens of other flourishing lodges, some ethnically oriented, some not. Of course, they also constituted a ripened home missions field.[5]

A second type consists of the immigrating sectarians, those who recently or in the immemorial past had expressed their dissatisfaction with comprehensive state churches by forming more rigorously disciplined communities of their own. The Mennonites are a classic example; and their history in America was profoundly altered in this very period by a large migration of German Mennonites from Russia. Having fled Germany earlier in the century to escape military service and other impediments, they were confronted in 1870 by the czar's revocation of their privileges in Russia. Given the alternatives of compromise or emigration, many of them found America's promise of peace and plenty decisive (as did even larger numbers of non-Mennonite Germans in Russia). Settling chiefly in the Midwest, from Kansas to Indiana, this group soon became the largest element in the General Conference Mennonite Church, which is somewhat more moderate in its belief and discipline than the older Mennonite church of Pennsylvania background.

Shaughnessy, *Has the Immigrant Kept the Faith?* (New York: Macmillan Co., 1925) adduced a fairly affirmative answer for Roman Catholics; but his problem was relatively simple. For Protestant immigrants one can do little more than hazard a guess that they did *raise* the incidence of church membership in the United States.

[5] Despite its obvious importance, the "lodge" as an American social and religious institution has been inadequately studied. The existing literature is largely designed either for polemical or defensive purposes.

Similar in many ways to the professed sectarians were many other deeply religious immigrants who were, in European terms, incipient sectarians, deeply dissatisfied with the formalism, the moral laxity, or the doctrinal indifference of an established church. Because their attitudes toward the church of their fathers were thus distinctly negative, they were eager to identify with the American free-church tradition. Their numbers were further increased by the active evangelism of various American churches. Two German-speaking Methodistic churches, the Evangelical Association and the United Brethren in Christ, were thus able to make large additions to their membership. Similar growth occurred among Baptists, Methodists, Presbyterians, and Congregationalists, who in various ways conducted active foreign-language evangelism, followed by organizational provisions for special ethnic conferences or synods of Germans, Scandinavians, Slovaks, Hungarians, and others. Walter Rauschenbusch's father, for example, was a professor in the "German Department" maintained by the Baptist theological seminary in Rochester, New York. The Congregationalists showed a special solicitude for the non-Mennonite Russian Germans whose churches in the Upper Midwest had adopted a congregational polity and set up a college and seminary at Yankton, South Dakota.

The fourth and fifth categories are constituted by those extremely numerous immigrants who belonged to various European state churches, and who wished to continue these affiliations in America. Most difficult to number are those of the fourth category. Their native loyalties simply led them to some branch or diocese of their home church. Great numbers of Anglicans, Presbyterians, Dutch Reformed, Lutherans, and others followed this course. Somewhat more visible are those of the fifth type who for various reasons organized new autonomous churches. They treasured the confessional heritage of their birth, and the churches they founded maintained close ties with a mother church in the old country, though only rarely did they receive substantial aid. Linguistic considerations were often an important factor in their choice. A great many in this category, however, were also church reformers of a sort, who used the opportunity for a new beginning in America to introduce important changes in liturgy, discipline, polity, and even doctrine. Because vigorous, new, and in some cases very large church bodies were brought into existence in this manner, three instances, the Christian Reformed Church (Dutch), Evangelical Church-Union of the West (German), and various Lutheran developments, merit more detailed consideration.

The Christian Reformed Church

The largest of several strictly "Reformed" churches in the United States, aside from the two large Presbyterian churches, is the Christian Reformed Church formed by a tiny group of Dutch immigrants in Zeeland, Michigan, on 8 April 1857. The decision of this frontier nucleus stemmed from dissatisfactions with the existing Dutch Reformed tradition which had been manifested almost simultaneously in both Holland and America. In the mother country a spirit of dissent rising during the revivals of the 1820s had by 1834 led to actual secession and the formation of a doctrinally strict free church, which in 1892 would be merged with another and larger secession. In America, Solomon Froeligh and four other ministers led a similar secession in 1822, forming the True Reformed Church. This group united in 1889 with the Christian Reformed Church of America, which at that time consisted of nearly ten thousand families, and by 1970 the church had about 400,000 members, most of whom are descendants of later nineteenth-century Dutch immigrants living chiefly in Michigan and nearby states. With a well supported church-school system and a strong intellectual and theological tradition nourished by Calvin College and Seminary in Grand Rapids, Michigan, the denomination has become perhaps the country's most solid and dignified bastion of conservative Reformed doctrine and church discipline.

German Unionists on the Frontier

The Evangelical Church-Union of the West (*Evangelischer Kirchenverein des Westens*), an immigrant church contemporary in its development with the Christian Reformed, represented the contrary tendency. This church founded on the Missouri frontier came closer than any other in America to achieving the union of Reformed and Lutheran confessions for which the king of Prussia had striven in 1817. In the mid-nineteenth century, Germans constituted perhaps a quarter of the population of the Saint Louis-Southern Illinois area; and they exhibited the full range of possible religious attitudes from ultra-orthodox Lutheran to anticlerical rationalist. Among them was a sizable number of pietistic evangelicals of both Reformed and Lutheran backgrounds, who in 1840 convened near Saint Louis to found a loosely organized union of pastors and laymen. In 1866, after the modest success of their early efforts, they made extensive constitutional changes in their polity, providing for a full-time president and a democratic synodical structure.

Nonsectarian and irenic in spirit, they always avoided a strict confessional basis for their synod, and at first authorized the use of both Luther's and the Heidelberg catechisms for instruction. In 1847, however, they showed their growing consensus by issuing their own Evangelical Catechism, based on both of the older catechisms but inclining in spirit toward the former. This Union catechism was "the ripest theological fruit" of the Union's early years. In 1862 they published an abridged version which was accepted as defining the church's official theological position. Even more important to the actual nurture of the members was the 242-page commentary on this Small Catechism written by Professor Andreas Irion (1823–67), a fervent, mystical product of Württemberg pietism with strong philosophical interests, whose early death robbed the church of an original "Union theologian."

Counting 122 pastors in nine different states at the time of reorganization in 1866, the synod steadily extended itself as German immigration continued to pour into the Midwest. Later, joined by four other churches of a similar nature, it became the Evangelical Synod of North America. In 1934, when its membership had reached 281,500, it further expressed its unionistic principles by merging with the German Reformed church, which then also included two Hungarian "classes." This process would be carried still further in 1957, when the Evangelical and Reformed church merged with the Congregational Christian church to form the United Church of Christ.

The New Shape of Lutheranism

If the Christian Reformed church represents the immigrant's doctrinal rigorism, and the German Evangelical Union his unionistic propensities, the Lutherans who poured into the country by the million in the period between the Civil War and World War I may be said to represent the entire span, from the strict confessionalism of the Missouri Synod (organized in 1847) to the moralistic revivalism of the Franckean Synod (organized in 1837 with probably more indebtedness to Charles G. Finney than to Martin Luther). Precisely this diversity had precipitated the crisis of 1855–69 and led to the division of the older eastern Lutheranism into two opposed formations, the confessional General Council, and the General Synod with its broader "American Lutheran" platform. By 1918, after the quadricentennial of the Reformation had been duly celebrated, a far more orderly situation would prevail, and the path to confessional fellowship among the Lutherans of America could be discerned. Between 1869 and 1918, however, lay the great immigration epoch of the church.

No Protestant communion was so thoroughly transformed by the later nineteenth-century immigration as was the Lutheran. Three million immigrants came from the diverse provinces of Germany, perhaps a half of them at least vaguely Lutheran, 1.75 million from Scandinavia, nearly all of them at least nominally Lutheran, and a heavy scattering of others from Finland, Iceland, and various parts of the Austro-Hungarian empire. They settled in every section of the country, in cities and on farms, but, of course, overwhelmingly in the North. It is hardly surprising that a communion which numbered a scant half-million in 1870 had almost quintupled by 1910, by which time they were outnumbered only by the Roman Catholics, Methodists, and Baptists.

Such an influx naturally contributed to the steady western expansion of the older Lutheran organizations, the General Council, the General Synod, and the United Synod of the South, though the latter two were hindered by their emphasis on the English language and by their lack of confessional concern. Most important for the reception of the immigrants were the independent new churches which the immigrants formed themselves. Oldest of these were the Buffalo Synod and the Missouri Synod, both of which date their American origins to 1839. One group of about a thousand had left Prussia because they could not accept the Prussian Union of 1817, when the king had celebrated the Reformation by forcibly uniting the Lutheran and Reformed into a single state church. Led by Johannes A. A. Grabau of Erfurt, they founded churches chiefly in the Buffalo, New York, area and around Milwaukee. Grabau held an extremely strict conception of Lutheran doctrine, a "high church" conception of ordination, and a very authoritarian understanding of the ministerial role. His alleged "Romanizing" tendencies soon brought his synod into conflict with other Lutheran bodies which, coupled with Grabau's ineffective leadership, led to the Buffalo Synod's loss of many of its ministers and members to other bodies. It remained very small until the time of its absorption by merger in 1930.

Equally strict confessional Lutherans from Saxony, centered in Missouri, figured most prominently in the controversies with Grabau, and they enjoyed an almost completely different destiny. They, too, had left their homes out of dissatisfaction with the state church, above all its rationalism and its indifference to vital religion. Led by Martin Stephan, a brilliant preacher from Dresden, they established a Lutheran "Zion on the Mississippi" around Saint Louis and in Perry County, Missouri. Though less than seven hundred in number at first, and though beset by the nearly disastrous necessity of deposing "Bishop" Stephan, they were able as the years went by to gather an ever increasing number of German immigrants into their fellowship. In 1847 they formed the "German Evangelical Lutheran Synod of Missouri, Ohio, and Other States" and by the time of World War I they had become the largest single synod in American Lutheranism. This remarkable growth was due to many factors, not least of which was the synod's situation in the heartland of German immigration. But the chief factor was the intense confessional loyalty of the Missourians, and the powerful esprit and evangelical zeal of its members, both ministerial and lay. Behind this zeal lay the intellect, erudition, piety, and personality of Carl F. W. Walther (1811–87), who very early made Concordia Seminary a strong center of influence. For a half-century he almost achieved an identification of his life and soul with that of his beloved synod.

Walther was the son and grandson of Saxon pastors, and a graduate of Leipzig University. He had served as minister for a time before joining the Stephanite exodus, but by this time his independent Luther studies, his readings in the literature of pietism, and his deep attachment to the Lutheran confessions had made him thoroughly dissatisfied with the easygoing status quo of the Saxon church. In America, after the expulsion of Stephan, Walther became the struggling colony's theological rallying point. And before many years his journal *Der Lutheraner* became a powerful influence among Lutherans throughout the country. As a preacher, professor, and theologian, Walther put an indelible mark on the life and faith of the Missouri Synod. Though two or three others might contend for the honor, he is probably the most influential figure in nineteenth-century Lutheranism in America.

The two predominant features of Walther's thought were pietism and confessionalism. Whatever else the Christian faith might be, it certainly involved a personal knowledge of forgiveness and justification by God's redeeming grace through faith in Christ; the rationalistic understanding of faith as simply "assent" was deficient. Yet his confessionalism stood opposed to all tendencies to reduce faith to feeling, as many pietists and, later, the romantic disciples of Schleiermacher tended to do. Another prominent aspect of Walther's thought was his emphasis on the "rule of faith" (*regula fidei*), which in fact constituted his resolution of the century's great struggle with historical relativism. He insisted that the Christian was committed to the testimonies of the Church given in the ecumenical creeds and the confessions of the Lutheran Reformation. The Gospel would be robbed of its power if it were not understood and preached in the light of this historic witness. Even among confessional Lutherans Walther stands out sharply for his attack on the prevailing tendency to consider a legalistic system of morality as the "essence of Christianity." In his most widely read work, *The Proper Distinction Between Law and Gospel* (published posthumously in 1897), Walther reveals himself as a truly "Neo-Reformation" thinker, for he insists upon this distinction as the central problem of theology.

In general Walther's views had the effect of isolating his synod from other Lutherans: against the Buffalo Synod and all other advocates of "high church" views, he committed the Missouri Synod to congregationalism and a "low" transfer theory of the ministry. In defining the Church he emphasized pure doctrine and greatly broadened the area in which clear theological consensus was demanded; as a result, controversy of all sorts became the lot of Missourians. Finally, he was led to so strong an emphasis on "grace alone" that he was widely accused of being a crypto-Calvinistic predestinarian. Out of this contention arose the most decisive controversial issue in later nineteenth-century American Lutheranism. Though many other factors were involved, this controversy did most to disrupt a burgeoning confessional entente—the Synodical Conference—which at its height included, under Missouri leadership, a large group of Norwegians and Germans in a great northern-swinging arc from Missouri to Ohio.

Isolation did not mean stagnation, however. Programs of parochial and higher education were instituted almost immediately; and Concordia Seminary at Saint Louis was set on its way to becoming one of the largest and most intellectually rigorous in the country. Missouri's sense of purpose and missionary zeal attracted new German immigrants, including many German-trained pastors; its explicitly conservative theological position also appealed to many pastors and congregations from older Lutheran bodies. Very soon "Missouri" anomalously designated a national church.

In the meantime other German Lutheran churches or synods were being formed in the West. The oldest in a strict sense, and soon to be one of the largest, was the Joint Synod of Ohio, whch had begun as a conference of the Pennsylvania Ministerium, but had separated from its parent in 1818 and begun its steady process of growth and subdivisión. Columbus, Ohio, became its headquarters and the seat of Capital University, its seminary and main college. In the Upper Midwest, chiefly in Wisconsin, another group of small synods took shape, the most important of which was the Wisconsin Synod organized in Milwaukee in 1850 by men sent out by missionary societies of the Prussian Union church. Gradually the explicitly Lutheran position of this synod was made clear, and Wisconsin soon began to coordinate its work with two other similarly minded synods in Michigan and Minnesota. By 1872 this group had moved far from its unionistic origins to an extremely rigorous kind of confessionalism. Its component synods even withdrew from the General Council to join Missouri in the still more rigorously confessional Synodical Conference.

Intertwined with these, and with many early congregations of the Missouri Synod, was another set of missionary impulses stemming from the great center at Neuendettelsau in Bavaria, which the eminent theologian, liturgical reformer, and missionary leader, Wilhelm Loehe, had made into an influential missionary agency. Though at first merely interested in extending the work of the church in the New World, men of this orientation grew fearful of the Missouri Synod's extreme congregationalism and strict demands for absolute consensus on all matters of doctrine. In 1854 they founded the so-called Iowa Synod, though like the Missouri, Ohio, and Wisconsin synods, it was by no means restricted to a single state. In fact, after 1895 "Iowa" even included an affiliation with the Texas Synod, a group which itself illustrates still another type of Lutheran origin in the United States. Organized in 1849, it had grown out of the response of the Saint Chrischona mission center near Basel, Switzerland, to the plea for pastors from German settlers in Texas.

By the diverse processes which have been sketched here with a few broad strokes, Lutheranism became a lively and extremely complex religious influence among the new German population of the country. Yet even this diversity among the Germans by no means reveals the whole fact, for during the same years, Scandinavian immigration reached flood tide, bringing nearly two million people to America, nearly all of whom were at least nominally Lutheran. The largest group was Swedish, whose earliest congregation was founded in Iowa in 1848. At first they affiliated themselves with the Synod of Northern Illinois, where ties with the General Synod actually established a sentimental relationship with the Old Lutheranism of New Sweden on the banks of the Delaware. In 1860 a separate Scandinavian synod was formed in this area, adopting the name Augustana (Latin for Augsburg) to proclaim its more explicit confessionalism. Ten years later the Danish-Norwegian elements in this synod went their own way, and the Danes later separated from the Norweigans as well. Between 1873 and 1884 the Swedish Augustana church also suffered the secession of a revivalistic, free-church element which formed the Evangelical Mission Covenant Church in 1884. Otherwise, Swedish Lutheranism during its entire first century was chiefly characterized by steady but relatively slow growth and nationwide expansion. Its greatest strength developed in Minnesota, though Rock Island, Illinois, remained the seat of its seminary and publishing house. Swedish people showed an unusual wanderlust, however, and the Augustana church became more national in scope than other Scandinavian synods.

Norwegian Lutheranism, by contrast, had an extraordinarily complex history during the same period. A strongly pietistic synod had formed in Wisconsin as early as 1846 and more or less on this foundation a synod named for the leader of Norway's religious awakening, Hans Nielsen Hauge, took form in the Upper Midwest, especially in Wisconsin and Minnesota. Another more confessional group, which also stood in closer relation the Church of Norway and the theological tradition of Royal Frederick's University in Oslo (Christiania), was centered in Iowa, particularly at Luther College in Decorah. This group in its early years worked closely with the Missouri Synod until the predestination controversy shattered the arrangement and divided the "Old Norwegian Synod." Between these two divergent groups was still a third "moderate" group consisting chiefly of those who had been in the Scandinavian Augustana Synod. In 1900 they joined with several other small center groups to form a "United" Norwegian church.

Danish and Finnish groups showed similar tensions and tendencies. Among the Danes two small churches grew up, one of them closely identified with the traditions of the Church of Denmark. These "happy Danes," as they were called, were also profoundly touched by the folk church and romantic high church ideas of the great Danish theologian, reformer, and hymn writer, N. F. S. Grundtvig. The "gloomy Danes," on the other hand, were of a more pietistic persuasion. Both of these Danish churches were strongest in the Midwest; yet both were severely handicapped by the sparsity and dispersion of those Danes who came to America. The Finns were similarly handicapped, and were more seriously, though similarly, divided. The largest group was in effect an extension of the Church of Finland. More inclined to extreme congregationalism and to pietistic emphases were those who followed the church reformer Lars L. Lästadius. In America they founded a separate Finnish Apostolic Lutheran Church in 1873. To the right of center, still another small Finnish group, the National Evangelical Lutheran Church, has grown up since 1900. Though at first a child of the Evangelical Society in Finland, it was led both by institutional factors and by a doctrinal disposition to emphasize free salvation and to deemphasize the proclamation of God's Law. It has gravitated toward the Missouri Synod.

The foregoing highly simplified account at least suggests the immense complexity of Lutheran institutional history, though it scarcely makes it crystal clear. At one time there were sixty-six independent church organizations. Yet the statistic alone is deceptive, for beneath this multiplicity—which was accounted for chiefly by linguistic differences, geographical separation, and varying degrees of Americanization—was an underlying unity of faith and practice which was probably unequaled among America's large communions except in the Roman Catholic church. Even the General Synod, where "American Lutheranism" had made its largest inroads, was steadily moving during these decades toward an understanding of the faith which was rooted in the Augsburg Confession, while the same loyalty kept the more pietistic synods in communication with those who maintained a closer tie to European state-church traditions. Furthermore, all of these groups felt a moral obligation to develop as inclusive a Lutheran fellowship as possible, and they constantly sought means of intersynodical coordination. Because of these centripetal tendencies the General Synod and General Council were able to bring several of the newer churches into the circle of their fellowship, while most of those who considered the General Council's discipline too lax found their way into the Synodical Conference which was organized in 1872 at Milwaukee with Professor Walther of the Missouri Synod as its first president.

Mergers and extensions of fellowship were a constant feature of the post-Civil War half-century. In 1917–18 a whole series of momentous reunions were consummated. In 1917 Norwegian Lutheranism with two or three small exceptions united to form a single Norwegian Lutheran Church, and a year later, stimulated in part by moves instituted during the four-hundredth anniversary of the Reformation, the General Synod, the General Council, and the United Synod of the South came together in the United Lutheran Church of America. The Iowa and Ohio synods established pulpit and altar fellowship, while in the same year the National Lutheran Council was formed, giving nearly all Lutheran bodies outside the Synodical Conference a basis for increased fellowship and collective endeavor. From that time forward the movement of the Lutheran churches toward full participation in the American religious life rapidly accelerated. In 1967, as a penultimate step, the Lutheran Council in the U.S.A. was formed as a coordinating agency for over 95 percent of the country's Lutherans.[6]

[6] While the reader has these relationships in mind, it may be appropriate to mention certain other steps in the movement toward

Lutheran unity. In 1930 the Ohio, Buffalo, Texas, and Iowa Synods came together to form the American Lutheran Church, and in the same year this new church also joined with nearly all of the midwestern Scandinavian churches in a looser federation named the American Lutheran Conference. Out of this conference came the associations from which grew the great merger of 1960, whereby the American Lutheran Church merged with the Norwegian church and the larger of the two Danish churches to form The American Lutheran Church. This act created the first corporate union of large churches of both Scandinavian and German background. Soon afterward, in 1962, another simliar union took place, by which the United Lutheran Church in America, Augustana (Swedish), the other Danish church, and the largest of the Finnish churches came together as the Lutheran Church in America. Since the more conservative Synodical Conference continued to exist, 95 percent of the once widely scattered Lutheran family had been brought within three rooms—connected by many doors and corridors, and well covered by a common confessional roof. The Lutheran Council in the U.S.A., formed by these large churches, had among its objectives both present-day cooperation and the achievement of future consensus (see John H. Tietjen, *Which Way Lutheran Unity?*).

46

THE GOLDEN AGE OF LIBERAL THEOLOGY

The nineteenth century was the "Great Century" in Christian history: so stands the assertion made, repeated, and substantiated in great detail by Kenneth Scott Latourette, America's most widely read church historian.[1] Yet his description of activity, fervor, popular strength, and global expansion is only half the story. The long epoch from the Second Awakening to the war with Spain was also a century of great tribulation, an "ordeal of faith" for churchgoing America. In an almost paradoxical manner, the religious impulse known as "liberalism" belongs to both sides of the century's picture. On one hand, it dealt responsibly with the social, moral, ecclesiastical, and above all, the theological issues of the crisis. On the other, it did so with such graceful ease and with such readiness to accommodate the spirit of the age that its effects were ambiguous. Alfred North Whitehead was even led to say in retrospect that "liberal theology . . . confined itself to the suggestion of minor, vapid reasons why people should go to church in the traditional way."[2] Viewed as a whole, however, American liberal theology was an impressive intellectual movement, and one that tends to confirm the idea of the Great Century.

The immediate background of liberalism's golden age was

[1] Kenneth Scott Latourette, *A History of Christianity*, chap. 45. His title for this section of the volume is "The Great Century: Growing Repudiation Paralleled by Abounding Vitality and Unprecedented Expansion."

[2] Alfred North Whitehead, *Adventures of Ideas* (1933); quoted by Sidney E. Mead, *Reinterpretation in American Church History*, ed. Jerald C. Brauer.

a profound social transformation which put the traditional content of preaching and teaching under severe duress. To these problems were added the intellectual difficulties provoked by scientific discoveries, religious scholarship, and pervasive shifts in moral and religious attitudes. On the intellectual level the new challenges were of two sorts. First, there was a set of specific problems that had to be faced separately: Darwin unquestionably became the nineteenth century's Newton, and his theory of evolution through natural selection became the century's cardinal idea. But the struggle over the new geology was a vital rehearsal in which new conceptions of time and process were absorbed. Historical research meanwhile posed very detailed questions about the Bible, the history of doctrine, and other world religions. Accompanying these specific problems was a second and more general challenge: the rise of positivistic naturalism, the cumulative result of modern methods for acquiring knowledge. In every discipline from physics to biblical criticism, myth and error were being dispelled, and the result of this activity was a world view which raised problems of the most fundamental sort. Are deterministic principles as applicable to human activities as to the natural world? Are all moral standards and religious beliefs simply behavioral adaptations of the most intelligent vertebrates? Are the Bible, the Christian faith, and the Church to be understood as having their existence entirely within history? Granted these naturalistic challenges, are Christians to save their faith by resort to the unbiblical solutions of romantic subjectivism and idealistic pantheism? These questions constitute the dilemma of America's postwar churches. We do well, therefore, to begin our consideration of the responses with those who considered scientific positivism itself to offer the most viable religious option.

CHALLENGES TO TRADITION

Organized religious radicalism had never flourished in the United States. Elihu Palmer failed almost completely in his efforts to institutionalize a religion of reason during the revolutionary epoch. As for the "Religion of Humanity" launched by the French positivist, Auguste Comte (1798–1857), its failure to develop a following in America was even more resounding, though there was a flurry of interest in Fourier's utopian notions. The one form of radical religion to show a little continuous life had its domestic origins in Transcendentalism. This movement for "Free Religion" had only a brief independent existence, though it did attain a certain continuity through its impact on the Unitarian tradition. Its martyr-hero was Theodore Parker, who died prematurely in 1860.

In 1865, when the National Unitarian Conference was organized with a constitution specifically committing the denomination to the "Lordship of Christ," the radicals of the membership felt themselves excluded. Almost immediately they laid plans for organizing a Free Religious Association; and in 1867 at their first convention in Boston they elected Octavious Brooks Frothingham (1822–95) as their president. Two years later the movement acquired a semiofficial organ when Francis Ellingwood Abbot founded the *Index* as a weekly journal. Abbot (1836–1903) had been a conservative Unitarian whose views began to shift leftward soon after his graduation from Harvard in 1859. As a seminary student, and later as a Unitarian minister in Dover, New Hampshire, his highly rationalistic and antiauthoritarian "scientific theism" began to take form, and for fifteen years he remained the chief philosophic figure in the movement. Acclaimed as the first American theologian to develop a system of religious thought in complete consonance with Darwinian evolution, Abbot was, however, too extreme to be popular, and his scientific emphasis alienated the Transcendentalists. He also organized the National Liberal League for the total separation of church and state and diverted much of the Free Religious Association's energies into that abortive campaign,[3] with the result that, in the 1870s, Frothingham became the movement's chief spokesman.

Frothingham, a very proper Bostonian by birth, was converted by Parker from a conservative Unitarian ministry to abolitionism and radical religion. During and after the Civil War he was a popular preacher n New York City. His book *The Religion of Humanity* (1872) best expresses the movement's effort to formulate a free and scientific religion for the

[3] The 1870s were a time of harsh interfaith contention and of controversy on the church-state question. Abbot's special target was the intensely evangelical National Reform Association which was working for a new Christian preamble to the federal Constitution.

American people. "The new Liberal Church," he declared, "has a consistent scheme of thought; it goes to the mind for its ideas; it admits the claim of spontaneity; its method of obtaining truth is rational; the harmony it demands is harmony of principles—the orderly sequence of laws."[4] Yet even Frothingham was unable to reach beyond a narrow circle of intelligentsia.

What Frothingham lacked, however, was possessed in great measure by Robert Green Ingersoll (1833–99), "the Dwight L. Moody of Free Religion," to borrow Abbot's label. Ingersoll had been a colonel in the Union army, a highly successful trial lawyer, and a political figure best remembered for the "Plumed Knight" oration with which he nominated James G. Blaine as Republican presidential candidate in 1876. The son of a conservative Protestant minister, he devoted his mature life to the cause of agnosticism in religion: "The rebellion of his boyhood became the crusade of his lifetime."[5] He made up for the very limited appeal of the Free Religious Association by ranging up and down the country, holding spellbound the many auditors who paid admission to hear his eloquent attacks on the clergy, the Bible, and the Christian faith. By 1880 there were very few Americans who did not recognize him as the nation's most outspoken infidel and a scourge of the churches. Beneath the rhetoric and the diatribes was a completely naturalistic message of confidence in man and hope for the future, derived more specifically from Thomas Paine and the earlier rationalism than from either Comte or Darwin.

Ingersoll left more than a trace on the religious life of a generation of Americans. Untold thousands found solace in their infidelity due to the glowing rhetoric of the widely reprinted oration which he delivered at his brother's grave. By such means free religion of various sorts reached far beyond the boundaries of organized movements. Social Darwinism, the philosophy of Herbert Spencer, and popular forms of naturalism also gained adherents without any kind of pseudoecclesiastical sponsorship. It was, in fact, with precisely this general tendency, coupled as it so often was with a distaste for evangelical revivalism that liberal theolo-

---

[4] Octavius Brooks Frothingham, *The Religion of Humanity* (New York, 1873), pp. 16–17.

[5] Ralph Henry Gabriel, *The Course of American Democratic Thought*, p. 179.

gians felt obliged to deal. The obligation led directly to specific questions, however, and one of the first of these had to do with the earth's own history.

Genesis and Geology

Scientific speculation as to the origins and history of the universe was one aspect of the intellectual ferment of the age, but it was not nearly so troublesome as the "new geology" that had been developing ever since James Hutton of Edinburgh had published his *Theory of the Earth* in 1788. By the time of Sir Charles Lyell's *Principles of Geology* (1830–32), it had become an organized scientific endeavor based, as he said, on the uniformitarian doctrine "that all former changes of the organic and inorganic creation are referrible [sic] to one uninterrupted succession of physical events, governed by the laws now in operation." In Lyell's works, moreover, the biblical account of Creation was called in question not only on geological grounds, but because of the fossil record which the rocks preserved. Controversy, needless to say, ensued.

In America the battle over Genesis would have been more sharply drawn than it was had not the country's leading geologist, Benjamin Silliman (1779–1864), sought to harmonize conflicting views. While a student at Yale, Silliman had been converted by the preaching of President Timothy Dwight. After graduation he was selected by Dwight to be a science professor, and dispatched to Edinburgh for advanced study. Although he returned as a man committed to a uniformitarian understanding of science, in 1836 he also argued that the Bible was not a scientific textbook, urging that the Hebrew word for "day" in the Creation story should be interpreted loosely as "aeon." Edward Hitchcock, his pupil, who became a professor and then president of Amherst College, took a still more positive stand in his important work *The Religion of Geology* (1851). An eminent geologist himself, Hitchcock explained the earth's long history as a further revelation of God's constancy and glory. Many problems remained, but in New England at least the Silliman-Hitchcock compromise opened the way to more constructive thought on the relations of science and religion. These relatively advanced views were accepted by only a very small minority, however, for most

Americans knew little and cared less about scientific method. Indeed the great alienation of large sectors of American Protestantism from the newer forms of modern thought had begun to accelerate with the revivals of 1800, while the surging westward movement and the advances of anti-intellectual revivalism made matters worse with each passing decade. Only in limited circles did the general type of solution advanced by Professor Hitchcock win acceptance.

The matter could not stop with geology—in part because of the fossil record and in part because geological estimates of the earth's great age made developmental theories of biological evolution increasingly plausible. In fact, a very strong tradition of evolutionary speculation already existed. Lamarck had announced his theory in 1801. Romantic naturephilosophers had given further encouragement to developmental views, and the historical movement also accentuated the idea of process, struggle, and emergent novelty. Herbert Spencer, who was to become the greatest popularizer of Darwinian notions in both Britain and America, had long been defending a view of cosmic progress from homogeneity to heterogeneity. By 1857 the time was so ripe for a theory of natural selection that it was formulated almost simultaneously by two remotely separated men.

In 1858 at a historic meeting of the Royal Society, two papers on the origin of species were read: one by Charles Darwin, the other by Alfred Russel Wallace. In the following year Darwin's *Origin of Species* appeared—the most important book of the century. After a decade of fierce controversy, Darwin in 1871 published *The Descent of Man*, in which he drew the human species within the same encompassing hypothesis. Never since the scientific revolution completed by Newton had the humanistic and religious traditions of the West been confronted by a greater need for adjustment and reformulation.

The Response to Darwin in the United States

Darwin did not expect or hope that his theory of evolution through natural selection would be acceptable to more than a small circle of specialists, but he sent a copy of *The Origin of Species* to the most famous of all American naturalists, Louis Agassiz (1807–73), hoping to be credited "for having carefully endeavored to arrive at the truth." The great paleontologist and glacial theorist, however, had by this time become chiefly a popularizer, a dogmatic philosopher of nature, and a museum organizer, and his rejection of Darwin was well-nigh absolute. Reaffirming his allegiance to the French zoologist Cuvier, Agassiz took his stand for "special creationism" as an explanation of both the fossil record and present state of all living things. Genesis, in his view, told of only one among many occasions of God's creative intervention in the world. At other times and places God had created other species and other human races. Although Agassiz showed considerable liberty in his interpretation of Scripture, he became, for obvious reasons, the white knight of the anti-Darwinians.

Fortunately for American science, Agassiz no longer held the respect of the four or five Americans most qualified to give a scientific evaluation of evolutionary theory. Asa Gray (1810–88), a colleague of Agassiz at Harvard, had publicly insisted on the single origin of plant and animal species even before Darwin's book appeared, and in March 1860, in the *American Journal of Science* (a journal founded by Silliman), Gray's favorable review appeared. Further support came from William B. Rogers, James Dwight Dana, and Jeffries Wyman, with the result that Agassiz began to lose the allegiance of his own students. The appointment of Charles William Eliot as Harvard's president in 1869, despite the opposition of Agassiz and many others, marked a turning point in American science.

Only after 1869 was the real impact of Darwinism felt in the American churches, partly because of the vast distractions of the Civil War and Reconstruction. The first response, naturally enough, was opposition, but this clerical resistance chiefly revealed the prevailing incapacity to grasp the dramatic transformation in world view that evolutionary theory occasioned. During most of the eighteenth century, Western Christendom had been engaged in a drawn-out encounter with the Enlightenment, including among other things, Newtonian physics, rationalism, and deism. This intellectual challenge had been almost magnificently surmounted. The firmament had been made to declare the glory of God. As the whole creation was conceived as a hymn to God's benevolent governance, the natural religion of the *philosophes* found its place in even the most revivalistic of evangelical theologies:

any Christian could look out of his kitchen window and behold a demonstration of God's marvelous design. Sun and clouds, trees and grass, seeds, cows, dogs, and insects—even manure—were all harmoniously interacting for man's well being! But after Darwin, what did the backyard reveal but a relentless struggle for existence, a war of all against all, with blood dripping from every bough, and man involved in the struggle not only against the locusts, but against other men, even other races of man, with victory for the fittest. No wonder that opposition to evolutionary doctrines arose. In this struggle, moreover, the Unitarian friends of Agassiz, having invested largely in the goodness and dignity of man, would join hands with the most strenuous conservatives. The Reverend Andrew Preston Peabody, a countercandidate for Harvard's presidency in 1869, was not far from Charles Hodge of Princeton Seminary when it came to attacking Darwinism.

Charles Hodge, in fact, soon published what many regarded as the orthodox repudiation. In his *What Is Darwinism?* (1874) he correctly isolated the essential factor, natural selection, and pronounced it to be in flat contradiction to the doctrine of an omnipotent, omniscient Creator. Christians, he insisted, must account for the facts in some other way. Professor Randolph S. Foster of Drew Seminary (later a Methodist bishop) took a lower route—one that was to be much more heavily traveled during the coming century—and sought to laugh evolutionary theory out of court: "Some future pup, Newfoundland or terrier, in the finite ages may," he said, "write Paradise Lost. . . . Therefore a pig is an incipient mathematician." Behind both Hodge and Foster lay a fundamental conviction that three decades later would still underlie Billy Sunday's confession that he did not believe "in a bastard theory that men came from protoplasm by the fortuitous concurrence of atoms."

There were serious Christian thinkers, however, who saw the conflict in less drastic terms, and by an unusual coincidence the two most impressive among them collaborated closely: George Frederick Wright (1838–1921), fervent evangelical, biographer of Finney, amateur geologist of distinction, and professor of science and religion at Oberlin; and Asa Gray of Harvard, America's most distinguished botanist and an amateur theologian adhering to a conservative Nicaeanic understanding of Christian orthodoxy. Issuing from the collaboration of these two men were the separate essays later published in Gray's *Darwiniana* (1876). In all of these essays, from his first review of Darwin to his more theological works, four important points stand out:

1. A deep respect for Darwin's empirical and theoretical contributions to the problem of species, and sharp criticism of dogmatic repudiation of the idea of evolution
2. A recognition that Darwin's theory lacked an explanation of variations (such as the science of genetics would later supply)
3. An insistence that scientific investigation continue without impediment
4. A conviction that Darwinian theory did not contradict Christian doctrine; that regardless of Darwin's or Spencer's beliefs, God's purpose in the Creation could be understood in evolutionary terms; and that orthodox views of man's sinfulness found corroboration in Darwin.

Darwin explicitly dissented from Gray's belief in divinely directed beneficent variations, but Gray's friendship with Darwin, as well as his demand for scientific autonomy, continued.[6]

During the 1870s President James McCosh of Princeton University and President Paul A. Chadbourne of Williams College added their prestige to the rapprochement of theology and evolutionary theory. Both thinkers introduced non-Darwinian elements which preserved the idea of beneficent design. They also strengthened the doctrine of progress by accenting Gray's idea that Divine Providence acts *"through* all time" rather than *"from* all time." More exuberantly optimistic than any was the prolific apologist for Darwin and Spencer, John Fiske (1842–1902). As early as 1872 Fiske had expounded a blend of evolution and idealism in his *Cosmic Philosophy.* Twelve years later, he ended his work *The Destiny of Man* with a hymn in which the full religious potentiality of evolutionism found expression. It deserves ex-

[6] Gray also continued his friendship with Alfred Russel Wallace (1823–1913), whose religious views were closer to his own than Darwin's. Wallace also shared William James's interest in psychical research and spiritualism.

tended quotation as a prime example of the optimistic heights
that nineteenth-century naturalism could reach:

> The greatest philosopher of modern times, the master and
> teacher of all who shall study the process of evolution for
> many a day to come, holds that the conscious soul is not
> the product of a collocation of material particles, but is in
> the deepest sense a divine effluence. According to Mr.
> Spencer, the divine energy which is manifested throughout
> the knowable universe is the same energy that wells up in
> us as consciousness. Speaking for myself, I can see no in-
> superable difficulty in the notion that at some period in the
> evolution of Humanity this divine spark may have acquired
> sufficient concentration and steadiness to survive the wreck
> of material forms and endure forever. Such a crowning
> wonder seems to me no more than the fit climax to a cre-
> ative work that has been ineffably beautiful and marvelous
> in all its myriad stages.
>
> Only on some such view can the reasonableness of the
> universe, which still remains far above our finite power of
> comprehension, maintain its ground. There are some minds
> inaccessible to the class of considerations here alleged, and
> perhaps there always will be. But on such grounds, if on
> no other, the faith in immorality is likely to be shared by
> all who look upon the genesis of the highest spiritual
> qualities in Man as the goal of Nature's creative work.
> This view has survived the Copernican revolution in sci-
> ence, and it has survived the Darwinian revolution. Nay,
> if the foregoing exposition be sound, it is Darwinism which
> has placed Humanity upon a higher pinnacle than ever.
> The future is lighted for us with the radiant colours of
> hope. Strife and sorrow shall disappear. Peace and love
> shall reign supreme. The dream of poets, the lesson of
> priest and prophet, the inspiration of the great musician, is
> confirmed in the light of modern knowledge; and as we
> gird ourselves up for the work of life, we may look forward
> to the time when in the truest sense the kingdoms of this
> world shall become the kingdom of Christ, and he shall
> reign for ever and ever, king of kings, and lord of lords.

When men outside the church could speak in this manner
of Darwinism, it goes without saying that many other liberal

Christian thinkers would sing evolutionary theophanies as
well. Horace Bushnell never could accept the "development theory," but his chief biographer, Theodore Thornton
Munger, in the prestigious pulpit of New Haven's North
Church, made up for his hero's lack. And the minister of the
neighboring church on the New Haven green, Newman
Smyth, after spending long hours in the Yale biological
laboratories, described his findings with equal fervor in
Through Science to Faith (1902). Undoubtedly, the two
successive ministers of Plymouth Church in Brooklyn did
more than most others to popularize the "New Theology."
Henry Ward Beecher was a fairly cautious pioneer. But
Lyman Abbott (1835–1922), a bolder exponent, in *The
Evolution of Christianity* (1892) sought to show that "in the
spiritual, as in the physical, God is the secret and source of
light." Accordingly, Abbott spoke of the evolution of the
Bible, the Church, Christian Society, and the Soul.

In at least two areas of thought, the debate over evolutionary theology pointed to much larger issues than the origin
of biological species or the descent of man. With new urgency it posed the question of "species" in general, that is, it
reopened the ancient debate over the "essential nature of
things" which had been at the heart of Western philosophy
since the time of Plato. Many of the classic structures of
traditional theology, as well as the post-Newtonian schemes
of natural theology, were thus disrupted. The static yielded
to the dynamic; stability to flux. History and Becoming
emerged as dominant categories of thought. In this way Darwin's works underlined what had been implicit in the great
romantic conceptions of the historical reason. The relativistic
implications of history—natural history and human history—
stood revealed. From this trend stemmed the second great
problem: the forms of developmentalism traceable to historical scholarship. Here indeed lay the burning question of the
age. Fossils and unimaginably remote developments in the
plant or animal kingdoms were academic abstractions compared with the direct impact of historico-critical studies on
the Holy Bible and sacred doctrine. Liberal theology in this
realm occupied its most important ground, while Fundamentalism arose to repulse the invader.

The Impact of History

The writing of history is as old as the Old Testament; but

in the nineteenth century it took on new vitality and in many ways transmitted this vigor to religious thought. In theology as in biology, a dynamic view of the past challenged traditional notions in at least five ways:

1. "Uniformitarian" principles were applied in the interpretation of past events to the exclusion of miracle and divine providence. As a consequence, the history of the Jews, the life of Jesus, and the rise of Christianity were treated no differently than "secular" events. Three famous studies, one in each of these subject areas, appeared in a single year (1835): Wilhelm Vatke's history of Israel's religion, David Friedrich Strauss's *Life of Jesus,* and Ferdinand Christian Baur's work on the place of the pastoral Epistles in the life of the early Church.

2. The Scriptures themselves were interpreted in the same manner as other important historical documents. Julius Wellhausen's questioning of both the Mosaic authorship and the literary unity of the Pentateuch (1878) made the implications of such methods fully manifest; and in New Testament criticism the results were even more troublesome. Nor could the problem be escaped by giving conservative answers to specific questions (such as the date of Daniel or the authorship of Second Peter), for the method itself undermined the idea of the Bible as the verbally inerrant Word of God.

3. Historical theology came into its own as a discipline; that is, anxiety about specific doctrines (such as the Atonement or the nature of Christ) came to be resolved by the scientific study of that doctrine in the history of Christianity. To the discomfiture of many, doctrinal truth seemed to depend on the "assured results" of critical scholarship. Some liberal scholars even insisted that the content of the faith had to be reduced to those few simple tenets which had been accepted in all times and places. This notion reached its fullest expression in 1900, when Adolph von Harnack, the great historian of dogma, in his famous lectures on the essence of Christianity, rested his case on a few central precepts of Jesus.

4. Comparative religion as an historical science was involved in each of the foregoing matters to a certain extent, notably in such questions as the relation of Hebrew religion to its ancient neighbors, or the Apostle Paul's indebtedness to Greek thought and the oriental mystery cults. In these pursuits many of the major disciplines for studying the history of

religions were first developed. But it was the Western discovery of the great "higher religions" of the Orient, above all Hinduism and Buddhism, that raised the more difficult questions, because these highly philosophical religions possessed an intrinsic appeal for an age already imbued wih idealistic philosophy and pantheistic theology. In Emerson's "Brahma" Americans savored the forbidden fruit in their parlors. Highly enthusiastic historical accounts raised more direct theological questions, above all, how is one to demonstrate the superiority and finality of Christianity? Even disclaimers raised the specter of religious relativism.

5. "Historicism" was a culminating and summary feature of the trend. This term is often used to designate two different philosophical positions, though they could be entertained together or separately. The first was basically an acceptance of the contextuality or interrelatedness of all human activities, thoughts, and concerns, and hence the insistence that all things human were inescapably historical. There is no nonhistorical vantage point for man, only the history of changing conceptions of absoluticity. There are no self-evident axioms in philosophical matters, only the history of changing views of self-evidence. The intellectual bedrock of today was the slimy ocean bottom of yore, and perhaps the mountaintop of tomorrow. In other words, "historicism" could refer to an all-encompassing relativism. Whether it was expounded by G. F. W. Hegel, Karl Marx, William Graham Sumner, or Ernst Troeltsch could make a vast difference in its social and religious implications, yet a disturbing insistence on the historicity of all things remained.

"Historicism" could also refer to the new kind of fatalism or determinism which historical studies induced—the conviction that what was, had to be; what is, must be. The nature of history's inexorable march was, of course, interpreted differently: some positivists thought in terms of physical causality rather than in terms of human action; Henry Adams could speak of a physics of history; Hegel early in the century and Marx in his train gave "dialectical" interpretations to the historical process; William G. Sumner as a "Social Darwinian" would take his cues from biological evolution. Some were pessimistic; others unbelievably hopeful. Yet by all of these men, chance and historical contingency, as well as freedom and human spontaneity, were regarded as extremely limited or entirely illusory. For weal or woe, man's fate was sealed.

In the end, regardless of how these five tendencies were used or interpreted, historical modes of thought became a powerful factor in the intellectual life of the age. Inasmuch as the categories of genetic explanation underlie geology and evolution as well, we may crown Clio, the muse of history, as the intellectual monarch of the century. Aided and abetted by other forces, this monarch very nearly succeeded in determining both the strategies and the content of liberal theology.[7]

The intellectual challenge with which liberal theologians grappled was awe-inspiring in its magnitude. From every sector the problems converged: the Enlightenment's triumphant confidence in science and in nature's law, the multiform romantic heresy that religion was essentially feeling or poetic exaltation, that nature was a cathedral and communing in it a sacrament; the disruption of the Creation story and the biblical time scale; the evolutionary transformation of the old notion that the world's orderliness bespoke God's benevolent design; the historical criticism of the Bible, the relativization of the Church and its teachings, the denial of human freedom and moral responsibility, and even the abolition of those eternal standards by which right and wrong, the false and the true were to be judged. All this had to be faced, moreover, in the new urban jungles of the Gilded Age, where Americans seemed to be chiefly bent on getting and spending and laying waste their powers. Never in the history of Christianity, it would seem, was a weak and disunited Christian regiment drawn into battle against so formidable an alliance, under such unfavorable conditions of climate and weather, and with so little information on the position and intent of the opposition. In such terms, at least, we must seek to understand the achievement of America's liberal theologians.

[7] Principal A. M. Fairbairn of Oxford described this historical revolution in an immensely influential work: "The most distinctive and determinative element in modern theology is what we may term a new feeling for Christ. . . . But we feel Him more in our theology because we know Him better in history. . . . The old theology came to history through doctrine, but the new comes to doctrine through history; to the one all historical questions were really dogmatic, but to the other all dogmatic questions are formally historical" (*The Place of Christ in Modern Theology* [New York, 1894], pp. 3–4).

THE VARIETIES OF RELIGIOUS LIBERALISM

The response of American Christianity to its crisis was as varied as its denominational texture. Roman Catholicism was so deeply involved in fending off the attacks of nativists and in solving its own institutional problems that the "modernism" of Europe which had provoked several major papal condemnations was almost—though not entirely—unknown. Lutheranism, too, was deeply engaged in solving the problems of immigration and church founding; synodical consolidation and confessional controversy were the main themes of its history. In the predominantly rural South, where the modern university and the German-trained seminary faculty were almost unknown, the response was negligible. And in countless congregations in the mainstream of American evangelical Protestantism, urban as well as rural, the older anti-intellectual patterns of revivalism held sway. The grappling with modern ideas obviously went on elsewhere.

In terms of denominations as a whole, only a few general statements can be made. Congregationalism, especially in the Northeast and in urban churches, now proved to be the most fertile soil for liberalism, just as it had been when Unitarianism struck down its roots. In Methodism, where religious experience rather than doctrine was the major concern, the liberal cause became almost as pervasive, and in Northern Methodism as nowhere in the nation it penetrated to the grassroots. In the Protestant Episcopal church, where the Enlightenment had made large inroads and where the evangelical resurgence had been rather restricted, liberalism also grew strong—except where it was countered by Tractarianism. The Northern Presbyterian church, the Northern Baptist Convention, and the Disciples of Christ all made important contributions to the liberal movement. These three were profoundly divided on the issues, however, and hence they were torn by the Fundamentalist controversy far more violently than other denominations.

Because the challenges to which the liberals responded were primarily intellectual, the seminaries were naturally crucial to the movement's development. Here again the importance of the Northeast was dramatized, for Harvard, Yale, and Union Theological Seminary (New York) played leading roles, and contributions of hardly less significance were made by Andover and Bangor (Congregational), Colgate, Rochester, and Crozer (Baptist), the Episcopal Theological School in Cambridge, Boston University (Methodist), and Lane Seminary (Presbyterian). After John D. Rockefeller's princely contributions to the University of Chicago, its Divinity School (Baptist) quickly became a great midwestern center of liberalism, around which Congregational Disciples, and Unitarian faculties were also gathered. So dynamic and accomplished was its faculty, and so great a regional need did it fill that Chicago remained throughout the first third of the twentieth century probably the country's most powerful center of Protestant liberalism. From all of these seminaries came a long line of distinguished parish ministers. The wealthy urban congregation was enjoying its heyday; and the "princes of the pulpit" had their hour, reaching memberships of great power and influence and attaining a high level of intellectual distinction. Indeed, liberalism was the last major impulse in American intellectual history in which the pastor-theologian played an extensive role.

The era when these seminaries and their eminent graduates in parish pulpits made theological liberalism a continuous and coherent movement extends for more than two long generations. William Newton Clarke (1841–1912) had served in the parish for two decades when he became a professor at Colgate Seminary in 1890; his most distinguished student, Harry Emerson Fosdick (b. 1878), wrote an autobiography that reflected on his long ministry in the parish and seminary in 1956. Newman Smyth (1843–1925) entered the ministry only after serving the Union army, published his most substantial book, *Christian Ethics,* in 1892 and his autobiography in 1926. The liberal movement maintained its inner unity through two wars and amid vast social changes.

Because the wide dispersion of liberal leadership and the absence of outstandingly influential American liberal theologians (aside from Emerson and Bushnell, whose careers belong to an earlier epoch) preclude concentration on individual studies in a general discussion of this sort, a review of the situation by denominations is probably most illuminating. Among the Congregationalists, liberals were legion in both seminaries and churches. In fact, this denomination's corporate stance underwent a nearly complete transformation between its basically traditional Burial Hill Declaration of

1865 (affirmed during a memorial assembly at the cemetery at Plymouth) and the liberal Kansas City Declaration of 1913. The spirit of Bushnell presided over this quiet revolution, but many men of national eminence furthered it. With the one important exception of Edwards Amasa Park, the entire Andover faculty led the way. At the Yale Divinity School the "new theology" did not become prominent until around the turn of the century and then chiefly through the work of an impressive group of biblical scholars: Harper, Bacon, and Porter. After World War I the Canadian Baptist and renowned pacifist D. C. Macintosh made Yale a center of empirical, realistic theology. Two other theologians with strong philosophic interests and wide influence were Louis French Stearns of Bangor Seminary and Eugene W. Lyman, who taught successively at Bangor, Oberlin, and Union theological seminaries. Reaching wider than any was Charles M. Sheldon, a pastor of Topeka, Kansas, who turned to the sentimental novel—and with *In His Steps* (1896) became a major apostle of not only the Social Gospel but of the broader liberal movement as well. The work of other pastors (Beecher, Smyth, Munger, Gordon, and Brooks) has already been mentioned.

The Presbyterian Church (North) also provided the liberal movement with both scholarly and popular leadership. Union Seminary of New York was the center from which radiated the influence of William Adams Brown, one of the movement's most widely read systematic theologians, A. C. McGiffert, an impressive historian of doctrine, and C. A. Briggs, the country's leading Old Testament scholar. Besides these intellectuals, the Presbyterians also claimed one of the era's most popular writers, Henry van Dyke, whose fiction and poetry were American parlor favorites for two generations, especially his famous Christmas story, "The Other Wise Man." He also wrote two extremely effective apologetical works: *The Gospel for an Age of Doubt* (1896) and *The Gospel for a World of Sin* (1899).

Among Methodists liberalism gained its most coherent philosophical expression in the idealistic "personalism" of Professor Borden Parker Bowne of Boston University. In later years A. C. Knudson at the Boston University School of Theology became personalism's chief systematic theologian, while his energetic contemporary Bishop Francis J. McConnell led the denomination in ecumenical affairs and as a social actionist.

The Baptists, like the Presbyterians, were preponderantly conservative. In several seminaries and many pulpits, however, extremely influential liberals made their mark not only upon the denomination but far beyond. Walter Rauschenbusch of Rochester Seminary, the Social Gospel leader, is now best remembered, but two other men made a much broader impact on their times. William Newton Clarke's *Outline of Christian Theology* (1898) became the most widely used of liberal texts in systematic theology. In rather sharp contrast to Clarke's modified evangelicalism was the far more radical speculation and scholarship of Shailer Mathews of the Chicago Divinity School, and somewhat later, the critical historical studies of his colleague, Shirley Jackson Case. Closely allied with the Baptists at Chicago were an influential group of Disciples of whom the philosopher, psychologist of religion, and theological radical Edward S. Ames, and the biblical scholar Herbert L. Willett were the most eminent. Immeasurably more influential was Charles Clayton Morrison, who in 1908 founded the *Christian Century* and made it a potent ecumenical, socially oriented journal.

In the Episcopal church, William P. DuBose of the Sewanee seminary (Tennessee) was probably his church's greatest theological mind. No Southerner of the period equaled his richness and depth of thought; yet his moderate, tradition-oriented liberalism was not widely noted, possibly because Catholic-Evangelical conflict consumed so much Episcopal energy. The Broad Church movement, however, did raise up at least one impressive liberal thinker, William Reed Huntington of New York, whose work *The Church Idea* (1870) remains a major ecumenical document. Phillips Brooks of Boston's Trinity Church was by all odds the most popular voice the Episcopal church has ever had. Brooks's influence was given a second life by the very widely read two-volume biography by Professor A. V. G. Allen, who in other ways as well made historical studies an evocative vehicle for liberal theological themes. *The Continuity of Christian Thought: A Study of Modern Theology in the Light of Its History* (1884) is Allen's most brilliant achievement.

Finally, the Unitarians, who had been the American vanguard of liberal Christianity, continued, though with less élan than formerly, to provide important and intellectual leadership. Francis Greenwood Peabody of Harvard achieved wide attention as the first seminary professor of social ethics. Minot J. Savage, the minister of Boston's West Church, wrote a major work on *The Religion of Evolution* (1876). But more important than individual instances was a major theological trend which John White Chadwick described in 1894: "The fifty years which have gone by since Channing died in 1842 have seen great changes. . . . The critical results which Parker reached and which his brother Unitarians could not endure, are now the commonplaces [not only of the Unitarians but] of the progressive orthodox."[8] As the century's turn approached, a kind of religious peace became manifest in New England. With the new historical, philosophical, and religious attitudes as common ground, Andover Seminary even returned to Harvard, where for over two decades the joint faculty achieved great distinction and influence.[9]

The chief proponents of liberalism in all of these denominations came from diverse backgrounds, yet most of them traced their roots to pious families where evangelical nurture had prevailed. Their spiritual history often resembled that which William Newton Clarke revealed in his moving personal account *Sixty Years with the Bible* (1912): "I am one of the men who have lived through the crisis of the Nineteenth Century, and experienced the change which that century has wrought. . . . Thus I am entering into the heritage of my generation, which I consider it both my privilege and my duty to accept." They usually studied in Germany or in American seminaries where Continental theology and scholarship was favorably regarded. Most of them had wide ecumenical sympathies, yet very few had cut loose from denominational loyalties. Although they took diverse positions on the social issues of the day and were often motivated by different concerns, several common themes and tendencies characterize their work.

[8] John White Chadwick, *Old and New Unitarian Belief* (Boston, 1894), pp. 31–32.
[9] In 1908 Andover Seminary moved to Cambridge, adjacent to the Harvard Divinity School; but in 1925 the virtual merger of the schools was voided in the courts. Andover then merged with the Baptist seminary in nearby Newton, leaving its faculty and most of its students at Harvard.

The Nature of Liberalism

Liberalism was, first of all, a point of view which, like the adjective "liberal" as we commonly use it, denotes both a certain generosity or charitableness toward divergent opinions and a desire for intellectual "liberty." Liberal theologians also wished to "liberate" religion from obscurantism and creedal bondage so as to give man's moral and rational powers larger scope. In this broad sense, liberals could be linked with a long Christian tradition extending from Abelard and Erasmus through Locke and Paley to Channing and the Transcendentalists. Actually, however, the "liberalism" of the nineteenth century was a positive and structured movement, not merely a vague tendency or an indefinite state of mind. Whether it was called the New Theology, Progressive Orthodoxy, Modernism, or some other name, it had a fairly definite doctrinal content.

In the language of historical theology, liberals were Arminian or Pelagian. With regard to human nature, they emphasized man's freedom and his natural capacity for altruistic action. Sin, therefore, was construed chiefly as error and limitation which education in morals and the example of Jesus could mitigate, or else as the product of underprivilege which social reform could correct. Original Sin or human depravity was denied or almost defined out of existence. As their predecessors of the Enlightenment had done, liberals tried to avoid deterministic conclusions by arguments for the creative and autonomous nature of the human spirit.

A strong emphasis on ethical preaching and moral education accorded with the liberal view of man. Ethical imperatives became central to the Christian witness, and the Sermon on the Mount was often regarded as the heart and core of the Bible. On the other hand, liberals tended to slight traditional dogma and the sacraments. Baptism came to be considered as an initiatory formality or as a dedicatory rite for parents, while the Lord's Supper was usually given only memorial significance and its importance to public worship was minimized. The sacramental character of ordination and of preaching was likewise deemphasized.[10] In New England, by the

[10] Preaching is sacramental when the preached Gospel of Christ's redeeming work is believed to be a means of grace and a mark of

same token, the traditional covenants of membership were forgotten or revised, and because liberals were usually non-denominational in spirit, the theological controversies and church divisions which had raged in former times were lamented as evidences of superstition and spiritual immaturity. Interest in the reunion of Christendom correspondingly flourished, with heavy emphasis on the scandal of the Church's being divided over essentially dead issues. To most liberals, however, the Reformation's blow to "medieval thralldom" was a providential boon, so that anti-Catholicism could still flourish, and sometimes did. Francis G. Peabody, despite his wide ecumenical interests, thought that the whole "Faith and Order" movement for church reunion was a hopeless throwback to a darker age.

Because of their revised estimate of man's nature and their tendency to interpret the entire evolutionary process as ultimately for mankind's benefit, liberals were fervently optimistic about the destiny of the human race. Supported by the apparent success of democratic governments and the evidence of scientific and technological advances, their confidence in the future outran even that of the Enlightenment's apostles of progress. The Kingdom of God was given a this-worldly interpretation and viewed as something men would build within the natural historical process. For them, in Reinhold Neibuhr's striking phrase, "History was the Christ."

Their interest in history caused the liberals to go even farther, radically altering the meaning and significance of revelation. The Old Testament was interpreted chiefly as a record of Jewish history, religiosity, and growing moral earnestness that culminated in the life and message of Jesus. The New Testament was placed in the same context, and the main aim of scholarship was to clarify the religion of Jesus. Because the New Testament consists exclusively of the history and testimony of the post-Easter church, it created many problems for liberals. Paul the Apostle became a very troublesome saint. On the divinity of Jesus and the inspiration of the Scriptures, therefore, widely divergent views arose. The dominant tendency was in the direction of a benign naturalism, although it was veiled by an extremely pious and time-

---

the Church. Liberals usually found it easier to preach duties and laws than to proclaim Good Tidings. To many critics this was the central issue: Does one have Good News (Gospel, Evangel) to preach?

honored vocabulary. Hence Jesus' divinity sprang from the fact that he spoke the most sublime truths and proclaimed the highest and (probably) the final religion. Creeds and dogmas about these matters were "human constructions" subject to evolutionary development and interpretation. Time had purged them of much error, and the process was still going on. The Bible thus had authority because, judged by standards outside of it (historical, philosophic, scientific, and experiential), it deserved to be so regarded.

Liberals tended strongly to monistic ways of construing many traditional problems of theology and philosophy. Wishing to see unity in all things rather than disjunction, they preferred to combine or merge the romantic inclination to see man and nature as alike infused with divinity and the Darwinian tendency to relate man to the natural world in a scientific way. Similarly, man and God were brought together. Liberals dwelt much more on the immanence of God than on his transcendence. As Bushnell had argued, the natural and the supernatural were consubstantial, observable in almost all forms of being. The supernatural and the spiritual tended to be identified; and the spiritual in turn was identified with consciousness—the conative, intellectual, emotive side of man. Finally, the ancient disjunctions between the subjective and objective, between the mental world and the "real" or "objective" world, were minimized philosophically by theories of reality which stressed the ideal nature of things and by intuitional or idealistic theories of knowledge. Not all liberals, by any means, believed that such matters were crucial, but when they did venture into philosophical realms, they usually regarded Plato, Kant, Hegel, Schleiermacher, Coleridge, and various mystical philosophers as very important and reliable guides.

A revised estimate of the purpose and power of religious education gave practical expression to so many articles of the liberal consensus that it must be singled out as a vital element of the movement's essence. Within the older Sunday school movement this new cause took a prominent place in the liberal understanding of church reform. The founding of the Religious Education Association in 1903 and the International Council of Education in 1922 gave it organizational focus; but the new educational philosophy probably owed most to George A. Coe, Harrison S. Elliott, and William C. Bower, all of whom were deeply interested in the psychology of religion, learning theory, and "progressive" views of education. The methods of Froebel and Pestalozzi were blended with John Dewey's social pragmatism, while Bushnell's *Christian Nurture*, republished by Luther A. Weigle of Yale in 1916, became the classic expression of the movement's underlying faith in the potency of education in the formation of Christian character.

Major Types of Liberalism

In the foregoing exposition of the liberal consensus, certain elements of dissent have been only faintly indicated. There were, however, fundamental disagreements on two large issues: on the nature of religion, and on the source of authority, which is to say, on the nature of revelation.

On religion the issue was twice drawn. In one school were the moralists who, like Rauschenbusch, insisted on "the fundamental truth that religion and ethics are inseparable, and that ethical conduct is the supreme and sufficient religious act."[11] This group's boundaries went far beyond the Social Gospel movement, however, to include thinkers with almost no concern for public affairs. In the other school were those who, with varying emphases, placed ethics within the context of a more comprehensive effort to deal with the general phenomenon of religion. Within this second school, furthermore, was another very marked division. One subgroup included those who stood in the tradition of Schleiermacher and William James (not to mention the Puritans and John Wesley), who put great value upon "being religious" and upon analyzing religious feeling. For them the religious consciousness and Christian experience were central, and in philosophy they often tended to intuitionism, subjectivism, and mysticism. Among them were Bushnell and many more or less romantic thinkers. Newman Smyth's "garland for Schleiermacher," *The Religious Feelings* (1877), is a fine representative of this position. The second subgroup was less interested in experience (though they might treasure it deeply and build upon it) than in metaphysics and the philosophy of religion. Josiah Royce and Bowne were outstanding examples of this tendency in the early period; but after World War I, as part of the "realistic revolt" from idealism,

[11] Walter Rauschenbusch, *Christianity and the Social Crisis* (New York: Macmillan Co., 1907), p. 7.

Macintosh and Henry Nelson Wieman represented a new philosophic tack. Throughout the period, each of these three major points of view on religion (ethical, experiential, and philosophical) continued to receive effective expression.

On the issue of revelation, thinkers parted ways over interrelated questions as to the authority of Scriptures, the Church, and formal creeds. Related to all of these concerns was the question of Christ's nature and mission. Here as in the controversy over religion, two distinctive tendencies emerged. The "Evangelical Liberals" were those determined to maintain the historical continuity of the Christian doctrinal and ecclesiastical tradition, except insofar as modern circumstances required adjustment or change. Biblical study remained central, "Back to Christ" became a familiar slogan, historical study of Christian doctrine was vigorously pursued, and theology was carried out so far as possible in the traditional context and vocabulary. The term "Progressive Orthodoxy," chosen by the faculty of Andover Seminary for its published manifesto in 1884, very accurately expresses the purposes of the Evangelical Liberals. Since the vast majority of churchgoing America shared these purposes, the spokesmen for this cause won a wide audience. W. N. Clarke, W. A. Brown, and Rauschenbusch were among the most widely known.

The term "Modernistic Liberalism," on the other hand, may be used to designate a much smaller group of more radical theologians, men who took scientific method, scholarly discipline, empirical fact, and prevailing forms of contemporary philosophy as their point of departure. From this perspective they approached religion as a human phenomenon, the Bible as one great religious document among others, and the Christian faith as one major religio-ethical tradition among others. With varying degrees of concern for the traditional topics of systematic theology, and with more or less sympathy for their native religious heritage, they sought to salvage what they could of traditional belief, piety, and ethics. Emerson could be regarded as a prototype. Perhaps the best example of a modernistic school was that which flourished at Chicago, where men like Mathews, Case, Ames, Wieman and their colleagues for several decades worked out the implications of such a stance in almost every branch of the seminary curriculum. William James and Josiah Royce are more famous examples.

THE SIGNIFICANCE OF LIBERALISM

During the later nineteenth century a self-conscious and intellectually distinguished movement of theological liberals gained many eloquent proponents in the Protestant churches. Yet its influence is very difficult to estimate. Even the author of a book on *The Impact of American Religious Liberalism* has great difficulty in defining its "impact"—not because the movement was without effects, but because its legacy was all-pervasive.[12] It is imposible to determine whether the people it influenced were called back to the faith, or whether they were merely assured that their minimal beliefs constituted the essence of Christianity. The single most vital fact, therefore, is that the liberals led the Protestant churches into the world of modern science, scholarship, philosophy, and global knowledge.[13] They domesticated modern religious ideas. They forced a confrontation between traditional orthodoxies and the new grounds for religious skepticism exposed during the nineteenth century, and thus carried forward what the Enlightenment had begun. As a result, they precipitated the most fundamental controversy to wrack the churches since the age of the Reformation.

Aside from performing this immense educative role, the liberal movement also made significant scholarly contributions. Most important were its manifold labors in the fields of religious history, social and psychological analysis, comparative religion, educational theory, philosophy of religion, and systematic theology. By sustained effort and creative thought, the liberals made a new place for religion in the modern world.[14] Because they remained in touch with the historical

[12] Kenneth Cauthen, *The Impact of American Religious Liberalism*. This is not criticism of an important book to which my distinction between evangelical and modernistic liberalism is indebted.

[13] "Modernism" performed a similar function in the Roman Catholic church during the same years, but its impact in America was slight (see pp. 310–17 below).

[14] These frequent references to the "modern" are not casually made (see Arthur C. McGiffert, *The Rise of Modern Religious Ideas*. Richard Ellmann and Charles Feidelson in *The Modern Tradition: Backgrounds of Modern Literature* (New York: Oxford University Press, 1965) pursue the question provocatively, yet affirm that "the modern awaits definition."

and romantic movements, they gave religious expression to the dynamic aspects of life and stood off the moral, social, and philosophical oversimplifications of scientific positivism. By raising problems for dogmatism, on the other hand, the liberals greatly enlivened the ecumenical movement.

It would be hard to deny that in doing these many things they sometimes stripped away the Church's spiritual armor. Often incredibly naïve in their evaluations of man, society, and the national destiny, they did little to prepare Americans for the brutal assaults of the twentieth century. In this respect they laid the ground work for tragedy and disillusion. One can accept H. Richard Neibuhr's harsh summary of their outlook: "A God without wrath brought men without sin into a kingdom without judgment through the ministrations of a Christ without a Cross."[15] In the face of many difficulties, however, they maintained standards of scholarly rigor, intellectual honesty, and moral responsibility that their successors often failed to appreciate. In the later twentieth century renewed demands that Christians be "honest to God" would enhance their reputation. To be sure, they may have been overly optimistic about human nature, but they were not fatuous; and those who entered the Social Gospel movement were effective critics of the American social order.

[15] *The Kingdom of God in America,* p. 193.

47

THE SOCIAL GOSPEL

When the Social Gospel movement began and when it came to a close are much disputed questions. But nearly everyone agrees that it was more fully represented by Walter Rauschenbusch than by anyone else, and that it gained classic utterance in 1907 with the publication of his *Christianity and the Social Crisis*. Let us read, then, the final page of this book, where the "lonely prophet" discloses his vision of God's coming Kingdom:

> If the twentieth century could do for us in the control of social forces what the nineteenth did for us in the control of natural forces, our grandchildren would live in a society that would be justified in regarding our present social life as semi-barbarous. Since the Reformation began to free the mind and to direct the force of religion toward morality, there has been a perceptible increase of speed. Humanity is gaining in elasticity and capacity for change, and every gain in general intelligence, in organizing capacity, in physical and moral soundness, and especially in responsiveness to ideal motives, again increases the ability to advance without disastrous reactions. The swiftness of evolution in our own country proves the immense latent perfectibility in human nature.
>
> Last May a miracle happened. At the beginning of the week the fruit trees bore brown and greenish buds. At the end of the week they were robed in bridal garments of blossom. But for weeks and months the sap had been rising and distending the cells and maturing the tissues which were half ready in the fall before. The swift unfolding was

the culmination of a long process. Perhaps these nineteen centuries of Christian influence have been a long preliminary stage of growth, and now the flower and fruit are almost here. If at this juncture we can rally sufficient religious faith and moral strength to snap the bonds of evil and turn the present unparalleled economic and intellectual resources of humanity to the harmonious development of a true social life, the generations yet unborn will mark this as that great day of the Lord for which the ages waited, and count us blessed for sharing in the apostolate that proclaimed it.[1]

This passage deserves close analysis not because it is extraordinarily difficult, but because beneath its blossoming rhetoric are three assertions which reveal the essence of the Social Gospel, a movement which has been widely hailed at home and abroad as the most distinctive contribution of the American churches to world Christianity.

The primary point of Rauschenbusch's conclusion is underlined by his central figure of speech: "now the flower and the fruit is almost here." The "great day of the Lord for which the ages waited" is at hand. The Social Gospel was a form of millennial thought; yet it was also an authentic "gospel" bringing good tidings of great joy to the people. Rauschenbusch's grounds for joy constitute the second point: "the immense latent perfectibility in human nature" has been revealed by the swift evolution of our country and by the progress that has been accelerating in Christendom ever since the Reformation. His third point is the moral demand, driven home by two conditional sentences that bracket the passage: men must gain control of social forces; the "bonds of evil" must be broken; and finally—and here is the insistence that makes the Social Gospel a movement in the churches— religious faith and moral strength must be directed toward these last great social tasks.

The Social Gospel must be understood as a transitory phase of Christian social thought. It was a submovement within religious liberalism, with a certain view of man and history governing its rationale. It reflected and depended upon the singular spirit of confidence and hope that prevailed for only

1 Walter Rauschenbusch, *Christianity and the Social Crisis* (New York: Macmillan Co., 1907), p. 422.

a few decades before the Great War and the Great Depression shattered the mood. Historians can record its rise and describe its aftermath, but efforts to see its persistence or revival during the 1930s involve serious distortions. Similarly, a single set of social problems stirred its passions: the urban dislocations occasioned by America's unregulated industrial expansion. The Gilded Age was a prerequisite. In this context its moral message consisted almost exclusively in applications, mild or severe, of the idea that the doctrine of laissez faire required Christian modifications. The Iron Law of Wages so dear to classical economics must be qualified by the Great Commandment. Between employer and employee brutality and conflict must yield to compassion and mutual respect. Even in this light, however, the historical problem of dealing with the Social Gospel remains very great, as four other important considerations will make clear.

SOME PRELIMINARY CONSIDERATIONS

In one sense, the Social Gospel was anything but new. The major element in America's moral and religious heritage was Puritanism, with its powerfully rooted convictions that the shaping and, if need be, the remaking of society was the Church's concern. American Protestantism was born in Holy Commonwealths and Holy Experiments. The Second Great Awakening and the great "theocratic" campaigns of the Evangelical United Front had intensified this tendency. Antebellum revivalism, in fact, was pervaded by concern for social reform and, beyond that, by the hope for a sanctified citizenry that would make this republic a model for the whole world. Lyman Beecher and Charles Finney were so fascinated by this vision that they almost forgot their quarrels about the "new measures" in revivalism. Unitarians and Transcendentalists also caught the contagious reforming spirit. During most of the nineteenth century, moreover, the professor of Christian morals and political economy became a stock figure in American colleges and universities. Until a very late date these men inculcated the old medieval principle that social, economic, and political theory is properly a branch of Christian ethics, a principle that the Social Gospel was to reaffirm.

The antislavery movement came to life within this matrix and gradually ate away the prevailing apathy and hostility in the churches. By 1860 Lincoln had at his back a crusading evangelical Protestantism so fervent that at times he feared it would trample him with the vintage that the grapes of wrath had stored. Abolitionism, with its hymns, slogans, and prophetic zeal, was a decisive prelude to the Social Gospel. Both were characterized by a readiness to harness the churches and a tendency to subordinate every other interest of the church to the one great national policy question of the day. The line from Theodore Dwight Weld and Elijah Lovejoy to Washington Gladden and Walter Rauschenbusch must never be ignored.

A second consideration is that by no means all opponents of the Social Gospel believed that public affairs and social questions ought to be put aside when a minister entered the pulpit. Even a social conservative like Henry Ward Beecher made freedom to speak out on social issues a condition of his accepting the call to Plymouth Church in 1847. During worship services in his church, Beecher not only "auctioned" slaves and raised money for Bleeding Kansas, but with the Bible before him, citing appropriate texts, he preached and published sermons on the whole gamut of social questions, including the problems of poverty and labor relations that worried the Social Gospelers. Although he took the opposing stand on nearly all of the issues, the social orientation which Beecher established at Plymouth Church enabled his successor, Lyman Abbott, to defend quite different economic views from the pulpit and to become the virtual chaplain of Theodore Roosevelt's Progressivism. This change in social outlook, moreover, did not involve Abbott in any basic departure from Beecher's form of the "New Theology." In other words, liberal preachers like Beecher (and at reduced scale they were legion) belong in the prologue to Social Gospel history despite their ideological opposition to men like Rauschenbusch.

Another phase of social protest that flourished during the Social Gospel's heyday was Populism and the great agrarian crusade. It, too, had a religious orientation. Its dominant leader was the Great Commoner, William Jennings Bryan, who was also the Joshua of American Fundamentalism. "Would you crucify labor on a cross of gold," he had shouted —at a time when Pastor Rauschenbusch was equally agonized by society's crucifixion of the poor. Yet historians never include Populism in the Social Gospel movement, for it lacked both an urban orientation and the presuppositions of theological liberalism. The same criteria apply to the varied activities of the Salvation Army and, somewhat later, to the Pentecostal rescue missions and similar institutions which brought the church into living contact with city slums.

Liberalism and the Social Gospel movement must not be identified, however, because liberalism often encouraged complacency and self-satisfaction. It throve mightily among the most socially conservative classes of people. The Social Gospel, on the other hand, was always a prophetic and unpopular impulse. Although it became a large and powerful minority in the early 1920s, even then its intradenominational battles were often bitter, and many were lost. Social Gospelers were usually theological liberals; but the statement cannot be reversed.

A third consideration involves the question of the Social Gospel's originality. Is it the most distinctive American contribution to world Christianity as is so often alleged? The facts are confusing. Although its Puritanic concern for the commonwealth is, as we have seen, embedded in an indigenous tradition which is unique, almost every major new element of the Social Gospel betrayed enormous indebtedness to two major foreign impulses. From Britain came a legacy of inspiration drawn from the Christian socialism of Charles Kingsley, Frederick D. Maurice, John Ruskin, William H. Fremantle, and the architects of Fabian socialism. From Germany came nearly its entire biblical and theological grounding, as well as the historical view of economic theory by which the social statics of *Manchesterismus* was to be overthrown. The key figure for the Social Gospelers as for so many other liberal theologians was Albrecht Ritschl (1822–89), whose Jesus-centered, antimetaphysical theology of the Kingdom of God provided the movement's chief integrative idea. Adolph von Harnack, the most famous of Ritschlians, formulated many of these views even more appealingly, especially through his disparagement of vain scholastic speculation and the exceedingly simplified ethical principles which he defined as the "essence of Christianity." And after Ritschl had come the rising Social Christian movement in Germany and Switzerland, not to mention the advanced social legislation of the new German Empire.[2] British and German devel-

---

[2] Karl Marx is a special case. His impact on German social and sociological thought extended far beyond socialist organizations. But in the Social Gospel movement, as in American thought generally, Marxian influence was slight and heavily filtered, even

opments, in short, provided a vital prologue to American Social Gospel history.

The final preliminary consideration calls attention to the opposition which the Social Gospel faced—the villain in the plot, as it were. What the Social Gospel had to combat was above all the American's basic contempt for poverty, the "hard shell of sanctified realism" fostered by the Puritan ethic in both its pious and secularized forms. This attitude had nothing to do with the immemorial assumption that a certain amount of poverty was inevitable, or with the notion of a Great Chain of Being which made the lowly an essential element in the Creation. The Puritan doctrine of vocation avoided a static interpretation of the dominical words, "You have the poor always with you" (Matt. 26:11). Because God called nobody unto mendicancy and inactivity, those who begged and did not work either were being or ought to be punished for their sins. Even in the complex urban surroundings of New York in the 1870s Henry Ward Beecher was willing to make this proposition axiomatic:

Looking comprehensively through city and town and village and country, the general truth will stand, that no man in this land suffers from poverty unless it be more than his fault—unless it be his *sin.* . . . There is enough and to spare thrice over; and if men have not enough, it is owing to the want of provident care, and foresight, and industry, and frugality, and wise saving. This is the general truth.[3]

William Lawrence, a Massachusetts Episcopal bishop, reduced this "gospel of wealth" to two "positive principles": "that man, when he is strong, conquers Nature," and that "in the long run, it is only to the man of morality that wealth comes." Beyond this, of course, lay "the privilege of grateful service" and Christ's "precepts on the stewardship of wealth."[4] One could fill book after book with similar hardshell quotations, from orthodox, liberal, and secular spokes-

---

among the Christian socialists on the Social Gospel's left wing (see James Dombrowski, *The Early Days of Christian Socialism in America*).

[3] Quoted by Sidney E. Mead, *The Lively Experiment: The Shaping of Christianity in America*, p. 160.

[4] "The Relation of Wealth to Morals," in *Democracy and the Gospel of Wealth*, ed. Gail Kennedy (Boston: D. C. Heath & Co., 1949), pp. 68–76.

men alike, all of them anxious, it would seem, lest someone accuse them of being "soft on poverty." Yet only when this attitude was called in question could American Protestantism produce the Social Gospel.

Two new circumstances served to intensify the American's prevailing hardness of heart. Simplest of these was the powerful evidence that Andrew Carnegie's faith in America's "Triumphant Democracy" had its warrants: "The old nations of the earth creep at a snail's pace; the Republic thunders past with the rush of the express." Carnegie's statistics were impressive; and his own rags-to-riches life story was more convincing than anything Horatio Alger was writing.

But the common view of poverty and wealth was given even greater plausibility during the Age of Enterprise by the doctrine of evolution through struggle and natural selection of the fittest. Darwin learned from Malthus, and the Malthusians, in turn, learned from Darwin. Social Darwinism thus gave the stock ideas of the Puritan ethic a new potency and the added dignity of "scientific" support. Herbert Spencer with enormous confidence extended Darwinian theories of development to human societies, and in the United States he won to his banner a Broad Church Episcopal minister of Morristown, New Jersey, named William Graham Sumner. In 1872 Sumner abandoned the pulpit for an academic podium at Yale, where he exchanged liberal Christianity for conservative Spencerianism, first as a professor of political economy, then increasingly as a sociologist. In these roles Sumner used his evolutionary determinism to bludgeon soft-hearted reformism and governmental intervention of all types (plutocratic as well as democratic). What little hope he saw for mankind he vested in a stern work-oriented moralism and the evolutionary process. Like a Henry Ward Beecher minus every shred of religiosity and teleology, Sumner made the task of the Social Gospel more difficult.

PREPARATORY DEVELOPMENTS

During the years after the Civil War, many Christian spokesmen in a variety of places began for the first time in American history to express serious doubts that the organized selfishness of a free enterprise economy would automatically solve the country's problems. Less theoretically, they openly lamented the fact that the laboring man was rarely understood and almost never defended in the Christian churches. Andover Seminary's famous journal, *Bibliotheca Sacra,* opened its pages to social commentary in 1866, and in 1868 it printed a series of articles entitled "The Natural Theology of Social Science," in which Professor John Bascom of Williams College criticized the conservatism of the Protestant pulpit. Bascom had no more sympathy for the poor and improvident than his contemporaries, but he did question the competitive principle, and advocated giving the workingman a "pecuniary interest" in the enterprises for which they worked. Later, after serving as president of the University of Wisconsin, he moved in his *Sociology* (1887) toward the more forthright "Kingdom theology" of the Social Gospel. Among Bascom's students was Washington Gladden, who in later years would earn his title as "the father of the American Social Gospel."

Two other pioneers of the movement merit brief mention, the first, a sensational preacher, widely known at the time but soon forgotten; the second, a typical champion of the workingman. Joseph Cook was an Andover graduate and an Orthodox Congregational minister who gained fame between 1875 and 1895 for his strenuous efforts to defend the Christian religion against biblical critics, evolutionists, and free thinkers. Cook was also a politically conservative enemy of vice and corruption of the fairly standard type. Less typically, he was concerned with working conditions, low wages, and child labor. Because his Monday Lectures in Boston attracted some of the largest audiences in that city's history, the Social Gospel's best historian can say of him that he "probably did more than any other individual or group in bringing the social implications of Christianity to the attention of Americans."[5]

The Reverend Jesse Henry Jones was a Boston Congregationalist of quite another order. As founder of the Christian Labor Union (1872–78) and editor first of *Equity: A Journal of Christian Labor Reform* (1874) and then of the equally short-lived *Labor-Balance* (1877), he defended a labor theory of value, advocated socialism, and made strident attacks on Henry Ward Beecher's truce between God and Mammon. Yet Jones was not simply a social radical with an

[5] Charles H. Hopkins, *The Rise of the Social Gospel in American Protestantism,* p. 39.

ordination somewhere in his past. In his book *The Kingdom of Heaven* (1871) he envisioned a perfect Christian society of separate socialistic communities. As Professor May remarks, he was of a type that is "common in the unfrequented byways of American social science. Religious radicals, spinning plans for a perfect society out of their reading of the Gospels and prophets or out of their own troubled consciences."[6] The views of such men had little to do with American realities, but their spirit was an important recurring ingredient of the Social Gospel, especially valuable as a reminder that the country's avid interest in utopian socialism during the antebellum period had some long-range effects.

Other Social Prophets

In addition to these anticipations of the later Social Gospel, a tradition of social criticism and "muckraking" opposed itself to the practices of the "robber barons" and the degeneration of political ethics that set in with the Grant administration. Civil service reform, government regulation of business, and antitrust legislation were its chief aims, and its accomplishments included the Civil Service Act, the Interstate Commerce Commission, and the regulatory legislation of the Progressive Era. With these later achievements the Social Gospel movement would have an especially close relationship. Contemporary with this eminently respectable reform tradition, however, were three more distinctive prophets who are related in special ways to social Christianity: Edward Bellamy, Henry George, and Lester Ward.

Bellamy (1850–98) was the son of a Baptist minister who during his short life moved from his father's faith to a "religion of solidarity" that took its inspiration in about equal measure from Christian liberalism, Transcendentalism, and Auguste Comte's "Religion of Humanity." "Living in the narrow grotto of individual life" he was "greedy of infinity." He yearned for a social order that would transcend the idea of "personality as an ultimate fact." Growing up in the industrial town of Chicopee Falls, Massachusetts, Bellamy became intensely aware of the "barbarity" and "monstrous cruelty" which were parts of the town's daily life. As a newspaper writer he vented some of his views, and as a novelist still

[6] Henry F. May, *Protestant Churches and Industrial America*, p. 79.

others; but his reputation rests almost entirely on his novel, *Looking Backward* (1888), in which he portrays the socialistic perfection of the nation in A.D. 2000. It soon became a best seller, and Nationalist Clubs began to be organized to bring about Bellamy's imagined world just as the Social Gospel was gaining self-consciousness as a movement. Both Bellamy's social organicism and his futuristic orientation became indispensable elements in the social optimism of the age.

Henry George (1839–97) "exploded into fame" nine years before Bellamy with his *Progress and Poverty* (1879)—so searing in its indictment of the American social system, so fervent in the millennial hope that it offered, that in America its author became the emotional equivalent of a Karl Marx. His panacea was the single tax, and around this program grew up a tight phalanx of orthodox followers, many of them from organized labor. Far more contagious and far broader in its influence was his root-and-branch critique of the American economic system and the theory that underlay it, as well as his enraptured vision of a perfected America. His religious passion and his tender concern for every human being put George in the Social Gospel tradition. In 1886, when he ran for mayor in New York with both the Roman Catholic Father Edward McGlynn and Walter Rauschenbusch supporting him, he revealed his true force in American life as an awakener of the slumbering Christian Social conscience. Although he died suddenly during his second New York mayoralty campaign, the hundred thousand mourners who filed past his bier paid homage to the powerful way in which he had taken economic theory out of obscure treatises and academic halls, making it a weapon in the social and political conflicts of a nation in crisis.

Lester Ward (1841–1913), unlike Bellamy and George, esteemed himself a scientist rather than a prophet or visionary. He was the first American to write a comprehensive sociological treatise, and his importance for the Social Gospel lies in the fact that in his sociology Ward challenged the reigning views of Sumner and Spencer. Though as interested as they in a cosmic scientific synthesis, and equally naturalistic in his premises, Ward distinguished human purposive action from all other natural processes, and attacked those Social Darwinians who used evolutionary theory to support the businessman's opposition to state intervention, charity, and all other "artificial" devices to preserve the "unfit" in the economic struggle for survival. For him sociology was an applied science to aid whole societies in bettering their condition. Ward was a liberal in politics; unlike George, he favored Populism and Bryan, and was "anxious to throttle the money power." He was too irreligious to affect the Social Gospel directly, but he did put on the record a formidable critique of Sumner's "Biological sociology."

THE SOCIAL GOSPEL

During the last two decades of the century the movement to awaken the social conscience of the churches moved far beyond the sporadic and uncertain forays of the 1860s and 1870s. It deepened the intellectual foundations of its work, broadened its focus, vastly increased its following, and began to make a positive impact in some theological schools, on certain major denominations, and no doubt, on the prevailing opinions of churchgoing America. Since these changes did not bring agreement in methods and aims, subdivisions of the movement took shape, some conservative, others moderate, still others frankly socialistic. Without becoming a hopelessly unreadable catalogue of names and dates, however, no brief account can touch on all of the many socially concerned Protestants who took part, or the myriad organizations which perpetuated these diverse impulses, or the innumerable projects, experiments, publications, and conventions which marked the movement. The account which follows will concentrate on a few of the most outstanding and representative leaders.

In the annals of the Social Gospel Washington Gladden (1836–1918) undoubtedly deserves first mention. He was among the earliest to be awakened, and he continued to be active until World War I. His gradual progress from abstract moral protest to a specific critique of American economic institutions typifies that of the movement as a whole, near whose ideological center he consistently remained. Gladden was reared on a farm near Owego, New York, and educated at Williams when Mark Hopkins was president and John Bascom a professor. After private study with Moses Coit Tyler, he entered the Congregational ministry in 1860. He was even then a pronounced liberal in theology, and he soon became an admirer of Bushnell. Throughout his life, Gladden was a popular expositor of the New Theology, writing three widely read books, *Who Wrote the Bible?* (1891), *How Much Is Left of the Old Doctrines?* (1899), and *Present Day Theology* (1913). In all of these works he showed his indebtedness to the leading liberal theologians and scholars, but unlike most of them he saturated his liberalism with social concern. His specifically Christian leverage came more from an appeal to the Great Commandment than from a legalistic interpretation of the "social teachings" of Jesus.

Very early in his career Gladden became interested in the struggles of labor and capital. After several brief pastorates and a few years as a religious journalist, he began in 1875 an important seven-year ministry at Springfield, Massachusetts, an industrial city where he soon had an opportunity to express his sympathy for unemployed workers. From 1882 to 1914 he served with great effectiveness as minister of the First Congregational Church of Columbus, Ohio. Adding thirty more to the six books he had already published, and lecturing far and wide, Gladden became one of the country's most influential clergymen. During this period he also pursued his analysis of the nation's economic situation, digging deeper into labor problems and the details of taxation, and gaining experience which formed the background for his insistence that the churches do more than attack personal sin and public corruption.

Over the years Gladden's criticism of American free enterprise became more severe. Though he never became a socialist, he did advocate public ownership of utilities and co-operative management of many industries. Among his most constructive works were *Tools and the Man* (1893) and *Social Salvation* (1902), both first presented as Beecher Lectures at Yale. His theology of social action, however, was very simple: he demanded that the churches concern themselves with social injustice, and that they help bring the economic aspects of American life under the laws of God's kingdom by example and by advocacy.[7] Yet this was no small matter in the Gilded Age, and Gladden is justifiably remembered as a major awakener of the American Protestant social conscience.

[7] Like most Social Gospel men, Gladden advocated interchurch cooperation. In *The Christian League of Connecticut* (1883) he presents a fictional scenario of churches working together to face social problems in a factory town. Many socially minded ecumenical leaders testified to its influence.

Francis Greenwood Peabody (1847–1936) represented the Social Gospel cause in another vital arena, the seminary. He had been deflected from the normal career of a Boston-born, Harvard-educated, Unitarian minister by a year at the University of Halle in Germany. When he was made a professor at the Harvard Divinity School in 1880, he very soon instituted what was probably the first systematic course in "social ethics" to be taught in an American theological school. Peabody understood himself to be living in "the age of the social question," and to promote an intelligent response, he implemented a program of undergraduate and graduate instruction in the subject at Harvard. His published volumes of chapel sermons and many treatises extended his influence far beyond his own university. *Jesus Christ and the Social Question* (1900) went through many editions and was translated into three languages. Rauschenbusch considered it, along with Shailer Mathews's similar work, to be definitive on the subject.

In theology Peabody drew heavily upon the tradition which Schleiermacher had inspired in Germany. His social advocacy was relatively conservative, with a strong emphasis on cooperatives, insurance, enlightened philanthropy, good planning, and a social security system on the Prussian model. In all of these areas, moreover, Peabody believed strongly in the value of factual knowledge. The Social Ethics department which he founded had an important library, introduced seminar methods, and laid the groundwork for future work in sociology at the university. Peabody also stands out as an important exception to the Social Gospel's prevailing lack of interest in Negro education and racial questions; and he is among the very few Americans of that period whose words on these matters could be read without embarrassment a half-century later. In addition, his career illustrates the two-way process by which liberal theology, historical studies, and the Social Gospel served for a time to bring Unitarianism back into the mainstream of American religious thought.

Social Science for the Social Gospel

The Social Gospel, needless to say, did not consist solely of biblical exegesis and theological elaboration; indeed those are the two elements it most definitely lacked. It was always chiefly concerned to find out the truth about society, and on the basis of that knowledge to chart programs for ameliorating the country's social woes. To this end it drew political science, economics, and sociology to its service and, whenever possible, sought to provoke in all social scientists a regard for the ethical implications of their work. In the fertile exchange of ideas that resulted, two social scientists, Richard T. Ely and Albion W. Small, are important not only for their efforts to advance the Social Gospel as a movement in the churches, but for their contributions to the conduct of their disciplines in America.

Richard T. Ely (1854–1943) grew up in rural New York State in a strict Presbyterian environment; but in the course of his life he became an advanced liberal in theology, an Episcopalian, a strenuous critic of neoclassical economic theory, and a strong advocate of reform in America's urban-industrial system. After a college education divided evenly between Dartmouth and Columbia, Ely went to Germany from 1876 to 1880 for advanced study. He spent a year in philosophy at Halle, then went to Heidelberg for a Ph.D. in economics. As a result of this experience he became—and remained—an admiring disciple of Karl Knies, the historical economist, Johann Bluntschli, and Rudolph von Ihering, all of whom repudiated the alleged laws of classical economics and emphasized the prior importance of differing cultural contexts, historical developments, national needs, and political realities. They underlined both the fact and the desirability of human solidarity, insisting that economic theory must deal with national culture as a whole. The relativistic implications of such doctrines are obvious, but these were counterbalanced by an emphasis on the need for goals in economic, social, or legal thinking. These historical theorists stressed normative considerations even as they exposed the unexpressed ethical presuppositions of classical or absolutist theories. Throughout his life, therefore, Ely was to oppose those who took "Back to Adam Smith" as their motto. Identifying himself with "the ethical school of economists," he insisted that it aimed "to *direct* in a certain definite manner, so far as may be, the economic, social growth of mankind. Economists of this school wish to ascertain the laws of progress, and to show men how to make use of them."[8]

8 Richard T. Ely, *The Social Aspects of Christianity* (New York, 1889), p. 122.

On returning to the United States, Ely was appalled both by the way economic theorists ignored the cultural, religious, and ethical norms of the nation, and by the widespread ignorance of alternative economic theories, Continental accomplishments in social reform, and the nature of the labor movement. During the next decade, while a professor at Johns Hopkins, he published books on each of these subjects, steeping all of them in his intense moral concern. In *Social Aspects of Christianity* (1889) he developed in more detail his understanding of the bearing of Christian ethics on social questions. With this book he became one of the most widely read of all American economists. To promote his large aims for America he led in the formation of the American Economic Association in 1885, also serving for a decade as its secretary or president. Through his participation in Episcopal social agencies and in many other conferences and commissions, as well as through his many writings, he became not only a "representative man," but an extremely influential theorist.

Albion W. Small (1854–1926) filled a very similar role as a reform-minded sociologist. He grew up in a pious New England Baptist home, attended Colby College in Maine and the Baptist Seminary in Newton, Massachusetts, and then proceeded to Germany, where at Leipzig and Berlin he became a convinced defender of the "historical school" in social thought led by Gustav Schmoller and Wilhelm Roscher. In later years he would add to this commitment a deep appreciation for the more positivistic sociological methods of Gustav Ratzenhofer and Ludwig Gumplowicz, thus becoming an important American pioneer of equilibrium theory in social relations.

After returning to America, Small became professor of political economy, then president of Colby College, gaining in the meantime his doctorate at Johns Hopkins. In 1892 he was called to the new University of Chicago to organize the sociology department. As the first person in the country to occupy a chair in this discipline, he played a major role in training the first generation of American-educated sociologists. His understanding of social science was, like Ely's, very comprehensive, involving an intense concern for its philosophic ground and its ethical implications. He believed that "the most worthy work of men is the effort to improve human conditions":

> If I am not mistaken, the most earnest seekers after God are . . . growing more and more in contact with the development of a science . . . of God's image, or the science of human welfare. . . . The ultimate value of sociology as pure science will be its use as an index and a test and a measure of what is worth doing.[9]

For these reasons, he was consistently critical of Sumner and Spencer, but very appreciative of Lester Ward. And through his active participation in many important conferences called by Social Gospel leaders, Small was able to keep empirical questions and the need for organized sociological knowledge before their minds.

The Apogee of the Movement

Josiah Strong (1847–1916) was the dynamo, the revivalist, the organizer, and altogether the most irrepressible spirit of the Social Gospel movement. Though of orthodox upbringing, he became an admirer of Bushnell's theological leadings; but more importantly, be came to regard the new industrial city as the central crisis for the nation and the church. In 1885, when Strong was a minister of the Central Congregational Church of Cincinnati, he expounded his views in what was almost certainly the most influential Social Gospel book of the nineteenth century, *Our Country: Its Possible Future and Its Present Crisis*. He then implemented his conviction that concerted interchurch action was necessary by convening an Interdenominational Congress at his church in Cincinnati, inviting many of the country's most outstanding social Christian spokesmen to attend. Future meetings and a series of urban surveys were projected. At once Strong became a national figure, and his appointment as general secretary of the almost moribund Evangelical Alliance in 1886 gave him an opportunity to maintain the momentum of these projects.

---

[9] *General Sociology* (Chicago, 1905), quoted in Cynthia Eagle Russett, *The Concept of Equilibrium in American Social Thought* (New Haven: Yale University Press, 1966), pp. 61–62; Albion Small, *The Significance of Sociology for Ethics* (Chicago, 1902), p. 4.

In 1887, 1889, and 1893, other congresses were held, all of them large, well-publicized, and followed up by publications and local conferences. The last of them, held at the Chicago World's Fair, had an especially powerful impact.

Two major results of these efforts were a revitalization of the country's main interdenominational agency and the focusing of ecclesiastical concern on the city. The Alliance meanwhile gave Strong a platform from which to proclaim his enormous confidence in America's destiny under Protestant leadership. That his fervor reached almost jingoistic proportions is undeniable, and there were also more than intimations of Anglo-Saxon racism in his message. In these respects he was clearly a spokesman for the "Protestant Establishment." Yet he was more than merely that, for he showed untiring concern for urban evangelism and for a linking of "fact and faith" in the churches' approach to industrial questions. Surveys and statistics informed his diagnoses and his prescriptions. When his advanced social views forced him out of the Alliance in 1898, he immediately organized the League for Social Service (later to become the American Institute of Social Service), which took social research and public education on social affairs as its primary tasks.

Strong's confidence in applied science and in guided evolution was boundless. His nationalism and his defense of imperialism have become almost infamous. Taken as a whole, however, his views were those which constituted the core program of the Social Gospel movement. In fact, without Strong's contribution, the very term "movement" would hardly be warranted. The latest and most thorough student of his work, moreover, rightfully stresses the way in which Strong's program parallels that of the political Progressives.[10] Josiah Strong, finally, almost personified the movement's culminating phase: the organization of an interdenominational agency of national scope. Certain other aspects of the movement need to precede an account of this chain of events, however.

Divergent Voices

Social Christianity could by no means be kept entirely within the liberal Protestant boundaries marked out by men

[10] See Dorothea R. Muller, "The Social Philosophy of Josiah Strong: Social Christianity and American Progressivism," *Church History* 28 (1959):183–201.

such as Strong or Gladden. The writings of Marx no less than the old native American tradition of utopian socialism made that unlikely. And indeed a considerable number of more radical spirits soon were heard, and a few new organizations were formed. These radicals were colorful personalities whose exploits and bold ideas frustrate the historian with space limitations, yet a few representative types may suggest the range of their accomplishments.

Among the most impressive was William Dwight Porter Bliss (1856–1926), a Congregationalist become Episcopalian, a follower of George, Bellamy, and British Christian Socialism, who in 1890 gave up his parish ministry in Boston and founded the Mission of the Carpenter, a socialist congregation which in turn became the nucleus for other organizations and activities, including a newspaper, *The Dawn*. In 1897 Bliss also published a huge and valuable *Encyclopedia of Social Reform*. More than any other prominent Christian reformer of the period, he anticipates the "secularized" urban mission of some mid-twentieth century activists. After 1906 Bliss became an active member of the Christian Socialist Fellowship as well as of the Socialist party.

The Minneapolis Congregational minister, George D. Herron (1862–1925), had an even more unusual career. Bursting on the scene in 1890 as a dynamic preacher, within three years he had won himself an endowed chair in applied Christianity at Iowa (Grinnell) College. A social critic from the first, Herron gradually became an outspoken socialist, though of a mystical, utopian sort; and between 1896 and 1900 his views were the inspiration for an unsuccessful communitarian experiment in Georgia. Suddenly in 1901 his influence in the American churches was ended by his divorce, his marriage to the daughter of his chief patroness, and accusations of his being a "free lover." Before his permanent departure for Italy, however, he played a brief but active role in the Socialist party, even giving the nominating speech for Eugene V. Debs at the party's Chicago convention of 1904.

Not surprisingly, the most durable impulses were those that led to more or less thoroughgoing versions of socialism, whether Marxian or Fabian. These movements possessed a degree of discipline and the guidance of a tradition. At that time, moreover, socialist leaders such as Henry D. Lloyd, Lawrence Gronlund, and even Eugene V. Debs showed a surprising measure of religious openness. The loosely organized Christian Socialist Fellowship, founded in 1906,

affiliated itself with the Socialist party, which in the startling
election of 1912 drew almost a million votes despite Wilson's
and Roosevelt's competitive bidding for the progressive vote.
Out of this milieu the Presbyterian minister Norman Thomas,
the Episcopalian Bernard Iddings Bell, Professor Vida
Scudder, and many others emerged as eloquent public
figures.

Walter Rauschenbusch

If Josiah Strong typified the organized mobilization of
social concern in the churches, Walter Rauschenbusch
(1861–1918) typified its passion and its soul. Nearly every
fundamental motif of the Social Gospel, including a strong interest in socialism, came to expression in his works. In theology, biblical interpretation, and church history he consistently expounded the major liberal themes. He subjected the
American social order to informed analysis and found it
wanting. He awakened compassion for human suffering and
proposed realistic reforms. He delineated the key concept of
the "Kingdom of God on earth" with persuasive clarity. And
finally, he overcame apathy and pessimism with a stirring
vision of the coming Kingdom. At one stage in his career
Rauschenbusch was, as Winthrop Hudson has shown, a "lonely
prophet," but before his death in 1918 and for almost a
decade thereafter, his growing reputation justified H. Shelton
Smith's assertion that he was "the foremost molder of American Christian thought in his generation."[11] Because of his
most atypical insistence on the power of the "kingdom of
evil," he is also one of the few liberal theologians who could
still be read after wars and depressions had dimmed men's
vision of a perfected social order.

Rauschenbusch was born in Rochester, New York, where
his father, an immigrant missionary, was professor in the
Baptist seminary's "German Department." Except for his
high school years in Germany, he was educated in Rochester;
and he taught church history in the seminary from 1897 until
his death. The decisive experience of his life was his eleven-
year ministry (1886–97) to a German Baptist congregation
situated in the proximity of New York City's notorious Hell's

---

[11] Winthrop S. Hudson, *The Great Tradition of the American
Churches*, pp. 226–42; Hilrie Shelton Smith, *Changing Conceptions of Original Sin*, p. 199.

Kitchen. In that blighted district "an endless procession of men 'out of work, out of clothes, out of shoes, and out of hope' wore down the threshold and wore away the heart of the sensitive young pastor and his wife."[12] Out of that experience came the Rauschenbusch whom America remembers. His Social Gospel career began almost immediately, during Henry George's mayoralty campaign of 1886. With Jacob Riis he labored for playgrounds and for better housing. The friendships he forged with a small company of other Baptist ministers grew, with the addition of a few non-Baptists, into the Brotherhood of the Kingdom, a fellowship that between 1893 and 1915 became an influential nucleus of devoted social concern, especially through its publications.

In his own denomination and among the movement's leading spirits, Rauschenbusch had become a well-known Social Gospel leader even before the century's turn. But in 1907, while he was on leave for a year of study in Germany, *Christianity and the Social Crisis,* the book that made him nationally famous, was published. Here in seven simple but eloquent chapters the whole Social Gospel was expounded: the social message of the Old Testament Prophets, the "social aims of Jesus," the subsequent decline of social concern in the church, the "present crisis" and the church's stake in it, and finally, "What To Do." Ringing through the whole is Rauschenbusch's doctrine of the Kingdom, a disparagement of older forms of piety and traditional theology, a thoroughly instrumental conception of the church, and an insistence that religion and ethics are one and inseparable. *Christianizing the Social Order* (1912) was more concerned with prescribing reforms for America's capitalistic system, which he deemed to be only "semi-Christian."

Then in 1917, and despite his conviction that "theology is the esoteric thought of the church," Rauschenbusch published *A Theology for the Social Gospel,* first presented as the Taylor Lectures at Yale. With the World War now undermining his hopes for the Kingdom of God, he found reason in this book to formulate more forcefully a doctrine of the "Kingdom of Evil." Having been stunned by the readiness of Americans to locate this kingdom exclusively in Germany, he traced the ultimate cause to "the lust for easy and unearned gain" of the "imperialistic and colonizing powers."

---

[12] Hopkins, *Rise of the Social Gospel,* p. 216. He quotes Ray Stannard Baker, *The Social Unrest* (1910).

He called for a "restoration of millennial hope," and declared that "after the war the Social Gospel will 'come back' with pent-up energy and clearer knowledge." He saw the "Christianizing of international relations" as the most acute sphere of concern.[13]

As it happened, military victory in "the War to End Wars" did stimulate social Christianity in America and lead to a great expansion of its machinery in the early postwar years. But we must first consider the prewar process by which the Social Gospel won an official, institutionalized place in American Protestantism.

Institutionalizing the Social Gospel

In 1907, when Rauschenbusch wrote the final lines of his first book (quoted in the opening of the present chapter), the fortunes of the movement he championed justified his enthusiasm. Josiah Strong, to be sure, had been routed from his commanding position in the Evangelical Alliance, but other agencies had been created. In 1901 the Episcopal and the Congregational churches both formed commissions to deal with labor issues; and in 1903 the Presbyterian Church (North) called Charles Stelzle to a "special mission to workingmen," and under his dynamic leadership its Department of Church and Labor became an outstanding success. In 1908 the Northern Baptists took a first step toward formal recognition of the movement, while the Methodist Church (North) went much further, making the Federation for Social Service an official agency and adopting as a church the very liberal "Social Creed" which the Federation had prepared. By 1912, when the Men and Religion Forward Movement was launched as an interdenominational campaign to win three million Americans to the church, a dozen other denominations had taken cognizance of the Social Gospel. The Social Service division, in turn, became the most active element in the Forward Movement.

At the same time that these advances were being made, the most portentous step of all was taken. Due largely to the efforts of the social action elements in several large denominations, the Federal Council of Churches was formally organized. Since the days of Josiah Strong's rejuvenation of the

[13] Walter Rauschenbusch, A Theology for the Social Gospel (New York: Macmillan Co., 1917), pp. 4, 15, 224.

Evangelical Alliance, a series of important preparatory organizations had been formed, one of them Strong's own privately sponsored League for Social Service. In 1894 the interdenominational Open and Institutional Church League was formed, and for a number of years Elias B. Sanford directed its campaign for enlarging the scope of unified social service work. Six years later Sanford also did much to found the National Federation of Churches and Christian Workers, a voluntary association based on precedents set in New York City in 1895. Its greatest achievement was to organize the Interchurch Conference on Federation which met with official delegates from twenty-nine denominations in Carnegie Hall, New York, in November 1905.

The Carnegie Hall Conference, besides issuing several statements on social issues, unanimously approved a plan of organization which, when adopted by denominations, would constitute the Federal Council of Churches of Christ in America. The proposed doctrinal basis was made brief and broad: no more than a reference in the preamble to "the essential oneness of the Christian Churches of America, in Jesus Christ as their Lord and Saviour." In Philadelphia in 1908 delegates from thirty-three denominations formally brought the Federal Council into existence. Although it possessed only advisory powers—or perhaps because of that fact—it turned to social issues at its first meeting, adopting a lengthy report on "The Church and Modern Industry" which clearly stated the church's responsibility for extending and applying "the principles of the new social order." This report also included a statement which virtually incorporated the Social Creed of the Methodists, including its bold assertion of the rights and objectives of the laboring man.[14] A Commission on the Church and Social Service was also established, with the liberal Presbyterian leader, Charles Stelzle, as "voluntary" secretary. One of its first tasks was an investigation of the Bethlehem steel strike in 1910. In its report it condemned both the twelve-hour day and the seven-day week as "a

---

[14] Many years later the last surviving delegate to that meeting described the mood in which this report was adopted: "Most vivid in my memory is our singing of Frank Mason North's hymn 'Where Cross the Crowded Ways of Life' after the presentation of his report. Most of us had tears running down our cheeks" (Samuel McCrea Cavert, *The American Churches in the Ecumenical Movement, 1900–1968*, p. 56).

disgrace to civilization," chiding ministers, as well as Christians generally, for aloofness from labor's problems and aims. The Federal Council thus began very early to establish a tradition of outspoken liberal advocacy which would survive both the World War and the "normalcy" which followed. Genuine ecumenical aspirations went into its founding and continued to inform many of its actions, but there is no denying the statement of its veteran general secretary in 1933 that throughout its existence the Federal Council's animating force had "come from men who were wrestling with the practical tasks of the churches in what was becoming a hostile or increasingly unaccommodating social order."[15]

In the Federal Council social Christianity finally won its place and gained a platform in American Protestantism. Yet because the council was founded through the efforts of men committed to the Social Gospel, it failed to become an authentic voice of Protestants. Underlying this circumstance was the hard fact that most American Protestants were conservative evangelicals who, despite massive provocations to change, strove chiefly to maintain the faith and practice of yore. They regarded the Social Gospel and the Federal Council as dangerous enemies.

On the other hand, the basic political thrust of the Social Gospel was by no means radical. In 1912, for example, its adherents probably avoided the Socialist Debs overwhelmingly, splitting their vote between Wilson and Roosevelt. And therein lies the essential fact: they supported the liberal impulses of the times. One might even revise D. C. Somervell's *mot*, and refer to the Social Gospelers as "the praying wing of Progressivism." To assert this parallel between the two movements, however, accentuates rather than diminishes the movement's significance. A major development of the period was the growing awareness that social change demanded new forms of social action and new conceptions of government. The Square Deal and New Freedom alike betoken the nation's shift. In the reinterpretation of old social

[15] Charles S. Macfarland, *Christian Unity in Practice and Prophecy* (New York: Macmillan Co., 1933), p. 53. The social emphasis of the Federal Council was greatly heightened by the fact that other cooperative concerns of the churches were at that time still being dealt with through other agencies such as the Foreign Missions Conference (1907) and the Home Missions Council (1908).

orthodoxies and in the storming of old conservative bastions, the Social Gospel movement simply took churchgoing America as its field of action and sought to convert the self-oriented Christian consciousness into one that was neighbor-oriented.[16] In reaching this wide and influential audience the movement played an important national role.

[16] Rauschenbusch stated the matter tersely: "The social movement is the most important ethical and spiritual movement in the modern world, and the social gospel is the response of the Christian consciousness to it. Therefore it had to be" (*A Theology for the Social Gospel*, pp. 4–5).

48

DISSENT AND REACTION IN PROTESTANTISM

American evangelical Protestantism was extraordinarily well adapted to the popular ideal and patterns of American life. Patriotism, manifest destiny, Anglo-Saxon self-confidence, the common man's social and economic aspirations, peaceful community life, the Declaration of Independence, and the Constitution—all were accommodated and supported in its capacious system of beliefs. During the later nineteenth century, however, at least five religious groups were left unsatisfied by this mainstream tradition and some were openly hostile.

Most obvious were those like Robert Ingersoll, Henry George, Edward Bellamy, Francis E. Abbot, and Clarence Darrow, who left the church despite their sometimes strong religious interests, becoming outspoken advocates of agnosticism, socialism, free religion, or at least total disestablishment. More moderate but similarly perturbed were the liberals and Social Gospelers, who sought to adapt Christian faith and practice to more urgent modern needs. A third group included those whose ethnic background or particular claims (or both) were not part of the old Protestant mainstream. Mormons, Christian Scientists, Mennonites, Unitarians, and other divergent movements belong in this category, but it consisted chiefly of Negroes, Jews, Roman Catholics, Lutherans, and a few other large communions that consciously resisted wholesale assimilation or were refused the opportunity. The fourth group was a vast interdenominational movement of those who protested against innovation in religion. Most of its adherents were troubled by the decline of the old-time religion. Most of its adherents were troubled by the decline of the old-time religion with its accent on conversion;

but their bonds were chiefly doctrinal. Whether rich or poor, educated or illiterate, rural or urban, Baptist or Presbyterian, they were troubled by the advance of theological liberalism and the passing of Puritan moralism. Fundamentalism is a name for the movement which its own leaders adopted and used.

The fifth and final group effected a more distinct separation from mainstream Protestantism than most Fundamentalists sought. A desire for a rebirth of life in the Spirit often led its adherents to schism and sectarian withdrawal. Its chief doctrinal concern was sanctification, and the "gathered" communities which it founded were Holiness or, if more radical in their innovations, Pentecostal churches. Finding its adherents chiefly among the disinherited and the uneducated, this movement was primarily a protest against birthright church membership and a Protestantism that had settled for a religion of conformity, middle-class respectability, and self-improvement. Since the Wesleyan emphasis on Christian perfection was very prominent in its teaching, the Methodist church was deeply involved in the attendant strife. Many of these sectarians, however, came to share the Fundamentalist's concern for biblical inerrancy, and Christ's Second Coming often loomed large in their thought.

All of these groups and movements have been considered elsewhere in this history, but the present chapter is chiefly concerned with the development of the latter two, which are such distinctive forms of evangelicalism that most Europeans regard them, along with baseball and wild-west movies, as American creations. Both of these movements are, in one sense of the term, conservative, yet they share a kind of radicalism that is unmistakably new. They arose in part because historical relativism and positivistic science threatened the heretofore unchallenged certainties of Scripture and dogma, and in part because materialism and religious indifference were infecting society as a whole. Popular attitudes were changing; social and ecclesiastical structures were being transformed; many old landmarks of church life were passing away. Equally irritating to them was the assertion of liberal theologians that orthodoxy itself could be "progressive." Yet the new trends affected much more than doctrine: just as lace, jewelry, and cosmetics were enticing the ladies, simplicity in the churches was yielding to organs, ornate furniture, and comfortable pews, while the passion for vital

Christian experience of sin and salvation was giving way to secular optimism. Even the clergy seemed vulnerable to the "inner revolution" of the Gilded Age.[1]

In charting the response to this new ethos, we begin at the most popular pole, where laymen who had almost no contact with the history of ideas rose up almost spontaneously against the prevailing religious ways and identified them with the great apostasy foretold in Scripture. Arthur T. Pierson in 1900 had no doubt that this was *the* culminating impulse among the evangelical "forward movements of the last half century." He described in detail "a general consensus of opinion that we are now on the threshold of that crisis, unparalleled in the history of the Church and the world, concerning which Christ bade us to 'watch and pray.' "[2]

RADICAL ADVENTISM

In the ensuing revival of millennialism the old Adventist bodies grew apace. The Bible was searched with renewed intensity for signs of the times; and champions of many new readings of "prophecy" arose. But of all the new chiliastic movements, the most successful and certainly the most publicized in subsequent years was the Jehovah's Witnesses. In its early years, the group embodied a vehement, thoroughgoing protest against the prevailing order. The bold, even lawbreaking, "publishers" of its message proclaimed that Satan's three great allies were false teachings in the so-called churches, the tyrannies of human governments, and the oppressions of business. They also attacked the pretensions of orthodox Christianity and questioned its two most central doctrines, the deity of Christ and the depravity of man. They appealed to the poor, outraged middle-class communities by violating their Sabbath quiet laws, and shocked "human governments" by refusing pledges, salutes, and military service to the devil's cohort.[3]

[1] See Thomas C. Cochran, *The Inner Revolution*, chap. 1.
[2] Arthur T. Pierson, *Forward Movements of the Last Half-Century* (New York, Funk and Wagnalls Co., 1900), p. 409.
[3] Between 1940 and 1943 the persistent refusal of Jehovah's Witnesses to perform patriotic rites brought three important civil liberties cases to the Supreme Court. In 1943 the Court upheld their right to such refusal.

The founder of this movement (it is expressly not a "church") was Charles Taze Russell (1852–1916), a haberdasher from Allegheny, Pennsylvania, whose independent Bible studies led first to highly successful preaching, then, about 1872, to the organization of his followers. The intricacies of his interpretation of prophecy cannot be given here; but its central point was that the Millennial Dawn had come. The Second Advent had already occurred (in 1874) and the end of all things was slated for 1914; hence the famous slogan of the early Russellites: "Millions now living will never die." But Russell did die in 1916, and his successor, Joseph F. Rutherford, was not only less specific in his dating of the Last Days, but more effective as an organizer and propagandist. After his death in 1942, Nathan H. Knorr became president, and under his leadership the Witnesses' immense publishing enterprises, missionary training schools, and evangelism programs became still more efficient and farflung. By 1965 the Watchtower Bible and Tract Society, with headquarters in Brooklyn, counted over a million "publishers" of its message in nearly every country of the world, more than three hundred thousand of them in the United States. Yet because of their exclusivism and proselytizing tactics, as well as their doctrinal departures on the Trinity and the means of salvation, Protestants generally have denied them fellowship.

THE RISE OF DISPENSATIONAL PREMILLENNIALISM

While highly individualistic adventist schemes of this sort were advancing at an unabashedly popular level, another similar movement of far more significance to the major church bodies was clarifying its testimony and more quietly gathering adherents. Several historians, in fact, would virtually *define* Fundamentalism as the creation of an interdenominational group of evangelical ministers, predominantly Presbyterian and Baptist, who after 1876 convened a series of annual meetings for Bible study, and who later organized two widely publicized Prophecy Conferences: in 1878 at Holy Trinity Episcopal Church in New York, and in 1886 at Farwell Hall in Chicago. The leaders of this group also met for fellowship and study at the annual Niagara Bible Conferences (so named for their most frequent place of meeting).

Animating this new impulse was a two-fold conviction that the whole Christian world, including the United States and Canada, was falling into apostasy and heresy so deeply and so decisively that it could only mean the approach of the Last Days; and that, therefore, nothing was more direly needed than preaching of the hard facts drawn from God's Word. The body of doctrine on which these men gradually converged, however, was more than "the precious doctrine of Christ's second personal appearing." They searched out God's whole "pattern for the ages," and gradually, a distinct system of dispensational, premillennialism unified this intense "bible study" movement and informed its conferences.

The idea of successive divine dispensations is, of course, immemorial, being implicit in the very terms Old and New Testament. The Swiss Reformer Heinrich Bullinger developed the idea of God's dealing with man through successive covenants, as did the Anglo-American Puritans and the great Dutch theologian of the covenants, Johannes Cocceius. But the modern form of this system, especially the radical separation of the present "age of the church" from the coming "Kingdom," had its effective origin in the teachings of John Nelson Darby (1800–82).

Darby was born in London and educated in Ireland for the bar, but instead he became a priest in the (Anglican) Church of Ireland in 1825. He soon became deeply distressed by political interference in ecclesiastical affairs. Yet finding the contention-ridden Dissenting churches no better than established Anglicanism, he became convinced of the "ruin of the church." By 1828 he had joined the Plymouth Brethren, and he soon became the foremost promoter of this new movement, traveling incessantly throughout Europe, calling men to separate from ecclesiastical "systems" and worldly pretensions and to carry on in simplicity while awaiting Christ's secret return. Darby believed that Christ would rescue all true Christians before the Tribulation soon to befall the earth, including apostate Christendom, just prior to His Coming in glory to establish His Israelitish Millennial Kingdom. Gradually he developed a periodization of all time and declared a radical distinction between the future of Israel and that of the Church. This overall scheme became known as dispensationalism.

Disagreements over this scheme and other matters split the Brethren in 1849 into the Open and Exclusive branches, the latter and much larger branch led unofficially by Darby. Many Brethren, as well as their writings, made their way to North America; and Darby himself joined them on seven different occasions between 1862 and 1876. Relatively few converts were won to Exclusive Brethrenism, but many Protestants, to Darby's consternation, accepted dispensationalism or parts of it while remaining within their denominations.[4] Very soon, moreover, various American dispensationalists began to elaborate and "improve" upon Darby's never very precisely defined scheme. Of special importance in this effort was James H. Brookes (1830–97), a Presbyterian minister in Saint Louis who was under strong Plymouth Brethren influence even before he became the leading force in the Niagra Conferences, and who edited a widely read dispensationalist magazine. Dwight L. Moody was also significantly impressed by Brethren teachings, and through him and others many dispensationalist notions (if not the complete system) persistently appeared in the Student Volunteer and Laymen's Missionary movements. Yet nowhere did Darbyism fall on more fertile ground than when it reached Cyrus Ingerson Scofield.

Scofield (1843–1921) was born of Episcopal parents in rural Michigan, but reared in Tennessee where he served in the Confederate army. Entering the legal profession in Kansas after the war, he acted for a time as United States attorney in that state, but later moved his practice to Saint Louis. Here he experienced a religious conversion in 1879, became a pupil of James H. Brookes, and soon entered the ministry. In 1882 Scofield accepted a call to a small Congregational church in Dallas, Texas, where he served until 1907, except for eight years (1895–1902) at the "Moody Church" in East Northfield, Massachusetts. After 1907 he propagated his scheme of dispensations and covenants by lecturing and through his Correspondence Bible School (which after his death continued as the Dallas Theological Seminary). The true monument to his lifelong efforts, however, is the Scofield Reference Bible, first published in 1909, but further amplified with the aid of various associates in 1919. For over

---

[4] In 1964 the United States had eight groups of Plymouth Brethren, identified by as many numerals and differentiated chiefly by their principles of fellowship within an otherwise commonly held body of beliefs. Plymouth Brethren 2, the largest group, claimed 15,000 of the total membership of 33,250.

half a century this Bible, with its explanations and annotations, has been a faithfully used resource of conservative Sunday school teachers, preachers, and churchgoers. It expounded the normative form of American dispensationalism, and for millions of people in diverse denominations its dogmatically phrased annotations became an indispensable guide to God's Word. In its time, few religious books equaled its influence, and the publication in 1966 of a new edition, revised by a committee of sympathetic dispensationalists, gave the book an extended term of influence.

At the heart of the matter, for Scofield as for rival interpreters, were two major themes: a "pattern for the ages" consisting of successive dispensations (usually seven in number, with the Millennium being the "Great Sabbath") and a radical distinction between Jews and Christians. Scofield understood these dispensations to be marked by, but not identical with, God's successive covenants:

1. *Innocency:* the Edenic covenant with Adam before the Fall
2. *Conscience:* the Adamic covenant, after man's explusion from the Garden
3. *Human Government:* the Noahic covenant, after the Deluge
4. *Promise:* the Abrahamic covenant with God's chosen, Israel alone; all other peoples remaining under Human Government
5. *Law:* the Mosaic covenant with Israel, extending through the ministry of Jesus to the Jews, until the crucifixion in which Jew and Gentile both participate
6. *Grace:* the covenant of grace in and through Christ, to Jews and Gentiles individually until Christ's Second Coming
7. *The Fullness of Time, or the Kingdom:* the Millennium when Christ shall restore the Davidic monarchy of Israel and rule for a thousand years.

Dispensationalist literature is complex and generalizations are risky, yet the movement's distinctiveness seems to arise in part from its dual insistence on strict inerrancy and a unitary view of the Bible. Hence both Old and New Testament apocalyptic texts (especially Daniel and Revelation) are interpreted as parts of one divine plan, with the result that Old Testament ideas on the course of history play a dominant role. This is accompanied by a clear distinction between

God's plans for Israel and for the Church, at least this side of eternity. The more common view has seen the Church as a new Israel, in which case New Testament eschatological ideas become dominant. On its own premises dispensationalist exegesis is difficult to assail. In this light one may see why the controversies were and are heated.

Dispensationalism, however, was much more than a partitioning of history, for its real appeal depended on its doctrinal foundations. In the first place it insisted undeviatingly on the absolute verbal inerrancy of the Bible as the "inscripturated" Word of the unchanging eternal God; every word and phrase was deemed capable of revealing not merely data for the historian and philologist, but divine truth. Its extensive use of typology, its commitment to numerology, and its dependence on highly debatable (not to say fanciful) interpretations of some obscure apocalyptic passages have led many to insist that its interpretation is anything but literal. Yet its repudiation of historical criticism was well-nigh total, except insofar as it was driven to textual problems in the original languages. During the nineteenth century it took little or no cognizance of geological or astronomic calculations, retained Archbishop Ussher's old dating of the Creation around 4000 B.C., and therefore placed the beginning of the seventh millennium around A.D. 2000.

The theological context of dispensationalism tended to be markedly Reformed or "Calvinistic." Methodists, for example, with their strong commitment to Arminian theology, found the atmosphere unappealing even though dispensationalists affirmed the characteristic American evangelical moral code and placed heavy emphasis on the experience of conversion. In a more general sense, however, this new system of prophecy aroused strongest resistance among American Protestants by denying what most evangelicals and all liberals firmly believed—that the Kingdom of God would come as part of the historical process. They could not accept the dispensationalist claim that all Christian history was a kind of meaningless "parenthesis" between the setting aside of the Jews and the restoration of the Davidic Kingdom. This claim aroused violent reactions because it provided a rationale for destructive attitudes and encouraged secession from existing denominations. Especially objectionable was the tendency of dispensationalists to look for the Antichrist among the "apostate churches" of this "present age."

As dispensationalist teachings developed, each system had many refined qualifications to meet as many equally refined objections, with the result that a whole new theological vocabulary came into being. This terminology, though alien to many deeply versed Christians, became the mark of a large band of Fundamentalist advocates, carrying with it many conceptions that earlier conservatives had never heard of. To many denominational traditionalists the new conceptions, far from being "fundamentals," were fundamental heresies. Name calling did not stop infiltration, however, and in 1927 the president of Princeton posed a question in his official report that was anything but merely rhetorical: "Shall Princeton Seminary . . . be permitted to swing off to the extreme right wing so as to become an interdenominational Seminary for Bible School-premillennial-succession fundamentalism?" This question leads us to consider the third level of Fundamentalist unrest, where Princeton Seminary played a leading role for over a century.

Presbyterianism and the Princeton Theology

Dispensational premillennialism was a vital factor in giving Fundamentalism a measure of interdenominational cohesion and esprit. It also gave a common body of theory to the many Bible study institutes which sprang up in every part of the country as training schools for missionaries and evangelists.[5]

[5] The first Bible college—later named the Nyack [New York] Missionary College—in the United States was founded in New York City in 1882 by A. B. Simpson, a former Presbyterian who in 1881 had founded the Christian and Missionary Alliance for the purpose of extending missionary work at home and abroad. (The Alliance has since then virtually become a denomination, with a strong Pentecostal tendency, encompassing more than a thousand churches in North America and a still larger constituency abroad.) A more influential school, however, was the Moody Bible Institute, which accepted its first students in 1889 under the auspices of the Chicago Evangelization Society, thus realizing a dream of Moody and Emma Dryer, who had operated a school of "Bible work" in the Chicago slums for sixteen years. The general idea of preparing "gapmen" to fill the breach between the laboring poor and the organized church gripped Moody during his revival activity in England. Ignoring charges that he was competing with seminaries and the professional clergy, Moody set out to "fit laymen" for the "practical work" of "learning how to

But the main forces of American conservatism did not believe that the Christian Church was a parenthesis. Indeed because they loved their denominations—often unduly—and wished to preserve them from liberal inroads, their resort was not in new schemes of scriptural interpretation but in shoring up old schemes; not in new doctrines, but in the official confessions and the writings of their own church Fathers.

The resultant Fundamentalist controversy occurred to a degree in all churches, though it was minor where liberalism was weak or nonexistent (Southern Baptist) or predominant (Congregational), or where doctrinal concerns had always been secondary (Methodist). A tripartite division in the Episcopal church—among high, low, and broad churchmen—reached schism-producing levels of acrimony in this period, but led finally to the acceptance of a live-and-let-live policy, whereby dioceses or parishes could move toward any of the prevailing options.[6] Lutherans were preoccupied with their own special problems, though by no means in the isolation often ascribed to them. In some denominations the intel-

---

reach the masses" (see James F. Findlay, Jr., *Dwight L. Moody: American Evangelist, 1837–1899*).

The Bible Institute of Los Angeles was founded in 1907 under R. A. Torrey (1865–1928), who had been the first head of the Moody school. Many other more strictly denominational schools were also established, so that by 1961 the number of Bible institutes and colleges had swelled to 194 in the United States and 54 more in Canada. In 1947 an accrediting association was formed, and by 1960 half of their number were degree-conferring colleges. About two-thirds of the institutions are denominational, the Churches of Christ and the Baptists controlling about two-thirds of these. In all, about twenty-five thousand day students and ten thousand others were enrolled in 1960. They provide nearly all the ministers for various small conservative denominations and many for the larger ones, and are a powerful factor in sustaining a Fundamentalist constituency in American and Canadian Protestantism (see S. A. Witmer, *The Bible College Story: Education with Dimension*).

6 A small schism did disrupt the Episcopal church in 1873 when Bishop D. G. Cummins of Kentucky led out an evangelical faction that organized the Reformed Episcopal Church, which held to conservative evangelical positions. More important was the General Convention's 1874 decision for "comprehensiveness" precipitated by James DeKoven, an Anglo-Catholic who insisted that he either be tried for heresy or be left unrestricted by church regulations.

lectual life had been so neglected by conservatives that the need for a new apologetic was very tardily recognized. When they did awaken, moreover, they discovered that their seminaries and great urban pulpits were in the hands of the enemy. It is this total circumstance that made Princeton Theological Seminary so important—not only for Presbyterianism, but for all the denominations that honored the Reformed tradition, and even for some that did not.

The centrality of Princeton and the Presbyterians was, of course, not accidental. Presbyterians were widely dispersed in the nation and often socially prominent. They also had a long tradition of learning and theological concern. Very soon after its founding in 1812, therefore, Princeton Seminary's leadership was recognized by conservatives in all denominations (even among conservative Unitarians when Transcendentalism arose in their midst). The Old School-New School controversy strengthened this reputation, and during the troubled decades which followed the reunion of northern Presbyterianism in 1869, Princeton's power increased as the former New School seminaries drifted away or closed their doors.[7] The Princeton Theology, expounded for a half-century by Charles Hodge and published in systematic form both by him and by his son, won acceptance far and wide as the strength and stay of embattled conservatism. And during the 1880s this dogmatic tradition gained further support from Benjamin B. Warfield (1851–1921), who brought great theological and historical prowess to the defense of the Reformed tradition, and a new rigidity into the doctrine of scriptural inspiration. Each of Warfield's great interests, Reformed doctrine and biblical inerrancy, provided a major theme in the "Fundamentalist Controversy" that raged within Northern Presbyterianism.

The always latent doctrinal question had been sharply posed as early as 1874, when Dr. David Swing, a prominent Chicago minister, despite acquittal by presbytery, left the denomination rather than face further judicial proceedings over his view that "a creed is only the highest wisdom of a particular time and place." In 1892 the General Assembly re-

---

[7] Union Theological Seminary (New York) declared its independence from Presbyterian control in 1892. Auburn Seminary joined forces with Union in 1939. In 1932 Lane Seminary merged with the Old School seminary which was founded in 1829 in Chicago with endowment from Cyrus McCormick.

sponded to a wide-spread demand for revisions of the West-minster Confession. The results were far short of those sought by the church's liberals, but they revealed that Presbyterians were approaching the American Protestant norm on double predestination and the salvation of infants. In order to ac-commodate Cumberland Presbyterian views in the merger of 1906, the church went still farther in this direction, taking an Arminian position on man's free will—a traumatic event for many Old School thinkers.

In questions pertaining to biblical inerrancy, on the other hand, the denominational majority was intransigent. During the 1880s the General Assembly on several occasions affirmed the strictest possible views, and in 1892 it issued the famous Portland Deliverance, which made official the Hodge-Warfield doctrine that the "inspired Word, as it came from God [that is, in the 'original autograph'], is without error." This position was reaffirmed in 1893, 1894, 1899, and then most decisively in 1910, when the assembly made it the key-stone of the Five Points that were to be regarded as "essen-tial and necessary" doctrines of the church. The other four points in this formulation—which with slight variations would ring through many Fundamentalist testimonies during subse-quent years—affirmed the Virgin Birth, the "Satisfaction The-ory" of the Atonement, the Resurrection "with the same body," and the miracles of Jesus.

Nor were these empty gestures. The deliverances of the 1890s were all directly connected with a series of sensational heresy cases which resulted in the extrusion of three of the country's very greatest Christian scholars from the Presby-terian ministry for neglecting to take a strict "doctrine" of inerrancy as the starting point for their biblical scholarship. Two were Old Testament men, C. A. Briggs, of Union Semi-nary (New York) and Henry Preserved Smith of Lane Semi-nary, while the other, A. C. McGiffert, also of Union Semi-nary, was an historian of the early Church who dealt with the New Testament literature. Each of them faced the issue head-on, Briggs most vigorously; but the preponderance of strict conservatives in the General Assembly was over-whelming. The first two were dismissed for heresy in 1893 and 1894; McGiffert reluctantly resigned from the Presby-terian ministry in 1900. Fundamentalism reigned in the de-nomination, and it would continue to reign, at least officially, for another quarter-century, though both scholarly and social pressures tended to modify the working theology of many ministers and church leaders.

A few men boldly persisted in proclaiming their liberalism, Henry Van Dyke (1852–1933) being especially outspoken. As a poet, short story writer, and literary critic, he is remembered as a very proper Victorian, but he was also a talented preacher, theologian, and controversialist. The son of an Old School minister and sometime moderator of the Presbyterian church, he was educated at Princeton College and Seminary. Up to that time he was a conservative, and very critical of the "vituperative theology" emanating from Germany. But a year in Berlin and studies under Isaak Dorner moderated his views. After becoming minister of the Brick Church on Fifth Avenue, he was a leader of the movement to revise the Westminster Confession. As for the famous Five Points, he declared one to be nonessential and the other four unbiblical; and he defended his judgment that the orthodox position on "prenatal election" was a "horrible" doctrine. In two widely read books, *The Gospel in an Age of Doubt* (1896) and *The Gospel in a World of Sin* (1899), he gave eloquent voice to a mediating theology that was remarkably attuned to the mood of the age, yet warmly evangelical. The popularity of his works demonstrated that he was not a solitary prophet. His literary fame and his position after 1899 as a professor of English at Princeton University rather than as a professor of theology in a seminary saved him from heresy proceedings.

Announcing the Fundamentals

The desire to arrest the drift from old moorings led to one other major event in the history of pre-World War Fundamentalism—an event, some would say, that gave the movement its name. Two wealthy Los Angeles laymen, Lyman and Milton Stewart, desiring to advance the cause of true religion in some decisive way, created a $250,000 fund in order that "every pastor, evangelist, minister, theological professor, theological student, Sunday school superintendent, YMCA and YWCA secretary in the English speaking world" might be given twelve substantial booklets in which the theological issues of the day would be addressed. These essays were to be written by a distinguished group of conservative Protestant theologians from Great Britain, Canada, and the United States. With Amzi C. Dixon, Louis Meyer, and Reuben A.

Torrey serving in turn as editors, *The Fundamentals* began appearing in 1910, and before the twelfth volume had been issued three or so years later, a total of three million booklets had been distributed.

The books had at least two important effects. First of all, by enlisting the efforts of eminent spokesmen such as James Orr of Scotland, Bishop H. C. G. Moule of Durham (England), Benjamin Warfield of Princeton Seminary, and President E. Y. Mullins of the Southern Baptist Seminary in Louisville, a great interdenominational witness was achieved. It is not inappropriate to say that the Fundamentalist *movement* was launched. This was done, moreover, with dignity, breadth of subject matter, rhetorical moderation, obvious conviction, and considerable intellectual power. If they had appeared in routine periodicals, few if any of these fourscore articles would have been long remembered; yet historians of Fundamentalism have deprecated them unduly. The conservative case was firmly and honorably made. The other important feature of the project was the way in which it created a kind of *entente* between two fairly incompatible conservative elements: a denominational, seminary-oriented group, and a Bible institute group with strong premillennial and dispensational interests. Since dispensationalism was highly esteemed by both the patrons and editors of the project, its message was prominent in every booklet, with R. A. Torrey, A. T. Pierson, Arno C. Gaebelein and even Scofield himself contributing one or more essays. Between these two groups there was a deep gulf, just as a cleavage of another sort and vintage separated Baptist and Anglican authors. Despite clashing interpretations of countless scriptural passages, however, the authors succeeded in forging an uneasy alliance to defend the doctrine of the Bible's literal inerrancy. The impact of this project, unfortunately, was interrupted in 1914 by a man-made Armageddon, but when peace had been established among nations, theological and ecclesiastical warfare would be resumed with even greater vehemence.

THE HOLINESS REVIVAL

Because certitude and peace are found in diverse ways, religious unrest takes many forms. In the premillennial movement Methodists were notable for their rarity. In the great surge of interest in Christian perfection and complete sanctification, on the other hand, the Wesleyan legacy was primary.[8] During the Gilded Age the Methodist churches, North and South, were swept by a great Holiness Revival, and the preaching and practice of this doctrine led to religious manifestations which most Methodist leaders tended to discountenance as disruptive and unseemly. Repression, in turn, led to defiance of discipline and then to outright secession. What had first been jubilantly welcomed as a Pentecostal blessing turned Methodism into a battleground; and out of the ensuing conflict a new denominational impulse emerged, much as Methodism itself (and before that, Puritanism) had arisen in the Church of England. As this newly released evangelical energy extended into foreign missions, its impact became literally worldwide. By World War I, however, the new current had itself divided into two distinguishable branches, one relatively moderate, the other extreme. Both branches prospered at cultural levels that hid their significance from the major middle-class churches, but their success nevertheless merits close historical scrutiny.

The first perfectionist secession, the Wesleyan Methodist Church of 1843, had been a by-product of the anti-slavery crusade, and it had been followed by the Free Methodist Church in 1859–60. But these were relatively minor incidents

[8] John Wesley had insisted that the doctrine of Christian perfection was "the grand depositum which God has lodged with the people called Methodist." He set forth his views most definitively in the fourth edition of his *Plain Account of Christian Perfection* (1777) which he then incorporated in the *Discipline* of 1789. Believing that Christ died for all and that the doctrines of election and predestination distorted the faith, Wesley distinguished between the experiences of justification and sanctification, insisted that "justified persons are to go on unto perfection," and felt confident that some Christians, through grace, would experience perfection or complete sanctification in this life as a culminating event in their spiritual development (see John L. Peters, *Christian Perfection and American Methodism*, p. 33 et passim. See also pp. 396–99 in Volume 1. The basic notion of going on to perfection was, of course, not new with Wesley. It was fundamental to Eastern Orthodox and Roman Catholic ethics, very prominent in most monastic movements, and in another form, a major theme in William Ellery Channing's Unitarianism. What most distinguished Wesley's version was his stress on two distinct works of grace and two equally distinct and separated personal experiences; both regeneration and sanctification were climactic events.

in the great surge of perfectionism that swept almost every denomination after 1835 and figured prominently in the great revival of 1858. Soon after the war, when the momentum of this movement was renewed, Methodists, North and South, were in the vanguard as before. A distinct "Holiness Revival" can be traced from the celebrations of Methodism's American centenary in 1866, and a year later a "Holiness camp meeting" at Vineland, New Jersey, was attended by such stirring results that the National Camp Meeting Association for the Promotion of Holiness was organized. Year after year its work was extended, and its conquests in Methodist circles were impressive. Many bishops rallied to the cause, as did the first presidents of the newly founded Drew Seminary and Syracuse University.

In a sense, however, the successes were too great, for many nondenominational Holiness associations were formed, and in these circles a separatistic "come-outer" movement began to arise during the 1880s. By 1888 there were 206 full-time Holiness evangelists in the field, though most of them lacked regular assignments from ecclesiastical superiors. An independent press was also flourishing, and many autonomous ministers were gathering independent congregations in all parts of the country, some in the rural South, most of them in the northern and far-western cities. Especially as they worked among the urban poor, these ministers discovered, as had the Salvation Army long before, that the needs of converts virtually required the organization of independent churches.

In the face of these trends Methodist bishops began to grow apprehensive. Theologians meanwhile became alarmed by the degree to which faith-healing, premillennialism, and other radical conceptions were gaining ground wherever Holiness flourished. Perhaps the most basic aspect of the antagonism, however, was the gradual drift of Methodist church practice away from the old Wesleyan landmarks and toward the sedate forms of middle-class Protestantism. The climax came in 1893 and 1894, when the truce between the Methodist churches and the Holiness associations ended. Secessions and expulsions became common during the turn of century decades. Since perfectionists are almost by definition censorious in their judgments of the worldliness of others, subschisms continued to occur.

Even as a disintegrative tendency accelerated, the need for

coordination and fellowship led to new kinds of reintegration within the Holiness movement. Gradually an ordering process began to dissipate the chaos of competing evangelists, independent congregations, and loosely organized non-denominational associations. The result was by no means a single denomination, but two tendencies did become noticeable: the moderate one which the term "Holiness" designates, and a more extreme alternative, which adopted the name "Pentecostal." The Church of the Nazarene best exemplifies the more moderate tendency; the Assemblies of God the more radical. Each is also the largest of its type.

The Church of the Nazarene came into existence in 1908 at Pilot Point, Texas, when two predominantly urban northern groups, the Association of Pentecostal Churches, whose center of gravity was New York and New England, and the Church of the Nazarene which stemmed from the work of Phineas F. Bresee[9] in Southern California, joined forces with the Holiness Church of Christ, a consolidation of rural southern congregations stretching from Tennessee to Texas. The components of this new church were rather diverse, for each was itself a federation with a complex history. Yet the action taken at Pilot Point dramatized the uniformity of conviction within this widespread Holiness Revival. It also revealed a trend away from interdenominational associations toward a more denominational understanding of the movement, and away from extreme congregationalism toward a connectional conception of the church that owed much to Methodism.

[9] Bresee (1838–1915) also became the new church's first general superintendent. His career was remarkable. Born in western New York, he grew up in Iowa, where he was "converted" in 1856. A year later he was assisting on a Methodist circuit, and in 1861 was ordained an elder. When only twenty-three he was assigned to a fine church in Des Moines and made an editor of the Iowa Conference paper. He was respected as a leader of his church in the area. During the winter of 1866–67 Bresee experienced complete sanctification. Moving to California in 1883, he became minister of the First Methodist Church in Los Angeles, as well as a presiding elder and a prominent civic leader. With the arrival of a hostile bishop, however, the Holiness movement ran into determined opposition, and in 1895 Bresee left the Methodist church rather than abandon a mission to the poor which he was conducting. This very mission could probably be regarded as the nucleus of the later Church of the Nazarene (see T. L. Smith's excellent history *Called Unto Holiness*).

Future years brought mergers with other equally complex groups. Nazarene evangelism, meanwhile, won many converts. Yet the church retained a character of its own. It gloried in the grace that was free to all men, and especially in the "second blessing" that came to the sanctified. On this score there is much truth to their claim that they adhere to Wesley's "grand depositum" with greater fidelity than mainline Methodism. In polity, the church reflects the overwhelming preponderance of Methodists among its early leadership, though it has introduced a larger measure of congregational autonomy and democratic government. From the first it has been a church of simple dedicated people who were eager to carry the gospel and a strict perfectionist code of morals to the strata of society which the older denominations were unable to reach despite the valiant efforts of their home mission boards. In theology they were, of course, conservative; and they were suspicious of higher learning. Nearly all of them were in a technical sense Fundamentalists, yet their passions and goals were oriented not so much toward doctrinal purity as toward true Christian experience. Social mobility would affect them as it did all other American groups; and by 1969, when they numbered 350,882 members, their primitive fervor was considerably attenuated and their interest in education much increased. Some Nazarenes were even thinking of reunion with the church that had treated perfectionism with such hostility in the 1890s. In this respect the Church of the Nazarene is a remarkable American instance of a nearly full sectarian cycle.

Pentecostalism and the Assemblies of God

Most Pentecostal churches are, like the Nazarenes, unions of like-minded groups that received their initial impulse from Methodism and the Holiness Revival. Yet their historian does not exaggerate when he states that through this movement "a new element was introduced into the religious life *of the world.*"[10]

Charismatic gifts had, of course, come to many in times past, not least to Saint Paul and the converts he addressed in his epistles. In revivals of all ages in church history, including the Holiness Revival, people had experienced the "latter rain" spoken of by the prophet Joel (2:21–32) and referred to by

10 Irwin Winehouse, *The Assemblies of God*, p. 11. Italics mine.

Saint Peter in the classic Pentecostal passage (Acts 2:1–20).
And on 1 January 1901, the gift of the Spirit came to Agnes
N. Ozman, a student in Bethel Bible College, recently
founded in Topeka, Kansas, by Charles F. Parham, a prominent Holiness evangelist. From this event can be traced a
powerful movement which by 1970 was claiming a worldwide membership of over eight million. Soon most of the
other Bethel students began to speak languages which they
could not understand. A period of quiescence and ridicule
followed, but after Parham's gifts of divine healing became
known in 1903, the movement spread to various scattered
Holiness groups.

In 1906, via Texas, Pentecostalism reached Los Angeles. A
great outpouring of the Spirit came to the Azusa Street Mission, which under the leadership of the black minister William J. Seymour became a radiating center of Pentecostalism.
From Azusa Street the message was soon carried to all parts
of the country. When the news reached North Carolina and
the Holiness movement consolidated by A. J. Tomlinson in
the area around Cleveland, Tennessee, the result was especially momentous. In 1908 Tomlinson himself received the
baptism of the Spirit, whereupon the Pentecostal seed was
soon sown in Alabama, Georgia, and Florida.[11] So it went
in other directions as well, though it moved chiefly where
Holiness movements were prospering, attracting in the process
many more non-Methodists, usually Baptists, than had the
earlier forms of perfectionism, and planting the seed for
much future contention on the issue of connectional as
against congregational church polity.

Speaking with tongues is not the only distinctive feature of
the churches in this fellowship. A strong belief in divine
healing, a distrust of medical care, and an extremely Puritanic
code of personal behavior are other marks. From the start,
moreover, Pentecostalists were also theological conservatives,
and in all phases of the Fundamentalist controversy they took

---

[11] Of the approximately two hundred religious groups named the
Church of God, five have their headquarters in Cleveland, Tennessee, a common origin in A. J. Tomlinson, and a general emphasis
on justification by faith, being born again, sanctification, baptism
of the Holy Spirit, speaking in tongues, fruitfulness in Christian
living, and a strong interest in the premillennial Second Coming
of Christ. Forty-four Protestant denominations are attributed to
Tomlinson's work.

a clear stand for scriptural infallibility. Their Methodist lineage, however, aligned them with Holiness groups in resisting the attempts of more distinctly Reformed denominations to make predestination one of the Fundamentals. They thus added a large militant faction to the Arminian wing of Protestant conservatism. The movement was also deeply marked by dispensational premillennialism; from the start it has interpreted the Pentecostal outpouring as a fulfillment of prophecy and a sign of the Last Days. The imminence of Christ's return is therefore believed and taught.

As the movement grew, the need for some kind of coordination became more and more apparent, especially to support missionaries already being sent to foreign lands by local groups. Almost the only persons to have some view of the whole movement, or a large part of it, were the editors of a growing number of periodicals, so it was appropriate that one of these, Eudorus N. Bell, who published *Word and Witness* in Malvern, Arkansas, should initiate organizational measures. In December 1913, Bell issued a call for all "saints who believe in baptism with the Holy Ghost" to meet in April 1914 in Hot Springs, Arkansas, for the purpose of providing means to coordinate and propagate Pentecostalism more effectively.

Three hundred enthusiastic delegates from every region of the country convened at the appointed time, and after three days of devotional services, they displayed remarkable unanimity in adopting a preamble and a statement of organizational purpose and in electing an executive presbytery. This presbytery was first intended to be merely a permanent committee to guide the affairs of autonomous local assemblies which would send delegates to an annual council, but it became the executive agency of a new fellowship, the Assemblies of God. The two leading periodicals were merged and moved to Findlay, Ohio, where within four months they had a joint subscription list numbering twenty-five thousand. A school was also founded, with former editors Bell and J. Russell Flower on the faculty. Bell was also president of the Incorporated General Council, and Flower was its secretary.[12]

12 Bell had gone to Stetson College in Florida, then to the Baptist Seminary in Louisville, before going to the University of Chicago Divinity School for his B.D. He was a Baptist minister when he received the baptism of the Spirit in 1908, and a year

By similar processes other Pentecostal organizations were formed, most notably the black movement which also stemmed from the Azusa Street outpouring and attained a membership as large as that of the Assemblies.[13] In 1949, when the Pentecostal Fellowship of North America held its second convention, it could claim eight denominations with a total membership of one million.[14] Two decades later Pentecostalists in the United States numbered over 1.5 million. By this time they had demonstrated an amazing capacity for both rural and urban evangelism. Inevitably, the sectarian cycle was also in evidence.[15] They were holding well-organized world conferences, and actively participated in the National Association of Evangelicals and were represented by two small Chilean churches in the World Council of Churches. They had become interested in advanced theological education, and had begun to experience internal dissension because of these accommodationist tendencies. As if to dramatize this trend, Oral Roberts, who rose to national fame as a Pentecostal preacher, healer, and television sensation, had become a Methodist in 1965.

In the later sixties, however, a surprising renewal of charismatic religion would take place and not only among the usual constituencies but in the very movements and age-groups that were most animated by counter-cultural aims. But this revival is treated below (pp. 605–7, n. 6) in connection with its broader social context.

---

later he became a Pentecostal minister in Malvern. Flower was Canadian-born but had grown up in Illinois. In 1913, when the Pentecostal movement was confronted by the rapid spread of a "Jesus Only" form of Unitarianism, the Assemblies of God lost 156 ministers, including Eudorus Bell, in a great defection.

[13] The place of Pentecostalism in the black churches is considered in chap. 62 below. The Pentecostal awakening is surely an important instance of the direct influence of Afro-American religion on American Christianity.

[14] John Thomas Nichol, *Pentecostalism*, p. 217.

[15] In a class by itself is the International Church of the Foursquare Gospel founded in 1927 by Aimee Semple McPherson (1890–1944). The declaration of faith professed by its ninety thousand members contains the Pentecostal distinctives, but her flamboyant ministry, her masterful fund-raising capacities, and the $1.5 million Angelus Temple which she built in Los Angeles make it a very atypical denomination. At her death the board of directors conveyed the leadership to her son.

The Churches of Christ

Around the turn of the century, when the Holiness and Pentecostal revivals were flourishing, still another expansive form of conservative Protestantism was differentiating itself from its more staid and accommodating parent denomination. The Churches of Christ, which at their request were counted separately in the federal religious census of 1906, were related to the Disciples of Christ much as the Holiness churches were to Methodism. Indeed, they considered themselves the only true restorers of the New Testament Church, and hence the only faithful followers of Thomas and Alexander Campbell, who had inaugurated the Restoration movement a century before.[16]

The state of affairs formally documented by this religious census had been slowly developing for a half-century, with Alexander Campbell's opposition to missionary societies and instrumental music nearly always the ostensible points of contention. Underlying these tensions, however, were economic and social cleavages. Conservatives were most numerous in the poor rural areas of the South where rustic forms of church life remained, and where a piano was a snobbish luxury. They were unspoiled by either middle-class manners or a seminary-educated clergy. In some broad sense these dissenters were Fundamentalists, especially on the question of biblical inerrancy and closely related issues, but for the rest, they were immured behind a Campbellian wall, going their own way without cooperation, consultation, or coordination with anyone but themselves, and as a result, they were relatively insulated from millennialism, perfectionism, and glossolalia. Most of their controversies and doctrinal questions involved points that only other Restorationists could understand.[17] So radically congregational were they, more-

[16] In 1809 Thomas Campbell had pointed the road away from sectarianism with his *Declaration and Address*. The leaders of the Cane Ridge revival of 1801 wrote *The Last Will and Testament of the Springfield Presbytery* in 1804; Alexander Campbell preached his *Sermon on the Law* in 1816; and representatives of Stonite and Campbellite parties in the "Christian" movement merged their efforts in 1832.

[17] This is not an innocent or hasty assertion. Despite their persistent demand for unity, the Disciples have found it very

over, and so opposed to hierarchies and human creeds, that they could make their secession official only by publishing lists of local churches which were in fellowship—or by a statistic in the Census Report. So it was that literal allegiance to Alexander Campbell's program for transcending Christian division resulted in one of America's most robust examples of rigorous exclusivism.

Neither apartheid nor the refusal to form official missionary agencies, however, prevented the Churches of Christ from expanding. They have proselytized with great earnestness and vigor, while demonstrating sufficient flexibility to keep the allegiance of socially mobile members desiring fine church buildings, good (but noninstrumental) music, graded Sunday schools, church-connected colleges, and well-educated preachers. They have become the most dynamic large denomination in the South, and have developed considerable strength in other sections and abroad.[18]

SUMMARY

No aspect of American church history is more in need of summary and yet so difficult to summarize as the movements of dissent and reaction that occurred between the Civil War and World War I. Even the reasons for the difficulty are obscure, though they surely are related to the differences between this period of ferment and that which preceded the

---

difficult to participate in ecumenical discussions unless they abandon their "landmarks." This applies with special force to the ultraconservative Churches of Christ. Of the nine critical issues that cause dissension within the Churches of Christ and separate them from other conservative Disciples, few if any have any important place in the controversies of other Christian churches, Catholic or Evangelical (see James DeForest Murch, *Christians Only: A History of the Restoration Movement*).

[18] Numbering only 159,688 members in 693 churches in 1906, they had probably exceeded 2 million members in 16,500 churches by 1969. By this time they had spread across the entire land—though the 4 churches in North Dakota must be compared with more than 2,000 in Texas. Four liberal arts colleges began to have an influence on the denomination's intellectual and theological attitudes (see Edwin S. Gaustad, "Churches of Christ in America," in *The Religious Situation: 1969*, ed. Donald R. Cutler, pp. 1013–33).

Civil War. The postwar era lacked the spiritual foundation provided by an aggressive and self-confident Protestant majority against which even Shakers, Mormons, and Oneida perfectionists, not to mention Roman Catholics and Jews, could orient themselves. After 1865 the problems of Reconstruction, urbanization, immigration, natural science, and modern culture destroyed the great evangelical consensus, leaving a situation wherein dissenters were merely angry and frustrated. Increasingly, conservatives and liberals simply lost contact with each other, both culturally and religiously. Social and economic factors also seem to loom larger as divisive forces. Even the patterns of anti-Catholicism reflected this change, in that nontheological factors became predominant.

The older middle-class churches, whether countrified or urban, often exhibited a kind of birthright complacency even when they rejected liberal theology. These staid and predictable church ways alienated many and simply failed to attract others—who then sought religious solace where more earnestness and old-time fervor prevailed. Others reacted directly against theological departures from tradition and sought to reverse the tide of "apostasy" within their own communions or by joining more militant groups. Whether these conflicts, secessions, and new church formations were occasioned by doctrinal or more institutional forms of discontent, they all revealed deep fissures in Protestantism which wartime patrioteering could briefly close over, but which would open again and widen disastrously in the years after World War I.

49

THE "AMERICANISM" CRISIS IN THE CATHOLIC CHURCH

In 1898 a book appeared in Paris with a provocative question in its title, *Father Hecker, Is He a Saint?* The author, Charles Maignen, a Vincentian priest, answered this question with a shrill negative. But his attack was only one element of a great campaign being waged against the perils of "Americanism." The American founder of the Paulists, more than a decade after his death, had become a vital factor in a French ideological conflict which shook the Third Republic down to its hastily constructed foundations. That the matter had still wider implications is suggested by the fact that the imprimatur for this polemic was issued not by the archbishop of Paris, but by Monsignor Alberto Lepidi, master of the Sacred Palace at the papal court in Rome—who was also having an English edition prepared. In the United States, meanwhile, an equally acrimonious controversy was involving the entire Roman Catholic church, from several very prominent archbishops down to many parish priests and laymen. Ultimately it would take a papal encyclical to quiet the international waters; but by that time a major chapter in American church history would have been enacted.

"Americanism" in one or another of its manifold forms has always been a problem for the rest of the world; and many Europeans, both before and since King George III, have wrestled with its mysteries. As noted in earlier chapters, both John Carroll, the first American bishop, and Orestes Brownson reflected the antitraditional impact of American conditions in their proposals for the Roman Catholic church. Fa-

ther Hecker's special concern for the American problem
became a matter for direct papal action. In this sense the
"Americanism crisis" has very early origins and a long eventful prehistory.

The climax of this long development occurred in the two
last decades of the nineteenth century—decades that were no
less critical for Protestants and Jews, and for similar reasons.
In addition to a complex of issues more or less peculiar to the
Roman Catholic church, the crisis involved many major
aspects of the national experience; but the basic circumstance
was increasingly rapid growth—in overall size, in ethnic
diversity, and in administrative complexity. And behind all
was the steady pressure of Catholic immigration and American nativism.

The decade of the 1850s marked a new order of magnitude
in the history of American immigration (see table, p. 208
above), and it understandably resulted in the high tide of political Know-Nothingism. During the Civil War, however,
American Catholics had loyally identified themselves with the
sections in which they lived. The war thus underlined the
truth of what the older group of Anglo-American Catholics
had always insisted, that membership in the Roman church
did not preclude participation in American life and a sharing
of the nation's culture. It is very significant that the overt
anti-Catholicism of the 1840s and 1850s passed from the
American scene, even though many grounds for contention
remained.

With the return of peace, the Second Plenary Council held
in Baltimore in October 1866 proceeded with the task of
unifying the ecclesiastical discipline of the reunited church.
The presence of seven archbishops and thirty-eight bishops
and the council's recommendations for two metropolitan sees
and ten new dioceses testified to the church's rapid growth.
The optimism that pervaded this great assembly as well as
the sense of identification with the national purposes that it
expressed was put to the test three years later, when Pope
Pius IX convoked an ecumenical council in the Vatican to
deal with the question of papal infallibility. Most of the
American bishops regarded further definition of this doctrine
to be inopportune, and they made no secret of their opinions
during the long deliberations that ensued. Only one American bishop stayed to register his opposition, but they all re-

turned home with a new apologetic burden to bear in democratic America.[1] Their known disposition, moreover, probably had some bearing on the decision of Rome to convoke the Third Plenary Council of the American hierarchy in 1884.

The agenda for this great ecclesiastical assembly was crowded with technical questions having to do with the jurisdiction of bishops, clergy, and religious orders, as well as many matters affecting relations between the Vatican and the American church, such as the procedures for naming or translating bishops, and the kind of supervision of American affairs which the Congregation de Propaganda Fide would continue to carry out. The need for a separate system of parochial schools was also stressed. In response to the pleas of the Americans, Archbishop James Gibbons of Baltimore, rather than a Roman prelate, was named as the apostolic delegate to the council. Also evidencing the fact that the church was not "foreign" were many fervently patriotic statements by those bishops who were most convinced that American circumstances were ideal for the flourishing of the Catholic church. There is little doubt that both the size and the decisions of the Plenary Council made many American prelates feel a need to demonstrate the church's solicitude for the spirit of American democracy.

Nor did the growth of the church during the three postwar decades contradict the optimism expressed in 1884. By 1895 the number of dioceses had risen to seventy-three and the number of provinces to fourteen. The Catholic population rose from about 3 million in 1860 to about 7 million in 1880 to an estimated 12.5 million in 1895.[2] While the attendant problems of expansion accumulated, however, the Vatican was beset by many difficulties of its own.

[1] Bishops Edward Fitzgerald of Little Rock, Arkansas, and Luigi Riccio of Cajazzo registered the only two negatives in the final vote on the council's constitution on papal infallibility.

[2] These estimates are interpreted in Thomas O'Gorman, *A History of the Roman Catholic Church in the United States* ACHS, vol. 9 (New York, 1895), pp. 493–500. The concluding portion of O'Gorman's history on the 1865–95 period is a remarkable instance of the uneasiness that was widespread in the church. He devotes many pages to a defense of the church's modes of jurisdiction and the problems of "foreign" Catholics, but, despite his own involvement in the events of the day, gives no account of the controversies that preoccupied both the American hierarchy and the Vatican.

THE EMBATTLED CHURCH OF ROME

Not since the Reformation had the Roman Catholic church been more seriously threatened than it was during the later nineteenth century. In 1870, without even allowing the Vatican council a decent adjournment, the armies of a united Italy, having long since taken possession of the Papal States, entered Rome and stripped the pope of his last vestige of temporal power, leaving him a prisoner of the Vatican until the Concordat of 1929. In 1878 an angry Roman mob impeded the funeral procession of Pope Pius IX and almost succeeded in throwing his bier into the Tiber. In France, meanwhile, the friendly regime of Napoleon III collapsed into the fierce anticlericalism of the Paris Commune, which was in turn followed by the Third Republic, in which the church's legal stake depended on a declining royalist tradition that would finally break down between 1904 and 1907 in the tumults of the Dreyfus affair and a harsh renewal of anticlerical legislation. Bismarck, on the other hand, followed his French victories with a campaign against Roman Catholic power in the newly proclaimed German Empire, while the multinational Austro-Hungarian Empire lumbered on, its rulers treating the church with a kind of cynical utilitarianism, as nationalistic minorities added anticlericalism to their diversified appeals for support. Everywhere in Europe the urban working classes—as Marxist and anarchist advocacy strengthened their self-consciousness—were singling out the church as the keystone of an outmoded social order. Even in Bavaria, where Catholic romantics had made Munich a center of revival, these tendencies were visible. In America, immigration steadily increased ethnic tensions within the church itself, while nativists of assorted hues conducted an anti-Catholic *Kulturkampf* of their own. "Americanism" became a critical issue during the years when the American Protective Association was at the height of its influence.

The American Problem

An institutional crisis usually involves conflict between radically opposed proposals for present and future action. The Roman Catholic Americanism crisis was no exception. The crisis, as we shall see, was a complex of at least a dozen interconnected questions, but it is punctuated by the clash of two opposing groups or factions. Inevitably, the largest was a traditional party that simply assumed Catholicism and the American way of life to be fundamentally at odds. Pope Pius IX with his detailed Syllabus of Errors (1864) had provided support for such a stand, and Leo XIII, surprisingly, would bolster this support in the 1890s. All that conservative Catholics hoped for, therefore, was a kind of mutually advantageous truce between two hostile cultures. Most militant in this regard were the Germans. Strengthened by the immigration of seven hundred thousand of their countrymen between 1865 and 1900, supported by powerful agencies in Europe, and possessing a rich and deep theological tradition, they were strong enough in many areas to be highly self-conscious. Yet at the same time they were a defensive minority in an Irish-dominated church. The Midwest was their stronghold, and Milwaukee, Chicago, and Saint Louis were powerful centers of influence. Polish Catholics tended to be of a similar mind, though they were not numerically strong.[3]

Allied with these groups was a large body of conservatives (clearly a majority) among the Irish clergy, who had so long defined themselves by their opposition to Anglo-Saxon culture that anything but the most utilitarian kinds of participation in American life seemed to imply a betrayal of their heritage. Indisputably at the head of this group was Archbishop Michael A. Corrigan (1839–1902), a former professor of dogmatics at Seton Hall (New Jersey) and a stern administrator of the New York archdiocese. Corrigan's constant adviser and supporter was the bishop of his suffragan see in Rochester, Bernard McQuaid (1823–1909), an older former president of Seton Hall whose great cultivation and intelligence did little to moderate either his theology or his ecclesiastical tactics. He was confident and articulate, and his parochial school system and seminary stood as models for the nation.

[3] Though small in the 1880s, the Polish minority would soon become large. The peak of Polish immigration came in 1912–13 when 175,000 arrived; during and after World War II 100,000 would arrive. Numbering 5 million by 1960, the Polish constituency had joined the Irish, Italian, and German as one of the four largest in the church. It had 500 priests, 7,000 nuns, and supported 585 elementary schools (See Aloysius J. Wycislo, "The Polish Catholic Immigrant," in *Roman Catholicism and the American Way of Life*, ed. Thomas T. McAvoy, pp. 179–87).

Among the Americanists four men consistently played leading roles. Chief among them was the archbishop of Baltimore, James Gibbons (1834–1921), after 1886 a cardinal. As the nominal primate of the American church he avoided a stridently partisan role, yet on almost every issue his very powerful influence was exerted in the progressive cause. Far more active was John Ireland (1838–1918), the outspoken and enormously energetic archbishop of Saint Paul. Metropolitan of a vast, rapidly growing midwestern province, he irritated eastern bishops by advertising western opportunities and even by arranging colonization projects with the railroads. His enthusiasm for the American system was boundless; his confidence in the nation's destiny well-nigh absolute. More avidly than any other American prelate, he sensed the advantages of full Roman Catholic participation in American politics and social affairs. He tended to the Republican party, for example, chiefly to prevent the Democrats from taking Catholics for granted. Having been sent to France by Bishop Cretin of Saint Paul for nearly all of his education, he remained a close observer of European affairs and never allowed his Americanism to be narrow or jingoistic. The other two leading Americanist voices were John J. Keane (1839–1918), the bishop of Richmond who became the first rector of Catholic University of America in Washington, D.C., and Monsignor Denis O'Connell (1849–1927), rector of the North American College in Rome, a later rector of Catholic University, and bishop of Richmond. Though occupying less lofty positions in the church, they made innumerable contributions, especially O'Connell, who served as a kind of Americanist agent at the Vatican.

Cardinal Gibbons was born five years after his father emigrated, but the other three Americanist leaders were born in Ireland to families which had felt the force of that island's woe. With deep personal memories of poverty and insecurity, they all showed marked solicitude for the immigrant and the laboring man. They were committed to democratic institutions and the full-scale participation of Catholics in American life, yet they also considered the theoretical questions of the day with a thoughtfulness not usually expected of ecclesiastical dignitaries. All four were more or less consciously moving along lines marked out by Father Hecker and the Paulists; and this commitment gave coherence to their advocacy on the whole complex of issues which are here brought under the single rubric of Americanism. So constantly interlaced were these controversies, however, that in the account which follows, chronological ordering must yield to a thematic discussion.

The German Campaign

The place to begin is with the conflict between Irish and German Catholics which had erupted repeatedly during the earlier struggle with trusteeism. After the Civil War, when many areas and, in some cases, whole dioceses became predominantly German, these tensions took on the character of cultural conflict. Not only were the Germans in general in a more favorable economic situation than the Irish, but they, like their Lutheran compatriots, were convinced that the Christian message could be safely conveyed only in their mother tongue. Despite Protestant resistance, they founded German-language parochial schools, accused the Irish of compromise and doctrinal laxity, and sought to end the subordination of German-speaking Catholics in the hierarchy and in the parochial organization of cities.

Several aspects of this problem as well as other questions relating to monasticism were raised by the arrival of the German Benedictines under Boniface Wimmer, who had already played a leading role in the reestablishment of his order in Bavaria. Receiving encouragement and land from Bishop Michael O'Connor of Pittsburgh, Wimmer founded Saint Vincent's Abbey in 1846. When the question of exempted status for this institution arose, conflict with the bishop occurred. Through their powerful friends in Bavaria, the Benedictines prevailed in Rome, and in 1855 the pope authorized a self-governing Benedictine congregation in America, naming Wimmer its abbot. Thereafter still other monasteries were founded, most notably in Minnesota, where Saint John's Abbey under its powerful abbot was soon creating problems for another Irish prelate, Archbishop Ireland of Saint Paul. Ireland seemed to share Father Hecker's reservations about traditional monasticism, and he made no secret of his displeasure at having semi-autonomous monasteries in his own province. At the installation of Thomas O'Gorman in Sioux Falls, South Dakota, in 1896, he publicly advised the new bishop to keep his diocese free of such institutions.

Not all Germans were monks; but nearly all of them drank beer, and Abbot Wimmer himself complained that only fanaticism could require monks to drink water. (Not even the Trappists do that, he maintained.) When Bishop O'Connor sought to close Saint Vincent's brewery, the abbot was also able to get papal authorization for its continuance. The incident, aside from the question of jurisdiction, aggravated a long-smoldering moral dispute. Before 1900 the Irish prelates generally and those of Americanist leanings in particular tended to be fervent temperance advocates. Interested as they were in the social welfare of their constituency, they saw the Irishman's drinking habits as a serious disability. The temperance controversy did not involve fundamental theological issues, but it caused much irritation and ill-feeling, and it continued to be a divisive factor until the political activities of the Protestant-dominated Anti-Saloon League and passage of the Eighteenth Amendment gradually created a nearly unified Catholic opposition to political prohibitionism.

Riding the crest of a great Catholic renaissance that was proceeding on the Continent, the Benedictines, on the other hand, agitated for far more than breweries. They reenlivened a monastic ideal that many had regarded as outmoded; their seminaries defended a rigorous theological tradition which gave prestige to German Catholicism. Through their influence in Europe, moreover, they won financial support from the Ludwig Missionsverein in Bavaria and the Leopoldinen Stiftung in Austria, and joined with others to convince powerful European Catholics that funds for missionary work among the Germans must bypass the Irish-dominated American hierarchy. As these efforts led to or coalesced with two other important developments, the "German question" assumed considerable significance in America.

Peter Paul Cahensly was a dedicated Roman Catholic businessman of Limburg-an-der-Lahn in Nassau who in 1871 organized the Saint Raphael Society to aid and protect German immigrants. Through these activities he also became linked with Catholic missionary movements in other countries. In 1890 the international convention of Saint Raphael Societies prepared a document which in the following year was presented to the Holy See. This memorial grossly exaggerated immigrant losses to the church and pleaded for arrangements that would make the institutions of the American church (parishes, schools, seminaries, bishops, etc.) formally multilingual and multinational. It also requested a cardinal protector in Rome to supervise the work of the Saint Raphael societies. In this way "Cahenslyism" brought European support to an American movement organized by the Germans to achieve the same ends.

The basic cause of dissatisfaction among German Catholics in America was the subordinate position to which their priests, parishes, and schools seemed to be relegated by the English-speaking (Irish) hierarchy. German priests in Saint Louis petitioned against these practices, but in 1886 the issue was drawn more sharply when Father Peter M. Abbelen, vicar general of the Milwaukee archdiocese, with the support of Archbishop Heiss, presented in Rome a memorial pleading not only for equal parochial status for German churches, but for regulations that would assign German laity to these churches regardless of parish boundaries. When the contents of this memorial became known, considerable public furor arose; but the counterstatement of four eastern archbishops and the representations of Ireland, Keane, and O'Connell, who happened to be in Rome, contributed to the memorial's rejection in 1887. German Catholics continued to resist and to criticize nearly all the projects and activities of the Americanist bishops.

Against the background of ethnic rivalry, the other old issue of public education and parochial schools continued to simmer. In fact, one of the irritations behind the Abbelen memorial was the silence of the Irish bishops in the Midwest when Wisconsin's Bennett Law of 1889 was passed, forcing all children to attend schools in their own districts rather than consolidated Catholic schools and requiring the use of English in all major subjects. Archbishop Ireland was a special irritant, not only because he advocated the use of English in churches and schools, but because he had publicly praised the work of the public schools, despite the demands of the last Plenary Council (1884) that parish schools be founded wherever possible. Ireland doubted that parochial schools were worth the outlay required, and he seemed convinced that the welfare of the immigrant would be improved by a free public educational system. For these reasons he tried to work out a scheme for the cooperation of church and state in education, the so-called Fairibault Plan, whereby the town took over parochial schools, paid approved Catholic teachers, and allowed religious education after school hours. By dint of extraordinary efforts and another trip to Rome in 1891, he gained papal permission for this plan, but Protestant opposition doomed it in any case. Here again was a perennial issue which remained alive to the end of the century and long after.

The school issue had only incidental ethnic overtones, and nearly all of the remaining issues divided "liberals" and "conservatives" on other grounds, a fact revealed very clearly by the agitation over the founding of Catholic University in Washington, D.C. Except within certain religious orders, American priests had usually received advanced training at the University of Louvain in Belgium or at the Propaganda College in Rome. In 1884, however, the Plenary Council had approved the founding of a university in the United States. Their decision resulted partly from the promise of a $300,000 gift, but it owed much to the eloquent plea made at the council by John Lancaster Spalding, the learned and philosophic bishop of Peoria. The opposition was strong: Bishop McQuaid in Rochester, Archbishop Corrigan in New York, and the Jesuits all feared a rival center of Americanist influence, and it took all that Spalding, Gibbons, Ireland, and Keane could do to win the assent of Pope Leo XIII. In 1889, its constitution approved, the pope appointed Bishop Keane of Richmond as rector. During the ensuing seven years Keane made the institution a powerful progressive force, but in 1896 his sudden removal from office came as a stunning blow to the liberal cause.

Keane's undoing as rector was probably related to still another matter on which he, Gibbons, and Ireland took a stand during his years of tenure: the church's relations with Protestantism. All three men clearly followed Father Hecker and the Paulists in seeking to improve relations and to open some kind of dialogue. In 1890, therefore, Keane accepted the invitation of President Eliot of Harvard to deliver the annual Dudleian Lecture in the college chapel. Bishop McQuaid refused to give him permission to address the Catholic Club at Cornell, however, and many conservatives were outraged not only by the act itself but by his very irenic lecture. When in 1893 the World Parliament of Religions was held in conjunction with the Chicago World's Fair, both Keane and Cardinal Gibbons participated, Gibbons even leading a recitation of the Lord's Prayer in the Protestant version at the opening session. On this occasion the conservative outcry was even more violent.

That this outcry did not remain simply a domestic controversy was due in part to still another incident connected with the world's fair. In Rome there had long been strong pressures for the assignment of an apostolic delegate to the United States, but because they were sensitive to Protestant charges of Catholic subservience to a "foreign potentate," and because they remembered Archbishop Bedini's catastrophic tour in 1853, the American bishops had always resisted such an innovation. The appointment of Archbishop Gibbons as apostolic delegate to the Plenary Council of 1884 was one result of their tact in this area. In 1892, however, the pope sent Francesco Satolli as a personal representative bearing certain memorabilia of Columbus to the Columbian Exposition. Satolli stayed on in America, and in due course he was invested as apostolic delegate and, after the termination of his office, was made a cardinal. His unfavorable estimate of the Americanists was almost certainly an element in the rising resistance to their program that became evident in Rome.

In the meantime a cluster of other issues was coming to a head, and Satolli became involved in them as well. These problems had to do with the economic predicament of immigrants, particularly the many Catholics employed as laborers in industries where working conditions required cooperative protection, organized bargaining, and political activity. In this context the question of secret societies arose. The Masonic order was, of course, anathema to European Catholics, and Pope Leo XIII had issued a new encyclical (*Humanum Genus*) on the subject in 1884. Conservatives naturally urged obedience to the letter, and Bishop McQuaid would even have banned the Ancient Order of Hibernians. The Americanists, however, were wont to recognize that societies such as the Odd Fellows, the Knights of Pythias, and many other similar lodges performed essential social and economic functions.

This issue soon was complicated by the emergence of the Knights of Labor as the country's first large labor union. Because its founder, Uriah Stevens, was addicted to secret practices and rituals, and because the counteractivity of employers almost made secrecy a necessity, the Knights of Labor undeniably was, among other things, a secret society. Archbishop Taschereau of Quebec took the lead as conservatives not only urged obedience to the papal encyclical, but sought explicit condemnation of the Knights. As usual it fell to Gibbons, Keane, and their cohorts to prevent this blow from falling on the American labor movement with its heavy Catholic constituency. In 1886, the very year in which the union was involved in a critical test of strength, they met with Terence Powderly, then head of the Knights and also a Catholic, and, having determined that the secret oath had been discontinued, they then convinced all but two of the American archbishops to oppose condemnation. Due to this lack of unanimity, the issue was referred to Rome, but a year later, while Gibbons himself was in Rome, he personally and successfully averted the embarrassment which condemnation would have brought.

Closely related to the labor issue was the problem of Henry George and the economic theories which he had expounded with such great effect in *Progress and Poverty* (1879). The Knights of Labor had absorbed much of his thought, and in 1886 they supported his campaign for mayor in New York, where Archbishop Corrigan had a very satisfactory arrangement with Tammany Hall.[4] To compound matters, one of George's most eloquent supporters was Father Edward McGlynn, a very popular parish priest. The Archbishop disciplined the priest and sought to have George's book put on the Index for its unorthodox views on property; and only when Gibbons pleaded that the church not proclaim itself an enemy of the poor was this extreme action avoided, though the pope did publicly condemn socialism. After an extended consultation with the apostolic delegate, Father McGlynn had his excommunication lifted in 1892. McGlynn subsequently attested his utter concurrence with Pope Leo's encyclical *Rerum Novarum* (1891), with its famously liberal but antisocialistic espousal of the workingman's cause. The George affair, in fact, seems to have helped precipitate the encyclical, and it may be more than a coincidence that two months after the reinstatement of McGlynn, Pope Leo issued his celebrated encyclical to the French church, calling for a Catholic *ralliement* to the Republic.

[4] In 1894 Archbishop Ireland himself entered Archbishop Corrigan's province, campaigned for the Republican party, and used his influence to have a liberal priest rather than Bishop McQuaid elected to the New York State Board of Regents. McQuaid's public condemnation of this invasion was so severe that he was reprimanded by the pope.

THE CRISIS

As it happened, Pope Leo's *ralliement* and the question of Catholicism in the French Republic provided the setting for the final climactic stage of the Americanism crisis. The ideological and theological questions at stake were in the strictest sense of the term fundamental. The very presence of the Roman Catholic church in the United States posed the bedrock question as to how a huge ecclesiastical institution, which had emerged from the wreck of the Roman Empire, slowly structured itself according to principles of canon law, consolidated its authority during fifteen centuries of tumultuous European history, and defined its faith at the Councils of Trent and Vatican I, was to be regulated in a pluralistic democratic state in which churches existed as one kind of voluntary organization among others, and in which its members were scattered at random so far as their social, economic, and political relationships were concerned. The successor of Innocent III, Boniface VIII, and Pius IX faced a situation such as Western Christendom had never before presented to a pope. In the United States, moreover, was a thoughtful and articulate group of prelates and theologians, as well as a considerable body of laity, who were convinced that their country provided an excellent, possibly even the ideal, circumstance for the church to accomplish the transition to a modern social order. Archbishop Ireland had proclaimed this conviction in a stirring oration at the Plenary Council in 1884:

> There is no conflict between the Catholic Church and America. I could not utter one syllable that would belie, however remotely, either the Church or the Republic, and when I assert, as I now solemnly do, that the principles of the Church are in thorough harmony with the interests of the Republic, I know in the depths of my soul that I speak the truth. . . .
> Republic of America, receive from me the tribute of my love and my loyalty. . . . *Esto perpetua*. Thou bearest in thy hands the hopes of the human race, thy mission from God is to show to nations that men are capable of highest

civil and political liberty. . . . Believe me, no hearts love thee more ardently than Catholic hearts, . . . and no hands will be lifted up stronger and more willing to defend, in war and peace, thy laws and thy institutions than Catholic hands. *Esto perpetua.*[5]

He stated the essence of this message again and again in his visits to France—almost a second homeland to him—and he repeatedly made his views known in Rome.

Then in 1891 Father Walter Elliott published his famous *Life of Father Hecker,* a ringing panegyric, so filled with Hecker's own writing as to make it a kind of *apologia pro vita sua* as well. All of Hecker was there: not only his fervent insistence that America must become Catholic to realize its destiny fully, but also his views on the Holy Spirit, on the active and the passive virtues, and the statements that had provoked the charges of "minimism" and pro-Protestant heresy. The book appeared, moreover, just when the international convention of Saint Raphael Societies in Lucerne was memorializing the pope with a most extreme statement of the German charges against the American church leadership and a demand for division of the hierarchy. Their petition was denied in Rome, but Archbishop Ireland and many others—including some congressmen—inveighed against it, accusing "foreign powers" of interfering with American internal affairs.

Against this background—as well as that provided by all the other controversies discussed above—Pope Leo XIII in 1895 addressed an encyclical to the American church, *Longinqua Oceani.* This remarkable document, in the traditional manner of such statements, contains warm felicitations to "the young and vigorous American nation, in which We plainly discern latent forces for the advancement alike of civilization and Christianity." Other praise follows, but "the prosperous condition of Catholicity" is attributed above all "to the virtue, the ability, and the prudence of the bishops and clergy"; and the "main factor, no doubt" is said to be "the ordinances and decrees of your synods," for it had been an early insistence of Pope Leo that a plenary council be convened in order to regularize the country's ecclesiastical ar-

[5] Quoted in James H. Moynihan, *The Life of Archbishop John Ireland,* pp. 33–34.

rangements. Then follows the famous reservation which American anti-Catholic diatribes have never ceased to quote. Despite the obvious prosperity of American Catholicism,

> it would be very erroneous to draw the conclusion that in America is to be sought the type of the most desirable status of the Church, or that it would be universally lawful or expedient for State and Church to be, as in America, dissevered and divorced. The fact that Catholicity with you is in good condition, nay, is even enjoying prosperous growth, is by all means to be attributed to the fecundity with which God has endowed his Church, in virtue of which unless men or circumstances interfere, she spontaneously expands and propagates herself; but she would bring forth more abundant fruits if, in addition to liberty, she enjoyed the favor of the laws and the patronage of public authority.[6]

Still later, in explaining his recent establishment of an apostolic delegation, he makes a related statement that must have rankled many: "We have wished, first of all, to certify that, in Our judgment and affection, America occupies the same place and rights of other States, be they ever so mighty and imperial." In the paragraphs which followed, other recent controversies were recalled by specific references: to respect for bishops and "mutual charity" among them; to moderation and respectful language in widely circulating periodicals; to the right of "the working classes . . . to unite in associations for the promotion of their interests," but on the other hand their duty to shun both those which have been openly condemned by the church and "those also which, in the opinion of intelligent men, and especially of the bishops, are regarded as suspicious or dangerous." As to social life in general, "unless forced by necessity to do otherwise, Catholics ought to prefer to associate with Catholics, a course which will be very conducive to the safeguarding of their faith." Elsewhere there were the expected admonitions to morality and religious duty; but it was, all told, an unusually —perhaps unexpectedly—severe and conservative message to have come from the author of *Rerum Novarum* and *Au Milieu des Sollicitudes*. One wonders if in 1895 the pope

[6] John Tracy Ellis, *Documents of American Catholic History*, pp. 514–27.

would have sent Ireland on a speaking tour of France as he had in 1892. Beyond speculation are the facts that in 1895 O'Connell was removed from his post at the American College in Rome, and in 1896 Keane was replaced as rector of Catholic University.

Whatever their response to such questioning, the progressives continued to press their cause. In 1897 Elliott's biography appeared in France, with a rousing introduction by Archbishop Ireland and a preface by the Abbé Felix Klein, a professor at the Institut Catholique of Paris. Klein stated that "probably no book in the last fifty years has cast so luminous a beam on the present condition of humanity, on the religious development of the world, on the intimate relationships of God and the modern soul, or on the present-day requirements for the advancement of the Church." Ireland, in his introduction, confessed that Hecker's was the most salutary influence in his own life, proclaimed him "the ornament and jewel [*joyau*] of the American clergy" and a man for the priests of the future to take as their model.[7] As in America, so in France: the book was both praised and condemned. From pulpit and press attacks were mounted by royalists and extreme theological conservatives who had important connections in the Vatican, which at that time was also a vortex of many reactionary pressures.

Then the Spanish-American War broke out, with the United States attacking one of the old imperial powers to which Pope Leo had alluded in *Longinqua Oceani*. Factions were pressing their claims in the Curia; speculation and rumor were providing grist for adventurous journalists. Not surprisingly, therefore, the pope reserved the question of Americanism for an encyclical, and on 22 January 1899, a few days before Archbishop Ireland arrived in Rome with hopes of staving off a conservative pronouncement, *Testem Benevolentiae* finally appeared. It was an important—even an epoch-making—document. Never before or since, as Monsignor Ellis says, has the orthodoxy of the Roman Catholic church in the United States been "called in question," though it must be added that rarely has heresy been more ambiguously assigned. Yet this very ambiguity probably heightened the long-term effect of the encyclical. The document does, to be sure, say that "certain things are to be avoided

[7] Walter Elliott, *Le Père Hecker, Foundateur des "Paulistes" Americains* (Paris, 1897), pp. ii, xxxix, xl, lv.

and corrected"; on the other hand the pope's wording gave good grounds for progressives to accept Cardinal Rampolla's assurance that the encyclical's real purpose was to quiet the French. It refers to the French translation of Elliott's *Hecker,* and makes clear that various doctrines are in error, without asserting that either Hecker or any Americans had taught these doctrines. It also commends religious orders and the so-called passive virtues. Its tone is well conveyed in its concluding summation:

> Hence from all that we have hitherto said, it is clear, Beloved Son [the letter was sent to Cardinal Gibbons], that we cannot approve the opinions which some comprise under the head of Americanism. If, indeed, by that name be designated the characteristic qualities which reflect honor on the people of America . . . there is surely no reason why we should deem that it ought to be discarded. But if it is to be used . . . to commend the above doctrines, there can be no doubt but that our Venerable Brethren the Bishops of America would be the first to repudiate and condemn it, as being especially unjust to them and to the entire nation as well. For it raises the suspicion that there are some among you who conceive of and desire a church in America different from that which is in the rest of the world.[8]

All considered, it is hard to avoid the conclusion that the pope sought a general pacification in *both* America and Europe (especially in France), and that he was also giving a tangential rebuke to modernism wherever it might be advancing.

Modernism is the usual Roman Catholic term for the movement condemned by Pope Pius X in the encyclical *Pascendi*

[8] Ellis, *Documents,* pp. 553–62. The specific doctrines condemned in *Testem Benevolentiae* were (1) that "the Church ought to adapt herself [and] . . . show some indulgence to modern, popular theories and methods"; (2) that some ancient doctrines should now be suppressed or passed over; (3) that individuals may decide how the church should adjust to changing circumstances; (4) that a larger liberty of individual interpretation should be introduced into the church; (5) that the promptings of the Holy Ghost can be rightly discerned without the help of external guidance; and (6) that natural virtues are more to be extolled than the supernatural virtues.

Gregis of 1907. The movement aimed, in the words of its greatest representative, Alfred Loisy, "to adapt the Catholic religion to the intellectual, moral, and social needs of the present time" (roughly 1890–1910). Basically modernists sought "to face and accept the general development of modern scientific knowledge, and, in particular, the results of biblical and historical criticism. . . . And it was from this approach that they proceeded . . . to broach wider philosophical and theological questions."[9] Given the near conjunction and vague overlapping in content of *Testem Benevolentiae* and *Pascendi Gregis,* the question of modernism's strength in America is often raised. In fact, conservatives often accused the progressives of modernism. When the Catholic University church historian Thomas O'Gorman was made a bishop in Archbishop Ireland's province, critics made reference to his having studied under Louis Duchesne, a French historian whose critical methods aroused consternation in many quarters. The same critics found fault with several of Bishop Keane's statements and with Bishop John Lancaster Spalding's effusive idealism, which sometimes verged on the "ontologism" of which Brownson had seen accused.

These complaints did address an undeniable liberal current. Cardinal Gibbons and many others, for example, approved of Salvatore di Bartolo's limitation of biblical inerrancy to dogmatic issues—only to have this work placed on the Index (1891). Far more publicized was the case of Father John A. Zahm, a professor at Notre Dame University. During the very years when the Americanism agitation was at its height, the Holy Office ruled that his pro-Darwinian *Evolution and Dogma* (1896) could not be translated into other languages, and for a time threatened to put it on the Index. Zahm was, in effect, silenced. And in 1898 Father George Zurcher of Buffalo, New York, had his *Monks and Their Decline* placed on the Index. But these incidents were relatively isolated.

[9] In *Providentissimus Deus* (1893) Pope Leo had taken a very conservative position on critical studies of the Bible; and in 1907 Pope Pius X condemned "modernism" in *Pascendi Gregis* and published a comprehensive Syllabus of Errors (*Lamentabili Sane*). Alfred Loisy (1857–1940), who was expelled from the church in 1908, is quoted in Alec R. Vidler, *The Modernist Movement in the Roman Church,* p. 6.

Three basic facts remain. First, despite the liveliness of many liberal tendencies, the essential demand of modernists (for a doctrinal or theological accommodation of modern science and critical studies) had few if any explicit defenders in the United States. American "liberals" were not doctrinal reformers. In fact, even the most outspoken Americanist prelates (Ireland, for example) held firmly to traditional views. The same could be said for Cardinal Gibbons's very widely read apologetic work *The Faith of Our Fathers* (1877). Except on the church and state question, their "liberalism" tended to be practical, not doctrinal.

Second, during the half-century after the Civil War, the faith, practice, church order, theology, and scholarship of American Catholicism was firmly in conservative hands. Knowing themselves to be supported in Rome, the great majority of the bishops and clergy saw no great threat and some obvious things to admire in "Americanism," though specific controversies often provoked bitter feelings and harsh words. The term "crisis" may indeed be too strong, unless it be applied to a profound inner contradiction between tradition and modernity that even most Americanists only dimly saw, and that would become widely recognized only in the later twentieth century.

Third, the doctrinal pronouncements of Leo XIII and Pius X had a distinctly stultifying effect on Roman Catholic intellectual life everywhere in the church. Americans, says Father Ong, "were so chastened . . . that they turned more industriously than ever to developing 'know-how' and letting theory be."[10] One great period of American ferment was over, and another was not to begin until 1958, when Pope John XXIII inaugurated a new epoch in Roman Catholic history.

In 1908 Pope Pius X at last terminated the mission status of the American church. Shortly after that, the World War gave the hierarchy further occasion to organize itself to deal with the urgent problems of the nation. Rapid social change, two wars, a depression, continued immigration, and virulent renewal of nativism provided American Catholics sufficient occasion to exercise their practical bent. In the mid-twentieth century, however, many circumstances, both na-

[10] Walter J. Ong, *Frontiers in American Catholicism*, pp. 21–22. See also his *American Catholic Crossroads*, chap. 3.

tional and international, would enhance the reputation of the Americanists; and in the light of this new situation, church reformers like Hecker, O'Connell, Keane, and Ireland would be remembered not as defeated semiheretics, but as foresighted pioneers.

50

THE PROTESTANT ESTABLISHMENT AND THE NEW NATIVISM

"The halcyon years of American Protestantism" is the phrase used by a sensitive historian reflecting on his own experience as a minister during the closing decades of the nineteenth century.[1] In view of the social and intellectual turmoil that wracked the nation in that period, the name seems ironic, or perverse, or both. Yet his judgment is sound, and the explanatory fact of the matter is that liberalism's wrestling with evolution and historicism, like the Social Gospel's anguish over the inhumanity of industrialism, involved only a small troubled minority of the nation's vast Protestant host. In the slowly changing yet tradition-bound mainstream of American evangelicalism, Darwin and Wellhausen were remote heretics to be ridiculed or condemned by every itinerant revivalist. As for poverty, slums, and strikes—a rabble of foreigners, drunkards, anarchists, and Roman Catholics were the troublemakers. If the "money power" was behaving indecently, it was the fault of a corrupt few with aid from conniving politicians—and then there were the Jews. In any case, Protestantism derived its power and had its firm foundations far from the teeming multitudes.

The ascendant Protestant tradition was becoming increasingly homogenized. Revivalists could be nonsectarian without cramping their style. The hard edges of doctrinal polemic were directed against Catholics and the more extreme liberals, while hymnody, religious journalism, Sunday school study aids, and popular devotional literature covered over

[1] Gaius Glenn Atkins, *Religion in Our Times,* chap. 2. A fine retrospective volume.

the old differences that had divided British Protestantism into Baptists, Episcopalians, Quakers, Presbyterians, Congregationalists, and Methodists. This composite entity was the "Protestant Establishment" which enjoyed special prestige and many privileges even though it was not supported or regulated by the government. The absence of a regular Catholic chaplain in the army until the Civil War and in the navy until 1888 is symbolic of the situation. This legal arrangement rested, of course, on colonial foundations which had not been destroyed by the American Revolution. The antebellum evangelical crusades had strengthened them. Then after the Civil War, especially during the 1870s, a minor revolution in church-state relations had actually strengthened the legal status of Protestantism in state after state, putting roadblocks in front of the Roman juggernaut, and routing the pagans who would keep religion out of the public schools. Rutherford B. Hayes had used these issues in Ohio along the route to the presidency. Garfield was a quondam preacher. And in 1896 either a Democratic or a Republican victory would have brought a testifying evangelical to the White House. The "common-core Protestantism" which was emerging by no means lacked internal variations; yet the developing consensus was highly relevant for American culture and for later church unity movements.

THE EVANGELICAL MAINSTREAM

Numerically and theologically, two vast, widely dispersed communions, Methodist and Baptist, provided the popular base of American Protestantism. Both of them had been relatively small fringe groups in 1800, but they had grown to denominations that numbered, respectively, 4,589,284 and 3,717,969 by 1890. The Presbyterians, though displaced from their proud position of other days, were next with 1,231,072 communicants. There were also 750,000 Christians and Disciples of Christ, and 540,000 Congregationalists. Many small groups and sects shared similar views, but even leaving these less influential bodies aside, the mainstream denominations constituted 80 percent of American Protestantism, and about 55 percent of America's religiously affiliated population in 1890. The figures themselves are relatively mute, however, unless various unifying factors are noted.

The distinguishing mark with deepest roots in the past was the basic Reformed or Calvinistic lineage of these bodies. Except among the Episcopalians, most of them accepted as virtually axiomatic the radical program of church reform that had been developed in Switzerland and elsewhere on the Continent, then matured with particular importance for America in Scotland and England. To England's long Reformation travail was owed the additional fact that Puritanism laid the chief foundations of American religious life in nearly every colony. This meant an even greater intensification of Reformed radicalism and a tendency to see the menace of popery at every turn. To be sure, many of the proudest hopes of the early Puritans had been shattered even during the seventeenth century, but their moralism and strict views of private behavior, as well as their conviction that America was a model for the world, remained.

Beyond the Reformed and Puritan legacy, American evangelical Protestantism had for the most part accepted as an essential part of its being the ideas and practices of revivalism. Puritan piety provided the basic theology for this great strategy of church extension, but the hero-founder of the tradition in America was George Whitefield. After him it was enthusiastically adopted by the Congregationalists, Presbyterians, Dutch Reformed, and other groups of colonial American strength; but no groups did so much to bring the revival spirit to every farm, way station, village, and city as the Methodists and the Baptists.

The crucial doctrine of revivalism was that which made a specific conversion experience the essential mark of a true Christian. This emphasis accounts for the radically individualistic accent of revivalism and its large role in extinguishing the Puritan's concern for the Holy Commonwealth as a whole. Concentration upon the individual sinner led inexorably to a preoccupation with exceedingly personal sins. The resultant erosion of social ethics was noted even in colonial times, but the full effect of this tendency was not manifest until after the Civil War, when the rise of huge corporate entities began to complicate the moral life of nearly all Americans. As exemplified in the preaching of Moody and Sunday, revivalism tended to become socially trivial or ambiguous to the point of irrelevance. It was precisely these tendencies which made pious Christians like Rauschenbusch so harsh in their judgments of evangelicalism.

Another element which became almost symbiotic with revivalism was Arminianism, a doctrinal tendency whose name stemmed from an intramural dispute of the Netherlands Reformed church but whose propagation in America owed most to Wesley and the Methodists. Because an emphasis on man's free will was intrinsic to revivalism, the doctrines of unconditional, election and limited atonement lost their vitality. Practice of the "new measures" led to "New School" theology. By the end of the century double predestination was the pet doctrine of only the Hard-shell Baptists, a declining number of Old School Presbyterians, and a few smaller groups. In 1906, upon receiving back the Cumberland Presbyterians after a century of separation on this issue, the Presbyterian Church (North) formally revised the Westminster Confession to an Arminian reading; and by 1911 most of the Freewill Baptists, after an even longer separation, found the offending doctrine too weak to prevent reunion. As God's predestinating decrees passed from favor, the floodgates of emotionalism and sentimentality in religion were opened, with the result that the doctrine of human depravity was also threatened with inundation. Because revivalists so often addressed interdenominational audiences, moreover, nearly all doctrinal emphases tended to be suppressed, not only by the famous spellbinders, but by the thousands upon thousands of local ministers and now-forgotten regional itinerants. Gradually a kind of unwritten consensus emerged, its cardinal articles being the infallibility of the Scriptures, the divinity of Christ, and man's duty to be converted from the ways of sin to a life guided by a pietistic code of morals. Revivalism, in other words, was a mighty engine of doctrinal destruction. "Are you saved?" became the central question of American Protestantism; and more and more it came to mean, "Have you decided to be saved?"

In conjunction with these distinctly theological or ecclesiastical features, other "secular" convictions had taken on religious coloring. The ideas of democracy and the rights of the common man strengthened Arminianism, encouraged the development of democratic, laity-centered polities, and further minimized ancient distinctions that had marked off the status of the clergy. More basic was the almost universal American conviction that the United States had a mission to extend its influence throughout the world. To mainstream Protestants a denial of America's manifest destiny bordered on treason. Translated into theological categories, this meant that the American was characteristically a "postmillennialist." He believed that the Kingdom of God would be realized in history, almost surely in American history. His thought was also strongly tinctured wtih perfectionism. To orthodox New Englanders this had been heresy when they heard it from the lips of William Ellery Channing, or from the Methodists, or from Charles G. Finney; but the old heresy became the new orthodoxy as American idealism soared to new heights during the nineteenth century. Progress was both a personal and a social fact. And this change did not witness so much to an augmented conception of grace as to a profound shift in the prevailing notion of human nature.

Professor Mead points out that the United States had two religious heritages, one denominational and divisive, the other patriotic, rooted in the Enlightenment, and unitive: "The high degree of amalgamation of these two faiths took place in the decades following the Civil War."[2] The cumulative effect of these several factors was that American evangelical Protestantism came to resemble nineteenth-century Methodism in nearly every way except with regard to its hierarchical form of church government. This may have been why Theodore Roosevelt said that he never felt so sure that he was speaking to a typical American audience as when he addressed a Methodist gathering.

The great reservoir of Protestantism lay in the middle-class churches of rural and smalltown America until long after 1920, when the census finally revealed that most Americans were city dwellers. And because the steady movement of people to the city had a continuous shaping influence on urban Protestantism, the chief characteristics of the mainstream heritage are nowhere better seen than in the individual churches of this rural reservoir. They were not, of course, strictly identical. Keepers of community social registers could make the subtle distinctions for which their antennae were attuned. There were also significant regional differences. Sociology rather than theology explains most of the variations. Yet the institution as such assumed classic, recognizable, highly predictable lines.

The American Protestant congregation of the later nine-

[2] Sidney E. Mead, *The Lively Experiment*, pp. 135–36.

teenth century was a friendly place which fitted naturally and securely into the needs of the community. A newcomer there would be greeted by some local variant of the unique American greeting, "Howdy stranger." If he came somehow to the wrong church and the greeting was cool, he would find another where the people put him at ease, where the forms of prayer and praise came in accents familiar to his ears, where the minister "fitted in" and gave understandable sermons, where the hymns and the choir put no new demands on his musical tastes, and where the social converse after Sunday services and on many other weekday occasions—for men, women, and children alike—would be free of jarring notes or unexpected demands.

Perhaps nothing better expressed the piety pervading these institutions than the new hymnody which swept much of Isaac Watts, the older Reformed "psalms," and even much of British Methodism's fine treasury into disuse and oblivion. In their place came the gospel tunes of the new piety: "What a Friend We Have in Jesus" (1868), "Jesus Keep Me Near the Cross" (1869), "Blessed Assurance, Jesus Is Mine" (1873), "Softly and Tenderly Jesus Is Calling" (1909), "I Come to the Garden Alone/While the Dew Is Still on the Roses" (1912), and hundreds of others, fitted to attractive tunes, lilting and easily syncopated or sweetly sentimental, rich in simple harmonies and sliding chromaticisms. Heard once, they would be remembered forever. Few ties were there that bound American Protestants so firmly together in a common popular tradition.[3]

The popularity and friendliness of these church ways exacted a price, however, for in drawing like to like they accentuated the social stratification of Protestantism. A prime characteristic of the ancient parish systems of Christendom, including those of Puritanism, was broken: judge, merchant, mechanic, and servant no longer had a common religious nurture. Although many denominations covered the whole social spectrum, this was rarely the case for a single congregation. Because each congregation had its characteristic constit-

---

[3] The Broadway musical *Say, Darling* (1958) contained a nice scene in which supposedly hardened New York theatrical producers are holding auditions. When the script calls for a revival hymn, they all reveal their midwestern origins by joining in every stanza and the refrain of "Let the Lower Lights Be Burning."

uency, a nation of socially mobile people developed patterns of church membership which were a radical departure from anything Christendom had seen. Abraham Lincoln's progress was typical: from a hard-shell Baptist background, through a "good" marriage and a successful law practice, to regular attendance on Presbyterian preaching. Yet the "progress" in Lincoln's case, as in millions of others, was by no means a matter of sheer social expediency; many such changes were required by maturing tastes and deepening intellectual interests. Denominational interchangeability was a feature of common-core Protestantism, and the movement of individuals within the system served to accentuate its overall homogeneity. The same end was served by the intense denominational rivalries which ensued. From 1870 to 1905 there was not a single large church merger in the country. As in commercial competition, the accent was on marginal differentiation.

The message and teaching of this increasingly homogeneous religious tradition and the attitudes it inculcated were closely adapted to what Americans wanted to hear and highly conducive to complacency and self-righteousness. The prophetic note tended to get lost. The sins most universally condemned were the middle-class "don'ts" applicable to any would-be self-made man. Positively, there was a "gospel of wealth" for the rich and a "gospel of work" for everyone. Henry May has stated the case accurately: "In 1876 Protestantism presented a massive, almost unbroken front in its defense of the status quo."[4] The leaders of the Social Gospel, whose history Professor May was writing, were an exception, but a numerically small one.

On more strictly ecclesiastical issues the prevailing bias was anticlerical in the good-natured American sense ("the minister should be a good fellow and one of us"), and antiliturgical in that it vented both an American love for spontaneity and a deeper anti-Catholic animus. Most pervasive of all was an anti-intellectual set of mind which was easily transferred from doctrinal or theological matters to more general areas. Theologians, intellectuals, professors, and the literati were rendered suspect. Richard Hofstadter in his *Anti-Intellectualism in America* points to revivalistic Protestantism as

[4] Henry F. May, *The Protestant Churches and Industrial America*, p. 91.

a primary source of this attitude; and a recent church historian makes the same case in more sympathetic terms:

> The "simple gospel" proclaimed by the American churches is not essentially a matter of rationalism or liberalism, but of grace for all. Nearly all the factors . . . contributing to the nontheological spirit of our faith are much older and run much deeper than the liberal tendency to discount the importance of dogma. The emphasis on simplicity is in part a Christian application of democracy. Our preachers have often quoted a saying attributed to Abraham Lincoln: "God must have loved the common people, he made so many of them." So the accent in our preaching has been not so much propositional as personal—an effort to commend to all men the Friend of Sinners.[5]

In such an ethos the troublesome facts and ideas propounded by the leading scientists, scholars, and philosophers of the nineteenth century were kept at safe distance or dismissed as unchristian. When an idea like biological evolution finally became almost axiomatic for large segments of the educated public, a wide sector of the religious community was still reacting with defensive ferocity. Revivalistic anti-intellectualism thus became one very important source of the Fundamentalist's anger and sense of betrayal. Already in the later nineteenth century this alienation was demonstrated by various movements of reaction which grew in strength with the passing decades, but these forms of dissent would have arisen sooner and with more disruptive force had it not been for the signs that the political and cultural power of Protestantism was being threatened.

THE RISING TIDE OF RACISM

After the Civil War, American fears of subversion had been turned, on a sectional basis, against Radical Republicans or the Southern "Redeemers" rather than against Catholics and foreigners. But in the Gilded Age the alarming increase of immigration and the growing concentration of unassimilated minorities in the cities provoked a revival of nativism.

[5] Ronald E. Osborn, *The Spirit of American Christianity*, p. 115.

For at least three reasons, moreover, the new forms of counter-subversion were often less theological and far more crassly racist. Because the old Puritan roots of antipopery were being steadily eroded by cultural compromises and liberal theology, nativism tended to lose its doctrinal animus and to become a function of folk Protestantism or secular prejudice. Evolutionary thought, meanwhile, brought a semblance of scientific support to old notions of "Nordic" superiority. These changes served to draw Northern attitudes on race closer to those which had received definitive formulation in the South. A growing consensus as to the "errors" of Radical Reconstruction was accompanied by an acceptance of Jim Crow laws. There was also widespread agreement that immigrant "hordes" were threatening the American dream.

The overt manifestations of this rising tide of racial pride, hostility, and fear were diverse. As usual, the country's "indigenous foreigners," the Indians, were among the first to feel the brunt of the white man's power. The most sensational aspect of the white man's dealings with the Indian, nearly to the end of the century, was continued armed conflict, a series of skirmishes and minor wars that became intrinsic to the American myth of the Wild West. Less celebrated were the efforts of missionaries, humanitarian reformers, and some government officials to create the conditions for peaceful co-existence, but even these well-meant efforts were seriously impaired by paternalism, racial stereotypes, sentimentalism, corruption, and very little awareness of the degree to which the cultural integrity of Indian life had already been hopelessly undermined.[6]

Another direction in which the new nativism was felt was foreign affairs. And as in the days when Puritan preachers had roused Queen Elizabeth to imperial action, so again the Protestant ministry proclaimed America's destiny in the world:

"It seems to me that God, with infinite wisdom and skill, is here training the Anglo-Saxon race for an hour sure to come in the World's future. . . . The time is coming when the pressure of population on the means of subsistence will be felt here as it is now felt in Europe and Asia. Then will the world enter on a new stage of its history—*the final*

[6] On missionary work and other involvements of the churches in the Indian question, see pp. 339-41, 568, n. 21 below.

*competition of races, for which the Anglo-Saxon is being
schooled.* Long before the thousand millions are here, the
mighty centrifugal tendency inherent in this stock and
strengthened in the United States will assert itself. Then
this race of unequalled energy, with all the majesty of
numbers and the might of wealth behind it—the representative, let us hope, of the largest liberty, the purest
Christianity, the highest civilization—having developed peculiarly aggressive traits calculated to impress its institutions upon mankind, will spread itself over the earth. And
can any one doubt that the result of this competition of
races will be the survival of the fittest?" Is it not reasonable
to believe that this race is destined to dispossess many
weaker ones, assimilate others, and mould the remainder,
until in a very true and important sense, it has Anglo Sax-
onized mankind?[7]

These are not the words of an editorial writer for some jin-
goist newspaper: they were written in 1893 by the general
secretary of the Evangelical Alliance, Josiah Strong, quoting
in large part from *Our Country,* the book that had made him
famous eight years before. No longer an obscure Ohio minister, he was now defining the world role of American Protestantism in his book *The New Era; or, The Coming Kingdom.*
Strong reveals in this passage the gifts that made him a
leader of the evangelical chorus which provided background
music for the war with Spain.

But Strong was not only an imperialist. A long chapter in
The New Era also elaborated the racist nuances of the passage just quoted. He described the providential way in which
the Christian church stood on Hebrew, Greek, and Roman
pillars, and, granting that each of these three peoples was
supreme in the characteristics required for its role in history,
he then went on not only to show how "all three unite in the
one Anglo-Saxon race," but how this thrice-blest race reached
still loftier heights. First, "The religious life of this race is
more vigorous, more spiritual, more Christian than that of
any other." Second, "The intellectual powers of the Anglo-
Saxon" have created not only the world's greatest literary
heritage, but the language which is better suited than any

[7] Josiah Strong, *The New Era; or, The Coming Kingdom* (New
York, 1893), pp. 79–80, including a quotation from *Our Country:
Its Possible Future and Its Present Crisis* (New York, 1885),
p. 222.

other to become a world language. Third, just as Rome possessed unequaled genius for law, organization, and government, "in the modern world the Anglo-Saxon occupies a position of like preeminence."

The Statue of Liberty was dedicated in 1886, between the publication of these two widely read books, but one can only imagine Strong and the readers he influenced wincing in disbelief as they read the lines of Emma Lazarus on the monument's base:

> Give me your tired, your poor,
> Your huddled masses yearning to breathe free,
> The wretched refuse of your teeming shore,
> Send these, the homeless, tempest-tost to me,
> I lift my lamp beside the golden door!

Yet the further fact must be faced: the American's attitude toward the foreigner was fundamentally ambivalent. Some have insisted that the national ideal of cosmopolitan optimism runs counter to human nature, while others have said that the doctrine of human equality was walled in by Anglo-Saxon pride. However formulated, the ambivalence remains. "We are the Romans of the modern world," declared the elder Oliver Wendell Holmes in 1858, "the great assimilating people." Yet forty years later John Fiske formulated a law that won some acceptance: "No ingenuity of legislation or of constitution making can evolve good political results out of base human material." Even the lines of Emma Lazarus vacillate between the masses "yearning to breathe free" and a condescending reference to "the wretched refuse of your teeming shore." American Protestantism in its best moods was capable of genuine charity, but in its average performance and typical expression, it strengthened nativism, contributing in many ways to extreme manifestations of intolerance, and even providing leadership for nativist organizations. But only a review of the way in which the period wrestled with this problem can show the difficulty of making an historical judgment.

THE "NEW" IMMIGRATION

The immense increase in European emigration during the later nineteenth century was not a single uniform movement of peoples. Americans at the time and architects of immigration laws in the 1920s all recognized that between 1880 and 1890 the ethnic makeup of the influx underwent a rather dramatic change. Northern European immigration tapered off, while that from eastern and southern Europe mounted at an unprecedented rate and remained dominant down to the closing of the gates in the 1920s (see tables, pp. 208–9 above). Numerous economic and cultural factors dramatized the change. Because the old immigration tended to include a large proportion of people who were not utterly destitute, it had distributed itself fairly widely across the country with an urban-rural balance that roughly approximated that of the nation. But the "new" immigration, overwhelmingly constituted as it was by the dispossessed, the persecuted, and the poverty-stricken from less developed countries, moved largely to the mines, the iron range, and the cities where jobs were most available. There were related contrasts in literacy and educational level, and, of course, obvious differences in dress, cuisine, language, and customs that tended to heighten the native American's awareness of "foreigners." Finally, there were marked religious differences. The "old" immigration, except during the Irish famine years, was about evenly divided between Roman Catholics and Protestants, though it included a considerable minority of German Jews, articulate rationalists, and religious radicals. The "new" consisted largely of Roman Catholics, Jews, and members of various Eastern churches; but even here important differences were apparent: the piety of Italian and Portuguese Catholics differed from Protestant norms far more dramatically than that of the Irish and Germans; the Orthodox Jewry of eastern Europe contrasted sharply with the increasingly sedate ways of Reform Judaism; the Eastern Orthodox churches, when noticed at all, seemed like so many odd historical relics. Most of the newcomers, moreover, tended to hold jobs where wages and working conditions were bad, and to live in ethnic enclaves. The immigrant's presence thus became identified with the gravest social problems of the age.

In light of all these circumstances, it is not surprising that the half-century after 1880 witnessed another tidal wave of intolerance and racist venom. A specifically theological rationale is far less apparent in this period than in the antebellum "Protestant Crusade," but its religious relevance remains very great. And Protestants, speaking and acting self-consciously as such, ministers and laymen alike, played an active role in bringing about the culminating accomplishment of the later nativism: the virtually complete restriction of immigration. This legislation in the 1920s would eventually mark an epoch in American history.

THE REVIVAL OF NATIVISM

The last recorded meeting of the Grand Executive Committee of the Order of United Americans, largest of the early nonpolitical nativist associations, was held during the Civil War. The Know-Nothing party had by that time collapsed, a victim of the sectional issue. And for some years after the war nativism languished. Men remembered Irish heroism on the field of battle. The absorptive powers of the Union seemed stronger than ever. Yet the Gilded Age was not a time for prejudice to die or for virtue to flourish; in Roger Burlingame's phrase, it was a time of "moral paralysis." Nor was insensitivity to the doings of the Politicos and the Robber Barons the only form which moral complacency took, for widely accepted principles of laissez faire economics and conservative Social Darwinism made complacency a public virtue. "Getting ahead in the world" was the thing that mattered; the Self-Made Man was the idol and the rags-to-riches myth the animating vision for a nation of people on the make. Against this tradition, though often subtly a part of it, was arrayed a celebrated band of reformers whose continuing efforts would culminate in the era of the Muckrakers, the Progressive movement, the New Freedom of Wilson, and the New Nationalism of Theodore Roosevelt. Their counterparts in the churches were the leaders and adherents of the Social Gospel. Yet even among the men and women who led this reform tradition and who seem to represent conscience incarnate, surprisingly few were sensitive to the moral implications of ethnic, racial, and religious prejudice. Indeed it appears that most of them (Josiah Strong, Lyman Abbott, and Walter Rauschenbusch as well as Theodore Roosevelt) were victims of such prejudice. Protests against overt intolerance or its underlying assumptions took a very subordinate place in the reformist literature of both the Progressive and Social Gospel movements. As for Populism or the tradition of agrarian radicalism, neither its anti-Semitism nor its anti-Catholicism was ever far beneath the surface.

Nativism, antipopery, and anti-Semitism, therefore, resumed their place in American life. As the Grand Old Party wearied of the Bloody Shirt, its leaders took up the cry. President Grant found occasion to assail parochial schools; running for governor in Ohio, Rutherford B. Hayes declared the Democrats to be subservient to Rome; Garfield blamed the railroad violence of 1877 on foreign radicals. The Reverend Samuel Burchard's famous outburst against the party of "Rum, Romanism, and Rebellion" revealed an important stream of Republican thinking. During the 1880s when cities like Boston and New York got their first Irish mayors, these nativistic sentiments grew. In the same spirit the Order of the American Union was formed on the old Know-Nothing model around 1870, its membership open to all Protestants regardless of birth. Although it fell to pieces after an exposé in 1878, subsequent events would revive the impulse. The Grand Army of the Republic, the veterans organization, served the same end.

The discovery of the "immigration problem" as an object of social concern added fuel to these fires, especially when accompanied by the ideas of cultural "solidarity" so dear to Richard T. Ely and the "historical school" of economic thought. By these means both humanitarian concern and economic "science" could be turned into antiforeignism. Reformers could champion labor unions and their interest in stopping the flow of "cheap labor." In this way the views of men as diverse as Henry George and James Blaine could converge.

Then in May 1886 came the Haymarket Affair, in John Higham's judgment "the most important single incident in late nineteenth-century nativism."[8] In the hysteria which followed, a short-lived "American party" was formed, as were a group of secret and "patriotic" fraternal organizations which were at once antiradical, anti-Catholic, and anti-Semitic. The most important organized expression of these fears was the American Protective Association (APA), formed in 1887 by Henry F. Bowers, a paranoid crony of the mayor of

8 John Higham, *Strangers in the Land: Patterns of American Nativism, 1860–1925*, p. 54. In May 1886, when the entire country was troubled by labor unrest, a bomb exploded amid Chicago police who were moving in on a meeting of anarchists in Haymarket Square. The furor over the legal disposition of the accused kept the issue alive for over a decade.

Clinton, Iowa, who had been defeated by the Irish labor vote. Members of its secret councils were sworn never to vote for a Catholic and if possible never to hire or strike with one. By 1890, when the APA held its first national council, it was flourishing from Detroit to Omaha, and although it accomplished almost nothing in terms of actual political or legislative action, it did serve to revive grassroots anti-Catholicism in many areas, especially after its reorganization under William J. ("Whiskey Bill") Traynor during the depression of 1893. As American nationalism heightened in the 1890s, the APA emphasized the subservience of Catholics to a "foreign potentate." In 1893 Traynor even fomented a bogus "Popish Plot" by publishing a false encyclical. In its singleminded concentration on Catholicism the APA neglected other "foreigners"; it even rallied much support among Protestant immigrants.

Anti-Semitism of one sort or another is much older than Christianity, but there can be little doubt that over the centuries Christians added a new kind of depth and intensity to it. Yet due to the Puritan's defiant rejection of popery and his identification with Israel, a softening of attitudes occurred which later American ideals were to foster. In addition, Jews were rare in the United States until very late in the nineteenth century. Longfellow's elegy "the Jewish Cemetery at Newport" struck a responsive chord with its tribute to all the Ishmaels and Hagars who have been "mocked and jeered, and spurned by Christian feet." Americans had, of course, appropriated the traditional literary stereotypes from Shakespeare, Walter Scott, and Dickens, but as Oscar Handlin observes, "Until the 1930's . . . there was no anti-Semitic movement in the United States that was not also anti-Catholic."[9] The Jew served, along with other foreigners, as the scapegoat (Lev. 16:20–28) for a vast variety of curses that many Americans would be rid of: city dwellers, peddlers, bankers, nonProtestants, non-Anglo-Saxons, anarchists, freethinkers, etc. What is important after the 1880s is that the Jews are explicitly included in antiforeign attacks, while previously this had rarely been the case. Again, the Haymarket Affair presents itself as a decisive incident.

The principles of racism added further ammunition to the

[9] Oscar Handlin, *Race and Nationality in American Life* (Boston: Little, Brown and Co., 1957), p. 43.

arsenal of American nativism. Up to this time, race theories had been applied only to the Negro, and then rather crudely, and usually in apologies for the institution of slavery and the Southern way of life. In general, however, racist notions had been throttled by the prevailing confidence in the assimilative and reformatory power of American Protestant culture. This confidence was buoyed by evolutionary optimism, the conviction that emigration was a winnowing process which brought the best and strongest to these shores, and a Darwinian environmentalism which saw American institutions as shaping these raw materials.

Gradually during the decades after 1880, however, urban corruption and social strife began to undermine the American's confidence and to raise racial questions. The tendency was especially noticeable in New England, where Anglo-Saxonism was strongest and Yankee dominance was most acutely threatened. James Russell Lowell struggled, though in vain, to maintain the antiracist radicalism and the anglophobia of his abolitionist days; but other cultural scions of New England's "Indian Summer" lacked even the restraining power of antislavery memories. Henry Cabot Lodge studied the Anglo-Saxon law; then as the "scholar in politics" worked in Congress to preserve his race, after 1895 making direct political use of Gustave le Bon's views on the tragedy of "racial" crossbreeding. President Francis A. Walker of MIT argued that, far from being superior peoples, America's newer immigrants were "beaten men from beaten races, representing the worst failures in the struggle for existence." Walker also perceived that the older American stock, as its birthrate declined, was being displaced by "the Latin and the Hun," whom he considered impervious to America's shaping power.

To this growing body of theory two other important scientific ideas were in due course added. America's leading eugenicist, Charles B. Davenport, pointed to the "biological issue," insisting that the admission of "degenerate breeding stock" was one of the worst, most suicidal sins that a nation could commit. William Z. Ripley of MIT in *The Races of Europe* presented the "anthropological issue," classifying Europeans into three races: Teutonic, Alpine, and Mediterranean, each with its characteristic physical constitution. The task of organizing this growing body of theory into an elaborate social argument was assumed by Madison Grant, a New York patrician, sportsman, and zoologist, whose book *The*

Passing of the Great Race (1916) is perhaps the classic of
American racism. It held the Teuton to be "the white man
par excellence," and maintained that races cannot crossbreed
without suicide or reversion, thus providing a "scientific" rationale for preserving racial purity and restricting immigration.

When Grant's book appeared, his beloved Teutons (German and English) were at war with each other, and American entry would soon require of him a revised edition. Yet
the war undeniably aided the nativist cause in two vital respects, by giving strength to the immigration restrictionists,
and by reviving the campaign for "100 percent Americanism." Until 1917 every effort of the Congress to pass a literacy
test had foundered on the presidential veto—Cleveland's in
1897, Taft's in 1913, and Wilson's in 1913—but in 1917
Wilson's second veto was overridden. The way lay open for
still greater victories under Harding, Coolidge, and Hoover.
Anglo-Saxonism would be weak at the League of Nations,
but strong on Capitol Hill.

The drive on "hyphenated Americanism" was in part an
opportunist use of the national emergency to achieve Anglo-
Saxonist ends. In this sense such acts as Iowa's ban on speaking foreign languages (even on the telephone) extended a
policy that many states had been implementing ever since the
late 1880s. All over the country the behavioral and linguistic
norms of the Anglo-Saxon were steadily enforced, often violently, with or without formal legislation. Labor leaders, civil
service reformers, and champions of clean government all
found such tactics convenient. The war and its aftermath are
the concern of a later chapter, but it must at least be noted
here that nativism, anti-Catholicism, and anti-Semitism prepared the ground for both the Immigration Restriction
League and the Anti-Saloon League. They were prominent
and functional features of the Protestant Establishment in
America during the last troubled decades of its hegemony.

51

CRUSADING PROTESTANTISM

The idea of the crusade is essentially medieval and Catholic in its connotations, but the Reformation, despite Luther's misgivings and Anabaptist refusals, soon unleashed crusades of its own. Zwingli died in battle. William the Silent, Gustavus Adolphus, and Cromwell all led armies in the Lord's name. And in antebellum America, the Evangelical United Front with unparalleled enthusiasm launched many of its own nonmilitary crusades against the forces of evil—most unitedly against popery, most dramatically against slavery. It is hardly surprising that in the decades after the Civil War fervent men and women, especially in the North, should strive again to awaken the Protestant host. And so they did, with "Onward, Christian Soldiers"[1] and the "Battle Hymn of the Republic" setting the cadence.

The diversity of these organized efforts was extreme. Some were dramatic and new, others were commonplace attempts to solve old problems. Those born of anxiety and fear—such as the nativist movement—contradicted both Christian and national ideals; others were conceived in confidence, charity, and hope. Some failed, others succeeded. To make matters still more complicated, they varied widely in their impact. Some of the boldest campaigns only illustrate a transient mood; some of the most humble had lasting effects on the country as well as on the churches.

Perhaps the strongest underlying cause of this renewal of

[1] The Anglican High Churchman Sabine Baring-Gould (1834–1924) wrote this greatest of Victorian crusading hymns in 1865. Arthur S. Sullivan (1842–1900) wrote the music to which it is usually sung.

organized activity was an awareness of momentum lost during the period of war and reconstruction and a half-conscious desire to counteract the gaping cleavages between North and South, East and West, country and city, liberals and fundamentalists. Rejuvenation, unification of spirit, and cultural leadership would at once be achieved. Beneath all, without a doubt, was the basic conviction that the church's message of salvation and righteousness was for the healing of the nations.

Among the less exalted movements was an interdenominational effort to revitalize the Sunday schools with a new kind of youth organization. In 1881 Dr. Francis E. Clark, a Congregational minister in Maine, founded the Christian Endeavor Society. Within six years there were more than seven thousand self-managed local societies with a half-million members, and by 1900 "Christian Endeavor," with its exciting international conventions and good organization, had become not only a significant ecumenical force, but had inspired emulation in almost every denomination not participating. The church had gained a new and effective means of nurture and extension, and youth had gained more distinct recognition.

More traditional in its method and aims was the Sabbatarian movement. Sabbath-keeping was a fundamental feature of Reformed religion, but industrialism and immigration had made heavy inroads upon the prevailing Puritan practices. Both old and new organizations sought to stem the rising tide of laxity, creating a furor, for example, by protesting the plan to keep the Centennial Exposition of Philadelphia (1876) open on Sundays so that workers on the six-day week could attend. It was opened, but without machine exhibits in operation. In 1893, the pressures for Sunday opening of Chicago's Columbian Exposition overwhelmed all Sabbatarian objections. The declining fortunes of Sabbatarianism do not accurately reflect the influence of evangelicalism in the nation, however, for there was widespread resistance within the churches to the Puritan conception of Sabbath keeping. Not only liberals looked back to the gloomy Sabbaths of their youth with sad revulsion and, like Richard Ely, wondered why—in light of Christ's word that the Sabbath was for man (Mark 2:27)—his father could piously sacrifice whole hay crops to the summer rain. Frances Willard of temperance fame was equally critical in her recollections of joyless, lonely Sundays on the Wisconsin farm where she grew up. But Protestant alarm over the decline in church attendance on the Sabbath did not become prominent until the 1920s.[2]

THE MISSIONARY IMPULSE

"One of the distinctive tokens of the Christianity and especially the Protestantism of the United States," writes Professor Latourette, "was the fashion in which it conformed to the ethos of the country." The energy and organizational resourcefulness of the American evangelical churches were another such token; in fact, they were a wonder of the world. By 1893 Philip Schaff had long since turned from his early hostility, influenced in part by his work as a secretary of the Evangelical Alliance, in part by his historical studies. American writers from Robert Baird in *Religion in America* (1844) to Josiah Strong in *Our Country* (1885) exhausted the language in expressing their enthusiasm and hope for the future of "Anglo-Saxon" Protestantism. For foreigners and natives alike, it was the activity, the bustle, and the lay support of the churches which seemed so distinctively American.

Nowhere was this activism more evident than in Protestantism's diverse missionary enterprises. These had begun almost immediately in the seventeenth-century colonies from Virginia to New England, with "foreign" missions to the Indians and "home" missions to increasingly scattered European settlers and their descendants. During the Interregnum Puritans had already chartered one society for this purpose, and a half-century later, Anglicans founded the famous SPG. The Second Awakening in America spawned a whole family of state, regional, and national societies. The American Home Missionary Society was of greatest domestic importance, while the American Board of Commissioners for Foreign Missions led the way abroad. Despite Presbyterian involvement in both of these interdenominational agencies, the Presbyterian General Assembly inaugurated home mission

[2] Despite its limited success, Sabbatarianism was by no means dead. All during the twentieth century its advocates were waging a strenuous, if losing, battle against the forces of urbanism, recreation, and leisure. Only after World War II did these reformers begin to encounter opponents who would defend their Sunday behavior by turning to the courts.

work of its own in 1802, and the Old School faction pressed this line of approach to the extent of dividing the denomination in 1837. After the schism, even the New School yielded to the rise of denominationalism, as did the reunited Northern Presbyterian church after its formation in 1869.

Among the Congregationalists the new forms of denominational self-awareness had direct and important consequences for home missions. They held their first national conference in two centuries in 1852 at Albany, and after proceeding by regular steps to organize themselves, in 1871 they formed a national council which thereafter prosecuted a fairly vigorous program of extension. By the end of the century the denomination stretched from coast to coast and had founded new seminaries at Chicago (1855) and Berkeley, California (1866).

Baptist growth was largely due to the semispontaneous expansion of the farmer-preacher system; but missionary societies were also organized in Massachusetts (1802) and in New York (1807). In 1814 a new General Missionary Convention was organized, inspired largely by the missionary efforts of Luther Rice. Among the Baptists, however, there was much suspicion of centralized authority, strong theological misgivings about "societies" in particular, and many doubts about missionary work in general. In fact, the antimission spirit helped to give birth to two new Baptist denominations: the Two-Seed-in-the-Spirit Predestinarian Baptists in the 1820s and the Primitive Baptists in the 1830s. But evangelism was inextinguishable, and Baptists, North and South, grew rapidly as the country expanded westward. The Disciples of Christ shared Baptist misgivings about extracongregational institutions like the societies, and they spent much energy (and newsprint, for they did not doubt the legitimacy of unofficial denominational journals) debating the implications of the New Testament church model for the present day. The missions controversy among them boiled on throughout the century, but evangelism continued nevertheless; and by 1865 this communion was poised for its greatest half-century of growth and geographic expansion.

Methodism had easily accepted the idea of home missions. Itinerant preachers were in fact a fundamental element of its polity, and circuits and bishops were added, North and South, as occasion demanded. Voluntary missionary societies performed a relatively unimportant role. After 1835 the Protestant Episcopal church conducted its home missionary labors chiefly as a church, appointing missionary bishops over remote or thinly populated districts.

In terms of church organization, perhaps the most important missionary development of the century was the gradual process, already alluded to, by which evangelism was made the task of the denomination as a whole, every member thus being at least theoretically a participant. At the heart of the change was a conception of the Church-as-mission which served to channel denominational self-consciousness and competitiveness while at the same time permitting closer control of the missionaries in doctrinal matters. Less commendable but certainly evident were the desires of denominational leaders for wider authority and the need, when zeal was flagging, to gain at least the financial support of every church member, regardless of his personal enthusiasm for the cause.

The end of the Civil War with its great burst in American population growth and accelerated westward expansion led to a resurgence of missionary activity. Baptist, Methodist, and Presbyterian churches were most successful in these efforts, in large part because so many of them migrated, and because they were the most natural affiliation for the average unchurched but nominally Protestant American. But all denominations continued to extend themselves—usually by methods developed on earlier frontiers. It is not necessary, therefore, to weary the reader with a sequence of denominational histories on the trans-Mississippi West. But in the West was also the Indian, and missionary heroes and martyrs had their roles in this momentuous confrontation just as did General George Custer. A century later, the problem of tarnished reputations arose in their case as much as in his.

The Indian and American Culture

During the decades after the Civil War the predicament of the American Indian demanded a shift in government policy. In 1871 Congress gave up the fiction that Indian tribes were independent powers, abolished the treaty system, and recognized that the Indians were in fact wards of the state. In retrospect, one can see that a process of cultural disintegration which had been set in motion by the European migrations of the sixteenth and seventeenth centuries was entering a critical stage. President Grant's announcement of a "peace policy," therefore, opened a new epoch in American Indian relations. The Indian reformer—after being ignored for so long—began to be heard. Helen Hunt Jackson culminated a long crusade with a stinging report to the nation, *A Century of Dishonor* (1881), and a powerful sentimental novel, *Ramona* (1884), while Senator Henry Laurens Dawes of Massachusetts marshaled the necessary congressional majorities. Conquest and removal yielded to a search for some means of "solving" the problem, whether by assimilation, protected isolation, or—it was advocated by a few—extermination.

Until the Civil War, Christian missions had been almost the only American institutions to deal constructively with the situation, although even they, like the Spanish and French, had always unabashedly sought to convert the Indian to Christianity and, in varying degree, to reshape his way of life according to Western norms. The Quakers and Episcopalians had been very vocal in their criticism of what passed for government policy, and when scandal and corruption in the Indian Service became a national disgrace, President Grant threw the doctrine of church-state separation to the winds and literally parceled out the task to the denominations. In their hands it largely remained until the Dawes Act of 1887 launched a new policy of individual land allotments that was frankly assimilationist in its intention though it became chiefly disintegrative in its effects. The churches also exerted considerable influence through the Board of Indian Commissioners, which functioned in an advisory capacity from 1869 to 1933; but public apathy and prevailing attitudes led to another long period of drift and neglect.[3] With the coming of the New Deal in the 1930s new efforts to reconstitute viable tribal life would be attempted. Yet in the 1970s the problem remained much as it had a century before. Although the churches by then were in no position to be active participants, their earlier search for ways to bring the Indian into

[3] Armed conflict aside, the inexorable force of white-red intercultural contact has been too little considered in discussions of missionaries, churches, and the Indian question (see Robert F. Berkhofer, Jr., *Salvation and the Savage: An Analysis of Protestant Missions and American Indian Response, 1787–1862;* Loring B. Priest, *Uncle Sam's Stepchildren: The Reformation of United States Indian Policy, 1865–1887;* R. Pierce Beaver, *Church, State, and the American Indians;* and Bernard W. Sheehan, "Indian-White Relations in Early America: A Review Essay," *William and Mary Quarterly* 26 [April 1969]: 267–86).

the mainstream of American life was by no means discredited.

Missions and Empire

Against this general background there were two major movements of combined pioneer settlement and missionary enterprise that had specific consequences for American expansionism. Most exciting were the exploits of the early missionaries to Oregon, an area which the British Hudson's Bay Company had kept very much for itself until 1834. In that year two Methodists, Jason and Daniel Lee, started a small mission there, which probably induced the American Board to follow their example. With the support of the board, Samuel Parker and three others made the trek west in 1835, to be joined later that year by Dr. Marcus Whitman (1802–47), a physician, the Reverend Henry H. Spalding, their wives, and a few other volunteers. They founded two missions in southeastern Oregon, and in 1838 they were assisted by the Reverend Cushing Eells, a graduate of Williams College and Hartford Seminary who had also been sent out by the American Board. Dr. Whitman died at Indian hands in 1847 along with his wife and a dozen other settlers. But by that time he had already made his famous trip back East in 1842, where his interviews with the president and the secretary of state probably stiffened American demands for Oregon. In returning to his mission as part of the great migration of 1843, he had again influenced future events by urging this company not to abandon its wagons at Fort Hall (Idaho) but to press on and open the road to Oregon. Eells, however, remained active in the ecclesiastical and educational life of the Northwest until his death in 1893. He was a missionary among the Spokane Indians for a decade and helped to found or strengthen six congregations and three colleges in the region.[4]

The American Board's semi-imperialistic projects in Hawaii belong in almost the same category as its earlier work in Oregon, since Hawaii, too, was ultimately annexed (1898) and made a state of the Union (1959). Both are examples of "foreign" missions that were, quite literally, domesticated.

Located about 2,100 miles west of California and 3,400

[4] On Roman Catholic missions on the upper Missouri and in Oregon, see pp. 653–54 in Vol. 1.

miles east of Japan, the Hawaiian (Sandwich) Islands became known to the West only when Captain James Cook
reported his "discovery" in 1778. A subsequent slow but
steady increase in Western contacts gradually altered the native Polynesian culture and undermined a fairly stable form
of feudal monarchy. The decisive event was the arrival in
1820 of a party of New England missionaries and three
American-educated Hawaiians sent out by the American
Board. Aided by later arrivals, these Americans had unexpected "success" in Christianizing a large majority of the natives, including numerous chiefs and members of the royal
family. They were also successful in introducing diseases that
decimated the native people (only 10 percent of the population was "native" by 1920), in developing the islands' economic potential, and in introducing constitutional reforms
that finally led to the overthrow of Queen Liliuokalani in
1893 and the proclamation of an independent republic as the
prelude to annexation. By this time the Yankees' economic
feudalism had replaced the old order.

As immigration continued, Filipinos, Portuguese, and diverse Americans brought Roman Catholicism almost to numerical equality with Protestantism, while the very large
influx of Japanese (43 percent of the population in 1920),
Chinese (9 percent), and Koreans introduced a large non-
Christian element. During the years preceding the American
Board's discontinuance of support in 1863, however, the missionary achievement was considerable. They reduced the native language to writing, provided the basis for an educational system, and introduced viable modern forms of
government and lawmaking. Nowhere else under the American flag, or any other flag, have the Orient and the Occident
met and blended with such goodwill and amity.

HOME AND WORLD MISSIONS

In the actual conduct of "home missions" the most important transformation came about not in the West but in the
East, not on the frontier but in the city. Here was a crisis that
required two drastic adaptations. In the first place, the traditional individualistic emphasis on soul-saving came up against
the fact that whole classes and ethnic groups needed saving.
Even the most conservative denominational home mission

boards had to concede that poverty, ignorance, and alienation posed problems with which rescue missions, revival campaigns, and Salvation Army methods could not cope. Next to the WCTU, the home missions movement was the most significant route by which social Christianity penetrated the conservative evangelical consciousness.

In the wake of this realization followed the second great adaptation: the resort to cooperative interdenominational planning and working. Charles L. Thompson (1839–1924) of the Madison Avenue Presbyterian Church in New York was a leader in both respects. After reorganizing his own denomination's board of home missions in the years after 1898 and developing relationships with parallel work in other churches, he had the satisfaction in 1908 of presiding at the organizational meeting of the Home Missions Council. Within a decade thirty-five boards were affiliated, and the Southern Baptist Convention was the only major evangelical denomination not represented. Its problems were vast, its resources and powers small, and the popular appeal of its cause could never match that of foreign missions during this period. But it did make important social surveys, develop methods of cooperation, and by joint promotional efforts, lay foundations upon which to build after World War I had enlarged the "home front" role of the churches.

"The Evangelization of the World in This Generation"

The closing two decades of the nineteenth century witnessed the climactic phase of the foreign missions movement in American Protestantism. This new surge of interest was due, above all, to the stimulus and inspiration of Dwight L. Moody, whose warm, optimistic evangelicalism shines through every phase of the activity which followed and was reflected in the hundreds and thousands of young men and women who committed themselves to the cause. The other essential contribution to this activity was that of the YMCA, which had, in fact, figured strongly in Moody's own life. This contribution can be traced to the YMCA's remarkable and spontaneous advance in American colleges and universities during the post-Civil War decades. At the YMCA convention of 1877 in Louisville, due largely to the zealous work of a student at Princeton University named Luther DeLoraine Wishard (1854–1925), the Intercollegiate YMCA movement was launched, with Wishard as corresponding secretary. His vigorous efforts brought the number of participating college associations from 21 to 96 in 1880, and to 258 by 1887. By this time the YWCA had also established a working relationship in a hundred or so women's collegiate associations.

The next stage involved Moody directly, first in a series of revivals at Princeton, Yale, Harvard, and Dartmouth that repeated his successes in Britain at Edinburgh, Oxford, and Cambridge. The meetings in England had resulted in the conversion of Charles T. Studd and Stanley Smith, who went on to careers in Hudson Taylor's famous China Inland Mission. It was Wishard's hope that a similar interest in foreign missions could be aroused in America. Climaxing the American college revival in 1886 was Moody's historic invitation of mission-minded college students to a month-long summer session at Moody's school in Northfield, Massachusetts. It turned out to be an occasion beyond anyone's dream, and before it was over an even hundred—the Mount Hermon Hundred—had taken the pledge to become foreign missionaries.

By the time of the next summer school, the number had reached twenty-one hundred (sixteen hundred men and five hundred women). President Seelye of Amherst called it the greatest missionary uprising in modern times. In 1888 the Student Volunteer Movement was organized, its almost unbelievable expansion due to the gifted leadership of another student, John R. Mott. Mott (1865–1955) was born of Methodist parents in New York State but brought up on an Iowa farm. In 1888 he was serving as the head of the YMCA at Cornell University. He was destined to become the leading American ambassador of missions and ecumenism for almost a half-century, and from 1890 to 1915 he served as the national college secretary of the YMCA. His impact on American Christian students during those years was phenomenal, and in due course the student community of the whole world became his parish.

The work among students was itself evangelism—a home missions work of sorts. But the growing student movement in turn gave impetus to the formation in 1906 of the Laymen's Missionary Movement, with a devout layman, John B. Sleman, providing the connecting link. The LMM owed its origins to a series of meetings held at Fifth Avenue Presbyterian Church to commemorate the "Haystack Meeting" at Williams College from which the American foreign missionary impulse had sprung. After long hours of prayerful discussion of a moving talk by J. Campbell White, the fifty men present resolved to set up a Committee of Twenty-Five to make plans for propagating missions and gaining financial support for the SVM's campaign to "evangelize the world in this generation." In 1908 the annual interchurch conference of foreign mission boards formally recognized the movement's "spontaneity and timeliness [as] evidence of the hand of God." Under the early leadership of Samuel B. Capen and, later, with J. Campbell White as general secretary, a large general committee and a network of subcommittees began its work: spreading the movement to Great Britain and Canada, organizing visits to mission fields followed by speaking tours in America, inaugurating education programs in local churches, and above all, stimulating generous gifts to the foreign missions cause.

The thousands of laymen awakened by the movement also became powerful agents in other crusades and campaigns during the World War and the twenties, illustrating what has always been the most important aspect of the entire foreign missions impulse: its reflex effect on the life and church activities of Christians at home. The missionary on furlough was the great American window on the non-Western world. Through him, the aims of the missionary movement, as well as the cultural stereotypes which underlay it, became fundamental elements of the American Protestant's world outlook. India, Africa, China, and Japan came to be regarded as spiritual provinces of the American churches from the Nebraska plains to New York's Fifth Avenue. Even in foreign policy the effects of this vast reservoir of popular interest and affection were registered. Statesmen could not treat these great "mission fields" as diplomatic pawns. The missionary's knowledge and experience also guided the State Department, and in due course missionary families furnished countless sons (John Foster Dulles being only the best known) to the diplomatic service and related scholarly pursuits.

The Crisis of the Missions

Alas, every movement has its crisis and the work of these mission-minded laymen was no exception. From the start the Laymen's Missionary Movement had been criticized as an escape and evasion. "Evangelization," so the critique ran, had come to mean no more than "presenting" Christ to the world so that prophecy might be fulfilled and a premillennarian expectation of the Second Coming provided. As early as 1911, Joseph E. McAfee, a Presbyterian with experience in urban home missions, defined the crisis:

> If the missionary maintains that the individualistic method is ultimate, and represents an individualistic scheme of salvation as final and complete, he runs counter to approved world tendencies and repudiates a social theory which schools of thought in all civilized lands are successfully establishing.[5]

By such a declaration the mission question was fatefully merged with the Fundamentalist controversy, and in this sense it points to larger aspects of the Protestant dilemma. But of more immediate concern to the development of missions was the remarkable degree to which McAfee's "conclusions" on missionary policy were adopted by the churches during World War I. The SVM itself would embrace a broader view of service at its convention of 1918, and thereafter the rift between liberal and conservative views widened year by year as increasing support accrued to a social and philanthropic rather than a narrowly evangelistic view of the Church's mission among non-Christians. The fact of crisis became undeniable; the "halcyon years" had blown up an unexpected tempest.

The ensuing debates made explicit what McAfee had implied. It began to appear that the foreign missions revival may well have arisen as a half-subconscious effort to divert Protestants from intellectual problems and internal dissensions by engaging them in great moral and spiritual tasks—only to have deeper problems and dissension reappear. And so it would be in the greatest and most unified of all Protestant crusades—that for temperance, a campaign whose suc-

[5] Joseph E. McAfee, *The Crisis of Missionary Method* (New York, 1911), p. 37. The issue which McAfee raised was central to the entire mission enterprise of the churches; it even posed the problem of the American Redeemer Nation's relation to the rest of the world. Inevitably, therefore, the debate intensified, finally coming to a head in 1932 with the immensely controversial report of an appraisal committee headed by the Harvard philosopher William Ernest Hocking, *Re-thinking Missions: A Laymen's Inquiry after One Hundred Years.*

cesses and failures, far more than those on far away mission fields, would affect almost every aspect of national life.

THE GREAT TEMPERANCE DEBATE

The "temperance movement" (as that most intemperate of reform impulses is usually called) hit America in three major waves. The first shared the great victories of the Evangelical United Front and the humanitarian crusades during the antebellum era. The famous "Maine Law" was passed in 1846, and in another decade thirteen northern and western states had followed suit. Yet these victories were fleeting; when the Civil War ended, only Maine and Massachusetts were in the dry fold, and the latter soon wandered out. To recoup these losses the Grand Lodge of Good Templars launched the Prohibition party in 1869. It gained attention slowly, and despite the broad vision of its leadership, it never became strong.

The really effective revival of the movement occurred five years later, through a sensational series of demonstrations and "pray-ins" that has not inappropriately been referred to as the Woman's Revolution. It all began on 24 December 1873, when Eliza Trimble Thompson of Hillsboro, Ohio, led more than seventy determined women from a prayer meeting to one of the town's liquor vendors. Though followed by hundreds of townspeople, they did no violence; but on one side or the other of the swinging doors they prayed, sang, pleaded, and in other ways besought the proprietor to close and desist. During succeeding days they dealt similarly with the twelve other saloons in town, and achieved almost complete (though impermanent) success. By this time, with wide press coverage and surprising public approval, the Woman's Crusade had begun to spread throughout Ohio and then to other states. In Minnesota the Singing Hutchinsons of abolitionist fame lent their talents to the cause, singing Julia B. Nelson's new battle hymn:

> And where are the hands red with slaughter?
> Behold them each day as you pass
> The places where death and destruction
> Are retailed at ten cents a glass.

Within a year the crusade lost steam, and its long-term results were in one sense small, for the great losses in liquor tax revenue reported during 1874 were soon matched by new gains. But the crusade did revitalize the temperance movement—and at the same time summoned women to a new role in public affairs. "That phenomenal . . . uprising of women in southern Ohio" declared feminist Mary Livermore, "floated them to a higher level of womanhood. It lifted them out of a subject condition where they had suffered immitigable woe." In November 1874 at Cleveland, delegates from seventeen states, many of them active in church missionary societies or "veterans" of war work in the Sanitary and Christian commissions, organized the Women's Christian Temperance Union. To the crucial post of corresponding secretary they elected Frances Willard, the woman who for two decades would not only make the WCTU her lengthened shadow, but who made it also the greatest women's organization of the century.

Frances Willard, as most Protestant school children once well knew, was born on 28 September 1839 to westering Vermonters then living near Rochester, New York. The family soon moved on to Oberlin, Ohio—where the child developed a lifelong distaste for Charles Finney's fearsome sermons—and then in 1846 further west to Wisconsin. Frances grew up on an isolated farm near Janesville under the stern rule of an ultra-Methodistic father. In later life she remembered standing on a rainy day huddled with her brother and sister in a barn doorway and exclaiming, "I wonder if we shall ever know anything, see anybody, or go anywhere." As it happened, she did all three, and by a fairly direct route. She went away to schools in Milwaukee and Evanston. After graduating in 1859, she spent the next decade teaching in various schools, serving as secretary to the Methodist Centenary Fund, and traveling in Europe and the Middle East for twenty-eight months. Shortly after her return she became president of the Evanston College for Ladies. When the college became part of Northwestern University, she was appointed its dean, but finding that arrangement unsatisfactory, she resigned in 1874. By that time she was already a vice-president of the Association for the Advancement of Women, and before the year was out she was elected an officer in the organization with which her name will always be linked, the WCTU.

The union's early years were marked, as she herself said,

by an ideological conflict "which became distinctly outlined under the names: 'conservative' and 'liberal.'" Its first president, Annie Wittenmyer (who in 1888 would also oppose Willard's efforts to get women accepted as delegates to the Methodist General Conference), led the conservatives, championing a focus on the single issue of prohibition. Dissenting from this narrow conception of the WCTU, Frances Willard resigned and in 1877 worked for a time on the evangelistic team of Dwight L. Moody. She disagreed with his policy as well, and after heavy western support brought her to the union's presidency in 1881, she began to implement her own ideas: a vigorous membership campaign, endless speaking tours to propagate the cause, spectacular annual conventions, a major emphasis on women's rights, including the vote, expansion of the union's concern for a wide range of social issues, including the traffic in young prostitutes which prudery had heretofore kept from public discussion, and finally, the development of diverse political strategies to gain these ends. Her success in carrying out this vast "Do Everything" program owed most, perhaps, to her amazing gifts of leadership; but it also depended on the way in which the WCTU, like Willard herself, remained committed to the ideals and spirit of evangelical Protestantism and to her shrewd policy of resting the whole cause on the two institutions where woman's "place" was assured: the home and the church.

Under Mrs. Hayes and Mrs. Garfield the WCTU had entered the White House almost immediately, leading one statesman to remark that at presidential receptions "the water flowed like champagne." But Frances Willard was disappointed when Garfield reneged on his preelection political commitments to temperance, and in 1884, having been spurned at the conventions of both major parties, she led the union to support the Prohibition party. Here she won a minor triumph, and she was plausibly accused of having diverted enough Republican votes in New York to elect Cleveland! Lest the lesson be forgotten, the union also developed its techniques of pressure politics and practiced them with an effectiveness never before equaled in America. By 1896 Frances Willard had become sympathetic to both Populism and the rising demand for urban reform. She commended both Henry George and Edward Bellamy to her ladies, having turned from "Gospel Politics" to "Gospel Socialism." And after failing to unite the Populist and Prohibition parties under a banner that included temperance and woman's suffrage, she was working with other thoroughgoing critics of the status quo to create a single great reform party. But by this time her health was failing. Even more ominously for one with her vision, the Anti-Saloon League had been founded; and soon after her death in 1898, the WCTU gradually became little more than the woman's auxiliary of that single-minded engine of political manipulation.

Before considering the league's place in Protestant history, however, it is well to underline the degree to which the union's later leadership hid the actual Frances Willard beneath a sentimental legend of Saint Frances of the White Ribbon. Americans generally, including church historians, have almost forgotten the single most impressive reformer to have worked within the context of the evangelical churches. When she died, someone observed that the death of no other woman except Queen Victoria could have so stirred the world. Frances Willard had given American womanhood a new place in society and in the churches. And beneath her zeal was the burning evangelical faith which she had always communicated with such unparalleled effectiveness. She could be inspired by anyone who sought holiness, from Marcus Aurelius to Emerson, and she was an eclectic in theology; but Christianity was her bridle. "I am a strictly loyal and orthodox Methodist," she said, and then in the idiom of her times, "Like the bee that gathers from many fragrant gardens, but flies home with his varied gains . . . so I fly home to the sweetness and sanctity of the old faith that has been my shelter and solace so long." In this spirit she made the WCTU a vast national organization with lively, growing roots in and amid the parishes of every state and territory. She succeeded, moreover, in making it the chief exception to the rule of evangelical social complacency during the "halcyon years."

The Third Wave of Temperance Reform

In Oberlin, Ohio, a town famous for its role in the antislavery crusade, the Anti-Saloon League was organized in 1893 as a church-oriented direct action political pressure organization. Due to the efforts of an Iowa Methodist minister, Alpha J. Kynett, the league was organized on a national basis two years later at a convention in Washington, D.C. Hiram Price, a former Republican congressman from Iowa, was elected president, and Wayne B. Wheeler, an Oberlin alumnus, was superintendent. Within a few years they had paid agents in nearly every state and an efficient staff in the national office. The league was well financed by men of wealth—S. S. Kresge was one of its most generous patrons— and before the goal of a constitutionally dry United States was reached, the league had spent $35 million. It had but one aim: to get dry laws, the drier the better, the more stringent and sweeping the better. Unlike the Prohibition party and the WCTU, it had no diversionary purposes and cared little or nothing about a politician's morals or political principles so long as he voted dry. It used hard-driving, tough-minded methods, and they worked. "We have got to kill the Anti-Saloon League and then lick the Republican and Democratic parties," declared the Prohibition party's presidential candidate in 1908; but by then the would-be slayer was all but slain. Although only three states had stood squarely in the dry category in 1903 (Maine, Kansas, and North Dakota), two-thirds of the states had taken action by 1916, and three-fourths of the population was living under some kind of prohibition law.

The campaign for an amendment to the Constitution was launched in 1913, and Superintendent Wheeler's machine began to roll immediately, heading first for the primaries, then for the congressional elections of 1914. When the House assembled, a dry majority was seated. Then came the bonanza—war—giving nativists a rationale for harassing the German brewers. After American entry into the war, a great stress on saving fuel (alcohol) and using grain for bread advanced the cause further. Finally on 18 December 1917 the Great Day came: the Eighteenth Amendment cleared the House 282 to 128, and with surprising speed received overwhelming approval in the states (only Connecticut and Rhode Island failed to ratify). On 16 January 1919, with Nebraska's ratification, the Noble Experiment began. Its history, of course, belongs to the twenties, but some consideration of the churches' role in its prewar preparation is called for.

The dry crusade in its third and triumphant phase was chiefly the work of the Anti-Saloon League; and Wayne Wheeler repeatedly insisted that the league was simply "the churches [and the "decent people"] organized against the saloon." But one can be more precise: Methodism, North and

South, gave the league its unanimous institutional support and supplied most of its most militant leadership. The Baptists and Presbyterians, North and South, were not far behind. Support came from everywhere, including at first some important Roman Catholics, but it was basically the last great corporate work in America of legalistic evangelicalism. Every major historian of the campaign, moreover, emphasizes other nontheological factors that identify this form of Protestantism more exactly. Most obviously it was rural or small-town; and its ancestry was British. Its deepest antipathies were directed toward city dwellers, foreigners, and Roman Catholics. Bigotry and nativism were often dry. Alphonso Alva Hopkins expressed a familiar combination of attitudes in his *Profit and Loss in Man* (1908):

> Our boast has been that we are a Christian people, with Morality at the center of our civilization. Foreign control or conquest is rapidly making us un-Christian, with immorality throned in power.
>
> Besodden Europe, worse bescourged than by war, famine and pestilence, sends here her drink-makers, her drunkard-makers, and her drunkards, or her more temperate but habitual drinkers, with all their un-American and anti-American ideas of morality and government; they are absorbed into our national life, but not assimilated; with no liberty whence they came, they demand unrestricted liberty among us, even to license for the things we loathe; and through the ballot-box, flung wide open to them by foolish statesmanship that covets power, their foreign control or conquest has become largely an appalling fact; they dominate our Sabbath, over large areas of country; they have set up for us their own moral standards, which are grossly immoral; they govern our great cities, until even Reform candidates accept their authority and pledge themselves to obey it; the great cities govern the nation; and foreign control or conquest could gain little more, though secured by foreign armies and fleets.
>
> As one feature of this foreign conquest, foreign capital has come here, and to the extent of untold millions has invested itself in breweries, until we are told that their annual profits at one time reached about $25,000,000 yearly, sent over seas to foreign stockholders, who shared thus in their conquest of America, while to them, in their palaces

and castles, American Labor paid tribute, and for their behoof American morals were debased, the American Sunday surrendered.[6]

By no means all temperance reformers and enemies of the saloon shared this syndrome. Kresge was chiefly interested in an efficient laboring force. Jack London lamented ruined lives, including his own. Socialists attacked a pernicious industry. Jane Addams spoke as a compassionate social worker. Yet few things Frances Willard said to the WCTU won more immediate criticism from the rank and file than her suggestion that poverty caused alcoholism, even though she also admitted the orthodox point that excessive drinking often caused poverty. Because it did give focus to so many fears and hopes, the temperance movement united Protestant Americans as nothing else ever had or would. By the same token, however, it diverted attention from many other social concerns and left the churches ill-prepared for great calamities that were in the offing.

[6] Born in Burlington Flats, New York, Alphonso Alva Hopkins (1843–1918) began in 1868 a long career as a lecturer and writer on temperance and economic topics. For three years he was vice-chancellor and professor of political economy at American Temperance University (Tennessee), and in 1882 he ran as a Prohibition candidate for governor of New York. His *Profit and Loss in Man* (New York: Funk and Wagnalls Co., 1908) elaborated the themes which he explored in *Wealth and Waste* (1896).

VIII

The Age of Faltering Crusades

I can remember, for I am a little older than the present century, when the first automobile rolled down the main street of my native village. . . . And I remember when the first motion picture invaded the town. No one took them seriously at first; it was useless to condemn them. They were too obviously innocent at that time, and though a few men of great imagination foresaw some of their serious consequences for business, morals, education, and religion, the great majority accepted them for no better reason than that they were inevitable. . . . What has speed to do with justice or cheap entertainment with kindness? Even to this day there are religious spokesmen who claim to disregard purely "secular" inventions. . . . But everyone knows by this time that these instruments have changed not only *how* we express ourselves but *what* we believe and do.

These innovations were products and signs of similar changes in our minds, of new discoveries, new history, new ideals, changed philosophies. . . . The range and focus of our interests have been revolutionized. Our religion itself, our love of the eternal, has yielded to the pressure of the times.

Herbert Wallace Schneider, *Religion in Twentieth-Century America* (1952)

Wartime excitements and postwar deflations of spirit have provided the rhythms for the religious climate of the United States during the greater part of the twentieth century. The rise of fascism in the thirties and the cold war after 1945 filled in the intervals. Yet beneath these alternations, a steady acceleration of uncontrolled economic growth, population movement, and governmental expansion had brought the United States by the later 1960s to a state of advanced technocratic crisis compounded by yet another war. Nor was this due only to critical developments within America's traditional households of faith. The old consensus about the country's destiny also collapsed; many came to doubt that the Redeemer Nation was capable of redeeming anybody, and wondered if it was capable of saving itself from urban rot, environmental pollution, racist conflict, poverty, and countercultural disaffection. Having become a victim of individualism, exploitation, and world-policemanship, the United States had become somehow the Old World—a lesson for less ravaged countries on the wages of sin.

The chapters which deal with this twentieth-century course of events are divided into two parts. The five chapters of Part VIII are chronologically arranged, proceeding by periods from the war with Spain through the years of religious revival which followed World War II. In Part IX the late modern development of six major religious traditions and communities is followed from their late nineteenth-century situation down to their rendezvous with the sixties. This decisive decade is then surveyed in the final chapter.

A view of the general religious situation down to the election of John F. Kennedy as president reveals the trend which this victory of a Roman Catholic candidate symbolizes: the crumbling of the Protestant Establishment and the emergence of more genuine pluralism. The crumbling, however, did not occur in November 1960; its origins lay far back in early English decisions on colonial immigration policy and their later reinforcement by the Declaration of Independence with its declarations of equality. Yet the twentieth century also played its role in the process through a complicated series of actions and reactions: Prohibition, the revival of the KKK, immigration restriction laws, the Depression, The New Deal, the election campaigns of Al Smith (1928) and Franklin Roosevelt (1932). Perhaps most basic were a set of value conflicts that reached an extreme phase during the twenties: the problems of the city, the revived Fundamentalist controversy, the implications of jazz, cocktail parties, and the movies. Rural America took its stand—and lost. And such experiences profoundly changed the ideals and inner character of all minorities, including white Protestants. Catholics and Jews gained a new place in American society, while black Americans migrated in large numbers to the cities.

Yet the Crash and the Depression did more than contribute to pluralism—they brought out new elements in every religious tradition, especially, perhaps, new kinds of critical thinking about the religious implications of the nation's domestic distress and the darkening political situation abroad. Those turbulent years also revealed that America's reservoirs of bigotry and fanaticism were by no means empty. Then with the war came a return to loyalty, cooperation, and relative singleness of purpose.

After World War II there was no return to the twenties, because the rising affluence was part of a social revolution out of which arose a new kind of industrial society. In this new ethos the hard edges of American religious life were corroded by a strange revival that had no precedent in American history. Unappreciated at the time was the degree to which the old-time religion was relegated to subcultural status. Even less appreciated was the degree to which the postwar concern for peace of mind was a foretaste, though an insipid one, of the radical theology which would grow out of the harsher confrontations that began to accumulate after President Kennedy's assassination in November 1963.

52

THE LITTLE WAR AND THE GREAT WAR

The Great War of 1914–18 left Europe shattered. The best part of its manhood was "missing in action." *La belle époque* was a tear-stained memory. The old order was gone. And more. When the retrospect of a half-century was at hand, historians would see that European civil war, that suicidal carnage, as the threshold of a post-European age in *world* history. Christendom might regain at least the outer semblance of health for two decades, or three; but the internal injuries sustained at the Marne, the Somme, and Tannenberg would not heal. World War II and all that came with it, before and after, would administer the coup de grace.

For Americans World War I was "over there"—a long, long way from Times Square. On the home front only a very few seemed to comprehend the tragic dimensions of the holocaust. During the twenties their numbers increased as participants and observers began to expose the reality and its aftermath. But only with the coming of the Great Depression did a fairly wide range of thinkers begin to see that bourgeois civilization was deep in crisis. And not until a quarter-century after that did the idea of a "post-Christian" world begin to dawn on the popular consciousness. All the more need, therefore, to approach the Great Crusade from the vantage point of the halcyon age—and to march into it, as it were, in the ranks of the Men and Religion Forward Movement, singing "Onward, Christian Soldiers." But before that, a glance at the Spanish-American rehearsal.

IMPERIAL AMERICA

Manifest Destiny as an American idea is probably as old as the "sea to sea" charters of the earliest colonies. The Puritan's sense of divine mission soon added a spiritual dimension to these grandiose ideas—a dimension that grew in importance after 1776, when nationalistic ambitions superseded the apocalyptic visions of an earlier day. In the antebellum decades evangelical dreams of a vast Christian republic brought prophetic certainty to the idea. Manifest Destiny became the catchword of an epoch.

John Quincy Adams, no less than John C. Calhoun, thought in continental terms. The vision extended not only "from sea to shining sea" but for some enthusiastic spirits from the snowy wastes of the Arctic to the tropical charms of the Isthmus. Journalists, railroad publicists, congressmen, and preachers exhausted the English language on the themes of America's destiny—until the question of slavery in the territories plus Northern fears of an enlarged "slavocracy" darkened the dream. For a quarter-century after the Civil War, Americans had other preoccupations. But in the 1890s the dream was enlivened again, partly because a kind of North-South compromise had been achieved, partly to hasten that process, and, of course, partly because a wide sector of the public anticipated real benefits from imperialism. With the Mexican and Canadian borders stabilized, men looked beyond the sea—especially to the Caribbean, the Pacific, and the Far East.

Behind these new impulses was advocacy of many kinds. Captain (later Admiral) Mahan was insisting on sea power as a condition of greatness, and his kind of logic led to acquisitions in Samoa and the annexation of Hawaii. Professor John W. Burgess and the Reverend Josiah Strong were proclaiming the destiny and duty of Anglo-Saxon civilization. Missionaries called for government furtherance of evangelism to the heathen, while nativists preached the liberation of oppressed peoples from Roman Catholic thralldom as a simple act of charity. With the horrors of the Civil War now gilded in memory, men like Theodore Roosevelt and others much less reserved celebrated the ennobling effects of war. Expansionism, in short, was popular—and perhaps *most* popular when surviving remnants of Spain's tottering empire hung nearby like ripened fruit.[1]

[1] The fruit had been both near and ripe for a long time, to be sure; and during Cuba's unsuccessful Ten Years War of 1868–78 the United States had had sufficient provocation. But at that time the country was sated with war.

In 1896 William McKinley was elected president with a Cuban independence plank in his platform, while Bryan and the Populists during the ensuing years hammered for action, raising the threat of a "Free Cuba—Free Silver" campaign in 1900. Not only for this reason, however, is the election of 1896 one of the great revelatory events in American religious history. As in no other election, both candidates virtually personified American Protestantism. Both William Jennings Bryan and William McKinley were reared in pious homes, educated in denominational colleges, and guided throughout their lives by the traditions and practices of evangelicalism. Yet the policy options they put before the nation in their campaigns were drastically at variance. McKinley took his stand for business, sound money, the tariff, and the myths of the city and the self-made man; Bryan for the farmers, laborers, and debtors, free silver, socialistic experiments, and the myths of rural virtue and the honest yeoman. In different ways each was at once nostalgic and forward-looking. Together they dispel the notion that Protestantism prescribed a specific program for America.

With regard to Cuba and Spain, the seemingly inevitable occurred in April 1898, when the president's war message to Congress expressed his pious hope that "our aspirations as a Christian, peace-loving people will be realized." As it turned out, America loved "the splendid little war" (19 April–12 August 1898), despite the gross mismanagement and ravages of disease in the armed forces. They also loved the gloriously simple victory of Commodore Dewey in the Philippines. "It was a little war," reflected Teddy Roosevelt a bit ruefully, "but it was the only one we had."

The churches reflected the American consensus—and then proceeded in the limited time available to convert the war into a crusade and to rationalize imperialism as a missionary obligation. President McKinley himself set the prevailing tone. To a meeting of fellow Methodists, he confided his deepest convictions:

I am not ashamed to tell you, gentlemen, that I went down on my knees and prayed Almighty God for light and guidance more than one night. And one night late it came to me this way. . . . There was nothing left for us to do but to take them all and to educate the Filipinos and uplift and civilize and Christianize them and by God's grace do the very best we could by them, as our fellow men for whom Christ also died.[2]

E. L. Godkin, the anti-imperialist editor of *The Nation*, was probably correct in his judgment that McKinley's own denomination was the most strident of the churches. "The fervent Methodists, at the beginning of the war, resolved that it was going to be a righteous and holy war because it would destroy 'Romish superstition' in the Spanish West Indies."[3] "This war is the *Kingdom of God coming!*" declared the *California Christian Advocate;* and its cry was echoed widely in the Protestant press. "Coming to poor Cuba—the sunrise of a better day for the Philippines! . . . Oppression, cruelty, bigotry, superstition, and ignorance must down, and give a Christian civilization the right of way."[4] Reflecting on the results of past experience in Hawaii and China, the *Pacific Advocate* minced no words: "The cross will follow the flag. . . . The clock of the ages is striking." Though of another mind himself, Gaius Glenn Atkins remembered the same pervasiveness of the martial spirit in the Protestant churches. Even in Massachusetts, where the Anti-Imperialist League led by Senator George F. Hoar had its greatest strength, Atkins was in a minority in his own Congregational church.[5] Kipling's words on "The White Man's Burden" became for a season the battle hymn of the republic. Never have patriotism, imperialism, and the religion of American Protestants stood in such fervent coalescence as during the McKinley-Roosevelt era.

For American Catholics, whose church during these very years was deeply involved in a severe institutional crisis, the war created special difficulties. Just when strenuous efforts were being exerted in Rome to prevent a papal condemnation of "Americanism," the United States ignored sweeping Spanish concessions and the conciliatory efforts of the pope— then declared war on one of the oldest and most steadfast Catholic powers in the world. Yet the action revealed the nation's dominant mood, and Catholics in general offered their

[2] Charles S. Olcott, *The Life of William McKinley* (Boston: Houghton, Mifflin & Co., 1916), 2:110–11.

[3] *The Nation*, 11 August 1898, p. 105; quoted by Kenneth M. MacKenzie, *The Robe and the Sword: The Methodist Church and the Rise of American Imperialism*, p. 66.

[4] Ibid., p. 72.

[5] Gaius Glenn Atkins, *Religion in Our Times*, pp. 188–89.

wholehearted support to the nation's leaders. Most Irish tended to identify Cuba's predicament with that of Ireland, and some spoke out strongly for a war of liberation. On the question of American imperialism Catholics again followed the prevailing views. What conflict there was arose over the disposition of Catholic properties in the new American empire—and on this matter the policies carried out won greater satisfaction among Catholics than among Protestants.[6]

ON TO A BIGGER CRUSADE

The churches moved from the little war to the Great War essentially without breaking the gait established in the 1880s and 1890s. Liberalism and the Social Gospel advanced in the spirit of Progressivism. The Fundamentalist controversy intensified; secessions of the disinherited from "common-core Protestantism" continued. Several new cooperative agencies were formed, and church-sponsored crusades followed one after another, while businessmen and perfected forms of promotionalism accounted for both the successes achieved and the limitations revealed. In 1911 the greatest prewar crusade of all was launched: the Men and Religion Forward Movement, with its across-the-board program for revitalizing the churches.

Even the peace movement enjoyed an unusually favorable Indian summer climate. Meetings were well attended and membership lists grew. "The times were so ripe," remembered John Dewey in 1917, "that the movement hardly had to be pushed."[7] Thirty-odd organizations and foundations were working for the cause, and in February 1914 Andrew Carnegie added another through his $2 million endowment for the Church Peace Union, showing his optimism by giving directions for alternative use of the funds should peace become "fully established." The Catholic Peace Conference in Liège and the Twenty-first International Peace Congress in Vienna, both scheduled for the summer of 1914, were canceled, however, by the outbreak of hostilities.

Archduke Francis Ferdinand, heir to the Hapsburg throne,

6 See the careful study of Frank T. Reuter, *Catholic Influence on American Colonial Policies, 1898–1904* (Austin, Tex.: University of Texas Press, 1967).

7 *New Republic* 11:297; quoted in Ray H. Abrams, *Preachers Present Arms*, p. 8.

was shot in Sarajevo on 28 June 1914. The sabre rattling of July was followed by the drums of August—the death march of the old order in Europe. Americans at the time thanked "the foresight exercised by our forefathers in emigrating from Europe." President Wilson urged strict neutrality. "We have nothing to do with this war," he insisted; its causes "can not touch us." Wilson even urged movie audiences not to reveal partisan views when newsreels were shown. But this was a futile admonition—as well bid the skylark not to sing. The flexing of national muscle begun in 1898 was still having its effect, and Theodore Roosevelt was still abroad in the land. The president himself was a fervent admirer of England, and he cooperated from the start with Britain's efforts to control the seas. By 1916 American commerce with Germany had fallen from $169 million to $1 million. Allied propaganda poured in, and the situation was aggravated by the sinking of the *Lusitania* in 1915 and all the diversely interpreted events that led to the raw, rainy day, 2 April 1917, when the president went before Congress to declare that a state of war existed.

But that was not all, for he went on—what else could he do with the knowledge of five hundred thousand Germans, four hundred thousand French, and two hundred thousand English dead on the Somme?—to proclaim a holy war. "It is a fearful thing," he said, "to lead this great peaceful people into war, into the most terrible and disastrous of all wars. . . . But the right is more precious than peace, and we shall fight . . . for a universal dominion of right by such a concert of free peoples as shall bring peace and safety to all nations and make the world itself at last free." Looking back on his decision, he would reaffirm this purpose: "We entered the war as the disinterested champion of right." Early on Good Friday morning (6 April) Congress did his bidding. This was not *Realpolitik*—very few Americans and no policy makers acted out of long-term concern for the nation's security—it was but a slightly revised version of a classic American sense of its chosen task in the world. William Leuchtenburg states the case:

American entrance into the war cannot be seen apart from the American sense of mission. The United States believed that American moral idealism could be extended outward, that American Christian democratic ideals could and should be universally applied. . . . The culmination of a long political tradition of emphasis on sacrifice and decisive moral combat, the war was embraced as that final struggle where the righteous would do battle for the Lord.[8]

Wilson, on the night before he asked for war, expounded for a friend the awful domestic consequences of putting the world *and the nation* on a "war basis." If we join with the Allies, he said,

> It would mean that we should lose our heads along with the rest and stop weighing right and wrong. It would mean that a majority of the people in this hemisphere would go war-mad, quit thinking and devote their energies to destruction. . . . A declaration of war would mean that Germany would be beaten, and so badly beaten that there would be a dictated peace, a victorious peace. It means . . . an attempt to reconstruct a peacetime civilization with war standards, and at the end of the war there will be no bystanders with sufficient peace standards left to work with. There will be only war standards.[9]

These were strong words, but events as they unfolded did not reveal Wilson as softheaded. Neither the nation's excesses, the overall military accomplishments, nor the complexities of peacemaking can be reviewed in detail here, however. Our purpose is to consider the religious aspects and consequences of the war; yet this alone is a vast subject, for like any traumatic national experience, this one had great transforming power. The churches discovered that in passing through the war they left one century behind and entered another. The experience, moreover, had both spiritual and institutional dimensions.

PREACHING THE GREAT CRUSADE

For a full century before the coming of war Germany had been America's tutor in the arts and sciences as well as in

[8] William E. Leuchtenburg, *The Perils of Prosperity, 1914–32* (Chicago: University of Chicago Press, 1958), p. 34.

[9] From Wilson's conversation with Frank Cobb of the *New York World*, as reported by Maxwell Anderson (Samuel Eliot Morison and Henry Steele Commager, *The Growth of the American Republic*, 2 vols. [New York: Oxford University Press, 1956], 2:466).

philosophy and theology. Educational institutions from the kindergarten to the graduate school seminar had been reshaped. Social and political theory, many leading ideas of the Social Gospel, and even the concept of academic freedom had been enthusiastically championed by thousands of men who had studied in German universities and research institutes. So deep did this influence penetrate that the president of the Hartford Seminary Foundation resorted to Wilhelm Hermann's *Ethics* and Johann Kaspar Bluntschli's theory of military force to justify the United States' entering the conflict.[10]

Yet despite such deep intellectual indebtedness, the outbreak of hostilities began almost immediately to sunder old attachments. Traditional distrust of "entangling alliances" at first inclined Americans against involvement. In his campaign of 1916 President Wilson was somewhat surprised that his having "kept us out of war" provided his liveliest argument for reelection. Churches of all types conspicuously supported the peace movement.[11] Running against the old isolationistic sentiment, however, was a rising demand for preparedness, ever more outspoken support for the Allied cause, and, among some prominent leaders including Theodore Roosevelt, a positive glorification of war. To advance the war cause the National Security League, the American Defense Society, and other similar groups were organized—some of them even arranging for military training camps for civilians. These or-

[10] W. Douglas MacKenzie, *Christian Ethics in the World War* (New York: Association Press, 1918), pp. 23–24. Bluntschli was Swiss, but he was educated in Germany and was a professor there during his most influential years.

[11] The Irish were not naturally disposed to spring to England's aid; and very early Cardinal Farley of New York returned from Europe with the diagnosis that all of the nations at war (perhaps especially France) were suffering justifiably for their abuse of the Roman church in recent years. England's brutal suppression of the Easter Rebellion in Ireland in the spring of 1916 further aroused Irish doubts about England's Holy Cause. German-Americans were also indisposed to accept the British interpretation of the war, and both intellectuals and church leaders (Lutheran and Roman Catholic) voiced their views. Under Pope Benedict XV the papacy was officially neutral, but diplomatic relations with France had been suspended since 1904, and Vatican sympathies tended to lie with the Central Powers. Wilson rejected the pope's peace proposals (summer 1917) as yielding too much to Germany.

ganizations flourished especially in the East among Americans of "Anglo-Saxon" descent, and they won increasing support from clergy of the denominations with strong and clear British rootage—Presbyterians, Congregationalists, Methodists and, most outspokenly, Episcopalians.

The steady pro-Allied pressure applied by many prominent spokesmen no doubt encouraged Wilson, despite obvious risks, to follow a policy that from the very first did not deny Britain the benefits of her naval superiority; and as the war settled down to a grim test of strength on the western front, he would not entertain "a single abatement of right" lest other "humiliations" ensue. Having settled upon this course, incidents such as the *Lusitania*'s sinking in 1915 with many Americans aboard were certain to happen. When they did, the stridency of anti-Germanism increased. The nation, therefore, was almost solidly behind the declaration of war when it came, and by this time the peace movement had been reduced to its hard core among the Quakers, Mennonites, and other conscientious objectors. Even these groups were subjected to such powerful patriotic pressures that many individuals defected.

Ray Abrams, who wrote in the isolationist atmosphere of the 1930s, has often been accused of exaggerating the wartime response of the churches in his *Preachers Present Arms.* But no successful refutation has been forthcoming—nor is one likely to appear. The simple fact is that religious leaders —lay and clerical, Jewish, Catholic, and Protestant, through corporate as well as personal expressions, lifted their voices in a chorus of support for the war. Every hideous term and image of the Allied and American propaganda offices found its way into official pronouncements. Even the Federal Council of Churches fell in line: "The war for righteousness will be won! Let the Church do her part." And indisputably, the church *did* her part. Randolph H. McKim, from his pulpit in the national capital, managed to pack all the standard crusading images into a single paragraph:

It is God who has summoned us to this war. . . . This conflict is indeed a crusade. The greatest in history—the holiest. It is in the profoundest and truest sense a Holy War. . . . Yes, it is Christ, the King of Righteousness, who calls us to grapple in deadly strife with this unholy and blasphemous power.

Amid such displays of chauvinism the Congregational theologian George Holley Gilbert declared that "this thought of divine favoritism looks strange indeed in the light of the twentieth century. We expect to find it among uncivilized peoples; it is part of the narrow intellectual outlook of barbarians." But Gilbert was not chiding his American brethren of the cloth; he was referring to the *Gott mit uns* of the kaiser, or (as the urbane Henry Van Dyke referred to that ruler), the "Potsdam Werewolf." "If the Kaiser is a Christian," echoed Courtland Meyers from Boston's Tremont Temple, "the devil in hell is a Christian, and I am an atheist."

Nor was it only the kaiser who came in for such violent language. Many refused so limited a target. Francis Greenwood Peabody, who had experienced his own religious awakening at the University of Halle in the 1890s and in 1910 had extolled the German intellectual heritage in connection with the opening of a Harvard-Berlin university exchange program, now found the German people "untamed barbarians." Newell Dwight Hillis, minister of Beecher's Plymouth Church in Brooklyn, spoke favorably of a plan for "exterminating the German people . . . the sterilization of 10,000,000 German soldiers and the segregation of the women." That Germans were all "swinish Huns" became a cliché of the American pulpit. With a remarkable combination of these views, Henry B. Wright, a warmly evangelical YMCA director and sometime professor in the Yale Divinity School, provided a Christian meditation for young soldiers with qualms about bayonet drill: "In the hour of soul crisis the [YMCA] Secretary can turn and say with quiet certainty to your lad and my lad, 'I would not enter this work till I could see Jesus himself sighting down a gun barrel and running a bayonet through an enemy's body.'" The Unitarian Albert C. Dieffenbach was equally sure that Christ "would take bayonet and grenade and bomb and rifle and do the work of deadliness against that which is the most deadly enemy of his Father's Kingdom in a thousand years." And so one could continue quoting bloodthirsty Americans from the books and magazines that, shelf on shelf, gather dust in any large American library.[12]

The basic message of such wartime offerings could be and was filtered through almost every kind of doctrinal net.

[12] Abrams, *Preachers Present Arms*, pp. 58, 55, 104, 105, 109, 70, 68, 31–32, 76, 100, 115, 150.

Shailer Mathews, the Social Gospel scholar of the Chicago Divinity School, made his book-length plea in the context of an extreme theological modernism. Mathews's central concern was the nature and interrelation of two great social forces, religion and patriotism. He argued for their substantial identity, but only after making clear that "the real expression of democracy in religious thinking is outside the field of orthodox theology. . . . Only where the spirit of democracy is working is there creative religious thinking. Only there is the union of patriotism and the religion of tomorrow. For in democracy alone can the immanence of God be expressed in the terms of human experience." He then expounded "the moral values of patriotism" in terms of America's destiny: "Our patriotism dares to glory in its outlook and its hopes because it knows that the triumph of our land is the triumph of the cause of a better humanity." Mathews believed that a conscientious objector should be spared persecution, "provided he does not speak with a German accent," but his positive moral counsel was unambiguously militant: "For an American to refuse to share in the present war . . . is not Christian." "A religion which will keep its followers from committing themselves to the support of such patriotism is either too aesthetic for humanity's actual needs, too individualistic to be social, or too disloyal to be tolerated." In a final chapter he expounded the manifold ways in which religion could serve patriotism, purging German influences from the country's teaching of sociology, history, political economy, and psychology, strengthening the people in times of trial, and above all, giving fervor and direction to the nation's moral life. The aims he proclaimed were an international extension of the Social Gospel and a world of democratic nations living in peace and justice. The first step in the achievement of these ends was the total defeat of the kaiser, the destruction of German *Kultur*, and the reeducation of the German people. He bade Christians, however, to oppose a "punitive" treaty and to encourage "the beginnings of a League of Nations . . . [that] already exist." Mathews thus concluded on a note of high idealism, but down to his final peroration he painted a world picture in solid blacks and whites and did his utmost to make religion an intrinsic component of national solidarity.[13]

[13] Shailer Mathews, *Patriotism and Religion* (New York: Macmillan Co., 1918).

At the opposite end of the theological spectrum, the conservative premillennialist S. D. Gordon of New York added a volume on "the deeper meaning of the war" to his long series of "Quiet Talks," attempting to fit Germany and the kaiser into his reading of the various "prophecies" that point to the Last Days. He found them, of course, and put special stress on the narrative of Moses, Joshua, and Amalek in Exodus 17:8–16. Germany in 1914, therefore, becomes "the modern Amalek through which Satan was renewing his old ambitious attempt. . . . The Satanic fingerprints are unmistakable. . . . The bloody footprints are beyond dispute."[14] They betray the Beast. Mathews, who was well aware of these interpretations among the organizers of the "prophetic conferences," dismissed their "fantastic expositions of scripture," their identifications of the kaiser as the Antichrist, and their predictions of war tanks found in the Hebrew prophets. He even condemned them for sapping "the springs of national courage" and leaving all to Christ and the angels. More remarkable, however, is the convergence of value judgments among modernists and premillennialists—and their agreement that in one sense or another, the war on earth was linked up with a war in heaven.

Speaking from what could be regarded as a rather central position in the evangelical Protestant doctrinal spectrum, W. Douglas MacKenzie, president of the Hartford Seminary Foundation, worked out what can fairly be designated as another characteristic rationale in his book *Christian Ethics in the World War* (1918). Like Mathews and a great number of other theologians who expressed their patriotism through ethical treatises, MacKenzie took great pains to counter the pacifist position which he himself had once supported. His argument, however, contrasted sharply with Mathews's message of religio-patriotic solidarity. He agrees with the German theologian, Isaak Dorner, that the nation-state, though a human institution, rests "on a divine basis," and hence must use physical force to restrain selfish and vicious men in order to secure the ends for which it exists. "Literal obedience to the outward phraseology [of the Sermon on the Mount] would actually cause the death or suicide of one institution after another." "In an unmoral

[14] Samuel Dickey Gordon, *Quiet Talks on the Deeper Meaning of the War* (New York: Fleming H. Revell Co., 1919), pp. 52–57.

world it is the moral duty of the State to use force." On the other hand, he sees on the horizon a time when even "the mightiest empires shall be brought under the control of a new international system" and justifies the war on the ground that a League of Nations will bring in a "new era in the moral development of humanity." Avoiding bloodthirsty maledictions of Germany, he contrasts it to the Allies in absolute terms: "The overthrow of German militarism will not only sweep away the supreme obstacle, but will compel the more rapid fulfillment of the age-long dream of seers and saints."

There were, of course, a few American pacifists who were not deflected from their stand. Those who came from the traditional "peace churches," Mennonite, Quaker, etc., suffered many public insults, but they were legally allowed to accept alternative forms of noncombatant service. The American Friends Service Committee (organized 1917) filled two important functions, assisting conscientious objectors at home and sending relief workers abroad. Christian Scientists also organized a service force.[15] Due to the enormous public pressures for loyalty, the workings of the Espionage Act, and the strong demands of most denominational leaders, dissenting views were only very rarely expressed. Even so, almost every communion had some representation among the several hundred who voiced conscientious objections to the war—or, as in most cases, to *all* wars. After a fairly rigorous survey Abrams documented seventy "nonconformist" ministers in the various non-German, nonpacifist churches. Most of them were socialists or showed pronounced Social Gospel leanings; Unitarians, Universalists, and Congregationalists made up slightly more than half of his list, while none came from the South or from the Roman Catholic church. Nearly all of them paid dearly for their antimilitaristic scruples.[16]

[15] In October 1914 the Mother Church solicited funds for the relief of Christian Scientists in Europe, an act which began their War Relief Fund. By 1915 the fund had widened its range of giving to non-Christian Scientists, and in 1917, with United States entry into the war, a Camp Welfare Committee was organized to meet the needs of inductees. All told, the church contributed $2 million through the War Relief Committee, of which $300,000 was devoted to Christian Science literature and its distribution, while the remainder went for housing, rest centers, recreation, salaries of workers, transportation, clothing for refugees, and knitted garments for military personnel.

[16] Abrams, *Preachers Present Arms,* pp. 21–23, 35, 177, 92.

German-Americans of almost every religious hue also became the objects of suspicion, discrimination, and in many
cases, even of violence. There were almost no signs of overt
resistance among them, even though a great many, probably
a majority, of them doubted that the Allied cause was an
unambiguous holy crusade. Walter Rauschenbusch spoke for
the many German-Americans during these years who recognized the near inevitability of American involvement. Given
the breakdown of world order and Germany's "excessive
power," he could justify the United States' course of action
and conscientiously support his government. In his 1917
Taylor Lectures at Yale, however, he held that "the ultimate
cause of the war was the same lust for easy and unearned
gain which has created the internal social evils under which
every nation has suffered. The social problem and the war
problem are fundamentally one problem." On other occasions
he pointed to great evils on both sides and suggested that
Germany "has not been the only power seeking geographical
and economic expansion." He recoiled from the "war spirit"
and "spiritual psychosis" that militarism was fomenting in
America. When Algernon Crapsey, an Episcopalian liberal
who had earlier gained national renown in a heresy trial,
"demanded" that he clarify his stand in a public statement,
Rauschenbusch dissented from the prevailing logic of American church leaders: "You assume that powers with such dis-
cordant interests as the present allies can be combined in a
perpetual league. . . . You offer a Utopian scheme as a
justification for emasculating and hog-tying one of the great
parts of humanity. . . . I am afraid of those who want to
drag our country in to satisfy their partisan hate, or because
they think universal peace will result from the victory of the
allies."[17]

In 1922 William Adams Brown reviewed the churches'
work during the war. He admitted that one of their main responsibilities had been "to keep alive the international spirit,
the spirit of brotherhood and good will, and in time of war to
prepare the world for the healing tasks of peace." Yet he also
knew from his experience as secretary of the General Wartime Commission that in this regard they had failed. "The
fact remains," he said, "that in the heat of the struggle the

[17] *Rochester Herald*, 23 August 1915; quoted in Dores R. Sharpe,
Walter Rauschenbusch (New York: Macmillan Co., 1942), pp.
378–79.

judgment of many a minister did not conspicuously rise above that of the average citizen. The Universal note, so signally sounded by Israel's prophets in times of similar crises, was less in evidence than we could have desired. Yet, thank God, the note of brotherhood was never entirely absent."[18] This is a just and accurate statement.

THE WARTIME WORK OF THE CHURCHES

As might be expected of groups so unquestioningly in support of American involvement in the war, the churches did everything in their power to strengthen the military effort. This involved them in two quite different campaigns: a ministry to the armed forces in the training camps and overseas, and participation in the countless tasks of the "home front."

When war was declared, the religious forces of the nation were unprepared. The military chaplaincy was moribund, and civilian agencies for ministering to soldiers and sailors, except for the YMCA, which at least stood ready as a national institution with interdenominational support, were almost nonexistent. As early as 8 May 1917, however, the Federal Council of Churches called a meeting in Washington to organize the General Wartime Commission, a coordinating agency consisting of official delegates of thirty-five different religious organizations including the Federal Council itself, the Home Missions Council and several other cooperative federations, the YMCA, YWCA, American Bible Society, and a representative group of Protestant churches.

This commission, in turn, created a Committee of One Hundred to carry out its tasks, with two Presbyterians, Robert E. Speer and William Adams Brown, as chairman and secretary. It included the heads of the large and aggressive war agencies which each denomination or group of related churches (such as the Lutheran) had organized. The committee thus was admirably suited to carry out its responsibilities as a source of reliable information, a liaison between the government and the churches, and a support for the military chaplaincy. Because morale was high and the need for

18 William A. Brown, *The Church in America*, pp. 94–97. He is less severe in *A Teacher and His Times* (New York: Scribners, 1940), pp. 223–50.

cooperation great, the committee demonstrated the social potentialities of organized Protestantism in an unprecedented way. As changing needs required, it created as many as twenty-five subcommittees for various tasks. One of the most important of these was that which organized the Interchurch Emergency Campaign for funds—not only to meet the $300,000 expenses of the commission itself, but also to supply the far vaster needs of individual denominations. Least practical and most forward-looking was the Committee on the War and Religious Outlook, which, with Brown as chairman, sought to evaluate the significance of the amazing release of ecclesiastical energy precipitated by the war and to lay plans for harnessing this power for postwar works of peace.

The chief contributions of cooperating churches were in answer to the perennial needs of armies. Once the War Department had improved the status of the chaplaincy, problems of recruitment and training ensued. A chaplain's school needed staff and support. Each denomination instituted procedures to gain chaplaincy volunteers sufficient to the ratio established by Congress of one for each twelve hundred men, and a joint commission was created to screen these ministerial candidates. The draft laws allowed seminarians to continue their theological studies so that a shortage of clergy would not develop, but each denomination, nationally and locally, did what it could to provide auxiliary ministries wherever military training was being conducted. Added to these needs was the enormous demand for Bibles, tracts, and general reading matter, as well as recreation facilities and rest centers at home and abroad. In response, the Red Cross, Library Association, American Bible Society, YMCA, and the newly constituted War Camp Community Service became major distributing agencies for Protestants. Particularly vital was the YMCA, which, with its agents in military uniform, became a semiofficial agency of the War Department to operate canteens and perform related services. The Salvation Army played a similar, less official role.

Jews and Catholics had less difficult organizational problems for obvious reasons, yet parallel agencies of coordination and direct activity were quickly formed or assigned wartime tasks: the Jewish Welfare Board, the Young Men's Hebrew Association, the National Catholic War Council, and the Knights of Columbus. For these groups, too, the wartime experience was to have an enduring impact, even though it was less complex, in one case for reasons of size, in the other because of existing institutional unity. In mobilizing Jewish resources the YMHA served a function like that of the YMCA among Protestants, while the Jewish Welfare Board coordinated other aspects of the task, including the arrangements for chaplains.[19] The great Roman Catholic fraternal order, the Knights of Columbus, appointed Patrick H. Callahan chairman of a new committee on war activities[20] and responded almost immediately to the needs for recreational and religious facilities, especially in southern military camps far from Catholic population centers. Later they would carry their work overseas. In several campaigns for funds the Knights raised over $14 million, and by Armistice Day they had nearly two thousand secretaries in active service. That it received over 80 percent of the Catholic share in the United Fund Drive of 1918 indicates its centrality in Roman Catholic war work.

The formation of the National Catholic War Council, however, had a more lasting impact on the church as a whole. It was organized at a large general convention gathered in August 1917 in Washington, D.C., where sixty-eight dioceses, twenty-seven national organizations already members of the American Federation of Catholic Societies, and the entire Catholic press were represented. As chairman of the council's Committee on War Activities, Father John J. Burke, then editor of the Paulists' *Catholic World,* began a long career as a shaper of Catholic social and political policy. When the council's large executive committee proved too cumbersome, the archbishops placed the council's administration in the hands of four bishops. During the war, the council undertook very much the same tasks as the Protestant General Wartime

[19] There were about 200,000 Jews in the armed forces (48 percent of those in the army being in the infantry), about 10,000 commissioned officers, twenty-five chaplains—and about 2,800 fatalities. The Jewish Welfare Board was organized in April 1917 by representatives of other Jewish agencies, with Colonel Harry Cutler of Providence, Rhode Island, as chairman. It had 500 workers in 200 different places at home, and 178 in 57 centers overseas. After the war, the board turned its attention to the development of community centers in the larger cities.

[20] Callahan was a Louisville industrialist who since 1914 had been head of the Knights' Commission on Religious Prejudices, an agency to counter nativist attacks.

Commission, among other things, arranging for the recruitment, training, and supervision (under a chaplain-general) of about a thousand military chaplains. Probably the most important side effect of the council's many activities was that it ended the neutrality or abstention of the bishops on specific quesions of public policy. In 1919 the Wartime Council was reorganized as the National Catholic Welfare Council, and thereafter the bishops assumed a new position of responsibility for national leadership in the realm of social affairs.

As a result of the gargantuan effort of America's religious forces, over eleven thousand civilian service personnel accompanied the armed forces in Europe, while an uncounted but far larger contingent served in and around the military camps and stations at home. Another important consequence was the unprecedented cooperation of Protestant, Catholic, and Jewish organizations, as well as nondenominational or completely independent agencies like the Red Cross. The United Fund Drive of 1918, for example, set an American fund-raising record with a yield of $200 million. All across the land, local congregations became rallying points for volunteers and organizational centers for war work. For denominations that were too small to maintain their own war agencies, the Protestant commission became a channel between willing hands and military needs.

American religious institutions, however, did not limit themselves to evangelistic and charitable ministries, but plunged directly into the war work. Ministers were steadily supplied with government propaganda, and they made their pulpits an important point of emission. Both directly and indirectly they labored to gain enlistments in the armed forces, and they hung service-star flags in their sanctuaries. Liberty Loan drives were conducted in the churches. Despite all of this activity, the English-born Presbyterian and sometime chaplain and war correspondent Joseph H. Odell stirred the nation in February 1918 with an article in the *Atlantic Monthly* entitled "Peter Sat by the Fire Warming Himself," in which he castigated the passivity of the churches! Needless to say, fervent and violent rebuttals soon found their way into print. The response of Methodist Bishop W. F. McDowell revealed their prevailing tone: "We do not intend that any church shall have more stars in its service flag than we have." All in all, the judgment of W. W. Sweet will stand:

"At least for the period of World War I the separation of church and state was suspended."[21]

ARMISTICE AND THE "NEW ERA"

On 11 November 1918 the news arrived: the war was over! A false report had sent the nation into a delirium of joy four days before, but President Wilson himself penned the three succinct sentences of this authentic report:

> My Fellow Countrymen: The armistice was signed this morning. Everything for which America fought has been accomplished. It will now be our fortunate duty to assist by example, by sober, friendly counsel, and by material aid in the establishment of just democracy throughout the world.

Jubilation reigned across the land, not always with sobriety. The "supreme obstacle" to the new era of international order was a battered ruin. The great opportunity was at hand. Only five days before, however, the Republican party had won control of both houses of Congress in the midterm elections. And all too soon the desire for "normalcy" would submerge the deep resolves that had been expressed since 1914. But before this trend could be discerned, the Protestant churchmen who had experienced the wartime triumphs of cooperative action resolved to find means for maintaining its momentum. In this access of euphoria a whole cluster of fund-raising campaigns were launched—all of them inspired by the astronomic attainments of wartime drives.

On the expected advent of a new era of world order, democracy, and peace, nearly every ethical and religious justification for American entry into Europe's war had rested. Almost every personal statement and official church pronouncement advancing the cause of war had anchored the argument in some plan for an international agency to outlaw war. What role, then, did the churches and the Presbyterian messiah in the White House play when the moment of truth arrived?

Even as churchmen were charting their ambitious cam-

21 William Warren Sweet, *The Story of Religion in America,* p. 402.

paigns, President Wilson, his selected peace commissioners, and a large group of technical experts were aboard the *George Washington,* moving toward their fateful rendezvous in Europe. These delegates of the American nation, and most assuredly their leader, were inspired by an even vaster vision: the delivery of Europe from the tyranny of history, the making of a world in which democracy would be safe and all peoples secure from war. But in one case as in the other, human nature and human history would soon reveal the undependability of visions. Indeed, the treaty and the League of Nations which Wilson hoped for were already doomed. The Wilson government had not made the relinquishment of the older Allied agreements a condition of American entry; Wilson's summons for a Democratic Congress in 1918 had not been heard by the electorate; the Republican party was alienated and hungry for power. Outraged by Wilson's decision to ignore the Senate in appointing his peace commissioners, powerful men like Henry Cabot Lodge and William Borah were determined to block Wilson's expected demand for unqualified American support. Finally and decisively, the American people had not been converted to a sense of international responsibility. Having been so long diverted from normal peacetime pursuits and pleasures, they were more isolationistic than ever. The long bombardment with war propaganda had probably served to cheapen and degrade popular idealism.

As for the churches and their memberships, the evidence is ambiguous. Robert M. Miller's careful canvass of both the denominational press and the official deliberations of the major churches has shown that by and large the attitude of ecclesiastical leaders was ideologically continuous with their wartime attitudes. Having supported a war to crush the Hun, they favored the treaty's harsh terms. "Within ten or fifteen years clerical criticism of the Treaty of Versailles became as common and as fashionable as denunciations of liquor, but in 1919 and 1920 only a very small minority of churchmen found the peace unjust."[22] On the other hand, approval of the treaty's harshness was accompanied by overwhelming support of the League without crippling reservations. According to every available index, whether editorials, official resolutions, or pronouncements by recognized spokesmen, the

[22] Robert M. Miller, *American Protestantism and Social Issues, 1919–1939,* p. 318.

Protestant churches supported the League. Even after its defeat they continued throughout the twenties to advocate American participation in the World Court and similar efforts to implement the idea of international order. As might be expected, the Federal Council of Churches—not to mention the Church Peace Union—was overwhelmingly in support, even to the point of sending five delegates to Paris to convey this message to the president in person. Wilson hardly needed their assurance, however; and since only 15 percent of the Senate was irreconcilably opposed to the League, it may be that support was not needed there either. Even the American people would have accepted American participation in 1919. News of the League's final defeat in the Senate was greeted in the religious press and in various ecclesiastical assemblies by a wave of outrage and disappointment, and by unspecific charges that men in high places were putting politics before principle. What was lacking during the critical months was not support, but presidential statesmanship. When that failed, the road to "normalcy" and national irresponsibility was open.

53

THE TWENTIES: FROM THE ARMISTICE TO THE CRASH

The decade of the twenties is the most sharply defined decade in American history. Marked off by the war at one end and the Depression at the other, it has a character of its own —ten restless years roaring from jubilation to despair amid international and domestic dislocation. It has also had a bad press, whether viewed from the Right or the Left. To conservatives it has always been the Jazz Age, a lamentable season of excess, ballyhoo, and moral degeneration. To liberal and radical interpreters, especially if they felt the pain of the Depression and the thrill of the New Deal, it was simply the culminating expression of bourgeois decadence, a demonstration that a social order dominated by businessmen was bankrupt. Religiously oriented critics of all parties have usually spoken of these ten years as a tragic display of obscurantism, superficiality, complacency, and futile conflict. What has been lost to mind is the fact that the twenties were an exciting time of social transformation, intellectual revolution, and artistic triumph.[1]

In the decade after the Armistice modern technocratic America came of age and began to be conscious of its newly

[1] In 1950 *Life* magazine looked back at the twenties with amused condescension: "It is startling to find the old headliners still looking as chipper as they do in these pictures taken in the past few months—startling and pleasant. They were the life of the party and everyone loves them, even though it was not a party that the nation can afford to throw again" (2 January 1950). It may be that the 1960s provide the standpoint for a more sympathetic judgment.

released potentiality. The United States became an urban nation not only in statistical fact but in its dominant mood.[2] The movies, the radio, and the automobile became commonplace. The standard of living took a great jump forward; leisure and play became the right of the many rather than the privilege of a few. Vacations with pay, golf, tennis, and spectator sports entered the American way of life. In Jack Dempsey, Babe Ruth, Knute Rockne, Paul Whiteman, Lowell Thomas, Rudolph Valentino, Charlie Chaplin, and, far above them all, in Charles A. Lindbergh, the nation found heroes cut from new kinds of cloth. The newly franchised American woman made her brazen appearance. And accompanying these highly visible cultural innovations were vast economic changes stimulated in part by national advertising and the mass media, but also reflecting important developments in technology, finance, and business organization. Given these circumstances, conflict was inevitable. Furious controversies, great debates, and wild fulminations were the order of the day. And nearly all of this conflict is part of the nation's religious history, either because the churches were active participants or because events impinged on their life.

THE PEACETIME CAMPAIGNS OF THE CHURCHES

Most appropriately, the first great peacetime campaign of the churches—Protestant, Catholic, and Jewish—received its impetus directly from the war. The United War Work Campaign directed by John R. Mott was conceived while the last great Allied advance on Germany's western front ground to its close. At their final victory banquet the campaign leaders listened to Mott's oration on "the Largest Voluntary Offering in History." He told them with unrestrained enthusiasm how "the entire American people—the rich and the poor, the members of all parties, races, and religious faiths—had united their gifts and sacrifices, and rolled up the vast sum of $200,000,000." Mott dwelt at length on the obstacles to success: hurried organization, high taxes, the competition of the government's Fourth Liberty Loan (itself a tribute to the newly developed art of high-pressure salesmanship), the congressional elections of 1918, the influenza epidemic, the

---

[2] The census of 1920 revealed that for the first time *most* Americans (51.4 percent) lived in "cities" of 2,500 or over.

"false" and then the "true" peace celebrations which, all across the nation, had disrupted the launching ceremonies, and finally, the very fact that the campaign had united the efforts of seven separate organizations and hence lost the power to capitalize on special interest groups. He did not exaggerate, however, in speaking of a "great triumph" and in insisting that "there has been nothing like it in the history of campaigns."[3] The event indicates the mood of America as it contemplated the return of peace and the discharge of three million soldiers.

Strictly in the realm of ecclesiastical history, the most important effort to propel wartime fervor and newly learned organizational techniques into the postwar situation was the Interchurch World Movement.[4] Professor William Adams Brown, who called it "the religious counterpart to the League of Nations," gives an inside account of the meeting at 25 Madison Avenue, New York City, on 17 December 1918, which had been called by the Board of Foreign Missions of the Southern Presbyterian church:

> No one who was present in the upper room on that momentous December day when the Interchurch World Movement was born can forget the thrill of expectation which stirred those who had gathered there. They were men of long experience—secretaries of church boards, professors in theological seminaries, veteran workers in the cause of home and foreign missions, and they knew the weaknesses and limitations of the bodies they served to the full. But they had seen a vision—the vision of a united church uniting a divided world; and under the spell of what they saw all things seemed possible. Difficulties were waved aside, doubters were silenced. In the face of an opportunity so unparalleled there seemed but one thing to do, and that was to go forward.[5]

What they attempted was a grand peacetime crusade which would unite all the benevolent and missionary agencies

[3] John R. Mott, *The Largest Voluntary Offering in History* (privately printed, 1919).

[4] See Eldon Ernst, "The Interchurch World Movement" (Ph.D. diss., Yale University, 1967) for a valuable interpretation of this great campaign.

[5] William A. Brown, *The Church in America*, p. 119.

of American Protestantism into a single campaign for money, men, and spiritual revival. Included in its scope were every phase of church work, domestic and foreign. In the words of its own general committee, it was to be "a cooperative effort of evangelical churches . . . to survey unitedly their present common tasks and simultaneously and together to secure the necessary resources . . . required for these tasks." A lavish prospectus, expensive offices, and elaborate promotional plans featured the movement's launching. Work went ahead to analyze worldwide needs, to inaugurate a broad educational program, to instruct the churches in wise planning and management of these vast responsibilities, to recruit personnel, and above all, by united efforts and modern methods, to raise astronomic sums of money, not only for the central agency itself, but for all the financial campaigns underway or to be launched by participating denominations.

On the eve of the big campaign in April 1920, they issued a nationwide bulletin concerning "the biggest business of the biggest man in the world":

> Christ was big, was He not? None ever bigger.
> Christ was busy, was He not? None ever busier.
> He was always about His Father's business.
> Christ needs big men for big business.

Three hundred million dollars was their first goal, but this was later raised to five hundred million and finally to a billion dollars. With such goals the result was perhaps inevitable; but a number of special factors help to explain the movement's collapse, not least the nation's postwar surfeit of idealistic financial campaigns. The prominence of liberal social thinkers among its leadership aroused already embattled conservatives to undermine the effort, and both Northern Presbyterians and Northern Baptists voted to withdraw their support in 1920. The obvious presence of Social Gospel tendencies also alarmed many potential donors, though the publicized pro-labor report of the commission set up to investigate the great steel strike actually appeared after the movement had begun to fall apart. Finally, a postwar resurgence of denominational loyalty left the IWM stranded, unable to meet even 15 percent of its indebtedness for expenditures. The "friendly citizens" outside the churches on whom the IWM's share of the take was to depend apparently lost their solicitude for the institutional church after the nation's martial spirit evaporated.

The Interchurch World Movement, a victim of its dreams and its overhead, failed completely and distributed its debts to the cooperating churches, who paid them in full. In financial terms the denominational campaigns were relatively more successful. By 1922 not less than $200 million in strictly denominational funds were raised or pledged, though the churches also suffered from excessive costs, unpaid pledges, and the general postwar letdown. In the qualitative sense, however, there was probably more loss than gain, for the promotional spirit that underlay these gigantic efforts corrupted and weakened the spiritual fiber of the churches. The methods used were artful, mechanical, and pragmatically effective; but the hard sell had a corrosive effect. It revealed the enormous toll of the wartime amalgamation of patriotic and religious objectives.

An excellent expression of this effect is William Adams Brown's *The Church in America, A Study of the Present Condition and Future Prospects of American Protestantism* (1922), an informative work by a great systematic theologian, a professor at Union Theological Seminary, and the liberal thinker most often praised for his great concern for the church. Yet the book rests its case on the utilitarian judgment that "American Protestantism contain[s] within itself the principle of improvement which warrants our hope that it will prove the unifying and inspiring influence which American democracy needs."[6] For Brown as for many others, the war seemed in retrospect to have been a tremendous stimulus to American piety, especially among Protestants. Never had the churches been better attended, never had so many members been busily involved in the country's life and work, never had the general public's judgments of religion been so affirmative or their generosity with money more apparent. Yet events were to reveal that these exhilarating experiences led the churches directly into the complacent culture-protestantism of the 1920s. The Great Crusade ended its march at the lawn socials of normalcy.

The indexes of denominational vitality show a prevailing downward trend for the next ten years.[7] Church attendance

6 Ibid., p. 11.
7 Robert T. Handy, "The American Religious Depression, 1925–1935," *Church History* 29 (March 1960): 3–16.

declined, not only in economically depressed rural areas, but throughout the country. The Foreign Missionary Conference of North America reported that only 252 students had offered themselves for foreign service in 1928, as against 2,700 in 1920. The income figures for the major mission boards also took a generally downward trend despite the nation's booming prosperity. Most serious of all, though almost impossible to quantify, was a pervasive thinning out of evangelical substance, a tendency to identify religion with the business-oriented values of the American way of life. Because of this prevailing spirit neither the widespread adoption of the Social Gospel by Protestant ministers nor the many social pronouncements of denominational assemblies had much popular impact.

All considered, however, "normalcy," "complacency," and "religious depression" do not adequately account for the many violent encounters of the twenties. One wonders if any decade was *less* normal, for it was a time of crisis for both the Protestant Establishment and the historic evangelicalism which undergirded it. It was the critical epoch when the Puritan heritage lost its hold on the leaders of public life, and when the mainstream denominations grew increasingly out of touch with the classic Protestant witness. Secular provocations, moreover, tended to speed up this estrangement—and this was especially true of the Red Scare.

RADICALS AND IMMIGRANTS

The Republican victory in the congressional elections of 1918 revealed an electorate surfeited with progressivism, sacrifice, and grand ideals. The war's enormous heightening of patriotic Americanism had also reduced the general tolerance for nonconformist behavior. Given the rise of world communism and the legacy of prewar nativism, therefore, the Red Scare was hardly a surprising response to the rash of strikes, bomb throwing, and radical advocacy that broke out after the Armistice. Nor were church members exempt from the pervasive hysteria. When the deportation of radicals was being proposed in 1919, Billy Sunday, who rarely failed to offer his conservative Protestant audiences the views they held most dear, offered a simpler solution. "If I had my way with these ornery wild-eyed socialists and IWW's, I would stand them up before a firing squad and save space on our ships." As for Reds, he would "fill the jails so full . . . that their feet would stick out of the windows." The vast promotional campaigns of the churches also supported the nation's anti-Red hysteria. Over and over they depicted religion as a valuable bulwark against radicalism.[8] Even the IWM voiced a remarkably agrarian version of the American dream and expressed alarm at its subversion, while rural America took a strong (if not quite its last) stand against an emergent urban civilization. Most Protestants, therefore, tended actually to accept, internalize, and perpetuate the major theories that animated the Red Scare.

On the other hand, church-related social action committees and many other persons and agencies provided more than their share of leadership in opposing the great witchhunt and demanding justice for the accused. The same can be said of their stand on the great *cause célèbres:* the Sacco-Vanzetti case in Massachusetts, the Mooney-Billings case in California, and the Centralia affair in Washington, all of which involved the criminal conviction of radicals under questionable circumstances. The postwar bearers of the Social Gospel not only opposed the illiberal spirit of the times, but often became themselves the objects of suspicion and censure.

The Roman Catholic church faced a totally different situation. Its constituency was heavily foreign-born and urban, deeply implicated in the labor movement, and frequently bore the brunt of nativist activities. The so-called Bishops' Program of 1919 was entitled "Social Reconstruction: A General Review of the Problems and Survey of Remedies," and in so many words it was a call for a social welfare state. During the twenties, therefore, Roman Catholicism exerted a mildly liberal influence in national affairs. That Jews were also as-

[8] "If the United States is to be one nation, with common feeling, language habits, customs and moral and spiritual attitude, the Americanization must center around the largest racial group, the old white stock. . . . The rural people, the agriculturists, have the least admixture of foreign blood of any portion of the population. . . . If American life is to have a tone, this tone must come not from the cities with their varied and heterogeneous racial groups, but from the villages and country districts. It is the task of the churches to see that this tone continues one of Godliness and pariotism, high ideals and clean living" (*New Era Magazine,* September 1919, p. 522).

sociated with liberal and radical causes gave many Protestants added inducement to campaign for immigration restriction.

When Attorney General A. Mitchell Palmer was winning wide popular applause for deporting aliens by the hundreds, legislative action on immigration was not hard to get. Woodrow Wilson, in one of his last presidential acts, declined to sign a bill setting 3 percent quotas based on the 1910 census; but under Harding the new Congress acted quickly and passed a bill in May 1921. In 1924 a still more stringent measure was passed, gauged to preserve the existing demographic balance, and thus to favor those countries which few wished to leave.[9] It was a "Nordic victory"—and it brought a long, colorful epoch in American history to a close. The country had somehow lost confidence in its assimilative powers. Nor did action stop with restriction, for many states passed laws which excluded aliens from a wide range of professional work, while suburban housing regulations, extralegal procedures, and new institutions like the increasingly numerous golf and country clubs accomplished the same ends. During the "tribal twenties" many colleges and even prestigious universities became noticeably restrictive in their admission policies.

More ominous still was the rapidly expanding activity of the Ku Klux Klan. It had been revived in 1915 by William J. Simmons, a camp-meeting revival convert and sometime preacher who retained the anti-Negro aims of the old Klan but soon broadened its scope to include anti-Catholicism and anti-Semitism. The Klan thus became a distinctly Protestant organization with chaplains and specially adapted hymns. "Never before," observes John Higham, "had a single society gathered up so many hatreds."[10] With agricultural depression, urban "immorality," and liberal religious ideas adding to popular discontent, the membership campaigns of the KKK became more successful, in the North as well as in the South. After 1921 D. C. Stephenson of Indianapolis rose to such prominence that he threatened the authority of Hiram Wesley Evans, the Texas dentist who had bought out Simmons's interest in the Invisible Empire. By 1923 the Klan had

[9] According to the 1924 law, quotas were to be computed on the basis of 2 percent of the 1890 population. Further restrictions were put in effect in 1927 and 1929.

[10] John Higham, *Strangers in the Land,* p. 289.

reached its peak of nearly three million members, and it was wielding great political power in a half-dozen states.

All of these campaigns—against radicals, immigrants, Negroes, Catholics, and Jews—revealed deep Protestant misgivings, and they elicited much overt support and participation in the churches. Compared with the problems of Prohibition, however, every public issue of the period took second place. Prohibition was *the* great Protestant crusade of the twentieth century—the last grand concert of the old moral order.

PROHIBITIONISM'S INTEMPERATE BATTLE

The aim of the Anti-Saloon League had always been to extricate the dry cause from its bondage to an obscure third party and a vast regiment of unenfranchised women. It had set out to organize the five hundred thousand crucial "public opinion makers" of the country and to get dry commitments from politicians at any and every level in the nation—from village councils in Kansas to the president of the United States. With the WCTU functioning as a women's auxiliary, the league was marvelously successful in giving direction and power to a rising tide of temperance sentiment in the nation.[11] Yet from the start it functioned as a semi-ecclesiastical movement, with denominational leaders in prominent positions and with local churches providing place and occasion for itinerant lecturers and tract distribution. Its leaders recognized that church membership lists constituted the real key to the situation. Virginius Dabney accurately refers to it as "virtually a branch of the Methodist and Baptist churches,"[12] but he neglects to emphasize the fact that with the exception of German Lutherans and Episcopalians, American Protestantism constituted an unprecedentedly solid phalanx that included evangelicals and liberals, Social Gospelers and conservatives, Democrats and Republicans. With remarkable unanimity the denominational press endorsed the antisaloon campaign.[13] Paul A. Carter does not exaggerate in calling the

[11] The organization of "Dry Power" in the 1912–28 period makes the "Black Power" of the 1960s seem very amateur indeed.

[12] Virginius Dabney, *Dry Messiah: The Life of Bishop Cannon*, p. 35.

[13] Many Episcopal leaders and parishes enlisted in the crusade, especially outside the cities and in the South. Scandinavian

dry cause "a surrogate for the Social Gospel." The gaining and maintaining of Prohibition became *the* crusade and *the* panacea for a whole generation of Protestants.

The great "Dry Messiah" of the decade was the Southern Methodist bishop, James Cannon, who reached the pinnacle of his crusading career in the election of 1928, when he played a key role in shattering the Solid South. James Cannon, Jr. (1864–1944) was born in Maryland, reared in the Southern Methodist church, and converted while a student at Randolph-Macon College. He entered the Methodist ministry in 1888 after taking a B.D. from Princeton Seminary, an M.A. from the neighboring university, and a wife from the household of Randolph-Macon's president. At age twenty-nine he became principal of a struggling academy for girls in Blackstone, Virginia, which at the time of his resignation in 1918 (to become a bishop) was a firmly established institution. In the meantime he had hitched his destiny to the Anti-Saloon League, helping to organize the Virginia branch in 1901 and becoming its president in 1904. In 1914, when a massive referendum victory brought statewide prohibition to Virginia, Cannon became a national figure and a dominant force in the Democratic politics of the South.

With such single-minded leaders at the helm the Prohibition movement marched to victory. In 1900 only about 24 percent of the population was living in dry territory; but in 1906, 40 percent. In 1913 the Webb-Kenyon Law provided the first great victory at the federal level by prohibiting the sending of liquor into dry states. By the time of Wilson's war message there were twenty-six prohibition states in the Union. More than half the population lived in no-license territory. After war had been declared against the kaiser, anti-German sentiments could be marshaled for a final assault on the "Beer Barons" with the alleged wartime needs for alcohol and flour as a rationale.

In 1917 came the deluge—or more accurately, the great drought. A tremendous effort by the league in the congressional elections of 1916 yielded the requisite number of dry victories. The Eighteenth Amendment was passed and sent to

---

pietistic Lutherans also joined in. Roman Catholics, though they had participated in the league's founding, dropped out as the crusade became more intemperate and nativistic. The northern and southern wings of the Democratic party were at odds on the issue.

the states for ratification, and other legislation soon followed. In 1918 laws were passed prohibiting the manufacture and sale of alcoholic beverages after 30 June 1919. The country was, in effect, dry without the Eighteenth Amendment. Then in October 1919, the amendment now ratified, Congress passed the Volstead Act as an enforcement measure, repassing it immediately over Wilson's veto, 176 to 5 in the House, 65 to 20 in the Senate. Prohibition became a fact on 16 January 1920.[14] Billy Sunday, who had for years been satisfying customer demand for his famous "booze sermon," held a mock funeral for John Barleycorn. Yet keeping John in the grave was a major Protestant task of the twenties.[15]

The greatest threat came in 1928, when the Democratic party's presidential candidate was Alfred E. Smith, a wet Roman Catholic from New York City who personified rural America's image of urban evil. Bishop Cannon and the Anti-Saloon Democrats were outraged, and on election day they broke the Solid South. Yet there was irony in that Protestant victory. The Dry Messiah could speak of "the kind of dirty people you find today on the sidewalks of New York . . . the Italians, the Sicilians, the Poles, and the Russian Jews."[16] But Al Smith, as he sang of those sidewalks, was forging a new

[14] Twenty-seven states were dry when Congress passed the amendment, but the ratification of the necessary thirty-six came more easily than expected. It was politically easier in many states to ratify the amendment than to vote and enforce a dry law. In addition, dry sentiment was growing, and ultimately only two states—Connecticut and Rhode Island—failed to ratify the amendment. The total votes cast in the lower houses of the forty-six ratifying states was 3,782 to 1,035. Votes on the amendment in the House of Representatives, both yeas and nays, were about evenly divided between the two parties.

[15] Each of the fifteen hundred federal agents, for example, would have had to prevent the liquor traffic along twelve miles of the international boundary, over two thousand square miles of American territory, and among seventy thousand people!

[16] One of Cannon's campaign utterances in 1928; quoted in Dabney, *Dry Messiah*, p. 188. After 1928 Cannon was involved in two ecclesiastical trials, one civil trial, three congressional hearings, and at least two libel suits. The accusations ranged from adultery and stock market gambling to the wartime hoarding of flour. He was "acquitted" in every case, but his influence as the Dry Messiah was negated as he became a symbol of puritanic hypocrisy.

Democratic coalition. The Crash provided a final blow, and after 1929 Prohibition's fragile supportive structure in American culture and politics collapsed. The election of 1932 would bring FDR to the White House and seal the doom of the Eighteenth Amendment. The temperance movement's greatest failure was its inability to accomplish an enduring reform.[17] In no previous crusade had the solidarity of Protestantism been so unbroken, its passion so aroused. Indeed, so great was the investment that the trauma of repeal would leave Protestantism itself transformed. This larger result, however, was due to the way in which the twenties also fomented strictly religious confrontations.

RELIGIOUS AND THEOLOGICAL MOVEMENTS

On the popular level a dominant theme of American religion was exhibited by a new wave of best sellers, often conservative or noncommittal on social issues but preoccupied with practical personal problems of health, harmony, and successful living. The genre was old, but it had its first great flowering in the twenties.[18] In 1922–23, when the Red Scare was waning, the French prophet of personal power through positive thinking, Émile Coué, made his American tour. He soon had thousands attending his institutes—and many more thousands repeating his famous formula: "Day by day, in every way, I am betting better and better." "Multitudes of people," said Harry Emerson Fosdick in his *Twelve Tests of Character* (1923), "are living not bad but frittered lives." And he, together with his immensely popular rivals Emmet Fox, Glenn Clark, and Ralph Waldo Trine, won millions of readers by providing inspirational paths to victorious living, constructive thinking, being in tune with the infinite, pushing to the front, and being a real person.

The decade's most popular work on Jesus was *The Man Nobody Knows* (1925), written by advertising executive Bruce Barton, who gives the Man from Nazareth front rank

[17] Given the nation's prevailing sentiment, a regulatory system that allowed the sale of beer and wine and put hard liquors under a government dispensary system, perhaps with rationing, might have endured.

[18] Later developments of positive thinking and aspects of its background are considered in chaps. 60 and 61.

among the world's business organizers.[19] Not only was President Coolidge declaring that America's business was business, but many were expounding the religious corollary. "The sanest religion is business," wrote Edward Purinton in the *Independent* in 1921. "Any relationship that forces a man to follow the Golden Rule rightfully belongs amid the ceremonials of the church. A great business enterprise includes and presupposes this relationship." This presupposition, it must be added, was safely held, for businessmen were at the apex of their public esteem in these golden years before the Crash. They had also become key elements in the promotional strategies and financial planning of the churches. Ministers meanwhile increasingly adopted the life styles and value systems of their more successful parishioners. Russell H. Conwell preached his "Acres of Diamonds" six thousand times before he died in 1925, reaching millions of listeners and readers with his amazingly frank equation of being rich and being good. He became a philanthropist on the proceeds.

Liberal theology in the more formal sense also flourished in the postwar years. Its defenders participated vigorously in the ecumenical movement, aroused the social concerns of many interchurch agencies at home, and developed new responses to the changed intellectual climate of the times. The liberalism of the twenties was thus by no means a static continuation of nineteenth-century attitudes. Most noticeable, perhaps, was the eclipse of philosophical idealism, the trend toward more realistic, more scientific, more empirical ways of thinking. The pragmatism of William James figured in this development, for it was directed against the various forms of idealism which at the turn of the century had been the mainstay of the "genteel tradition" in religion and morals. Yet James was a subjectivist himself, and his classic, *The Varieties of Religious Experience,* became a popular apologia for religion. Faith that "worked" was true; given the "will to believe," it would work. Neither James nor Emerson would have been happy about it, but both of them figured prominently in the popular peace-and-harmony books of the period. Men like John Dewey and others of the "Chicago school," on the other hand, turned the pragmatic arguments

[19] Unbelievable as it may seem, the volume's epigraph was the query of the boy Jesus when he was found in the temple, "Wist ye not that I must be about my Father's *business?*"

into secular channels, above all toward social and educational problems.

The new currents of philosophical realism had an even more direct impact on theology. In this context, Douglas Clyde Macintosh (1877–1948) and Henry Nelson Wieman (b. 1884) were especially influential. Macintosh came to Yale from Canada and carried his pacifistic refusal to bear arms in defense of the Constitution to the Supreme Court. He lost the case and never became a U.S. citizen, but his defense of the reasonableness of Christianity won wide attention. God, for him, was an objective, verifiable reality; and the essentials of the Christian faith could be established quite apart from any historical evidence. Macintosh was a moral optimist for whom salvation was within human grasp:

> As a result of acting intelligently on the hypothesis of the existence of a God great enough and good enough to justify our absolute self-surrender and confident, appropriating faith, there comes a religious experience of spiritual uplift and emancipation in which, as a complex of many psychological elements, there can be intuited empirically, or perceived, the operation of a Factor which we evaluate and interpret as divine, because of its absolute religious and spiritual value. It is here then, and not in traditional creeds or sacred books as such, that we find revelation.[20]

Eight years later he stated the realist case even more tersely:

> I will not mince words in this connection. . . . If in proclaiming the Christian gospel we can predict and promise that whosoever will fulfill the prescribed conditions of repentance and faith . . . will experience ethico-religious salvation, then it cannot be denied that there is in the Christian message a nucleus of essentially or potentially scientific generalization.[21]

Wieman, like Macintosh, was a critic of subjectivism and a champion of empirical theology. He was far less concerned with religious experience, however, and drew much inspira-

[20] *The Pilgrimage of Faith in the World of Modern Thought* (Calcutta, 1931), pp. 223–24.
[21] "Empirical Theology and Some of Its Misunderstanders," *Review of Religion* 3 (May 1939): 398.

tion from the metaphysics of Alfred North Whitehead. From 1927 to 1947 he was perhaps the dominant figure at Chicago, but several of his colleagues added much to the institution's fame (and notoriety) as a center of "modernism." Edward Scribner Ames, chairman of the Chicago philosophy department and minister to the University Disciples Church, became the country's most widely read psychologist of religion. Shirley Jackson Case carried positivistic methods into scholarship on the New Testament and the early Church; and Gerald B. Smith defined Christianity almost entirely in terms of social concern. In the spirit of these men and their many influential students, realism became the new watchword of religious liberalism.

A natural corollary of these trends was a growing dissatisfaction with the older type of Sunday school instruction, its accent on evangelism, its uncritical use of the Bible, and its lack of interest in scientific educational theory. In response to this uneasiness the Religious Education Association had been organized on an interfaith basis in 1903. John Dewey was a charter member, and the development of progressive theory in secular education was a constant spur to its work.[22] Due to the energetic direction of Henry F. Cope (1870–1923), the association's impact was enormous; and it became even greater through the participation of many of its members in the International Council of Religious Education, where churches were directly represented. As early as 1904 George A. Coe (1862–1951) had provided a basic programmatic statement in his *Education in Religion and Morals*, followed in 1917 by *A Social Theory of Religious Education*, in which reverence for personality and democratic life are the key principles. The other great theorist of the new views was Coe's successor at Union Seminary and Columbia, Harrison S. Elliott (1882–1951), who placed even more confidence in discussion and fellowship as instruments of moral and religious education.[23] In 1940 he would forthrightly ask, *Can*

---

[22] The great American pioneer in scientific psychology, G. Stanley Hall, had in 1882 already announced views on religious nurture and child development which were to have widespread effects in later years (*Princeton Review* 58 [1882]: 32). Horace Bushnell, however, was the movement's American patriarch, and his *Christian Nurture* (1849) was its primary inspiration.

[23] As early as 1908 Elliott had addressed an essay to the question, "What Does Modern Psychology Permit Us to Believe in Respect to Regeneration?"

Religious Education Be Christian? By that time various countercurrents were leading Christian educators to the opposite question: Can Christian education be religious? But in 1928, at the movement's zenith, Gerald B. Smith could say with complete justice that in religious education as nowhere else "we see the direction in which religious thinking is moving."

The Social Gospel must be seen as another well-traveled road, however, for the prevailing complacency of the twenties did not prevent spokesmen of the church or denominational conclaves from "speaking out" on public issues with monotonous regularity. According to its closest student, "The most striking single fact which comes out of intensive reading in the denomination weeklies for the year 1920 is that their pages were filled with articulate and vigorous social criticism."[24] In that year, despite the Red Scare, the Interchurch World Movement report on the steel strike of 1919 was published, and it probably received more publicity than had any similar findings in the preceding half-century. The same sources reveal persistent criticism of isolationism and support of the League of Nations despite the countercurrents exposed in successive national elections. In large part this development was a reaction from the churches' uncritical role in World War I; and this remorse deepened as evidence of the war's failure to resolve the world's problems accumulated. Harry Emerson Fosdick, who had enthusiastically "presented arms" in 1917, took a vow that he would never again come to the support of war. But it is also true, as Professor Carter has emphasized, that again the churches were simply providing biblical texts and "Christian" arguments for a secular trend that had put a Quaker in the White House and made a former conscientious objector prime minister of Great Britain.[25] Pacifism was in fact so popular in the late twenties and early thirties that serious concern for totalitarian threats to world peace were long delayed.

The ecumenical movement also made strong advances during these years. At home interdenominational cooperation continued to expand along lines laid down before the war, as the Federal Council of Churches, serving as a central coordinating agency, gained steadily in membership. And the movement had set even larger international goals. The vision

[24] Paul A. Carter, *The Decline and Revival of the Social Gospel,* p. 19.
[25] Ibid., pp. 136 ff.

of church reunion had been awakened at the great missionary conference held at Edinburgh in 1910 and discussed at three smaller international conferences, one just before, one during, and one just after World War I. Out of these, in turn, came the invitations that led to the historic Stockholm Conference of 1925, where six hundred delegates from thirty-seven countries, including some from the Eastern Orthodox churches, laid the foundations for the ecumenical Life and Work movement, which urged a unified Christian approach to the world's social problems. While these arrangements went forward, another movement animated by concern for the issues of faith and order among Christendom's divided churches gathered momentum. Charles Brent, the Protestant Episcopal missionary bishop in the Philippines and a delegate to Edinburgh in 1910, provided the impetus that finally led in 1927 to another historic ecumenical gathering, at Lausanne, Switzerland. Out of these two major elements the world Council of Churches would be formed in 1948; but even in the 1920s Americans played important roles in world ecumenism, offering a strong witness to their own practical concerns and receiving, in turn, a deepened awareness of traditions and theological issues that were rarely encountered at home.

Yet notes of liberalism and church unity by no means dominated the religious scene. What brought a sense of discovery and progress to some brought anxiety and a sense of betrayal to others. The great disorienting forces of the decade aroused a "silent majority" of deeply disturbed conservatives. We must turn our attention, therefore, to circumstances that threw American Protestantism into a state of disarray from which it would never recover.

THE FUNDAMENTALIST CONTROVERSY

The theological issue at stake in the twenties was, of course, immemorial, and it had aroused intense conflict for a century. After the wartime moratorium on internal conflict was lifted, the old issues were rekindled. This militancy took two distinct forms: first, as an effort to prevent public schools and universities from teaching scientific theories which were deemed incompatible with traditional interpretations of the Bible; and second, as an effort to block the advance of liberal theology and modern scholarship in the churches. Of these two movements, the former has received far more publicity, shed far more discredit on the churches, and won remembrance among many who know little or nothing of the church-oriented struggles. The latter, on the other hand, constitutes a more intrinsic element of ecclesiastical history and requires more detailed consideration.

Of Men and Monkeys

In the course of a few days in July 1925 two million words of newspaper reportage were telegraphed from Dayton, Tennessee. The occasion for this historic flood of publicity was the confrontation of William Jennings Bryan and Clarence Darrow at the trial of John Scopes, who was under indictment for teaching evolution contrary to the laws of the state. The trial itself bore more resemblance to a camp meeting (or a prize fight) than to a legal process, and the State Supreme Court of Tennessee rejected its finding on a technicality. In an age of ballyhoo it became something of a national joke. Scopes was no Galileo, only a recent college graduate struggling through his first year of high school teaching, yet the event exposed fears that pervaded every section of the country. It pointed to a poignant dilemma of American evangelicalism.

The trouble in Tennessee began, appropriately, on a farm; and, as Ray Ginger remarks, "with a sincere effort to do good."[26] George Washington Butler was perturbed by the spread of modern scientific teachings, and as a member of the Tennessee legislature he proposed "An Act prohibiting the teaching of the Evolution Theory in all the Universities, Normals, and all other public schools of Tennessee." Because he had many sympathizers, and because even those who championed better education did not wish to risk a fight on this issue, the Butler Act was passed. Yet Tennessee was not unique in its efforts to hold back the advance of science and learning. Oklahoma's law in 1923 was the nation's first. Bryan himself helped draft the anti-evolution resolution passed by the Florida legislature later that year. Mississippi passed a law in 1926, and Arkansas in 1927, and in Arkansas a case

[26] Ray Ginger, *Six Days or Forever? Tennessee v. John Thomas Scopes*, p. 7.

came into court as late as 1966. In Louisiana and North Carolina similar measures were defeated by only a small margin.

This campaign to halt the teaching of evolution and kindred theories in the schools was not only a movement of the rural South. Ministers of great city congregations in the North also provided leadership. Through the World's Christian Fundamentals Association led by William Bell Riley of the large First Baptist Church in Minneapolis, the Fundamentalist movement gained nationwide scope. At the association's ninth annual convention in 1927—with representatives of several allied organizations present—it made plans for a coordinated approach to all state legislatures. Its publications, special conferences, and organized efforts served not only to unify the movement, but to keep it oriented toward the premillennial dispensationalism being advanced in many churches and Bible institutes. Especially in its efforts to gain anti-evolution laws in the states, it was supported by the Bible Crusaders of America, almost the personal agency of a single wealthy founder, George F. Washburn of Florida. From Wichita, Kansas, Gerald B. Winrod led his Defenders of the Christian Faith. The existence of many of these organizations depended on a single dynamic leader; yet they did maintain contact with a vast constituency of conservative Protestants and win countless local victories. In the process, no doubt, innumerable Americans were convinced that modern science was not only incompatible with Christian orthodoxy, but destructive to the moral order. Despite local successes, however, conservatives could not gain organizational control in the various denominations. It was this circumstance that underlay the second major phase of the Fundamentalist controversy.

The Battle within the Churches

The Fundamentalist controversy, properly speaking, was not fought out in courts of law and legislative halls but within the churches. It was, in fact, a struggle for ecclesiastical control whose intensity varied in direct proportion to the strength of theological liberalism in a given denomination, unless (as in the cases of Congregationalism and Northern Methodism) the liberals were unassailably strong. The situation remained relatively peaceful among the Lutherans and in the southern churches, especially in the Southern Baptist Convention, where liberals constituted no threat.[27] It was disputed with greatest fury among the Northern Presbyterians and the Northern Baptists, with the Disciples of Christ perhaps the next most agitated.

The Presbyterian church, because of its closely knit polity and and its rigorous doctrinal tradition, had already been deeply riven in the later nineteenth century. After the war, conflict broke into the open again with William Jennings Bryan playing an important role. Presbyterian withdrawal from the Interchurch World Movement and mounting conservative criticism of the Presbyterian New Era Movement were more than straws in the wind. During the war (1916) the General Assembly had required ministerial candidates to subscribe to its Five-Point Deliverance of 1910, and this gave conservatives leverage for future battles.

The chief provocation to renewed conflict was provided, oddly enough, by a Baptist, Harry Emerson Fosdick, who had come to Union Seminary in New York first as a student, then in 1908 as a professor. Shortly after the war he became a regular "guest preacher" at the First Presbyterian Church of New York. In that role he made known his objectives to the exclusivistic tactics of ultraconservatives, especially among the premillennialists who were increasing their strength in the foreign mission fields. "Shall the Fundamentalists Win?" he asked in 1922 in a widely read article in the *Christian Century*. In terms of concrete acts the answer returned, "We will if we can." First they attempted to expel this liberal Baptist from his Presbyterian pulpit. This was accomplished—though with an untoward result. Fosdick's next call, to the Park Avenue Baptist Church, led directly to John D. Rockefeller's offer to build an interdenominational church on Morningside Heights, and in 1931 Fosdick was installed in that great architectural and institutional eminence.

During the next fifteen years Fosdick was the nation's most influential Protestant preacher. For countless tourists the chance to hear Fosdick in Riverside Church fulfilled a life's ambition. Meanwhile, a whole generation of Presbyterian preachers were forced to quote from his many books with the innocent introduction, "As someone has said . . ." Their reti-

[27] In the Episcopal church there were several widely publicized cases involving individual priests, but Catholic-Evangelical tensions continued to provide the chief doctrinal controversy.

cence stemmed not from the Fosdick affair, but from the furor provoked by the Auburn Affirmation of 1924. This statement, signed by over twelve hundred people, condemned the denomination's official biblical literalism and the extraconfessional character of the Five-Point Deliverance. In the next few years it became increasingly clear that moderate forms of evangelical liberalism were acceptable to at least a narrow majority in the church, but this fact only increased the violence of Fundamentalist attacks.

Inevitably, Princeton Seminary moved to the center of this theological conflict, as its brilliant professor of New Testament, J. Gresham Machen (1881–1937), provided intellectual leadership for the conservative cause. Machen's *Christianity and Liberalism* (1923) even after a half-century remains the chief theological ornament of American Fundamentalism. His thesis—like the book as a whole—was uncompromising and crystal clear, stating that "despite the . . . use of traditional phraseology, modern liberalism not only is a different religion from Christianity but belongs in a totally different class of religions." By the late 1920s, however, Machen's refinement of the old Hodge-Warfield position on scriptural inerrancy was being challenged in the seminary itself. This fact finally led in 1929 to a reorganization of the seminary and to three secessionist moves by the conservatives: first, the formation of Westminster Seminary in Philadelphia, then the organization of an independent foreign missions board, and finally, the founding of the Orthodox Presbyterian Church as a new denomination.[28] All of these actions, it must be added, were accompanied by much debate, many polemical publications, and harsh personal recriminations. But the steady drift of sentiment in the denomination (among laity, ministers, and theologians) was toward a broadened evangelicalism and away from the strict, propositional orthodoxy that had held at least up to 1916, or even 1922. That the denomination was seriously scarred (as indeed it had been by the schisms of 1741, 1805–10, 1837, 1957, and 1860) nobody denied.

[28] After an Independent Board of Missions had been barred from the church, the new denomination was formed (1936). The word "orthodox" was added only after litigation required a change of corporate name (1939). By that time the new conservative church had itself divided (1937)—premillennialism having been a major divisive issue. On the earlier phase of this struggle see pp. 282–86 above.

In the Northern Baptist Convention the Fundamentalist controversy involved wider extremes than among the Presbyterians. On one hand, the Baptists' anticreedal congregationalism left the way more open to theological departures. An unusually large number of leading liberal theologians were Baptists—Clarke, Rauschenbusch, Fosdick, Mathews, and Macintosh, to name only the more prominent. And financially independent Baptist seminaries such as Newtown, Colgate, Rochester, Crozer, and, above all, the Chicago Divinity School made the denomination famous for its sponsorship of learning. On the other hand, the prominence of anti-intellectualism and revivalism had produced a membership (both clerical and lay) that was unresponsive to the problems created by scholarship, science, and social change. Baptists thus provided the chief leadership for the more important national Fundamentalist organizations and were prominent in premillennialist circles. They also founded more conservative "counter-seminaries" than any other denomination.[29]

As in the Presbyterian church, Baptist conservatives succeeded in leading their denomination out of the Interchurch World Movement in 1920. Of larger future significance, however, was the preconvention conference of that year at which Fundamentalists consolidated their forces. Out of this grew the National Federation of Fundamentalists of the Northern Baptists, with John Roach Straton of New York, Jasper C. Massee of Brooklyn, and Amzi C. Dixon, editor of *The Fundamentals*, leading its many-pronged assault on modernism and evolution. William Bell Riley meanwhile guided the Baptist Bible Union toward similar ends. Due to the efforts of these organizations, most of the annual meetings of the Convention were torn by violent debates. Three issues predominated: the need for a formal declaration of doctrine, heresy

[29] In the Boston area, where Newton Institute was showing signs of liberalism, A. J. Gordon had led off in 1889 with a Missionary Training School (in Boston), later Gordon College and Seminary (in Wenham, Mass.). In Chicago, Northern Baptist Seminary was founded in 1913 to counter the influence of the university divinity school; and in 1925 Eastern Seminary took up this role vis-à-vis Crozer Seminary in Philadelphia. The latter two retained a relationship to the convention, however. The non-denominational Moody Bible School in Chicago, like its sister institute in Los Angeles and Scofield's school in Dallas, was frequently attended by Baptist conservatives who had strong premillennial and dispensationalist convictions.

among foreign missionaries, and liberalism in the seminaries. On all these matters conservatives scored victories, but they were invariably qualified and in some cases rendered almost nugatory by amendments. At the end of the decade the denomination was very much where it had been in 1920.

During the bottom years of the Depression something like denominational peace prevailed among Northern Baptists. As many historians of Fundamentalism seem not to have realized, however, the peace was only temporary.[30] During the 1930s conservative revivalistic Christianity would flourish. The number of Bible institutes grew from 49 in 1930 to 144 in 1950; radio evangelists prospered (most sensationally, Charles E. Fuller's "Old Fashioned Revival Hour" emanating from Los Angeles), and independent Fundamentalist congregations became increasingly numerous. In 1932, as the chances for asserting the Fundamentalist program in the Convention grew slimmer, the General Association of Regular Baptists was organized, and by 1946 it had grown to include five hundred churches. A second secession occurred in 1947, when the Conservative Baptist Association was formed, though it was not at first a separatistic organization. By 1969 it had become a strong Fundamentalist body with affiliated seminaries, a large foreign missionary society, and 315,000 members.

The restorationist movement which looks to Barton W. Stone and the Campbells as its founders had even less organizational structure than the Baptists to give focus to the Fundamentalist controversy. By 1906 its most conservative elements, largely in the rural South, had already separated themselves as the Churches of Christ, but even in the 1890s the remaining (and larger) part of the denomination had begun to be polarized. Among churches where magazine editors wielded extraordinary influence and power, the *Christian-Evangelist*, edited in Saint Louis by James H. Garrison, upheld the cause of moderate inclusivism and emphasized the Disciples' traditional concern for Christian unity. Setting a stricter restorationist tradition was the *Christian Standard*, edited by Isaac Errett from 1866 to 1888. Sharply accentuat-

[30] Norman K. Furniss, in *The Fundamentalist Controversy, 1918–1931*, revealed this tendency to premature obsequies in his concluding pages. This is surprising, since by 1954, when his book appeared, Fundamentalism was enjoying a rather sensational resurgence of influence and power.

ing this trend between 1893 and 1912 were the weekly columns of John W. McGarvey. He demanded baptism by immersion and the older methods of biblical study while inveighing against open membership, ecumenism, and a more centralized church order.

At the heart of this controversy, however, was the issue of liberal theology and biblical criticism, especially as it had been defended and propagated by Herbert L. Willett, a professor of New Testament at the Chicago Divinity School and for thirty years an indefatigable participant in denominational controversies. Willett supported the Divinity School and the Disciples House affiliated with it, encouraged those who would extend its scholarly ideals in other colleges and seminaries, urged the revision of Sunday school materials, and advocated participation in the ecumenical movement. As the possibility of halting or reversing these several trends diminished, the conservatives took the important step in 1927 of organizing the North American Christian Convention. No formal separation took place, but two quite distinct fellowships arose and the denomination's leading historian would subsequently speak of the conservatives as constituting a second group of "Churches of Christ."[31]

The Fundamentalist controversy neither began nor ended in the twenties, but the decade did witness the climactic confrontation of American evangelical Protestantism and modern thought. After the decade's turmoil the more extreme forms of doctrinal conservatism would continue to grow, notably among the Pentecostalists. Yet it would occupy an increasingly restricted place in the nation's life. Certain large denominations would continue to resist the advance of science and biblical criticism, but they would never again be able to alter the content of scientific education or hinder serious scholarship except in institutions they controlled. Hereafter Fundamentalism was in retreat.

THE CRISIS OF THE PROTESTANT ESTABLISHMENT

The Protestant churches of America did not lose their historic hegemony during the troubled twenties, but they were

[31] Alfred Thomas DeGroot, *New Possibilities for Disciples and Independents, with a History of the Independents, Church of Christ Number Two.*

made sharply aware that their ancient sway over the nation's moral life was threatened. Even as modern religious ideas steadily advanced or as concern for social issues increased, the churches tended to lose their capacity to shape and inform American opinion. The debacle of Prohibition functioned both as evidence and cause of the churches' loss of authority in a culture where urban values became primary. The decline of the Puritan Sabbath despite strenuous campaigns in its behalf, the emergence of new attitudes toward recreation despite old Puritanic suspicions of play, and the expansion of the amusement industry served meanwhile to weaken the disciplinary aspects of church membership. Modern thought and social change were slowly bringing down the curtains on the "great century" of American evangelicalism.

A greatly diminished hold on the country's intellectual and literary leadership was another important sign of change. This meant in turn that ministerial candidates were turning to other vocations. Nor were they dissuaded from this decision by the assorted hypocrites and boobs that marched through Sinclair Lewis's *Elmer Gantry*. Dr. Arrowsmith's vocation seemed a more effective means for saving Main Street from Babbittry.[32] Offended as much by the obscurantism of the Fundamentalists as by the cultural accommodations of the churches, intellectuals, young and old, were leaving the church—with H. L. Mencken piping the tune and providing the laughs. "Every day," he said, "a new Catholic church goes up; every day another Methodist or Presbyterian church is turned into a garage." "Protestantism is down with a wasting disease."[33] And Mencken thought he knew why, though he ignored matters of urban ecology and spoke chiefly of regions where Catholics were scarce.

Any literate plowhand, if the Holy Spirit inflames him, is thought to be fit to preach. Is he commonly sent, as preliminary, to a training camp, to college? But what a college!

[32] Sinclair Lewis was the first American author to receive the Nobel Prize, in 1930. *Elmer Gantry, Dodsworth, Babbitt, Arrowsmith,* and *Mainstreet* all appeared in the 1920s. *The Good Earth* (1931) by Pearl Buck received the Pulitzer Prize in 1932, and the Nobel Prize in 1938. For her views on missions she was much criticized by Presbyterian conservatives.

[33] From a review of Wilbur C. Abbott, *The New Barbarians,* in *Prejudices,* 5th ser. (New York: Alfred A. Knopf, 1926), p. 157.

You will find one in every mountain valley of the land, with its single building in its bare pasture lot, and its faculty of half-idiot pedagogues and brokendown preachers. One man, in such a college, teaches oratory, ancient history, arithmetic and Old Testament exegesis. This aspirant comes in from the barnyard, and goes back in a year or two to the village. His body of knowledge is that of a street-car motorman or a vaudeville actor. But he has learned the clichés of his craft, and he has got him a long-tailed coat, and so he has made his escape from the harsh labors of his ancestors, and is set up as a fountain of light and learning.[34]

More disturbing than the revolt of highbrows and middle-brows were more readily experienced social realities. Immigrant "hordes" were corrupting the old ways of life and upsetting the political order. New methods and ideas were invading the schools. The cities were ruling the nation. Hard work and sobriety were no longer honored. New temptations were disrupting the family and leading youth astray. Any number of public statements reveal the unsettlement and despair which many American Protestants inwardly felt. But none, oddly enough, better revealed the underlying pathos than Hiram Wesley Evans, the Imperial Wizard of the Ku Klux Klan. His lengthy defense of the Klan's course of action, published in the *North American Review,* deserves extended quotation and close reading.

Nordic Americans for the last generation have found themselves increasingly uncomfortable and finally deeply distressed. There appeared first confusion in thought and opinion, a groping hesitancy about national affairs and private life alike, in sharp contrast to the clear, straightforward purposes of our earlier years. There was futility in religion, too, which was in many ways even more distressing. . . . Finally came the moral breakdown that has been going on for two decades. One by one all our traditional moral standards went by the boards, or were so disregarded that they ceased to be binding. The sacredness of our Sabbath, of our homes, of chastity, and finally even of our right to teach our own children in our own schools fundamental facts and truths were torn away from us. Those who maintained the old standards did so only in the face of constant ridicule.

Along with this went economic distress. The assurance for the future of our children dwindled. We found our great cities and the control of much of our industry and commerce taken over by strangers, who stacked the cards of success and prosperity against us. . . .

So the Nordic American today is a stranger in large parts of the land his fathers gave him. . . . Our falling birth rate, the result of all this, is proof of our distress. We no longer feel that we can be fair to children we bring into the world, unless we can make sure from the start that they shall have capital or education or both, so that they need never compete with those who now fill the lower rungs of the ladder of success. We no longer dare risk letting our youth "make its own way" in conditions under which we live. . . .

We are a movement of the plain people, very weak in the matter of culture, intellectual support, and trained leadership. We are demanding . . . a return of power into the hands of the everyday, not highly cultured, not overly intellectualized, but entirely unspoiled and not de-Americanized, average citizen of the old stock. Our members and leaders are all of this class—the opposition of the intellectuals and liberals who held the leadership, betrayed Americanism. . . is almost automatic.

This is undoubtedly a weakness. It lays us open to the charge of being "hicks" and "rubes" and "drivers of the second hand Fords." We admit it. . . . Every popular movement has suffered from just this handicap, yet the popular movements have been the mainsprings of progress, and have usually had to win against the "best people" of their time.[35]

For Roman Catholics, Eastern Orthodox, Lutherans, Jews, Negroes, and other large groups who often bore the brunt of nativistic intolerance, the twenties were also decisive, but in very different—even opposite—ways; and later chapters

[35] "The Klan's Fight for Americanism," *North American Review* 213 (March-April-May 1926): 33–63; quoted by Richard Hofstadter, *The Age of Reform: From Bryan to FDR* (New York: Alfred A. Knopf, 1956), pp. 293–94.

will deal with these developments. For most churchgoers in the Protestant mainstream, however, the promise of American life—despite jazz, flappers, speakeasies, and gangsters—seemed never to have been greater.

Then in October 1929, the Crash. And in the darkening months and years that followed, the Depression. The promise evaporated. But during the hard times there came no great revival of religion such as had followed the panic of 1857. Indeed, for a long time there were not even many signs of popular social reformism; long addiction to make-believe delayed the general awareness that a national catastrophe would require a national solution. In due time an upsurge of realistic self-awareness would occur. A renewal of theology was also in the offing, even a considerable expansion of church membership, and after another great war, a religious revival. But the renewal would take place on a smaller stage, and the revival would be utterly discontinuous with America's earlier awakenings. In retrospect, it becomes clear that the decade of the twenties marked a crucial transition in American religious history.

54

THE THIRTIES: FROM THE CRASH TO PEARL HARBOR

The thirties, in effect, began with the Crash and ended with the outbreak of World War II. But in American memory this tumultuous decade always passes under the name of the Depression or the New Deal, and it is inextinguishably associated with Franklin Delano Roosevelt. His solemn predecessor in the White House, who presided over almost a third of the decade, is a leftover of the twenties. Under whatever name, the thirties were momentous times. Heinz Eulau ventured to say that the New Deal's impression on the American experience "in the long run can only be compared with the birth of the nation itself and the fratricidal blood-letting of the Civil War."[1] During these years the third great stride in the formation of the federal Union was taken; and the American people as a whole participated in this time of turning—in its sufferings and satisfactions, in its verbal and physical conflict, and in its profound discoveries.

THE IMPACT OF THE DEPRESSION

Like every great experience of any people, the Depression had wide-ranging religious ramifications. Moral tradition and church affiliation counted heavily in the politics of the day. Theological issues underlay several of the most heated controversies, while churchmen often led the corresponding crusades. And of course the churches were filled with echoes of

[1] "Neither Ideology nor Utopia: the New Deal in Retrospect," in *The New Deal*, ed. Bernard Sternsher (Boston: Allyn and Bacon, 1960), p. 168.

the decade's momentous debates on the responsibilities of government for social welfare and the issues of war and peace. Just as the spiritual and intellectual life of the nation was matured by the decade's hard lessons, so were the churches forced to deeper levels of understanding. It would be no exaggeration to apply Professor Eulau's strong statement about the New Deal to the American religious experience of the thirties. Hence this chapter will deal with its institutional and social implications, while the next will consider its impact on theology.

Without doubt, much that went on in the churches followed immemorial custom. Clergymen went their rounds, baptizing, marrying, and burying—and preaching on Sundays according to their style. Controversies over the Atonement or the inerrancy of Scripture waxed and waned; liberals and conservatives continued the struggles of the previous decade. Among both Northern Presbyterians and Northern Baptists, controversies that had intensified during the twenties resulted in open schism. Among Roman Catholics the gap between social conservatives and progressives widened. Sectarian movements arose and strange new cults came into existence—some for the rich, others for the poor. On revisiting "Middletown" in 1935, ten years after their first survey, the Lynds found the "same serious and numerically sparse Gideon's band" inside the churches.[2] Yet they thought that the congregation looked older on the average, and we know now that baptisms were less frequent, since the population increase was only half as great as during the preceding decade. It was not a time for great confidence in the future. In the western dustbowl there were more prayers for rain; and as the decade wore on, prayers for world peace became more numerous everywhere. In other words, the historian's old problem of change and continuity also pertains to the thirties. Consequently, many developments of these years are dealt with in other more thematic chapters. The emphasis here will be upon the newer movements that arose most directly out of this decade's particular experience.

The Crash came as a shock to many Americans—like a "firebell in the night" to denizens of all allegedly fireproof building. Many wanted to believe that it was a false alarm,

[2] Robert S. and Helen Merrell Lynd, *Middletown in Transition* (New York: Harcourt Brace, 1937); quoted in Frederick L. Allen, *Since Yesterday*, p. 156.

that prosperity was just around the corner. But there was no mistaking the Great Depression as actuality. It broke the mood of the twenties once and for all. The national income dropped from $83 billion in 1929 to $40 billion in 1932, while the number of unemployed began to approach fifteen million in early 1933.

> Fear, hunger, and finally desperation became the inevitable facts of life in an emergency that had no precedent in United States history. Across America and across class lines spread privation. Men stood on bread lines, selling apples on street corners, sleeping in subways and parks and city incinerators. Armies of homeless youth roamed the land while relief agencies, running out of money and morale, had to stand helplessly by while thousands suffered. Violence erupted in some communities, as men chose to steal rather than watch their children starve.[3]

Americans of every type sought and found scapegoats and panaceas; racist attitudes and ethnic animosities intensified; class antagonisms sharpened. Political and religious views gravitated to the extremes; and demagogues, often with the Cross of Christ on their banners, began to gather their followers. Old popular beliefs collapsed, confidence in the redemptive power of the American way of life faltered, the "religion of business" lost votaries in droves, faith in automatic progress evaporated.

Yet amid these fallen idols a many-sided revival of spirit also occurred. Realizing that the whole country was in trouble, Americans gained a new kind of national self-awareness. Mutual distress drew people together. As neighbor discovered neighbor, a great many Americans found a new sense of solidarity. A nation of rugged individualists found reasons for group activities; laborers, farmers, small business men, the aged, and many others banded together. Ethnic and racial ties became more meaningful. And this sense of urgency ineluctably took on a religious aspect.

The nation by no means fell to its knees in penitence and supplication—though there were jeremiads enough. Among the Fundamentalists and in the Holiness and Pentecostal churches, something like a revival took place, perhaps be-

[3] David H. Bennett, *Demagogues in the Depression: American Radicals and the Union Party, 1932–1936*, p. 4.

cause the Depression so enlarged their constituencies among the disinherited. Between 1926 and 1936 for example, the Church of the Nazarene grew from 63,558 to 136,227 and the Assemblies of God from 47,950 to 148,043, and this at a time when the large mainstream denominations were experiencing a drastic decline in congregational giving and were barely holding their own in membership. Most pointedly ecumenical was the process by which various "Fundamentalist" churches, due largely to their dissatisfaction with the liberalism and the social actionism of the Federal Council of Churches, felt a need for federation. This impulse led to the formation of the highly combative American Council of Churches in 1941 and the less exclusivistic National Association of Evangelicals in 1942–43.

In the older denominations a convergence of these factors —declining vitality, national awareness, ethnic solidarity— led to several important church mergers. Southern and Northern Methodists ended their old alienation, drew in the smaller Protestant Methodist Church, and in 1939 formed a reunited church. The two African Methodist churches were not included, however; and even the black conferences of Northern Methodism were segregated in a Central Jurisdiction. Four smaller German churches—the old German Reformed, the Evangelical Synod, the Evangelical Church, and the United Brethren—held merger discussions. But they discovered too great a difference between the first two, whose origins were in the Reformation, and the latter two essentially Methodistic bodies, which had sprung from the Second Awakening revivals between 1800 and 1810. As a result, two separate mergers were carried out, producing the Evangelical and Reformed Church in 1934 and the Evangelical United Brethren Church in 1946. Of a similar nature was the merger in 1931 of two churches with very different origins, the Congregational churches of old New England background and the so-called Christian churches which had come together out of three separate secession movements between 1790 and 1810.[4] Perhaps coincidentally, all nine of these

4 The oldest element in the "Christian churches" was the so-called Christian Connection which had withdrawn from the New England standing order under the leadership of Abner Jones and others; the second, led by James O'Kelley, had left the Methodist church to protest its hierarchicalism; the third was made up of followers of Barton W. Stone who chose not to merge with Alex-

merging groups would merge again after World War II. The United Church of Christ was formed in 1957 to include the Congregational-Christian and Evangelical-Reformed groups. In 1968 the United Methodist Church was broadened to include the Evangelical United Brethren.

The Social Gospel Revival

As the fact of social catastrophe was gradually driven home to churchgoing America, Prohibition, Sabbatarianism, and the questions of personal morality occasioned by the rise of the movies and "ballroom" dancing yielded to larger issues. In significant portions of the church leadership the Social Gospel was revitalized. At their national meeting of 1931 the Northern Baptists had already virtually endorsed what the New Dealers would later propose. In 1932 the Northern Presbyterian Committee on Social and Industrial Relations reported to the General Assembly that the country faced "an emergency of unprecedented magnitude" that had been brought on by "incompetency and wrong-headedness." They went on to raise questions about the capitalistic principles "upon which it was assumed general prosperity was based." Episcopalians received even sterner warnings from the *Churchman,* the denomination's most steady advocate of social Christianity. Its diagnosis would have justified far more thoroughgoing reforms than the New Deal would ever undertake.

In no large denomination were social concerns more forcefully expressed than among the Methodists. In 1932 the Committee on the State of the Church delivered to the General Conference a wholesale condemnation of the social order and the acquisitive principle on which it was based. Its semiofficial Federation for Social Service consistently took positions in advance of most other American church agencies, due to the strenuous leadership of such men as Professor Harry F. Ward of Union Seminary and Bishop Francis J. McConnell. In 1934 the National Council of Methodist Youth at its first national convention endorsed socialism, chided the New Deal for its halfway measures, and circulated a pledge that began: "I surrender my life to Christ. I renounce the

---

ander Campbell's very similar but more narrowly defined Restoration movement. These three had subsequently agreed to articles of union (see Robert Lee, *The Social Sources of Church Unity,* p. 112).

Capitalist system . . ." In nearly all the churches, one could note how periodicals, special policy committees, and general deliberative bodies showed an increased willingness to speak out on social issues in a distinctly critical manner. Utopian platitudes about industrial peace and international order gave way to a more realistic concern for proximate causes of economic distress and the actualities of power.

When denominational pronouncements went to such lengths, the Federal Council of Churches naturally went as far—or farther. In 1932 it drastically revised the social creed which it had adopted in 1912, now affirming the need of government action and social planning. In early 1933 the *Christian Century* complained that the president-elect would probably be as hopelessly conservative as Hoover had been. Later in the year, after FDR's famous "hundred days," Benson Y. Landis, a leading Congregational social actionist who had also played a major role in the Federal Council, published his trenchant book *The Third American Revolution*. Is the New Deal, he worried, "more the expression of provincial America than of international cooperation?" Is its concentration on economic recovery "the enemy of revolution?" Yet he was proud that the "federal government was applying many of the policies which the churches [or "liberal churchmen," for he also used this more accurate term] had advocated for two decades."[5]

Interdenominational groups bent on a more radical critique of the status quo were also active. The Fellowship of Reconciliation, founded during World War I to strengthen the pacifist witness, shifted its interest markedly toward social affairs after 1928, when it absorbed the Fellowship for a Christian Social Order; and by 1933 it was so committed to the cause of labor that it had to poll its membership on the question of using force when social justice was at stake. Despite constant tension on this question it gave strong support to liberal and socialistic policies. The Fellowship of Socialist Christians, in which Reinhold Niebuhr was a leading voice, was formed in 1930; its manifesto of the following year spoke frankly of "class struggle" and warned that "class war" would result if the inequities of the social order were not removed. In the early thirties it was highly critical of Roosevelt's kind of "whirligig reform" and contemputous of liberals

[5] Benson Y. Landis, *The Third American Revolution*, pp. 128–33.

who would merely patch up the old system. As with the earlier Social Gospel, however, racial inequities had a minor place in most protest literature of the period. Few seemed to share Niebuhr's grimly realistic view that "the white race in America will not admit the Negro to equal rights if not forced to do so. Upon that point one may speak with a dogmatism which all history justifies."[6]

In November 1936 the United Council for Christian Democracy was formed in order to coordinate liberal and radical groups in the various churches and to organize such groups in denominations that lacked them. But by this time questions of pacifism and violence were dividing the coalition, first with regard to industrial class conflict, then later over matters of defense and foreign policy. The Depression unquestionably obtained for Social Christianity a voice in the churches which it had not had before. The men who felt deeply about issues and platforms in the churches where they could speak, organize, publish, and act. How positive a response they got from the rank-and-file membership is another question. The revival of social concern and the great increase in liberal pronouncements by church groups of various types seems not to have brought Protestant churchgoers to a position in advance of the American electorate, though it probably brought many to a broader understanding of the issues and of the need for social change.

The Conservative Response

Social conservatism, sometimes of an extreme sort, continued to flourish in the great middle-class denominations in which liberal advocacy was most audible. Few active parish pastors rose to prominence in the social reform agencies. Angry rebuttals and expressions of mass displeasure greeted the Federal Council's new social creed, and in many churches there were organized countermovements. In 1935 James W. Fifield, the ultraconservative minister of a large and well-financed Congregational church in Los Angeles, organized Spiritual Mobilization to promote the cause of Christian individualism. In 1936 the Layman's Religious Movement was launched to perform a similar service in the Methodist church. In the South the tradition of ecclesiastical silence on

[6] *Moral Man and Immoral Society* (New York: Charles Scribner's Sons, 1932), p. 253.

social issues (aside from Prohibition) was so strong that conservatives rarely had cause for complaint. The Southern Baptist Convention in 1938 termed the American economic system the "best in the world." "There ought to be no room for radical Socialism and for atheistic Communism in the United States of America, and the widespread propaganda now carried on in their interest should be as speedily as possible and in every way possible prevented and counteracted."[7] In pietistic or revivalistic churches in all parts of the country the counsels of patience, prayer, and belt-tightening usually prevailed. How men voted was regarded as a private civic affair.

Robert M. Miller, who surveyed all of the Protestant periodicals, gained the distinct impression that in 1932 almost all of them were favorable to Hoover. In 1936 they were for Landon, though less distinctly. Comparing their advocacy in 1928, 1932, and 1936, he found it very clear that Protestant editors were far more inclined to support candidates on the issues of Prohibition or Catholicism than on unemployment and hunger. The *Literary Digest* poll of 21,606 clergymen in 1936 revealed that 70.22 percent of them were opposed to New Deal policies. A poll conducted in 1936 showed that a majority of Protestant church members voted for Landon in the Roosevelt landslide. Interestingly, it also showed that Congregationalists were 78 percent for Landon and Southern Baptists 65 percent for FDR.[8] The evidence seems to support the generalization that, outside the Solid South, the economic well-being or social status of church members had more effect on their voting than their church's pronouncements.

Both North and South, moreover, the times were leading many to believe that President Roosevelt's emergency measures were not the answer the country needed. Adding greatly to the uneasiness of churchgoing Americans of all classes was the continued advance of those changes in manners and mores that had made the 1920s a nightmare for rural America. Despite the Depression, urban civilization continued to make its conquests. Jazz, dancing, feminism, and the Hollywood star system mocked the older moral standards, both Catholic and Protestant. Hard times notwith-

[7] Quoted in Robert M. Miller, *American Protestantism and Social Issues, 1919–1939*, p. 118.

[8] Ibid., 117–23.

standing, the automobile continued to transform traditional modes of living and loving. Sabbathkeeping was losing ground. All over the country racketeers and bank robbers seemed to prosper—even if Bonnie and Clyde and Dillinger were shot down. With millions hungry, the government was destroying livestock and ploughing under corn. WPA workers leaned on their rakes; hoboes and tramps were everywhere; prosperity manifested itself very slowly. The times seemed out of joint.

In this decade of desperate responses Protestant-Catholic relations were put under serious strain by the very fact that the resounding Democratic victories of 1932, 1934, and 1936 rested on the coalition that Alfred E. Smith had begun to forge in 1928. A new era in American power relationships was at hand. Among the many signs of this changing balance was the fact that only 8 of the 214 federal judges appointed by Harding, Coolidge, and Hoover were Catholic, as against 51 of 196 under Roosevelt. Nor were Protestant feelings assuaged in 1939, when the President sent Myron Taylor as his "personal representative" to the pope. With the Jewish vote in crucial urban areas also breaking the hold of the Protestant Establishment, anti-Semitism became sharper and more explicit.

Between 1929 and 1933, furthermore, the precarious state of Prohibition was a major source of Protestant anxiety. In this cause the churches had achieved unprecedented unity; and in this crusade they had triumphed. Yet now they beheld the great victory being undone by scorn, racketeering, and nonenforcement. Then with Utah's ratification of the Twenty-first Amendment in December 1933, came the dreaded calamity: Repeal. It was the greatest blow to their pride and self-confidence that Protestants as a collective body had ever experienced. Not even the comforting charm of FDR's fireside chats could prevent many from believing that only drastic reversals could save the country from aliens and radicals.

In the midst of this swirling contention about America's proper course of action at home and in the world, a religious movement with ostensibly no other interest than "changed lives" became for a time a strong, even sensational, conservative force. Its founder and charismatic leader was Frank Buchman (1878–1961), a Lutheran pastor of pietistic background. Buchman was a "Lecturer in Personal Evangelism" at Hartford Seminary en route to the World Disarmament

Conference in Washington, D.C., when he received from God a commission to convert the world—through a program of Moral Re-Armament (MRA). Even on that trip he was using a strategy that his so-called Oxford Group or First-Century Fellowship would always employ, whether on the college campus or in the world's capitals—that of concentrating on the successful, the "up-and-outers," the people with prestige, influence, and power. By organizing "houseparties" in comfortable or lavish places, on the theory that "good food and good Christianity go together," he would gather like-minded people and in an informal way bring them through the "Five C's" (confidence, conviction, confession, conversion, continuance) to a "God-guided" life under the "Four Absolutes" (honesty, purity, unselfishness, and love).

During the twenties, amid much controversy Buchman developed followings not only at various eastern colleges in the United States, but in China and Britain as well (like Saint Paul, he had a chronic itching foot). During the 1930s, with Queen Marie of Romania and many other dignitaries as patrons, the movement became famous (or notorious) the world over. The tension-filled atmosphere of those years also politicized the pious evangelicalism that Buchman had absorbed from Moody and the Student Volunteer Movement. Anticommunism became a major theme in the increasingly thronged MRA assemblies, as did its reverse, a friendliness to fascism. Buchman revealed both his political attitudes and his missionary strategy in an interview in 1936:

> I thank heaven for a man like Adolf Hitler, who built a front line of defense against the Anti-Christ of Communism. Think what it would mean to the world if Hitler surrendered to the control of God. Or Mussolini. Or any dictator. Through such a man God could control a nation overnight and solve every last bewildering problem.[9]

During World War II MRA gained a more favorable image through its patriotic efforts, but by this time it had become a rich and complex organization and had lost the intimacy that accounted for its early strength. In the postwar era the applicability of its slogans and the health of its founder would decline together. Conservative evangelicals, however, would

[9] Walter Houston Clark, *The Oxford Group: Its History and Significance,* p. 16.

continue to use strategies very similar to those of early Buch-
manism, especially in their college and university work.

Demagogues on the Right

Frank Buchman was hardly a demagogue in the usual
sense of that term, though he was an elitist with great faith in
simple formulas. In the later 1930s he organized vast MRA
mass meetings tinged with conservative social ideology and
far removed from traditional revivalism. Much more potent
were various religio-political movements of the Right which,
during these years, were being organized for the first time in
American history. Most of them showed at least some
influence from European fascistic and corporatistic thinking,
though a certain continuity with Populism was even more in
evidence, especially its addiction to radical monetary panaceas. Also visible was the racist and nativist bigotry which
had motivated the Ku Klux Klan.

Gerald B. Winrod (1898–1957), a Baptist evangelist and
militant premillennialist with headquarters in Wichita,
Kansas, saw himself as the man to rally the Fundamentalist
host. Honored in that constituency during the 1920s as the
organizer of the Defenders of the Christian Faith to combat
the spread of evolutionary teaching in the schools, he now
towered above his many midwestern rivals. Through the *Defender Magazine* he was by 1938 reaching into a hundred
thousand households. After 1933 he began to wage war on
Roosevelt's "Jewish New Deal," and after a trip to Europe in
1934 he became more respectful of Hitler and more pro-
nouncedly anti-Semitic. For his services to religion he was
made an honorary doctor of divinity by Los Angeles Bible Institute in 1935. His aspirations to national leadership were
groundless, for he was soundly beaten in the primary for the
Kansas senatorial nomination in 1938. But throughout the
thirties he nourished a huge constituency on a diet of bigotry
and fear, as well as Fundamentalist theology, rugged individualism, and anticommunism.

Vying with Winrod was the less orthodox William Dudley
Pelley, who published *Liberation* magazine and founded a
college for the study of "Christian Economics" in Asheville,
North Carolina. His Legion of Silver Shirts, organized in
1933, never amounted to much, despite its gaudy uniforms.
And although Pelley's campaign for the presidency in 1936 as

the Christian party's candidate was also a total failure, his pro-Nazi and violently anti-Semitic propaganda did its part to enlarge the "Paranoid" element in the country. His religious message was a mixture of theosophy and astrology (see chap. 61, n. 7), but he wanted to disfranchise Jews and allow only Protestant Christians to lead the country. After Pelley ran afoul of the law, the "I AM" movement of Guy and Edna Ballard cut in on the Silver Shirts' constituency until it, too, ran into legal difficulties in 1941. Like Pelley, the Ballards stressed theosophical doctrines, but they added an emphasis on healing, personal self-fulfillment, and success that appealed to people in higher income levels. They also gave an elitist and "100 percent American" tone to their teaching and attacked every threat to the status quo. The huge public meetings which they sponsored in city after city took on heavy political overtones.

More significant than Winrod, Pelley, or the Ballards—not to mention dozens of lesser "apostles of discord"—was Gerald L. K. Smith (b. 1898), whom H. L. Mencken rightly judged to be the greatest oratorical "boob bumper" of his time. Wisconsin-born and relatively well-educated, Smith was a successful minister in Indianapolis until he took a church in the South for his wife's health. In Shreveport, Louisiana, as minister of the largest Disciples of Christ congregation in the state, he soon established a reputation for oratorical gifts and reformist interests. Then after the elections of 1932 he became one of Huey Long's chief lieutenants. He was especially active in promoting the Share-Our-Wealth Society and other schemes by which the Louisiana Kingfish sought to gain a national constituency. After Long's assassination in 1935, Smith delivered a memorable funeral oration and transferred his political base to Michigan. He was an orator in need of an organized cause when he allied himself and the Share-Our-Wealth Society with the Union party, a party which was at that time little more than the radio audience of the decade's greatest church-related demagogue.

Charles E. Coughlin was born in Hamilton, Ontario, in 1891 and grew up in a lower middle-class Irish Catholic environment. After distinguishing himself in college and seminary, he was ordained in 1916 and moved to the Detroit area in 1923. There he soon distinguished himself again as a preacher and parish organizer, especially after being assigned to a new church in the suburb of Royal Oak which was to be a shrine to the recently canonized Saint Theresa of the Little Flower. His work in that cause gained him local prominence as a radio preacher—and in 1929 the Crash provided a major topic for his sermons. Industrial management and the Hoover administration soon felt the brunt of his impassioned attacks. Coughlin also began to develop a distinct point of view on social matters which drew, first, on the papal social encyclicals of 1891 and 1931, persistently emphasizing their criticism of unchecked free enterprise and their openness to the idea of the "corporate state." Beyond this, however, Coughlin followed his own intuitions as to what would gain a response from his Depression-hit audiences. In 1932 the message was "Roosevelt or Ruin," but by 1934 he had cooled on FDR (who in turn had given very little attention to Coughlin's monetary nostrums). By 1936, with 145 clerks handling the mail and money that was pouring in from his ten million weekly listeners, Coughlin was in strident opposition to the New Deal and searching for a national political constituency.

The "sixteen points" of his Union for Social Justice summarized a reasonably coherent position. The key demands were for "nationalizing public necessities," replacing the Federal Reserve System with a "Government owned central bank," and allowing the government to facilitate the unionization of all laborers. They were not far removed from the "Blueprint for Economic Planning" which Catholic oil executive Michael J. O'Shaugnessy had proposed, or from the spirit of Pius XI's *Quadragesimo Anno*, or, indeed, from the ideas that underlay the National Industrial Recovery Act of 1933. But Father Coughlin's actual influence stemmed from his amazing capacity to manipulate the rhetoric of hate and fear. His basic opportunism is revealed by the senior partners he chose for the Union party: Dr. Francis E. Townsend's old age revolving pension movement, Smith's Share-Our-Wealth Society, and the farm refinancing reform movement that Lynn Frazier and William Lemke of North Dakota were rallying. With Lemke as the presidential candidate, with discontented urban Catholics, old people, and impoverished rural Protestants being held together by anti-Semitism, fears of atheistic communism, the lure of cheap money, and the oratorical power of Coughlin and Smith, the party hoped to be an influential factor in the election.

To entertain such hopes in 1936, however, was not to reckon with FDR. The Union party's campaign organization, moreover, soon fell into nearly total disarray. Roosevelt lost only Maine and Vermont, while the Union party garnered 892,378 votes and promptly fell to pieces, though not without some retrospective satisfactions. It had exceeded the 873,000 Socialist votes that Norman Thomas had garnered in 1932 and far surpassed Thomas's 188,000 votes in 1936. What may be most significant was the movement of the country's "protest vote" from the Left to the Right.[10] The election result hardly justified the alarm Sinclair Lewis had shown in his novel and play *It Can't Happen Here* (1935). But if a well organized Union party had faced a less formidable opponent than Roosevelt, it might have rallied the vast discontented audiences of its demagogues with heavy political effect. Of more enduring significance is the fact that ever since those years, the religio-political Right has remained a potent factor in American public affairs.

FACING THE DICTATORS: PEACE OR WAR?

The election of 1936 also marks the return of foreign policy issues to haunt the American scene. Japan had begun its occupation of Manchuria in 1931 and by 1936 was extending its control in China proper. Italy had fallen to the fascistic blandishments of Mussolini in 1922, and in 1936 its conquest of Ethiopia was being completed. Hitler had risen to power in Germany even before Hoover left the White House, and in 1936 he occupied the demilitarized Rhineland. In July 1936 the rising of the Nationalists had brought civil war to Spain. Franklin Roosevelt confessed in private that the situation was blacker than any he had ever known—though the isolationistic disposition of the American people required him to minimize his concern. In the face of alarming events the basic commitments of Americans to peace and nonintervention were put to the test. Intellectual neutrality among the harsh

[10] See Bennett, *Demagogues in the Depression,* pp. 263–72 Coughlin received very little official Catholic support and was opposed by many prelates, editors, and intellectuals in the church. Ideologically these several demagogic leaders drew more on America's nativist, anti-subversionary, and populist traditions than on the fascistic "Extreme Right." Embattled Fundamentalism, aroused Catholic anticommunism, and deep dissatisfaction with the New Deal were also basic components.

alternatives of Soviet communism, the stricken democracies, and the rising dictators was impossible. Indeed, men like Winrod, Pelley, G. L. K. Smith, and above all, Father Coughlin, had abandoned neutrality. Anti-Semitism, extreme nationalism, and frantic anticommunism dominated their oratory. Other voices were declaring Western civilization to be at the crossroads—and calling America to rally to the democratic cause.

The effect of all this on the leadership of the mainstream Protestant churches was traumatic. Their remorse for the excessive militarism exhibited during World War I had led to a widespread commitment to dogmatic Christian pacifism. In 1929 the Federal Council of Churches had greeted the United States Senate's consent to the Kellogg-Briand Peace Pact with jubilation: "Let church bells be rung, songs sung, prayers of thanksgiving be offered and petitions for help from God that our nation may ever follow the spirit and meaning of the Pact."[11] Countless Protestant ministers had sworn that they would never again support a war. Three of the most prominent preachers (Fosdick, Ernest F. Tittle, and Ralph W. Sockman) were taking pacifist positions, many wondered if even police forces could be justified, and among radicals the question of justifying violence in the class struggle became divisive. The Fellowship of Reconciliation flourished in such an atmosphere, especially in the seminaries. The Oxford Union peace pledge was gaining countless signers in the universities. Undergirding this fervency were two almost contradictory assumptions: that civilized nations would not again resort to war, and that the United States could with a clear conscience ignore the aggressions of the dictators.

As the world situation darkened, however, the pacifist consensus began to weaken. What had been an almost academic debate on the legitimacy of always turning the other cheek began to yield to the question of collective security versus nonintervention. And this new phase created the anomaly of Christian socialists and Social Gospel liberals, because of their pacifism, joining voices with the Silver Shirts and Father Coughlin in a demand for isolation, neutrality, and Amercia First. The anomaly proved unbearable for many

11 *Federal Council Bulletin*, February 1929, p. 24. The Peace Pact of Paris had been signed in August 1928; it was approved by the United States Senate in January 1929.

Christian spokesmen but reasonable to as many others. In the churches the result was especially cacophonous and even divisive, perhaps because they felt obliged to speak when they did not even have a consensus to report, much less a clearly formulated Christian position. Editorial staffs, unofficial groups, and official church agencies were split. Even peace groups such as the Church Peace Union and the World Alliance for International Fellowship offered contradictory counsel.

The arguments, needless to say, did not always rest securely on logic or biblical exegesis. Phobias and irrational loyalties also gained voice or sought rationalization. Easterners tended to be less isolationistic than westerners. Jews regarded Hitler as diabolical; anti-Semites considered him farsighted and wise. Germans, Italians, and Irish saw little reason for aiding Britain or France; Anglo-Saxons usually inclined to the Allied cause. Catholics tended to support Franco in Spain, as well as his allies, and, following the pope, to consider communism as the world's chief threat. And so the "debate" continued even after Hitler's invasion of Poland. In 1940 Roosevelt in his campaign for a third term still pledged to keep our boys at home. As for the churches, Professor Miller had good grounds for a negative judgment:

> History affords no sadder tale than the impact of [these] events . . . upon the followers of the Prince of Peace in America. . . . The response . . . was pathetically confused, halting, divided, and uncertain. It is a heartbreaking record of alternating deep despair and naive optimism, of timid vacillation and blind dogmatism. . . . To put it bluntly, confusion over war and peace seemed more starkly extreme in the Protestant churches than in American society as a whole—and this is a damning comparison.[12]

Then on Sunday, 7 December 1941, a Japanese decision brought America's indecision to an end. The New York Philharmonic Symphony's broadcast of Schubert's *Unfinished Symphony* was interrupted by the solemn announcement that Pearl Harbor had been treacherously attacked. America was at war—and the Depression decade passed into history. In a strict sense it did not pass away, however, for the decade of

[12] Miller, *American Protestantism and Social Issues*, pp. 333–34.

the "third American Revolution" had made a permanent mark on the mind and face of America. Especially important for Protestantism was a remarkable renewal in theology which had a quickening effect in the seminaries and churches. An examination of Neo-orthodoxy, therefore, can illuminate the inner meaning of the decade's adventure.

55

NEO-ORTHODOXY AND SOCIAL CRISIS

When events at Pearl Harbor embroiled the United States in World War II, the circumstances were as unambiguous to most Americans as such things ever are. Without warning or immediate provocation a "peace-loving nation" had become the object of sudden, carefully planned aggression. It was in President Roosevelt's words a day that would "live in infamy." Furthermore, the ideological grounds for a declaration of war could not possibly have been less ambiguous. Faced by Hitler's enormities, Mussolini's unprovoked aggression in Ethiopia, and their joint contribution to Franco's victory in Spain, the rhetoric of justification was virtually unassailable from a democratic standpoint. Yet the churches did not "present arms" with the disgraceful lack of charity and proportion they had displayed during World War I, nor were they so naïve and vainglorious when it came to talk of peace and the United Nations. What has been called "the Protestant search for political realism," had not been entirely in vain. A sense of the sinfulness of man, the finitude of nations, the actualities of power, and the limitations of American virtue was more in evidence.

Within the leadership of the Protestant churches another change was apparent: Fundamentalism had lost the support of the great "moderate middle" which even during the twenties and thirties had remained latently if not aggressively conservative in its doctrinal stand. Gradually a new way of conceiving biblical authority and the doctrinal tradition had taken hold. It was no longer necessary for "orthodox" Christians to regard scientific freedom, biblical criticism, urban mores, and the critique of social or economic structures as inimical to their faith. And in one case as in the other, the Neo-orthodox movement in theology was an essential aspect of the transformed situation. If one looks to the remarkable way in which theology and theologians loomed up during the forties in the nation's moral, intellectual, and cultural life, again Neo-orthodoxy becomes essential to an adequate explanation. The cultural and religious revolutions of the 1960s and the still more circumspect view of the churches toward American imperialism and the war in Vietnam are also relatively inexplicable if Neo-orthodoxy is not taken into consideration. This intellectual phenomenon of the thirties, therefore, deserves fairly detailed consideration. Although its heyday was relatively brief, it involved a major reassessment of the Church's entire tradition. It was by no means a unified movement, and its influence in the denominations varied greatly. But its overall impact was powerful.

PREPARATION IN EUROPE

For over a century the American churches had been profoundly stimulated by Continental scholarship and theology, especially as it took shape in Germany. On religious liberalism German influence had been especially strong. It was only natural, therefore, that Americans should also respond to the new currents of thought which were evoked by the military and cultural catastrophe of 1914–18. This meant that some attentive Americans very soon began to share in the discovery of a whole literature of religious prophecy which had been widely ignored during the halcyon decades of the nineteenth century. Voices from the underground such as Sören Kierkegaard and Fëdor Dostoevski were heard again, and now their demand for a deeper kind of Christian earnestness was better understood.

There was also a parallel line of secular prophets, men like Schopenhauer, Jacob Burckhardt, the historian and philosopher of culture, and, most piercing of all, Friedrich Nietzsche, who either sadly or triumphantly had proclaimed the decadence of bourgeois culture, the coming of the "mass man," the end of Western civilization, and the death of God. From his listening post in Basel, Switzerland, Burckhardt had seen the Franco-Prussian War as premonitory of the new caesarism:

The military state must become one great factory. Those hordes of men in the great industrial centers will not be left indefinitely to their greed and want. What must logically come is a fixed and supervised stint of misery, glorified by promotions and uniforms, daily begun and ended to the sound of drums. . . . Long voluntary subjection under individual *Fuehrers* and usurpers is in prospect. People no longer believe in principles but will, periodically, probably believe in saviors. . . . For this reason authority will again raise its head in the pleasant twentieth century, and a terrible head.[1]

During the ensuing decades, however, the cultural climate in Europe and America was not responsive to Nietzschean prophecy. Except among the socialists, profound social and spiritual criticism had a small audience. Not until after the Great War of 1914 did the full tragedy of Western history stand exposed. Oswald Spengler's *Decline of the West* may not be an enduring classic, but in 1918 it could not easily be ignored. Also in 1918 Karl Barth, an obscure Swiss pastor, sent into the world a commentary on Saint Paul's Epistle to the Romans. In its enlarged edition of 1921 this became a veritable "bombshell on the playground of the theologians" (as Karl Adam, a Roman Catholic, put it). Its impact derived from the evangelical intensity with which Barth drove home the Kierkegaardian axiom as to "the 'infinite distinction' between time and eternity."[2] Addressing the predicament of the preacher on Saturday night, he proclaimed God's transcendence. He turned with a new seriousness to the Word of God, a Word from beyond all human possibilities. He attacked every effort to accommodate the faith: the scholars who treated the Scriptures as so many runes to be deciphered, the liberals who merely provided an ideology for the middle classes, and the social Christians who made the Christian ethic a platform for reforming the world. With an immense and constantly growing emphasis on the victory of Christ, he called men back to the "strange world of the Bible." He also called attention to the classic theology of the

[1] Burckhardt to F. von Preen, 1872, quoted in Karl Löwith, *Meaning in History* (Chicago: University of Chicago Press, 1949), p. 24.

[2] Karl Barth, *The Epistle to the Romans*, trans. Sir Edwyn Hoskyns, 2d ed. (New York: Oxford University Press, 1933), pp. 10, 27 (preface). The prefaces to the first six editions are an interesting commentary on the book's reception—and significance.

Reformation. Then in the 1930s he began to publish his monumental *Church Dogmatics*.

In the meantime, the "theology of crisis," or dialectical school, had developed an articulate following: Georg Merz and Friedrich Gogarten in Germany and, most important so far as America was concerned, Emil Brunner of Zurich. Brunner was in fact much more than a mediator of Barthian views. Having studied in the United States and taught in England, he sensed the American situation better than Barth and made a very important impression as a guest professor at Princeton Seminary in 1938–39. Through his quickly translated and widely read books he was until after World War II the most influential of the European dialectical theologians.

Yet the theology of crisis was only one facet of the theological renaissance then stirring Europe. Equally basic was the increasing seriousness in evangelical exegesis of the Old and New Testaments. The playground of the biblical scholars had also had its bomb: Albert Schweitzer's *Quest of the Historical Jesus* in 1906, followed in 1912 by *Paul and His Interpreters*. Taking the form of critical surveys of the previous century's massive scholarly efforts to discover the historical Jesus, the young Strasbourg professor (who would later become famous as a Kant scholar, theologian, philosopher of civilization, authority on Bach and baroque organs, and medical missionary to Africa) pronounced the liberal tradition of New Testament study a failure. In effect, he found the scholars peering down the 2,000-year-long shaft of history and seeing their own bourgeois faces reflected from the bottom of the well. Schweitzer, on the contrary, saw the New Testament pervaded by an intense apocalyptic concern that ruled out liberalism's optimistic view of the Kingdom of God.

Schweitzer himself never joined the "school" which he founded, but the decades which followed were marked by a constantly growing current of scholarship and exegesis that took seriously his basic contention. Christian hope was revived as a living doctrine. (In 1954, to the great irritation of many liberals, it would be the theme of the World Council of Churches Assembly in Evanston, Illinois.) In a more general way, studies of the apostolic preaching began to replace the quest for the religion of Jesus. Barth himself was responding to this broad impulse. Among many others were Martin Dibelius, Karl Ludwig Schmidt, and the young Rudolf Bultmann, whose *Jesus and the Word* (1926) was a study of the synoptic gospels which gave new clarity to a postliberal conception of the *Kerygma* (message, proclamation) of the New Testament community. During the next four decades, by means of ever more intense scholarship as well as by theological interpretation, Bultmann would give added meaning and clarity to a wonderfully succinct sentence in his first chapter: "When we encounter the words of Jesus in history, *we* do not judge *them* by a philosophical system with reference to their rational validity; *they* meet *us* with the question of how we are to interpret our own existence."[3]

A third stream of renewal is commonly designated as the "Luther renaissance" though actually its interests were far broader. Theodosius Harnack, father of the famous historian of dogma, stands close to its source in the midnineteenth century. Karl Holl of Berlin, an outspoken critic of Adolf von Harnack and Ernst Troeltsch, was also important. Werner Elert at the University of Erlangen articulated another subcurrent. Destined to be best known in America was the Swedish impulse stemming from Lund University. All of these scholars and theologians were determined to deepen the liberal notion of Luther as merely a pioneer of intellectual liberty. In 1900 Einar Billing of Lund had already published his corrective *Luther's Doctrine of the State*. Most influential of all were Bishop Anders Nygren's historical study of the Christian doctrine of love, *Agape and Eros* (1930, 1936), and Bishop Gustav Aluén's study of the Atonement, *Christus Victor* (1930). One of the remarkable results of the Luther renaissance was the way in which the Reformer became an intensely relevant contemporary theologian again. Other scholars, meanwhile, were performing a similar office for John Calvin—and at the same time giving new relevance to the issues that had long divided the Lutheran and Reformed traditions.

A fourth trend to be noted was the new urgency being given to "social Christianity" in many quarters. An uneasiness about the social situation of the church lurked in all of the views under discussion, but in some men it became a dominant concern. Appalled by the apostasy of Europe's working classes, incensed by official unconcern for social injustice, and

[3] Rudolf Bultmann, *Jesus and the Word* (Charles Scribner's Sons, 1958), p. 11. Bultmann's theology would not begin to have wide influence in America until after his controversial work on demythologizing of 1941—and hence not until after World War II.

considerably affected by official unconcern for social injustice, and considerably affected by the Marxian analysis of the modern economic order, a new breed of theologians tried to undo the churches' long commitment to middle-class values. There was, to be sure, a Continental "social gospel" to build on; indeed, the American movement of that name owed more to Albrecht Ritschl than to any other theologian. But the newer movement wished to be free of liberal theological assumptions, to be more existentially evangelical, and, above all, to be more realistic in assessing the waning "Protestant Era" in European civilization. For Americans none of these men would become so well-known and influential as Paul Tillich. H. Richard Niebuhr expounded Tillich's critique in an important essay of 1930, and two years later he published a translation of Tillich's *The Religious Situation*. The impact of this cluster of influences helps to explain why the theology of crisis in America led not to a decline, but to a revival of the Social Gospel's historic concerns.

British contributions to the changing theological climate were considerable though less influential than their quality warranted. Scotland, due to its many contacts with the Reformed family of denominations on the Continent and in North America, had a larger impact than England, especially through scholarship and translations pertaining to the Calvinistic tradition.[4] Anglican theology, meanwhile, tended to preserve its insularity and to concern itself with the tensions inherent in its ambiguous Reformation heritage—especially as these had been reawakened in 1928 by Parliament's rejection of a new revision of the Book of Common Prayer. In William Temple (1881–1944), however, there arose one monumental exception. As archbishop of York and later of Canterbury, Temple became an influential world figure. As a theologian he sought to expound the Christian faith in relation to man's scientific knowledge, moral light, and rational powers. In *Christus Veritas* (1924) and in his famous Gifford Lectures, *Nature, Man and God* (1934), he revealed his indebtedness to Alfred North Whitehead and to the liberal Catholicism of Bishop Charles Gore (1853–1932). His importance was not chiefly due to his philosophical apologetics,

[4] Two Reformed theologians in England, P. T. Forsythe (1848–1921) and John Oman (1860–1939), did move from liberalism to profound reappropriations of classical theological insights; yet both of them were only belatedly discovered in the United States.

however, but to the compelling way in which he, as a church leader in England and as a major voice in the ecumenical movement, united a strong social concern with a profound conception of the Church. "Let the Church be the Church," the resounding slogan of the 1937 Life and Work Conference, can stand as an epitome of Temple's most enduring impact on America.

Temple's influence also serves to underline the importance of the ecumenical movement for American theology throughout these decades. In innumerable committees, commissions, and conferences of that worldwide movement, a wide range of American church leaders and theologians had their decisive personal confrontation with European theology and with church traditions that had previously been left out of consideration. They learned, for example, that Barthianism was not simple German fundamentalism. They also became church reformers in a new sense. Paul A. Carter rightly reminds us that the American delegates who came to the Oxford Conference "talking about *our churches*" went home "talking about the Church."[5]

THE AMERICAN RESPONSE

To most Americans of the 1920s the notions of "crisis" and "despair" could arise only in the frightened and diseased minds of those who stalked the remote European ruins, the world of yesterday—or in the minds of expatriate intellectuals who preferred the ruins to the world of Cal Coolidge. Yet this façade of confidence began to crack with the passing years. As hope for peace and world democracy guttered out, the American dream was increasingly interrupted by nightmares. T. S. Eliot published *The Waste Land* in 1922 and *The Hollow Men* in 1925. In 1923—the year of Hitler's Beerhall *Putsch*—Professor Lee M. Hollander of the University of Texas brought out a volume of selections from Kierkegaard in an obscure bulletin series of the University of Texas. David L. Swenson of the University of Minnesota was able to review it discerningly and perhaps to lay plans for the translation projects and further essays that were to make him virtually the father of American Kierkegaardian studies.

[5] *The Decline and Revival of the Social Gospel, 1920–1940,* p. 195.

In the meantime, what is in retrospect recognized as American Neo-orthodoxy began to take shape piecemeal. The contributors came from all over; some traveled widely, some stayed at home, some were refugees from Hitler. Some of the new voices witnessed to conversions of one sort or other; many had radically changed their minds. They drew their inspiration from thinkers of the most diverse sorts and from many lands; they were themselves provoked to new kinds of thinking by Russian Orthodox, Jews, Roman Catholics, and Protestants of all sorts, by ancient Greek tragedians and by contemporary atheists. They spoke as confident heralds or as self-questioning diarists, as historians, exegetes, or systematic theologians. They were troubled by diverse problems: social injustice, political and churchly utopianism, routine complacency, and ecclesiastical passivity. Some protested against apostasy and heresy; others condemned orthodox pride. Yet to take account of all these variations would result in either a sterile catalogue or a long book. In a single chapter one can only discuss a few of the more influential thinkers and make some effort to represent their major theological interests.

Walter Lowrie (1868–1959), a Philadelphia-born and Princeton-educated Episcopalian, was rector of Saint Paul's American Church in Rome from 1907 to 1930. Liberal theology had saved him, like so many others, from skepticism; but the introduction to his translation of Schweitzer's *Mystery of the Kingdom of God* (1925) marks a transition that gradually deepened into fullscale revolt as he began to contact the dialectical theologians and to immerse himself in the German translations of Kierkegaard. In 1932 came his major outcry—with one of the century's longest titles: *Our Concern with the Theology of Crisis, the Fundamental Aspects of the Dialectical Theology Associated with the Name of Karl Barth, Appreciatively Presented with the Query Whether It Be Not Our Only Positive Possibility, The Crisis of Society and of the Church Understood as the Crisis of the Individual before God.* Kierkegaard looms larger than Barth in this book, so the groundwork was well laid for Lowrie's great lifetime achievement as a biographer of Kierkegaard and translator of a dozen of his works.

Douglas Horton (1891–1968) was an American-born Congregationalist who, after an education in four countries, was serving as a parish minister in the Boston area when he chanced upon an early volume of Barth's essays on the Harvard Divinity School new-book shelf. He determined that very afternoon to translate the work—and in 1928 appeared *The Word of God and the Word of Man,* Barth's first book in English. Thirty years later Horton, then dean of the Harvard Divinity School, reflected on that early experience:

> It was a generation ago that I ran across the German text, published under the title *Das Wort Gottes und die Theologie.* . . . Only those who are old enough to remember the particular kind of desiccated humanism, almost empty of other-worldly content, which prevailed in many Protestant areas in the early decades of this century, can understand the surprise, the joy, the refreshment which would have been brought by the book to the ordinary and, like myself, somewhat desultory reader of the religious literature of that time. To question evolutionary modes of thought in that day was something like questioning the Ptolemaic theory in the time of Copernicus, with the stupendous difference that Copernicus seemed at first to shut the transcending God out of the world and Barth seemed immediately to let him in.[6]

In addition to these and many other Americans who contributed to the rise of a new theological temper in America, two Germans who came to America permanently made especially vigorous contributions. Wilhelm Pauck (b. 1901) entered the University of Chicago Divinity School as an exchange student in 1925 and stayed on as a professor of historical theology in that great center of liberalism. In 1931 he published an informative and enthusiastic study of Barth. Pauck's many students moved on to faculties elsewhere inspired by his vast learning and, above all, by his expositions of Reformation theology. Paul Tillich (1886–1965) began his enormously influential second career as a professor at Union Theological Seminary in New York in 1934. Though basically a speculative religious philosopher in the German idealistic tradition, Tillich's strong ontological interests were powerfully informed by existential thought, a modified Marxian analysis of the Western cultural predicament, and a conviction that the church's middle-class orientation was a

[6] Douglas Horton, Foreword to Karl Barth, *The Word of God and the Word of Man* (New York: Harper & Brothers, Torchbooks, 1957), pp. 1–2.

fatal shortcoming. His wide interests in art and culture and in the problem of history were vital factors in the great renewal of interest in theology which he stimulated even among intellectuals who had decided that that "ghostly enterprise" was void of interest and relevance.

The Niebuhrs

Despite all the varied contributions that make up the phenomenon of American Neo-orthodoxy, the fact remains that its dynamics, nature, and purposes are best revealed in the lives and works of Reinhold Niebuhr (1892–1970) and his brother H. Richard Niebuhr (1894–1962). Both men were born in Missouri, educated in the college and seminary of the German Evangelical church in which their father was a minister; both did further study at Yale.[7] After varied service in their own denomination—Reinhold for thirteen years as a pastor in Detroit, Richard as a professor and college president—they both entered upon careers as professors of ethics, Reinhold at Union Theological Seminary (New York) in 1928 and Richard at the Yale University Divinity School in 1931. For more than a quarter-century both men, with many congenial if not always like-minded colleagues, made these two institutions lively and influential centers of theological ferment.

The two brothers were by no means indentical in interest or tendency. Richard was more a theologian's theologian and a moral philsopher; Reinhold was more involved with practical problems in social ethics. Yet both were learned historians, deeply concerned with the whole course of Western thought, and both brought formidable analytical powers to the theoretical questions of the day. Despite differences in approach they both also dealt with the problems raised on one side by the historicity and finitude of man, the social accommodation of the Church, the temptation to absolutistic moral judgments; and on the other side by the threat of moral emptiness and formality, the dangers of human arrogance, and the menace of idealistic naïveté. Although neither was an apologist for Christianity in the overt manner of, say,

---

[7] Hulda Niebuhr, a sister, was also an influential professor of Christian education at McCormick Theological Seminary in Chicago. The mother of these three distinguished children was very appropriately awarded an honorary doctor's degree by Lindenwood College in 1953.

Archbishop Temple, both demonstrated the profundity and relevance of Christian views far more effectively by involving a whole generation of readers and listeners in their creative reexamination of the heritage and in their realistic relating of this heritage to contemporary dilemmas.

In 1937 H. Richard Niebuhr reversed his earlier judgment of Jonathan Edwards. With "Sinners in the Hands of an Angry God" in mind, he spoke of Edwards's "intense awareness of the precariousness of life's poise, of the utter insecurity of men and mankind which are at every moment as ready to plunge into the abyss of disintegration, barbarism, crime, and war of all against all, as to advance toward harmony and integration. He recognized what Kierkegaard meant when he described life as treading water with ten thousand fathoms beneath us."[8] This was a considerable change of mood from Niebuhr's first major work. In *The Social Sources of Denominationalism* (1929), he had followed Adolf von Harnack in seeking to liberate traditional Protestantism from "that strange interpretation of the faith which has prevailed since the days when Greek disputants carried into it the problems and methods of Greek philosophy."[9] Even at this date, however, he had participated in certain intellectual movements that prepared him for his future role as a Neo-orthodox prophet. D. C. Macintosh, Niebuhr's mentor at Yale, was a vigorous realist who demanded an objective basis for religious faith. The sociological analysis of religious institutions which liberal scholarship encouraged also began to shake the ground beneath the feet of many confident churchmen. Indeed, Niebuhr's *Social Sources of Denominationalism* worked to the same end. Using the insights of Marx, Weber, and Troeltsch, he exposed the changing historical involvements of the Church, showing how class, race, nationality, and economic factors had divided the churches, and how deeply involved in middle-class presuppositions was the American religious mainstream.

In the same year, 1929, Reinhold Niebuhr published his *Leaves from the Notebooks of a Tamed Cynic* and revealed

[8] *The Kingdom of God in America*, pp. 137–38.

[9] *The Social Sources of Denominationalism*, pp. 11–12. Harnack, the great historian of Christian dogma, had stated this view of early doctrinal controversies in his famous lectures on the essence of Christianity in 1900 (published in English as *What is Christianity?* in 1901).

that his burgeoning protest had roots trailing back to 1915. Here he did not merely condemn specific social abuses and industrial cruelty; he pointed to a more ominous kind of handwriting on the wall, finding the current faith in religious education "the last word in absurdity." Then came the Crash —after which many Americans began to raise doubts about the positive identification of Christian hope and the national dream. But in 1932 (the year of Franklin Roosevelt's election) both brothers again issued important books. Richard Niebuhr published his translation (with an introduction) of Paul Tillich's *The Religious Situation,* a very sober statement, deeply informed by Marxian analysis of the values of middle-class civilization. Reinhold Niebuhr, meanwhile, published *Moral Man and Immoral Society,* his single most important book and probably the most disruptive religio-ethical bombshell of domestic construction to be dropped during the entire interwar period—the major document in that "Protestant search for political realism" which Donald Meyer has so brilliantly described. Niebuhr distinguished between the ethical potentialities of individuals and organized groups and insisted that both in criticism and in advocacy the severe limitations of the latter be kept in mind. Labor unions, corporations, and sovereign states, he said, are *by their nature* all but completely incapable of altruistic conduct. Social ethics, therefore, require a dialectical rather than an absolutistic moral stance. Given the immensely practical bent of American Protestantism and the staggering policy questions of the Roosevelt era, one may wonder if the degree to which American Neo-orthodoxy's history is enmeshed with the biography of Reinhold Niebuhr does not prove that a revision of the Social Gospel was the primary purpose of the movement.

Reinhold Niebuhr's views were further developed and explicated in a long series of important books and countless articles and reviews during the next quarter-century; but they took their basic shape in *The Nature and Destiny of Man* (1941–43), which was first delivered as the Gifford Lectures shortly after the outbreak of World War II. Throughout these years Niebuhr attacked the idea of progress and the notion that "history is the Christ." He saw man as "at once saint and sinner," as both creature and creator, as in and yet transcending history. Above all, he sought to make men fully aware of the depths of human sinfulness. Critics who found his message more prophetic than evangelical could hardly be denied their point; but no American did more to transform the old liberal Social Gospel movement and to demonstrate the relevance of biblical insights and Christian affirmations.

Two more books of great prescriptive value were published in 1935. Reinhold Niebuhr's *Introduction to Christian Ethics* appeared, with its famous Niebuhrian critique of the "illusion of liberalism that we are dealing with a possible and prudential ethic in the gospel." "The ethic of Jesus," he insisted, "does not deal at all with the immediate moral problem of every human life. . . . It transcends the possibilities of human life . . . as God transcends the world." Almost simultaneously, Richard Niebuhr joined Wilhelm Pauck and Francis P. Miller to issue what was in effect a Neo-orthodox manifesto to the churches: *The Church Against the World.* Niebuhr in his essay dwelt characteristically on the need of the Church, not to march out to battle (it had been marching to too many drums), but to withdraw from the world's embrace awhile and find itself, to rediscover its gospel, and then perhaps to fulfill its mission. Characteristically, during the 1930s and 1940s he was emphasizing the need for the Church to realize itself as a confessing community—an idea that would be more fully expounded in his classic, *The Meaning of Revelation* (1941.)

Before proceeding to the constructive task of that book, however, Richard Neibuhr had to settle his accounts with the American church tradition, and that he did profoundly in *The Kingdom of God in America,* a masterpiece of reassessment in which the prophetic stance of Puritanism and Jonathan Edwards, as well as the great evangelical enterprises of the nineteenth century, were appreciatively reconsidered. Liberalism was then weighed and found wanting. In this book Harnack yields to Jonathan Edwards as a major source of Niebuhr's thought, and so it remains to the very end.[10] Nowhere is the living relationship of *Neo*-orthodoxy and *Paleo*-orthodoxy better illustrated—unless in Reinhold Niebuhr's continual invocations of Saint Augustine.

Annus Mirabilis

An account of the Niebuhrs must not be allowed to veil other vital aspects of the Neo-orthodox resurgence, though it has already led past the movement's most remarkably productive year, 1934, the year, let us not forget, in which Hitler

[10] Compare *The Kingdom of God in America* (1937), pp. 113–16, with *Radical Monotheism* (1960), pp. 37–42.

settled down to the *Aufbau* of a national socialist state in Germany; the year, too, when the murder of Kirov set off the great purge trials in Russia. Not inappropriately, therefore, Reinhold Niebuhr published his *Reflections on the End of an Era* and delivered the Rauschenbusch Lectures on Christian ethics.[11] But other very important writings expanded the scope of the movement. Walter Marshall Horton of Oberlin Seminary published his *Realistic Theology,* a forceful work that described both a collective and a personal change of mind. The Methodist theologian Edwin Lewis of Drew Theological Seminary expanded an earlier essay, "The Fatal Apostasy of the Modern Church," into a book-length *Christian Manifesto* which underlined the same point. George W. Richards of the German Reformed Seminary of Mercersburg memory struck a very important note with *Beyond Fundamentalism and Modernism, The Gospel of God.* In the same year he and Elmer G. Homrighausen brought out the first volume of Barth's sermons in translation, an important event considering the degree to which the new movement championed a restoration of the preaching office in the church.

From this time forward books, articles, visits, and ecumenical conversations become so numerous that detailed narration becomes impractical. But taken together they do constitute a collective transformation of the theological situation: the beginning of a distinctly postliberal period in American theology. In 1939, when a series of autobiographical articles by the country's leading theologians appeared in the *Christian Century* (since its refounding in 1908 the chief organ of interdenominational liberalism), a genuine change of mood was made manifest.[12]

THE ESSENCE OF NEO-ORTHODOXY

Neo-orthodoxy was not greeted with joy in every quarter. To countless liberal preachers and theologians it seemed merely an erudite form of the very Fundamentalism that they

---

[11] They were published as *An Interpretation of Christian Ethics* (1935).

[12] The difference which the passage of seven years had made is revealed by comparing this series with the volume of essays *Contemporary American Theology,* ed. Vergilius Ferm (1932).

had shaken off in the bolder days of their youth.[13] To the more learned Fundamentalists, on the other hand, Karl Barth's theology (not to speak of American Neo-orthodoxy) was but a confusing form of modernism, especially dangerous because it had cut itself loose from religious experience, natural theology, philosophic rationalism, and a propositional view of biblical revelation. Because they perceived no return to a strict doctrine of scriptural inerrancy, they could take little comfort from the changes occurring in the old liberal seminaries. Given these claims and counterclaims, it is important to make some generalizations about the new movement as a whole.

The first step toward such a general view of Neo-orthodoxy must be a recognition of its doctrinal diversity, which was at least as great as that of the Orthodox Presbyterians and Pentecostalists bound together in the Fundamentalist movement. The translators of Kierkegaard alone included Lutherans, Anglo-Catholic Episcopalians, and Quakers. Participation in a movement of theological reform did not mean the relinquishing of other commitments on the historic points of controversy—the Church, the ministry, baptism, and Eucharist, predestination, and free grace. Neo-orthodox theologians differed from liberals, however, in regarding these questions as important, even as crucial. They differed from Fundamentalists and the older conservatives in that they wished to face them directly in the new context provided by contemporary thought and the ecumenical movement.

In the second place, Neo-orthodoxy was a critical movement, an attack on certain prevailing assumptions of liberalism. Neo-orthodox theologians criticized with special vehemence liberalism's optimistic doctrine of man and hence its doctrine of historical progress. The radical historicity and finitude of all things human must not be ignored, they said; nor should the opaque aimlessness of human history be minimized. The small solicitude of the universe for man must be recognized. The tragic sense of life must be apprehended. Closely related was an assault on both the great romantic doctrine that the religious and/or moral consciousness provides the proper starting point of theology and the philosophical idealism that often figured in theologies of that sort. The genteel tradition must go; metaphysics cannot do duty for the revealed Word of God. The Word, moreover, cannot

13 See Henry N. Wieman et al., *Religious Liberals Reply.*

be reduced to a literal concern for the teachings of Jesus and the virtual abandonment of Saint Paul's witness to the Christ. Man needs and the New Testament brings more than new rules, they would say. This critique as a whole adds up to the single complaint that theological liberalism left men spiritually naked and morally unprepared in an age of depression, despair, and international violence. Certainly not all liberals were as naïve as this critique suggested, but an aggressive new movement is not always fair, and Neo-orthodoxy was no exception.

In the third place, the essential consensus of Neo-orthodox theologians was not in specific doctrines, but, primarily, in a sense of urgency and a demand for moral and intellectual humility. The renewed interest in Kierkegaard was no accident. Just as such medieval theologians as Aquinas, Averroës, and Maimonides (Christian, Moslem, and Jew) were united by a commitment to Aristotelian rationalism, so Neo-orthodox thinkers responded affirmatively to the existentialism of the Catholic Gabriel Marcel, the atheist Jean-Paul Sartre, the Jew Martin Buber, or the Spaniard Miguel de Unamuno and his classic, *The Tragic Sense of Life* (1912).[14] This existential mood may have had more to do with their distaste for an ethic based on the rules of Jesus than with their exegesis of the New Testament, though the revival of evangelical exegesis did make their attack double-barreled. In any event, a situational-contextual "love ethic" became the positive part of a widespread critique of legalism and code morality. The existential commitment also made them suspicious of ambitious metaphysical systems, natural theology, and natural law concepts.

Neo-orthodoxy was pervaded by a dialectical mood; paradox and the contradictions of history figured strongly in its expositions. Hegel, Marx, and Kierkegaard in various ways supported this tendency, but not in any single way. The best explanation of this dialectical tendency may well be there further consensus as to the all-enveloping nature of human history. Neo-orthodox thinkers stressed the problem of histor-

[14] They were well aware of their great remove from scholasticism, however; which is to say that their existentialism virtually assumed the critical work of Immanuel Kant. Time and again they affirmed their Kantian lineage. At the same time Roman Catholic theologians with various non-Catholic allies were developing a strong Neo-Thomist movement.

ical relativism not because they liked it, but because they could not escape it. They were heirs of the whole historical movement. Everything had its history: every religion, every idea of the "absolute," every doctrine, every moral principle, every book of the Bible, every planet and solar system, every star—and every man. Small wonder that every problem didn't "come out even." Antinomies, paradoxes, and contradictions were conditions of existence. So the existential, historical, and dialectical moods mingled—to the consternation of Americans who wanted their theology simple and straightforward.

Despite all, however, Neo-orthodoxy was pervaded by a hopeful mood. It was neither cynical, pessimistic, nor nihilistic. Due to its concern for social issues, it absorbed the positive spirit of the New Deal. It never counseled resignation or passivity. Theologically it also recovered an eschatological sense of hope, one that rested on faith in the God who was beyond, beneath, and above all human possibilities. Because it did not rest its ultimate faith in human arrangements, it could bear—or even advocate—the shaking of cultural foundations.

Also partaking more of mood than of doctrine was Neo-orthodoxy's deep respect for the scientific, scholarly, and artistic achievements of men. Its great difference from fundamentalistic conservatism lay in its respect for these diverse activities. Indeed, Neo-orthodox thinkers not only continued the liberal attack on obscurantism in the churches, but made major contributions to the critical study of Scriptures, the sociological understanding of religious institutions, and the historical enterprise as a whole. Reformation and Puritan studies were especially meaningful to them; and they rescued many movements, writers, and thinkers from oblivion or obloquy. The newer tendencies in painting, music, and literature were not merely accepted, but explored for their theological significance.

Finally, in two ways Neo-orthodoxy undeniably did have positive doctrinal implications. For many, the doctrine of the Church, so slighted by liberals and fundamentalists, assumed a central place due to the convergence of several factors: (1) the new emphasis among biblical scholars on the message and tradition of the New Testament community; (2) the full scale emergence in both Roman Catholic and Protestant traditions of a liturgical movement that criticized many aspects of medieval ceremonialism and sought to restore the Reformation's emphasis on the corporate role of the laity in worship; (3) the persistent way in which the ecumenical Faith and Order movement revealed questions of the Church, the sacraments, and the ministry as key factors in the dividedness of Christianty; and (4) Neo-orthodoxy's own critique of culture-protestantism and its demand for a prophetic church that would recognize its continuity with the New Testament community and, therefore, its distinctness from the world in which it proclaims the Word and to which it ministers. It would be wrong, of course, to say that there was a Neo-orthodox doctrine of the Church; but the movement did much to make ecclesiology a major object of concern.

The other doctrinal effect of Neo-orthodoxy was its overall revival of interest in theology per se, and hence in the great ages of theological construction. The new concern for "biblical theology" was perhaps primary, above all the full restoration of Saint Paul as the first Doctor of the Church. Yet the early Fathers, the early councils, Saint Augustine, and, above all, the master theologians of the Reformation also gained new currency. Nor was it simply that they became objects of historical attention (though that they emphatically did) but that they were taken seriously rather than dismissed in the liberal manner as outmoded stages in the evolution of pure religion.

All considered, there are many reasons for regarding Neo-orthodoxy as an ambiguous prelude to the theological radicalism of the 1960s. Yet the interest in traditional doctrine which the movement stimulated—especially when Karl Barth was being heeded—did undeniably lead to a revival of supernaturalistic ways of thinking. And because they ignored many intellectual difficulties, Neo-orthodox theologians have been justifiably accused of putting down only a very thin sheet of dogmatic asphalt over the problems created by modern critical thought. Rudolf Bultmann was to protest this very tendency in 1941 with his call for "demythologizing" the biblical message. The implications of this protest, however, would not be exposed until well after the mid-twentieth century.

THE SCOPE AND DURATION OF NEO-ORTHODOXY

Neo-orthodoxy was primarily an intellectual movement. Like many another theological reform movement (from Aquinas

through Luther to John Henry Newman and Rauschenbusch) academic professors played a dominant role in
giving it shape and force. Its leaders were highly articulate,
and in due course they set in motion a tidal wave of
published articles and books which broke over the beaches of
liberalism and cultural complacency with considerable effect.
Due to the practical bent and anti-intellectual propensities of
the American clergy, however, enduring changes in American
parish life could result only as seminary graduates moved
into the churches as ministers and denominational leaders.
The distractions of the Great Depression followed by the terrible disruptions of World War II greatly retarded this movement to the grassroots, but even so, its influence was considerable. A new note of evangelical urgency became noticeable
even among great liberal preachers like Harry Emerson Fosdick and Ernest Fremont Tittle. The widely read *Christian
Century* reflected the movement's spreading influence. Christian education boards in nearly every denomination where
liberalism had made deep inroads were subjected to demands
for revised lesson materials, and in the Northern Presbyterian
church forces were set in motion which led to the election of
a new board and the launching of a totally reconceived educational program.

Neo-orthodoxy achieved its most direct influence on the
churches precisely in the area where men like Reinhold
Niebuhr had made their most original contributions—with a
reshaped Social Gospel. The dire condition of the economy
and a steady succession of international crisis had in any
event made a quantitative increase of social concern almost
inevitable. But Neo-orthodoxy gave men a more realistic
awareness of institutional power, social structures, and
human depravity. It made men at once more biblical in their
standpoint and less utopian in their advocacy. Most important, perhaps, it built bridges that opened communications
not only with modernists who had all but decided that Christianity was obsolete, but also with conservatives who had all
but decided that true Christians must repudiate modern
modes of thought and action.

56

WORLD WAR II AND THE POSTWAR REVIVAL

The peace settlement after World War I was the prelude to a tragically unsettled twenty years in European history. And the United States participated in that unsettlement, actively or passively hastening the political crises, intensifying the underlying economic disaster, and sharing the period's drastic ideological impasse. On Sunday, 7 December 1941, therefore, as a result of Japan's assault on Pearl Harbor, Americans awoke to the massive irony of national consensus in the actuality of war. In a day the situation had changed. What had been confused became clear. The great debates were at an end. An "army" of pacifists dwindled to about twelve thousand (or about 1 percent of those who registered for the draft). About $4 million was raised during the war to support various forms of alternative service.

The churches shared in this *renversement;* whether Protestant, Catholic, or Jewish, they showed no reluctance in supporting the national effort. All became engaged in the characteristic tasks of war, providing about eight thousand chaplains, raising money and volunteers for war service agencies, distributing Bibles, prayerbooks, and devotional literature, maintaining contact with servicemen, consoling and aiding those left behind.[1] Even with the provocations which Hitler provided, however, the churches did not repeat the unrestrained capitulation to the war spirit which had left them disgraced after 1918. Many factors help to explain this

[1] The government in turn showed its solicitude for religion by maintaining a uniformed chaplain corps (one chaplain for each twelve hundred men), building over six hundred interfaith chapels in training camps and posts, and providing many lesser services.

change, but most important by far was the chastening experience of the decade 1925–35. In theological terms. Neoorthodoxy is a large part of the explanation.

In more practical terms, one further effect of the social transformations wrought during the interwar decades was a distinct decline in the relative moral force of the churches. They simply were not as important a factor in the molding of public attitudes as they had been in 1916. The pulpit and church press had lost their preeminence among the mass media. Most conservative evangelicals had become committed to being noncommittal on public issues, while modernists, with their deemphasis of "divine" sanctions, had undermined the authority of the churches to speak on any issue. On the institutional plane, cooperative interchurch agencies had become so extensive that the war itself had nothing like the innovative impact of the 1916–18 experience. As the war dragged on, however, and especially as it drew to a victorious close, signs of increased religious interest multiplied. Events soon made clear that a revival was in the offing.

THE REVIVAL AND ITS SOCIAL SOURCES

The religious depression of the twenties had sunk to new depths after the Great Crash of 1929. Unemployment and hunger proved inconducive to a revival of popular religion, though they did cut away much superficiality and self-assurance from American church life. With the return of national confidence under the New Deal, something like an upturn in ecclesiastical prosperity also became noticeable. The collapse of European order, the rise of Hitler, and other ideological challenges led Americans to a new concern for their national heritage, including its religious tradition. Wartime mobilization interrupted the movement of renewal which Neo-orthodoxy had inspired, yet the anxieties of scattered families and the social dislocations of the "war effort" did stimulate an unmistakable rise of interest in religion. "There are no atheists in the foxholes," was the word from the theaters of military action. In millions of blue-star and gold-star households and in thousands of home churches the same could be said. In this sense, the "post-war revival" began long before the fighting ceased.

The atomic bombs, the final surrender, and the return of peace mark a new era in world history. Every major aspect of human affairs was involved, and American religious life was no exception. Yet three basic reminders seem essential to an understanding of American religious history during the fifteen-year period which ensued.

Most basic for the United States, which alone among the Western nations would experience a resurgence of religion during these years, was the dawn of an "age of affluence." After nearly two decades of depression and war, the nation's unsatisfied demands for the things of this world could now be supplied. The industrial expansion begun during the war accelerated afterward, making it possible between 1947 and 1957 for Americans to earn 2.6 trillion dollars and yet divert only 160 billion to savings and 290 billion to taxes. Along with these economic changes came an equally momentous transformation in the balance, structure, and dynamics of American life. By 1950 two-thirds of the American population had moved into metropolitan regions. In a great crescendo of migration, Negroes and Puerto Ricans moved into the inner cities. Orchards, woods, and open fields yeilded to the bulldozer to accommodate an expansion of suburban population that was three times greater than that of the central cities. In the meantime, the mechanization of agriculture, the improvement of roads and automobiles, and the postwar explosion of the television industry tended to bring vast areas which were still statistically "rural" into a quasi-suburban ambiance. Due to a trend to organize industry and business on a national basis and a large numerical increase in managerial personnel, geographical mobility became as prominent a feature of the new industrial society as social mobility. The organization man, the "lonely crowd," and the suburban status seeker became new features of the religious situation.

As a direct result of these social trends, virtually all of the churches were confronted with vast new responsibilities for "home missions." Migrants from the farms, villages, and inner cities of America were populating a vast new suburban mission field. Many of them were moving around within this "field" with unprecedented frequency—either because a pay raise enabled them to occupy a slightly more expensive housing development, or because opportunities for white collar promotions often involved transfers to other parts of the country. Problems of adjustment and anxieties over status and "acceptance" were ever-present. Churches were obviously the sort of family institution that the social situation required.

The chief international accompaniment of this sensational increase in national production and per capita income was the cold war, the postwar confrontation between what was usually referred to as the "Communist bloc" and the "free world," but which meant chiefly the emergence of the USSR and the U.S. as the colossuses of world politics. A corollary of this development was the collapse of the old European empires and the rapid emergence of new nations in Africa and Asia. Between 1950 and 1953, moreover, the United States was deeply involved in a hot war in Korea. The chief religious result of the international standoff was twofold. Consciously and subconsciously, with and without governmental stimuli, the patriotism of this "nation with the soul of a church" was aroused. Being a church member and speaking favorably of religion became a means of affirming the "American way of life," especially since the USSR and its Communist allies were formally committed to atheism. The other side of this process—and to a degree its result—was a long drawn out repetition of the Red Scare of 1919–20. Senator Joseph McCarthy of Wisconsin had his heyday, and being an active church member became a way to avoid suspicion of being a subversive influence. It seemed understood that a church member would not be a serious critic of the social order.

In a rapidly changing intellectual and spiritual environment, there also arose an urgent need for the consolations of religion that was quite independent of prudential considerations. Grave international uncertainties became more oppressive in the dawning age of nuclear fission. New scientific views forced adjustments of older conceptions of the natural world. A profoundly alerted social system brought changes in moral values that robbed old habitudes of their comfort.

Against this background of rapid change American religious communities of nearly every type (Protestant, Catholic, and Jewish; churches, sects, and cults) were favored during the postwar decade and a half by an increase of commitment and a remarkable popular desire for institutional participation. This popular resurgence of piety was a major subject of discussion in newspapers, popular magazines, and learned journals. Many books were published—some critical, some laudatory, some analytical. Publishers' lists, book sales, even the juke boxes and disc jockeys provided evidence of a change in public attitudes. In 1957 the Census Bureau reported that 96 percent of the American people cited a specific affiliation when asked the question: "What is your religion?"[2] And the statistics of church membership revealed that this always religious nation was in fact becoming affiliated at an increased rate.[3]

Church Affiliation in the Twentieth Century

Year	Percentage of Total Population
1910	43
1920	43
1930	47
1940	49
1950	55
1956	62
1960	69
1970	62.4

Accompanying this numerical growth was a very distinct increase in church attendance and even more remarkable acceleration of church-building construction.

Postwar Church Construction

Year	Amount Spent
1945	$ 26,000,000
1946	76,000,000
1948	251,000,000
1950	409,000,000

[2] Winthrop Hudson, Religion in America, p. 383.
[3] Roy Eckardt, The Surge of Piety in America, p. 22; augmented from Yearbook of the American Churches. Church membership statistics are notoriously inaccurate, but the basic trend is clear. See also Winthrop Hudson, "Are the Churches Really Booming?" Christian Century 72 (1955): 1494–96.

Postwar Church Construction

Year	Amount Spent
1954	$ 593,000,000
1956	775,000,000
1958	863,000,000
1959	935,000,000
1960	1,016,000,000

These figures are not corrected for monetary inflation, and the reader must bear in mind the degree to which depression and wartime restrictions had held back church construction for over fifteen years. To a large extent, moreover, the churches were responding to needs for new churches created by the geat postwar migration to suburbia. The increased tempo of construction provides evidence, nevertheless, of remarkable willingness by Americans to support local religious institutions.

Monetary support, increased church attendance, and even membership growth are by no means unambiguous demonstrations of religious commitment in the historical sense of that term. But the problem of interpreting the phenomenon is put in clearer light if five distinguishable but overlapping types of revival are recognized:

1. An accent on new forms of the civil religion which had always been a constituent element in American patriotism
2. A vast increase of popular interest in generalized forms of religion which, though discontinuous with the older revival tradition, were rooted in a long and lively American tradition
3. A resurgence of traditional evangelical revivalism which was also linked with serious intellectual efforts to update the older "fundamentalist" theology
4. The penetration into many congregations of a movement for liturgical renewal
5. A theological revival which was in fact a continuation of the Neo-orthodox impulse.

These separate, contemporaneous revivals must all be borne in mind if the religious character of the postwar "surge of piety" is to be understood.

THE ENLIVENED CIVIL RELIGION

Writing in the middle fifties about America's "triple melting pot" (Protestant, Catholic, and Jew), Will Herberg spoke of the American way of life as "the characteristic American religion, undergirding life and overarching American society despite indubitable differences of religion, section, culture, and class."[4] More important for the country's actual religious life was the propagation of a new form of patriotic piety that was closely linked to the "cold war." Finally, there seemed to be a consensus that personal religious faith was an essential element in proper patriotic commitment. In all of these modes, religion and Americanism were brought together to an unusual degree. This was especially true of the 1950s, when President Dwight D. Eisenhower served for eight years as a prestigious symbol of generalized religiosity and America's self-satisfied patriotic moralism. The president even provided a classic justification for the new religious outlook. "Our government," he said in 1954, "makes no sense unless it is founded on a deeply felt religious faith—and I don't care what it is."[5]

This "piety on the Potomac" was not limited to the president's private life, however, nor even to the prayer breakfasts and other religious activities in which many members of the Eisenhower administration participated. In the halls of Congress a whole series of legislative enactments actually extended the previous century's "quasi-establishment" of religion, with proponents of these measures sometimes showing a utilitarian conception of religion far more crass than the president's. When in 1954 the phrase "under God" (as used by Lincoln in his Gettysburg Address) was added to the Pledge of Allegiance, this important American pledge of loyalty came to include a theological affirmation which

[4] Will Herberg, *Protestant, Catholic, Jew,* p. 77. Characteristic of white analyses of the 1950s, this work shows almost no awareness of race or of Black America as a "melting pot" by itself.

[5] *Christian Century* 71 (1954), quoted in *Christianity Today,* 8 May 1961. The postwar form of civil religion debased the older tradition which had reverenced the Union as a bearer of transcendent values and summoned citizens to stewardship of a sacred trust. See Bibliography, sec. 8, especially the works of Paul C. Nagel.

millions of American humanists could not honestly make. In 1956 the venerable statement, "In God We Trust," was raised from the semiofficial place it has had since 1865 as a device on our coinage to become the country's official motto. Such patriotic uses of religion were also employed by the American Legion in its organized Back to God movement, and by countless other organizations. Yet they were not forced upon an unresponsive people by a few pious political leaders. Given the temper of the electorate, it is more likely that even impious congressmen found it expedient to vote for God.

PEACE OF MIND AND THE PLACID DECADE

The most characteristic religious feature of the period had little to do with either church membership or patriotism. The generalized kind of religiosity which predominated in the postwar years had "faith in faith" as its material principle and pious utilitarianism as its leading characteristic. Peace of mind and confident living were the promises it held out in the "age of anxiety," especially to those who were caught up in the stress and busy-ness of the business world and/or the insecurity and tensions of residential life in suburbia. The religion which answered to these needs was in fact a trans-denominational phenomenon with a long and distinctive history. So important is it that a later chapter is devoted to harmonial religion in America; but we must at least take passing note here of some of the major peace givers.

The first to establish himself as a postwar best seller was Joshua Loth Liebman, a Reform rabbi of Boston. His *Peace of Mind* (1946) was not simply another work of inspirational mind-cure, but a thoughtful adaptation of Freudian insights to problems of personal composure. Liebman accomplished his ends so effectively, moreover, that his successors would not be able to ignore the rising public interest in depth psychology.[6] At the far pole from Rabbi Liebman both in the-

[6] This psychological genre, due to its semi-religious function and appeal, would also be immensely popular, as Harry A. Overstreet's *Mature Mind* (1949), Smiley Blanton's *Love or Perish* (1956), Erich Fromm's *Art of Loving* (1956), and Eric Berne's *Games People Play* (1964) would demonstrate. Dr. Blanton popularized Freudian conceptions with great effectiveness and avoided

ology and in literary manner was a Presbyterian minister of Washington, D.C., whose posthumously published sermons gained a response so huge that a mass-audience movie of his life, *A Man Called Peter,* was also produced.[7] Within this range a great many others made highly varied efforts.

All of these writers and preachers, however, were but as forerunners to Norman Vincent Peale, the inspirationalist who indeed reached the height of his powers in the fullness of time. As minister of the Marble Collegiate Church on Fifth Avenue in New York, Peale moved into the field with such astounding success and with such a keen awareness of the potentialities of the mass media that he almost created a crisis in American Protestantism. He was as important for the religious revival of the fifties as George Whitefield had been for the Great Awakening of the eighteenth century. His "new measures" aroused as much criticism as Charles Finney's had in the nineteenth century. Although he by no means brought

---

Peale's simplism (see Donald Meyer, *The Positive Thinkers,* chaps. 21–23).

Another popularizer who cashed in on the interest in psychology and analysis was Lafayette Ronald Hubbard (b. 1911), a native of Helena, Montana, who in 1940 organized the Hubbard Association of Scientologists International. In recent years he has divided his time between a mansion in Sussex, England, and an oceangoing ship. Scientology (or dianetics), which was brought to popular attention in 1950 by Hubbard's best seller, *Dianetics: The Modern Science of Mental Health,* purports to be "the common people's science of life and betterment." Based on a theory of the brain as a virtually perfect calculating machine, it helps a preclear ("one who is discovering things about himself and who is becoming clearer") to become a clear ("one who has straightened up this lifetime") through sessions with a trained "auditor," who uses an "E" meter or "truth detector." Although some scientologists claim only to raise the I.Q. and develop personality, others have claimed the ability to cure all psychoses, neuroses, psychosomatic illnesses, coronary diseases, arthritis, and other ailments. In December 1963 scientology became the source of much controversy in Australia, with the state of Victoria setting up a special board of inquiry. In August 1968, despite considerable opposition, a World Congress of Scientology composed of delegates from twenty countries was held in London. In 1963 it was reported that there were fifty to a hundred thousand practicing scientologists in the United States.

[7] Peter Marshall, *Mr. Jones, Meet the Master* (New York: Fleming H. Revell Co., 1949); Catherine Marshall, *A Man Called Peter* (New York: McGraw-Hill Book Co., 1951).

about the postwar renewal of religious interest, he rode its crest, and more than any other, he set the tone and guided the interests of the popular revival. When Peale's *Guide to Confident Living* (1948) and *The Power of Positive Thinking* (1952) succeeded in reaching a reading audience of millions, Monsignor Fulton J. Sheen had almost no recourse but to produce his own *Peace of Soul* (1949), and Billy Graham his *Peace with God* (1953). Then in 1955 Anne Morrow Lindbergh topped them all with her *Gift from the Sea*, a remarkable little book addressed to those Americans, especially housewives, who were distraught with the emptiness of their lives.[8] Ignoring the specific institutional appeals that Peale, Sheen, and Graham were wont to make, she drew on the timeless resources of mysticism. Her book in many ways looked beyond the revival. And this may indeed be a sign of her profundity, for during 1957 and 1958 historians and social critics began to speak of that phenomenon in the past tense.

THE REVIVAL OF REVIVALISM

Popular evangelicalism had been making a slow retreat for a century, but it still flourished in all parts of the country, especially among those who were least affected by modern intellectual currents. In rural areas, particularly in the West and South, in small towns, and in many of the older urban neighborhoods, the more revivalistic denominations and sects held intact the oldtime religion with its accent on experientialism, pietistic code morality, gospel hymns, and simple preaching. Dwight L. Moody would have found himself at home in these constituencies, while they in turn longed for the kind of national leadership which Moody—or even Billy Sunday—had provided. Against this background we consider the rise of Billy Graham, the handsome and strangely solitary hero who answered this mid-twentieth century longing for a restoration of revivals to their former glory.

William Franklin Graham was born in 1918 near Charlotte, North Carolina, the son of a strict, revival-favoring dairy farmer who belonged to the very conservative Associate Reformed Presbyterian Church (General Synod). Billy was

[8] *Gift from the Sea* (New York: New American Library, Signet Books, 1957), p. 54.

converted at a revival led by Mordecai F. Ham in 1934, and
in 1936 he entered Bob Jones College (then in Cleveland,
Tennessee), only to transfer a semester later to the Florida
Bible Institute near Tampa, where he underwent a deeper
conversion, was rebaptized, and ordained as a Baptist minister. In 1940 he enrolled in Wheaton College (Illinois), and
after receiving his B.A. in three years, he began a combined
parish and radio ministry in the Chicago area in close association with the Moody Bible School and men who were organizing the National Association of Evangelicals and the
Youth for Christ movement. As a field representative for the
latter, Graham began after 1945 to establish his reputation as
a preacher and evangelistic team leader, but it was a Los Angeles tent-meeting revival in 1949 which catapulted him into
national prominence.

By 1956 the Billy Graham Evangelistic Association (incorporated, 1950) was using almost all available mass media—
advertising, television, radio, paperback books, and cinema—
and had an annual budget of two million dollars. Graham
had become a rallying point for the National Association of
Evangelicals, and he was doing much to alleviate the identity
crisis of conservative evangelicalism. He made all Americans
aware of the fact that the urban revival tradition in America
was anything but dead.[9] At the same time, however, Graham's well-organized "success" served to conceal the degree
to which time had eroded the old mainline constituencies to
which Moody and Sunday had appealed. To be sure, it was
his policy not to undertake his citywide crusades unless supported by local church councils[10]; yet his huge audiences did
not come from the mainstream Protestantism to which Moody
had preached. The chief source of Graham's strength was the
conservatives within the larger Protestant denominations or
in churches opposed to the ecumenical movement.

[9] It is surprising that so knowledgeable a Methodist as W. W.
Sweet in his *Revivalism in America: Its Origin, Growth and
Decline* (1944) should have ended his book with a kind of
funeral sermon—"Revivalism on the Wane." There were no doubt
hundreds of local revivals in progress on the day his book was
published, especially in the South. Had there not been, the career
of Billy Graham would have been impossible.

[10] This policy estranged the ultraconservative evangelicals,
though Graham's pronouncements on social and political issues
were sufficiently individualistic, pietistic, and conservative to
keep this estrangement to a minimum.

An important key to this "neo-evangelicalism" of the postwar years is the National Association of Evangelicals. It was founded in 1942 by a group of diverse conservatives who were dissatisfied with the politically oriented and rabidly exclusivist American Council of Churches which Carl McIntire had organized during the preceding year. Though agreeing with McIntire that conservatives needed to counter the Federal Council of Churches with some corporate expression, many evangelicals wanted a less divisive and more constructive association.[11] The NAE, therefore, replaced the moribund agencies of the old Fundamentalist movement and drew into its increasingly diversified activities a growing number of churches. By 1956 it claimed over a million and a half members, and spoke ambiguously of "service connections" with ten million more.[12] Though at this time the editor of the association's official organ estimated that half of the country's sixty million Protestants were still of Fundamentalist tendency, the actual membership of the NAE was heavily shaded toward the Holiness and Pentecostal churches, and only a quarter of its constituent elements exceeded twenty thousand members, while four members made up over two-thirds of its total.[13] It did, nevertheless, give a voice to conservative Protestants on questions pertaining to church-state relations, radio time, the military chaplaincy, and similar matters. It also gave something like denominational status to the "third force" in American Christianity. An additional measure of cohesiveness resulted from the founding in 1956 of *Christianity Today*, a fortnightly magazine of news and opinion edited by C. F. H. Henry, a former professor of New Testament at Northern Baptist and Fuller seminaries. By 1967 the magazine claimed 150,000 paid subscribers.

Still another aspect of this "new evangelicalism" which

---

[11] McIntire had already been involved in a complex series of schisms among ultraconservative Presbyterians, many of whom were offended by his vituperative emphasis on anticommunist militancy. The NAE did not admit whole denominations that belonged to the Federal Council of Churches, but it would admit disaffected subdivisions thereof.

[12] Louis Gasper, *The Fundamentalist Movement*, pp. 38–39.

[13] The four largest member churches were the Assemblies of God (400,000), the Church of God of Cleveland, Tennesse (200,000), the National Association of Free Will Baptists (400,-000), and the Church of the Four Square Gospel (88,000).

gained public notice during the fifties was its effort to over-come the powerful anti-intellectual and antiscientific spirit that had discredited the older Fundamentalism. This did not involve much (if any) modification of the movement's commitment to scriptural infallibility or its emphasis on the conversion experience. Nor, for the most part, did it involve an effort to transcend the many serious doctrinal issues that divided the "third force." But it did result in a considerable body of critical and apologetic literature attacking modernism, exposing Neo-orthodoxy as but another form of modernism, and defending conservative theology as a rational option for modern man. Less learned was its running critique of the World Council and the National Council of Churches as doctrinally lax, pro-Catholic, institutionally aggressive, and—on economic and political issues—too outspokenly in support of liberal causes. This concern for social issues betokened a highly significant shift among Protestant conservatives—a departure from the doctrine that the only proper concern of the church was the salvation of sinners. The tendency of "evangelicals" to align themselves with conservative, nationalistic, and racist politics had been noticeable in the interwar period, but it became more obvious and more nearly "official" in the postwar period.

By the end of the 1950s it had become clear that the old fundamentalist controversy was by no means a thing of the past. Conservative "evangelicalism" was a rapidly growing force in American Christianity. It included both a vast, inchoate multitude of earnest Christians and a much more dynamic and exclusivistic "third force." The churches in the latter category—chiefly those discussed in an earlier chapter on dissent and reaction—increased their membership from 400 to 700 percent during the two postwar decades, as against 75 to 90 percent for the older Protestant denominations. Yet these conservatives continued to be deeply troubled by the ways in which scholarship, science, technology, and rapid social change were destroying the old religious landmarks. Most of them had broken with the mainline denominations between 1890 and 1920 when liberalism and the Social Gospel were responding to new intellectual and social forces, and they remained committed to the individualism and morality of that bygone era. Both their consequent tendency toward conservatism in politics and their immense emphasis on foreign missions reflect their alienation from the domestic American scene.[14] In 1965 only 308,370 of the 1,040,386 Jehovah's Witnesses lived in the United States, while three-fourths of the Seventh-Day Adventists were overseas. Pentecostalism was surging in Latin America. During the later 1960s the situation of conservative evangelicalism in a pluralistic "nation of minorities" would have to be defined again in times of even greater urgency. It was becoming a major—and little understood—subculture. As if to confound supercilious observers, moreover, evangelicals, especially those who stressed charismatic gifts, would in the late 1960s experience a revival that made striking headway in new constituencies. Youthful, socially concerned "Jesus people" would even play a distinct kind of counter-cultural role.

THE MOVEMENT FOR PARISH RENEWAL

Practical concern for the worship and the religious life of local congregations had not been a major problem for most Neo-orthodox theologians. But after the war a pronounced awakening took place in this area, not just in abstract theological terms, but with concrete proposals for renewing worship, awakening the laity to its priesthood, invigorating the preaching office, and reforming parish education. In many ways the reformers sought to halt the inroads of patriotic piety and success-oriented religion. In this work the seminarians educated under Neo-orthodox auspices performed a vital function both in parishes and in denominational offices, though perhaps their most comprehensive achievements were made in the area of Christian education. In several denominations, notably the Episcopal and the Northern Presbyterian, an entirely new lesson system for all ages was prepared and instituted.

The postwar years also witnessed a rather remarkable flowering of the so-called Liturgical Movement. Its origins can be traced to the romantic religious revival of the nineteenth century in both Great Britain and on the Continent among both Roman Catholics and Protestants. In the twentieth century a long-developing movement of liturgical re-

[14] See William G. McLoughlin, "Is There a Third Force in Christendom?" *Daedalus* (Winter 1967): 43–68; and Henry P. Van Dusen, "The Third Force's Lessons for Others," *Life,* 9 June 1958.

form in several Benedictine abbeys began to take on ecumenical implications due to the surprising way in which major emphases of the Catholic tradition and those of the Reformation began to merge, as they had once abortively done in the work of Philip Schaff and John W. Nevin at Mercersburg Seminary.[15] Corporate worship was subjected to serious rethinking, as were the liturgical relationships of word and sacrament. Culminating the development was a renewal of concern for the royal priesthood and the active participation of the laity in the worshiping community. In this context the worshiping parish came to be a central fact of the Church's presence in the world. The effects of this new emphasis became prominent not only in the so-called liturgical churches (Catholic, Episcopalian, and Lutheran), but in various branches of the Reformed tradition as well. Church building, which was proceeding at an unprecedented rate, thus became not only a major means of expressing the country's architectural renaissance, but a visible expression of a theological movement. Stone, concrete, and glass were often enlisted in the protest, against the trivialization of the gospel. The slogan of the Faith and Order movement, "Let the Church be the Church," was taken to heart in many localities.

THE CONTINUATION OF NEO-ORTHODOX THEOLOGY

Many of the men who had inaugurated the Neo-orthodox period in modern theology—whether they were European or American—lived to produce some of their most important works in the postwar period. Karl Barth, for example, not only continued to add volumes to his monumental *Church Dogmatics,* but he saw these great works translated into Eng-

[15] Dom Prosper Guéranger (1805–75), abbot of Solesmes and leader of the Benedictine Order's return to France, was one major source of renewed interest in worship. More directly pertinent to the United States was the restored abbey at Metten in Bavaria. From it came the founders of Saint Vincent's Abbey in Pennsylvania, and from Saint Vincent's, in turn, came the founders of Saint John's Abbey in Minnesota, which became almost the national center of the movement. Behind its work, and of special theological importance for the twentieth century, was the liturgical and theological pioneering of the Benedictine abbey at Maria Laach in Germany (see pp. 1012–15).

lish. After the war, American seminarians could study the powerful christological interpretations of the "later Barth." Paul Tillich also brought his *Systematic Theology* to completion. Reinhold Niebuhr never accepted Barth's extreme conception of God's otherness nor Tillich's strong philosophical interest, but he, too, continued to address public issues in his characteristic dialectical way. In 1959 he published *The Structure of Nations and Empires: A Study of the Recurring Patterns and Problems of the Political Order in Relation to the Unique Problems of the Nuclear Age.* At a quarter-century's remove, it became an important sequel to *Moral Man and Immoral Society,* which had first established his reputation as a realistic analyst of politics and international relations.

H. Richard Niebuhr was even more significantly active, counterbalancing, as always, the theological fashions of the time. His *Christ and Culture* (1951) again exhibited his dual interest in social forces and prophetic theology in a masterly discussion of the available options in relating the church to the world. In 1960 he published his *Radical Monotheism and Western Culture,* the last book he was to see through the press before his death in 1962. The revolutionary implications of this short work make it in fact a requiem for the Neo-orthodox period, and an opening into the secular theology and non-religious interpretation of Christianity for which the 1960s would be remembered.

During the postwar decade and a half no new theologians arose either to eclipse the public eminence or to challenge the leading ideas of the older generation, though there did ensue a considerable extension of themes and methods that had come to prominence during the two previous decades. The World Council of Churches also inspired considerable groundbreaking in an international context, above all, on the nature of the Church.[16] In the United States the most provocative new concern of religious thinkers was the place of the Negro in American society. But this issue did not result so much in new thinking as in the activation of old ideals. President Truman's executive order desegregating the armed services (1950) and the Supreme Court's famous decision on the schools (1954) provided the basic response to the rising tempo of black demands. In focusing Protestant attention on

[16] Claude Welch, *The Reality of the Church,* provides both an example of and an introduction to these ecclesiological concerns.

civil rights, the National Council of Churches played a major role. Probably the most important religio-ethical event of the decade came in 1957, when the National Guard of Arkansas stood off the assault of a few black children on the segregated Central High School of Little Rock. Since that confrontation —which finally led President Eisenhower to order the army into Little Rock—neither the country as a whole nor the churches have been able to keep the question of racial justice in a closet. But only in the 1960s, in a radically altered context, would these questions begin to be squarely faced. Before long a new theology and a new ethics—and a new breed of thinkers and doers—would gain popular attention. Reformers would speak of secularity, poverty, political power, economic priorities, and Marx, often without awareness of how Neo-orthodox realism had led the way.

During 1958 and 1959, in any case, discerning observers began talking about the postwar revival in the past tense. By 1960 this view was generally accepted. The significance of the postwar revival, however, is not adequately indicated by an observation that it ended. More important is the fact that it failed to sustain human religious needs. The churches by and large seem to have done little more than provide a means of social identification to a mobile people who were being rapidly cut loose from the comfort of old contexts, whether ethnic or local. Yet with new multitudes entering their portals almost unbidden, the churches muffed their chance. Put more analytically, the so-called revival led to a sacrifice of theological substance, which in the face of the harsh new social and spiritual realities of the 1960s left both clergy and laity demoralized and confused. A loss of confidence occurred. Quantifiable aspects of the situation (church membership, attendance, and giving; seminary enrollments; demissions from the clergy, etc.) began to register decline. Thinkers who for some years—or decades—had been speaking of the "death of God" and of a "post-Christian era" began to be heard. Forces of cultural change, subtle, pervasive, and ineluctable —far less tangible than wars, depressions, and political campaigns—were altering the moral and religious ethos. The postwar revivals came more and more to be interpreted as the epilogue to an epoch.[17] Americans began to sense the

[17] See Martin E. Marty, *Second Chance for American Protestants*.

dawn of a new age in their spiritual history, a time of reorientation and beginning again, in which the past experience and present situation of every tradition would be opened for reexamination.

IX

Toward Post-Puritan America

Genuinely radical monotheism has . . . affirmed not only all mankind but all being. It has involved men not only in battle against the wrongs that afflict men but set them into conflict with what is destructive and anarchic in all accessible realms of being. Its religion has found holiness in man, but also in all nature and in what is beyond nature. It has believed in the salvation of men from evil, but also in the liberation of the whole groaning and travailing creation. Its science has sought to understand men, yet for it the proper study of mankind has been not only man but the infinitely great and the infinitely small in the whole realm of being. Its art has reinterpreted man to himself but also re-created for man and reinterpreted to him natural beings and eternal forms that have become for him objects of wonder and surprise.

Radical monotheism as the gift of confidence in the principle of being itself, as the affirmation of the real, as loyalty—betrayed and reconstructed many times—to the universe of being, can have no quarrel with humanism and naturalism insofar as these are protests against the religions and ethics of closed societies, centering in little gods—or in little ideas of God. But insofar as faith is given to men in the principle of being itself, or insofar as they are reconciled to the Determiner of Destiny as the fountain of good and only of good, naturalism and humanism assume the form of exclusive systems of closed societies. A radically monotheistic faith says to them as to all the other claimants to "the truth, the whole truth and nothing but the truth," to all the "circumnavigators of being" as Santayana calls them: "I do not believe you. God is great."

H. Richard Niebuhr, *Radical Monotheism and Western Culture* (1960)

America has endured many crises, but the moment of truth which the country began to experience in the 1960s was made uniquely critical by the convergence of several developments. Most serious were the military and domestic events that led to a loss of that kind of corporate commitment that a nation of unusually heterogeneous minorities desperately needed. This loss of national self-assurance was made more poignant by the declining incidence of dedication to the moral and doctrinal message of the churches and to the religious institutions that had sustained these traditions. An increasing awareness of public violence and environmental overexploitation, meanwhile, extended popular misgivings to the economic and social system itself, and thus also to the entire educational enterprise. The idea of America as a Chosen Nation and a beacon to the world was expiring. The people had by no means become less religious, and their sense of moral urgency was, if anything, heightened. Yet unmistakably at the heart of the prevailing anxiety was the need for reexamining fundamental conceptions of religion, ethics, and nationhood.

The chapters of Part IX deal with major aspects of this developing crisis. They first trace the more recent history of Judaism and Catholicism, and the whole course of the ancient Eastern Churches in America. In all of these contexts the new awareness of pluralism and the changing situation of the Protestant establishment is observed. This theme is then given additional emphasis by an account of black religion and the rise of the militant protest movement. In this chapter the centrality of America's racial dilemma is exposed. Two chapters are also devoted to two major streams of "harmonial religion" which have a long American history but which were enlivened almost simultaneously by Mary Baker Eddy's *Science and Health* in 1875 and Madame Blavatsky's *Isis Revealed* in 1877, and which after World War II gained increasing attention from religious seekers in all walks of life. During the 1960s these ancient religious traditions became highly significant elements of the American scene, in part because of the widespread rejection of the exploitive and competitive stress of the Puritan ethic and the questioning of Judaeo-Christian beliefs. Also very apparent was a serious awakening of interest in perennial forms of mysticism and various streams of Eastern religion.

How these and many other developments converged in the decades of the sixties and seventies is the explanatory task undertaken in the concluding chapter, wherein some grounds are given for the view that the great Puritan epoch in America's spiritual history was drawing to a painful and tumultuous close.

57

TWENTIETH-CENTURY JUDAISM

President Harding's signature on the immigration restriction act of 1921 marked the end of one period in American history and the beginning of another. As rendered more decisive by the acts of 1924 and 1927 and by President Hoover's executive order of 1930, this policy reversal was also a turning point in the history of American Jewry—as of many other ethnic groups. Mass immigration became a thing of the past; ahead lay only varying modes of Americanization for different immigrant groups in the population.

The generation before 1920 had, of course, experienced the deluge; nearly two million Jewish immigrants had arrived between 1870 and the outbreak of World War I. During the four postwar years a quarter-million more had come. After 1925 the American Jewish community's future was linked no longer to Ellis Island but to New York City, where half the country's Jews resided, and to the other cities of the country —the larger the city the greater the proportion of Jews. The Jewish population continued to grow, from nearly 3.5 million in 1917 to 4.2 million in 1927 to 4.5 million in 1937 to perhaps 5.5 million in 1964.[1] The number of Americans nam-

[1] The change in immigration volume was sharply defined: in the seven years before 1914, 656,400 Jews entered the country; in the seven years after 1924, only 73,378. Only about 170,000 Jews came to the United States during the twelve years between Hitler's rise and fall. Between 1933 and 1943 there were 341,567 unfilled places in quotas from Germany and countries it occupied, and 900,000 unfilled places from other quotas during these years; but the regulations were so strictly enforced that refugees could not claim these places. The political pressures against admitting Jews came chiefly from veterans organizations, "patriotic" societies, and overtly anti-Semitic movements.

ing Yiddish as their mother tongue, however, reached its
peak of 1,222,658 in 1930, and this fact points to what is
perhaps the major shaping force in twentieth-century Judaism. Without the great influx of Yiddish-speaking Orthodox
Jews from Eastern Europe, not even the Hitlerian Holocaust
nor the founding of Israel would have had the impact they
later did.

FROM EASTERN EUROPE TO THE AMERICAN GHETTO

Certainly no religious group in America was more
thoroughly transformed by the later immigration than the
Jewish community. The Reform rabbis who announced their
spiritual emancipation in the famous Pittsburgh Declaration
of 1885 spoke for most of the approximately 250,000 Jews
then associated with the synagogues (or temples) of America. There were two small exceptions, however. One was the
small group of synagogues along the East coast with a few
thousand members who maintained the "dignified Orthodoxy"
of the old Sephardic tradition. The other exception was the
larger and rapidly growing group of East European Jews.
As early as 1852 they had organized a synagogue in New
York City, and after the czarist pogoms of 1881–82 their
rate of immigration had been steadily increasing. They were
also fleeing from poverty and intensified persecution in
various regions of the rambling Austro-Hungarian Empire
and Romania. And after 1918 the plight of Jews in most of
these areas became still worse. Hence the number of synagogues grew from 270 in 1880 to 533 in 1890 (with over 130
in New York City alone), to 1,901 in 1916 and 3,100 in
1927. These dramatic changes are not merely quantitative,
however, for the new immigration came quite literally from a
world of its own—the world of Eastern Ashkenazi Orthodoxy, a vast "nation" numbering from six to eight million at
its height. These people were gathered in rural villages and
urban ghettos, in the midst of a dozen other dominant nation-

Ever since the Jews in czarist Russia were divided nearly in
half by the restoration of Polish and Lithuanian independence
after World War I, American Jews have been the largest national
Jewish community. Before the war the Russian Empire extended
westward to the German border and the Baltic Sea.

alities in the huge, backward, predominantly agricultural region extending from the Baltic Sea to the Black Sea. By the time Hitler's Third Reich had been smashed in World War II this vast Jewish world had been almost utterly extinguished; but its history and character are vital to American religious history because 90 percent of those who emigrated came to the United States.

The Yiddish (*jüdisch*) language of these Eastern Jews, though spoken with many local variations, was a medieval German dialect written in Hebrew characters and containing various Hebrew words. As this fact betokens, German Jews had been moving eastward for a long time. In fact, a slow trickle had begun at latest in the thirteenth century, and it gradually increased in volume century by century due both to new legal restrictions in Germany and to encouragement from Polish or Russian rulers. After the defeat of Napoleon, however, most of Poland and Lithuania fell under Russian rule, and Jews were limited to a "pale of settlement" that tended to keep them out of Russia proper. The nineteenth century also brought great distress—persecution, famine, inequitable conscription laws—and most basically, a gradual collapse of the old peasant economy in which the trades and vocations of Jews had taken an important place. With the rise of industrialism a movement to the city had begun, with heavy de-Judaizing consequences.[2]

Yet until the 1880s the old ways of Orthodox observance were maintained, especially within the defined limits of each agricultural village (or *shtetl*), where a genuinely communal existence could continue. Here, where the gentile world did not intrude on Torah-centered living, the Sabbath could truly be a foretaste of heaven. The old system of nurture assured the raising up of new students of the Scriptures, the Talmud, and the rabbinic commentaries. The more promising students could be sent on to some respected center of studies for further training. Given a common language, moreover, great revivals of piety could take place, as they had since the mid-

[2] Lodz, the Russian Manchester, was a village with 11 Jews in 1793; a city with 98,677 Jews in 1897 and 166,628 in 1910. Warsaw's Jewish population numbered 3,532 in 1781; 219,141 in 1891. Along with urban life came contact with Western philosophical and social ideas which often undermined Jewish modes of life and belief.

eighteenth century when Hasidism, with its joyous mystical devotionalism, had arisen.[3] It is not surprising, therefore, that on arrival in America these Jews would try to re-create the old institutions and, if possible, found a synagogue where the familiar dialect would be spoken. In old age, even if they had "made it" to a life of affluence and comfort, they would cherish their memories of life in the *shtetl*.[41]

Until the later nineteenth century the ghetto—an urban quarter where an observant Jewish life could be lived—had not figured strongly in American life. The migration of Eastern Jews changed that, and in every large northern city ghettos arose, but on the most massive scale in New York, "the Promised City." The immediate problem was survival in the intensely competitive atmosphere created by the cresting tide of the new immigration. It was solved through merchandizing in street and store, through innumerable crafts and trades, and, above all, through "the great Jewish métier"—the making of clothes. The Jewish home and family became a workshop. As one reporter on the New York ghetto commented:

You are made fully aware of it before you have travelled the length of a single block in any of these East Side streets, by the whir of a thousand sewing-machines, worked at high pressure from earliest dawn till mind and muscle give out together. Every member of the family from the youngest to the oldest, bears a hand, shut in the

[3] Hasidism was a pietistic movement founded by Israel Baal Shem Tob (1700–60), a mystic, cabalist, and healer who, with the aid of several equally dedicated disciples, attracted numerous followers, first in the Polish Ukraine, then more widely. By the early nineteenth century half of Eastern Jewry, especially the poor and uneducated, were profoundly affected. By intention Hasidism was Orthodox, even intensely so; but due to its emphasis on the divine immanence and on communion with God, it tended to threaten those who stressed only rabbinical study and strict observance of the Law. To the oppressed it brought a message of God's love, a sense of joy, and a gift of hope that was reflected both in worship and in daily life.

[4] After World War II a group of anthropologists through interviews with immigrants in America developed a remarkably colorful and detailed account of Eastern Jewish village life (see Mark Zborowski and Elizabeth Herzog, *Life Is with People: The Culture of the Shtetl*).

qualmy rooms, where meals are cooked and clothing washed and dried besides, the livelong day. It is not unusual to find a dozen persons—men, women, and children —at work in a single small room.[5]

Yet the household was held together and a measure of self-respect retained. As the garment industry became more organized, so did labor. And the old emphasis on education remained. All of these factors made the Jewish "ghetto" a place of rapid turnover, social change, and religious unrest.

JUDAISM IN THE TWENTIES AND THIRTIES

In 1927 probably 80 percent of the Jews in the United States were of Eastern European origin and Orthodox in background. They or their parents had been arriving in the country for over a half-century; but they were no longer crowded into the teeming ghettos of New York and a few other larger cities. Most of them (nobody agrees as to what percentage) had improved their economic status and were now living in houses or apartments of residential areas. Ordinarily these neighborhoods were also predominantly Jewish, but strict Orthodox observance was gradually yielding to a reliance on close-knit family life, participation in Jewish organizations, the best possible education of children, and close attention to economic advancement in a rapidly expanding country. The obvious success of preceding immigration waves, the German Jews in particular, provided both example and grounds for hope.

Genuinely Jewish communal life still went on in the old areas of first settlement, where kosher food stores and restaurants, Yiddish and Hebrew newspapers, and Orthodox synagogues of every description could still be found. But all of this was now carried on at a reduced scale. The important fact was that most Jews in America, including most of the latest immigration wave, were either becoming alienated from their religious heritage, or had already become so. Especially in the second generation, Jews were drifting away from the synagogue by the thousands. A survey made of New York City youth in 1935 revealed that 72 percent of the young

[5] Quoted in Moses Rischin, *The Promised City: New York's Jews, 1870–1914*, p. 61.

Jewish men (between the ages of fifteen and twenty-five) and 78 percent of the women had not attended services for a year, and 89 and 94 percent not in a week. In other large cities the situation was probably not different. Two-thirds to three-fourths of these young people had probably had some kind of Jewish education during their school years; but only a tiny fraction had been schooled with Orthodox thoroughness. A larger percentage had been influenced by the Yiddish school movement which was socialistic, antireligious in spirit, and, after 1929 especially, inspired by the militant "proletariat" of the garment industry. Secular Zionism attracted others.

Undoubtedly, most young Jews were chiefly involved in the basic process of Americanization, for the public schools and secular universities played a major role in translating them into the professions (at three times the rate for non-Jews) and into white-collar occupations. In this context, Orthodox schooling and strict observance seemed to be a hindrance, irrational or meaningless once the bonds of thoroughly Jewish communal life were broken. The story—sometimes agonizing, sometimes exhilarating—of how the edifice of strict observance could be suddenly or protractedly toppled has been told many times; but the classic account is Abraham Cahan's autobiographical novel *The Rise of David Levinsky* (1917). Cahan shows how the process could begin even during a young boy's rabbinical training far away in Russia, and then accelerate rapidly in New York City. He confessed that "the very clothes I wore and the very food I ate had a fatal effect on my religious habits." "If you . . . attempt to bend your religion to the spirit of your new surroundings, it breaks. It falls to pieces." His decision to shave his beard became a traumatic turning point in his life.[6] American Jews were rapidly becoming an ethnic rather than a religious minority in America.

Forces were at work, however, which would maintain or

[6] Abraham Cahan, *The Rise of David Levinsky*, pp. 110–11. In real life Cahan became the publisher of the *Jewish Daily Forward*, the most widely read Yiddish paper in the world. He was an outspoken liberal leader of Yiddish-speaking America. The world he lived in is memorably described in Hutchins Hapgood, *The Spirit of the Ghetto* (1902) with drawings by Jacob Epstein and additional commentary by Harry Golden (New York: Schocken Books, 1965). Michael Gold describes the next generation in the ghetto in *Jews without Money* (1930).

even strengthen the solidarity of American Jews. One of these factors was the anti-Semitism which had first emerged in the 1870s and then been persistently fanned by nativistic organizations and the immigration restriction movement. In these campaigns Jews were marked off for discrimination on vaguely racial grounds or for contradictory linkages with the urban "money power," social radicalism, commercial aggressiveness, and freethinking. Zionism was in part a response to anti-Semitism and persecution, and it, too, became an agent of solidarity.

Zionism, in one or another sense of the term, had been an intrinsic element of Jewish hope ever since the Babylonian Captivity of the sixth century B.C.E. It was renewed after the destruction of the Jewish commonwealth in 70 C.E. and the end of temple worship in Jerusalem. During the nineteenth century more than one movement of emancipation through colonization in Palestine had been set in motion by Jews in Eastern Europe. Most notable was Judah Pinsker's Love of Zion movement with headquarters in Odessa.[7] The effective origins of modern Zionism, however, must be traced to the zeal of Theodore Herzl (1860–1904), a completely secularized Jewish journalist of Vienna. After witnessing the degradation of Alfred Dreyfus in Paris in 1895, Herzl was converted to the Zionist cause, and in 1896 he published his manifesto *Der Judenstaat* (the Jewish State). As the sole solution of the anti-Semitic problem he demanded an international treaty-supported act of indemnification; and despite the hostility of Orthodox leaders, Reform Judaism, socialists, and emancipated Jews of great prominence, the first Zionist Congress was held in Basel in 1897. Other congresses followed and Herzl became a renowned international prophet and diplomat. In America the response to Zionism was immediate, and a federation was organized in 1898 with Rabbi Stephen S. Wise of New York as secretary.[8] Yet the opposi-

[7] Emma Lazarus (1849–87), the Jewish poet, famed for her lines on the Statue of Liberty, wrote one of the more popular Zionist anthems ("O for Jerusalem's Trumpet Now"). Several American Christians also projected settlement plans. One which resembled earlier Negro colonization schemes was prepared by the Reverend William E. Blackstone of Illinois, signed by J. P. Morgan, J. D. Rockefeller, Philip D. Armour, and others, and submitted to President Harrison in 1891.

[8] Wise was in many ways atypical, however. He declined a call to Temple Emanu-El—the New York "Cathedral of Judaism"—

tion was also strong. The German Jews, often wealthy and thoroughly Americanized, saw Zionism as challenging a major tenet of their faith and as jeopardizing their status in the United States. The conference of Reform rabbis consequently stood in firm opposition. Labor leaders and socialists regarded Zionism as bourgeois, escapist, romantic, and chauvinistic. Orthodox leaders saw it as a secularist misunderstanding of Jewish hope.

Yet gradually Zionism began to gather a certain inchoate strength, chiefly among those of the Eastern Jewish poor who had been unattracted by labor radicalism. After 1903 "Zionist socialism" began increasingly to attract the workers.[9] Around the same time an allied federation of Orthodox Zionists was formed, and a few distinguished and scholarly supporters

---

and in 1907 founded the Free Synagogue, which was very similar in spirit to the nonsectarian Ethical Culture Society which Felix Adler had founded in 1876. Both Adler and Wise were active social reformers, though Adler dissociated himself from Judaism almost completely.

[9] The destiny of Golda Mabovitch was hardly typical, but her life sheds light on the American movement. Born in Kiev, Russia, in 1898, she came with her parents at the age of eight to Milwaukee. During her high school years she became interested in the Labor Zionist movement, and soon she was teaching in a Yiddish school and working with a group of intense Zionists. In 1917 she married Morris Myerson, with whom she sailed to Palestine in 1921 and joined kibbutz Merhavia, ten miles south of Nazareth. (They had a son and a daughter but eventually separated; he died in 1951.) After moving to Jerusalem, Mrs. Myerson began a long and distinguished public career. By 1928 she was secretary of the Women's Labor Council, and soon thereafter she assumed a lifelong role of leadership in the Jewish Labor Party (Mapai). As a department head in the Jewish Agency for Palestine (1946–48) she made a major contribution to the establishment of a Jewish state through her highly successful fund raising in the United States. After statehood she served as ambassador to the USSR (1948–49), as minister of labor (1949–56), and as minister of foreign affairs (1956–66). When in 1956 Ben-Gurion requested cabinet members to take Hebrew names, she chose Meir, which means "illuminates." After succeeding Levi Eshkol as prime minister in 1969 she pursued a hard line against Israel's foes. While on a state visit in October 1969 she paid a nostalgic visit to her elementary school in Milwaukee. The pupils of the school, all of them black, greeted her by singing in Hebrew the Israeli national anthem.

from the Reform group rallied to the cause. Still others came from the newly emerging movement of Conservatism, notably its spiritual father in the United States, Solomon Schechter, who left England to become head of the Jewish Theological Seminary in 1902. In the meantime the "official" Federation of American Zionists began to take shape, and by 1920 it had become the movement's chief organized focus amid a large number of other Zionist orders and associations. In 1925 the United Palestine Appeal was established to aid the cause.

The thirties brought other, more important stimuli, and a more complete sense of solidarity among American Jews than they had ever shown or known before. The largest and most horrible cause was Adolf Hitler and the rise of the Third Reich in Germany. Closer at hand was the emergence of militant anti-Semitism in the United States, incited most popularly by Father Charles E. Coughlin, the radio priest at the Shrine of the Little Flower near Detroit, but advanced as well by the reorganized Ku Klux Klan, the German-American Bund, Protestant Fundamentalist Gerald Winrod of Kansas, the Silver Shirts, and a number of other secret and semimilitary terrorist organizations. As a result, the leaders of the three great "Jewish defense agencies"—the American Jewish Committee, the American Jewish Congress, and the Anti-Defamation League—came to appreciate the significance of Zionism. By 1935 the Jewish National Fund had raised $5 million for the purchase of land in Palestine. The number of American Jews involved in Zionist groups rose from 150,000 in 1930 to 400,000 in 1940. As the world moved closer to World War II, especially after Great Britain's pro-Arab White Paper of 1939, and with the Jewish community in Palestine genuinely threatened with extinction, a great majority of American Jewry began to sympathize with the Zionist cause.

The basis of this new solidarity in the American Jewish community was not "religious" in the historic Judaic sense, nor was it Torah-centered. Challenged on an ethnic basis, they responded as an ethnic group. A certain non-traditional religious element was present, however, and this would have large consequences for the postwar revival. Equally important to these later developments were gradual changes taking place in the older forms of American Judaism and the rise of specific new movements.

THE DIVISIONS OF JUDAISM

Orthodox Judaism was the most important sector of Judaism, if for no other reason than that it was overwhelmingly the largest, its numbers having grown to between 1 and 1.5 million by 1937. The constituency of Orthodox Judaism had always been relatively unprosperous, and its places of worship were unpretentious. It had also been slow to organize on a national basis. But for a few remnants of Sephardic Orthodoxy (chiefly in New York City) it would have been almost leaderless and without an effective link to the non-Jewish world. Rabbi Henry Pereira Mendes of the old Spanish and Portuguese synagogue in New York did provide some leadership, however, and in 1898 he organized the Union of Orthodox Jewish Congregations. Four years later the Union of Orthodox Rabbis was formed, a group instrumental in founding the Rabbi Isaac Elchanan Theological Seminary in New York City. On this foundation Yeshiva College, later University, was built. In this institution and in similar ones elsewhere a new English-speaking Orthodox rabbinate was trained, who in 1930 organized the Rabbinical Council of America. The Young Israel movement (founded in 1912) gave further scope to such activity.

Due to these organizational efforts the continuity of Orthodoxy was assured; indeed, it showed remarkable vigor and adaptive power. By the time of World War II the major problems of transition had been solved. Steps had been taken to eliminate aspects of Orthodox worship which often made disaffiliation from the synagogue a first step toward Americanization. Some of the intellectual concerns of the Reform were also entertained. In the mid-1950s it was estimated that about half of the country's 5.5 million Jews were religiously affiliated, and that about a third of them were associated with somewhat over seven hundred Orthodox synagogues. Orthodox strength was declining, but not rapidly.

In Reform Judaism the opposite tendencies were observable. During the period 1885 to 1915 it had become increasingly disengaged from historic normative Judaism. Many congregations had adopted the forms of liberal Protestant worship and had even shifted their public services to Sunday. Of considerable significance for this Americanizing tendency was the fact that Hebrew Union College and Seminary, the intellectual center of the Reform, was isolated in Cincinnati, whereas the great concentration of Eastern European immigrants, with whom the future of American Judaism necessarily lay, were concentrated in other larger cities, particularly in New York. During and after World War I a number of forces began to reverse the assimilationist tendency, notably the increasing responsibilities of immigrant aid, the gradual movement of upward-mobile Eastern Jews into Reform congregations and the Reform rabbinate, and finally, the process by which anti-Semitism, fascistic harassment at home, and Nazi terrorism abroad combined to awaken the Reform's slumbering concern for Judaism. Intellectual trends and world-historical developments were also undermining the rationalistic optimism of the older theology. The Reform, in other words, underwent a chastening very similar to that of Protestant liberalism; and out of this experience came a rediscovery of the power and existential relevance of prophetic religion and those very Jewish attitudes which the Enlightenment had quite summarily rejected. Before World War II the full significance of these various forces could not be appreciated, but during the postwar decade important shifts in temper and practice were very much in evidence. This awakening to the values of the tradition seems to have helped the Reform to maintain its hold on about a third of the religiously affiliated Jews. In 1955 they were gathered in slightly more than five hundred congregations, many of them exceedingly prosperous. By this time, however, a newer religious movement was threatening their primacy in the American Jewish community.

Conservative Judaism has claimed the title of "authentic American Judaism"—a claim that need not be adjudicated here. Less controversial is the quip that it is "the lengthened shadow of Jewish Theological Seminary in New York." This school was founded due to serious dissatisfactions with the Reform trend, and because a number of Jewish leaders in New York recognized an educational responsibility for the vast numbers of immigrants who were pouring into the city. Nothing much came of the school, however, until 1902, when Solomon Schechter (1850–1915), a great Romanian-born scholar, powerful teacher, and deeply religious thinker, came from Cambridge University to become its president. Around him were gathered a learned faculty of biblical, talmudic, and historical scholars who made the institution a famous center of Jewish studies.

In substance the "Conservatism" that took shape in America was very similar to the secession from radical Reform led in late nineteenth-century Germany by Zechariah Frankel. Its hope was to unite American Judaism; and in the long run this aim may be realized. In the near term, however, a new and distinctive religious impulse began to be institutionalized. In 1913 Schechter led in the founding of the United Synagogue of America, a federation of congregations sympathetic to the school's objectives and paralleling the Rabbinical Assembly of America, which had been in existence since 1901 as a uniting bond of the school's graduates. Gradually a new Judaic movement came into existence, one that more or less accepted the Reform's openness to scientific research and its demand that Judaism continue as in the past to reinterpret its fundamental loyalty in terms of changing historical circumstances. In public services, too, certain desires for change were accommodated: mixed choirs, family pews, organ music, and the like. As the platform of the United Synagogue made clear, however, its objectives also included genuine efforts to preserve the tradition. Among its aims were—

1. to assert and establish loyalty to the Torah and its historical exposition;
2. to further the observance of the Sabbath and dietary laws;
3. to preserve in the service the references to Israel's past and the hopes for Israel's restoration;
4. to maintain the traditional character of the liturgy with Hebrew as the language of prayer.[10]

Not asserted as an "aim" but important as a fact was the tendency of the professors at the seminary to expound the Bible and the rabbinical writings essentially in the traditional manner and not to engage in the higher criticism of the Scriptures or to wrestle with modern problems of observance. This was to create a rift between the Conservative rabbis and their congregations, because it forestalled the nominal purpose of the movement, namely, to reinterpret and adjust the Law to the realities of the American scene. The movement helped to maintain the continuity of Judaism under circum-

[10] Rufus Learsi, *Israel: A History of the Jewish People*, p. 206.

stances of great difficulty and transitional stress, however, and it shaped a form of Judaism that was well adapted to American religious needs. A half-century after Schechter's arrival in the United States, Conservatism embraced 450 rabbis and over five hundred synagogues.

"Reconstructionism" also had Jewish Theological Seminary as its point of origin. Some interpreters, in fact, see it as a radical extension of Conservatism's interest in the "totality" of Jewish experience. By extending its concern to Jewish art and culture it sought to attract those who desired no participation in any kind of synagogue. Far more than Conservatism, moreover, Reconstructionism owed its organized existence in America to one man, Mordecai M. Kaplan (b. 1881). Kaplan was born in Russia and raised in the traditions of Orthodoxy. After coming to New York and attending City College, he became an Orthodox rabbi. His advanced studies, especially in philosophy at Columbia University, led to a change in his religious outlook, which came strongly to resemble the naturalism of John Dewey, Edward Scribner Ames, and Horace Kallen. Kaplan became an instrumentalist in religion; God was a name for man's collective ethical ideal. In 1918 he founded the Jewish Center in New York and set up a broad cultural program. During the 1920s he also served as a professor at Jewish Theological Seminary, where the convergence of scholarly studies and the secular cultural interests of Zionist students gradually gave content and purpose to his developing ideas. In 1934 he published his diagnosis and prescription, *Judaism as a Civilization,* in which he expounded not only his philosophical views, but a program for utilizing the study of Hebrew history, culture, and language in order to win back the loyalty of religiously alienated Jews.

In actuality, Kaplan was providing a rationale for the Jewish center movement which had been making considerable advances during the twenties and would continue to do so during the thirties. The centers were taking over functions similar to those assumed by the old German Jewish YMHA's and YWHA's and by various settlement houses that had been founded in immigrant communities. But in most cases these institutions had become little more than middle-class recreation centers. Even though occasionally connected with a synagogue, they were less interested in Judaism than in "Jewishness." It was precisely this broad tendency that Kaplan wished to provide with a deeper self-understanding and purpose. But because his "rationale" contained important elements that offended each of the three main movements in American Judaism, it never served as a unitive force. Organizationally it has become instead a very small and unpromising federation of a half-dozen or so Reconstructionist synagogues.

Kaplan's significance, however, was very great. He personified the major conflicts and uncertainties of his tradition and gave voice to the unarticulated conviction of many that Jewishness was a significant and sufficient basis for assuring the survival of the Jewish people in America, and, negatively, that Judaism, to the degree that it was Torah-orientated, would be an instrument of alienation. Kaplan's philosophical views became increasingly unattractive to intellectuals who had witnessed or endured the holocaust which began in the very year his book appeared. Yet he was deeply sensitive to popular needs as well as to modern religious trends. After the postwar religious revival had waned, his views would again be regarded as relevant.

JUDAISM IN THE AGE OF AFFLUENCE: THE POSTWAR REVIVAL

Will Herberg is 1955 commented on the great transformation of Judaism which had occurred largely within the last quarter-century:

> American Jewry first established itself in this country as an ethnic-immigrant group. . . . But unlike the rest, it somehow did not lose its corporate identity with advancing Americanization; instead . . . it underwent a change of character and turned into an American religious community, retaining, even enhancing, its Jewishness in the process.[11]

This participation of Judaism in the postwar "upswing in religion" is what Nathan Glazer has called "the Jewish Revival."[12]

The postwar revival probably had a more marked effect on Judaism than on any other religious faith in America. No-

---

[11] Will Herberg, *Protestant, Catholic, Jew,* p. 172.
[12] Nathan Glazer, *American Judaism,* p. 106.

where had disaffiliation and alienation been so prominent a religious trend during the first three decades of the twentieth century as among the Eastern Jews who had entered this country since 1870. After 1945, however, neither Protestantism nor Roman Catholicism experienced so marked an increase in formal religious identification and institutional support. For a generation the process of denationalization was almost brought to a halt. The Jewish response, of course, bore many similarities to that of Americans in general, except that Jewish needs were, if anything, more poignant. In universities and residential areas alike they were awakened to a new kind of ethnic self-awareness which was accompanied by an unmistakable return to religious affiliation. Jewish ethnicity and religiosity, of course, have always been famously tangled, and new snarls were created by the establishment of the republic of Israel in 1948 and the subsidence of domestic intolerance in the 1950s. But a trend was clear.

That the future of this trend rests largely with the Eastern Jews is one of the truisms of American Judaism, but two other factors are almost equally vital. This first was documented with special force by Marshall Sklare in his *Conservative Judaism*, though it was anticipated by Louis Wirth's study, *The Ghetto*, in 1928. Both of these sociologists emphasize the fairly consistent pattern of movement by which Eastern Jews first took up their American abode in urban ghettos where, so far as possible, they reproduced the life they had left behind. Then gradually the more upward mobile members of the second generation, who were offended by such milieux and by the unedifying cacophony of synagogue worship, led a steady outward movement to "areas of second settlement." These areas also became "Jewish neighborhoods," but in a more generalized and outwardly "American" way. Even the rabbi of an Orthodox synagogue would, in the American mode, take on increasingly professional ministerial functions, and worship would be made more orderly and decorous. The religious losses during this phase of Jewish Americanization, however, were enormous. It was the great "secularizing time" during which the foundations were laid for a highly significant "humanist" sector in the American population.[13]

[13] John Courtney Murray speaks of the familiar three faiths plus this "humanist-secularist" sector as America's four great "conspiracies" (see John Cogley, ed., *Religion in America* [New York:

In the postwar "age of affluence" the broad reaches of metropolitan suburbia became the "third area of settlement," and in this environment the return to institutionalized religion was largely made. Leaving behind vast inner-city neighborhoods to new in-migrants (largely Negro and Puerto Rican), Jews now joined other ethnic minorities as part of the suburban "lonely crowd" which David Riesman so memorably described. In this environment, fertile with its own anxieties and insecurity, Jews had to solve their problems of religion and child nurture in constant encounter with Roman Catholics and Protestants—who then, as earlier, were generally far more faithful in their formal religious obligations. In 1947 a national public opinion poll showed that 18 percent of the Jews attended services once a month, as against 65 percent of the Protestant respondents and 85 percent of the Roman Catholics. In addition to all the other religious pressures of postwar America, it may be legitimately supposed that staus consciousness, the special pressures of "suburbanized Americanization," and the ordinary comforts of conformity have at least no less impact on Jewish modes of life than on others. Emulation, thus, is at least one factor in the revival.

A second factor of large importance has been underlined by Will Herberg through his invocation of "Hansen's law," the formulation of the great immigration historian, Marcus Lee Hansen: "What the son wishes to forget, the grandson wishes to remember."[14] Herberg saw a relation between the succession of generations and the dynamics of religious revival. Stressing certain anxieties which seem to be inherent in the process of Americanization, he interpreted the *second* generation, in its desire for acceptance and outward acculturation, as striving to cast off every habit or custom that would remind others of its "foreign" origins. By the

---

Meridian Books, 1958]). Jews have provided this "fourth faith" with many of its finest defenders ever since the days of Felix Adler and Stephen Wise. Horace Kallen in his *Secularism Is the Will of God* (1954) gave strong expression to it.

[14] Quoted in Herberg, *Protestant, Catholic, Jew*, p. 186. Even the distinguished writers who during the postwar decades made the "Jewish novel" a major genre in American literary history tend to substantiate Hansen's law (see Irving Malin, *Jews and Americans*, which considers Delmore Schwartz, Saul Bellow, Philip Roth, Bernard Malamud, Leslie Fiedler, and others).

thoroughly Americanized *third* generation, however, these insecurities are less sharply felt; they are replaced, in fact, by a certain nostalgia for ancestral tradition and perhaps a measure of guilt and shame for having abandoned it. A general shift in national religious mores supported this trend by applauding affiliation with any one of democracy's "three great faiths." Over and above such popular encouragement is a value-oriented desire for meaning, inspiration, and moral guidance in a world where many of the older assurances seemed empty or fatuous. It is this last dimension of the revival that theologians and other serious religious thinkers have addressed.

Theological renewal was a prominent feature of the entire Atlantic community after the devastations of World War II. Jews, whose participation in this shattering experience had been the most tragic of all, made a large intellectual and artistic contribution, one that both responded to and developed the tendencies of thought expressed in other traditions. Leo S. Baeck, Franz Rosenzweig, Martin Buber, and Abraham Heschel are at least partially representative of these intellectual currents.

Rabbi Leo S. Baeck (1873–1956) was a profound spokesman for the tradition of Reform universalism whose great book *The Essence of Judaism* (1905) nevertheless sought to define the special vocation of the chosen people. Having endured the concentration camps of the Third Reich, he emerged after World War II as a peculiarly effective interpreter of Judaism for the postwar generation. Sensitive to the tensions of modern culture and profoundly aware of man's creatureliness, Baeck sought to combine a concern for man's religious consciousness with the conception of Judaism as fundamentally a religion of commandment. It is in deeds of moral dedication, despite the immensity of the task and the this-worldly hopelessness of the hope, that he finds the essence and strength of Judaism.[15]

[15] In his strong ethical emphasis, Baeck, like many of his contemporaries, was deeply indebted to Hermann Cohen (1842–1918), the famed Neo-Kantian philosopher of Marburg University, especially to his posthumous *Religion of Reason Out of the Sources of Judaism* (1919). The Marburg school was firmly antimetaphysical, logical, and disinclined to concede authority to particular historical movements. Cohen shared this cosmpolitan outlook despite his self-conscious Jewishness.

If Baeck can be said to speak in a manner that is especially congenial to Reform Judaism, Franz Rosenzweig (1886–1923) and Martin Buber (1878–1965) developed themes more properly associated with Conservatism, though Buber especially can be said to speak to all men, and he has undoubtedly had a larger influence on Christian thought than any other Jewish thinker of the twentieth century. Buber was born in Vienna, where, before going to the university, he lived with his grandfather and became thoroughly steeped in the Hasidic Judaism of Galicia, acquiring the mystical interests that colored his thought to the end. In later years Wilhelm Dilthey, Kierkegaard, Dostoevsky, and Nietzsche became important to his social and religious outlook, yet he never abandoned his role as an interpreter of Judaism. Like Rosenzweig, with whom he collaborated on a new translation of the Scriptures, he was also a brilliant participant in Jewish-Christian dialogue.[16] Rosenzweig's *Star of Redemption* (1921) and Buber's classic *I and Thou* (1923) are masterly statements of an existential and dialogical understanding of both human relationships and the divine-human encounter. Of the two, it was Buber who for a very wide range of thoughtful Americans—Jewish as well as gentile— contributed to the developing seriousness with which religious commitment was taken.

In the United States it was perhaps Abraham Heschel who addressed these several concerns most effectually. Heschel was born in Warsaw to a distinguished Hasidic family and educated at the University of Berlin on the eve of Hitler's takeover. He worked unflaggingly in Poland, England, and after 1940 in the United States to combine rigorous historical research with a fervent affirmation of traditional Judaism— though always with the dual emphasis on legal observance and inner piety that is the hallmark of Hasidism. Probably no Jewish thinker of his time so nearly warrants comparison

[16] Jewish-Christian dialogue has been an important aspect of modern religious thought ever since the Enlightenment. Hegel's dialectical conceptions were a spur to the enterprise, as was the rise of the history of world religions. A translation of Rosenzweig's profound exchange with Rosenstock-Huessy has recently been published (*Whom Money Cannot Buy* [University, Ala.: University of Alabama Press, 1969]). In recent years Christians have been forced to ask if some of the most fundamental motifs of classic Christian nurture do not conduce to anti-Semitism and ethnocentrism.

with Karl Barth, the great scholar-theologian of Protestant
Neo-orthodoxy. Intensely alert to social issues, deeply aware
of the need to address the religious predicament of all men
(not just Jews), and constantly involved in interfaith discussions, he nevertheless constantly strove to make biblical religion a vital reality and to lead modern Jews toward a serious
encounter with their classic tradition.[17]

As in Protestantism and Roman Catholicism, so in Judaism
there is a vast chasm between serious religious thinkers and
American congregational life. Practicality and social activity
predominate at the local level. Yet it would be wrong to let
matters rest at that. Later developments would show that the
"Jewish Revival" was a significant *religious* phenomenon.
Glazer, for example, though accurate in many of his judgments, overlooks those Jews who shared his dissatisfaction
with prevailing trends of the mid-fifties:

> The pattern of middle-class respectability becomes the pat-
> tern that all Americans wish to follow. . . . The syna-
> gogues have become "synagogue centers" . . . Mordecai
> Kaplan's view of the future of Judaism has triumphed. . . .
> The Jewish law is now (except in Orthodox congregations)
> generally neglected, and the rabbi is no longer called upon
> to act as judge and interpreter. He can keep himself busy
> running his expanded synagogue and school and going to
> interfaith meetings.[18]

Again, as in Protestantism and Catholicism, even in the
deepest reaches of darkest suburbia there was a counter-
vailing revival—a revival against the revival, as it were—
which did get beneath the superficialities of mere religious
interest and peace-of-mindism. Even Herman Wouk's popular novel *Marjorie Morningstar* (1955) shows how a middle
range of awareness came to many twentieth-century Jews
who had lost touch with their heritage. And there were many
others whose external religious observance was accompanied
by great intellectual and moral seriousness.

Yet the postwar mood and the trend to religious affiliation
would change in unexpected ways. For one thing, Jews, like

[17] See Fritz A. Rothschild's systematic anthology of Heschel's
huge corpus, with an introduction, *Between God and Man: An
Interpretation of Judaism* (New York: Free Press, 1959).

[18] Glazer, *American Judaism*, pp. 116, 124–25.

other Americans, would discover that the religious revival had provided very feeble preparation for the social and spiritual tumult of the 1960s. In addition to these violent domestic confrontations, secularization, increased social mobility, and the decline of anti-Semitism tended to erode the Jewish sense of particularity. College students in considerable numbers repudiated the establishment's culture, constituting themselves, as it were, in a new category of "fourth generation" Jews. The rate of interfaith marriages rose so markedly that the question of the "vanishing Jew" became a subject of public debate. Radical secularists compounded the problem with denials of the possibility for theological inquiry "after Auschwitz." The situation of Judaism—as indeed of nearly all traditional forms of organized religion—would become unexpectedly critical.[19]

[19] For a penetrating survey of contemporary Judaism, see Jacob Neusner, *American Judaism: Adventure in Modernity* (1972). He stresses how support of the great national organizations is a major mode of Jewish identification and finds that "checkbook Judaism" is everywhere the norm (p. 15). His analysis of the meaning and implications of modern Zionism is a vital element in his conclusion that the "distintegration of the archaic religious and ethnic unity of the 'holy people' [is] the most important Judaic testimony about what it means to be a modern man" (p. 153).

58

THE ANCIENT EASTERN CHURCHES IN AMERICA

The Federal Council of Churches at its organization in 1908 was a Protestant agency, in effect a successor to the Evangelical Alliance. By 1961 its character had been fundamentally transformed: the Greek, Romanian, Russian, Serbian, Syrian, and Ukrainian Orthodox churches, as well as the Armenian church and the Polish National Catholic church had become active members and were asking that their historic views be recognized in the council's pronouncements. Winthrop S. Hudson could rightfully observe that this broadened participation had "effectively deprived the Protestant community of its one surviving institutionalized symbol."[1] On the other hand, this fact also symbolized the emergence of the "ancient Eastern churches" as an important component of American Christianity. The ecumenical participation of the Eastern churches, hesitatingly begun in 1927 at the Lausanne Faith and Order conference, was explicitly recognized as an invaluable enrichment at the 1963 conference in Montreal. At that Faith and Order assembly the Orthodox delegation for the first time involved itself at every level of discussion and shared responsibility for the final reports.[2]

For most Americans, nevertheless, these churches had been

[1] Winthrop S. Hudson, *American Protestantism*, pp. 169–70. In 1950 the Federal Council was reorganized as a consolidated interchurch agency and renamed the National Council. In 1948 the World Council of Churches had been formed in a similar manner.

[2] The encyclical *Unto All Churches of Christ Wheresoever They Be* issued by the Holy Synod of the ecumenical patriarch in January 1920 no doubt helped prepare the road to Lausanne.

—or still are—a closed book. A Greek was a restaurateur, not a bearer of a rich and ancient Christian tradition. A Russian is variously suspected as White or Red. The historic testimony and ways of about one hundred thousand Unitarians or four hundred thousand Christian Scientists or a handful of surviving Shakers are better known, even in many seminaries, than the faith and practice of America's nearly three million Orthodox.[3] Following the same pattern, most histories of American Christianity devote only three or four pages to the subject.[4] In the future, however, these churches may have an important role to play—not only due to the antiquity and richness of their heritage, but because they did not participate in the tumultuous events that have separated Catholics and Protestants since the Reformation. In a way, the long silence of Orthodoxy increases its ecumenical potential. Most markedly will this be true if the movement for a unified American Orthodox church achieves its end.

The ancient Eastern churches naturally had a long pioneering period in the United States, a time of small and isolated beginnings. The records of the early Virginia Company note that a certain "Martin the Armenian" came out to the colony in 1618–19, but not until 1866 was the first Orthodox parish in America organized, in New Orleans. The real expansion of these churches is a twentieth-century development, the years 1900–14 being a particularly important time of organization and reorganization. Only after World War II, in a manner somewhat similar to the Roman Catholics and Lutherans, have the Orthodox begun to experience the full implications of Americanization. They themselves began to point out the futility and inutility of making the church an agency for the perpetuation of Old World ties, languages, and folk traditions; and their impact on American religious life and the

[3] In 1944 the Greek archbishop of New York claimed 5 million Orthodox in the U.S., but this is little more than a totaling of nominally Orthodox ethnic groups. According to the 1936 federal census, there were only 100,000 effective Russian members and 189,000 Greek members. These figures are no doubt too low, but not exceedingly (see n. 16 below).

[4] In 1936 a typical work on American religion would allot chapters to six kinds of Protestantism and three kinds of Judaism, plus Unity, Theosophy, and Spiritualism—and include nothing on Eastern Orthodoxy (Charles S. Braden, ed., *The Varieties of American Religion*). Winthrop S. Hudson's *Religion in America* (1965) is an exception to the pattern of neglect.

thought of the nation began to be felt. Essential to an understanding of this impact is a brief consideration of the historical background of the Eastern churches.

A GLANCE AT THE EARLY HISTORY

One astute historian has declared the "formal principle" of Eastern Orthodoxy to be "its tenacious adherence to the old," and nearly all of its own theologians also emphasize the unbroken continuity of their church and its undeviating commitment to the first seven ecumenical councils of the "undivided" Church. Elsewhere in Christendom, the Orthodox tend to see only defection and unauthorized innovation, considering themselves to be the organic continuation of the apostolic Church, or in Bulgakov's phrase, the "elect from among the elect."[5] In terms of developmental logic, moreover, this claim is well supported: the patriarchs of Jerusalem and Antioch do indeed stand in a venerable succession. Yet the anomaly and perhaps the tragedy of this commitment is the fact that by the time John of Damascus (ca. 675–749), the last of the great Eastern Fathers of the Church, had rendered the teachings of the councils into semisystematic form, the Church was no longer undivided.[6] During the fifth and sixth centuries, the so-called Lesser Eastern churches, from Syria, Armenia, and Egypt on to Persia and India had separated themselves, partly for cultural and political reasons, but also out of dissatisfaction with certain doctrinal tendencies of the councils.

By the time the "Seventh Pillar" of Orthodoxy had been raised at the Council of Nicaea (787), not only had the Asiatic and African churches gone their ways or fallen under the sway of Islam; but the Western church under the bishop of Rome had long since developed its characteristic form, shaped and inspirited by Augustinian theology, Benedictine

[5] "Not the whole of the human race belongs to the Church, only the elect. And not all Christians belong, in the fullest sense, to the Church—only Orthodox" (Sergius Bulgakov, *The Orthodox Church*, p. 18).

[6] The Seventh Council, to be sure, met long after John's death, in 787; but in approving the veneration of icons, it took a position he had defended. The Seventh Council is peculiarly vital to the Eastern Orthodox churches, who celebrate the final victory for holy images in 843 as "the Triumph of Orthodoxy."

monasticism, and a rigorously unified hierarchy. In the West Greek became an almost unknown tongue. And the separation deepened with the passing centuries as each area endured its own vicissitudes.[7] Limited exchanges of influence would continue, and at the Council of Florence in 1439 a reunion was even temporarily achieved. Yet so distinctive did the Greek and Slavic church tradition become, that in 1846 a Russian theologian could declare that "all Protestants are Crypto-Papists," and that for Western Christians "a passage to Orthodoxy seems like an apostasy" from their past, their science, their creed, and their life.[8] A half-century later Adolf von Harnack, the great German historian of dogma, would exhibit the liberal Protestant view of "Eastern Catholicism":

> There is no sadder spectacle than this transformation of the Christian religion from a worship of God in spirit and in truth into a worship of God in signs, formulas, and idols. To feel the whole pity of this development, we need not descend to such adherents of this form of Christianity as are religiously and intellectually in a state of complete abandonment, like the Copts and Abyssinians; the Syrians, Greeks, and Russians are, taken as a whole, only a little better. . . . As a whole and in its structure the system of the Oriental Churches is foreign to the Gospel.[9]

Since 1900 prejudice has declined and knowledge increased, but Western noncomprehension of the Eastern churches is still very widespread.

THE CHARACTER OF ORTHODOXY

Aside from their utterly different historical experience since the sixth century at latest, the Orthodox churches are distin-

[7] Although A.D. 1054 is the traditional date of the Great Schism, political, cultural, and religious differences were already perceptible in the lifetimes of Saint Augustine (354–430) and Saint Benedict (480–543). During the seventh and eighth centuries Islam not only conquered vast regions of the Eastern church, but of the Western church as well—in North Africa and on the Iberian Peninsula.

[8] Alexis Khomiakov, quoted in Timothy Ware, *The Orthodox Church*, p. 9.

[9] Adolf von Harnack, *What Is Christianity?* (New York: G. P. Putnam's Sons, 1901), pp. 204–05, 210; see also pp. 187–210.

guished by a strong propensity for Neoplatonic metaphysics, especially its confidence in reflection and its reliance on human consensus as a pathway to knowledge. Given this intellectualist traditionalism, Christ, the Trinity, and Redemption are defined in very complex philosophical terms.[10] The distinctive world of thought that lives on in the Eastern churches was thus a product of the Hellenistic age that extends from Alexander the Great to Constantine the Great. These five or six centuries were pervaded by an awareness that the old political and religious traditions had crumbled, and hence by a search for new grounds of certainty. Among both Christians and pagans one notes a rise of asceticism, mysticism, and pessimism, a despair of patient inquiry and social reconstruction, a desire for infallible revelation and for salvation *from* the world, a turning to mystery cults and religious ideas from Egypt, Anatolia, Syria, and Babylon. For many people religion replaced politics as a primary concern.[11]

Into this Hellenistic world came the Christian gospel, preached and accepted by men who in varying degrees were part of that world of thought, and who proceeded to formulate the implications of Christianity in the philosophical terms of the day, and by means of those same terms to distinguish Christian teaching from pagan speculation. In the East doctrinal expression became increasingly Platonic and mystical in spirit. The West, during the ensuing centuries, maintained the letter of the early councils (with some very controversial exceptions); but unlike the Eastern churches, it lost touch with the religious spirit and nonjuridical attitudes that had informed them.[12]

[10] The great controversies on the Trinity and the Person of Christ were essentially Eastern and with two exceptions "all the great writers and teachers of that wonderful age of theological dialectics were in the Greek Church" (Walter F. Adeney, *The Greek and Eastern Churches* [New York: Charles Scribner's Sons, 1908], pp. 1–2).

[11] See Gilbert Murray, *Five Stages of Greek Religion* (1925; New York: Doubleday & Co., Anchor Books, 1955). I have paraphrased some passages of chap. 4.

[12] The sharpest controversy between the Eastern and Western churches had to do with the primacy, infallibility, and ecclesiastical authority of the bishop of Rome, and derivatively other questions of ecclesiastical polity. In Eastern Orthodoxy the ecumenical patriarch of Constantinople is *primus inter pares,* though he shares

As in many other churches, worship provides a vital key to the nature and spirit of Orthodoxy. Any sympathetic observer of the Divine Liturgy will sense (and "sense" is the word) the otherworldly glory which pervades the place and ceremony, whether in a great cathedral or in a remodeled building bought from some now departed Protestant congregation. To the Orthodox the sacraments are sacred mysteries, not logical riddles, and this, too, will be borne out by all that is done, seen, and heard. The Eucharist is the constituting reality of the church; and when it is celebrated locally, the whole church in its fullness is present—as, indeed, the icons attest. Especially striking to most Westerners are these icons that bedeck the churches, especially on the *iconostasis* (icon wall) separating the chancel and the nave—and the kisses bestowed on them by each entering believer. The icons, in fact, do suggest the essence of Orthodoxy, for these stylized images are, in the words of Ernst Benz, "a kind of window between the earthly and the celestial worlds" through which each beholds the other.[13] In the same way, the church itself is an icon of heaven, while man ("in the image of God") carries the icon of God within himself. Christ is the New Adam —in and through whom the original image of God is restored.

---

a position of special honor with the three other ancient patriarchates (Alexandria, Antioch, and Jerusalem). After the Fall of Constantinople in 1453, the patriarch of Moscow assumed a very high but never precisely defined honor. There are also twelve autocephalous churches, at least four autonomous churches, and several other provinces that in various ways depend on one or more of the above jurisdictions. All but those in the last category elect and consecrate their own bishops or patriarchs and adjudicate all ecclesiastical conflicts. Remaining in communion with all of the autocephalous churches is the chief criterion of a church's "orthodoxy" or legitimacy, though many great churches (e.g. the Russian and the Greek) for longer or shorter periods have lacked such acceptance. By comparison, the Church of Rome is far more unified and far more given to precise juridical regulation of authority and practice. Among other controversies with Rome, the most celebrated are those pertaining to the procession of the Holy Spirit from the Father (East) or from the Father and the Son (West) and to when and how the miracle of the Eucharist takes place.

[13] Ernst Benz, *The Eastern Orthodox Church: Its Thought and Life*, pp. 5–19.

The Westerner (especially if Protestant) may be surprised, or even repelled, by the casual way in which believers participate in these glories (the men ambling out for a smoke in the middle of the service, for example); yet another fundamental aspect of Orthodox religion is its blending with the common life as a kind of "natural religion" of the people. Nationality and religion became inseparable aspects of existence. If the civil government was destroyed or hostile, the church through its clergy spoke for the people. Autochthonous religion of this sort could outlast centuries of persecution and foreign rule. On the other hand, a church with these strengths was very poorly adapted to the realities of mass immigration and the situation of ethnic minorities in the United States. Confusion and ecclesiastical inattention were often the rule. In the mid-twentieth century, therefore, institutional division remained a dominant characteristic of Orthodoxy's vast constituency in America. Over a score of Orthodox and other Eastern churches share this American experience, but only a few of the more representative ones can be considered here.

Russian Orthodoxy

In 1448, just five years before Constantinople fell to the Turks, a Russian council of bishops elected its own metropolitan. In 1472 Czar Ivan the Great married Sophia, niece of the last Byzantine emperor, and proclaiming Moscow to be the Third Rome, he declared Russia to be the protector of Orthodox Christendom—a grand consummation of the mission to the Slavs begun by Saints Cyril and Methodius in 863. In 1741 under Peter the Great the landing of Captain Vitus Bering on Kayak Island symbolized another vast missionary and imperial achievement—a reach beyond even the distant limits of Siberia. The first permanent settlement in Alaska followed in 1784, and a decade later the Holy Synod dispatched ten monks to establish a mission there. So successful was their evangelism that an Alaskan diocese was created in 1799 and Joasaph Bolotov, the mission's head, was consecrated as bishop—only to drown on his return trip. Finally in 1840 Ivan Venyaminov (1797–1879), "the greatest Russian missionary of the nineteenth century," became Alaska's first resident bishop. In 1848 he built at Sitka the Cathedral

of Saint Michael which still stands.[14] In 1868, a year after
the United States acquired Alaska, Venyaminov (an archbishop since 1850) became metropolitan of Moscow and
primate of Russia. In this capacity he strengthened the
Alaskan diocese by separating it from its Siberian province
(1870) and by moving the see to San Francisco (1872). At
this time the diocese numbered twelve thousand communicants—making it one of the most thriving Indian missions
to be established north of Mexico.

The next major change in Russian church affairs came in
1891, when the membership of this Russian church in the
United States was suddenly enlarged by an event that also
required the extension of the diocese to include the entire
country. This large accession of members consisted of Ruthe-
nian "Uniates" who had emigrated from the Carpathian area
of central Europe.[15] In America they objected to the loss of
special concessions granted in Europe (e.g. the right of
priests to marry), and Father Alexis Toth of Minneapolis led
a secession movement for a reunion with the Russian church
which ultimately involved about 120 parishes, many of them
in mining and steel areas of Pennsylvania and Ohio. By 1909
half of the membership of the Russian church consisted of
this and other similar transfers. Some of these churches
gained diocesan status as a separate Carpatho-Russian church
in 1938. In response to still other developments, Archbishop
Tikhon Belavin transferred his see from San Francisco to New
York in 1905. Up to this point the Russian church provided
what general Orthodox oversight there was—not only for the
Russians, but also for other Orthodox groups that were emigrating in large numbers from Russia, Central Europe, and

[14] Serge Bolshakov, *The Foreign Missions of the Russian Orthodox Church*, p. 86; Chauncey Emhardt et al., *The Eastern Church
in the Western World*, p. 52.

[15] Ruthenians (Latin for Russians) are in effect Ukrainians or
Russians who were living in areas governed by Poland or the
Austro-Hungarian Empire. "Uniate" constituencies were those
which at various times (notably by the Council of Brest in 1596)
had been brought under the authority of the pope, but with permission to use Eastern liturgical rites and to continue certain
other practices. Similar constituencies do or did exist from Lithuania through the Middle East to India. They often lack strong
popular support and hence constitute a Roman thorn in the
Orthodox side. On the other hand, their existence conduced to a
measure of flexibility in the Roman church.

the Balkans. By 1916 this constituency was approaching a half-million, with Ukrainians the largest element everywhere but in the Far West.

After World War I the religious leadership of the Third Rome was shattered, primarily by dissension resulting from the Communist "reorganization" of the church. In 1918 the Romanians in America organized separately; they were soon followed by the Serbs, and in 1922 by the Greeks. In 1927 both the Ukrainians and the Syrians withdrew from Russian jurisdiction, but they were quickly overtaken by various kinds of factionalism. The Syrian Orthodox attained unity in 1933. The Ukrainians, on the other hand, remained divided among four different jurisdictions in addition to the Carpatho-Russian diocese. The Russian Orthodox church as well was rent by bitter controversies after the "exarchate" of the patriarch of Moscow gained control of the New York cathedral in 1925. The vast majority of Russian Orthodox in America resisted this jurisdiction, however, and since 1924 had been organized in a manner that made them more nearly an autonomous church that any other Orthodox communion in America. In 1970 the patriarch of Moscow healed this schism and declared the reunited church to be autocephalous. By this time, Saint Vladimir's Seminary in New York had become an important intellectual force not only among Russians, but in the world ecumenical movement. John Meyendorff and Alexander Schmemann, and before them George Florovsky, have become important twentieth-century interpreters of the Orthodox tradition.[16]

Greek Orthodoxy

The largest single Orthodox constituency in the United States is the Greek, though the history of the Greek Orthodox

16 See Alexander A. Bogolepov, *Toward an American Orthodox Church: The Establishment of an Autocephalous Orthodox Church*, p. 100. The Albanian Orthodox Church in America is also technically a Mother Church, but its constituency of about twelve thousand is too small to assume full autocephalous status. In her *Guide to Orthodox America*, Anastasia Bespuda lists 336 parishes in the Russian Orthodox church, 32 in the Patriarchal Exarchate, and 89 in the Russian Orthodox Church Outside of Russia, an international jurisdiction organized in Europe by exiles who hope for a return of the old czarist order. The reported membership in 1970 for these three churches was, respectively, 700,000, 160,000, and 60,000.

churches in the United States is relatively brief. The great migrations from Greece, the Mediterranean islands, and Asia Minor began in the 1890s, reached a peak between 1900 and 1910, and continued unabated down to the restriction laws of the 1920s. By 1940 perhaps five hundred thousand had come. The first parish in New York was organized in 1891, and many others followed in other parts of the country. The church grew only very slowly, its overall expansion hindered by the overwhelming predominance of male immigrants (95 percent between 1899 and 1910) who often returned to Greece, by the violent polarization of royalists versus Venizelists both in Greece and in America, and by the absence of any fully recognized ecclesiastical authority in the United States until 1930. In that year the ecumenical patriarch in Constantinople arranged to have Metropolitan Athenagoras of Corfu undertake the difficult task of restoring order to a long embattled constituency. In this the new archbishop eminently succeeded; the price of order, however, was a drastic centralization of power in the new archbishop of North and South America. Other bishops, now without dioceses, served as his assistants. In 1949, after Athenagoras had been flown to Istanbul in President Truman's airplane and enthroned as ecumenical patriarch, Archbishop Michael was appointed. Under Archbishop Michael (1950–58) a still larger measure of order and advancement was established in the archdiocese, which increasingly became the recognized spokesman for the Greek minority in the United States. Under Archbishop Iakovos, who was appointed in 1959, the basic organization of the church was not altered, but far more aggressive efforts to meet the needs of an essentially English-speaking constituency were inaugurated.[17] Early

[17] These adjustments to the American scene were much needed; with only 2.3 percent of the third generation Greeks being able to speak Greek, Americanization was obviously proceeding rapidly. This situation is due in no small part to the unusually high ratio of men to women among Greek immigrants (193 to 100, as against, for example, 115 to 100 among Russian immigrants), (see Constantine Volaitis, "The Orthodox Church in the United States as Viewed from the Social Sciences," *Saint Vladimir's Seminary Quarterly* 5 [1961]:74, 77). For other statistics and detailed accounts of Greek-American ecclesiastical turmoil, see Theodore Saloutos, *The Greeks in America*.

efforts to found seminaries had faltered, but in 1937 another was founded in Pomfret, Connecticut. Under more favorable conditions it was moved to Brookline, Massachusetts, in 1947. In 1968 the church had gained a liberal arts college; and by 1970 the Holy Cross School of Theology had graduated 321, founded an important theological journal, and become a flourishing center of Orthodox study.

AMERICAN ORTHODOXY IN RETROSPECT

In the history of Eastern Orthodoxy in the United States four features stand out. First and most obvious is its multiethnical character. Its constituency, in the language of its own canon law, has almost a dozen "Mother Churches" in Europe; but of these some have almost expired, others are suspected of having lost either their freedom or their orthodoxy, and almost all are entirely incapable of offering material support to their American counterparts. Given this practical motherlessness, the second feature becomes explicable; namely, that serious conflicts have ensued within almost every ethnic group, and in many cases separate jurisdictions have been the result. The Greeks were long riven by royalist-democratic issues in their homeland. Among the Ukrainians there were five separate groups, among the Russians (until 1970) three, and even the little Albanian group was divided in two.

The third feature has to do with the fact that Orthodox religion, due to its close identification with the land, culture, language, folk customs, and political structures of a specific country, does not easily follow the immigrant to a religiously neutral republic. Even greater difficulties stemmed from the hurly-burly of a rapidly changing industrialized and pluralistic social order. Religion and ethnicity could not long remain coterminous in the face of social mobility, geographical scattering, public education in the English language, and an inherited reliance on a hierarchy immobilized in the Old World and without autonomy in the New. As a result, these ethnic minorities were often "Orthodox" in the same way that countless unaffiliated Americans identify themselves as "Protestant." Due to the lack of a unified hierarchy and of strong missionary methods, the vast Orthodox constituency in

America—estimated in purely ethnic terms as exceeding five million—has been waning steadily ever since the Great Migration ceased.[18]

Important for the future of the Orthodox churches in America was a fourth feature: their noticeably increased attention to the problems of an Americanized constituency during the quarter-century after World War II. Among the Russians this was especially marked, in part because this church had been in vigorous, even brilliant dialogue with Western thinkers since early in the nineteenth century, and in part because it most nearly approached ecclesiastical autonomy. In the largest group of all, the Greek, on the other hand, such concern was less evident. Very early in the century Archbishop Tikhon (later to become patriarch of Moscow) gained authorization for an English liturgy for his jurisdiction, which then included members from seven or eight language groups. Such liturgies and English language preaching have since become widespread in the Russian, Syrian, and Albanian churches, as has lay participation in parish affairs or at even higher organizational levels. In 1927 Metropolitan Platon of the Russian church drew up a plan for a unified autocephalous American Orthodox Church, complete with a proposal that the Syrian Archbishop Aftimios be president of the synod of bishops. But this plan also came to naught. Whether the grant of autocephalous status to the Russian church in 1970 would conduce to future unification was at best uncertain. In the meantime the Standing Conference of Canonical Orthodox Bishops, founded in 1960 with Archbishop Iakovos of the Greek church presiding, filled many important functions. Through eight commissions and regular meetings it began to deal with contemporary problems in a concerted way. In 1971 the Greek church began work on an English liturgy despite strenuous opposition.

[18] Federal census figures tend to be about a fourth as large as official claims. According to L. M. Gray's analysis in *Commonweal*, 13 April 1932, three fourths of baptized Orthodox children are inactive by age sixteen. Among those of the Greek Orthodox church who were baptized and actively church-related at age fifteen, half were in churches other than the Greek Orthodox (see Donald Atwater, *The Christian Churches of the East*, 2 vols. [Milwaukee: Bruce Publishing Co., 1948], 2:148–55).

THE SEPARATE EASTERN CHURCHES

"Is it not tragic," asks Professor Schmemann, "that one of the main reasons for the rejection of Orthodoxy by almost the whole non-Greek East was its hatred for the empire? . . . This was the price the Church paid for the inner dichotomy [of the union of church and state] under Constantine."[19] In less than a century after the condemnation of Monophysitism at the Council of Constantinople (553), the Syrians and Copts would greet their Mohammedan conquerors almost as saviors. The Lutheran historian Rudolf Sohm asks and answers a similar question regarding the pope's leadership of the secession of Western Christendom: "Was there any power in the Church ready and able to withstand the Empire, and to defend the self-government of the Church through a supreme spiritual head against the ruler of the world? That was the great place in the world's history which was filled by the Bishop of Rome."[20] Nobody need be told what issued from the Roman bishop's rebellion from the empire's temporal authority; but the story of the Eastern churches has been lost in the shadows of imperial, Islamic, and Orthodox history. It is perhaps fortunate, therefore, that America possesses reminders of the great spiritual empires that once stretched from the Mediterranean south to Nubia and Abyssinia and east to Persia, India, and China. Even these vast ecclesiastical realms were not united in their opposition to Constantinople, however.

"No decree of a council has ever destroyed a powerful heresy," writes Adeney, who then points out how the Council of Ephesus (431) gave Nestorianism its opportunities for eastward expansion. Theological centers developed in Byzantine Syria at Edessa and in Persian territory at Nisibis where the disfavor of the empire was a boon. Perhaps as a concession to Zoroastrianism, the Nestorians moderated their Hellenistic asceticism and allowed priests to marry. Yet they remained true to the basic witness of the Patriarch Nestorius, and even truer to Theodore of Mopsuestia, who was, in fact,

19 Alexander Schmemann, *The Historical Road of Eastern Orthodoxy*, p. 157.
20 Rudolf Sohm, *Outlines of Church History*, pp. 60, 65.

chief theologian of the christological tendency which Nestorianism emphasizes—the humanity of Jesus, the importance of his earthly life, and his brotherly concern for mankind. They also perpetuate Nestorius's objections to the veneration of Mary as the Mother of God, forbid icons in their churches, and strongly object to the doctrine of purgatory.

In 498 the head of the Nestorian church took the title "Patriarch of the East," and with headquarters at Seleucia and Ctesiphon began sending missionaries to the Far East over the caravan routes. At its height this church was said to have had 80 million members—which seems improbable. Yet heavy blows were to fall; and ultimately Islam, Chengis Khan, and Tamerlane would reduce the Nestorian church to a few scattered remnants. In 1551 one of these remnants east of the Tigris appealed to Rome for the consecration of a dissident bishop. Julius III obliged, and subsequently these so-called Chaldeans became a kind of Uniate church. In 1843 the Kurds massacred four thousand Nestorians, and in 1915 a small group that had taken refuge in Anatolia was driven into neighboring countries by the Turks. It was due to these woes in the Middle East that a few Nestorians began emigrating to the United States in 1911. In 1940 the 119th patriarch of the Church of the East and Assyrians (Mar Eshai Shimun XXIII) took residence in the United States among the 3,000 or so of his coreligionists in this country. All over the world perhaps as many as 250,000 other Nestorian faithful have in some way recognized his authority.

The Nestorian offshoot dating from the Council of Ephesus formulated the doctrine of the Person of Christ so succinctly that new fears arose: in correcting Nestorius, had Saint Cyril of Alexandria led the council too far in the opposite direction? At the so-called Robber Council, also held at Ephesus (449), these fears were substantiated, for it approved the extreme position of Eutyches that the person of Christ was of one nature only, that the body of Christ was by union with the divine made different from that of other men. This "monophysite" doctrine was so widely unacceptable that the emperor convoked another council at Chalcedon (451), whose formulations unambiguously stated the doctrine of two natures, the divine and human, in one "person," which has ever since been accepted both in the Orthodox and the Roman churches as well as in the major Reformation churches.

In Syria and Egypt, however, Chalcedon met massive opposition. This led to the formation of separate national churches, which launched very successful missionary ventures of their own. The Monophysite cause was least disputed in Egypt, and under the patriarch of Alexandria it vigorously extended itself southward to Nubia and Abyssinia. Bishop Jacob Al Bardi, a former monk, became the great apostle of Syrian Monophysitism, to whose credit also falls the great Syriac version of the Bible. Ultimately this church, like that of the Nestorians, reached out through Mesopotamia and Persia to India, where the church of Malabar (Kerala) still perpetuates the Jacobite tradition. They suffered from the same great invasions as the Nestorians, however, and by 1900 their numbers (aside from Malabar) were reduced to 150,000, gathered chiefly in Mesopotamia but with a scattering in and around Damascus and Jerusalem. In the 1890s the intensity of Turkish persecution forced many of them into flight, and some came to America.

Still a third area of Monophysite strength was the so-called Gregorian Church of the semiautonomous Kingdom of Armenia, which never really accepted the Council of Chalcedon and in 491 finally anathematized it. This stand was formalized in its national council of 535, a date deemed so important that the Armenian calendar was reckoned from it. In addition to the common woes of Middle Eastern Christians, the Armenians finally had visited upon them the terrible Turkish massacres of 1895, when a hundred thousand or more were slain, most of them Gregorians or modern Protestant converts. The rest of the nation scattered; but in the United States the Armenian Apostolic Church became the largest and most prosperous of the Monophysite churches. Organized in 1899, in 1970 it consisted of about 275,000 members and nearly ninety congregations divided into two jurisdictions, one under the catholicos in Soviet Armenia, the other with its head in Lebanon.

Among the many who since the 1890s have escaped the violence and economic dislocations of the Middle East by emigrating to the United States, there were still other thousands who belonged to Monophysite churches. The Syrian Jacobites in America, probably not exceeding ten thousand in number, are organized under the jurisdiction of the patriarch of Syria in three separate churches. In 1970, when the Ethiopian Orthodox Church dedicated its headquarters in New

York, it claimed ten thousand members. On a few feast days even a group of scattered members of the Malabar Church of India celebrate the liturgy together in New York City.

In the context of American religious history as a whole, these several separated Eastern churches obviously do not loom large. But they do pose the question of group existence and demonstrate the tenacity of certain forms of doctrinal commitment. They are thus living witnesses to the substantial nature of such controversies as the often ridiculed "battle over an iota" which agitated the Council of Nicaea in A.D. 325.[21] By the same token, all of these Eastern churches, including the Orthodox, exhibit the process by which the ancient Graeco-Roman religious legacy was transmitted to European Christendom. In this sense, even the most battle-scarred of these churches are reminders of theological issues which are intrinsic to a definition of Christianity.

[21] The reference is to terms current in the Arian controversy: *homoöusion* and *homoiusion*, which characterized the Son of God respectively as being "of one substance" with the Father, or as "like" or "similar to" the Father.

59

ROMAN CATHOLICISM IN THE TWENTIETH CENTURY

Before Pope Paul VI had taken his stand athwart the tide of Roman Catholic reform, even before the Second Vatican Council and the revolutionary pontificate of John XXIII, and well before the United States elected a Roman Catholic president, the Jesuit scholar-theologian Walter J. Ong observed that "American Catholicism is in a state of intellectual and spiritual crisis."[1] He was pointing to the profoundly transformed social situation which no longer allowed Roman Catholicism to regard itself as an "immigrant faith." In the age of affluence presided over by Dwight D. Eisenhower, a vague, homogenizing civil religion had supplanted the old forms of interfaith strife. The Protestant Establishment was passing into history and a new age of pluralism was at hand. Though there were still vast untapped potentialities for bigotry and intolerance beneath the surface of the American mind, Roman Catholics had to abandon the defensive posture that constant immigration and wave after wave of nativism had provoked. Standing on the threshold of a new period of participation and responsibility, Catholics were justifiably pondering the circumstances that had brought about this change in their situation.

THE "NEW" IMMIGRATION OF CATHOLICS

During the later nineteenth century the main ethnic tensions in the church had arisen between the English-speaking

[1] Walter J. Ong, *Frontiers in American Catholicism: Essays on Ideology and Culture*, p. 2.

Irish majority and a large, highly self-conscious German minority with great strength in the Midwest. After 1880, however, this situation began to be altered by a steady stream of immigration from eastern and southern Europe. By 1920 there were about 3.3 million Americans of Italian parentage and about 3 million Polish, as well as many Hungarians, Portuguese, Croatians, Bohemians, and Ruthenians. During the intervening half-century the church had faced difficult problems of expansion as these poor, unskilled, and often illiterate people formed separate ethnic enclaves, usually in the cities. In their basic religious attitudes the new immigrants varied widely, but the total phenomenon had an enormous impact on the situation of Catholicism in America. Most obvious were the flamboyant celebrations of a new galaxy of saints' days. More basic were vast institutional problems involving schools, seminaries, hospitals, and convents, as well as agencies for immigrant aid. Less tangible, but equally important, was the way in which immigration prolonged the church's role as a protector of new Americans and thereby prevented it from assuming the constructive role in public affairs which "Americanist" leaders like Archbishop Ireland had long advocated.

For the Italians who came to America the church had always been an accepted fact of life amid the grinding poverty of the cities and villages of Sicily and southern Italy whence most of them came. Since the quest for national unity and social reform had led to open conflict with the papacy, the church was often associated with oppression, and relatively benign forms of anticlericalism were fairly widespread. Although in the Italian quarters of America the parish church did become a major agency of cultural identity and continuity, in neither the old nor the new country was the attachment marked by strong popular fervor; and even a proud historian concedes "some truth" to the view "that the Italian immigrant has not been generous toward his Church."[2] The presence of roughly five million Italian-American Catholics in 1960 indicates that apostasy was relatively rare. But in America, where economic opportunities beckoned, there was a relatively small movement of men and women into the

[2] Juvenal Marchsia, "The Italian Catholic Immigrant," in *Roman Catholicism and the American Way of Life*, ed. Thomas T. McAvoy, p. 175.

priesthood and religious orders, and little avidity for the financial sacrifices that parochial schools required. Very few Italians have entered the hierarchy or become prominent church leaders in other ways. The great preponderance of men—over a million of whom returned to Italy between 1900 and 1916—also contributed to this circumstance. In urban politics the Italians and the Irish have frequently been at odds, but the kind of religious intensity that led German Catholics into ecclesiastical conflict has rarely been manifested, even in New York where nearly a quarter of the nation's Italians lived.[3]

Arriving in only slightly fewer numbers than the Italians were the Polish, but the fervency of their devotion to the Catholic church contrasted sharply. Repeatedly invaded, dismembered, or partitioned out of existence, and constantly menaced by Protestant Germany or Orthodox Russia, Poland has linked its national identity with Roman Catholicism for centuries, and never more devotedly than during the century of Russian repression preceding World War I. In America the parish church and the parochial school became a surrogate for the unfettered national existence that had been denied them since the Congress of Vienna in 1815. For first generation immigrants the Polish language "became the cornerstone that would maintain solidarity. They firmly believed that when the language was lost—all was lost."[4] In this spirit, whether in small farming communities or in the cities where most of them gathered in closely knit neighborhoods, they made great personal sacrifices for the institutions that would maintain their cultural heritage. During the nineteenth century they had been too few in number to affect the course of the Americanism controversy, but as their number passed the five million mark—as it did by 1950—over eight hundred identifiably Polish parishes constituted perhaps the largest self-conscious ethnic group in the church. Only after World War II, despite another considerable influx of émigrés, did

[3] In 1930, 1,700,355 out of a total of 4,651,195 Italian-Americans lived in New York, a number that then exceeded the population of Rome. About 3.5 million Italians immigrated between 1900 and 1925.

[4] Aloysius J. Wycislo, "The Polish Catholic Immigrant," in McAvoy, *Roman Catholicism and the American Way of Life*, p. 183. In 1897–1904 the Polish National Catholic Church, led by Father Joseph Hodur, gave form to such dissent.

urban change and the ineluctable processes of acculturation
gradually disperse the great Polish communities that had
arisen in Chicago, Buffalo, Detroit, Milwaukee, Cleveland,
and many other cities.

The latest major Roman Catholic constituency to achieve
large numerical importance and a degree of self-consciousness was in fact the oldest element in the American
population—older than Virginia's first families, older even
than the Spanish conquerors through whom the Spanish language and Catholicism became enduring elements of their
culture. In 1970 the Spanish-speaking population of the
United States numbered about nine million—though tran-
sients, illegal entrants, those with non-Spanish names, or
Puerto Ricans who were erroneously counted as blacks may
add up to another million. The largest part of this minority
(about 60 percent) is constituted by Mexican Americans,
most of whom have migrated during the twentieth century,
and who live for the most part in Texas, the Southwest, and
California. The other main component stems from Puerto
Rico (about 20 percent), and to a much lesser extent from
Cuba and other Spanish-American countries. They are concentrated heavily in the New York metropolitan region and in
other eastern cities, notably Miami with its many Cuban
émigrés.

About 95 percent of this Spanish-speaking population is at
least nominally Roman Catholic. (In a decade or two Puerto
Ricans may become the largest Catholic group in New York
City, since the Irish and Italians are gradually moving out of
the city.) Yet because Spanish-speaking peoples, regardless
of origin, tend to come from the least churched classes and
areas of their respective countries, share a common tendency
to anticlericalism, and have usually been extremely poor,
their participation in Catholic church life has been very
slight. Almost never have they on their own initiative formed
and supported parish churches as so many other immigrant
communities did, and the number of men entering the
priesthood in the United States has been very small. Due to
various ethnic tensions, moreover, existing parish churches,
even when favorably situated, have been unable to extend an
adequate ministry. The most effective work has been accomplished by various monastic orders and by special diocesan projects; but even these efforts, whether in Los Angeles

or New York, have often been ambivalent in their cultural aims and hesitant to mobilize activistic programs. The institutions of Catholicism, therefore, have not played the crucial roles in the acculturation of these minorities that they have for other immigrant groups.

Protestant evangelism, on the other hand, has found a surprisingly strong response among both Mexicans and Puerto Ricans. As in Latin America generally, the Pentecostalists have been especially successful; and in these fervently evangelical contexts Spanish Americans have produced their own clergy and given relatively strong financial support to their churches. These churches, though rarely concerned with social issues per se, have through their nurture and moral discipline conduced to a pronounced pattern of upward mobility among their members. Yet the basic ecclesiastical problems of this minority are social and economic in origin; and only in the 1960s, when black militancy provided an important model, and in the 1970s, when a protracted strike by grape pickers in California became a national catalyst, did Puerto Rican and Mexican Americans begin to develop a kind of solidarity and militancy that could awaken the nation and its churches to their plight as grossly underprivileged minorities.

The Maturation of the Catholic Minority

The unsensational yet revolutionary process that underlay the new situation of most Roman Catholic Americans was social mobility, a function of modern society which had always been especially pronounced in the United States. For individual Catholics it had always gone on—though at a slower rate due to the repressive attitudes and actions of the Protestant majority. But for Catholic church members as a group it had been greatly retarded by a constant incoming tide of immigration which actually reached its peak in the early twentieth century. For this reason, World War I and the immigration restriction legislation of the 1920s had especially drastic consequences, the first of which was a virtual stabilization of the relative size of the Protestant and Catholic communities. From 1916 to 1955 the membership of 128 Protestant bodies increased by 94.2 percent, the Roman Catholic church by 92.4 percent. The following table reveals the steady but relatively similar increases in the percentage of the total population in the two groups:[5]

	Protestant	*Roman Catholic*
1926	27.0	16.0
1940	28.7	16.1
1950	33.8	18.9
1955	35.5	20.3
1958	35.5	20.8

The second consequence was that after 1930 the acculturative process had a more enduring effect; due to the sudden cessation of immigration, the Catholic community as a whole was transformed. The disruptions of the American social order wrought by the Depression and the New Deal, then by World War II, and finally by America's great postwar "industrial revolution" greatly accelerated the normalization of the country's vast Catholic minority. It could no longer be categorized as an "immigrant faith." Will Herberg described the situation in 1955:

> Increasingly the great mass of Americans understand themselves and their place in society in terms of the religious community with which they are identified. . . . The only kind of separateness or diversity that America recognizes as permanent, and yet also as involving no status of inferiority, is the diversity or separateness of religious community. . . .
>
> All this has far-reaching consequences for the place of religion in American life. . . . For being a Protestant, a Catholic, or a Jew is understood as the specific way, and increasingly perhaps the only way, of being an American and locating oneself in American society. . . . Not to be a Catholic, a Protestant, or a Jew today (1955) is for increasing numbers of American people not to be anything, not to have a *name;* and we are all, as Riesman points out, "afraid of chaotic situations in which [we] do not know [our] own names, [our] brand names."[6]

[5] Will Herberg, *Protestant, Catholic, Jew,* p. 160.
[6] Ibid., pp. 36–40. Herberg quotes David Riesman, *Individualism Reconsidered* (Glencoe, Illinois: Free Press, 1954), p. 178. Herberg does not deal with Negroes as a distinct community, ex-

It is this maturation of the American Roman Catholic minority that America was experiencing in the 1950s. Essential to our understanding of how it could result in the "crisis" to which Father Ong alludes, however, is an account of the major phases of the Catholic experience during these twentieth-century decades.

THE LEGACY OF THE AMERICANISM CONTROVERSY

When the century began, the church was faced with the warning issued by Pope Leo XIII in 1899 in his encyclical on "Americanism." *Testem Benevolentiae* was an ambiguous document, but coming at a time when it could hardly be dissociated from a series of stern papal moves against "modernism," the encyclical had a dampening effect on creative thought and churchmanship in America. It tended to heighten the constant temptation of Americans to concentrate on practical matters. The Progressive Era went its way, therefore, without creating many important positive responses to the social and theoretical challenges of the day.

Catholics were extremely active and remarkably effective in attaining positions of power and influence in the Democratic party, especially in the cities. Political activities, in fact, were woven into the web of religious charitable institutions that sheltered people from an alien world. As Daniel Moynihan has written, Catholic politicians "never thought of politics as an instrument of social change—their kind of politics involved the processes of a society that was not changing."[7] Politics was conceived in essentially conservative terms—as a device for taking the risk and uncertainty out of urban life. In labor relations a similar situation obtained. Since Roman Catholics were the largest element among the country's genuinely distressed workers, they were a mainstay of unionism. The hierarchy had tended to view unionization

---

cept in passing. He also ignores the many humanists whom Duncan Howlett identified as a group in *The Fourth American Faith.*

[7] Nathan Glazer and Daniel P. Moynihan, *Beyond the Melting Pot,* p. 229. See also David J. O'Brien, *American Catholics and Social Reform: The New Deal Years,* pp. 30–33.

efforts with favor; and during the 1880s Cardinal Gibbons stirred up considerable nativist wrath by defending Henry George, the Knights of Labor, and various nonmasonic secret societies when the Vatican threatened condemnation. In the realm of social and economic theory, however, the hierarchy did little more than indicate a general approbation of labor unions so long as they were not socialistic, hostile to religion, or given to violence. Priests who actively identified themselves with social reform and labor radicalism were very rare. Father Thomas J. Hagerty did work with socialist unionists, and in 1905 he was one of the architects of the IWW, but he had left the priesthood in 1902. Father Thomas McGrady of Kentucky also defended socialist policies, but in 1903 when his bishop asked for a retraction, he left the church.

First in the mind of most Catholic leaders were the problems of reaching the immigrant and strengthening an independent Catholic educational system. Opposed to socialism and an environmental analysis of poverty, the church concentrated on the rescue and rehabilitation of individuals, and by 1910 it was operating nearly twelve hundred charitable institutions. "Though lip service was paid to Leo XIII's *Rerum Novarum*, leading Catholics for nearly two decades [after its publication in 1891] failed to emphasize its meaning: they expounded it as a 'bulwark' of the *status quo* and not as a charter of social justice."[8]

In matters of theology and philosophy, the church was in general even less adventurous. Seminaries and institutions of higher learning were providing only the minimum essentials for the priesthood and laity despite the great social and intellectual transformations which were in progress. Handbooks and compendia sufficed. The "Sulpician tradition" of the nineteenth century perpetuated itself uncreatively.[9] The Thomistic revival promoted by Pope Leo XIII made slow advances. The vast problems of history, culture, science, and

[8] Aaron I. Abell, "Preparing for Social Action: 1880–1920," in *The American Apostolate*, ed. Leo R. Ward, pp. 18–19.

[9] "Sulpician tradition" is simply a term to designate the tradition in which the continuing influence of the French Sulpicians was strong. Without denying the sacrificial contributions of the many Sulpicians who came to the United States and who served with distinction as professors, priests, and prelates, one may suggest that rarely during the nineteenth century were their intellectual efforts distinguished or imaginative.

the social order—realms in which nineteenth-century thinking had left a revolutionary legacy—were left not only unresolved but unapproached. Even among the leaders of Americanism few went beyond a call for accommodating the church to American ways, and those who did were warned against dangerous innovations in Pope Leo's encyclical. Hecker and Brownson won few disciples; and Father John A. Zahm of Notre Dame University, whose *Evolution and Dogma* (1896) attempted a rapprochement with Darwinism, was silenced. Though founded in a moment of educational idealism, the Catholic University of America lacked the resources to become the great center of learning of which its founders had dreamed.

WORLD WAR I AND THE TWENTIES

The later years of World War I saw the beginnings of at least a partial resurgence, particularly in the realm of social thought. In this sense the war's effect on Roman Catholic thought was quite the reverse of its effect on Protestantism, for only then did the Catholic bishops of the country begin to exercise direct responsibility for thought and action in the social field. In August 1917 a General Conference of Catholics representing sixty-eight dioceses and twenty-seven national Catholic organizations created the National Catholic War Council with a large representative executive committee. Administrative responsibility was assigned to four bishops, and John J. Burke, former editor of the *Catholic World* and founder of the Chaplain's Aid Association, was appointed chief director of operations. After the Armistice, this group continued to function, its attention now turned to problems of citizenship, education, rehabilitation, and postwar social problems.

In February, 1919, the Administrative Committee of Bishops published an almost epoch-making document: "Social Reconstruction: A General Review of the Problems and a Survey of Remedies." It was written largely by Father John A. Ryan, who had been widely known as a progressive since 1906 when he published his treatise *A Living Wage*, justifiably remembered as a major contribution to the minimum wage law movement. In the superheated years of the postwar Red Scare and the revived Ku Klux Klan, the "Bishops' Program," as it came to be known, was far more often attacked than defended, even by Catholics. The program was, nevertheless, the first expression of Catholic social progressivism to be given at least semiofficial status in America. This was a triumph for Ryan, who a few years earlier, while he was a seminary professor in Saint Paul, Minnesota, had complained that he could not name five bishops in the country who had spoken out for social reform. Progressives were soon to be disappointed, however, for "not a single remedial or transforming proposal in the Bishops' Program was adopted [in the United States] during the 1920s."[10]

Yet movement in this direction did not cease. In 1919 the War Council was reconstituted as the National Catholic Welfare Council with a similar organization, with Burke as executive director and with Ryan as director of the Social Action Department. Though certain bishops strenuously objected to its encroachment on their authority, and still others to the liberal hue of its pronouncements, the National Catholic Welfare Conference (its name was changed to avoid misunderstanding) rapidly became the most effective agency in the country for acquainting Catholics with the social doctrines of Leo XIII. After 1920 it also provided the largest support given to the rural life movement led by Father (later Bishop) Edwin V. O'Hara.[11] In these and many other efforts the National Council of Catholic Men and a parallel organization for women, both coordinated by the NCWC, became channels of communication to the Catholic laity and a valuable means of gaining support for various projects and programs. The scope of the NCWC's concern became well-nigh total, ranging from the publication of scholarly monographs to Father Burke's personal negotiations with the revolutionary government of Mexico in 1928.[12] In all realms its

[10] Aaron I. Abell, *American Catholicism and Social Action: A Search for Social Justice, 1865–1950*, p. 204.

[11] O'Hara became director of the Rural Life Bureau of the NCWC in 1920 and the first executive secretary of the National Catholic Rural Life Conference in 1923. During the first half of 1922 the council was in suspended animation because Pope Benedict XV had withdrawn his approval. Pius XI reversed this decision. In 1923, to avoid confusion as to the organization's authority, its name was changed to the National Catholic Welfare Conference.

[12] During the years of Spanish rule the church had become a powerful force in Mexican life. It owned much of the land, con-

social consciousness was evident; and despite the fact that it was organized as a voluntary and unofficial agency with whose advocacy bishops frequently disagreed, it performed an important service in shaping Catholic thought and bringing it to bear on American problems.

The idealistic fervor frequently found in the NCWC or in the rural life movement, however, was not contagious. The 1920s was by no means a period of vital and adventurous advance for the Roman Catholic church. Its parishes, like the local congregations of other faiths, were invaded by the complacency of the times. Even more unfortunate was the defensive stance forced upon the church by the organized bigotry of the Ku Klux Klan and and the anti-Catholic hostility promoted by the temperance crusade and the campaign for restricting immigration. Drawing all of these impulses to a focus was the bitterly fought national election of 1928,

---

trolled the educational system, and enjoyed many legal immunities. After independence was gained in 1822, a series of Mexican governments sought to divest the church of much of its power and privilege; and with the outbreak of revolution in 1910 an especially bitter struggle began. The most determined persecution was carried out by Plutarco Elías Calles (1924–28), who even promoted the founding of a schismatic church. Catholics, in turn, organized the Liga de Defensa de la Libertad Religiosa, which engaged in boycotts, protests, and propaganda. When Calles moved to crush all resistance, the so-called Christero Rebellion erupted. Father John J. Burke held private discussions with President Calles at Veracruz in the spring of 1928, and a truce of sorts was signed in June of the following year; but hostilities resumed in December 1931. So persistent was Mexican anticlericalism that in 1937 Pius XI promoted the establishment of the Seminario Nacional Pontificio in Montezuma, New Mexico.

Many American Catholics were dismayed by the widespread apathy of their countrymen towards religious persecution in Mexico, and they were particularly alienated by President Roosevelt's refusal to become involved, even though he was given further provocation in 1938 by Mexico's nationalization of the petroleum industry. During the Roosevelt years, when Mexican secularization of education was at its peak, Josephus Daniels, the American ambassador to Mexico (1933–41), became the focus of controversy. Although a devout Methodist who in no way sympathized with Mexico's religious persecution, he provoked the wrath of many Catholics with certain of his statements on education. Daniels did, however, work quietly and effectively for greater religious freedom in Mexico (see E. David Cronon, *Josephus Daniels in Mexico* [Madison, Wis.: University of Wisconsin Press, 1960]).

when the Democratic nomination of Governor Alfred E. Smith of New York dramatized the "religious issue" in politics as no event heretofore had done. Smith at this stage of his career proclaimed a humane, undogmatic liberalism that had grown out of his experience of New York's Lower East Side. He also stated in no uncertain terms how he could, as a Roman Catholic, take the oath and carry out the functions of the presidency as he had already done as governor of New York. Despite bitter and often fiercely bigoted opposition, he drew a large popular vote (40.7 percent), gained more votes than the Democratic party had ever before received, altered the trend set in the Democratic debacle of 1924, and laid important groundwork for the kind of majorities which Franklin Delano Roosevelt would marshal in 1932 and 1936. In this sense Smith played an important role in American Catholic history. He also revealed an important fact about the social liberalism of Ryan, Burke, and the Bishops' Program: that it was not merely the facade of an inevitably reactionary constituency.[13]

The immigration legislation of the 1920s made the decade the end of an epoch for Catholics. Nativism, Al Smith's defeat, and American indifference to anticlericalism in Mexico helped to maintain old Catholic attitudes during the decade. But the 1930s would see a turning of the tide—greater acceptance in public life, more concern in the church for national problems, and the beginning of a long process of adjustment to a situation in which the newly arrived immigrant no longer determined the church's basic stance.

DEPRESSION AND THE NEW DEAL

The New Deal was, in one sense, an enactment of the Bishops' Program; and Catholics contributed much to the electoral majorities of Roosevelt and the congressmen who made the social welfare state an actuality. On the other hand, the fact that Catholics came to constitute about two-thirds of the American union membership accentuated the labor movement's basic conservatism and weakened the advance of socialist ideas. The sympathy shown for laboring people by

[13] Gerhard Lenski's studies in Detroit bear out the view that Catholics tend to support social welfare legislation more than do white Protestants (*The Religious Factor,* pp. 135–42).

both the higher and lower clergy served meanwhile to maintain the goodwill, confidence, and Christian fidelity of the laboring classes far more effectively than has the Roman Catholic church on the Continent, the Anglican church in England, or mainstream Protestantism in the United States. In America the church has continued to draw its clergy and its prelates from the ranks of the working class. In the 1940s Archbishop Cushing of Boston, in an address to the CIO, could report that not a single bishop or archbishop of the American hierarchy was the son of a college graduate.

The Crash and the Great Depression were, of course, the efficient causes of increased popular support for social reform during the 1930s. For Roman Catholics as for other Americans the travail of unemployment and economic collapse stimulated a resurgence of both thought and action. A powerful additional stimulus was provided in 1931 by *Quadragesimo Anno,* the great encyclical on social reconstruction with which Pope Pius XI commemorated the fortieth anniversary of Pope Leo's *Rerum Novarum.* In that very year, in fact, the hierarchy itself petitioned the government to assist the unemployed and to reform American economic life along lines suggested in the Bishops' Report of 1919. One of its first fruits in America was the publication in 1935 by the Social Action Department of the NCWC of a programmatic pamphlet, *Organized Social Justice—An Economic Program for the United States Applying Pius XI's Great Encyclical on Social Life.* Prepared under Father Burke's direction and probably written in large part by Father Ryan, it was signed by 131 other prominent Catholic social thinkers. Ryan called it "the most fundamental, the most comprehensive, and the most progressive publication that has come from a Catholic body since the appearance of the Bishops' Program."[14] Touched off by the Supreme Court's invalidation of the National Industrial Recovery Act, it declared for a constitutional amendment to effect those same purposes. Its objective was a "new economic order," wherein the chaos and violence of the existing system would yield to integration under government auspices along industrial and occupational lines. Lamenting "the inadequate organization of some of the most important social classes," it called for fuller unionization of labor, the expansion of farmer and consumer cooperatives, and some creative way of organizing the urban middle

[14] Abell, *American Catholicism and Social Action,* p. 251.

classes, probably on vocational lines. Over and above these structures, the federal government would function somewhat in the manner suggested by the NRA.

Some Catholic theorists, such as Father Aloysius J. Muench (later bishop of Fargo) and Father Francis J. Haas of Catholic University (later bishop of Grand Rapids), argued that fuller unionization, probably under government auspices, must precede further organization. Haas, indeed, blamed the Depression itself on the fact that only 10 percent of American labor was unionized. Generally speaking, social thought based on the encyclicals tended toward the idea of the corporate state.[15] But the influence of "Encyclical Catholics" was often modified by conservative business interests, pragmatic city politicians, humanitarian reformers, and old-line unionists. By far the most widely known of all the "Encyclical Catholics" was Father Charles E. Coughlin, the "radio priest" of Royal Oak, Michigan, who has already been discussed in connection with the politics of the 1930s. After his break with FDR, however, Coughlin began getting his signals from strange corners of the political universe and ceased to be a Catholic thinker in any significant sense. On election day in 1936 it became evident that his vast radio audience was not a political following.

THE NEW CATHOLICISM

That the situation of the Catholic in American life was changing was indicated by the passing of Coughlin as the nation's great "radio priest" and the ascent of Monsignor Fulton J. Sheen to that role. Sheen had made his mark as a defender of the Thomistic viewpoint in 1925, but not until the 1940s, as the reigning celebrity of "The Catholic Hour," did he

[15] In corporatistic theory the state takes an active role to assure social justice and harmony by organizing and regulating all the major elements of society, including both laborers and employers. Mussolini's reorganization of the Italian social order was frequently seen as exemplary. "It is manifestly in the pontifical teachings," a textbook would declare, "that a Catholic statesman like Salazar, Prime Minister of Portugal, has found the inspiration that made it possible for him to lift up his country from an abyss of confusion and misery, and lead it to order and well-being" (Daniel A. O'Connor, *Catholic Social Doctrine* [Westminster, Md.: Newman Press, 1956], p. 81).

become widely known as a preacher and as an extremely evocative apologist for a total Catholic world view. Claire Booth Luce and Henry Ford II were only the most prominent of the many converts who responded to his boldly expressive yet basically conservative social and theological views. After the war, when Peale and Graham were the popular Protestant voices, Sheen continued to demonstrate that Catholicism had become a live option for many religiously inclined Americans.[16]

Within the church itself there were also stirrings that anticipated not only a time when Catholicism would occupy an undisputed place as one of America's "three great faiths," but when Christians generally would have to redefine their relationships to the secular order. One of the most appealing leaders of this new breed was Dorothy Day (b. 1899). A former Socialist who had become a Catholic, Day set out in 1932 as a journalist and social worker to refute the Communist charge that Catholicism was indifferent to the social aspirations of labor. Her monthly paper, the *Catholic Worker*, first issued in 1933 (appropriately on May Day), soon achieved a phenomenal circulation of over a hundred thousand. She persistently gave papal social doctrines their most liberal, even radical interpretation. Intellectually and spiritually her movement owed much to the personalism of Emmanuel Mounier in France, with its emphasis on individual charity and direct participation, and to the liturgical thought of Virgil Michel, with its accent on the priesthood of all Christians.

Most directly influential was her teacher and collaborator,

16 Fulton John Sheen was born in El Paso, Illinois, in 1895. He was educated in Catholic institutions, and after his ordination in 1919 he completed his education at the Catholic University of America and at Louvain (Ph.D., 1923). Sheen served as a member of the faculty of the Catholic University of America (1926–50), as national director of the Society for Propagation of Faith (1950–67), and as bishop of the Rochester Diocese (1967–69). (He had been consecrated titular Bishop of Caesariana and auxiliary bishop of New York in 1951.) Bishop Sheen achieved his greatest fame as preacher on NCB's popular "Catholic Hour" (1930–52) and on the radio and television program, "Life Is Worth Living" (1951–57). His numerous publications, which have ranged from *God and Intelligence* (1925) to *Guide to Contentment* (1966), have been read by millions of people of all religious faiths.

Peter Maurin (b. 1877), a French expatriate who lived for a social order that would truly recognize the image of God in every person. Convinced of the intrinsic inhumanity of industrial society and accepting the proposals of the English distributists (G. K. Chesterton, Hilaire Belloc, and Eric Gill), he sought in every possible way to mitigate the depersonalizing effects of the factory system. The lay apostolate which the Catholic Worker movement inspired was thus marked by intense sacramental piety, self-abnegation, and prayer. It involved itself directly in the plight of the poor and the unemployed, opening houses of hospitality in thirty cities, founding in 1936 a farming commune, participating in strikes, counteracting the Communists directly with a Christian philosophy of labor, and opposing the reactionary activities of the "Christian Front."[17] The broad program for social reconstruction which Dorothy Day and Peter Maurin inspired would still be a strong but subdued Catholic force in the 1960s, when nuclear testing, race relations, capital punishment, urban problems, and militarism had become national preoccupations.

Closely related to the Catholic Worker group in origin and spirit, though far less hostile to the industrial order itself, was the Association of Catholic Trade Unionists, formed in 1937 with the direct aims of supporting the CIO and the cause of responsible industrial unionism and helping Catholics to function effectively in the labor movement. As this work was augmented by dozens of labor schools which drew upon a wide array of talent for giving systematic instruction, Roman Catholics gained new prominence in the nonpolitical leadership of labor movement.

More broadly influential than either of these labor-oriented movements in giving direction and intellectual force to "liberal Catholicism" in America was the magazine *Commonweal*, which was founded in 1924 by Michael Williams (1877–1950), a layman who guided its policy until 1938, when Edward Skillen and two associates took over its direction. The long-term effect of their broad and vigorously liberal advocacy was to make "Commonweal Catholicism" a meaningful social position.

Like the Catholic Worker movement by which it was much

---

[17] The Christian Front was an alliance of ultraconservative and anti-Semitic elements that had been prominent in Father Coughlin's movement until the Union party's debacle of 1936.

influenced, Commonweal Catholicism found the American economic and social order in many ways unchristian. But Commonweal Catholics rejected the distributists' solution, for they believed that the industrial order could gradually be made compatible with a personalist Christian democracy. Asserting that Christian industrialism had not failed, but had never been tried, Commonweal Catholics found in the papal encyclicals a program which would supplant competition with cooperation by bringing workers and owners into a mutual community of interest. Laborers were to form unions, share in profits, and participate in the management of industries, which were to be decentralized. This approach, it was contended, would escape the twin evils of egoistic individualism and bureaucratic socialism. The attention of Commonweal Catholics, however, was frequently diverted from the full program to the immediate first steps required by it. The focus was on the struggle of indigent groups seeking to unionize rather than on plans to widen the worker's voice in management. The result was often an advocacy not immediately distinguishable from that of non-Catholic liberals, yet *Commonweal's* success in keeping the newly suburbanized church at least somewhat aware of the inadequacies of the nation's social system was no small achievement.

The revitalization of Roman Catholic thought was not restricted to social theory, however. The post-Depression years also witnessed important changes in other areas of concern. Most apparent and perhaps earliest was a long overdue response to the admonition given by Pope Leo XIII in his *Aeterni Patris* (1897) that Saint Thomas Aquinas be taken more seriously as a theological and philosophical norm. Probably no thinkers did more to extend Thomistic influence in America than two Frenchmen, Étienne Gilson (b. 1884), a great scholar of medieval thought, and Jacques Maritain (b. 1882), a prolific convert whose works began to be widely published in America during the 1930s. Both men spent much time lecturing and teaching in the United States and Canada. Fulton J. Sheen also contributed to this movement. Having felt the rejuvenating influence of Neo-Thomism at Louvain, Sheen published in 1925 his *God and Intelligence in Modern Philosophy: A Critical Study in the Light of the Philosophy of Saint Thomas*, with an introduction by G. K. Chesterton, the English convert, who in his own journalistic manner also did much to advance the Thomist cause. Aided by many translations from European theologians and by increasingly mature scholarship at home, Neo-Thomism became a self-conscious and critical tradition, showing far greater sophistication and depth than the scholasticism which had dominated the manuals and handbooks. It also became a philosophic mainstay of Anglo-Catholics; and secular thinkers, too, found it attractive, most notably President Robert M. Hutchins of the University of Chicago, and Mortimer Adler. The so-called Humanist movement in literary criticism led by Professor Irving Babbitt of Harvard also appealed to Saint Thomas and Aristotle as bulwarks against romantic irrationalism.

During and after World War II still other influences, some of which had been gestating for decades and even centuries, began to be felt, among them an accentuation of the realistic and existential dimensions of Thomism such as Maritain had advanced in a moderate form. For others this shift showed itself in a renewed interest in Saint Augustine, or Pascal, or Sören Kierkegaard, or contemporary French thinkers such as Gabriel Marcel and Emmanuel Mounier. Inevitably, too, the profound critique of traditional philosophy carried on by logical positivists, scientific empiricists, and the English analysts introduced a certain caution in the use of language and speculation, especially in those realms where modern physics and historical studies weakened or invalidated the presuppositions of medieval Aristotelianism.

Far more important theologically than this process of philosophical tempering were three less strictly philosophical impulses that began increasingly to be felt: a renewed concern for the Church as the Body of Christ, a revival of biblical studies, and an awakened historical consciousness. The third of these was half-implicit in the second, and the first two were much implicated in what is known, rather ambiguously, as the liturgical movement; but they may advantageously be discussed separately.

The Rediscovery of the Church

To speak of the Church's "rediscovering" itself is, to be sure, only a manner of speaking; what the term designates is a new awareness of the corporate nature of the *ekklesia* (assembly) of God and its status as an organic entity, the Body of Christ, in which men are, in the Pauline phrase, "members one of another." In America, where atomistic or individualistic conceptions of the Church were so widespread (in both Protestantism and in the Roman church), this new emphasis was almost radical. Its most significant modern roots were probably in the thought of the great nineteenth-century German theologian, J. A. Moehler (1796–1838); they were taken up effectively by Karl Adam and given enormous practical significance by the liturgical movement. Especially after the issuance of Pius XII's momentous encyclical on the subject (*Mystici Corporis,* 1943) the movement functioned as a quiet but effective leaven in the practical and intellectual life of the church. One of its most pronounced effects was its promotion of serious concern for the place of the laity. In 1959 Professor Leo R. Ward could say that this new attitude toward the laymen, though "hardly yet out of the baby stage," was, except for the church's emergence from its "ghetto-period," the most important new direction to be observed in contemporary American Catholicism.[18] Ramifying in almost every direction, the "lay apostolate" came increasingly to be felt in social action, retreat centers, interracial relations, and local parishes. Mitigating "spectator attitudes," it was giving the laity a deepened sense of participation in the life and work of the church.

Biblical Renewal

The real or supposed hesitancy of the Roman church to encourage Bible reading by the laity was increasingly put to rest in the twentieth century. The encyclical *Spiritus Paraclitus* of Benedict XV (1920) was one factor, the inevitable effects of the revision of church thinking another; but perhaps most influential was the advocacy and action of men such as Father Pius Parsch, leader of the *Bibelbewegung* in Austria (who made his personal discovery of the life of Jesus and the world of the Bible while a chaplain in World War I). American bishops such as Edwin V. O'Hara of Kansas City, and influential parish priests such as Monsignor Hellriegel of Saint Louis made forthright biblical preaching an important part of their ministry. That this "Bible movement" was paralleled by a revised attitude toward scholarly study of the Scriptures promised even larger consequences. Dating in one

18 Leo Ward, *Catholic Life, U.S.A.: Contemporary Lay Movements* (Saint Louis: Herder & Herder, 1959), p. 7.

sense to an encyclical of Leo XIII in 1893, but gathering new momentum after Pius XII's epoch-making *Divino Afflante Spiritu* of 1943, this scholarly "revolution" rapidly brought Roman Catholic scholars into the midst of the biblical renaissance so prominent in Protestant thought during this period. Not only was a whole range of critical questions opened to research, but biblical theology took its place as a formative factor in Catholic thinking, often giving it a strong "evangelical" spirit and serving simultaneously as an important corrective to scholastic modes of theological expression.

Historical Consciousness

The great nineteenth-century resurgence of interest in history had left Roman Catholics relatively untouched, especially in America. "Modernism" was, to be sure, such a movement, but it had been condemned; and the papal admonition on "Americanism" had made Roman Catholics in the United States doubly wary. After World War II, however, a distinct shift in attitude became evident. It resulted not only in far more serious historical research, but in a heightened awareness of the way in which the past inheres as a vital reality in the present. The renewed appreciation for Cardinal Newman's approach to "the development of Christian doctrine," and the reconsideration of "tradition" which began to emerge from ecumenical discussions were other manifestations. Perhaps most provocative of all was the comprehensive evolutionary theology of Father Pierre Teilhard de Chardin (1881–1955), the great Jesuit paleontologist whose works received widespread attention after his death.

Liturgical Renewal

Infusing the renewed interest in both the laity and the Bible and partaking also of the new historical concern was the many-sided liturgical movement, which began to put its mark on parish life and worship during the 1950s. The origins of this movement are traditionally seen in the efforts of the French Benedictine Abbot of Solesmes, Dom Prosper Guéranger (1805–75), to reappropriate the Church's full liturgical heritage. On the eve of World War I, Abbot Ildefons Herwegen of the German Benedictine Abbey of Maria Laach began the labors which were to make this institution a world center of the movement. Soon after the war the first of Romano Guardini's many works began to appear in Germany. The Augustinian Father Parsch carried on the work in Austria while still others advanced it in Belgium and France.

Since Benedictines were by far the most prominent in this work, it was natural that Saint John's Abbey in Minnesota should become the center of the movement in America. It was there that Father Virgil Michel, after studies in Europe, founded the pioneer organ of the liturgical apostolate in the English-speaking world, *Orate Fratres* (later renamed *Worship*). The Liturgical Press at Saint John's has also provided a steady flow of literature on the subject. Without doubt, however, the most powerful impetus to the renewal of worship stemmed from Pope Pius XII's encyclical *Mediator Dei* (1947), in which the implications of the Church as the Mystical Body of Christ were expounded in liturgical terms.

The liturgical apostolate was an effort to make the total worship (*leitourgia*, service) of the Christian Church a living reality in the believer. This involved an awakening of concern for the world and fellow men, for the corporate reality of the Church, for the biblical sources of faith, for a deeper and more relevant theology, and above all, for the involvement of the laity in a lively and meaningful way. Most centrally, the renewal of liturgical concern was directed toward the Great Prayer of the Church, the Mass, the Holy Eucharist. The need arose not only for intensified study in the seminaries, but for a deepening of the laity's understanding through the publication of English translations of the missal, for the encouragement of congregational participation, for the reconceiving of liturgical ceremony and church architecture to make this possible, for the wider use of the vernacular and preaching in worship, and for the renewal of private devotional life. Another aim was to increase among the faithful the actual reception of Holy Communion rather than mere regularity in attending Mass. Some indication of the movement's impact is provided by the fact that whereas in the 1920s English missals for the laity were being sold only a few thousands per year, during the 1950s the number in use rose to many millions. The real fulfillment of the movement's aims came in the 1960s after the Second Vatican Council made sweeping liturgical reforms. Yet even before that these several trends began to open up channels of conversation between long-separated churches and faiths.

THE NEW AGE OF THE CHURCH

This chapter began by describing a dispirited church: the new immigration was overwhelming its institutional structures, "Americanism" was deflated and liberal thinking intimidated. Yet almost all that followed has dealt with new signs of promise: progressive organizational reform, creative responses to the Depression, and a series of awakenings and renewals led by a generation of impressive thinkers, scholars, and reformers of church life. It is ironic, therefore, that during the later 1950s the church should have been disturbed by the problem of intellectualism: not the excess of it (though voices in high places did complain of this), but the dearth. Through widely disseminated public statements it became known that former president John J. Cavanaugh of Notre Dame, the eminent historian of American Catholicism, John Tracy Ellis, and the Jesuit theologian Gustave Weigel were alarmed by the fact that Catholics were lagging far behind the national average in science, scholarship, and other forms of intellectual leadership. Then in 1958 appeared *The Catholic Dilemma*, by lay sociologist Thomas O'Dea, who had been asked to study the situation. His book not only confirmed the facts, but suggested that the causes lay in long established Catholic patterns of formalism, authoritarianism, clericalism, moralism, and defensiveness. The appearance of his book in the very year in which Pope John XXIII began his memorable pontificate thus illustrates the coincidence of reformist thinking on both sides of the Atlantic.

In 1959 the recently elected pope proclaimed Elizabeth Seton, the American-born convert from the Episcopal church, a "venerable servant of God." He also took occasion to say of the American Catholic church that its "time of development" was past and its "full maturity" at hand. And in the following year Monsignor Ellis made those words the text for a very important essay. The "heroic age" of the American church, he said,

is now a matter of history, and we stand on the threshold of another act in the ceaselessly unfolding drama of the Church's life in this land. . . . Today's world and today's America have a right to expect from the third most numerous body of Catholics in the universal Church . . . a positive contribution to a remedy for the ills that beset them in the atomic age.

Pointing out how unprepared they had been for the social upheavals of the twentieth century, primarily because "Catholic energies had been concentrated on the frantic race to keep ahead of the immigrant flood," Ellis called Catholics to a "realistic and constructive" approach to their responsibilities "within a pluralistic society."[19]

The circumstances that account for the transition which Ellis dramatizes are diverse. Most tangible were the end of the immigrant "flood" and the movement of Catholics into more favorable places in American social and economic life. A corollary to this change was the decline of suspicion and hostility among non-Catholics. Yet there were also the important inner changes that this chapter has touched upon, the several simultaneously developing movements of discovery and renewal which were made more profound by the adversities of war, economic distress, and tumultuous social change. One may even speak of the adversities of affluence. All of these developments were preparing the ground for "Pope John's Revolution." This fact could be only dimly apprehended in 1958 when the elderly John XXIII began his short but illustrious pontificate. Yet as the new pope's profoundly gracious personality began to be manifested, all of these reform movements were enlivened. Just about four centuries after the Council of Trent, the Counter-Reformation epoch in Western Christendom virtually came to an end. Within the church the influence of John's two great encyclicals, *Mater et Magistra* (1961) and *Pacem in Terris* (1963), would combine with the many-sided work of the Second Vatican Council (1962–65) which he convoked. Together they would release responses to the modern world which had been stifled for a century. In the United States hardly a village or city neighborhood failed to experience a transformation of interfaith relationships. The church itself, meanwhile, was shaken by forces of change more powerful and fundamental than those which had been advanced by the Protestant Reformation.

[19] John Tracy Ellis, "American Catholicism in 1960: An Historical Perspective," *American Benedictine Review* 11 (March-June 1960): 1–20.

The remaining chapters of this book all deal with the diverse ways in which the moral and religious life of Americans has been profoundly shaken during the twentieth century, and in a more drastic way since the 1960s. And Roman Catholicism, with the largest single religious constituency in the nation, has been deeply involved in this onrush of modernity. In fact, it has been more severely shaken than any simply because its doctrines, social attitudes, and institutional structures had been progressively rigidified after the Reformation, again after the French Revolution, and still again by the Vatican Council of 1869. With a large independent school system, and with a clergy and teaching force that was for the most part educated all the way to the doctorate within that system, it had separated itself from many general problems. The impact of the Second Vatican Council could not possibly have been gradual and mild, even though it did release much energy and enthusiasm. One may even wonder if many of the bishops at the Council understood the full scope of the transformation they were initiating.

In 1969 when lay journalist John O'Connor reported on his tour of the new movements and the new modes of action and worship that flourished all across the country, he entitled his report *The People versus Rome: Radical Split in the American Church.*[20] He was not exaggerating, for conflict was intense and consternation widespread. Priests and religious were complaining of oppression and demanding their rights—even their right to marry. The laity called for a voice in church affairs, and women, in and out of orders, were asking to be freed from a caste system. Married couples complained about regulations on birth control and abortion imposed by a celibate clergy. Eminent moral theologians, meanwhile, con-

[20] "Rome is under siege again," wrote O'Connor. "Today it is Rome as center of an ecclesiastical establishment that is being besieged. . . . And the assailants are neither Goths, Huns, nor Yanks, but Roman Catholics themselves, priests and laymen, conditioned for too long to a velvet-gloved Renaissance terror, but now determined that the church of their childhood, the church as it is now understood, will in their lifetime be radically renewed. . . . For one camp the church is a movement to fully humanize man as a brother of Jesus in history and the Christ of faith. For the other the church is an institutionalized sanctuary where one can feel alone with God" (*The People versus Rome: Radical Split in the American Church,* pp. ix, xi).

tinued to stress the claims of conscience despite the firm language of the encyclical *Humanae Vitae* (Of Human Life) issued by Pope Paul VI, in 1968. This last-mentioned subject of contention was especially serious in that it was linked to the world's population explosion and hence to ecological issues. Some observers even rank the encyclical's significance with that which excommunicated Martin Luther. Thomas O'Dea in *The Catholic Crisis* made a carefully measured understatement:

> The reception of the encyclical of Pope Paul VI on birth control testifies to the breakdown of two long-standing pillars of popular Roman Catholicism: mistaking fear of sex for spirituality, and mistaking subservience to authority figures for membership in the *laos theou* [people of God].[21]

These controversies became facts of everyday life during the years after 1965, though, of course, not only for Catholics. Less susceptible to wide public discussion but equally revolutionary were corresponding movements in theology and philosophy. The full significance of these difficulties, however, became inseparable from other larger changes, moral, social, and political, that were slowly being felt in the nation as a whole.

[21] Thomas O'Dea, *The Catholic Crisis*, p. vii. For a profound and thorough history of Catholicism and birth control, see John T. Noonan, Jr., *Contraception: A History of Its Treatment by the Catholic Theologians and Canonists.*

60

HARMONIAL RELIGION SINCE THE LATER
NINETEENTH CENTURY

"If we tire of saints," wrote Emerson in his profoundly confessional essay on Emanuel Swedenborg, "Shakespeare is our city of refuge. Yet the instincts presently teach, that the problem of essence must take precedence of all the others." He goes on to quote from a Persian poet: "Go boldly forth, and feast on being's banquet." And with these words he is well prepared to discuss the great Swedish mystic as a Representative Man, the seer whose insights, "take him out of comparison with any other modern writer, and entitle him to a place, vacant for some ages, among the lawgivers of mankind." Emerson also names the great predecessors in this mystic succession: Plato, Potinus, Porphyry, Boehme, Fox, Guion, and others. This list of heroes, to be sure, does not identify a narrow party, but it calls attention to a tradition that enjoyed a powerful revival in the nineteenth century, one with which he emphatically associated himself. And it merits clarification as a major force in modern religion.

Harmonial religion encompasses those forms of piety and belief in which spiritual composure, physical health, and even economic well-being are understood to flow from a person's rapport with the cosmos. Human beatitude and immortality are believed to depend to a great degree on one's being "in tune with the infinite." Specific instances of such religion frequently have very unusual features: charismatic founders, complicated institutional structures, secret doctrines, or elaborate rites and rituals. Despite their distinctive characteristics, however, these religious movements possess a kind of harmonial kinship among themselves. Their fundamental claims involve a persistent reliance on allegedly rational argument, empirical demonstration, and (when applicable) a knowledge of the "secret" meanings of authoritative scriptures.[1] Even those of very recent origin show similarities with the syncretistic religions that were challenging Judaism and Christianity two millennia ago, and many claim an even more ancient lineage.

Despite the problem of definitions and boundary lines, this chapter deals with certain major modes through which this tradition has found expression in America. This is emphatically not done, however, as a concession to a few odd people "who also believed." Harmonial religion as here conceived is a vast and highly diffuse religious impulse that cuts across all the normal lines of religious division. It often shapes the inner meaning of the church life to which people formally commit themselves. As earlier chapters have indicated, some of its motifs probably inform the religious life of most Americans. During the 1960s, moreover, one could note a steady growth in the strength of this general impulse, while those closely related but more esoteric forms of religion discussed in the next chapter seemed to thrive even more vigorously.

THE SCIENCE OF HEALTH

Phineas Parkhurst Quimby (1802–66) was a blacksmith's son born in Lebanon, New Hampshire, who later established himself in Belfast, Maine, as a clockmaker. Though successful in this trade, he began in the early 1830s to be impressed by the psychic dimensions of disease, attended some of New England's earliest demonstrations of "animal magnetism," and later became a traveling mesmerist himself, using an hypnotic subject to make diagnoses and prescriptions.[2] His success in

---

[1] Modern forms of pantheism, for example, generally employ a rationalistic apologetic, as does mysticism in its main tradition. Occultist movements point to empirical evidence such as communications with the dead or fulfilled prognostications. When scriptural support is desired, these movements tend to find allegorical and other secret meanings that "transcend" the literal import of given passages.

[2] Animal magnetism, mesmerism, hypnotism, and somnambulism had, under various names, figured in the history of religion, magic, and occultism long before Mesmer and Puységur began to

healing led him to abandon mesmerism and to search for the "one principle" that would explain such cures. He finally concluded that disease was an error of the mind. After 1859 Quimby lived in Portland, Maine, treating the sick with great success and further developing his theories. His mature thought emphasized that man was a spiritual being, that the wisdom common to all men is God in man, and that the soul, thus, stands in an immediate relation to the divine mind. He was interested in the Bible, used the terms "Christian science" and "science of health," and said his healings were similar to those of Jesus.[3] Yet Quimby would be all but forgotten had he not healed a very remarkable woman in 1862.

Christian Science is one of at least five large and easily differentiated religious movements that bear the stamp "made in America." (Mormonism, Seventh-Day Adventism, Jehovah's Witnesses, and Pentecostalism are the others.) Statistically it is the smallest of these, yet it is the institutionalized part of a huge popular movement involving millions of people who in largely unorganized ways resolve their personal problems through almost the same form of harmonial religion. Because Mary Baker Eddy was for many years a religious seeker of this sort, it is probably more important to trace the troubled course of her long life than the relatively uneventful history of the church she founded.

Mary Morse Baker (Eddy) (1821–1910) was born on a farm in Bow, New Hampshire.[4] She grew up in a relatively pleasant and normal household, but spinal and nervous ailments made her unable to attend school regularly. Yet her

---

control and explain the phenomenon in the later eighteenth century. Charles Poyen had become convinced of its value in 1832 while studying medicine in Paris; and after coming to New England in early 1836, he soon became a leading practitioner and defender of the new "science." In 1837 he published in Boston his *Progress of Animal Magnetism in New England.* The resultant furor naturally stimulated interest in faith healing. (Mary Baker Eddy, for example, regarded animal magnetism as a rival.) In 1899 Sigmund Freud would also gain valuable therapeutic insights from hypnotic work being done in Paris.

[3] Horatio W. Dresser, *History of the New Thought Movement* (New York: Thomas Y. Crowell, 1919), p. 35.

[4] This account of Mrs. Eddy and Christian Science is based in large part on my article, "Mary Baker Eddy," in Edward T. James, ed., *Notable American Women,* 3 vols. (Cambridge, Mass.: Harvard University Press, 1971).

education was not neglected; and by her twelfth year she was writing verse, as she continued to do off and on throughout her life, and pondering matters of life, death, and immortality. Everything we know of her early years makes them an understandable prelude to an adult life of ceaseless search for health, religious certainty, and communion with God on the one hand, and for attention and fame on the other.

In 1836 the family moved to a farm in the more populous town of Sanbornton Bridge, where she became a member of the Congregational church and in 1843 married George Washington Glover, an old friend and neighbor. He died a year later, forcing her back to a frustrating nine years in Sanbornton Bridge as an impoverished and dependent widow. Her nervousness, chronic ailments, and signs of infantilism returned in acute form, especially after the birth of a son in September. Morphine certainly and possibly mesmerism were also resorted to without more than temporary avail. In 1853 she ended her widowhood to begin a miserable twenty years as the wife of Dr. Daniel Patterson, an itinerant dentist. For the next decade her health deteriorated further as they moved from place to place. She departed for Portland as an invalid in October 1862, and after being treated by Quimby, she almost immediately became vigorous enough to climb the 182 steps of the city hall tower. Thereafter she studied with her healer, praising him in print and expounding his theories in public lectures. But in 1866, while living in Lynn, Massachusetts, she received the crushing news of Quimby's death. Hard on this tragedy came the famous incident from which she herself, many years later, would date the birth of Christian Science. She slipped on the ice and hurt her back—but "on the third day," after reading the words of Matthew 9:2, she arose from her bed, healed.

Perhaps in the next few months it came to her that she must carry on in Quimby's place. In any event, at the age of forty-five, she became a woman with a vocation as teacher and healer. The decade 1866–75 was a time of homeless wandering, contention, estrangement, poverty, and intermittent exultation, lived out in a religious and cultic subculture now almost unrecoverable. In 1870 she returned to Lynn and formed a partnership with one Richard Kennedy, whom she had won to her views two years before. "Dr. Kennedy" began practice as a healer while Mrs. Patterson conducted her school.

Although this partnership soon collapsed, Mrs. Patterson seems to have gained from it a clarified sense of mission. She now began to see herself and her theories within the larger vision of a Christian Science church. In 1875, therefore, she bought an unpretentious house in Lynn, which became the "Christian Scientists' Home," and on 6 June she held the first public Christian Science service. In the fall she brought out the first edition of *Science and Health*. A Christian Science Association was formed in 1876, and in 1879 the Church of Christ (Scientist) was formally chartered. In 1881 she obtained a charter for the Massachusetts Metaphysical College. In the same year, following a disruption in her following which climaxed a series of defections and lawsuits, a faithful remnant ordained her as pastor, and a few weeks later, at the age of sixty, she moved her church to Boston. Asa Gilbert Eddy, whom she had married in 1877, helped her in these new ventures until his death in 1882.

Her college soon opened its doors in a house on Columbus Avenue; and by 1889 she would have received perhaps $100,000 in tuition for teaching the lower and higher elements of her science to at least six hundred students. The chief clue to her success was her capacity for transforming run-of-the mill students, the great majority of them women, into dedicated followers who would go out across the nation as practitioners of Christian Science, organizing societies where they could. In 1886, when the National Christian Scientist Association was founded, the church was a nationally significant phenomenon. In 1882 it had consisted of one fractious fifty-member congregation; in 1890, twenty churches, ninety societies, at least 250 practitioners, thirty-three teaching centers, and a journal with a circulation of ten thousand. It was a unique institution, and at its heart was the college on Columbus Avenue with an intense little lady on the lecture platform. Her hold on a rapidly growing constituency was a marvel of the times.

The written word was also a major instrument for propagating Christian Science. In 1883 Mrs. Eddy founded the monthly *Christian Science Journal* to which she contributed regularly until 1889. In 1898 the weekly *Christian Science Sentinel* was added, and in 1908, the great daily newspaper, the *Christian Science Monitor*. *Science and Health*, meanwhile, was not allowed to languish. After the third edition of 1881 new editions appeared with dizzying speed, reaching a total of 382 before her death. By 1891 this personally controlled and very profitable publication had sold 50,000 copies and by 1910, 400,000.

Growth during the decisive decade of the 1880s caused many changes in the church's organizational structure, of which none was more significant than Mrs. Eddy's decision to seclude herself, first to a house on Commonwealth Avenue in Boston, then two years later to "Pleasant View" on the outskirts of Concord, New Hampshire, with a view of the distant hills where she had been born, and finally, in 1908, to a mansion in Brookline, Massachusetts. During the last nineteen years of her life, she was to visit Boston but four times, not even attending the dedication of the Mother Church in January 1895, nor of its vaster "Extension" in June 1906. She concentrated on the long-range problem of creating a fixed and enduring institution, and the result was a sharp concentration of ecclesiastical power. In 1889 Mrs. Eddy surrendered the charter of her college, and in 1892 she "disorganized" the National Christian Science Association. In the meantime, the Boston church itself was reorganized, and Mrs. Eddy gained control through twelve "Charter Members" and twenty "First Members" of her own selection. Christian Scientists everywhere were then invited to apply for membership. The Mother Church thus took the place of the national association. The whole organization was crowned by a self-perpetuating board of directors appointed by Mrs. Eddy. Measures were also taken to limit the independence of branch churches: pastors were replaced by "readers" on three-year terms; while assigned passages from *Science and Health* and the Bible supplanted preaching as the central element of public worship. Unauthorized expositions of the faith were forbidden. Even before 1910 an "authorized" version of Christian Science history was in existence; and since then great quantities of historical source material have been removed from the public domain and sequestered in the church's archives.

During her last years, Mrs. Eddy could claim not only an amazingly devoted following but also wealth, power, and fame. Yet her life was anything but peaceful. As her health declined and attacks of renal calculi grew more frequent, morphine had to be administered at regular intervals. Darkest of all was her continuing dread of malicious animal magnetism (MAM), the destructive streams of telepathic influence which she had dreaded ever since the turbulent 1870s. It now became necessary to have a coterie of students around her to ward off the mental malpractice of real or imagined enemies. Only death brought relief from the pain, insecurity, and lifelong fears. It came on 3 December 1910: "Natural causes—probably pneumonia," said the medical examiner. She was eighty-nine years old. After modest ceremonies she was buried in Mount Auburn Cemetery, Cambridge, Massachusetts. Her estate was valued at well over $2 million, nearly all of which she left to her church. She had made no special provision for the succession of authority, but the board of directors readily assumed control. Mrs. Eddy's desire to have things stay as she left them was in this way gratified.

Besides a church structure, Mrs. Eddy left behind a body of doctrine, which is set forth primarily in *Science and Health with Key to the Scriptures*. She had, like Swedenborg, "discovered the key" which unlocked the previously hidden meaning, the "spiritual sense," of the inspired Word of God. Her book is thus an authoritative interpretation of the Bible. She insisted on the divine origin of her discovery: "the spiritual advent of the advancing idea of God as in Christian Science" was "unquestionably" the Second Coming of Jesus. The basic postulate of Christian Science, variously stated, is that God is All, the only Being, Mind. Man—the real man, not the seeming or "mortal man"—is a divine reflection of God. The so-called objective world of the senses is unreal, or mere "belief." "Matter and death are mortal illusions," as are sin, pain, and disease.

Christian Science, however, was not primarily a philosophy or a theology, but a "science of health." Mrs. Eddy began by training doctors of a sort, and the history of Christian Science down to 1910 can be understood as a continuous effort to explain the phenomenon of healing in specific metaphysical, religious, and biblical terms, and to give ecclesiastical structure to the result. The church appropriately marked the centenary of Mrs. Eddy's "discovery" with a volume of testimonies, *A Century of Christian Science Healing* (1966). In practice Christian Science has also focused on peace, comfort, and success in this life; indeed, worldly affluence is held to "demonstrate" its truth. The idea of God as Love did figure in Mrs. Eddy's thought, but humanitarianism, philanthropy, or social ethics did not have a prominent place.

Christian Science can thus be described only in somewhat paradoxical terms: it can inspire lofty morals and the religious fervency of classic pantheism, yet it more ordinarily manifests itself as a this-worldly, health-oriented immaterialism and as a dogmatic denial of medical and pharmaceutical science, of many public health measures, and hence of a scientific search for knowledge.

At the same time, it must be seen as growing out of a great religious disquietude that was spreading through New England—and the rest of America—during Mrs. Eddy's lifetime. Her dissatisfaction with evangelical revivalism and orthodox dogmatism was shared by the Universalists, Spiritualists, Transcendentalists, and Swedenborgians as well as the mesmerists, faith healers, and health seekers with whom her life was entwined. Even thinkers such as Emerson and William James, who lived in quite a different intellecutal world, shared much of her unrest and developed views that have important similarities to hers. Certain social trends are also relevant. The growth of cities seems to have created new anxieties to which these forms of religion brought a meaningful message. Christian Science and its competitors also gave a religious role to women which American Protestantism had characteristically denied.

Of the many new religious impulses which emerged amid these shifting circumstances, Christian Science was the most clearly defined and best organized. It proved attractive in ever-widening circles, especially to women. Of large American denominations it came to have the highest percentage of urban, female, and adult membership, and probably the greatest wealth per capita. By 1906 the federal religious census showed a membership of 85,717; by 1926, 202,098; by 1936, 268,915.[5] Its size in later periods can only be estimated, but it would appear to have leveled off between .2 percent and .25 percent of the national population. Because of its cultic sobriety and nonemotional concern with health and well-being, its status, character, and size are not likely to change rapidly.

Mrs. Eddy and her message have undoubtedly brought health, serenity, and prosperity to many people. She dramatized a new approach to religion and biblical interpretation,

---

[5] Christian Science has made considerable advances in Great Britain, Australia, New Zealand, Switzerland, and other countries whose social development parallels that of the United States.

and she clearly stimulated much interest in the ministry of healing which the Protestant churches had virtually abandoned, despite its prominence in the New Testament. During the early years of her ministry at least, she performed a great service by reducing the number of Americans who were exposed to an unregulated and largely uneducated medical profession. During a critical age of transition in Western conceptions of body and spirit, physiology and psychology, health and sickness, she and her church also demonstrated the importance of will, mind, and religious faith for personal health and well-being.

Yet the largest significance of Christian Science lies neither in its sensational growth before 1930 nor in the durability of its authoritarian ecclesiastical structure, but in its clear revelation that Americans in large numbers were developing a new kind of religious interest. "A new continent has arisen . . . in the wide world of human thought and life," wrote one observer in 1911, while other writers spoke of a "new age in religion."[6]

NEW THOUGHT

The religious leadership of this "new age" was by no means conceded to Mrs. Eddy. Even while she lived, a strident group of Quimbyites challenged her directly. Both before and after 1910, moreover, many others sponsored parallel movements, criticizing her dogmatism, denouncing the authoritarianism of her church, and expounding modifications of the underlying theory. The term New Thought came to designate this variegated impulse. Besides Quimby, its adherents also honored Charles Poyen, the French mesmerist, Andrew Jackson Davis, the "Poughkeepsie seer" (a healer with Swedenborgian overtones in his message), and many others, including of course, Swedenborg himself. The first effective publicist of these views was Warren Felt Evans (1817–89), a man with New Church ideas who was healed by Quimby in 1863. A year later he championed Swedenborg in *The New Age and Its Messenger,* followed by *The Mental Cure* (1869), *Mental Medicine* (1872) and several other

[6] John Benjamin Anderson, *New Thought: Its Light and Shadows, an Appreciation and a Criticism* (Boston: Sherman, French & Co., 1911), preface.

works. Evans was a thoroughgoing idealist who also showed a considerable interest in occultism and what he called "esoteric Christianity." For a time he maintained a healing sanatorium in Salisbury, Massachusetts. But his greatest distinction, according to the chief historian of the movement, "lies in the fact that he was the first of a long line of exponents of New Thought ideas and methods to set them forth in published book form."[7]

New Thought began to take organized shape in the 1880s when Julius A. Dresser and his wife came to Boston, opened a controversy with Mrs. Eddy on the Quimby question, and began a competitive movement of mental healing. It soon had many followers. The Church of the Higher Life was founded in Boston, while numerous periodicals took up the idea in various places across the country. The term "New Thought" began to win acceptance after 1890 with the founding of a periodical of that name and with the organization of the [Boston] Metaphysical Club in 1895 and the International Metaphysical League four years later.

The movement's basic spirit is suggested by the constitution of the International New Thought Alliance, organized in 1915: "To teach the infinitude of the Supreme One, the Divinity of Man and his Infinite possibilities through the creative power of constructive thinking and obedience to the voice of the Indwelling Presence, which is our source of Inspiration, Power, Health, and Prosperity."

Two years later the alliance published a comprehensive set of "Affirmations" which constitute an almost classic summary of this form of harmonial religion.

We affirm the teaching of Christ that the Kingdom of Heaven belief. . . .

The essence of the New Thought is Truth, and each individual must be loyal to the Truth as he sees it. . . .

We affirm the Good. . . . Man is made in the image of the Good, and evil and pain are but the tests and correctives that appear when his thought does not reflect the full glory of this image.

We affirm health. . . .

We affirm the divine supply. . . . Within us are unused resources of energy and power. . . .

[7] Charles S. Braden, *Spirits in Rebellion: The Rise and Development of New Thought*, p. 92.

We affirm the teaching of Christ that the Kingdom of Heaven is within us, that we are one with the Father, that we should judge not, that we should love one another. . . .
We affirm the new thought of God as Universal Love, Life, Truth and Joy.[8]

On this broad platform a host of preachers, healers, writers, organizers, and publishers took their stand, reaching out into every corner of the land.

People who left the Christian Science church but not the main lines of its teaching were a strong element in the New Thought movement. Many apostates simply continued to practice, teach, and preach on their own; but others founded churches. Augusta Stetson, the leader of an extremely prosperous Christian Science church in New York City until she was excommunicated by Mrs. Eddy in 1909, was among the first of these. Annie C. Bill led another dissenting movement out of Christian Science just after Mrs. Eddy's death. Then in 1929–30 her Parent Church, as it was called, abandoned its old allegiance entirely, and with Mrs. Bill's *Science and Reality* as its textbook, became the Church of the Universal Design.

Another very consequential exile from Christian Science was Emma Curtiss Hopkins, who was for a time editor of Mrs. Eddy's *Journal.* In 1887 she founded her own Christian Science Theological Seminary in Chicago and soon made it a major fountainhead of New Thought. Through a woman she healed, her influence also reached Nona L. Brooks in Colorado, who with two other women founded the Divine Science movement in Denver. Mrs. Hopkins in her old age also had a strong influence on Ernest S. Holmes, who with his brother founded a flourishing Religious Science movement in Los Angeles.

Most successful of all these offshoots was the Unity School of Christianity founded in 1889 in Kansas City, Missouri, by Charles and Myrtle Fillmore, who also received the harmonial message from Mrs. Hopkins. After dedicating themselves to this cause in 1892 they gradually became its major exponents in the Midwest. Their magazine *Thought* (earlier *Christian Science Thought*) was a vital part of an immense publishing enterprise that would claim two million correspondents. The main themes of Unity theology, a modified form of Christian

Science, are expounded in Mr. Fillmore's two widely circulated books *Christian Healing* (1912) and *The Twelve Powers of Man* (1930). Unity does not deny the material world or emphasize self-help so strongly as to jeopardize or inconvenience the lives of its adherents. On the other hand, Fillmore could push his notion of latent human power to the edge of occultism:

> The spiritual ethers are vibrant with energies that, properly released, would give abundant life and health to all God's people. The one and only outlet for all these all-potential, electronic, life-imparting forces existing in the cells of our body, is our mind unified with the Christ mind in prayer.[9]

As this statement suggests, prayer lies at the center of Unity's extensive communications network. The need for prayer attracts potential converts, while an elaborate computerized system which sends out seven hundred thousand answers a year gains and maintains the movement's vast constituency. The Unity School has never stressed institutional development; but even so there are over five hundred local Unity Centers in which "members" hold regular services. Conventions take place annually, and lavish headquarters designed by the founders' son have been built outside Kansas City. Only in a very loose sense, however, could this organization be considered a church or religious body. In 1970 Unity was under the executive management of the founders' grandson, Charles Fillmore, a graduate of the University of Missouri School of Journalism. The emphasis now was on the central institution and the effective maintenance of a system for reaching and helping as many correspondents as possible. Despite turbulent and revolutionary changes in the public's religious outlook, the inward flow of six thousand letters a day indicated that Unity's message still answered the needs of America for peace of mind and inner harmony.

POSITIVE THINKING

As early as 1831 Alexis de Tocqueville had said of American preachers that "it is often difficult to ascertain from their

[9] Quoted by Charles S. Braden, ed., *Varieties of American Religion*, p. 150.

discourses whether the principal object of religion is to procure eternal felicity in the other world or prosperity in this." Even while Tocqueville toured the country, the major exponent of religious self-reliance, Ralph Waldo Emerson, was shaping the Transcendental gospel which he would soon be teaching the nation. The tougher and profounder elements in Emerson's thought make it almost blasphemous to link his name with positive thinking, yet the continuity of popularized Transcendentalism and later expositions of utilitarian piety is unmistakable.[10] William James's writings, too, especially as developed in "The Will to Believe," were also easily vulgarized. They seemed to justify religion on grounds of its personal utility, for its "cash value." His pragmatic apologetic for religion thus became a vital element in the inspirational literature of the twentieth century.

In tracing the lineage of the "positive thinkers," Donald Meyer singles out Dr. George Beard, a New York neurologist, as the pioneer diagnostician of the malaise which had to be cured. Beard's *American Nervousness* (1881) described nervous exhaustion as an inevitable concomitant of industrial society:

> The force in the nervous system . . . is limited; and when new functions are interposed in the circuit . . . there comes a period, sooner or later . . . when the amount of force is insufficient to keep all the lamps actively burning.[11]

Such negative thinking, however, could not prevail in the land of Emerson and James. "Neurasthenic" Americans demanded and received in abundance a more hopeful message. Kate Douglas Wiggin's *Rebecca of Sunnybrook Farm* (1903) and Eleanor Porter's *Pollyanna* (1913) gave optimistic counsel in fictional form, and a vast stream of sentimental novels carried the message to an older audience. Ella Wheeler Wilcox reached into ordinary households with her sentimental stories, novels, poems, and autobiographical writings. "Laugh and the world laughs with you;/ Cry and you cry alone" are undoubtedly her best known lines—and they suggest the tone of her counsel. In the 1920s Émile Coué and his autosug-

---

[10] When *Science and Health* was published in 1875, Emerson's neighbor and fellow spirit Bronson Alcott provided Mary Baker Eddy almost the only positive encouragement she received from a major American intellectual.

[11] See Donald Meyer, *The Positive Thinkers*, chaps. 21–23.

gestive proposals had a brief triumph in America, and in later years the novels of Lloyd C. Douglas had a very similar impact, especially *The Magnificent Obsession* (1929), which as a popular film reached an even wider audience. Other New Thought advocates, meanwhile, provided a more theoretical literature.

The patriarch of the modern health and harmony tradition is Ralph Waldo Trine (1866–1958), whose parents, if indeed they did so christen their son, must be credited with prophetic powers, for no man so successfully adjusted the great Ralph Waldo's message to the needs of troubled Americans. Trine stated the substance of his philosophy and religion most specifically in the two best sellers with which he, in effect, opened his career: *What All the World's A-Seeking, or, The Vital Law of True Life, True Greatness, Power, and Happiness* (1896); and *In Tune with the Infinite, or, Fullness of Peace, Power, and Plenty* (1897). In the latter volume, his "classic," he puts the matter succinctly:

The great central fact of the universe is that Spirit of Infinite Life and Power that is back of all, that animates all, that manifests itself in and through all; that self-existent principle of life from which all has come, and not only from which all has come, but from which all is continually coming. . . . The great central fact in human life . . . is the coming into a conscious, vital realization of our oneness with this Infinite Life, and the opening of ourselves fully to this divine inflow. . . In essence the life of God and the life of man are identically the same, and so are one. They differ not in essence, in quality; they differ in degree.[12]

This "mighty truth," said Trine, "is the golden thread that runs through all religions." The differences between them are laughable absurdities. Buddhists, Jews, and Christians can worship "equally as well" in each other's temples:

Let us not be among the number so dwarfed, so limited, so bigoted as to think that the Infinite God has revealed Himself to one little handful of His children in one little quarter of the globe, and at one particular period of time.[13]

[12] Ralph Waldo Trine, *In Tune with the Infinite* (New York, 1897), pp. 11, 16, 13.
[13] Ibid., pp. 205–07.

Through fifty eventful years, in dozens of books and count-less articles he wrote in this vein, making practical applica-tions of his basic doctrine, showing its resources for personal peace, power, and plenty. Yet he always remained a frank and consistent champion of generic universal religion as the key to these benefits.

Looking about him in 1897, noting the popular reception of his works as well as those of many rivals and, no doubt, aware of the surging expansion of Christian Science during these years, Trine could speak with confidence of the "great spiritual awakening that is so rapidly coming all over the world, the beginnings of which we are so clearly seeing in the closing years of this, and whose ever increasing proposi-tions we are to witness during the early years of the coming century." He then invoked the master spirit of his thought: "How beautiful if Emerson, the illumined one so far in ad-vance of his time, . . . were with us today to witness it all!"

In effect, a new genre of American religious literature had been created—one that by 1960 would have become as com-mon as aspirin. Between 1900 and 1960 writer after writer found himself "in tune with Trine," as did millions of readers. So mighty was the stream of this optimistic inspirational liter-ature, in fact, that it is almost unwise to speak of individual writers; the books seem almost to have written themselves. Yet certain practitioners of inspirational art revealed not only unusual gifts for attracting traders, but developed person-alized varieties of the genre. Especially eminent are Emmet Fox (1886–1951), Glenn Clark (1882–1956), and E. Stan-ley Jones (1884–1973).

Fox was ordained as a minister in the Church of Divine Science, and for years his "congregation" in New York City filled first the old Hippodrome, and later Carnegie Hall. Of the popular writers, Fox stood most clearly in true New Thought tradition, hitting his peak with *The Lord's Prayer* (1932), *The Power of Constructive Thinking* (1932), *The Sermon on the Mount* (1934), and *Make Your Life Worth-while* (1942). His message was that "things are thoughts," evil a false belief, and external reality an "outpicturing of our own minds." He was exceedingly technique-oriented, and given to a vocabulary that was strange to those unacquainted with Christian Science and New Thought literature. The broader interests of Glenn Clark are revealed in such best-selling books as *The Soul's Sincere Desire* (1925); *The*

Lord's Prayer, and Other Talks on Prayer, From the Camp Farthest Out (1932); *I Will Lift Up Mine Eyes* (1937); and *How to Find Health Through Prayer* (1940); though Clark is distinguished by his radical confidence in the mental healing of physical ailments. He even diagnosed the World War I influenza epidemic as due "to a great inflooding of wrong thinking and wrong feeling of entire nations." Jones, an influential Methodist missionary in India, was by no means merely a "inspirationalist," yet such works as *Victorious Living* (1936), *Abundant Living* (1942) and *The Way to Power and Poise* (1949) have proved beyond doubt that liberal theology, deep respect for other world religions (especially modern Hinduism), strong ecumenical interests, and active participation in Methodist church life by no means need keep a man from publishing a large literature on personal peace and power.[14]

Other more practical teachers moved away from devotional themes to a much more explicit, even crass, concern for wealth and success. In this field the prolific Orison Swett Marden (1850–1924) had once been the undisputed leader. While he lived, he was one of the most widely read American writers. His "classic" treatise, *Pushing to the Front: or, Success Under Difficulties* (1894), was translated into twenty-five languages, and his *Success Magazine* attained a phenomenal circulation of nearly a half-million. In 1928 fifty-one of his books were in print. Bruce Barton dealt with the same themes, but Marden was without a true successor until Dale Carnegie's meteoric rise as a teacher of friend-winning and business success.[15]

---

14 Harry Emerson Fosdick's case is similar. Though an eminent churchman and intellectual, several of his most widely sold titles belong in this genre. He, like Jones, took care to keep his counsels within the bounds of Christian theology in its liberal form. Most relevant of Fosdick's many works is *On Being a Real Person* (1943), though his very widely read *Twelve Tests of Character* (1923) and *As I See Religion* (1932) show the continuity of his thought.

15 Born in Maryville, Missouri, Dale Carnegie (1888–1955) was educated first at the State Teachers College at Warrensburg, Missouri, then at the Columbia School of Journalism, the New York University School of Journalism, and the Baltimore School of Commerce and Finance. In 1912 he began to conduct courses in effective speaking and applied psychology, a labor which, during the next thirty-three years, took him into several foreign countries. He became known nationally through his daily syndi-

Applied psychology was yet another very practical interest that for obvious reasons had always flourished in these circles. Indeed, the notion of functional illness had figured strongly in New Thought literature long before depth psychology entered American folkways. The most important pioneers in this field were two clergymen, Dr. Elwood Worcester and Samuel McComb of Emmanuel Episcopal Church in Boston. Recognizing the need to diagnose organic ailments, they associated a board of physicians with their work. Then in 1906, by special worship services, counseling, and pastoral visitation, they began a broad program in which ministers, doctors, and psychotherapists cooperated. With the publication of *Religion and Medicine* in 1908 and other books soon after, the leaders of the Emmanuel movement made their influence nationwide. During the next half-century these not always compatible interests in spiritual healing and psychotherapy became a powerful new element in the pastoral work of many denominations. The "revival" of the 1950s provided an especially favorable climate for such emphases. In the more troubled sixties, the development of "sensitivity training" promoted still another psychotherapeutic revival.

THE PHENOMENON OF PEALE

In terms of sheer capacity for exploiting the many-sided interests of the New Thought tradition, the unrivaled leader in the period after World War II was Norman Vincent Peale (b. 1898). Peale was born into a Methodist parsonage in Ohio, attended Ohio Wesleyan University and the Boston University School of Theology, and conducted increasingly successful pastorates in Methodist churches before being called in 1932 to the Marble Collegiate Church on Fifth Avenue. This move involved a transfer from Methodism to the Dutch Reformed church, but the austere predestinarianism of the Belgic Confession does not seem to have been the attrac-

───────────

cated newspaper column and his radio programs in the 1930s and '40s, but he gained his widest audience through three enormously popular books: *Public Speaking and Influencing Men in Business* (1926), *How to Win Friends and Influence People* (1936), and *How to Stop Worrying and Start Living* (1948). After his death, a large organization carried on his work, and the "Dale Carnegie Course" virtually became an American institution.

tion. Indeed, only in these new surroundings did he begin to test his powers as a prophet of positive thinking. *You Can Win* (1938) was his first major effort, and though its sales were relatively small, its preface gave the clue to his entire message: "Life has a key, and to find that key is to be assured of success in the business of living. . . . To win over the world a man must get hold of some power in his inward or spiritual life which will never let him down." Naming this key, detailing procedures for using it so as to achieve various personal ends, and recounting anecdotes of people who had done so became the highly successful business with which Peale, according to his own rather low estimate, had "reached" thirty million Americans by the mid-1950s.

No medium of communication was overlooked as Peale presented his message in sermons and lectures to crowded assemblies, on the radio, phonograph records, and television. Most important, however, was his use of the printed word: sermons, books, articles in the mass circulation magazines, a newspaper column, testimonies and further articles in his own widely distributed *Guideposts,* booklets, tracts, and even little "How Cards" in which his procedures were tersely summarized for those who read while they run. Probably his most significant audience was reached with his two best sellers: *A Guide to Confident Living* (1948) and, above all, *The Power of Positive Thinking* (1952), which hit the two-million mark during the Eisenhower years. All considered, it was appropriate that the story of Mr. and Mrs. Maurice Flint's great success should appear in Peale's most successful book. This enterprising couple, after being reached by Peale, had built up a successful business marketing "Mustard Seed Remembrancers" to be worn as a kind of charm or amulet, calling to mind the parable of the mustard seed (Matthew 17:20)—from tiny beginnings, large results can flow. Of Peale it could certainly be said that he made very much out of very little. By comparison, Trine was an abstruse philosopher.

Yet the exposition of mind-cure was not Peale's only work. In an external way he took psychiatry seriously, and he collaborated with Dr. Smiley Blanton both in books and in a clinic affiliated with the Marble Church.[16] He was also active in support of conservative political causes. In the fall of 1960, Peale closed out the decade by presiding in New York City

16 See chap. 56, n. 6.

over an ad hoc conference of conservative Protestants who injected an acrid stream of anti-Catholicism into the presidential campaign of John F. Kennedy.

Pealeism, as it spread abroad in the land, was strenuously criticized in many quarters despite the fact that Peale himself was, like Billy Graham, remarkably adept at disarming his potential critics. Theological liberals attacked his accent on techniques and his reactionary social views. Theological conservatives objected to his Pelagian reliance on self-help. Neo-orthodox critics found his optimism fatuous. And all of these critics were embarrassed by the image of Christianity that he conveyed.

At least one immensely popular exponent of religion-in-general who escaped such criticism was Anne Morrow Lindbergh, whose *Gift from the Sea* appeared in 1955. The shells she had gathered by the ebbing and flowing sea became symbols of her themes as she invoked a tradition that was both ancient and modern, Catholic, Protestant, and pagan. As a woman who had borne her share of woe, she brought quiet counsel to Americans—especially women—through a discussion of selfhood, inner growth, and fully personal relationships. She too recognized the threat of the overcharged life, "the *Zerissenheit,* the torn-to-pieces-hood" of modern living. "The space is scribbled on, . . . the time has been filled." She then dwelt upon Rilke's insistence that solitude "is not something that one can take or leave. We *are* solitary . . . even between the closest human beings, infinite distances continue to exist." Yet to her it was that inner space which enables each person to become "a world to oneself" and thus become whole. "Two solitudes will surely have more to give each other than when each was a meager half." "To the possession of the self the way is inward, says Plotinus. The cell of self-knowledge is the stall in which the pilgrim must be reborn, says St. Catherine of Siena." So woman is called to be the pioneer in bringing "extrovert, activist, materialistic Western man . . . [to] realize that the kingdom of heaven is within."[17]

Unlike most of the popular soothsayers, Mrs. Lindbergh, far from deepening the "suburban captivity of the churches," was seeking to release the captives. The immense popularity of her book, moreover, reveals the degree to which Ameri-

[17] *Gift from the Sea* (New York: New American Library, Signet Books, 1957), pp. 23, 56–58, 93–97. See also p. 453 above.

cans have fundamental religious needs that the churches do not answer. When old-time revivalism seemed anachronistic, Neo-orthodoxy too austere, neighborhood parishes too wrapped up in togetherness, and Pealeism too superficial, she provided a thoroughly modern guide to a deeper harmonial current. Evelyn Underhill once said that some men and women run away to God as boys used to run away to sea. And it is well to remember that a long and deep tradition does flow beneath even the most utilitarian perversions. Indeed, Underhill, through her many widely read writings on mysticism, is only one of many who have helped chart the way to the more enduring expressions of the *philosophia perennis*. In 1946 Aldous Huxley served the same end with an excellently conceived and widely read anthology of this great tradition.[18]

But the American who brought the mystical tradition to full expression in a way that won the attention of young and old alike and who reached into the 1960s with surprising force was Thomas Merton (1915–68). Born to artist parents in France, educated in France, at Cambridge and at Columbia University, he became a Catholic in 1938 and entered the Trappist silence of Gethsemani Monastery at Bardstown, Kentucky, in 1941. In many widely read books he then expounded the mystic way, showing not only great learning and philosophical insight, but also a sensitive understanding of contemporary spiritual dilemmas and, what is more unexpected, a deep concern for American social and political problems. Yet it must be added that his best-selling autobiography, *The Seven Storey Mountain* (1948), does much to make Merton's keen sense of relevance less surprising.[19]

[18] Evelyn Underhill, *Mysticism: A Study in the Nature and Development of Man's Spiritual Consciousness,* 12th ed. (Cleveland and New York: World Publishing Company, 1969); Aldous Huxley, *The Perennial Philosophy* (London: Chatto and Windus, 1946). Huxley's opening words define the term: "PHILOSOPHIA PERENNIS—the phrase was coined by Leibniz; but the thing—the metaphysic that recognizes a divine Reality substantial to the world of things and lives and minds; the psychology that finds in the soul something similar to, or even identical with, divine Reality; the ethic that places man's final end in the knowledge of the immanent and transcendent Ground of all being—the thing is immemorial and universal."

[19] Merton's father was a New Zealander, his mother American. His education, in addition to much traveling and reading, in-

In harmonial religion as in so many other traditions, one can thus discern a wide spectrum of ideas ranging from the prudential to the profound. Yet the full richness and variety of this religious current cannot be perceived unless we proceed to consider a parallel stream of esoteric thought which, though equally ancient, has been much rejuvenated in very recent times.

---

cluded an interrupted novitiate as a Franciscan and a period of service with Friendship House (founded by Catherine de Hueck in Harlem during the 1930s), which burned lessons on white oppression and black suffering deep into his consciousness. Among his later works were *Conjectures of a Guilty Bystander* (1966), *Mystics and Zen Masters* (1967), and *Contemplative Prayer* (1969).

61

PIETY FOR THE AGE OF AQUARIUS: THEOSOPHY, OCCULTISM, AND NON-WESTERN RELIGION

On 6 October 1962 a disc by the Beatles—"Love Me Do" and "P.S. I Love You"—first hit the English popularity charts. The date, according to their biographer, is one which "some maintain should be an international celebration, a parade-picnic holiday." Before the decade was out the Beatles were clearly among the world's leading cultural subversives, irreverently, joyously, and pensively filling the air with freedom, exposing social cruelty, asking deeply personal questions. Yet by a strange paradox they were also both leading and reflecting a new religious impulse, not only in their music, but with their lives. One of their press agents said in 1964 that "they are so anti-Christ they shock me, which isn't an easy thing." But four years later, to the great surprise of many, they were gathered by the banks of the Ganges, seeking spiritual peace through the ancient but modernized disciplines of Hindu religion.[1]

This turning away from the religious traditions of the West was a major sign of the times. Simultaneously, the displays of countless novelty shops were providing evidence that a lively religious counterrenaissance was advancing under the sign of Aquarius. A popular revival of astrology was in progress, and with it renewed prestige for the Cabala and the Thrice-Greatest-Hermes. Because all of these interrelated movements are very old, and because America has long provided them a hospitable environment, an historical view is illuminating.

[1] Anthony Scaduto, *The Beatles* (New York: New American Library, 1968), pp. 1–27.

Nineteenth-century scholars and philosophers were understandably obsessed with the problem of classifying religions. Because they invariably found religions to exist in distinct institutional, cultural, and linguistic contexts, they tended to stress the uniqueness of each. Yet scheme after scheme of classification proved unacceptable for reasons John Baillie has suggested:

> The more closely we study these seemingly exclusive and diverse systems and the more intimately we come to understand them from the inside, the more they appear to us as but partially divergent expressions of a common impulse and principle.[2]

So it is with the religious movements discussed in this chapter. They do have much in common with those grouped in the preceding chapter—indeed, the concept of harmonial religion embraces both. Yet a distinction can be made. The impulses now to be considered either explicitly place themselves outside of the Judaeo-Christian tradition, or they claim to absorb the truths of all historical religions. They tend to relate themselves positively to the great Eastern religions. (For this reason the religions of Asian Americans are also considered here.) Despite strong rational and empirical interests, they emphasize esoteric doctrines, astrology, flamboyant symbolism, occult powers, and/or secret organizational structures. Yet time and again one is impressed by similarities to Christian Science and New Thought as well as to many venerable traditions of Christianity and Judaism.

THEOSOPHY

The origins of Western theosophical religion are as obscure as its ramifications over the centuries are diverse. Some Rosicrucians trace their brotherhood to the reign of Thutmose III in ancient Egypt, while Madame Blavatsky considered Lao-Tzu and the Buddha to be relatively late "transmitters" of "the one Primeval, universal wisdom" that she, after "long aeons and ages," was unveiling; and undoubtedly some elements of esoteric religion are very ancient. But a more

[2] John Baillie, *The Interpretation of Religion* (New York: Charles Scribner's Sons, 1928), p. 414.

basic source is the great flowering of Neoplatonic and Gnostic speculation which occurred during the first three Christian centuries, in which the body of writings attributed to the legendary Thrice-Greatest-Hermes (Hermes Trismegistus) holds a central place. This "Hermetic" corpus of syncretistic religious thought has in fact been a great religious and cosmological alternative to Christianity ever since apostolic times. It dealt with all the classic topics: God, the Divine powers, Creation, the ordering of the universe, the nature of the elements, man, soul, sin, salvation, and the symbolic interrelationships of all things. From earliest times even orthodox Christians and Jews have taken it into account, incorporating what they could, denouncing what was unacceptable, and disagreeing as to which was what.

Throughout the Middle Ages this enormously imaginative and unitive view of reality maintained itself. Though constantly held suspect, it provided a lively dialogue with Christian and Judaic orthodoxy. It is the chief Western fountainhead of theosophy, that viewpoint which holds divinity or God to be the decisive and pervading force in the universe, and which makes special mystical insight into the divine nature and its constitutive moments and processes the key to religious, philosophical, and scientific knowledge. This wisdom is given to adepts or initiates by divine illumination or perceived by them due to the operation of higher faculties.[3]

[3] In her "Proem" to *The Secret Doctrine* Madame Blavatsky, in her own distinctive way, sets forth the three basic ideas of theosophy: "(1) An Omnipresent, Eternal, Boundless and Immutable PRINCIPLE, on which all speculation is impossible, since it transcends the power of human conception. . . . (2) The Eternity of the Universe *in toto* as a boundless plane; periodically 'the playground of numberless Universes incessantly manifesting and disappearing, called the 'Manifesting Stars,' and the 'Sparks of Eternity.' . . . The absolute universality of that law of periodicity, of flux and reflux, ebb and flow, which physical science has observed and recorded in all departments of nature. (3) The fundamental identity of all Souls with the Universal Over-Soul, the latter being itself an aspect of the Unknown Root; and the obligatory pilgrimage for every Soul. . . . The pivotal doctrine of the Esoteric Philosophy admits no privileges or special gifts in man, save those won by his own Ego through personal effort and merit throughout a long series of metempsychoses and reincarnations."

An Adept is one "who has reached the power and degree and also the purification which enables him to 'die' in his physical body,

As passed on and elaborated, it constitutes a vast "Secret Tradition" with ramifications into alchemy, astrology, necromancy, magic, and the "black arts" as well as into highly creative forms of theology, philosophy, mysticism, and science.

As a world view the hermetic tradition tended toward an idealistic form of pantheism which saw divine meanings and correspondences in every natural thing and found celestial wisdom in the most outwardly prosaic passages of Scripture. It blended with many forms of mysticism and sometimes inspired or informed whole philosophical systems. The Jewish Cabala, compiled from both Christian and Jewish sources in the later Middle Ages, was a major vehicle for transmitting this heritage to various Christian thinkers. During the age of the Renaissance men like Pico della Mirandola, Paracelsus, and Reuchlin stimulated a veritable "hermetic" and "Cabalistic" revival which was advanced still farther in each succeeding century by both Protestants and Catholics. Jacob Boehme, the Protestant mystic, was a vital link in the tradition; Swedenborg was at least an offshoot from it; and some of the nineteenth century's greatest minds (Schelling, Novalis, Victor Hugo, Balzac, Franz Baader, and Joseph de Maistre) showed deep continuous interest in it. Masonic lodges and other secret fraternal orders often provided an institutional setting. Spiritualism, mesmerism, and faith healing aroused further interest in the spiritual unity of all things and hence in man's latent powers.

In modern times this syncretistic approach to religion inevitably appealed to those who were fascinated or troubled by the increase of knowledge about other world religions. Emerson and his Transcendental friends inspired a revival of serious scholarly study of the Eastern religions. Later in the century, both in Europe and in America, the alluring message of the Hindu and Buddhist scriptures began to be known—

───────────

and *still live and lead a* conscious life in his Astral Body." In the Judaeo-Christian tradition "Enoch is the type of the dual nature of man—spiritual and physical." Theosophists thus prize the biblical book of Jude for recognizing Enoch, and the Fourth Gospel for at least seeming to. Interestingly, theosophists (like Anabaptists) regard the Emperor Constantine as an archvillain; but their complaint is that he throttled "the old religions in favor of the new one, built on their bodies" (H. P. Blavatsky, *The Secret Doctrine*, 3 vols., 3d ed. [New York, 1893–95], 1:42–45, 27, 559–61).

especially after Max Müller's multivolume edition of Eastern scriptures (1875–1901) became available. Not only did "reincarnation," "Karma," and "nirvana" enter the American religious vocabulary, but one or another of the Eastern religions often became a live alternative for those who were dissatisfied with or untouched by the more traditional forms of Judaeo-Christian religion.

Theosophy took shape in America as a specific organized religion in 1875, with the founding of the Theosophical Society in New York, but the wide dispersion of theosophic teaching resulted chiefly from the indefatigable efforts of two remarkable women: Madame Helena Petrovna Blavatsky (1831–91) and Annie Wood Besant (1847–1933). Madame Blavatsky had left her first husband and her native Russia by the time she was twenty, and for the next two decades she was a wanderer. By her own account she visited every continent, including South America. Questions as to what she did during these formative years, and how decorous her behavior was, are much debated; but it is certain that when she appeared in New York in 1872 she had become steeped in esoteric lore and was widely known as a wonderworker and a medium of spiritual communications from the mahatmas. By this time her legendary beauty (which seems to have figured in many amatory adventures) had yielded to a very considerable obesity; yet her charismatic powers in matters esoteric had suffered no diminution. Her apartment soon became a theosophic center, and out of the resulting associations came the decision to unveil and to organize the "secret" theosophic tradition.

An illumination suggesting to Madame Blavatsky that she form an organization like the Rosicrucian or Masonic lodges may have been the occasion. In any event, Colonel Henry S. Olcott (1832–1907), a sometime spiritualist leader of New York City, at her instigation took the formal steps in 1875 and became the first president of the Theosophical Society Brotherhood, with HPB as secretary. Its constitution, as well as HPB's *Key to Theosophy* (1889), states the purpose of modern theosophy: to establish a nucleus of the universal brotherhood of humanity, to promote the study of comparative religion and philosophy, and to make a systematic investigation of the mystic potencies of man and nature. Spiritualism had been a strong interest of Olcott, and up to then of HPB as well; but she soon repudiated its claims in her influential book *Isis Revealed* (1877). In the same work she also expounded the chief new emphasis of modern theosophy—its concern for the Hindu and Buddhist traditions of India and Ceylon—and her belief that direct illumination was received from a hierarchy of Hindu masters of the past and present. It was in response to this Oriental interest that HPB and Colonel Olcott departed for India in 1878, leaving the society's American chapter to flounder without leadership. The two founders maintained the society in India, however, until accusations of fraud led to their departure in 1885. Madame Blavatsky retired in Europe, studying and writing; then in 1888 she published her major work, *The Secret Doctrine,* a vast compendium of theosophic teaching. She remained in Europe and devoted herself to theosophy and the "Blavatsky lodge" or Esoteric Society, leaving the exoteric society and its organizational problems to Colonel Olcott.

After HPB's death in 1891 the movement's second great leader soon moved to the fore. Annie Wood Besant was the daughter of an Anglican priest and a sometime adherent of the Oxford Movement. She had turned to atheism, secularism, feminism, and socialism; and then after becoming interested in spiritualism, had been captivated by Madame Blavatsky and her *Secret Doctrine.* In 1893 Mrs. Besant and a representative of the society from India made a strong impression at the World Parliament of Religions in Chicago, but she returned to India to become head of the society after Olcott's death in 1907. During the next twenty years the society's membership grew to forty thousand, scattered in forty-three different countries, including over seven thousand in the United States, with headquarters in Wheaton, Illinois. During these years Mrs. Besant also strengthened the bond between Hinduism and theosophy and became a significant proponent of Indian nationalism.

In America, however, strong resistance to this oriental emphasis developed. Division followed, with the American group reorganizing itself on a more universal basis. This group, whose headquarters were in Point Loma, California, enjoyed considerable growth under their successive presidents William Q. Judge and Katherine Tingley. In Germany similar resistance developed; and Rudolf Steiner (1861–1925) led most of its Theosophical Society membership into a separate Anthroposophical movement, which he understood as "the Esoteric Movement of the Reformation." As its name suggests, this movement stressed the *natural* accessibility of divine wisdom. Indeed, Goethe was Steiner's hero—and the "Goetheanum" was the name for its central temple, near Basel, Switzerland. Most of Steiner's works appeared in American editions, and his intellectual impact among theosophists was considerable.[4] In Germany this movement achieved a fairly solid institutional base which survived Hitler's efforts to suppress it. There is also a small Anthroposophical movement in America.

Aside from the divided Theosophical Society, still another movement stemmed from Madame Blavatsky's efforts. Oddly enough, its name is the Liberal Catholic Church. Its founders were Charles W. Leadbeater, a longtime associate of Mrs. Besant, and James I. Wedgewood, an English bishop of the Old Catholic Church who, after becoming a convinced theosophist, consecrated Leadbeater as a bishop of this church. His purpose was to give a positive ecclesiastical form to the theosophical impulse.[5] In "Liberal Catholicism" the historic ceremonial and vestments of the church were taken over in detail but given theosophical meanings. The chief substance of its eclectic and extremely tolerant doctrinal stance follows the same pattern. It thus became possible for an "orthodox" theosophist to worship in the precise forms of high Anglo-Catholicism. Bishop George S. Arundale of the Liberal Catholic Church succeeded to the international presidency of the Theosophical Society in 1933; and C. Jinarajadasa (Leadbeater's protégé) succeeded *him* in 1945; but the church and the society remained separate. By that time, however, the theosophical movement in all of its institutional manifestations was losing its force, becoming more a current of thought than an organized religion. The basic ideas of theosophical religion thus flowed far beyond organizational boundaries. Isis had, indeed, been unveiled, and occultism in various forms became the sparetime preoccupation of hundreds of thousands of Americans. Some, as we shall see, were organized in distinctive groups; but very many others pursued

4 See Ernst Boldt, *From Luther to Steiner;* and Steiner's *Theosophy* (New York: Rand-McNally and Co., 1910).

5 The Old Catholic Church was formed by Roman Catholics who dissented from the proclamation of papal infallibility by the Vatican Council of 1869–70. The Liberal Catholic Church, therefore, looks upon the ordination of its clergy as being more clearly in the apostolic succession than that of the Anglicans.

the subject alone, some as passionate believers, others as dabblers and hobbyists, yet all together they constituted a huge reservoir of interest which able organizers could rally.

Aside from the Theosophical Society and its offshoots, there are many other movements that are or claim to be based on the wisdom of the mahatmas. They conceptualize reality in similar terms and offer the same promises of greater personal power, health, and composure to their adherents. The "I Am" movement, founded in 1930 by Guy and Edna Ballard, was certainly not the most impressive or durable of American movements, but it demonstrated the prevalence of a certain kind of religious hunger in the United States, as well as the appeal of theosophic doctrines. Both of the Ballards had had longtime connections with innumerable forms of occultism before Guy Ballard published *Unveiled Mysteries* in 1934, in which he claimed to have received revelations from Saint Germain, the "ascended master" who continuously held the place of honor (along with Jesus, who is also an ascended master) in the writings and public ceremonies of the Ballards.[6] Through excellent organization, press-agentry, and theatrical meetings that filled the largest halls in one city after another, the Ballards may have reached as many as three million people with their message. They organized "classes" of thousands of interested followers. Like Christian Science, their program emphasized healing; like the later New Thought, it stressed the vast powers latent in man by virtue of his unity with Being (I AM) and the aid to be received from ascended cosmic beings. Guy Ballard's death in 1939 and a succession of lawsuits for fraudulent use of the mails brought to an end the sensational success of the movement.[7]

[6] The real Comte de Saint-Germain (1710?–80?), a figure to stir anyone's imagination, was an adventurer in a half-dozen courts of Europe who reached his apogee of influence while in the confidence of Louis XV of France. He was a chemist, alchemist, and wonder worker, the alleged founder of freemasonry, the initiator of Cagliostro thereinto, and an authority on the Secret Tradition. Invocation of his name would ring bells for knowledgeable occultists everywhere.

[7] The notorious Legion of Silver Shirts initially had much the same appeal during the 1930s. William Dudley Pelley (1885–1965) was a Hollywood screen writer and real estate promoter who in a sensational article in the *American Magazine* in March

ROSICRUCIANISM

If poetic justice had prevailed, this chapter on the Secret Tradition would have begun with Rosicrucianism, for that half-legendary fraternity and its possibly nonexistent "founder" constitute ideal material for beginning the history of modern occultism. In 1618 Johan Valentin Andrea (1586–1654), a Lutheran pastor-theologian of Württemberg, obviously fascinated by esoteric lore, published an account of one Christian Rosenkreuz, who had culminated an adventurous life (strongly resembling that of Paracelsus) by founding the Fraternity of the Rose Cross in 1408. Whatever may have been Andrea's purpose, he aroused widespread interest in occultism and provoked a revival of the hermetic tradition, especially among German Protestants of pietistic inclination.

1929 claimed that he had died and been reborn after "seven minutes in Eternity." From then on he became a medium of the wisdom of the mahatmas. Convinced that Hitler was the leader to whom his divine instructions pointed, he shaped his following to very outspoken fascistic and anti-Semitic ends. After legal problems disrupted Pelley's organization, the Ballards drew away many of his adherents. Upon release from prison Pelley resumed his earlier religious interests, and in 1954 he published a message he had allegedly received from Mary Baker Eddy. In an interesting way it affirms the unity of harmonial religion: "What I should like to see achieved is the extension of Christian Science as an earth-study of Matter and Materialisms into realms of the psychically abstruse, if I may use that term. I am not a Spiritist in the popular sense of the term. I am not a therapeutic religious teacher, even. I am a contrite and devout woman who wishes to transfer to my brothers and sisters on the earth-plane an agenda of what I believe to be true in respect to the eternal survival of the human spirit for great and greater performings in flesh and out of it as the age progresses into the Millennia of Beauty" (W. D. Pelley, *Why I Believe the Dead are Alive* [Noblesville, Ind.: Soulcraft Chapels, 1954], p. 285).

The remarkable little movement which Professor Festinger and his associates infiltrated in the 1950s and then described in a brilliant book showed again how a similar set of interests, augmented by the issue of flying saucers, could hold a group together despite great adversities (see Leon Festinger et al., *When Prophecy Fails* [Minneapolis: University of Minnesota Press, 1956]).

Secret lodges were also founded, and after 1750 Rosicrucianism found an important institutional "home" in many of the Masonic lodges.

Rosicrucianism came to America with considerable éclat in 1694 when Johann Kelpius (1673–1708), a student of Jacob Boehme and other sources of hermetic wisdom, arrived from Germany at the head of a party of pietistic millennialists. Their settlement on the Wissahickon Creek near Philadelphia attracted much attention and exerted a strong influence on the surrounding community. The claims of later Rosicrucian leaders of a secret succession of Rosicrucian councils running back to Kelpius can be neither proved nor disproved, but there is no doubt whatever that a fairly lively interest in theosophical and cabalistic doctrines was maintained by private enthusiasts, in the Masonic lodges, among Swedenborgians, and elsewhere, and that a renewal of interest occurred during the nineteenth century. To this end General Ethan Allen Hitchcock (1798–1870) became an especially effective expositor of the serious philosophical and religious views that underlay the occult tradition.[8] One pioneer organizer of this revived interest was R. Swinburne Clymer of Quakertown, Pennsylvania, who published a history of Rosicrucianism in 1902 and then founded the Fraternitatis Rosae Crucis, which has continued to sponsor a considerable literature on the subject. In 1915 another American expositor of the tradition, H. Spencer Lewis, founded the Ancient Mystical Order Rosae Crucis (AMORC) in San Jose, California. Still a third arose in Oceanside, California, through the efforts of Max Heindel, a German follower of Steiner whose elaborate and very widely read tome, *The Rosicrucian Cosmo-Conception; or, Mystic Christianity* (1909; 3d ed., 1911), provides both a major textbook on the tradition and a doctrinal norm for the Rosicrucian Fellowship which he founded. All three of these groups, and several lesser ones, maintain the concept of membership in an "order," "fraternity," or "fellowship"; but

---

[8] Hitchcock was a Vermont-born grandson of Ethan Allen whose half-century of distinguished military service did not prevent wide-ranging research on alchemy and many related subjects (see especially his *Swedenborg, a Hermetic Philosopher . . . with a Chapter Comparing Swedenborg and Spinoza* [1858]). On the Wissahickon Hermits, see Julius F. Sachse, *The German Pietists of Provincial Pennsylvania, 1694–1708.*

they are usually anything but secretive in their efforts to create a constituency. National advertising and the distribution of literature have become major modes of "evangelism."

It is as propagandists for the venerable tradition of theosophical wisdom that Rosicrucians are most significant. In this role they join other theosophical organizations and the broad New Thought impulse in sustaining throughout America a vast amorphous constituency that overlaps other denominations and faiths. Leading Rosicrucian themes are evident in the following passages from *Mastery of Life,* a booklet that AMORC sends free to the inquirer:

> Since we are part of an orderly universe, with its majestic and immutable laws, *above and below,* then there also exists for man as part of this great cosmic scheme, a true purpose in life. By knowing this purpose, by relating it to his existence each day, man discovers himself. He becomes the rightful master of his dominion—this world—and relegates suffering, misery, and ignorance to their proper places—and apart from himself. . . . Those who continuously suffer misfortunes and whose lives are not as progressive or inspiring as they would want them can experience marked changes when [the] cosmic blueprint is followed.[9]

Then with an accent on its rational and scientific character, the booklet partially unveils the ancient Egyptian wisdom on the nature of cosmic law and the hidden powers of man.

COSMIC CONSCIOUSNESS AND THE SCIENCE OF SPIRITUAL MAN

In 1901 Richard Maurice Bucke, a Canadian-born wanderer and self-educated seer, expounded the results of his study of the literature of ecstatic illumination in a large volume entitled *Cosmic Consciousness.* With evidence drawn from Buddha, Jesus, Paul, Boehme, Saint John of the Cross, Balzac, and various unidentified Americans, he delineated the experience of Cosmic Consciousness as a "new plane of existence" that results from an "illumination" of cosmic life

[9] *Mastery of Life* (San Jose, Calif.: Department of Publication, Supreme Grand Lodge of the Ancient and Mystical Order Rosae Crucis, 1965), p. 7.

and order and a sense of immortality.[10] Bucke thus sought, like so many before him, to counteract and absorb scientific materialism in a highly generalized form of mysticism. He does not seem to have founded any organization to perpetuate his teaching, but the ancient impulse he represented was later given institutional form by Dr. Walter Russell (1871–1963), who received his illumination in 1921, and his wife Lao Russell (b. 1904), who received hers in 1946.

With the motto "World Peace through World Balance" the Russells founded their University of Science and Philosophy in 1957 with its headquarters in Swannanoa, a neorenaissance palace in the Virginia Blue Ridge. An important aspect of the university's teaching is indicated in a tribute written by Lao Russell in 1957:

> My husband, Dr. Walter Russell, is a consummate Illuminate. God gave him an innersensory perception which reaches around the entire 360 degrees of the light spectrum. He can "see" within the atom without need of microscope or cyclotron—or within all the stars and nebulae of space without need of telescope or spectroscope. More than that he can see and know the geometry of space and the means by which the invisible universe absolutely controls the visible universe. That means that the riddle of the universe which no man has ever solved, regarding the mystery of the emergence of matter from space, and of its being swallowed by space, is as clear to him as the light of the sun is clear.[11]

In 1926 Walter Russell first presented to the world the two periodic charts of the elements which underlay his cosmological conceptions. This intuitional scientific interest in the natural order, however, is complemented by a more directly religious message that Dr. Russell described in an answering tribute:

> It was [my wife's] destiny to search from early childhood for the illusive secret which alone would free man from

[10] Richard M. Bucke, *Cosmic Consciousness* (Philadelphia: Innes & Sons, 1905), p. 2. On Bucke, see also William James, *Varieties of Religious Experience,* pp. 308–09.

[11] Walter and Lao Russell, *Atomic Suicide?* (Waynesboro, Va.: University of Science and Philosophy, 1957), p. xxv.

his belief in EVIL, which seemingly enslaved. . . . She looked only into the Light of [man's] illumined Soul. And it was there . . . she found the Holy Grail. . . . For behold! all that she found was GOOD—naught but GOOD.[12]

The moral and religious implications of these discoveries were more fully expounded by Lao Russell in her magnum opus of 1953, *God Will Work With You But Not For You:*

The new way of life, which is based upon God-awareness within, is now necessary, else we perish. . . . Your divine immortal Soul is ONE with the Creator of the Universe. . . . You are the spiritual Intelligence of the ONE mind of the Creator of all things, which centers your body as a seat of Consciousness. . . . That is why you eventually become what you think. When you have finally reached the stage of complete unity with your God-Self you will become One with God and lose your desire to manifest individuality. However, this state may be thousands of lives ahead, for it is the Ultimate.[13]

These familiar central doctrines of the harmonial tradition she associates with Emerson and Whitman, who, she says, "were both cosmic conscious Illuminates." More distinctive was the Russells' belief in the coequality of man and woman, caused by a balance of elemental forces based on Dr. Russell's philosophy of nature.

The Russells' outlook is also marked by a fairly strident apocalypticism, which, along with their stand on women's rights, even won them a hearing in the student protest movements of the 1960s. They designated 1960 as "the crucial year" for reversing man's way of life "to serving man instead of preying upon him," and they regarded 1963 as the "point of no return" in this race with time. The white race they considered "on the eve of its downfall" and in need of drastic transformation, despite its persistent belief in itself as the "world master." For instruction in this religious outlook the Russells maintain an extensive and rather expensive home-study course. Adherents in any one locality may be brought in contact with each other by their common religious interests,

[12] Lao Russell, *God Will Work With You But Not For You* (Waynesboro, Va.: Walter Russell Foundation, 1955), p. xi.

[13] Ibid., pp. 13–20.

but there are no organized "churches" to unite the hundreds of thousands who thank the Russells for having given them religious peace in a troubled world.

One of the perennial features of harmonial religion, as we have seen, is its intense interest in Eastern religion. Some scholars of India trace this Western fascination for the light of Asia back to ancient times. Through Plato and the Neoplatonists, they claim an influence on the entire mystical tradition, and thus see the West's modern interest in Hinduism and Buddhism as a kind of religious nostalgia.[14] Be that as it may, American interest in Oriental wisdom has mounted steadily since the days of Transcendentalism. In the twentieth century both Vedanta and Buddhism had not only eloquent expositors but an increasing number of converts. The enormously complex religious history of India, Iran, China, and Japan cannot even be touched upon here, but some channels by which Asia's religions came to America can be at least briefly considered.

Vedanta

Though emigrants from India have moved in large numbers to Africa and British Guiana, very few have come to the United States. Their religions, however, have gained a significant foothold. A very impressive missionary of Hindu religion, the Swami Vivekananda (1862–1902), who came to the World Parliament of Religions in 1893, was a disciple of the great mystic theologian Ramakrishna (1836–86), and the Vedanta Society which he founded in 1897 has continued to maintain centers in many American cities. By its publications and lectures this society has not only created a dedicated constituency, but has given many Americans a larger appreciation of Indian religion generally. The poetry of Rabindra-

[14] The "fundamental truth" of the Upanishadic religion of India on the eve of Buddhism's rise, writes Kenneth K. S. Ch'en, is the doctrine that "Brahma, the inner essence of the universe, is the same *atman*, the inner essence of man" (*Buddhism: The Light of Asia*, pp. 8–9). Here are the key concepts of the harmonial tradition which led so many of its followers to embrace the Hindu logic of future existence and the transmigration of souls.

nath Tagore (1861–1941) also helped to accommodate Vedanta to Western ways of thought. But it was Mohandas Gandhi (1869–1948), the spiritual leader of Indian nationalism, who with unprecedented success made Hindu religion a significant theological and ethical option the world over, but especially in Christian countries. In American Martin Luther King, Jr., underlined Gandhi's significance for the racial justice movement. Aldous Huxley has probably been the most widely read Western advocate of a philosophy which, though not expressly Vedantic, does stress the essential unity of the world's great mystical religions.

Considerably less elevated in its aims is the Self-Realization Fellowship organized in 1914 by another Indian swami, Paramhansa Yogananda. In contrast to the austere Ramakrishna monastery near Laguna Beach, Yogananda's interpretation of Yoga had its institutional center in a former luxury hotel near Los Angeles. Like the Vedanta Society, it posits the essential unity of all religions, but its message has a practical accent on peace, health, and greater personal power. By the 1960s the fellowship claimed two hundred thousand members. No small part of its success and prosperity was due to the efforts and largesse of a Kansas City millionaire who became not only a convert, but the successor of Yogananda.

Transcendental Meditation was the name by which still another wave of American interest in Vedantic wisdom came to be known. Its widespread following was due almost entirely to one remarkable guru, the Maharishi Mashesh Yogi, who belongs to the order of Shankara (or Shankaracharya) and is the leader of the International Meditation Society or Spiritual Regeneration Movement, with headquarters in Rishikesh, Uttar Pradesh, India. The Maharishi continued to hold longer, more advanced classes in Rishikesh, but he made his reputation as the "chief guru of the Western world" by dint of an extraordinarily busy itinerary in Europe and America and by founding hundreds of meditation centers in dozens of countries.

Shankara, the eighth-century philosopher and commentator on the Hindu scriptures, is known for his doctrine of absolute monism: Brahma alone is real; the phenomenal world is mere illusion. He stands, thus, at the opposite extreme from those dualistic and theistic forms of Hindu thought which have often interested ecumenical Christians. The Maharishi claims only to have modernized this ancient philosophy and to have developed modes of meditation that enable people to find the secret of life so that their living can be full and complete. No small part of his success stemmed from his having interested the Beatles in his message and method. That his name was also linked with many other popular figures helped to win him a large following among university students. Yet Transcendental Meditation was by no means limited to the counterculture of a protesting generation. It was simply a modern form of the recourse to Eastern harmonialism. Emerson and Thoreau were among its most distinguished American prophets, but for two thousand years it has been embraced in one form or another by those who found little solace in orthodox forms of the Judaeo-Christian tradition.

Bahá'i

The religion now known as Bahá'i or Bahaism arose within a messianic sect of the Shiite Islam of Iran. It began with the announcement by 'Ali Muhammad (1819–50) that he was a divine messenger, or the Báb (Gate). He then claimed that he was the last successor of Muhammad who would lead the way into the messianic kingdom; but later he declared that he, like Muhammad himself, was a manifestation of God, that the laws of Muhammad's dispensation were abrogated, and that he was the founder of a new religion. During the long period of turmoil that followed the Báb's death, one of his disciples, Husayn 'Ali (1817–92), took the title Bahá'u'lláh (Glory of God), and while exiled at Acre in Turkish-ruled Palestine, won increasing acceptance of his claim to be the one whom God would manifest. He left behind a large body of writings which defined the religious outlook of his following. He was succeeded by his son, 'Abdu'l-Bahá (1844–1921), who had been born on the date designated at the time of the new dispensation. It was he who through lecturing and writing gave most definitive expression to Bahá'i teaching and established it as an independent and worldwide religious movement. After 1921 his grandson, Shoghi Effendi, became the guardian of the faith.

Bahá'i teachings are syncretistic by intention, emphasizing the essential similarity of the great world religions, conceding the inspiration of the prophet or messiah of each, and ostensibly providing only a more perfect indication of the basis or nature of their essential unity. Bahá'i is thus committed to seek rational harmony in religion and the unity of mankind. Its aim is the establishment throughout the world of peace, equality, mutual love, and personal holiness. Its means for achieving a synthesis of world religions are monotheistic, and its basic theology expresses the major themes of Judaism, Christianity, and Islam in a modern, somewhat philosophic mode that deemphasizes the more sharply distinctive features of these religions.

Bahá'i was first brought to America through the World Parliament of Religions in 1893. It gained a significant number of adherents in the Chicago area, which was visited by 'Abdu'l-Bahá in 1908 and again in 1912, when he broke ground in suburban Wilmette for the ambitious nonagonal temple which was finally dedicated in 1953. This temple is projected as a center for educational and welfare institutions as well as a national headquarters. The World Center is in Haifa, Israel. In 1947 Bahá'i membership in the United States was numbered at five thousand; but during the 1960s it has shown marked growth, especially among thoughtful, ethically concerned people who desire a religious affiliation free from dogmatism and the sectarian spirit. In 1969 there were 440 local assemblies in the United States and members in 2,570 cities.

Buddhism

Asia's religious heritage has often come to America through Buddhism—and in a form that reflects the passage of that impulse from India to China and then to Japan. No other "Eastern religion" is maintained in the United States by an ethnic minority so large as that constituted by Japanese-American Buddhists. Dominant among this group is the Jodo Shinshu school founded by Shinran Shonin in the twelfth century and now the most widespread form of Buddhism in Japan. The arrival of two priests in San Francisco in 1898 marks its American beginnings, and by 1970 it had a membership of about one hundred thousand served by eighty active ministers, a publishing house, and magazines in both English and Japanese. Though it is organized on a national basis, nearly three-fourths of its churches are located in the

Pacific coast states.[15] Among America's half-million Japanese as among its quarter-million Chinese, the tendency to Christian affiliation has been very strong. Especially since 1945 ethnic religious commitments have not figured prominently in their self-consciousness as peoples. White antioriental hostility has also markedly waned.

After World War II, and especially during the 1960s, Zen Buddhism began to command the interest of many nonoriental Americans. The reasons for this unmistakable tendency were diverse. A half-articulated countercultural animus undoubtedly accelerated the trend, notably among college students. Yet the so-called Zen boom was not just a protest movement, nor was it just an exotic fad.[16] As many distinguished thinkers came to realize, Zen answered to very important religious needs of a secular age. It was direct, practical, and nonmetaphysical. In the words of one of its most effective Japanese expositors,

> Zen has no God to worship, no ceremonial rites to observe, no future abode to which the dead are destined, and, last of all, Zen has no soul whose welfare is to be looked after by somebody else and whose immortality is a matter of intense concern.[17]

[15] Bishop Kenyru T. Tsuji, *The Buddhist Churches of America* (San Francisco: Buddhist National Headquarters, n.d.). Probably not more than 10 percent of the country's Japanese Americans maintain an active relationship to Buddhism.

[16] William Johnston refers to the "Zen boom" in *The Mysticism of "The Cloud of Unknowing"* (New York: Desclee Co., 1967), p. 12. See also Aelred Graham, *Conversations: Christian and Buddhist;* Heinrich Dumoulin, *A History of Zen Buddhism.*

[17] Daisetz T. Suzuki, *An Introduction to Zen Buddhism,* pp. 35–39. Zen (Chan) Buddhism is usually traced to Bodhidharma, who around A.D. 520 came from India to China, where his teachings were significantly influenced by Taoism. During the twelfth century it became a strong influence in Japan, especially among the military, who found in it a method of self-discipline. In Japan, whence its influence in the West has chiefly stemmed, it tended increasingly to free itself from the complex and otherworldly metaphysics of Indian Buddhism. During the last century this trend toward secularity has accelerated. The object of its discipline, as expressed through seemingly cryptic sayings or stories (*koans*) posed by its teachers, was the experience of enlightenment (*satori*), that is, a new viewpoint for looking into the essence of things (ibid., pp. 88–89).

At the same time, however, Zen is a way of bringing men to know the absolute oneness and allness of God by acquainting them with the real nature of their own minds. Christian theologians and psychoanalytical theorists could enter into meaningful dialogue and find a profound complement to Western mysticism.

Far less demanding and hence far more popular as manifestations of the countercultural spirit were several other ancient religious impulses. Most important, perhaps, both as symptom and as substance, was a sweeping resurgence of astrological interest. Separating dabblers from true believers is impossible, but the existence of over 10,000 full-time and 175,000 part-time astrologers indicates that this most ancient of sciences was exerting a powerful influence on the outlook and life styles of Americans.[18] Quite different in form but similarly popular was a revived interest in spiritualism.[19] Of at least equal significance to either of these was the greatly increased use of LSD and other hallucinogenic drugs and the rise of "psychedelic mysticism." LSD was practically unknown to the public until 1963, when Timothy Leary and Richard Alpert, both psychology professors at Harvard, were discharged for involving students in questionable experiments. In 1966 Leary founded the League for Spiritual Dis-

[18] As the one clearly predictable phenomenon in a mystery-filled universe, the movement of heavenly bodies has always figured prominently in the religious life of mankind. Theosophy and astrology, moreover, have almost always been closely linked. Christianity's swift growth in the Roman Empire is in part explained by the freedom it promised from astrological determinism. The prison-like character of modern technocratic society, on the other hand, conduces to the revival of this determinism, computerized horoscopes included. On the other hand, the Age of Aquarius, calculated from the westward procession of the equinoxes to begin sometime in the twentieth century, is variously interpreted by astrologists to be a time of peace, joy, love, and freedom—which, if true, might, by an interesting irony, bring mankind's release from the fateful power of the stars as well as from man-made tyrannies.

[19] Perhaps the most sensational convert to spiritualism during the 1960s was the Episcopal Bishop James Pike. Spiritual Frontiers Fellowship, founded in 1956 with its offices in Evanston, Illinois, is one of many organizations fostering these interests, but nobody knows how many million Americans take spiritualist claims more or less seriously.

covery and became the drug movement's most famous advocate. By 1970 drugs had become a national concern, and the religious states which some of them could induce had become the experience of thousands, though by that time Leary himself was warning against the use of drugs (aside from marijuana) and urging the disciplines of Eastern religion. Drugs nevertheless continued to be at once a powerful element in the search for religious peace and a path to the destruction of both peace and personhood.[20] For the American Indian, however, the peyote cult gained a special kind of cultural significance.[21]

Lonely housewives and overworked businessmen were as much a part of the harmonial tide as hippies and protesting students. Statistics on these seekers can never be gathered, but the way in which many people are reached by prophets of inner peace is suggested in a simple yet poignant letter

[20] In addition to Leary's league at least two psychedelic churches have been founded: in 1963 the Church of the Awakening in New Mexico, which has a conservative but activistic membership, and the Neo-American Church, which professes a frank "drop out and turn on" otherworldliness (see William Braden, *The Private Sea: LSD and the Search for God,* pp. 90, 174).

[21] The most significant church to stress psychedelic experience arose from the peyote cult of the American Indians. Its immediate background was the powerful and syncretistic Ghost Dance movement led by the prophet Wovoka, a Nevada Paiute who envisioned an apocalyptic return to a kind of Indian golden age. His movement, however, led to the Sioux Outbreak of 1890–91 and a terrible massacre by federal troops. By this time two other prophets of the Southwest, Quanah Parker and John Wilson (both part white), were setting another, more distinctly Christian, pan-Indian movement in motion—one in which peyote had a central sacramental place as a gift of God. As further shaped by former students of Carlisle and Haskell institutes, it became a strong post-tribal and hence "modernizing" impulse. After 1910 it spread widely in the trans-Mississippi region, and in 1918 it was incorporated in Oklahoma as the Native American Church. In 1934 an interstate federation under that name began to be achieved. In 1970 it was "the most influential, most important, and largest Indian religious body, directly involving more Indians than any other pan-Indian group" (Hazel W. Hertzberg, *The Search for an Indian Identity: Modern Pan-Indian Movements,* p. 295).

sent by an elderly lady to the editor of a small Ohio newspaper in 1970:

I hope this letter will help someone.

Our only son was killed in Vietnam in September, 1968. The time since has been very difficult but as Jim wrote from Vietnam when real lonely, "Life is too important to let loneliness get the best of you. That's why we take each day as it comes and make the best of it We must do that for our little grandson.

My mother found help in Rosicrucian teachings, including reincarnation. Since 1950 I have read psychic books. My mother left me her books and many new books are being written by doctors, ministers, psychologists, psychics and many others. Surely God is trying to get some new beliefs to the world since so many people are having psychic experiences. The Bible is full of psychic occurrences. Jeane Dixon is able to read people's thoughts and make future predictions. Many thoughts surely are not for the good of the world.

Recently Jeanne Gardner from Elkins, W.Va., has appeared on TV. A voice has given her information and future predictions since 1961. The proceeds from songs, books and TV appearances are to be used to build a million dollar cathedral for all faiths near Elkins. The voice has given her specifications for this temple. Each part in it will have a meaning to the world.

Lao Russell had a vision of Christ and with her husband Walter sculptured this vision at Swannanoa in Waynesboro, Va., at their University of Science and Philosophy. A home study course and their books are available from there. Both had Cosmic Consciousness (they talked with God), which is very, very rare (That happened to Paul in the Bible.) Walter Russell could do everything. He died not long ago at 92. Lao Russell is younger and lectures and writes to help people know God.

Some ideas from their books follow. Love is Mind (God) and this cannot die—and we are all extensions of that one Great Mind. All knowledge exists. Man is what he thinks, what he desires to be. When man comprehends God's ways and processes and lives them, he has all the power of his Creator. God will work with you but not for you.

I challenge youth to read and study psychic books and see if they can't find a help for our world. Many books are available in paperback. Don't use alcohol and drugs but keep your mind alert so we can be proud of our future leaders. Love one another! Help one another![22]

Not to appreciate the distress exposed in a letter such as this is to miss a fundamental aspect of modern technocratic society. Not to see that the spiritual impulses that sustained this woman were an ascendant aspect of American religion is to overlook a major historical fact.

[22] *Wilmington* (Ohio) *News-Journal*, 22 January 1970. Jeane Dixon (b. 1918) is the Wisconsin-born daughter of well-to-do German immigrants, and a Roman Catholic. She divides her time in Washington, D.C., between a very successful real estate business and well-publicized crystal-ball prophesying. Her predictions showed little more than average prescience, but due to their conservative political slant and persistent religious tone, her great popularity was an important sign of the times (see Ruth Montgomery's highly uncritical account, *The Gift of Prophecy: The Phenomenal Jeane Dixon;* and James Bjornstad, *Twentieth-Century Prophecy: Jeane Dixon and Edgar Cayce*).

Jeanne Gardner (b. 1930) teaches a broad religious message through all available media, including her book *A Grain of Mustard* (New York: Trident Press, 1969), which she summarizes in a sentence: "We have two wills: our will, which leads to nowhere, and God's will, a bumpy, rocky road which leads to peace of mind and happiness." Following the VOICE that first spoke to her mother and then to her, she seeks to build a large cathedral for all faiths near Elkins, West Virginia (quoted from a letter to the author, 15 July 1970).

62

BLACK RELIGION IN THE TWENTIETH CENTURY

The rise of the black churches in the half-century after the Civil War was accompanied by a steady erosion of the nation's will to make the Emancipation Proclamation a meaningful document. The collapse of the Freedman's Bureau, the Compromise of 1877, the Supreme Court's virtual invalidation of the Civil Rights Act in 1883, and President Wilson's extension of racial segregation to the federal civil service in 1913 are milestones on the road away from liberty and equality. The Fourteenth and Fifteenth amendments—and in a sense even the Thirteenth—became dead letters.

The twentieth century has witnessed a double transformation of this history. First of all, the scene was changed by an immense movement of people from southern farm lands to the cities of both the North and the South. Second, the civil rights movement became a more potent force. Around 1900 a more militant mood began to appear in the black community, and within fifty years it had become a decisive factor in the life of the entire country. Each of these trends has had profound consequences for Afro-American religious history.

THE GREAT MIGRATION: NORTHWARD AND CITYWARD

Migration and urbanization have been the major social facts of the twentieth century for Americans generally. But for no part of the population was the change so drastic as for the southern blacks who moved not only to the city but to the North. This migration was chiefly the result of the nationwide growth of industrialism and sweeping technological changes in southern agriculture, with the relative unattractiveness of southern race relations a strong contributing factor. The Negro population in the rural South was, of course, declining even before 1914 (77 percent in 1890; 72 percent in 1900; 66 percent in 1910), but World War I and generally changing employment patterns accelerated the trend. During the Depression the greater availability of public relief in the North introduced still another incentive. The second, third, and fourth decades of the century involved respectively 440,000, 680,000, and 403,000 blacks in the movement northward. World War II and the great economic expansion which followed brought a further increase. Between 1950 and 1960 a million Negroes left the South. By 1965 three-fourths of the black population was living in cities, and about half of it was in the urban North.

This gigantic transformation of location, occupation, and status was, if anything, a more traumatic experience for black Americans than the Civil War and emancipation. One way of life, its social system and economic setting, its moral and spiritual atmosphere, was exchanged for another. Family structures lost the reinforcement provided by familiar neighbors, the local church, and the necessities of domestic agriculture. Despite the constant crushing fact of discrimination, many new possibilities for employment presented themselves, and a new kind of class structure emerged. Black Americans also discovered the scope and variety of American life, though they could obtain few of the means for participation. Since 1900 nearly every new development in black religion has been a corollary of the great migration and the resulting shift of life styles. Even in the South, cities like Montgomery, Little Rock, New Orleans, and Birmingham became the chief arenas of conflict and change.

THE CHANGING SHAPE OF EVANGELICALISM

With a migrant people came a migrant church. The Baptist and Methodistic traditions which had held sway in the old rural situation of the South continued to predominate. Even the storefront and single-residence churches that sprang up on crowded city streets bore these denominational affiliations overwhelmingly. Almost two-thirds of the black church membership continued to be Baptist, and nearly one-third reflected Wesleyan origins. The prevailing piety of the members and the theology of the preachers witnessed to the same continuities. As with the other masses of migrants in America's growing cities, including whites from American rural areas and foreigners from abroad, the Negro strove to preserve and to duplicate the spirit and forms of his traditional religious institutions. Yet inevitably there were changes proportionate to the vast shift of social circumstance. What these former rural folk experienced is perhaps best understood it we consider two very basic trends: secularization and social differentiation.

The term "secularization" has recently undergone profound shifts of meaning, but it is here used to designate some unmistakable city-bred pressures on rural religion. Put simply, twentieth-century city life was not church-centered; the alternative opportunities for diversion, recreation, cultural satisfaction, and social grouping were far more diverse and seductive than in the country. Complex institutions, machines, the mass media including metropolitan newspapers and radio, more varied types of education, and wider ranges of entertainment all served to diminish an otherworldly view of life. In the environment itself the works of man closed out the mysteries of the natural world and the more elemental human confrontations with nature and nature's God. The supernatural lost its immediacy. In this strange new urban world with its hurried tempo and its anonymous crowds, the fixed norms of the older moral order also disintegrated. They appeared now as but one way of life among several others, and they lost their authority.

Nothing illustrates the changed situation better than the way in which jazz and public dancing took America by storm in the twenties. In this realm Negroes played a continuously creative role, greatly enriching American culture in the process. As New Orleans competed with Harlem for primacy, a new kind of popular music emerged, and with it exuberant new forms of dancing and the commercial "ballroom." Indeed, could anything in Harlem vie with the Savoy in its heyday? Ministers and prohibitionists, both black and white, wailed and railed; but with assists from radio and phonograph, jazz "gave the Negro his first victory in America."

Yet there are important bridges connecting "Steal Away to Jesus" with "The Saint Louis Blues." William C. Handy, the "father of the blues"—as well as the son and grandson of black preachers—alternated the publication of spirituals and blues all through his career. A rich background of experience in the small towns of the Mississippi Delta and the big southern and northern cities had taught him that the two genres were related:

> I think rhythm is our middle name. . . . When darktown puts on its new shoes and takes off the brakes, jazz steps in. If it's the New Jerusalem and the River Jordan we're studying, we make the spirituals. . . . In every case the songs come from way down deep. . . . The dove descended on my head just as it descended on the heads of those who got happy at camp meeting. The only difference was that instead of singing about the New Jerusalem my dove began to moan about high-brown women and the men they tied to their apron strings.[1]

Charles Keil points both to a vital spiritual relationship and to the importance of religious institutions when he insists that "every contemporary blues singer, with perhaps a few exceptions, has received his musical socialization in the church and sees little or no conflict between the secular and sacred musical traditions."[2]

As a result of such forces, however, not only did the old folk religion lose its unchallenged claim on people's lives; but that powerful personage in the Negro's "free" past, the folk preacher, experienced a steady decline in his authority. To maintain a semblance of his power he would have to develop his showmanship or his sophistication; but even these strategies could only retard an inexorable process. Secularization, then, may be understood as a general atmospheric aspect of city life that did not conduce to the flourishing of traditional piety.

Social differentiation as the Negro experienced it in the city was, on the other hand, a rather hard objective circumstance. In contrast to the rural South, urban conditions produced a fairly definite class structure, though with rather marked differences among individual cities. The major sociological studies tend to agree in charting the emergence of a

[1] William C. Handy, *Father of the Blues,* ed. Arna Bontemps (New York: Macmillan Co., 1941), pp. 31, 83.
[2] Charles Keil, *Urban Blues* (Chicago: University of Chicago Press, 1966), p. 40.

relatively small upper class (largely professional, well edu-cated, and usually with considerable white ancestry), a some-what larger middle class (skilled laborers, clerical personnel, and salaried government employees of various types), and a very large lower class (unskilled laborers, service employees, and those only partially employed or on welfare). As residen-tial patterns and standards of behavior varied among these classes, so did each class have its characteristic religious affiliations. The upper class tended strongly toward mem-bership in churches of predominantly white denominations, especially the Episcopal, Presbyterian, or Congregational. The Negro middle class also made these affiliations, but remained far more loyal to the independent black denomi-nations, the African Methodist churches, and to a somewhat lesser degree, the Baptist. The individual congregations of these churches differed widely; but those with middle-class orientation tended to become more sedate in their worship, to have better educated ministers, to show a stronger interest in social reform, and to be less strict in enforcing pietistic moral taboos. The highly developed organizational life of most congregations tended to sharpen the status consciousness of nearly everyone.[3]

The more dramatic changes in the black religious tradition occurred among the newer migrants to the city and among the very poor. To them was due the rapid increase of small storefront and residential churches. In the study of Mays and Nicholson (1933) 45 percent of the churches in Detroit and 72 percent of those in Chicago were of this type. Obvious economic factors go far to explain the rise of such churches; but their small size and intimate atmosphere was an impor-tant attraction.[4] Also important was the outlet they provided for imaginative leadership. From apostolic times on through the Middle Ages the Church had provided leadership oppor-tunities for the lowly born. In America, among Protestants and Catholics alike, the clerical role was always an important route to social advancement. Because blacks in the growing urban ghettos had far fewer opportunities to exercise their diverse talents, the institutions of religion became especially important.

[3] See the comparative pyramidal charts in E. Franklin Frazier, *The Negro in the United States,* pp. 293-97.

[4] See Benjamin Elijah Mays and Joseph William Nicholson, *The Negro's Church.*

BLACK PENTECOSTALISM

Between 1906 and 1908 at a church on Azusa Street in Los Angeles occurred the great outpouring of the Spirit from which the twentieth-century revival of Pentecostalism flowed. The pastor of that Apostolic Faith Gospel Mission, whose influence spread across the nation and even abroad, was William J. Seymour, a Negro. Seymour thus personifies a process by which black piety exerted its greatest direct influence on American religious history, for the gift of tongues came during those years to black and white alike. Just as Pentecostal doctrines and church ways answered to the spiritual and social needs of blacks, so did they to other disinherited or suppressed people all over the world, most notably the underprivileged people of Latin America. During the later 1960s yet another Pentecostal revival would come to the United States. In the America of 1908, however, a new religious movement was not likely to remain more than momentarily integrated, and Pentecostalists soon began to organize segregated churches and associations. Given the extraordinary tendency of a "charismatic" movement to develop charismatic leaders, Pentecostalism from the first provided an especially fertile field for sensational and highly independent preachers to develop a distinctive following. As in white Pentecostalism, the gift of tongues conduced to extreme subjectivism. As a result, many Spirit-favored leaders proclaimed themselves to have received special revelations. This often led to the founding, not only of new congregations, but in cases where an effective organizer was at hand, of new sects or denominations. The very tendencies that accentuated radical congregationalism and a powerful laity also provided opportunities for self-proclaimed bishops to develop strong and financially lucrative bases of ecclesiastical power (see pp. 286–94 above).

The resultant situation among black Pentecostalists was chaotic. Yet certain representative bodies merit mention. Probably largest is the Church of God in Christ, founded by Charles H. Mason, a former Baptist who joined the Holiness movement in the 1890s. After participating in the movement in Los Angeles, Mason converted his Holiness congregation in Memphis to Pentecostal views and made it the nucleus of a rapidly expanding circle of churches. In its teaching on doctrine and morals this church stands near the center of normative Pentecostalism. By 1965 its general assembly reported 4,150 churches and nearly 420,000 American members, plus a sizable foreign constituency located largely in Africa and the Caribbean.

The Ethiopian [later, Apostolic] Overcoming Holy Church of God was founded in Alabama in 1916 by a former Methodist, W. T. Phillips. It followed standard Pentecostal lines except that Bishop Phillips retained an unusual degree of authority. He appointed the ministers of the denomination's three hundred churches and even received the tithes of his membership, which had reached seventy-five thousand by 1965.

In addition to these various large, medium, and small organizations there were literally countless independent congregations. Taken as a whole, the black Holiness-Pentecostal impulse probably included a million adherents. It constituted perhaps the most dynamic and socially functional element in black Protestantism; and its strict pietistic moral demands made it a considerable factor in the upward social mobility of its members. On the other hand, as these churches began to have a second generation membership, they tended toward greater sobriety and less otherworldliness in their faith and practice. Such accommodation to the standards of historic evangelicalism, however, led to the continuous founding of new gatherings as the flow of in-migrants continued, or as competition with the city's other attractions required more unrestrained forms of worship. During the later 1960s, however, black militancy was creating an atmosphere which was less favorable to ecstatic and otherworldly forms of religion.

THE FLOWERING OF CULTS

Pentecostalism was by no means the only religious impulse that took institutional form in the urban ghettos. The desperate circumstances of a people so incarcerated also led to far more drastic innovations, in particular, to the founding and development of unusual and sometimes brilliantly organized cults. Whether or not "Jack-leg preachers," sensational "healers," purveyors of spiritualistic frauds, and other types of religious showmen have found more avid constituencies among blacks or whites would be hard to say. Yet the "black

gods of the metropolis" have undoubtedly had a character
and appeal of their own. They have also tended to justify the
disdain that Ira Reid displayed in a widely read and often
quoted article, "Let Us Prey!"

> The whole group is characterized by the machinations of
> impostors who do their work in great style. Bishops with-
> out a diocese, those who heal with divine inspiration, pray-
> ing circles that charge for their services, American Negroes
> turned Jews "over night," theological seminaries conducted
> in the rear of "railroad" apartments, Black Rev. Wm. Sun-
> days, Ph.D., who have escaped the wrath of many commu-
> nities, new denominations built upon the fundamental doc-
> trine of race—all these and even more contribute to the
> prostitution of the church. And there seems to be no end to
> their growth. Already have five new institutions been
> opened for business. One thinks of the much advertised
> cinema production "Hell Bent for Heaven."[5]

Some of the references in this passage are to groups that do
not even pretend to be Christian, yet their charismatic leadership and institutional form link them with many of the
more radical evangelical organizations. The "cult" phenomenon, therefore, deserves separate discussion, even though a
meaningful distinction between sects and cults is notoriously
difficult to establish and maintain. To summarize definitions
made in a previous chapter,[6] one may use the term sect to
designate a restoration or intensification of certain emphases
in an older or larger tradition. The term cult, on the contrary,
refers to more radical departures, often vitually new religions with new doctrines and new grounds for authority,
including new scriptures and even new messiahs. In the Afro-
American tradition cults are important not only for their
direct influence on many people, but also for the light they
shed on the actualities of race in America.

Father Divine

By far the most widely publicized of the black cults was
the Father Divine Peace Mission. This movement serves to

[5] Ira de A. Reid, "Let Us Prey!" *Opportunity* 4 (September
1926): 274–78. See also his *In a Minor Key* (Washington: American Council on Education, 1940).

[6] See pp. 290–92 and 571–77 (in Volume 1).

illustrate the way in which various motifs taken from Holiness, New Thought, Perfectionist, and Adventist movements could be combined with utterly new elements so as to constitute, in effect, a small but distinct religion which could maintain itself even after the founder had "passed." George Baker, later known as Major J. Morgan Divine, and later still as Father Divine, was born on a Savannah River island around 1878–80. He showed religious interests very early, but the decisive turn came when he was about twenty and serving as a part-time Baptist minister in Baltimore. There he met Samuel Morris, an itinerant preacher who declared that he *was* the Father Eternal (1 Cor. 3:16). As Father Jehoviah, Morris founded a church of his own, and then associated George Baker with him as his "Messenger," or second person. In 1908 one Saint John the Vine Hickerson joined them, but the trio soon broke up because of quarrels over their places in the Godhead.

Around 1912 Baker alone gathered a following in Valdosta, Georgia, but three years later he was forced to move north to Brooklyn, then to Sayville, Long Island. Here for twelve years (1919–31), with an evangelism strategy that consisted of offering bountiful chicken dinners free, the movement's popularity increased, while the world wondered how the bounty was paid for. Then in 1931, with the Depression almost at its worst, Baker moved to Harlem, where the Peace Mission enjoyed a decade of expansion. "The part-time hedge-keeper of Baltimore had become a full-time heaven-keeper in New York." After 1941 legal problems required a transfer of Father Divine's residence and headquarters to Philadelphia, but the Peace Mission continued to thrive. When he died in 1965, the major heavens of his kingdom were still in New York and Philadelphia, but there were farms in New York State and other "extensions" in various northern and western cities.

The tenets of the Peace Mission issued chiefly from two sources. Most important was Father Divine's flamboyant personality, his free-flowing prodigality, and his alleged divinity. He was the incarnation of God, whose words, transcribed by secretaries and published in *New Day*, were sacred scripture. Heaven is now on earth; Holy Communion is celebrated at banquets with God himself; the age of the Church and of baptism by water is over. In theory, no hierarchy divided the blessed, except that God's two wives, *seriatim*, held a privileged position. His widow continued to lead the movement after his death as Mother Divine. (Edna Rose Ritchings was a golden blonde of twenty-one whom Father Divine married in 1946, to the consternation of many followers. Born in Vancouver, Canada, she had joined the Peace Mission, and as "Sweet Angel," had become a dedicated Rose Bud in Father Divine's entourage.) As a practical matter, membership of two sorts did evolve in the Peace Mission: an inner circle of those who gave over all their worldly possessions and became a sort of company of heaven entirely at the Father's bounty, and a wider membership of those who continued their worldly occupations.

A vital yet secondary source of Peace Mission teachings were theological principles with marked similarities to New Thought, though they were modified by perfectionist doctrines stemming from the Holiness impulse. Sin, sickness, and death are consequences (and signs) of unfaith; true faith is victorious and holiness is within reach:

> PEACE shall flow like a river [said Father Divine in 1939], and shall continue to extend this way, and sorrow and misery shall no longer be, when you all wholeheartedly accept ME and live exactly according to MY teaching universally. . . . You have to harmonize with ME in opposition to your sense of feeling.[7]

The moral implications of such "harmonizing" were clearly and, according to most observers, effectually laid down:

> One must refrain from stealing, refusing to pay just debts, indulging in liquor in any form, smoking, obscene language, gambling, playing numbers, racial prejudice or hate of any kind, greed, bigotry, selfishness, and lusting after the opposite sex.[8]

[7] Quoted from banquet messages given in Joseph R. Washington, Jr., *Black Religion: The Negro and Christianity in the United States*, pp. 122–25. "Christian Science is the half-truth, and Father Divine is the whole truth," declared one admiring convert (quoted in Sara Harris and Harriet Crittenden, *Father Divine, Holy Husband*, p. 287). These authors also found that most of the devoted members interviewed had a long history of experimenting with Christian Science, Unity, yoga, etc.

[8] Arthur H. Fauset, *Black Gods of the Metropolis: Negro Cults of the Urban North*, p. 64.

Most distinctive among these rules were the prohibitions of racial bigotry (the words "Negro" and "white" were not even to be used) and of lust (dancing, copulation, and marriage were forbidden since they would only increase the amount of misery in the world). Father Divine has been criticized as the sponsor of an essentially escapist movement; yet he did sponsor a Righteous Government Convention in 1936, worked for the election of Mayor LaGuardia and President Eisenhower (not least because Eisenhower had once quoted Father Divine's slogan, "Peace, It's Wonderful"), actively sought to modify racial conflict, and successfully brought order and dignity into the lives of many adherents. Considerably less can be said of a rival cult often compared with the Peace Mission.

Sweet Daddy Grace

The United House of Prayer for All People (Isaiah 56:7) was the creation of Bishop Charles Emmanuel "Sweet Daddy" Grace, who, as his assumed name implied, invested himself with almost as much importance as Father Divine.

> Never mind about God [he said]. Salvation is by Grace only. . . . Grace has given God a vacation, and since God is on His vacation, don't worry Him. . . . If you sin against God, Grace can save you, but if you sin against Grace, God cannot save you.[9]

Grace's origins were humble; as his speech betrayed, he had come from Portugal or the Azores. He alleged himself to be white and often spoke patronizingly of the blacks who were baptized into his church. In 1925 he left a railroad job to begin preaching in the poorest urban districts of the Atlantic states, first in the South, later in the North. Over the years his wealth increased, as did the splendor of his living and the exaltedness of his place in the worship of his congregations as he toured from city to city, maintaining discipline, performing acts of healing, receiving gifts, collecting money, and selling a wide range of wonder-working Daddy Grace commodities.

The basic tenet of the House of Prayer is the sovereign power of its bishop, from whom all blessings flow. But the

[9] Quoted, ibid., p. 26.

blessings (unlike Father Divine's) were intangible: healings on occasion, but more predictably ecstasies of the spirit, various ceremonial honors, and the vicarious pleasures of "sharing" Sweet Daddy's sumptuous life in a mansion-studded realm. What vestiges of Christianity remain suggest an extreme form of Pentecostalism. Worship services consist chiefly of frenzied dancing to very lively instrumental music —catalepsy, jerks, and the award of a white robe being the desired culmination. The House of Prayer demanded of its members only abject obedience and a willingness to part with money; consequently it had very little moral or social impact. Its success seemed to depend on the psychic needs of the more depressed elements of the black ghetto communities and the ability of a charismatic leader to satisfy those needs, in part by providing frequent lively meetings as well as splendid parades, public baptismal services with fire hoses, and monarchical pomp in worship.

The great crisis in the House of Prayer came in 1960 when Daddy Grace died. For a time it appeared that tax litigation and conflicts between rival successors would end the cult's history and disperse its twenty thousand or so followers. After a year or two, however, Bishop Walter McCollough succeeded in extending its life, and in 1969 he dedicated a splendid new headquarters with an adjacent old people's home in Washington, D.C. At the national conclave there in 1969 a great parade and fire-hose baptisms in the street indicated that the church continued to win a lively following. Yet by this time the changing temper of the ghetto and the rise of black militancy were subjecting such forms of religious organization to increasingly severe criticism. Extensive future growth seemed improbable unless considerable changes in spirit and practice were effected.[10]

[10] At the time of Daddy Grace's death on 12 January 1960, the newspapers reported the membership of the House of Prayer as from three to six million; but Marvin A. Eisengart doubts that there were more than 25,000 regular members ("The House of Prayer" [Scholar of the House essay, Yale University, 1962]). Walter McCollough, who had joined the House of Prayer in 1930 at the age of fifteen, was in 1956 appointed by Daddy Grace as the pastor of the mother House of Prayer in Washington, D.C. At a meeting of the General Assembly on 6 February 1960, he was elected bishop, but Elder John McClure challenged the legitimacy of the election and declared himself bishop—a claim which he pressed for more than a year (see Eisengart, pp. 29–30).

Cults such as the Peace Mission and the House of Prayer are unusual chiefly for their relative success and extreme individuality; but similar groups, often ephemeral and local, are constantly arising whenever some leader with the necessary gifts gathers a following. Some of them, but for their unusually charismatic leadership or extreme emphasis on faith healing, might be regarded simply as Holiness or Pentecostal churches. Like all such manifestations, white or black, they tap large reservoirs of human insecurity and anxiety. Yet students of black religion tend to stress three particular factors: their appeal to the special frustrations of the poorest and most culturally deprived elements in the ghetto; their response to the need of the more recent in-migrants for small, intimate contexts where the full range of feeling can find expression; and finally, their provision of a realm in which natural leaders can exercise organizational and entrepreneurial skills without white hindrance or competition.

Until or unless profound social changes occur, so that the energies and aspirations of urban blacks can find more meaningful expression, the cults (and kindred Christian movements) will no doubt continue to find many devoted adherents. The future of larger independent churches, however, as well as that of the rapidly growing Holiness-Pentecostal sects, depends on the larger question of the continued strength of Christian commitment in the black community as a whole. Since World War II problems of race relations and urban existence have become so intense that this question cannot even be addressed without prior consideration of the protest movement, which during the 1960s put the whole question of black religion in a new perspective. And mediating between the realm of cultic religion and the protest movement was the "protest cult" itself.

BLACK NATIONALISM AND THE BLACK MUSLIMS

The Nation of Islam, to give the Black Muslims their proper name, belongs in a class by itself among black religious movements. Not only has it been unusually successful in combining an appeal to blackness with an affirmation of Islam, but more than any other cultic religious movement it became a potent, even seminal, element in the rising protest movement. Its complex history, however, is so hidden from public view that it may never be entirely freed of confusion and controversy.

In its present form the Nation of Islam stems from two converging lines of influence. One of these can be traced to the "African dream" of Bishop Henry Turner, as well as to the later efforts of Marcus Garvey (1887–1940), a Jamaican who in 1914 founded a Universal Negro Improvement Association and African Communities League, with the motto "One God! One Aim! One Destiny!" Garvey's aim was to awaken the self-esteem of blacks everywhere and to redeem Africa for all Africans at home and abroad. Between 1916 and 1923 he recruited members in the United States with phenomenal success, using every means at his command, from flashy military parades to an extensive network of cooperative business ventures. His measures even included the organization of an African Orthodox church, with a militant Episcopal priest, George Alexander McGuire, being consecrated as its bishop by Archbishop Vilatte of the Syrian Orthodox church. McGuire bade the faithful to "forget the white Gods" and provided them with pictures of a black Madonna and Child.[11] Garvey meanwhile concentrated on more tangible objectives, and at a convention in 1920 he was elected the provisional president of Africa. Numerous frauds led to his deportation in 1927, yet far more effectively than earlier colonizationists, he had awakened the spirit of African nationalism among the urban masses. Like the organizations and churches of many ethnic minorities, Garvey's also contributed powerfully to the self-respect and group-consciousness of his followers and in the process exposed the degree to which many Afro-Americans were alienated from the white culture around them. After he had demonstrated the potentialities of this appeal, countless smaller movements, some more esoteric than others, most of them with strong religious overtones, stressed Ethiopian, Abyssinian, or more generally African themes. It is not surprising, therefore, that Black Muslims recognize Garvey as a forerunner in black nationalism.

More direct links seem to exist between the Black Muslims

11 See E. David Cronon, *Black Moses: The Story of Marcus Garvey and the Universal Negro Improvement Association.* In 1960 the African Orthodox church still had a membership of about seven thousand (C. Eric Lincoln, *The Black Muslims in America,* p. 65).

and the Moorish Science Temple of America, though they are by no means clear or undisputed. Its founder was a North Carolinian named Timothy Drew (1866–1929), who had somehow developed an interest in Islamic religion and become convinced that American "Negroes" should abandon that name and declare their "Asiatic" origins as Moors or Moorish Americans. To advance these interests he took the name Noble Prophet Ali Drew (Noble Drew Ali) and published *The Holy Koran,* a small pamphlet containing Islamic, Christian, and Garveyite passages along with his own interpretations. The basic message has had far-reaching implications, for it departed from Garvey's form of black nationalism in its insistence that the designations Negro, colored, Ethiopian, etc., be abandoned, that an Asiatic or Moorish identity be affirmed, and that the self-defeating life styles of the back subculture be abandoned. For those who took this new allegiance, salvation and self-respect were assured. The first Moorish Science Temple was founded in Newark in 1913, and others were planted elsewhere. In Chicago the movement flourished best, but with success came factionalism and violence. In 1929 one of Drew's major deputies was murdered, and shortly thereafter the prophet himself was killed. The Moorish Temple continued, however, and thirty years later his followers still maintained an expectant vigil at his grave in Lincoln Cemetery, Chicago.[12]

After Drew's death, a struggle for the succession to leadership and a splintering of the movement ensued. Among the claimants was Wallace D. Fard (or Wali Farad Muhammad), who began to gather a following in Detroit in 1930. Claiming (it is said) to be a reincarnation of Drew and a sometime visitor in Mecca, he preached a message very similar to that of Noble Drew Ali, founded a Temple of Islam in Detroit with possibly eight thousand members, and then a second in Chicago, where his most trusted lieutenant took charge. Farad's mysterious disappearance in 1934 opened another period of very slow growth. But amid the contention among rival elements of the black Islamic impulse, the leader

[12] The Church of God (Black Jews), founded in Philadelphia by the Southern-born prophet F. S. Cherry, holds Adam, Jacob, and Jesus to have been black. Its cultic sobriety, moral teachings, and use of a Semitic language and scriptures resemble various Moorish and Islamic movements (see Fauset, *Black Gods,* chap. 4).

of Temple Number Two in Chicago gradually became dominant. He was Robert Poole (b. 1897), the son of a Baptist minister in Georgia, who had taken the name Elijah Muhammad. Having led the faction ascribing the most exalted status to the departed Farad, he now became the movement's leader, though the founding of Detroit's Temple Number One in 1931 was still accepted as the movement's beginning and Farad's birthday, 26 February, was in due course appointed as Saviour's Day.

Elijah Muhammad's authority rested on a unique claim that the will of Allah himself had been communicated to him and published in *The Supreme Wisdom* and successive issues of *Muhammad Speaks.* According to these teachings the Negroes of North America (the Black Nation) are to be led into their true inheritance as members of the ancient tribe of Shabazz, which looks to Abraham as its patriarch and to which all the world's nonwhite peoples belong. They will be led by the Nation of Islam, the followers of Elijah Muhammad. Caucasian people are an inferior, latter-day offshoot of the Black Asiatic Nation. The American Negro's self-hate (his negative estimate of blackness) is thus replaced by a strong sense of triumphant peoplehood. Black Muslim eschatology teaches that God has come; there is no life after this life; heaven and hell are only two contrasting earthly conditions; the hereafter (which will begin to appear about A.D. 2000) is but the end of the present "spook" civilization of the Caucasian usurpers, including the Christian religion. It will be followed by the redemption of the Black Nation and their glorious rule over all the earth.

Because of his refusal to kill on any orders but Allah's, Elijah Muhammad and a number of followers went to prison during World War II, while the movement languished—except behind bars, where it has always recruited effectively. The Nation of Islam, therefore, dates in a practical way to 1946, when Elijah Muhammad resumed leadership of a membership that had fallen to a thousand or less. In the changed atmosphere of the later 1950s the Black Muslims' outspoken message began to gain a new kind of relevance. Official membership statistics are not released, but responsible estimates made around 1960 spoke of a hundred thousand disciplined, relatively young, and predominantly male followers of whom was expected unquestioning obedience to the Messenger of Allah, regular attendance at meetings, and at least a tithe in money. Affiliated with the Chicago temple were many small business enterprises and the University of Islam, which provided a complete education through high school and beyond. Plans were projected for a major Islamic center and the acquisition of extensive farmlands.

The man who most effectively brought this message to the black multitudes of the urban ghettos and to the world at large was Malcolm X (1925–65). Malcolm Little was born in Omaha, Nebraska, the son of a Baptist preacher who had supported Marcus Garvey. He spent most of his youth in Michigan, but he really discovered the black community only after completing the eighth grade and moving to the Boston area. He went to prison on a burglary charge in 1946. While he was in prison the Muslim's message came to him as a veritable gospel, and for over a decade after his release in 1952 he was an untiring apostle of the movement in New York and across the nation. Then in March 1964 he left the Black Muslims, founding first the Muslim Mosque, Incorporated, and later the nonreligious Organization of Afro-American Unity, both of which aimed to awaken and unify the movement for black liberation. He was assassinated in New York on 21 February 1965, but through his posthumously published autobiography and speeches he continued to be one of the decade's most prophetic voices.[13]

The appeal and importance of the Black Muslims, according to E. U. Essien-Udom, depends not so much on their "esoteric" doctrines and cultic practices as on their "exoteric" moral and social teachings, especially their rigorous standards of personal behavior, family responsibility, and occupational stability.[14] Robert Vernon made a related point five years

13 See *The Autobiography of Malcolm X* and *Malcolm X Speaks,* ed. George Breitman.

14 *Black Nationalism* (Chicago: University of Chicago Press, 1962). Its prohibitions of alcohol, narcotics, and sexual profligacy, like its demands of respect for womanhood in the context of a strong patriarchal family, of occupational responsibility, and of quiet, decorous behavior, are precisely those of the traditional Puritan-American mainstream. Black Muslims are thus summoned to the moral standards of the Caucasian devils; in this sense it is a "cultural sect" calling Negroes out of their subculture.

The relations of Black Muslims with traditional Islam are controversial. Many followers of the original Muhammad (A.D. 570–632), a large proportion of whom are Caucasian, insist that the racism of the Black Muslims as well as their leader's claim to

later:

> So long as the movement had meaning to the ghetto poor
> in terms of their own experiences, and provided psycho-
> logical and material therapy against the ravages of a white-
> dominated hell called America, the religion could have
> been Black Buddhism or Black Brahmanism or Black Any-
> thing with equal effect.[15]

The growth of the movement thus testifies to the alienation
and despair bred by America's racial discrimination. In this
sense the Black Muslims are a kind of bridge between the escapist cults and the main tradition of black militancy. In
theory, the movement offers a message of deliverance for
blacks the world over; in reality, it is an island of disciplined
security that is at once radical and bourgeois. Whether the
esoteric features of the Black Muslims will survive the death
of the movement's charismatic leader or whether the movement will move toward the social-political goals that Malcolm
X advocated during his last days remains to be seen. Crucial
to the denouement will be the protest movement on whose
success not only black religion but the future of American democracy may be said to depend.

THE RISE OF THE PROTEST MOVEMENT

On 4 July 1881 Booker T. Washington called to order
Tuskegee Institute's first class in a battered AME Zion
church. Only three years later he addressed the National Ed-

---

authority contradict the basic nature of this most widely propagated
and most interracial of world religions. Yet certain Arab leaders
have shown some deference to Black Muslim leaders and their
University of Islam in Chicago. On the other hand, Malcolm X's
personal experience of the Islam of Mecca itself seems to have
alienated him from the Chicago version (see *The Autobiography
of Malcolm X*, pp. 323–88).

[15] Robert Vernon, "Malcolm X: Voice of the Black Ghetto,"
International Socialist Review (Spring 1965); quoted in George
Breitman, *The Last Year of Malcolm X: The Evolution of a Revolutionary* (New York: Merit Publishers, 1967), p. 7. This does
not mean, of course, that Malcolm's conversion, like any number
of others, did not have a deep religious dimension.

ucation Association on "The Educational Outlook in the South," and from that time until his death he was the chief American spokesman for the Negro. His most celebrated statement was made in 1895 at the Atlanta Exposition, where he bade the whites of the New South "Cast down your bucket where you are":

> Cast it down among the eight millions of Negroes whose habits you know, whose fidelity and love you have tested in days when to have proved treacherous meant the ruin of your firesides. . . . While doing this you can be assured in the future as in the past that you and your families will be surrounded by the most patient, faithful, law-abiding, and unresentful people the world has seen. . . . In all things that are purely social we can be as separate as the fingers, yet one as the hand in all things essential to mutual progress.[16]

Accepting political inequality and social segregation (though not the denial of constitutional rights), he pleaded to all men everywhere to help make the Negro a trained, literate, and useful component of the new society. Though no churchman himself, he thus accepted and strengthened the arrangements which nearly all of the major Negro denominations and sects, including their educational leaders, then accepted—and which they by and large continued to accept down to World War II, and even after.

Ever since the days of the antislavery crusade, however, there have been men and women, black and white, who took a more radical view; and during the racial-justice nadir of the Progressive Era the first important challenge to the Washingtonian view of things came from W. E. Burghardt DuBois (1868–1963), a Massachusetts-born Harvard Ph.D. who had become a professor of sociology at Atlanta University in 1897. In *The Souls of Black Folk* (1903) DuBois condemned the "Atlanta Compromise" and the whole notion that the pre-Civil War strategy of the free Negroes should now be changed "from a by-path into a veritable Way of Life." He saw, too, that religion was a fundamental part of this way of life, and in the same year published *The Negro Church,* the

[16] Given in full in August Meier et al., eds., *Black Protest Thought in the Twentieth Century,* pp. 3–8.

first scholarly work in the field. Except for his heavy emphasis on the need for liberal (as against technical) education and his emphasis on the leadership role of the "Talented Tenth," his words and ideas strike a trenchant contemporary note even a half-century later. Besides leading the anti-Bookerite "Niagara Movement," DuBois also helped to found the National Association for the Advancement of Colored People in 1909. As the only Negro on the national staff, he became editor of its magazine, the *Crisis*.

By 1915 DuBois had repudiated the notion that "God or his vice-gerent the White Man" should define the Negro's goals, and was seeking to awaken the self-consciousness of the Negro masses. In this sense he was frankly a "race man"; and in 1934 he broke with the NAACP by taking a position on the "segregation issue" which was then held by only a small black minority and almost no whites:

> There should never be an opposition to segregation pure and simple unless that segregation does involve discrimination. . . . Never in the world should our fight be against association with ourselves, because by that very token we give up the whole argument that we are worth associating with.[17]

During the next three decades the court battles of the NAACP brought considerable progress in the realms of integration, civil rights, and economic opportunity. World War II, to be sure, was fought by an utterly segregated army and navy, but the efforts of Adam Clayton Powell, Jr., in Harlem, a new wave of organized protest, and a series of urban riots had significant effects.[18] In 1949 two executive orders of President Truman integrating the armed services and the federal civil service achieved some of the most decisive reforms since the Reconstruction amendments were passed. Then in 1954 the Supreme Court culminated a long series of important decisions with its epoch-making unanimous ruling

[17] W. E. B. DuBois, "Segregation," *Crisis* 41 (January 1934); quoted by Meier et al., *Black Protest Thought*, pp. 159–60.
[18] See Powell's *Marching Blacks: An Interpretive History of the Rise of the Black Common Man*. In 1941 he was elected to the New York City Council, and in 1944 to Congress. Succeeding his father, he was minister of the Abyssinian Baptist Church from 1937 to 1971.

against "separate but equal" public schools. In one sense Ralph Bunche's pessimistic observation that Negroes were "wards of the Supreme Court" became more appropriate than in 1935 when he uttered it; but in the 1950s a new awakening of the national consciousness began to manifest itself, and a more general protest movement took shape.

THE WHITE REVOLUTION AND THE BLACK REVOLUTION

The revolutionary stage in the movement for racial justice in America has two relatively distinct aspects, both of them with great importance for religious history. The first may well be called the White Revolution because it involved a dramatic shift of viewpoint by leaders of the white community and a very considerable shift in public opinion. As complacency began to yield to guilt and concern, the basically racist character of American institutions came to be recognized to an unprecedented degree. The depth of this response should not be exaggerated, for reactionary movements also gained strength, yet doubts of the gravest sort began to corrode the old assumption that American ideals of equality had been achieved and that increased production would painlessly make all Americans happy. Especially effective in jogging the public conscience was President Eisenhower's decision in 1957 to move federal troops into Little Rock, Arkansas, in support of a court order integrating that city's Central High School. This widely publicized confrontation rallied the civil rights movement as had no other event for over a century. As a result, the churches slowly awoke from the complacency induced by the postwar revival. The National Council of Churches wrote a new chapter in the history of its concern for social issues. The "silent generation" of students began to be heard. But the chief impetus for change stemmed from an awakening in the black community.

The Black Revolution came into existence almost apart from organized efforts as sudden unanticipated events gradually transformed a hopeless passive minority into a self-conscious force. Blacks grew impatient with the almost imperceptible gains made through the strategies of Tuskegee, the Talented Tenth, or the NAACP. Direct action by the many rather than inductive research and legal maneuvers by the few became the order of the day. Due to this momentous shift of strategy, a long list of leaders, organizations, campaigns, and historic confrontations entered the annals of American history. And out of it all came a new sense of racial identity and purpose.

The real heroes of these many events—those who marched, picketed, protested, went to jail, and suffered pain and inhuman indignities—are innumerable and anonymous. They registered their courage, however, at places that deserve remembrance along with Valley Forge and Gettysburg. Hence Americans remember Montgomery, where Rosa Parks's exasperation with Jim Crow buses led to a successful transportation boycott and the emergence of Dr. Martin Luther King, Jr., as a racial leader. In February 1957 King became the first president of the Southern Christian Leadership Conference. Later that year came the events at Little Rock. The student sit-in movement dated back as far as 1943 when the newly organized Congress of Racial Equality (CORE) began its work in Chicago; but in 1960 this movement of passive resistance spread throughout the South despite more than a thousand arrests. In that year the Student Nonviolent Coordinating Committee (SNCC) began its "Jail, No Bail" activities and together with students in CORE began to make "freedom rides" so as to eliminate segregated interstate transportation facilities. The first bus was bombed and burned near Anniston, Alabama, on 14 May, and the National Guard was called into Montgomery. Through 1962 the voter registration drive was increasingly pressed, despite resistance and violence; and in October, after many legal maneuvers and a night of rioting in which two lives were lost, James H. Meredith registered as the first Negro student of the University of Mississippi. Incidents multiplied during 1963 with Birmingham, Alabama, most prominently in the news; but the culminating event was the peaceful convergence on Washington, D.C., of over 250,000 freedom marchers. Martin Luther King's moving depiction of his dream to this vast audience did not bring peace and equality to America, however; and in 1964 the chief centers of activity were in the North, as riots in New York, Jersey City, and Rochester set the stage, as it were, for the devastating outbreak in the Watts district of Los Angeles in the summer of 1965.

The year 1965 also witnessed the culminating demonstration of the civil rights movement, when twenty-five thousand people from all over the country converged on Selma, Alabama. This event brought President Johnson himself to declare that "We shall overcome." For the many who were there it took on almost pentecostal significance. Yet it also marked the beginning of the end of joint interracial protest. In the following summer, on 9 June, the shooting of James Meredith as he walked from Memphis to Jackson led to a convergence of black leaders on that highway march—and from that time forward a new sense of *black* responsibility became manifest. CORE dropped the term "multiracial" from its statement of purpose, and SNCC became even more black in its makeup and orientation. Both organizations lost their force, moreover, as opposition to the war in Vietnam began to absorb the attention of white student protests. New strategies came to the fore in the black liberation movement as the ideas of Malcolm X, who had been assassinated on 21 February 1965, began to replace those of Martin Luther King, who would be assassinated on 4 April 1968.

"Black Power" became the chief slogan during the next cycle of years. One notable example of the new spirit was the July 1966 meeting of forty Negro churchmen in the Bethel AME Church of Harlem. Responding to the changed temper of the times, they issued a powerful statement on the nature and promise of Black Power. They conceded that "too often the Negro church has stirred its members away from the reign of God in *this world* to a distorted and complacent view of *an otherworldly* conception of God's power." They insisted that black religion must no longer function as an institutional accommodation of white supremacy. Then without apology they compared their demands to Irish, Polish, Italian, and Jewish efforts at achieving group leverage in both public and private affairs. They pledged themselves to advance this cause and bade their white brethren regard it as a contribution to the future health of the American social order.[19]

Neither leaders nor spokesmen were much in evidence during the summer of 1967, when pent-up frustration and rage erupted in fire and violence in Newark and Detroit. After this "long hot summer," however, a three-day conference of black leaders was convened in the Episcopal Cathedral of Newark, again with the Reverend Nathan Wright as chairman. Among

[19] The statement is explained and presented as an appendix in Nathan Wright, Jr., *Black Power and Urban Unrest.*

the several resolutions they issued was one which urged a boycott of all churches not working for the "black revolution." Yet this seemingly clear warning left many dilemmas even for those black churchmen who actively sought to rectify the entire American "system" of racial oppression. In part, the black churches faced the question of which road to follow.[20] For decades they had been accused of retarding the achievement of equality. "When one encounters the Negro church," the sociologist E. Franklin Frazier had declared, "one encounters the most important barrier to integration and the assimilation of members."[21] But by 1967 these same black churches were on the defensive for the opposite reason. They could proudly accept Frazier's statement and point to the fact that from time immemorial it was religion (organized and unorganized) that had held the Afro-American heritage together and preserved black solidarity.

At the same time, candid observers wondered if the churches could still perform that cultural function in the later twentieth century. Joseph R. Washington, for example, declared that the two large Baptist conventions merely "maintain church chaos via dictatorship perpetuated for personal gain" and that dictatorial regimentation in the Methodist bodies "inspires mediocrity."[22] Given the modern radical revolution, Vincent Harding wondered if the leaders of the black church hierarchy could "hold on to their already shaky grounds."[23] The otherworldly preoccupations of the sects and cults, meanwhile, despite their continued growth, seemed to in-

[20] Needless to say, the white churches faced the same dilemma, especially as they responded to the "inside" demands made by their own black laity and clergy for special funds and separate organizational status. Still more provocative were the "outside" demands for "reparations" pressed upon them by James Forman and the Black Economic Development Conference. Born in Chicago (1929) and educated at Roosevelt University (degree in Public Administration, 1957), Forman worked at the Institute for Juvenile Research (Chicago) and taught school before being appointed executive director of the Student Nonviolent Coordinating Committee, 1961–66. After leaving SNCC he became active in the Black Economic Development Conference, and in April 1969 presented a Black Manifesto which demanded $500,000,000 in reparations from the churches and synagogues of America.

[21] *The Negro Church*, pp. 70–71.

[22] Joseph R. Washington, *Black Religion*, pp. 67–69, 76–77.

[23] Vincent Harding, "The Religion of Black Power," in *The Religious Situation: 1969*, ed. Donald R. Cutler, p. 13.

crease both the chaos and the mediocrity. Church attendance and affiliation were declining just as they were in the white churches, except that they had started from a lower level and were proceeding at a swifter pace. The crisis was aggravated by the widening gap between the educational level of the clergy and that of the laity, with no improvement of the theological seminary situation in sight.[24]

In addition to the new social, economic, and intellectual factors which affected all churches, the black churches were profoundly involved in a reassessment of their particular theological and ideological situation. Among the options before them were, first of all, the two extremes: a single-mindedly pious concern for the development of a church that preached only a message of otherworldly salvation, or a secularist outlook in which the institutional church was regarded as no more than an assembly-point for community action. Between these extremes, however, diverse positive conceptions of the church's role were expounded by several very thoughtful men.

Most in accord with America's Reformed and Puritan heritage was that view which saw the Church's orthodox, pietistic, and moral message as the proper guide to constructive living in the social and political order. When coupled with pride of race and a strong concern for social justice, this might well be taken as the characteristic theology of most participants in the churches' civil rights effort. "We shall overcome" could be taken as its theme song. Yet it could

24 Reliable comparisons of black and white church membership in recent years are lacking; but the United States religious censuses of 1926 and 1936 indicated that the differences were very small, and that among men the black percentage was lower. In 1936 the overall figures were 44 percent (black) and 42.4 percent (white). In 1963 the Harris poll found that among Negroes regular church attendance (once a week) stood at 49 percent. Since the average congregation numbered two hundred, as against five hundred for whites, at least a thousand new ministers a year would be needed for the fifty-five thousand black churches; but only about a hundred a year were being graduated from seminaries (see William Brink and Louis Harris, *The Negro Revolution in America;* H. Richard Niebuhr et al., *The Advancement of Theological Education* [New York: Harper & Row, 1957]; and Fauset, *Black Gods,* chap. 10). *Theological Education* 4 (Spring 1970), with supplement, surveys black theological education. It reports 665 seminarians enrolled for a black membership of 10 million gathered in forty thousand congregations (p. S-10).

draw on both the spirituals and traditional preaching tradition. From the lips of Ralph Abernathy, who succeeded Martin Luther King, Jr., as head of the SCLC, it would have great power and effectiveness.

Dr. King himself drew heavily on these same rich evangelical resources; yet the uniqueness of his theology owed much to the idealistic personalism and the Hegelian view of history which he studied while seeking his doctorate at Boston University. With further reading in Paul Tillich, the existentialists, and, at some point, Mohandas Ghandi, King developed a profound view of the office of black suffering and the meaning of historical travail, and a faith in God's ultimate victory. This standpoint suggested to him that Christian love must always be at the heart of the struggle. Yet he never failed to keep these "liberal" views in touch with the Baptist nurture of his youth. Almost the last words he uttered on the motel balcony in Memphis where he was assassinated were a request that Thomas Dorsey's gospel song, "Precious Jesus, Take My Hand," be on the program for that evening's scheduled rally. As his coffin was borne to its last resting place through the streets of Atlanta in a mule-drawn farm wagon, a sad and distracted America would remember the day five years before when a vast throng stretching out before the steps of the Lincoln Memorial had heard of his dream—that "We will be free one day":

> This will be the day when all of God's children will be able to sing with new meaning, "let freedom ring." . . .
> When we allow freedom to ring—when we let it ring from every city and every hamlet, from every state and every city, we will be able to speed up that day when all of God's children, black men and white men, Jews and Gentiles, Protestants and Catholics, will be able to join hands and sing in the words of the old Negro spiritual, "Free at last, Free at last, Great God a-mighty, We are free at last."[25]

In retrospect, it would seem that his theology went far to clarify his role as leader during a crucial decade of American history.

When Martin Luther King, Jr., died, one stage in the history of American race relations also ended, though to many

[25] Martin Luther King, Jr., *I Have a Dream* (Los Angeles: John Henry and Mary Louise Dunn Bryant Foundation, 1963).

(possibly to most) Americans, both black and white, his way was still the best road to amity and justice. The more militant and separatistic spirit of the later sixties had no single theologian with anything like King's steady sustaining power. Black nationalism has from time to time had strong Christian support ever since the founding of the AME church in 1816. The Reverend Adam Clayton Powell, Jr., added his eloquent voice to the tradition for two decades, and very notably in March 1966; but in subsequent years his place in the black liberation movement became very uncertain. In 1968 the Reverend Albert B. Cleage, Jr., pastor of Detroit's Shrine of the Black Madonna (a church associated with the UCC), published *The Black Messiah*, a series of forceful sermons addressed to black Christians.[26] In these addresses Cleage contended that Jesus was a "revolutionary black leader" and that blacks should not look to "the Resurrection of the physical body of Jesus but the Resurrection of the Black Nation which He started." Here was a message in which a major accent of Garvey's African Orthodox church and even the Black Muslims was echoed.

James H. Cone, on the other hand, was far more effective in developing a theology that would give Christian substance to black consciousness and provide an ethical basis for Black Power:

It is not my thesis that all Black Power advocates are Christians or even wish to be so. Nor is it my purpose to twist their language or to make an alien interpretation of it. My concern is, rather, to show that the goal and message of Black Power is consistent with the gospel of Jesus Christ. Indeed, I have even suggested that if Christ is present among the oppressed, as he promised, he must be working through the activity of Black Power. This alone is my thesis.[27]

26 Born in Indianapolis in 1911, Cleage attended Wayne State University (Detroit) and Oberlin Graduate School of Theology (Ohio). After serving as pastor of churches in Lexington, Kentucky, San Francisco, and Springfield, Massachusetts, he returned to Detroit in 1952 to serve as minister of the Central Congregation Church. Cleage became active in the NAACP, but in the 1960s his church was linked more explicitly with the cause of black liberation.

27 James H. Cone, *Black Theology and Black Power*, p. 48; see also pp. 32–35.

Cone poses urgent questions: "Is there a message from Christ to the countless number of blacks whose lives are smothered under white society? Is it possible to be *really* black and still feel any identity with the biblical tradition expressed in the Old and New Testaments?" Against those who would abandon the faith as an opiate of the people, he provides a theology of revolution that begins and ends with the man Jesus —his life, death, and resurrection." He professes his faith in the One who was sent "to proclaim release to the captives and recovering of sight to the blind, to set at liberty those who are oppressed, to proclaim the acceptable year of the Lord" (Luke 4:18–19). Without depriving the gospel of its comfort, Cone would animate the black churches—and the white churches, too, if they would listen—with grounds for faithful social action.

A final consideration is the religious dimension of Black Power itself, which Vincent Harding has so profoundly articulated. He describes the movement as an apocalyptic awakening to the fact that "now is the fulness of time . . . a day of destruction demanded by a just God," a time when armed and marching black saints conceive of their task no differently than those Puritans "who cut off unrepentant heads in old England or now burn 'suspected' children in Vietnam." He also sees—and calls for—a more positive religious response to the oft-reiterated affirmation that "We are a spiritual people," wondering if a broader identification with the world's oppressed will not lead Black Power to a rediscovery of Africa's religion "which seeks unity and harmony with the forces of God in the universe."[28]

The search for religious roots that are unrelated to the middle-class technocratic culture of Christendom goes on among white Americans as well—and for similar reasons that are discussed in the next chapter of this book. Yet these trends in black religion, like the revolutionary aims that accompany them, will depend on the nation's progress in abating racial oppression. No one can speak confidently of the future. What is certain is that the awakening of black America which became so prominent a fact of the sixties did more than anything else to make that decade a turning point in American religious history.

[28] Harding, "The Religion of Black Power," pp. 3–38.

63

THE TURBULENT SIXTIES

The decade of the sixties seems in many ways to have marked a new stage in the long development of American religious history. Not only did this intense and fiercely lived span of years have a character of its own, but it may even have ended a distinct quadricentennium—a unified four-hundred-year period—in the Anglo-American experience. A Great Puritan Epoch can be seen as beginning in 1558 with the death of Mary Tudor, the last monarch to rule over an officially Roman Catholic England, and as ending in 1960 with the election of John Fitzgerald Kennedy, the first Roman Catholic president of the United States. To underline the same point, one might note that the age of the Counter-Reformation began in 1563 with the adjournment of the Council of Trent and ended in 1965 with the closing of the Second Vatican Council. Histories of the rise of organized Puritanism begin their accounts with the decisive first decade in the reign of Queen Elizabeth; and the terms "post-Puritan" and "post-Protestant" are first popularly applied to America in the 1960s.

This is not to say that only the vicissitudes of Puritanism are vital to an understanding of the intervening years; but it *is* to say that the exploration and settlement of those parts of the New World in which the United States took its rise were profoundly shaped by the Reformed and Puritan impulse, and that this impulse, through its successive transmutations, remained the dominant element in the ideology of most Protestant Americans. To that tradition, moreover, all other elements among the American people—Catholic, Orthodox, Lutheran, Jewish, infidel, red, yellow, and black—had in some

way, negatively or positively, to relate themselves. Or at least
they did so *until the 1960s,* when the age of the WASP, the
age the melting pot, drew to a close. Let us then look more
closely at this momentous decade, this seeming watershed
and alleged turning in American history, this moment of
truth for "the nation with the soul of a church."

THE RADICAL TURN IN RELIGION AND MORALS

Like many of its elegant, gay, or roaring predecessors, the
decade of the 1960s will probably gain a name or two. Men
will, of course, identify it with President Kennedy's New
Frontier and President Johnson's Great Society (though not
without irony), and with the war in Southeast Asia. Adjec-
tives like "secular" or "permissive" will probably commemorate other aspects of these ten eventful years. The decade
may also be remembered for the "death of God" or the
"Great Moral Revolution"; and these terms will rest on actualities far more pervasive than, say, the gaiety of the
troubled nineties or the elegance of the eighties. New cosmic
signs *were* being read in the sixties. The decade *did* experience a fundamental shift in American moral and religious attitudes. The decade of the sixties was a time, in short, when
the old foundations of national confidence, patriotic idealism,
moral traditionalism, and even of historic Judaeo-Christian
theism, were awash. Presuppositions that had held firm for
centuries—even millennia—were being widely questioned.
Some sensational manifestations came and went (as fads and
fashions will), but the existence of a basic shift of mood
rooted in deep social and institutional dislocations was anything but ephemeral.

There were also many specific events which registered a
traumatic impact. A Roman Catholic was elected to the
presidency of the United States—and then at the peak of his
public favor was struck down and laid to rest while the nation and the world, half stupefied by the succession of events,
joined in a concert of grief such as human technology could
never before have made possible. In the meantime, an aged
cardinal who had been elevated to the papacy in 1958 was
carrying out a revolution in the Roman Catholic Church
whose reverberations rumbled back and forth across the
Christian world with implications for the future that defy

human calculation. In 1967 Israel's Six-Day War brought about not only a dramatic renewal of Jewish self-consciousness, but a marked deterioration of Jewish-Christian relations—and at a time when Negro-Jewish relations were being put under severe strain by population shifts in the cities.

At the same time, the Protestant Establishment was absorbing the shock of two epoch-marking Supreme Court decisions. In 1962 a ruling on the one man-one vote principle cut deep into the rural strongholds of Protestant political power. In 1963 the Court dealt even more decisively with long established and prevailingly Protestant practices by ruling religious ceremonies in the public schools unconstitutional. Then, as if to demonstrate the revolutionary import of the nation's pervasive pluralism, the civil rights movement itself was transformed. The culmination of its interracial phase was the great demonstration in Selma, Alabama, in March and April 1965; yet the virtual end of that movement and the emergence of Black Power as an organizing principle lay only a year away—on the other side of the Watts riot in Los Angeles and the Meredith march from Memphis to Jackson. Finally, as if fate were determined to make the decade a turning point in history, President Johnson authorized the bombing of North Vietnam in February 1965, and by the end of the year escalated the American troop strength there to two hundred thousand men. By 1969 this figure had passed the half-million mark, and the war had become America's longest. By 1970 the nation's sense of unity had fallen to its lowest point since 1861.

The full significance of these several compound events will not be knowable until the end of time, but it was perfectly clear to any reasonably observant American that the postwar revival of the Eisenhower years had completely sputtered out, and that the nation was experiencing a *crise de conscience* of unprecedented depth. The decade thus seemed to beg remembrance for having performed a great tutelary role in the education of America, for having committed a kind of maturing violence upon the innocence of a whole people, for having called an arrogant and complacent nation to time, as it were, and for reminding it that even Mother Nature is capable of dealing harshly with her children when they desecrate and pollute her bounty. There are good reasons for believing that the decade of the sixties, even at the profoundest ethical and religious levels, will take a distinctive place in American history.[1]

Given this situation, the historian is obliged to accept his traditional twofold task: first, to clarify the new elements which came to pervade America's moral, intellectual, and religious atmosphere; and then to suggest why the country found itself in such revolutionary circumstances at this particular time. Much that will be said would of course apply, *mutatis mutandis,* to Western civilization generally or even to the whole world. This sense of global unity, indeed, is a fundamental feature of the times. Our chief focus, nevertheless, shall be on the American scene, where the transition seems to have come first and been especially abrupt.

Lest the reader's expectations become too exorbitant, however, a warning is in order. The truth is that phenomena of this scope could be "explained" only if one had a "God's-eye view" of the whole past and the whole future. Teilhard de Chardin rightly observed that "not a thing in our changing world is really understandable except in so far as it has reached its terminus."[2] In the strict sense, our situation is historically inexplicable. We face the *mysterium tremendum.* We can only speculate as to the place of the sixties in some ultimate roll call of decades. Yet we know that these years were turbulent—that they brought excitement and liberation to some, bewilderment and pain to others. Nearly every American at some time or other wondered why this "almost chosen people" should have encountered so much unsettlement at just this juncture in history. No law can explain why a New World nation experiences such an upheaval in the thirty-sixth decade of its life; but perhaps a telling of the many-stranded

[1] The nature and impact of the sixties are discussed in three overlapping essays of my own: "The Radical Turn in Theology and Ethics: Why It Occurred in the 1960s," in *The Sixties: Radical Change in American Religion,* ed. James M. Gustafson; "The Moral and Theological Revolution of the Sixties and Its Implications for American Religious Historiography," in *The State of American History,* ed. Herbert Bass; and "The Problem of the History of Religion in America," *Church History* 39 (June 1970): 224–35.

[2] Pierre Teilhard de Chardin, *Panthéisme et Christianisme* (Paris, 1923), p. 8. Arthur C. Danto makes the same point in his *Analytical Philosophy of History* (Cambridge: At the University Press, 1965), chap. 1. See also Marcus Cunliffe, "American Watersheds," *American Quarterly* 13 (Winter 1961).

histoire that led up to this crisscross crisis of the sixties can have more explanatory value than the characteristic findings of more scientific disciplines.

WHAT'S NEW?

The most widely publicized aspect of the decade's religious history was the emergence of a radical movement in theology which betokened (even if it did not cause) a major reappraisal of the most assured grounds of the historic Judaeo-Christian consensus. From beyond the grave Dietrich Bonhoeffer's demand for a "secular interpretation" of biblical language was answered by a deluge of serious efforts to meet the needs of a "world come of age." In America it was H. Richard Niebuhr who, at the age of sixty-six, delivered the crucial inaugural address to the sixties with his great essay *Radical Monotheism* (1960); but it was Gabriel Vahanian who first brought Nietzsche's famous phrase into public currency in his book *The Death of God: The Culture of Our Post-Christian Era* (1961). Far more conspicuous were three startlingly popular best sellers: Bishop J. A. T. Robinson's *Honest to God* (1963) in Great Britain, Pierre Berton's *The Comfortable Pew* (1965) in Canada, and Harvey Cox's *The Secular City* (1965) in the United States. Equally provocative were the works of three or four rather diverse thinkers who either proclaimed the "death of God," or insisted on an entirely "secular" interpretation of the gospel, or thoroughly "demythologized" the biblical message.[3] In the meantime, the same themes were being popularized in the mass media—and rendered more erudite in the treatises of a wide range of writers, both lay and clerical, of all faiths. A critical, some-

[3] See Dietrich Bonhoeffer, *Letters and Papers from Prison* (New York: Macmillan Co., 1953), especially the later letters; Schubert M. Ogden, *Christ Without Myth* (New York: Harper & Row, 1961); Paul Van Buren, *The Secular Meaning of the Gospel* (New York: Macmillan Co., 1963); Thomas J. J. Altizer and William Hamilton, *Radical Theology and the Death of God;* Van A. Harvey, *The Historian and the Believer* (New York: Macmillan Co., 1966); Edward Farley, *Requiem for a Lost Piety;* William A. Beardslee, ed., *America and the Future of Theology;* Brevard S. Childs, *Biblical Theology in Crisis;* and, as indicative of related matters, William Braden, *The Private Sea: LSD and the Search for God;* and Jacob Needleman, *The New Religions.*

times exceedingly hostile literature of equal proportions soon arose, yet the movement won support both at the grassroots and in the halls of learning. A massive credibility gap in matters of faith and religion opened up.

Contemporaneous with this development, and closely related to it, was a tidal wave of questioning of all the traditional structures of Christendom, above all, of the so-called parish church. After Peter Berger's sounding of an early tocsin in *The Noise of Solemn Assemblies* (1961), "morphological fundamentalism" became the key concept of the new critics. Local churches, they said, were irrationally and stubbornly committed to structures and strategies inherited from the Middle Ages. Relevant and effective social action was almost impossible. Even more seriously, traditional methods of nurture were forcing laymen to divorce faith and theology from the modes of thought by which they dealt with other problems of life and work in the world. With cities in crisis, men accepted Gibson Winter's diagnosis of *The Suburban Captivity of the Churches* (1961). Recognizing the moribund state of the old institutions and traditions, Martin Marty wrote of *The Second Chance for American Protestants* (1963). This profound self-examination was not restricted to Protestants, moreover. Thomas O'Dea, among many others, wrote of *The Catholic Crisis* (1968). Jews, too, were soon involved in an equally drastic process of theological and institutional reformation. In *After Auschwitz* (1966), Rabbi Richard Rubenstein denied that religion as usual was any longer possible.

The ecumenical significance of these trends was considerable but in some ways untoward. Secularizing trends, even if moderate, tended to undermine old confessional commitments and make interchurch cleavages anachronistic. At the same time, the urgency of the social crisis made interchurch and interfaith cooperation imperative—even involuntary. Between 1960 and 1970, therefore, the officially supported Consultation on Christian Union (COCU) was able to propose highly acceptable terms of reunion for ten major denominations as widely separated as the Protestant Episcopal, the African Methodist Episcopal, and the Disciples of Christ. Catholic-Protestant dialogue proceeded so favorably that the president of Notre Dame predicted in 1970 that church reunion would come before the century's end. Even with such ecumenical "progress," however, the quality of theological dialogue deteriorated and the laity's concern for reunion diminished. The National Council of Churches was cutting its budget for lack of support. Astonishingly little feeling either for or against the COCU proposals arose—except among Fundamentalists and Neo-evangelicals, who regarded all of these trends as demonstrations of flagging commitment. Since these conservatives also opposed the rising current of social concern evinced by the mainstream churches, the old liberal-conservative polarization was intensified and also given a strong socio-political dimension.

An equally significant shift could be noted in both ethical theory and actual behavior. Not only did the mass media devote much time and space to a "new morality," but even in doing so they often exploited a new permissiveness by dealing frankly with long-forbidden subjects. In schools, colleges, and universities, this "moral revolution" first took the form of opposition to the traditional doctrine that schools and colleges operate *in loco parentis*. Students demanded and received greater freedom, and then moved on, often with strong faculty support, to question the structures and value priorities of higher education generally. Questions of loyalty and obedience to constituted authority, even to the national state itself, were also opened with new intensity. Ethical thinkers, meanwhile, tended toward less legalistic, more situational modes of guiding the moral life.[4] As a corollary of these developments nearly every church body in America (as well as many in Europe, including the Vatican) decided that the time had come to appoint a commission for the reexamination of positions on sexual ethics that had been relatively unchallenged for two thousand years.

Far more fundamental than the revising of various sexual attitudes and prohibitions was the new vitality that came into the movement for women's liberation. As in so many cases, the churches felt the first effects as pressure to ordain women to the ministry became a steady feature of the decade—with widespread positive results. Then late in the sixties the movement took on broader and more truly revolutionary dimensions both by renewing the older (but widely ignored) demands for equality and by posing deeper questions about

4 See Joseph Fletcher, *Situation Ethics: The New Morality* (Philadelphia: Westminster Press, 1966); Paul Lehmann, *Ethics in a Christian Context* (New York: Harper & Row, 1963); Harvey Cox, ed., *The Situation Ethics Debate;* James M. Gustafson, *Christ and the Moral Life* (New York: Harper & Row, 1968).

the moral structure of Western culture. Out of this new perspective for considering male and female values emerged a line of inquiry and action whose implications were at least as profound as that which stemmed from the black revolution.

No account of the decade's radicalism, especially at the ethical level, is complete, however, unless it also takes cognizance of a vast and long overdue moral renewal. A revolt against the hypocrisies and superficiality of conventional moral codes by no means resulted in nihilism or libertinism, though both of the latter were defended and practiced by some especially alienated groups. Much of the violence and organized protest of the sixties arose from intense moral indignation, a deep suspicion of established institutions, and a demand for more exalted grounds of action than social success, business profits, and national self-interest. America's patriotic "civil religion," which Will Herberg in the mid-fifties had quite rightly designated as the basic faith of most Americans, was subjected to extremely severe criticism.[5] The old nationalistic rhetoric was widely repudiated as hollow and deceitful. Nor did this civic faith die only in youthful hearts, for superannuated legislators were at the same time transforming the calendar of national holy days into a convenient series of long or lost weekends. On the other hand, there arose a veritable "great awakening" to the threat of environmental pollution and of the widespread depredations of nature which were robbing "America the Beautiful" of its truth. Yet it was in connection with governmental priorities that sharpest conflict developed. Probably nothing did more to divest "The Star-Spangled Banner" of its unifying power than the subordination of social and economic needs to those of war and military might. Even flag-flying became a divisive symbol of the debates on law-and-order versus social justice.

In summary, one may safely say that America's moral and religious tradition was tested and found wanting in the sixties. For Protestants the theological solutions which Neo-orthodoxy had developed ceased to satisfy, with the result that problems of science and biblical criticism returned. For Roman Catholics the same fate overcame the stern condemnations of liberalism and "modernism" propounded by the Vatican Council of 1869–70 and a long series of encyclicals

[5] See pp. 450–51 above.

extending from Pius IX's *Quanta Cura* (1864) to Pius XII's *Humani Generis* (1950). After Pope John's call for *aggiornamento* had made its mark, and increasingly after the vernacular liturgies and other innovations of Vatican Council II had been absorbed, a new spirit manifested itself among the laity and clergy alike. When Pope Paul VI in July 1968 issued *Humanae Vitae,* his fateful encyclical condemning artificial methods of birth control, he was confronted by an unprecedented resistance. Many devout Catholics seemed more inclined to follow the counsel of theologians and moral philosophers than simply obey the popes instruction. Everywhere the need for greater intellectual honesty and deeper foundations of belief was exposed.

Of course, one must not exaggerate the depth and extent of change whenever the reference is made to a whole national population—or even to all churchgoers. If common observation were not enough, there are surveys to prove that most adult Americans, though deeply troubled, still held—in some outward formal sense—to the religious convictions of earlier years.[6] On the other hand, the declining growth rates and

[6] See Andrew M. Greeley et al., *What Do We Believe? The Stance of Religion in America;* and Greeley, *Religion in the Year 2000.* Superficially my statement about the continuity of majority attitudes may seem to be contradicted by the incontestable growth of interest in astrology, spiritualism, and the occult. The contradiction, however, is more apparent than real (on the harmonial and theosophical traditions, see chaps. 60 and 66 above). The revival of these "esoteric" traditions is more "rational" than it seems, especially when they are understood as corollaries of cultural and institutional alienation.

Equally relevant was the many-faceted evangelical revival that manifested itself in the late 1960s. Appearing first was a charismatic revival that soon flowed beyond the Pentecostal churches into staid middle-class denominations and the student population. By 1971 there were even ten thousand or more Roman Catholic Pentecostals, with both clergy and nuns among them. Appearing somewhat later, chiefly among those of student age, was the so-called Jesus Movement, and it too was highly variegated. The more spontaneous groups showed little interest in clerical leadership or doctrinal fine points, took Jesus as an example, worked for peace and social justice, stressed love and charity in warmly personal terms, rescued derelicts of the drug culture, founded communes, adopted counter-cultural life styles, and flouted many legalistic forms of code morality. Expressive of their theology and outlook were the music and lyrics of two young Englishmen, Andrew

widespread budgetary problems of all the large denominations clearly revealed a loss of institutional vitality—though this loss was also experienced by every other institution as well. Parallel to these trends was a marked tendency among the clergy and religious of all faiths to leave their churchly callings for work in the world. Among seminary students the same tendency was noticeable. Between 1966 and 1969 the number of Roman Catholic sisters decreased by fourteen thousand and the number of seminarians by 30 percent. At the same time, youth of high school and college age were showing a strong sense of estrangement from traditional forms of Christian and Judaic nurture. In the same circles marrying outside one's faith became more prevalent, and Catholic regulations on mixed marriages were made less inflexible. The prospect, of "the vanishing Jew" heightened rabbinic stringency, but the trend nevertheless continued.

The three basic but closely intertwined elements that pervade or characterize this steady rise of religious antitraditionalism are profound matters of outlook; they seem to involve a deep shift in the presuppositional substructures of the

---

Lloyd Webber and Tim Rice, whose rock opera, *Jesus Christ Superstar,* appeared as an enormously popular record album in 1969 and as a Broadway stage production in 1971.

Other groups were of more orthodox—or even Fundamentalist and Pentecostal—tendency. These often evidenced somewhat more continuity with older American revival movements, picketed *Jesus Christ Superstar* on both moral and doctrinal grounds, often attended conservative Bible institutes and seminaries, and frequently participated in local churches and in organized evangelistic efforts. They remained critical of the older leadership, however, and accepted many elements of the youth culture, including individualistic apparel, the bearded, long-haired look of conventional portraits of Jesus, new forms of poster art, and a penchant for guitars and rock music. They could thus be very effective missioners among those who were thoroughly disillusioned with ecclesiastical institutions.

The Jesus People soon gained widespread attention and provoked a deluge of published commentary, but their long-term significance cannot be known. Whether they should be considered in a footnote (as here) is a question which only the future will answer. To grim, tormented times they brought the blessings of joy and love; but there is no apparent reason for seeing them as an exception to the larger generalizations attempted in this chapter. Yet surprises are the stuff of history.

American mind. One can designate them as metaphysical, moral, and social:

1. A growing commitment to a naturalism or "secularism" and corresponding doubts about the supernatural and the sacral
2. A creeping (or galloping) awareness of vast contradictions in American life between profession and performance, the ideal and the actual
3. Increasing doubt as to the capacity of present-day ecclesiastical, political, social, and educational institutions to rectify the country's deep-seated woes

Rich natural resources, technological marvels, vast productive power, great ideals, expanding universities, and flourishing churches seem to have resulted only in a country wracked by fear, violence, racism, war, and moral hypocrisy. Nor was this simply the diagnosis of a few black militants and campus radicals. The sense of national failure and dislocation became apparent to varying degrees in all occupational groups and residential areas.

The question returns: Why should a moral and intellectual revolution that was centuries in the making have been precipitated in the 1960s? Why should the complacency and religiosity of the Eisenhower years have faded so swiftly? Why did shortcomings of American society that had aroused reformers since the eighteenth century suddenly become explosive? Why, in summary, did so many diverse processes drop their bomb load on the sixties?

THE DEVELOPING PROBLEM

Radical theology, whether Catholic, Protestant, or Jewish, is fundamentally an adjustment of religious thought to an ordered understanding of the natural world that had been gaining strength at an accelerating rate for over four hundred years. The most basic element in this process is the attitude toward the physical universe typified by Galileo's telescopic observations of the moon's rocky surface in 1610. Three centuries later, when Henry Adams reflected on the intellectual revolution that separated the age of the Virgin of Chartres from the age of the dynamo, he became one of America's early death-of-God theologians: "The two-thousand-years failure of Christianity roared upward from Broadway, and no Constantine the Great was in sight."[7]

Even more troubling was the steady advance of knowledge in the biological realm, especially after Charles Darwin placed the "descent of man" within that area of intensified investigation. Until the nineteenth century the idea of providential design had easily turned man's knowledge of the animate as well as of the inanimate world to the uses of natural theology. With the rise of evolutionary theory, however, this grand structure of apologetical theory began to crumble before the incoming tide of naturalism. As the twentieth century wore on, the full force of still another long effort began to be felt: the attempt of historians, anthropologists, sociologists, and psychologists to explain the *behavior* of man in scientific terms.

In the churches there were more specific sources of intellectual consternation. Serious threats to the inerrancy of Scripture had been raised by the "Copernican revolution" which Isaac Newton had consolidated; other threats provoked the Genesis-and-Geology controversy. But these problems were mild compared to the impact of biblical criticism, the history of world religions, and developmental studies of religion and doctrine. In the churches of the United States the crisis of relativism which these investigations portended was staved off by liberalism's roseate world view, by widespread certainty of America's glorious destiny, and by the tendency of popular evangelical revivalism to ignore the problems. A new flourishing of idealistic philosophy also blunted the force of this new impulse for a time. Americans were even spared the devastating blows which World War I brought down upon the notion of Christendom's triumphant world role. Even in 1929, when the great economic collapse did finally bring this message home, the resurgent forces of Fundamentalism and Neo-orthodoxy—each in different ways to separate constituencies—staved off the accounting for yet another generation. During the Eisenhower years Norman Vincent Peale, Monsignor Fulton J. Sheen, Rabbi Joshua Loth Liebman, and Billy Graham could link hands, as it

[7] *The Education of Henry Adams* (Boston: Houghton Mifflin Co., 1918), p. 500.

were, and preside over an Indian summer of confident living and renewed religious interest. Beneath the affluence and the abundant piety, however, a vast range of unresolved issues remained. Since these were the very years in which the mass media, notably television, were having an unprecedented effect upon the popular awareness of social and intellectual change, and in which a college education was becoming an expected, even necessary, stage in the life of every moderately ambitious American youth, the day was fast disappearing when traditional religious views would be accepted without serious questioning.

Almost as basic to the rise of radical theology as the cultivation of the modern mind was the inexorable development of what was often referred to as modern technocratic society. Max Weber performed a great office by turning men's attention to the ways in which the Judaeo-Christian world-view in general and the Protestant Reformation in particular accelerated the rationalization of social and economic life which underlies the rise of organized technology.[8] The United States, moreover, provided a living demonstration of the fact that, if unhindered by medieval notions of class and status, if animated by sufficiently powerful belief in the virtues of work and exploitation, and if blessed with natural resources in sufficient abundance, a "nation of immigrants" could outstrip the world in achieving technocratic maturity. Yet because of the strongly agrarian terms in which the American idea of the good life has been couched, as well as the relentlessness with which industrialism fostered the growth of cities, American history, especially during the last century, has necessarily experienced harsh confrontations of urban and rural values. In the sectional crisis of the 1860s, again in the 1890s, and still again in the 1920s, these value conflicts were exceedingly severe. In the 1960s the clash became especially intense.

In 1940 Waldo Frank predicted the intensification of these conflicts in *A Chart for Rough Waters:* "The collectivising trend of society under machine production, whether that society calls itself democratic, fascist, or socialist, is irrevocable." Roderick Seidenberg reiterated this warning a decade later in his work on *Posthistoric Man* (1950). He found "the full

8 See Benjamin Nelson. "Conscience, Revolutions, and Weber,' *Journal for the Scientific Study of Religion* 7 (Fall 1968) 157–77, which cites much of the recent literature.

implications of science, technology, and the world of machinery . . . so vast as to defy . . . the possibility of sensing their ultimate meaning or their final impact upon our ways of life and thought."[9] Since then technological inroads on old ways of life have steadily advanced all over the world, from Arkansas to China. Regardless of governmental forms, this process has destroyed primordial social structures and modes of understanding human existence, and despite protest and violence it was proceeding apace to make "organization men" of the entire human race, with that portion of the race living in the United States and Canada feeling every major transition first.

In addition to these two worldwide trends—one intellectual, the other technological—there is another major transformatory process which the United States shares with few, if any, other countries, namely, the eclipse of the Protestant Establishment which presided over its early colonial life, its war for independence, and its nineteenth-century expansion. In theory, the federal Union has been from its origins a nation of minorities, a land of freedom and equality. But it has never been so in fact. Radical inequality and massive forms of oppression have been features—fundamental features—of the American Way of Life. The election of the first American legislature and the first importation of African slaves took place in Virginia in 1619, and from that time forward the rhetoric of American democracy has been falsified by the actualities of racism and bondage. Catholics were subjected to disabilities, intolerance, and violence from the earliest times; and anti-Semitism began to grow virulent as soon as the Jewish immigration rate started to rise during the 1880s. The American Indian has been excluded from American life from the start, while Spanish-speaking citizens, whether gained by annexation of their territory or by immigration, have been consistently relegated to subordinate status. During the past century, however, the social structures, legal arrangements, patterns of prejudice, and power relationships that maintained the older establishment have been gradually undermined. The steady acculturation of the newer ethnic commu-

[9] Roderick Seidenberg, *Posthistoric Man* (Chapel Hill: University of North Carolina Press, 1950), pp. 1, 95. Herbert W. Richardson's *Toward an American Theology* (New York: Harper & Row, 1967) addresses the intellectual problems of the "sociotechnic age."

nities contributed much to this denouement, but the largest single factor in effecting the changed relationships was the urban explosion of the twentieth century.

A final long-term factor stems from the very dominance of Puritanism in the American religious heritage. One *can* imagine a different turn of affairs, for example, if English authorities, in the manner of the French, Spanish, and Dutch, had kept their dissenters at home and peopled the New World colonies only with orthodox conformists. But it was not so, and the future United States was settled and to a large degree shaped by those who brought with them a very special form of radical Protestantism which combined a strenuous moral precisionism, a deep commitment to evangelical experientialism, and a determination to make the state responsible for the support of these moral and religious ideas. The United States became, therefore, the land *par excellence* of revivalism, moral "legalism" and a "gospel" of work that was undergirded by the so-called Puritan Ethic. The popular revivalistic tradition of America tended, moreover, to be oblivious to the intellectual and social revolutions of the modern world. In its church life, as in its forms of popular democracy, intellectualism was deprecated and repressed. Since higher education was under the control of these same forces, many of the most powerful sources of modern thinking lagged far behind those of continental Europe, even though America's cash outlay for education led the world. And due to the strength of these ideas in overrepresented rural constituencies, they had a kind of illicit hold on the national life even after their actual strength had waned. By the mid-twentieth century, therefore, the circumstances were such that a pluralistic post-Puritan situation could rapidly develop.

None of these several long-term developments, however, explains why the 1960s should have experienced anything more than the same gradual adjustments that befell each preceding decade. Processes that are centuries old hardly constitute a sufficient account for the outbreak of a revolution. One is led, therefore, to the more immediate question: What precipitated so violent and sudden a moral and theological transformation in this particular decade? To satisy such questioning one must point to special contingencies and partly accidental convergences which together might plausibly be designated as catalytic in their effects.

THE CATALYSIS OF THE SIXTIES

Each of the long-term processes already discussed was brought to a critical stage by the enormous economic expansion and rapid social change that the United States experienced and, for the most part, thoughtlessly enjoyed during the affluent years that followed World War II. Here again the phenomenon can be subdivided for clarity's sake by reference to five diverse but very familiar sequences.

1. The long-developing problems of rampant, unregulated urban and industrial growth began to create social conditions with which American political and fiscal practices could not cope. Problems of bureaucratic organization, political process, crime, medical care, education, sanitation, communication, housing, pollution, and transportation rendered American cities barely capable of sustaining minimum levels of existence and popular acquiescence. This situation had a timetable of its own, and crises were developing even in cities where race conflict was almost nonexistent.

2. Technological developments in agriculture and industry produced migrations of people that led the national electorate to repudiate many of the arrangements that had hindered equality of participation in American life. And what voters did not do, the Supreme Court accomplished. The John F. Kennedy family in the White House and Pope John XXIII in the Vatican symbolized or brought about a drastic alteration of old interfaith relationships. Between 1954 and 1963 the Supreme Court removed crucial legal supports from the power structure of the Protestant Establishment. The legal and political basis of equality, liberty, civil rights, censorship, and freedom from arbitrary arrest were greatly strengthened. Most important by far, black America first in the context of the civil rights movement and then after 1966 under the banner of Black Power began to seek rectification of the historic inequalities that had featured its situation. For the first time in American history, in other words, the traumatic implications of true pluralism began to be realized. As a result of these traumas, radical discontent, militancy, and violence became as never before common features of American life. John Kennedy, Martin Luther King, Jr., and Robert Ken-

nedy—all of them men on whom vast multitudes pinned their hopes for a better world—were assassinated.

3. Rapid technological development and widely publicized advancements in science also contributed to creating the national mood. Their impact was enormously increased by sensational accomplishments that aroused the popular imagination. Successful trips to the moon, for example, capped a decade of technical triumphs, while genetic discoveries dramatized progress in the study of human life. In this way the cumulative educative effects of television and of vastly expanded enrollments at the college level were suddenly magnified. Modern science and technology seemed to have no conceivable bounds. For many the idea of the supernatural lost its force, while these and still others came to doubt that human existence had any transcendent reference.

4. Less benign achievements, on the other hand, mitigated whatever remained of humanistic optimism in its older liberal forms. Nazi extermination camps and American atomic bombs on Japan, writes Robert Jay Lifton, inaugurated a new era in human history—a time in which man is devoid of assurance that he will live on as a species. His "self-destructive potential" seemed to be without limit. And in the 1960s not only was the memory of Auschwitz and Hiroshima renewed, but its implications were interiorized and expanded. "A "New History" was being shaped.[10] The Cuban missile crisis, continued nuclear testing, indecisive attempts to achieve international control of nuclear armaments, and the construction of vast offensive and defensive missile systems underlined the tentativity of mankind's earthly existence. Meanwhile the alarming facts of overpopulation and environmental pollution called attention to still other ways in which mankind's future was threatened.

5. And finally, as the supreme catalyst, President Lyndon Johnson in 1965 began a drastic escalation of the war in Southeast Asia. This not only prevented an assault on the problems of poverty, racism, and urban dislocation, but it also exposed the terrible inequities of selective service regulations. When added to other signs that military considerations were determining American priorities, these policies not only

[10] See Robert Jay Lifton, "Notes on a New History," *New Journal* 3, no. 1 (September 1969): 5–9; and idem, *Death in Life: Survivors of Hiroshima* (New York: Random House, 1968).

activated the student protest movement, but led to an unprecedented loss of confidence in American institutions, even among those charged with their custody and extension. As the viability of the entire "system" came into question in ever-widening circles, the population as a whole became increasingly polarized. Traditional patriotism and the American dream lost their credibility among several large minority groups, one of which was defined by its youthfulness.

THE SPIRITUAL RESULT

In the area of religion and morals the catalytic power of these converging developments proved to be enormous. The sharp crescendo of social strife seemed to demonstrate that the time-honored structures of American church life were "irrelevant" to the country's actual condition. By many critical observers, moreover, churchgoing America—both black and white—came to be regarded not as a moral leaven but as an obstacle to change. The seeming social irrelevance of the church brought profound and widespread disillusion to the ministers in nearly all denominations, but especially to those in whom the Social Gospel tradition was strong. Yet even to conservatives who believed that the mission of the church was to "save souls" and not to save society, very grave problems were evident. Not only did the universe seem unmindful of man's plight, but man's best achievements—including the educative measures on which so much effort and money had been lavished—rather suddenly began to produce an intellectual atmosphere in which the traditional faith did not flourish. Evil seemed triumphant. There seemed to be no place under the sun, or beyond the sun, for a "God who acts." Evidence of God's love for the world was hard to find.

As the decade of the sixties yielded to the 1970s, dissensus was more visible than consensus. The profound depth of racism lay open and exposed. Doubts, despair, and moral confusion were endemic. One great portion of the population wondered if a just society could ever be achieved; another portion felt that law and order had been needlessly and foolishly sacrificed. Among those "under thirty" and their many allies a counterculture struggled to be born, with the accent on spontaneity and freedom from dogma—whether theological or social. Yet militancy in the student movement and among the oppressed seemed to have become counterproductive. In the misnamed Bible Belt of the South and Midwest, in the lower middle classes, in organized labor, and among ethnic minorities whose economic and social status seemed (to them) very insecure, an inchoate conservative tendency could be noted, though no one could say what this frightened and preplexed multitude portended as a political force.

Americans, whether conservative, liberal, or radical, found it increasingly difficult to believe that the United States was still a beacon and blessing to the world.[11] Even less were they prepared to understand themselves as "chosen" to suffering and servanthood. Amid fears of genocide and the advent of a police state, a new kind of secular apocalypticism gained strength. In this context, the inducements to nihilism were strong. Because the national situation looked hopeless, and because so many hopeful leaders lay prematurely in their graves, the tendency to irrational destructiveness or withdrawn communalism was also very strong. Otherworldliness arose in many new forms. Radical theology, meanwhile, sent down its roots and drew its nourishment from the yearnings that underlay these responses and these temptations. It sought to bring a measure of transcendence, hope, and community to those who were alienated from technocratic society generally, from the American "warfare state," and from outworn forms of churchly life and pactice. Religious interest and moral intensity were by no means waning in the Age of Aquarius; but neither the rejuvenated profession of astrology nor the burgeoning "science" of futurology were very definite about the prospects. One could only be assured that radically revised foundations of belief were being laid, that a drastic reformation of ecclesiastical institutions was in the offing, and that America could not escape its responsibilities as the world's pathbreaker in the new technocratic wilderness.

11 An unusually thorough public survey conducted from January through April 1971, *The Hopes and Fears of the American People* (New York: Universe Books, 1971), revealed "new and urgent concern over national unity, stability and law and order." Of those questioned, 47 percent feared "a real breakdown." The average American for the first time believed that the United States had "slid backwards" during the previous five years and that the trend would continue (*New York Times*, 27 June 1971).

CONCLUDING REFLECTIONS ON THE PREDICAMENT OF THE
WRITER AND THE READER OF HISTORY

"It is one of the great charms of books," observes Frank
Kermode in his essay on eschatology and fiction, "that they
have to end."[12] And so this book, too, has its charm. It ends,
however, in a rather somber mood, for we have been considering a time of calamities. As the American people moved
toward the bicentennial of the nation's independence, they
could see few living signs of the self-confidence and optimism
that had marked the centennial observances of 1876, and
even less of the revolutionary generation's bold assurance.
Still more attenuated was the Puritan's firm conviction that
America had a divine commission in the world. The nation's
organic connections with the sources of its idealism and hope
were withered.

The demarcation of historical periods, to be sure, is a
heuristic, semifictional device. It is almost always a way of
calling attention to the rise and fall of important ideas,
beliefs, and institutions. But the historian who describes his
own times as the *end* of an epoch makes a more daring venture. Because he finds the present to be in some sense a turning point in history, his words also acquire faintly apocalyptic
connotations. He thus risks future disconfirmation. We know,
furthermore, that the idea of a Puritan Epoch cannot be
universally applied. To a large degree it refers only to the
United States. In other parts of the globe—notably in the
Third World—the present time of crisis is linked, not with
Puritanism, but more broadly with the rise and fall of Western imperialism, colonialism, and capitalism. Yet for nearly
everyone the impulse to see the present as the end of a
period stems from an awareness of living in a time of radical
transition. We survey the national experience from the kind
of pseudo-future that a sense of crisis provides. As Kermode
says, "We project ourselves—a small humble elect, perhaps
—past the End, so as to see the structure whole, a thing we
cannot do from our spot of time in the middle."[13]

[12] Frank Kermode, *The Sense of an Ending: Studies in the
Theory of Fiction* (New York: Oxford University Press, 1967),
p. 23.
   [13] Ibid., p. 8.

The concept of a Puritan Epoch, however, does not release us from the constant obligation to reinterpret the American past. Because each morning's newspaper adds new events to the historian's agenda and hence alters his angle of vision, it joggles the past a little. For this reason historical work is an endless, Sisyphean task. And which events—if any—will turn out to be decisive for the spiritual history of the future, and hence also for interpreting the past, is intrinsically unknowable.[14] Yet the provocations of this predicament remind the writer and reader alike of the ways in which the historical enterprise is fundamentally relevant to nearly every major question of human existence. A history book that comes down to our own time is thus a tantalizing challenge—and an invitation.

As an active participant in contemporary history, the reader can hardly escape the responsibility for seeking to understand his present circumstance. Beyond that, as an observer of continuity and change in the conditions of his own existence, he may exercise the privilege that Carl Becker underlined when he spoke of "Everyman his own historian."[15] In this exciting role he will soon discover that the American

[14] In April-May 1970 the final two weeks of my course on American religious history were swallowed up in the turmoil of demonstrations and protest related to a widely publicized trial of several Black Panthers in New Haven, the American invasion of Cambodia, the National Guard's killing of four students at Kent State University, and the police slaying of two more at Jackson State College. The course, in other words, merged with the subject matter of this concluding chapter. In subsequent discussions as to what had actually happened in New Haven, the impossibility of producing an historical account of the events became manifest. Too few introspective diaries were kept, too many levels of action were proceeding at once, too many conflicting forces impinged on the university community. It meant too many different things to various groups of people; and from beginning to end the events had no physical or spiritual boundaries. Only with the passage of time, if ever, will it become clearer which elements of the situation had the most enduring effects and which ones, therefore, should have registered their impact on would-be historians. How much more impossible is it to account for a whole nation's turmoil during an entire decade!

[15] Carl L. Becker, *Everyman His Own Historian* (Chicago: Quadrangle Books, 1966), pp. 233–55. This was his presidential address to the American Historical Association in 1931. The book of essays bearing this title appeared in 1935.

experience does not explain itself. Whether as amateur or as professional, he will be a pioneer on the frontiers of post-modern civilization. Even his life style and moral stance will be elements in an interpretation of the religious situation—and hence of the past. Beyond all thoughts of epochs and endings and turning points, moreover, one may hope that such future interpreters, as well as later readers of these words, will see increasing evidence that the American people, in their moral and religious history, were drawing on the profounder elements of their traditions, finding new sources of strength and confidence, and thus vindicating the idealism which has been so fundamental an element in the country's past.

BIBLIOGRAPHY

§ 1, Bibliographies. § 2, General Histories of Religions. § 3, Catholic Europe, New Spain, and New France. § 4, The European Protestant Background. § 5, The Reformation and Puritanism in England. § 6, General Works of American History. § 7, General Works of American Religious History. § 8, Church and State and Civil Religion in America. § 9, Indians, Indian Policy, and Indian Missions. § 10, Roman Catholicism: General American and Colonial Histories. § 11, Judaism in America. § 12, Eastern Orthodoxy in America. § 13, Protestant Denominational Histories and Studies. § 14, Long-Term Themes in Protestant History, § 15, Early Colonial Religion. § 16, American Puritanism. § 17, Later Colonial Religion. § 18, Jonathan Edwards and the New England Theology. § 19, Antebellum Protestantism. § 20, Transcendentalism and Other Romantic Currents. § 21, New Movements in Religion: Nineteenth Century. § 22, Sectional Issues and the Civil War. § 23, Slavery, the Negro, and the Black Churches. § 24, Roman Catholicism in the Nineteenth and Twentieth Centuries. § 25, Protestantism since the Civil War. § 26, Liberal Trends in Nineteenth-Century Religious Thought. § 27, Ecumenical and Inter-Faith Developments. § 28, Religious History from World War I to the Vietnam War. § 29, Twentieth-Century Theological Currents. § 30, Black Movements and Voices in the Twentieth Century. § 31, Spanish-Speaking Americans. § 32, Religion in the 1960s and 1970s. § 33, Biographies and Autobiographies.

One is staggered by the thought of a bibliography of American religious history that would include all of the relevant documents, published primary materials, periodicals, historical works, and scholarly articles. Fortunately, it is not necessary to undertake anything of this sort, since guides to the literature of nearly every major period, theme, and subject exist. Most important is Nelson R. Burr's two-volume *Critical Bibliography of Religion in America* (1961), which provides information on other bibliographical aids, has a table of contents, and includes a complete author index. Older but still valuable are Peter G. Mode's *Sourcebook and Bibliographical Guide for American Church History* (1921) and the *Bibliographical Guide to the History of Christianity* (1931) edited by Shirley Jackson Case, with an American section by William W. Sweet. Of the older bibliographies, none are more valuable than those which accompany each of the denominational histories contained in the thirteen-volume American Church History Series (ACHS, 1893–97) edited by Philip Schaff et al., volume 12 of which contains a general bibliography. (See below, sec. 1, for full titles of works mentioned here as well as other bibliographies.)

Due to the availability of these works as well as other compilations referred to in section 1, the suggestions for further reading provided in this volume, though comprehensive, are relatively modest. The bibliography which follows includes only a small fraction of the works consulted. Of the titles mentioned in footnotes, it usually repeats only recent secondary works which serve the purposes described below. Emphasis, with rare exceptions, has been placed upon important book-length secondary works in English, most of them recent, which themselves contain extensive and critical introductions to the primary and secondary literature of the subjects they treat. These titles are gathered in thirty-three sections, beginning with general topics and proceeding to more delimited areas in a broadly chronological manner. Because historians do not write with such classification schemes in mind, the reader with some special interest is advised to consult several related sections. Since nearly all of the works included are deemed to be of great value both for their substantive content and for their bibliographical contribution, comments on individual items are very rarely made.

Biographies, though they exist in immense profusion and constitute one of the most valuable approaches to periods and movements, have not been included in great number because of their accessibility through the catalogues of any good library, and because the *Dictionary of American Biography,* general and specialized encyclopedias, and other similar reference works provide critical guidance in this area. Yet because biographies and autobiographies provide a unique form of illumination, a few representative works in this important genre are given in section 33.

Relatively few histories of individual denominations and other smaller groups are included, but they are listed in most general works on American religion (sec. 7), in encyclopedias of several sorts, and, again, in library catalogues. Also of great value in this regard are the several general works or handbooks which deal systematically with churches, denominations, sects, and cults. Especially to be recommended is that of F. E. Mayer.

This bibliography does not contain a section on theory and method, despite the fact that the intersection of historical investigation and religious subject-matter has always raised formidable theoretical questions which have often provoked scholars, philosophers, and theologians to profound intellectual innovation. The reasons for my negative decision are quickly stated: the literature on this subject is not only vast and variegated but it is almost by definition controversial. Any brief list of books would be misleading or tendentious or both. Every item in this bibliography, moreover, does exemplify one or another methodological position to some degree, while some of them (such as those by Weber and Troeltsch) have exerted great influence on how historians have dealt with matters of religion and on what aspects they have chosen to study. In part to illustrate the multiplicity of ways in which a religious movement can be fruitfully studied, sections 5 and 16 on English and American Puritanism have been somewhat expanded. Not only has Puritanism in the broad sense of the term received more careful and mature concern than any other subject in the American field, but it is an area in which many historians have posed fundamental questions of theory and method and produced works of lasting significance.

It has taken much inner restraint to keep this bibliography within reasonable bounds; and countless deeply prized books —not even to mention articles—have been painfully omitted. Yet I believe that easily followed paths to the whole terrain have been marked out by those which are listed. My concluding hope is that some of the excitement and seriousness of purpose that motivated the many historians who are represented will be contagious, and that those who consult these books will find their interest in American religious history enlivened. To anyone so responding it can be guaranteed that he will find problems of intense human consequence at every turn, and that only very rarely, if ever, will he find a subject that has been definitively treated. For the analytical historian answers become questions.

1. BIBLIOGRAPHIES

Burr, Nelson R. *A Critical Bibliography of Religion in America.* 2 vols. Princeton, N.J.: Princeton University Press, 1961. [Part One, pp. 3–84 on bibliographical guides.]

Cadden, John Paul. *The Historiography of the American Catholic Church, 1785–1943.* Washington, D.C.: Catholic University of America Press, 1944.

Ellis, John Tracy. *A Guide to American Catholic History.* Milwaukee: Bruce Publishing Co., 1959.

Handlin, Oscar, et al. *Harvard Guide to American History.* Cambridge, Mass.: Harvard University Press, 1955.

Mode, Peter G. *Source Book and Bibliographical Guide for American Church History.* Menasha, Wis.: George Banta Publishing Co., 1921.

Rischin, Moses. *An Inventory of American Jewish History.* Cambridge, Mass.: Harvard University Press, 1955.

Schaff, Philip, et al., gen. eds. *The American Church History Series.* 13 vols. New York: Christian Literature Co., 1893–97. [Each denominational history contains a bibliography; general bibliography in vol. 12.]

Vollmar, Edward R. *The Catholic Church in America: An Historical Bibliography.* 2d ed. New York: Scarecrow Press, 1963.

2. GENERAL HISTORIES OF RELIGIONS

Baron, Salo W. *A Social and Religious History of the Jews.* 12 vols. New York: Columbia University Press, 1952–67.

Chadwick, Henry, ed. *The Pelican History of the Church.* 6 vols. Baltimore: Penguin Books, 1960–70.

Ch'en, Kenneth K. S. *Buddhism: The Light of Asia*. Woodbury, N.Y.: Barron's Educational Series, 1968.

Dolan, John P. *Catholicism: An Historical Survey*. Woodbury, N.Y.: Barron's Educational Series, 1968.

Dumoulin, Heinrich. *A History of Zen Buddhism*. Boston: Beacon Press, 1969.

Guttmann, Julius. *Philosophers of Judaism, from Biblical Times to Franz Rosenzweig*. New York: Holt, Rinehart and Winston, 1964.

Latourette, Kenneth Scott. *A History of Christianity*. New York: Harper & Brothers, 1953.

———. *A History of the Expansion of Christianity*. 7 vols. New York: Harper & Brothers, 1937–45.

Margolis, Max, and Marx, Alexander. *History of the Jewish People*. New York: Meridian Books, 1960.

Schaff, Philip, ed. *The Creeds of Christendom*. 3 vols. New York, 1877.

Smart, Ninian. *The Religious Experience of Mankind*. New York: Charles Scribner's Sons, 1969.

Sohm, Rudolf. *Outlines of Church History*. Boston: Beacon Press, 1958.

Trepp, Leo. *Eternal Faith, Eternal People: A Journey into Judaism*. Englewood Cliffs, N.J.: Prentice-Hall, 1962.

Troeltsch, Ernst. *The Social Teaching of the Christian Churches*. Translated by Olive Wyon. New York: Macmillan Co., 1931.

Walker, Williston. *A History of the Christian Church*. Rev. ed. New York: Charles Scribner's Sons, 1959.

3. CATHOLIC EUROPE, NEW SPAIN, AND NEW FRANCE

Bolton, Herbert E. *The Mission as a Frontier Institution in the Spanish American Colonies*. Academic Reprints. El Paso, Tex.: Texas Western College Press, 1960.

———. *The Spanish Borderlands: A Chronicle of Old Florida and the Southwest*. New Haven: Yale University Press, 1921.

Bouyer, Louis. *The Roman Socrates: A Portrait of Saint Philip Neri*. Translated by Michael Day. Westminster, Md.: Newman Press, 1958.

Braden, Charles S. *Religious Aspects of the Conquest of Mexico*. Durham, N.C.: Duke University Press, 1930.

Bremond, André. *A Literary History of Religious Thought in France from the Wars of Religion to Our Own Time.* 3 vols. London: Macmillan & Co., 1928–36.

Brodrick, James. *The Origin of the Jesuits.* London: Longmans, Green and Co., 1940.

———. *The Progress of the Jesuits.* London: Longmans, Green and Co., 1947.

———. *Saint Ignatius Loyola: The Pilgrim Years, 1491–1538.* New York: Farrar, Straus and Cudahy, 1956.

Brou, Alexandre. *Saint Madeleine Sophie Barat: Her Life of Prayer and Her Teaching.* Translated by Jane Wynne Saul. New York: Desclee Co. 1963.

Burns, Edward M. *The Counter-Reformation.* Princeton, N.J.: Princeton University Press, 1964.

Elliott, J. H. *Imperial Spain, 1469–1716.* New York: Saint Martin's Press, 1963.

Hallet, Paul H. *Catholic Reformer: A Life of Saint Cajetan of Thiene.* Westminster, Md.: Newman Press, 1959.

Janelle, Pierre. *The Catholic Reformation.* Milwaukee: Bruce Publishing Co., 1949.

Kennedy, John Hopkins. *Jesuit and Savage in New France.* New Haven: Yale University Press, 1950.

Ozment, Stephen. *The Reformation in Medieval Perspective.* Chicago: Quadrangle Books, 1971.

Picón-Salas, Mariano. *A Cultural History of Spanish America, from Conquest to Independence.* Translated by Irving A. Leonard. Berkeley and Los Angles: University of California Press, 1966.

Talbot, Francis X. *Saint Among the Hurons: The Life of Jean de Brébeuf.* New York: Harper & Brothers, 1949.

Walsh, Henry H. *The Christian Church in Canada.* Toronto: Ryerson Press, 1956.

Wright, J. Leitch. *Anglo-Spanish Rivalry in North America.* Athens, Ga.: University of Georgia Press, 1971.

Wrong, George M. *The Rise and Fall of New France.* 2 vols. New York: Macmillan Co., 1928.

4. THE EUROPEAN PROTESTANT BACKGROUND

Bainton, Roland H. *Here I Stand: A Life of Martin Luther.* Nashville, Tenn.: Abingdon Press, 1950.

———. *The Reformation of the Sixteenth Century.* Boston: Beacon Press, 1952.

Bergendoff, Conrad. *The Church of the Lutheran Reformation: A Historical Survey of Lutheranism.* Saint Louis: Concordia Publishing House, 1967.

Courvoisier, Jacques. *Zwingli: A Reformed Theologian.* Richmond: John Knox Press, 1971.

Dillenberger, John, and Welch, Claude. *Protestant Christianity Interpreted through Its Development.* New York: Charles Scribner's Sons, 1954.

Green, Robert W. *Protestantism and Capitalism: The Weber Thesis and Its Critics.* Boston: D. C. Heath, 1959.

Grimm, Harold J. *The Reformation Era, 1500–1650.* New York: Macmillan Co., 1965.

Heppe, Heinrich. *Reformed Dogmatics.* Introduction by Karl Barth. London: G. Allen and Unwin, 1952.

Hunt, George L., ed. *Calvinism and the Political Order.* Philadelphia: Westminster Press, 1965.

Jones, Rufus M. *Spiritual Reformers in the Sixteenth and Seventeenth Centuries.* New York: Macmillan Co., 1914.

Littell, Franklin H. *The Origins of Sectarian Protestantism: The Anabaptist View of the Church.* New York: Macmillan Co., 1960.

McNeill, John Thomas. *The History and Character of Calvinism.* New York: Oxford University Press, 1954.

Niesel, Wilhelm. *The Theology of Calvin.* Philadelphia: Westminster Press, 1956.

Ong, Walter J. *Ramus: Method and the Decay of Dialogue.* Cambridge, Mass.: Harvard University Press, 1958.

Schmid, Heinrich. *The Doctrinal Theology of the Evangelical Lutheran Church.* Translated from the 5th ed. by Charles A. Hay and Henry E. Jacobs. Philadelphia, 1876.

Schwiebert, E. G. *Luther and His Times.* St. Louis: Concordia Publishing House, 1950.

Spitz, Lewis W. *The Renaissance and Reformation Movements.* Chicago: Rand-McNally, 1971.

Tawney, R. H. *Religion and the Rise of Capitalism.* 1926. Reprint. New York: New American Library, 1947.

Torrance, Thomas F., ed. and trans. *The School of Faith: The Catechisms of the Reformed Church.* New York: Harper & Brothers, 1959.

Walton, Robert C. *Zwingli's Theocracy.* Toronto: University of Toronto Press, 1967.

Watson, Philip S. *Let God Be God! An Interpretation of the Theology of Martin Luther.* Philadelphia: Muhlenberg Press, 1947.

Weber, Max. *The Protestant Ethic and the Spirit of Capitalism.* London: G. Allen and Unwin, 1930.

Wendell, François. *Calvin: The Origins and Development of His Religious Thought.* New York: Harper & Row, 1963.

Whale, John Selden. *The Protestant Tradition.* Cambridge: At the University Press, 1955.

Williams, George H. *The Radical Reformation.* Philadelphia: Westminster Press, 1962.

Wilson, Charles. *The Dutch Republic and Its Civilization of the Seventeenth Century.* New York: McGraw-Hill Book Co., 1968.

5. THE REFORMATION AND PURITANISM IN ENGLAND

Ames, William. *The Marrow of Theology.* Translated from 3d Latin ed., 1629, and edited by John D. Eusden. Boston: Pilgrim Press, 1963.

Barbour, Hugh. *The Quakers in Puritan England.* New Haven: Yale University Press, 1964.

Cragg, Gerald R. *From Puritanism to the Age of Reason: A Study of Changes in Religious Thought within the Church of England, 1660–1700.* Cambridge: At the University Press, 1950.

Donaldson, Gordon. *The Scottish Reformation.* New York: Cambridge University Press, 1960.

George, Charles and Katherine. *The Protestant Mind of the English Reformation, 1570–1640.* Princeton, N.J.: Princeton University Press, 1961.

Haller, William. *The Elect Nation: The Meaning and Relevance of Foxe's Book of Martyrs.* New York: Harper & Row, 1963.

———. *The Rise of Puritanism.* New York: Columbia University Press, 1938.

Hill, Christopher. *The Century of Revolution, 1603–1714.* New York: W. W. Norton & Co., 1961.

Hughes, Philip. *The Reformation in England.* 3 vols. London: Hollis and Carter, 1954.

Knappen, Marshall Mason. *Tudor Puritanism: A Chapter in the History of Idealism.* Chicago: University of Chicago Press, 1939.

Little, David. *Religion, Order, and Law: A Study in Pre-Revolutionary England.* New York: Harper & Row, 1969.

MacCaffrey, Wallace. *The Shaping of the Elizabethan Regime.* Princeton, N.J.: Princeton University Press, 1968.

Moorman, John R. H. *A History of the Church in England.* London: A. and C. Black, 1953; New York: Morehouse-Barlow, 1959.

Morgan, Irvonwy. *The Godly Preachers of the Elizabethan Church.* London: Epworth Press, 1965.

Notestein, Wallace. *The English People on the Eve of Colonization.* New York: Harper & Brothers, 1954.

———. *The Scot in History: A Study of the Interplay of Character and History.* New Haven: Yale University Press, 1947.

Nuttall, Geoffrey F. *The Holy Spirit in Puritan Faith and Experience.* Oxford: Basil Blackwell, 1946.

———. *Visible Saints: The Congregational Way, 1640–1660.* Oxford: Basil Blackwell, 1957.

O'Connell, Marvin R. *Thomas Stapleton and the Counter-Reformation.* New Haven: Yale University Press, 1964.

Parker, Thomas M. *The English Reformation to 1558.* New York: Oxford University Press, 1950.

Powicke, Frederick M. *The Reformation in England.* New York: Oxford University Press, 1941.

Prall, Stuart E., ed. *The Puritan Revolution: A Documentary History.* Garden City, N.Y.: Doubleday & Co., Anchor Books, 1968.

Ridley, Jasper G. *Thomas Cranmer.* Oxford: Clarendon Press, 1962.

Rowse, A. L. *The Elizabethans and America.* New York: Harper & Row, 1959.

Trinterud, Leonard J., ed. *Elizabethan Puritanism.* New York: Oxford University Press, 1971.

Walzer, Michael. *The Revolution of the Saints: A Study of the Origins of Radical Politics.* Cambridge, Mass.: Harvard University Press, 1965.

Wright, Louis B. *Religion and Empire: The Alliance between Piety and Commerce in English Expansion, 1558–1625.* Chapel Hill: University of North Carolina Press, 1943.

6. GENERAL WORKS OF AMERICAN HISTORY

Bailyn, Bernard. *Education in the Forming of American Society.* Chapel Hill: University of North Carolina, Press, 1960.

Bancroft, George. *History of the United States.* 6 vols. 2d ed., rev. Boston: Little, Brown and Co., 1876.

Bass, Herbert, ed. *The State of American History.* Chicago: Quadrangle Books, 1970 [Historiographical essays.]

Bernstein, Barton J., ed. *Towards a New Past: Dissenting Essays in American History.* New York: Random House, 1968.

Blau, Joseph L., ed. *American Philosophical Addresses, 1700–1900.* New York: Columbia University Press, 1946.

———. *Men and Movements in American Philosophy.* Englewood Cliffs, N.J.: Prentice-Hall, 1952.

Blum, John Morton, et al. *The National Experience: A History of the United States.* 2d ed. New York: Harcourt, Brace & World, 1968.

Clark, Thomas D. *Frontier America.* New York: Charles Scribner's Sons, 1959.

Cremin, Lawrence A. *American Education: The Colonial Experience.* New York: Harper & Row, 1970.

Curti, Merle. *The Growth of American Thought.* New York: Harper & Brothers, 1943.

Davis, David B. *The Fear of Conspiracy: Images of UnAmerican Subversion from the Revolution to the Present.* Ithaca: Cornell University Press, 1971.

Gabriel, Ralph Henry. *The Course of American Democratic Thought.* New York: Ronald Press, 1940.

Handlin, Oscar. *The Uprooted: The Epic Story of the Great Migrations that Made the American People.* New York: Grosset & Dunlap, 1951.

Hofstadter, Richard. *Anti-Intellectualism in American Life.* New York: Alfred A. Knopf, 1963.

Kraditor, Aileen, ed. *Up from the Pedestal: Writings in the History of Feminism.* Chicago: Quadrangle Books, 1968.

Parrington, Vernon L. *Main Currents in American Thought.* 3 vols. New York: Harcourt, Brace & Co., 1927, 1930.

Pochmann, Henry A. *German Culture in America: Philosophical and Literary Influences, 1600–1900.* Madison, Wis.: University of Wisconsin Press, 1957.

Potter, David M. *People of Plenty: Economic Abundance and the American Character.* Chicago: University of Chicago Press, 1954.

Schlesinger, Arthur M., and Fox, Dixon R., eds. *A History of American Life.* 13 vols. New York: Macmillan Co., 1927–48.

Schneider, Herbert W. *A History of American Philosophy.* New York: Columbia University Press, 1946.

Wittke, Carl. *We Who Built America: The Saga of the Immigrant.* New York: Prentice-Hall, 1939.

7. GENERAL WORKS OF AMERICAN RELIGIOUS HISTORY

Ahlstrom, Sydney E., ed. *Theology in America: The Major Protestant Voices from Puritanism to Neo-orthodoxy.* Indianapolis: Bobbs-Merrill Co., 1967.

Bach, Marcus. *They Have Found a Faith.* Indianapolis: Bobbs-Merrill Co., 1946.

Bacon, Leonard W. *A History of American Christianity.* New York: Christian Literature Co., 1897.

Baird, Robert. *Religion in American.* 1844. Critical abridgement with introduction by Henry W. Bowden. New York: Harper & Row, 1970.

Braden, Charles S., ed. *Varieties of American Religion.* Chicago: Willett, Clark and Co., 1936.

Brauer, Jerald C. *Protestantism in America: A Narrative History.* Rev. ed. Philadelphia: Westminster Press, 1965.

———, ed. *Reinterpretation in American Church History.* Chicago: University of Chicago Press, 1968.

Clark, Elmer T. *The Small Sects in America.* Rev. ed. New York: Abingdon-Cokesbury Press, 1949.

Clebsch, William A. *From Sacred to Profane America: The Role of Religion in American History.* New York: Harper & Row, 1968.

Gaustad, Edwin S. *Historical Atlas of Religion in America.* New York: Harper & Row, 1962.

———. *A Religious History of America.* New York: Harper & Row, 1966.

Hudson, Winthrop S. *American Protestantism.* Chicago: University of Chicago Press, 1961.

———. *Religion in America.* New York: Charles Scribner's Sons, 1965.

Marty, Martin E. *Righteous Empire: The Protestant Experience in America.* New York: Dial Press, 1970.

Mead, Frank S. *Handbook of Denominations in the United States.* 5th ed. Nashville, Tenn.: Abingdon Press, 1970.

Mead, Sidney E. *The Lively Experiment: The Shaping of Christianity in America.* New York: Harper & Row, 1963.

Moberg, David O. *The Church as a Social Institution: The Sociology of American Religion.* Englewood Cliffs, N.J.: Prentice-Hall, 1962.

Olmstead, Clifton E. *History of Religion in the United States.* Englewood Cliffs, N.J.: Prentice-Hall, 1960.

Smith, Hilrie Shelton, Handy, Robert T., and Loetscher, Lefferts A. *American Christianity: An Historical Interpretation with Representative Documents.* 2 vols. New York: Charles Scribner's Sons, 1960–63.

Smith, James W., and Jamison, A. Leland, eds. *Religion in American Life.* 4 vols. Princeton, N.J.: Princeton University Press, 1961. [Two of these volumes contain topical and thematic essays on American churches and religious thought. The other two are bibliographical.]

Sontag, Frederick, and Roth, John K. *The American Religious Experience: The Roots, Trends, and the Future of American Theology.* New York: Harper & Row, 1972.

Sweet, William W. *The Story of Religion in America.* New York: Harper & Brothers, 1950.

Weigle, Luther A. *American Idealism.* New Haven: Yale University Press, 1928.

8. CHURCH AND STATE AND CIVIL RELIGION IN AMERICA

Cherry, Conrad. *God's New Israel: Religious Interpretations of American Destiny.* New York: Prentice-Hall, 1971.

Drinan, Robert F. *Religion, the Courts, and Public Policy.* New York: McGraw-Hill Book Co., 1963.

Healey, Robert M. *Jefferson on Religion in Public Education.* New Haven: Yale University Press, 1962.

McLoughlin, William G. *New England Dissent, 1630–1833: The Baptists and the Separation of Church and State.* 2 vols. Cambridge, Mass.: Harvard University Press, 1971.

Nagel, Paul C. *One Nation Indivisible: The Union in American Thought, 1776–1861.* New York: Oxford University Press, 1964.

———. *This Sacred Trust: American Nationality, 1798–1898.* New York: Oxford University Press, 1971.

Pfeffer, Leo. *Church, State, and Freedom.* Boston: Beacon Press, 1953.

Smith, Elwyn A., ed. *The Religion of the Republic.* Philadelphia: Fortress Press, 1971.

Stokes, Anson Phelps. *Church and State in the United States.* New York: Harper & Brothers, 1950.

Tuveson, Ernest Lee. *Millennium and Utopia: A Study in the Background of the Idea of Progress.* Berkeley and Los Angeles: University of California Press, 1949.

———. *Redeemer Nation: The Idea of America's Millennial Role.* Chicago: University of Chicago Press, 1968.

9. INDIANS, INDIAN POLICY, AND INDIAN MISSIONS

Beaver, R. Pierce. *Church, State, and the American Indians.* Saint Louis: Concordia Publishing House, 1966.

Benedict, Ruth. *Patterns of Culture.* Boston: Houghton Mifflin Co., 1934.

Berkhofer, Robert F., Jr. *Salvation and the Savage: An Analysis of Protestant Missions and American Indian Response, 1787–1862.* Lexington, Ky.: University of Kentucky Press, 1965.

Brown, Joseph E. *The Sacred Pipe: Black Elk's Account of the Seven Rites of the Oglala Sioux.* Norman, Okla.: University of Oklahoma Press, 1953.

Carroll, Peter N. *Puritanism and the Wilderness: The Intellectual Significance of the New England Frontier.* New York: Columbia University Press, 1969.

Driver, Harold. *Indians of North America.* Chicago: University of Chicago Press, 1961.

Harrod, Howard L. *Mission among the Blackfeet.* Norman, Okla.: University of Oklahoma Press, 1971.

Hertzberg, Hazel W. *The Search for an American Indian Identity: Modern Pan-Indian Movements.* Syracuse, N.Y.: Syracuse University Press, 1971.

Hinman, George W. *The American Indian and Christian Missions.* New York: Fleming H. Revell Co., 1933.

Jackson, Helen Hunt. *A Century of Dishonor.* 1881. Reprint. Edited by Andrew F. Rolle. New York: Harper & Row, Torchbooks, 1965.

Osborn, Chase S. and Stellanova. *"Hiawatha" with Its Original Indian Legends.* Lancaster, Pa.: Jacques Cattell Press, 1944.

Pearce, Roy Harvey. *The Savages of America.* Baltimore: Johns Hopkins Press, 1953.

Priest, Loring B. *Uncle Sam's Stepchildren: The Reformation of United States Indian Policy, 1865–1887.* New Brunswick, N.J.: Rutgers University Press, 1942.

Vaughan, Alden T. *The New England Frontier: Puritans and Indians, 1620–1675.* Boston: Little, Brown and Company, 1969.

10. ROMAN CATHOLICISM: GENERAL AMERICAN AND COLONIAL HISTORIES

Burns, James A. *The Growth and Development of the Catholic School System in the United States.* New York: Benziger Brothers, 1912.

Ellis, John Tracy. *American Catholicism.* 2d ed., rev. Chicago: University of Chicago Press, 1969.

———. *Catholics in Colonial America.* Baltimore: Helicon Press, 1965.

———. *Documents of American Catholic History.* Milwaukee: Bruce Publishing Co., 1956.

Gleason, Philip, ed. *The Catholic Church in America.* New York: Harper & Row, 1970.

———. *Contemporary Catholicism in the United States.* Notre Dame, Ind.: University of Notre Dame Press, 1969.

Greeley, Andrew M. *The Catholic Experience: An Interpretation of American Catholicism.* Garden City, N.Y.: Doubleday & Co., 1967.

Maynard, Theodore. *The Catholic Church and the American Idea.* New York: Appleton-Century-Crofts, 1953.

Melville, Annabelle M. *John Carroll of Baltimore: Founder of the American Catholic Hierarchy.* New York: Charles Scribner's Sons, 1955.

Shea, John Gilmary. *The Catholic Church in Colonial Days.* 2 vols. New York, 1886.

11. JUDAISM IN AMERICA

Blau, Joseph L. *Modern Varieties of Judaism.* New York: Columbia University Press, 1966.

———, and Baron, Salo W. *The Jews of the United States, 1790–1840. A Documentary History.* 3 vols. New York: Columbia University Press, 1966.

Eisenstein, Ira, and Kohn, Eugene, eds. *Mordecai M. Kaplan, An Evaluation.* New York: Jewish Reconstructionist Foundation, 1952.

Finkelstein, Louis. *The Jews: Their History, Culture, and Religion.* New York: Harper & Brothers, 1949. [Includes section on the United States.]

Gay, Ruth. *Jews in America: A Short History.* New York: Basic Books, 1965.

Glazer, Nathan. *American Judaism.* Chicago: University of Chicago Press, 1957.

Handlin, Oscar. *Adventure in Freedom: Three Hundred Years of Jewish Life in America.* New York: McGraw-Hill Book Co., 1954.

Hapgood, Hutchins. *The Spirit of the Ghetto,* with drawings by Jacob Epstein, 1902. New edition with commentary by Harry Golden. New York: Schocken, 1965.

Heschel, Abraham Joshua. *Between God and Man: An Interpretation of Judaism.* Edited with introduction by Fritz A. Rothschild. New York: Free Press, 1959.

Hirshler, Eric E., ed. *Jews from Germany in the United States.* New York: Farrar, Straus and Cudahy, 1955.

Karp, Abraham J., ed. *The Jewish Experience in America: Selected Studies from the Publications of the American Jewish Historical Society.* 5 vols. New York: Ktav Publishing House, 1969.

Learsi, Rufus. *Israel: A History of the Jewish People.* Cleveland: Meridian Press, 1968.

Levy, Beryl Harold. *Reform Judaism in America.* New York: Bloch Publishing Co., 1933.

Malin, Irving. *Jews and Americans.* Carbondale, Ill.: Southern Illinois University Press, 1965.

Philipson, David. *The Reform Movement in Modern Judaism.* New York: Macmillan Co., 1931.

Rischin, Moses. *The Promised City: New York's Jews, 1870–1914.* Cambridge, Mass.: Harvard University Press, 1962.

Rose, Peter I., ed. *The Ghetto and Beyond: Essays on Jewish Life in America.* New York: Random House, 1969.

Sherman, Charles B. *The Jew within American Society.* Detroit: Wayne State University Press, 1961.

Sklare, Marshall. *Conservative Judaism: An American Religious Movement.* Glencoe, Ill.: Free Press, 1955.

Wirth, Louis. *The Ghetto*. Chicago: University of Chicago Press, 1956.

Wischnitzer, Mark. *To Dwell in Safety: The Story of Jewish Migration since 1800*. Philadelphia: Jewish Publication Society of America, 1948.

Zborowski, Mark, and Herzog, Elizabeth. *Life Is with People: The Culture of the Shtetl*. New York: International Universities Press, 1952.

12. EASTERN ORTHODOXY IN AMERICA

Benz, Ernst. *The Eastern Orthodox Church: Its Thought and Life*. Translated by Richard and Clara Winston. Chicago: Aldine Publishing Co., 1963.

Bespuda, Anastasia. *Guide to Orthodox America*. Tuckahoe, N.Y.: Saint Vladimir's Seminary Press, 1965.

Bogolepov, Alexander A. *Toward an American Orthodox Church: The Establishment of an Autocephalous Orthodox Church*. New York: Morehouse-Barlow Co., 1963.

Bolshakov, Serge. *The Foreign Missions of the Russian Orthodox Church*. New York: Macmillan Co., 1943.

Bulgakov, Sergius. *The Orthodox Church*. Milwaukee: Morehouse Publishing Co., n.d. [ca. 1935].

Emhardt, Chauncey, et al. *The Eastern Church in the Western World*. Milwaukee: Morehouse Publishing Co., 1928.

Saloutos, Theodore. *The Greeks in America*. Cambridge, Mass.: Harvard University Press, 1964.

Schmemann, Alexander. *The Historical Road of Eastern Orthodoxy*. New York: Holt, Rinehart & Winston, 1963.

Ware, Timothy. *The Orthodox Church*. Baltimore: Penguin Books, 1964.

13. PROTESTANT DENOMINATIONAL HISTORIES AND STUDIES

Albright, Raymond W. *A History of the Evangelical Church*. Harrisburg, Pa.: Evangelical Press, 1942.

———. *History of the Protestant Episcopal Church*. New York: Macmillan Co., 1964.

Bacon, Margaret Hope. *The Quiet Rebels: The Story of the Quakers in America*. New York: Basic Books, 1969.

Baxter, Norman A. *History of the Freewill Baptists: A Study in New England Separatism.* Rochester, N.Y.: American Baptist Historical Society, 1957.

Bloch-Hoell, Nils Egede. *The Pentecostal Movement: Its Origin, Development, and Distinctive Character.* New York: Humanities Press, 1964.

Bucke, Emory Stevens, ed. *The History of American Methodism.* 3 vols. Nashville, Tenn.: Abingdon Press, 1964.

Drury, Augustus W. *History of the Church of the United Brethren in Christ.* Dayton, Ohio: Otterbein Press, 1924.

Garrison, Winifred E., and DeGroot, Alfred T. *The Disciples of Christ: A History.* Saint Louis: Christian Board of Publication, 1948.

Jones, Rufus. *The Quakers in the American Colonies.* London: Macmillan & Co., 1911.

Kromminga, John Henry. *The Christian Reformed Church: A Study in Orthodoxy.* Grand Rapids: Baker Book House, 1949.

Lewis, Arthur J. *Zinzendorf, The Ecumenical Pioneer: A Study in the Moravian Contribution to Christian Mission and Unity.* London: SCM Press, 1962.

Loetscher, Lefferts A. *The Broadening Church: A Study of Theological Issues in the Presbyterian Church since 1869.* Philadelphia: University of Pennsylvania Press, 1954.

McConnell, S. D. *History of the American Episcopal Church, 1600–1915.* 11th ed. Milwaukee: Morehouse Publishing Co., 1916 [First edition appeared in 1890.]

Manross, William Wilson. *A History of the American Episcopal Church.* 2d ed., rev. and enl. New York: Morehouse-Gorham, 1950.

Meuser, Fred W. *The Formation of the American Lutheran Church.* Columbus, Ohio: Wartburg Press, 1958.

Murch, James D. *Christians Only: A History of the Restoration Movement.* Cincinnati: Standard Publishing Co., 1962.

Nelson, Eugene C. *The Lutheran Church among Norwegian Americans.* Minneapolis: Augsburg Publishing House, 1960.

Nichol, John Thomas. *Pentecostalism.* New York: Harper & Row, 1966.

Olsson, Karl A., ed. *The Evangelical Covenant Church.* Chicago: Covenant Press, 1954.

Peters, John L. *Christian Perfection and American Methodism.* Nashville, Tenn.: Abingdon Press, 1956.

Schaff, Philip, et al., eds. *The American Church History Series,* 13 vols. New York: Christian Literature Co., 1893–1898. [Eleven of these volumes contain histories of major denominations.]

Schneider, Carl E. *The German Church on the American Frontier.* Saint Louis: Eden Publishing House, 1939.

Smith, Timothy L. *Called unto Holiness: The Story of the Nazarenes, The Formative Years.* Kansas City, Mo.: Nazarene Publishing House, 1962.

Stephenson, George M. *The Religious Aspects of Swedish Immigration: A Study of Immigrant Churches.* Minneapolis: University of Minnesota Press, 1932.

Sweet, William W., ed. *Religion on the American Frontier:* Vol. 1, *The Baptists* (New York: Henry Holt & Co., 1931). Vol. 2, *The Presbyterians* (New York: Harper & Brothers, 1936). Vol. 3, *The Congregationalists* (Chicago: University of Chicago Press, 1939). Vol. 4, *The Methodists* (Chicago: Univeristy of Chicago Press, 1946). [These works consist of documents with introductions by the editor.]

Thompson, Ernest T. *Presbyterians in the South.* Richmond, Va.: John Knox Press, 1963.

Tietjen, John H. *Which Way to Lutheran Unity? A History of Efforts to Unite the Lutherans of America.* Saint Louis: Concordia Publishing House, 1966.

Torbet, Robert G. *A History of the Baptists.* Philadelphia: Judson Press, 1950.

Wentz, Abdel R. *A Basic History of Lutheranism in America.* Philadelphia: Muhlenberg Press, 1955.

Winehouse, Irwin. *The Assemblies of God.* New York Vantage Press, 1959.

On groups claiming a distinct break with the Protestant tradition, see section 21: Christian Science, Jehovah's Witnesses, Mormons, New Thought, Shakers, Swedenborgians, Theosophy, etc.

14. LONG-TERM THEMES IN PROTESTANT HISTORY

Ahlstrom, Sydney E. *The American Protestant Encounter with World Religions.* Beloit, Wis.: Beloit College, 1962.

Bailey, Albert B. *The Gospel in Hymns: Background and Interpretation.* New York: Charles Scribner's Sons, 1950.

Baltzell, Edward Digby. *The Protestant Establishment: Aris-*

tocracy and Caste in America. New York: Random House, 1964.

Brumm, Ursula. *American Thought and Religious Typology.* New Brunswick, N.J.: Rutgers University Press, 1970.

Handy, Robert T. *A Christian America: Protestant Hopes and Historical Realities.* New York: Oxford University Press, 1971.

Hudson, Winthrop S. *The great Tradition of the American Churches.* New York: Harper & Brothers, 1953.

Latourette, Kenneth Scott. *Missions and the American Mind.* Indianapolis: National Foundation Press, 1949.

Lynd, Staughton, ed. *Nonviolence in America: A Documentary History.* Indianapolis: Bobbs-Merrill Co., 1966.

McLoughlin, William G. *Modern Revivalism: Charles Grandison Finney to Billy Graham.* New York: Ronald Press Co., 1959.

Marty, Martin E. *The Infidel: Freethought and American Religion.* Cleveland, Ohio: Meridian Books, 1961.

Meyer, Donald B. *The Positive Thinkers: A Study of the Quest for Health, Wealth, and Personal Power from Mary Baker Eddy to Norman Vincent Peale.* Garden City, N.Y.: Doubleday & Co., 1965.

Mode, Peter G. *The Frontier Spirit in American Christianity.* New York: Macmillan Co., 1923.

Niebuhr, H. Richard. *The Kingdom of God in America.* New York: Harper & Brothers, 1937.

———. *The Social Sources of Denominationalism.* New York: Henry Holt & Co., 1929.

Osborn, Ronald E. *The Spirit of American Christianity.* New York: Harper Brothers, 1958.

Perry, Ralph Barton. *Puritanism and Democracy.* New York: Vanguard Press, 1944.

Shea, Daniel B., Jr., *Spiritual Autobiography in Early America.* Princeton, N.J.: Princeton University Press, 1968.

Smith, Hilrie Shelton. *Changing Conceptions of Original Sin: A Study in American Theology since 1750.* New York: Charles Scribner's Sons, 1955.

———. *Faith and Nurture.* New York: Charles Scribner's Sons, 1941.

Stewart, Randall. *American Literature and Christian Doctrine.* Baton Rouge: Louisiana State University Press, 1958.

Sweet, William W. *Revivalism in America: Its Origin, Growth and Decline.* New York: Charles Scribner's Sons, 1944.

Weisberger, Bernard A. *They Gathered at the River: The Story of the Great Revivalists and Their Impact upon Religion in America.* Boston: Little, Brown and Co., 1958.

15. EARLY COLONIAL RELIGION

Andrews, Charles M. *The Colonial Period of American History.* 4 vols. New Haven: Yale University Press, 1934–38.

Bailyn, Bernard. *New England Merchants in the Seventeenth Century.* Cambridge, Mass.: Harvard University Press, 1955.

Baird, Charles W. *History of the Huguenot Emigration to America.* 2 vols. New York, 1885.

Bertelson, David. *The Lazy South.* New York: Oxford University Press, 1967.

Condon, Thomas J. *New York Beginnings: The Commercial Origins of New Netherland.* New York: New York University Press, 1968.

Craven, Wesley F. *The Southern Colonies in the Seventeenth Century, 1607–1689.* Baton Rouge: Louisiana State University Press, 1949.

Davidson, Elizabeth H. *The Establishment of the English Church in the Continental American Colonies.* Durham, N.C.: Duke University Press, 1936.

Johnson, Amandus. *The Swedish Settlements on the Delaware.* 2 vols. Philadelphia: University of Pennsylvania Press, 1911.

Sachse, Julius F. *The German Pietists of Provincial Pennsylvania, 1694–1708.* Philadelphia, 1895.

———. *The German Sectarians of Pennsylvania.* 2 vols. Philadelphia, 1899–1900.

Tolles, Frederick B., and Alderfer, E. Gordon. *The Witness of William Penn.* New York; Macmillan Co., 1957.

Wertenbaker, Thomas J. *The Founding of American Civilization.* 3 vols. New York: Charles Scribner's Sons, 1938–47.

16. AMERICAN PURITANISM

Erikson, Kai T. *Wayward Puritans: A Study in the Sociology of Deviance.* New York: John Wiley & Sons, 1966.

Foster, Stephen. *Their Solitary Way: The Puritan Social Ethic in the First Century of Settlement in New England.* New Haven: Yale University Press, 1971.

Hall, David, ed. *The Antinomian Controversy: A Documentary History.* Middletown, Conn.: Wesleyan University Press, 1968.

Langdon, George D., Jr. *Pilgrim Colony: A History of New Plymouth, 1620–1691.* New Haven: Yale University Press, 1966.

Miller, Perry. *Errand into the Wilderness.* Cambridge, Mass.: Harvard University Press, 1956.

———. *The New England Mind; From Colony to Province.* Cambridge, Mass.: Harvard University Press, 1953.

———. *The New England Mind: The Seventeenth Century.* New York: Macmillan Co., 1939.

———. *Orthodoxy in Massachusetts, 1630–1650.* Cambridge, Mass.: Harvard University Press, 1933.

———. *Roger Williams: His Contribution to the American Tradition.* Indianapolis: Bobbs-Merrill Co., 1953.

———, and Johnson, Thomas H., eds. *The Puritans: A Sourcebook of Their Writings.* Bibliographies revised by George McCandlish. 2 vols. Rev. ed. New York: Harper & Row, 1963.

Morgan, Edmund S. *The Puritan Dilemma: The Story of John Winthrop.* Boston: Little, Brown and Co., 1958.

———. *Roger Williams: The Church and the State.* New York: Harcourt, Brace & World, 1967.

———. *Visible Saints: The History of a Puritan Idea.* New York: New York University Press, 1963.

Morison, Samuel Eliot. *Builders of the Bay Colony.* Boston: Houghton Mifflin Co., 1930.

———. *The Founding of Harvard College.* Cambridge, Mass.: Harvard University Press, 1935.

Murdock, Kenneth. *Literature and Theology in Colonial New England.* Cambridge, Mass.: Harvard University Press, 1949.

Pettit, Norman. *The Heart Prepared: Grace and Conversion in Puritan Spiritual Life.* New Haven: Yale University Press, 1966.

Rutman, Darrett B. *American Puritanism: Faith and Practice.* Philadelphia: J. B. Lippincott Co., 1970.

———. *Winthrop's Boston: Portrait of a Puritan Town.* Chapel Hill: University of North Carolina Press, 1965.

Schneider, Herbert W. *The Puritan Mind*. Ann Arbor: University of Michigan Press, 1958.

Simpson, Alan. *Puritanism in Old and New England*. Chicago: University of Chicago Press, 1955.

Walker, Williston. *The Creeds and Platforms of Congregationalism*. Introduction by Douglas Horton. Boston: Pilgrim Press, 1960.

Winslow, Ola E. *Master Roger Williams: A Biography*. New York: Macmillan Co., 1957.

———. *Meetinghouse Hill, 1630–1783*. New York: Macmillan Co., 1952.

17. LATER COLONIAL RELIGION

Akers, Charles W. *Called unto Liberty: A Life of Jonathan Mayhew, 1720–1766*. Cambridge, Mass.: Harvard University Press, 1964.

Aldridge, Owen. *Benjamin Franklin and Nature's God*. Durham, N.C.: Duke University Press, 1967.

Bailyn, Bernard. *The Ideological Origins of the American Revolution*. Cambridge, Mass.: Harvard University Press, 1967.

Baldwin, Alice M. *The New England Clergy and the American Revolution*. Durham, N.C.: Duke University Press, 1928.

Boorstin, Daniel J. *The Lost World of Thomas Jefferson*. New York: Henry Holt & Co., 1948.

Bridenbaugh, Carl. *Mitre and Sceptre: Transatlantic Faiths, Ideas, Personalities, and Politics, 1689–1775*. New York: Oxford University Press, 1962.

Bushman, Richard L. *From Puritan to Yankee: Character and the Social Order in Connecticut, 1690–1795*. Cambridge, Mass.: Harvard University Press, 1967.

Carroll, Peter N., ed. *Religion and the Coming of the American Revolution*. Waltham, Mass.: Ginn & Co., 1970.

Cassirer, Ernst. *The Philosophy of the Enlightenment*. Princeton, N.J.: Princeton University Press, 1951.

Cousins, Norman, ed. *In God We Trust: The Religious Beliefs and Ideas of the American Founding Fathers*. New York: Harper & Brothers, 1958.

Cross, Arthur L. *The Anglican Episcopate and the American Colonies*. New York: Longmans, Green and Co., 1902.

Gaustad, Edwin Scott. *The Great Awakening in New England.* New York: Harper & Row, 1957.

Gay, Peter. *The Enlightenment: An Interpretation, The Rise of Modern Paganism.* New York: Random House, 1966.

Gewehr, Wesley M. *The Great Awakening in Virginia, 1740–1790.* Durham, N.C.: Duke University Press, 1930.

Goen, Clarence C. *Revivalism and Separatism in New England: Strict Congregationalists and Separate Baptists in the Great Awakening.* New Haven: Yale University Press, 1962.

Heimert, Alan E. *Religion and the American Mind from the Great Awakening to the Revolution.* Cambridge, Mass.: Harvard University Press, 1966.

Henry, Stuart C. *George Whitefield: Wayfaring Witness.* New York: Abingdon Press, 1957.

Koch, Gustav A. *Republican Religion: The American Revolution and the Cult of Reason.* New York: Henry Holt & Co., 1933.

Loveland, Clara Olds. *The Critical Years: The Reconstruction of the Anglican Church in the United States of America, 1780–1789.* Greenwich, Conn.: Seabury Press, 1956.

McLoughlin, William G. *Isaac Backus and the American Pietistic Tradition.* Boston: Little, Brown and Co., 1967.

Maxson, Charles H. *The Great Awakening in the Middle Colonies.* Chicago: University of Chicago Press, 1920.

Morais, Herbert M. *Deism in Eighteenth-Century America.* New York: Columbia University Press, 1934.

Ray, Sister Mary Augustina. *American Opinion of Roman Catholicism in the Eighteenth Century.* New York: Columbia University Press, 1936.

Tanis, James R. *Dutch Calvinistic Pietism in the Middle Colonies: A Study in the Life of Theodorus Jacobus Frelinghuysen.* The Hague: Martinus Nijhof, 1967.

Thompson, Henry P. *Into All Lands: The History of the Society for the Propagation of the Gospel in Foreign Parts, 1701–1950.* London: SPCK, 1951.

———. *Thomas Bray.* London: SPCK, 1954.

Tolles, Frederick B. *Meeting House and Counting House: The Quaker Merchants of Colonial Philadelphia 1682–1763.* Chapel Hill: University of North Carolina Press, 1948.

Trinterud, Leonard J. *The Forming of an American Tradition: A Re-Examination of Colonial Presbyterianism.* Philadelphia: Westminster Press, 1949.

18. JONATHAN EDWARDS AND THE NEW ENGLAND THEOLOGY

Boardman, George N. *A History of the New England Theology*. Chicago, 1899.

Carse, James. *Jonathan Edwards and the Visibility of God* New York: Charles Scribner's Sons, 1967.

Cherry, Conrad. *The Theology of Jonathan Edwards: A Reappraisal*. Garden City, N.Y.: Doubleday & Co., Anchor Books, 1966.

Davidson, Edward H. *Jonathan Edwards: The Narrative of a Puritan Mind*. Boston: Houghton Mifflin Co., 1966.

Delattre, Roland A. *Beauty and Sensibility in the Thought of Jonathan Edwards*. New Haven: Yale University Press, 1968.

Elwood, Douglas J. *The Philosophical Theology of Jonathan Edwards*. New York: Columbia University Press, 1960.

Faust, Clarence H., and Johnson, Thomas H., eds. *Jonathan Edwards, Representative Selections*. Rev. ed. New York: Hill & Wang, 1962.

Foster, Frank H. *A Genetic History of the New England Theology*. Chicago: University of Chicago Press, 1907.

Haroutunian, Joseph. *Piety versus Moralism: The Passing of the New England Theology*. New York: Henry Holt & Co., 1932. Reprint. Introduction by Sydney E. Ahlstrom. New York: Harper & Row, Torchbooks, 1970.

Levin, David, ed. *Jonathan Edwards: A Profile*. New York: Hill & Wang, 1969.

Mead, Sidney E. *Nathaniel William Taylor, 1786–1858: A Connecticut Liberal*. Chicago: University of Chicago Press, 1942.

Miller, Perry. *Jonathan Edwards*. New York: William Sloan Associates, 1949.

Winslow, Ola E. *Jonathan Edwards*. New York: Macmillan Co., 1940.

19. ANTEBELLUM PROTESTANTISM

Ayres, Anne. *The Life and Work of William Augustus Muhlenberg*. New York, 1380.

Billington, Ray A. *The Protestant Crusade 1800–1860: A Study of the Origins of American Nativism.* New York: Macmillan Co., 1938.

Bodo, John R. *The Protestant Clergy and Public Issues, 1812–1848.* Princeton, N.J.: Princeton University Press, 1954.

Cleveland, Catharine C. *The Great Revival in the West, 1797–1805.* Chicago: University of Chicago Press, 1916.

Cole, Charles C., Jr. *The Social Ideas of the Northern Evangelists, 1826–1860.* New York: Columbia University Press, 1954.

Cross, Whitney R. *The Burned-Over District: The Social and Intellectual History of Enthusiastic Religion in Western New York, 1800–1850.* Ithaca: Cornell University Press, 1950.

Eaton, Clement. *The Mind of the Old South.* Rev. ed. Baton Rouge: Louisiana State University Press, 1967.

Ekirch, Arthur. *The Idea of Progress in America, 1815–1860.* New York: Columbia University Press, 1944.

Elsbree, Oliver W. *The Rise of the Missionary Spirit in America, 1790–1815.* Williamsport, Pa.: Williamsport Printing Co., 1928.

Ferm, Vergilius. *The Crisis in Lutheran Theology: A Study of the Issue between American Lutheranism and Old Lutheranism.* New York: Century Co., 1927.

Foster, Charles I. *An Errand of Mercy: The Evangelical United Front, 1790–1837.* Chapel Hill: University of North Carolina Press, 1960.

Goodykoontz, Colin B. *Home Missions on the American Frontier, with Particular Reference to the American Home Missionary Society.* Caldwell, Idaho: Caxton, 1939.

Griffin, Clifford S., *Their Brothers' Keepers: Moral Stewardship in the United States, 1800–1865.* New Brunswick, N.J.: Rutgers University Press, 1960.

Howe, Daniel W. *The Unitarian Conscience: The Harvard Moral Philosophers, 1805–1861.* Cambridge, Mass.: Harvard University Press, 1970.

Johnson, Charles A. *The Frontier Camp Meeting: Religion's Harvest Time.* Dallas, Tex.: Southern Methodist University Press, 1955.

Keller, Charles Roy. *The Second Great Awakening in Connecticut.* New Haven: Yale University Press, 1942.

Krout, John Allen. *The Origins of Prohibition*. New York: Alfred A. Knopf, 1925.

Ludlum, David M. *Social Ferment in Vermont, 1791–1850*. New York: Columbia University Press, 1939.

Marsden, George M. *The Evangelical Mind and the New School Presbyterian Experience*. New Haven: Yale University Press, 1970.

Mathews, Lois Kimball. *The Expansion of New England: The Spread of New England Institutions to the Mississippi River, 1620–1865*. Boston: Houghton Mifflin Co., 1909.

Miller, Perry. *The Life of the Mind in America: From the Revolution to the Civil War*. New York: Harcourt, Brace & World, 1965.

Miyakawa, T. Scott. *Protestants and Pioneers: Individualism and Conformity on the American Frontier*. Chicago: University of Chicago Press, 1964.

Ratner, Lorman. *Antimasonry: The Crusade and the Party*. Englewood Cliffs, N.J.: Prentice-Hall, 1969.

Rice, Edwin W. *The Sunday School Movement and the American Sunday School Union*. Philadelphia: Union Press, 1917.

Rosenberg, Carroll S. *Religion and the Rise of the City: The New York City Mission Movement*. Ithaca: Cornell University Press, 1971.

Silverman, Kenneth. *Timothy Dwight*. New York: Twayne Publishers, 1969.

Smith, Timothy L. *Revivalism and Social Reform in Mid-Nineteenth-Century America*. Nashville, Tenn.: Abingdon Press, 1957.

Smith, Wilson. *Professors and Public Ethics: Studies in Northern Moral Philosophers before the Civil War*. Ithaca: Cornell University Press, 1956.

Stephenson, George M. *The Puritan Heritage*. New York: Macmillan Co., 1952.

Sweet, William W. *Religion in the Development of American Culture, 1765–1840*. New York: Charles Scribner's Sons, 1952.

Taylor, William R. *Cavalier and Yankee: The Old South and American National Character*. New York: George Braziller, 1967.

Tewskbury, Donald G. *The Founding of American Colleges and Universities before the Civil War, with Particular Ref-*

erence to the Religious Influences Bearing on the College Movement. New York: Columbia University Press, 1932.

Tyler, Alice F. *Freedom's Ferment: Phases of American Social History to 1860.* Minneapolis: University of Minnesota Press, 1944.

Wright, Conrad. *The Beginnings of Unitarianism.* Boston: Beacon Press, 1955.

20. TRANSCENDENTALISM AND OTHER ROMANTIC CURRENTS

Bishop, Jonathan. *Emerson on the Soul.* Cambridge, Mass.: Harvard University Press, 1964.

Brown, Jerry W. *The Rise of Biblical Criticism in America, 1800–1870: The New England Scholars.* Middletown, Conn.: Wesleyan University Press, 1969.

Carpenter, Frederic I. *Emerson Handbook.* New York: Hendricks House, 1957.

Cross, Barbara M. *Horace Bushnell: Minister to a Changing America.* Chicago: University of Chicago Press, 1958.

Crowe, Charles. *George Ripley: Transcendentalist and Utopian Socialist.* Athens, Ga.: University of Georgia Press, 1967.

Easton, Loyd D. *Hegel's First American Followers: The Ohio Hegelians.* Athens, Ohio: Ohio University Press, 1966.

Fairweather, Eugene R., ed. *The Oxford Movement.* Library of Protestant Thought. New York: Oxford University Press, 1964.

Frothingham, Octavius Brooks. *Transcendentalism in New England: A History.* 1876. Reprint. Introduction by Sydney E. Ahlstrom. Philadelphia: University of Pennsylvania Press, 1972.

Furst, Lilian R. *Romanticism in Perspective: A Comparative Study of Aspects of the Romantic Movements in England, France, and Germany.* London: Macmillan & Co., 1969.

Hochfield, George, ed. *Selected Writings of the American Transcendentalists.* New York: New American Library, 1966.

Hutchison, William R. *The Transcendentalist Ministers: Church Reform in the New England Renaissance.* New Haven: Yale University Press, 1959.

Matthiessen, F. O. *The American Renaissance.* New York: Oxford University Press, 1941.

Miller, Perry, ed. *The Transcendentalists: An Anthology.*
Cambridge, Mass.: Harvard University Press, 1959.

Nichols, James Hastings. *Romanticism in American Theology:
Nevin and Schaff at Mercersburg.* Chicago: University of
Chicago Press, 1961.

———, ed. *The Mercersburg Theology.* New York: Oxford
University Press, 1966.

Rusk, Ralph L. *The Life of Ralph Waldo Emerson.* New
York: Charles Scribner's Sons, 1949.

Stanton, Phoebe B. *The Gothic Revival and American
Church Architecture 1840–1856.* Baltimore: Johns Hopkins
Press, 1968.

Swift, Lindsay. *Brook Farm: Its Members, Scholars, and Visi-
tors.* New York: Macmillan Co., 1900.

White, James F. *The Cambridge Movement.* New York:
Cambridge University Press, 1962.

Williams, Norman P., and Harris, Charles, eds. *Northern Catholicism: Centenary Studies in the Oxford and Parallel
Movements.* New York: Macmillan Co., 1933.

21. NEW MOVEMENTS IN RELIGION: NINETEENTH CENTURY

Andrews, Edward D. *The People Called Shakers.* New York:
Oxford University Press, 1953.

Bates, Ernest Sutherland, and Dittemore, John V. *Mary
Baker Eddy: The Truth and the Tradition.* New York:
Alfred A. Knopf, 1932.

Bestor, Arthur Eugene, Jr. *Backwoods Utopias: The Sectarian
and Owenite Phases of Communitarian Socialism in America, 1663–1829.* Philadelphia: University of Pennsylvania
Press, 1950.

Block, Marguerite. *The New Church in the New World: A
Study of Swedenborgianism in the New World.* New York:
Henry Holt & Co., 1932.

Boldt, Ernst. *From Luther to Steiner.* London: Methuen &
Co., 1923.

Braden, Charles S. *Spirits in Rebellion: The Rise and Development of New Thought.* Dallas, Tex.: Southern Methodist
University Press, 1963.

———. *These Also Believe: A Study of Modern American
Cults and Minority Religious Movements.* New York: Macmillan Co., 1949.

Brodie, Fawn. *No Man Knows My History: The Life of Joseph Smith, the Mormon Prophet.* New York: Alfred A. Knopf, 1945.

Cole, Marley. *Jehovah's Witnesses: The New World Society.* New York: Vantage Press, 1955.

Dresser, Horatio W. *History of the New Thought Movement.* New York: Crowell, 1919.

Ferraby, John. *All Things Made New: A Comprehensive Outline of the Bahá'i Faith,* New York: Macmillan Co., 1958.

Flanders, Robert Bruce. *Nauvoo: Kingdom on the Mississippi.* Urbana, Ill.: University of Illinois Press, 1965.

Fornell, Earl Wesley. *The Unhappy Medium: Spiritualism and the Life of Margaret Fox.* Austin, Tex.: University of Texas Press, 1964.

Holloway, Mark. *Heavens on Earth: Utopian Communities in America, 1680–1880.* 2d ed. New York: Dover Publications, 1966.

Kennedy, Hugh A. Studdert. *Mrs. Eddy: Her Life, Her Work, and Her Place in History.* San Francisco: Farallon Press, 1947.

Kuhn, Alvin Boyd. *Theosophy: A Modern Revival of Ancient Wisdom.* New York: Henry Holt & Co., 1930.

Leopold, Richard W. *Robert Dale Owen.* Cambridge, Mass.: Harvard University Press, 1940.

McMurrin, Sterling M. *Theological Foundations of the Mormon Religion.* Salt Lake City: University of Utah Press, 1955.

Mayer, Frederick E. *Jehovah's Witnesses.* Saint Louis: Concordia Publishing House, 1952.

Martin, Walter R. *The Truth about Seventh-Day Adventism.* Grand Rapids, Mich.: Zondervan Publishing House, 1960.

Miller, William M. *Bahá'ism: Its Origin and Teachings.* New York: Fleming H. Revell, 1931.

Mullen, Robert. *The Latter-Day Saints: The Mormons Yesterday and Today.* Garden City, N.Y.: Doubleday & Co., 1966.

Nichol, Francis David. *The Midnight Cry: A Defense of the Character and Conduct of William Miller and the Millerites.* Washington, D.C.: Review & Herald Publishing Association, 1944.

O'Dea, Thomas. *The Mormons.* Chicago: University of Chicago Press, 1957.

Peel, Robert. *Mary Baker Eddy: The Years of Discovery.* New York: Holt, Rinehart & Winston, 1966.

Porter, Katherine H. *Through the Glass Darkly: Spiritualism in the Browning Circle.* Lawrence, Kans.: University of Kansas Press, 1958.

Schneider, Herbert W. *A Prophet and a Pilgrim: Being the Incredible History of Thomas Lake Harris and Laurence Oliphant.* New York: Columbia University Press, 1942.

Spaulding, W. W. *A History of Seventh-Day Adventists.* 2 vols. Washington, D.C.: Review & Herald Publishing Association, 1949.

West, Ray B. *Kingdom of the Saints: The Story of Brigham Young and the Mormons.* New York: Viking, 1957.

22. SECTIONAL ISSUES AND THE CIVIL WAR

Barnes, Gilbert H. *The Antislavery Impulse, 1830–1844.* New York: D. Appleton-Century Co., 1933.

Blied, Benjamin J. *Catholics and the Civil War.* Milwaukee: Privately Printed, 1945.

Duberman, Martin, ed. *The Antislavery Vanguard: New Essays on the Abolitionists.* Princeton, N.Y.: Princeton University Press, 1965.

Dumond, Dwight L. *The Antislavery Origins of the Civil War in the United States.* Ann Arbor: University of Michigan Press, 1965.

Dunham, Chester F. *The Attitude of the Northern Clergy toward the South, 1860–1865.* Toledo, Ohio: Gray Co., 1942.

Filler, Louis. *The Crusade Against Slavery, 1830–1860.* New York: Harper & Row, 1960.

Fredrickson, George M. *The Inner Civil War: Northern Intellectuals and the Crisis of the Union.* New York: Harper & Row, 1965.

Korn, Bertram W. *American Jewry and the Civil War.* Cleveland: Meridian Books, 1961.

Mathews, Donald G. *Slavery and Methodism: A Chapter in American Morality, 1780–1845.* Princeton, N.J.: Princeton University Press, 1965.

Pressly, Thomas J. *Americans Interpret Their Civil War.* New York: Collier Books, 1962.

Silver, James W. *Confederate Morale and Church Propaganda.* Tuscaloosa, Ala.: Confederate Publishing Co., 1957.

Stampp, Kenneth M. *And the War Came: The North and the Secession Crisis, 1860–61.* Chicago: University of Chicago Press, 1950.
———. *The Era of Reconstruction, 1865–1877.* New York: Alfred A. Knopf, 1967.
Staudenraus, P. J. *The African Colonization Movement, 1816–1865.* New York: Columbia University Press, 1961.
Wolf, William J. *The Almost Chosen People: A Study of the Religion of Abraham Lincoln.* Garden City, N.Y.: Doubleday & Co., 1959.
Zilversmit, Arthur. *The First Emancipation: The Abolition of Slavery in the North.* Chicago: University of Chicago Press, 1967.

23. SLAVERY, THE NEGRO, AND THE BLACK CHURCHES

Bardolph, Richard. *The Negro Vanguard.* New York: Random House, 1959.
Bracey, John H., Jr., Meier, August, and Rudwick, Elliott, eds. *Black Nationalism in America.* Indianapolis: Bobbs-Merrill Co. 1970.
Davie, Maurice R. *Negroes in American Society.* New York: McGraw-Hill Book Co., 1949.
Davis, David B. *The Problem of Slavery in Western Culture.* Ithaca: Cornell University Press, 1966.
DuBois, W. E. Burghardt. *The Souls of Black Folk.* 1903. Reprint. New York: Fawcett World Library, 1961.
———. *The Negro Church.* Atlanta, 1903.
Franklin, John Hope. *From Slavery to Freedom: A History of Negro Americans.* New York: Alfred A. Knopf, 1967.
Frazier, E. Franklin. *The Negro Church in America.* New York: Schocken Books, 1964.
———. *The Negro in the United States.* New York: Macmillan Co., 1949.
Gossett, Thomas F. *Race: The History of an Idea in America.* Dallas: Southern Methodist University Press, 1963.
Johnson, Clifton H., ed. *God Struck Me Dead: Religious Conversion Experiences and Autobiographies of Ex-Slaves.* Philadelphia: Pilgrim Press, 1969.
Jordan, Winthrop D. *White over Black: American Attitudes toward the Negro, 1550–1812.* Chapel Hill: University of North Carolina Press, 1968.

Lapides, Frederick R., and Burrows, David, eds. *Racism: A Casebook*. New York: Thomas Y. Crowell, 1971.

Mays, Benjamin E. *The Negro's God, as Reflected in His Literature*. New York: Atheneum Publishers, 1968.

———, and Nicolson, Joseph W. *The Negro's Church*. New York: Institute of Social and Religious Research, 1933.

Meier, August. *Negro Thought in America, 1880–1915*. Ann Arbor: University of Michigan Press, 1963.

Murray, Andrew E. *Presbyterians and the Negro: A History*. Philadelphia: Presbyterian Historical Society, 1966.

Nelsen, Hart M., Yokley, Raytha, and Nelsen, Anne. *The Black Church in America*. New York: Basic Books, 1971.

Pelt, Owen D., and Smith, Ralph Lee. *The Story of the National Baptists*. New York: Vantage Press, 1960.

Pipes, William H. *Say Amen, Brother! Old-Time Negro Preaching: A Study in Frustration*. New York: William-Frederick Press, 1951.

Redkey, Edwin S. *Black Exodus: Black Nationalist and Back-to-Africa Movements, 1890–1910*. New Haven: Yale University Press, 1969.

Reimers, David M. *White Protestantism and the Negro*. New York: Oxford University Press, 1965.

Rose, Arnold. *The Negro in America*. Boston: Beacon Press, 1956 [A condensation of Gunnar Myrdal. *The American Dilemma, 1944*.]

Washington, Joseph R., Jr. *Black Religion: The Negro and Christianity in the United States*. Boston: Beacon Press, 1964.

Weinstein, Allen, and Gatell, Frank O. *American Negro Slavery: A Modern Reader*. New York: Oxford University Press, 1968.

Woodson, Carter G. *The History of the Negro Church*. 2d ed. Washington, D.C.: Associated Publishers, 1921.

Woodward, C. Vann. *The Strange History of Jim Crow*. 2d rev. ed. New York: Oxford University Press, 1966.

24. ROMAN CATHOLICISM IN THE NINETEENTH AND TWENTIETH CENTURIES

Abell, Aaron I., ed. *American Catholic Thought on Social Questions*. Indianapolis: Bobbs-Merrill Co., 1968.

———. *American Catholicism and Social Action: A Search*

for Social Justice, 1865–1950. Garden City, N.Y.: Hanover House, 1960.

Bell, Stephen. *Rebel, Priest, and Prophet: A Biography of Dr. Edward McGlynn*. New York: Devin-Adair Co., 1937.

Browne, Henry J. *The Catholic Church and the Knights of Labor*. Washington, D.C.: Catholic University of America Press, 1949.

Callan, Louise. *Philippine Duchesne: Frontier Missionary of the Sacred Heart, 1769–1852*. Westminster, Md.: Newman Press, 1957.

Cross, Robert D. *The Emergence of Liberal Catholicism in America*. Cambridge, Mass.: Harvard University Press, 1958.

Flynn, George Q. *American Catholics and the Roosevelt Presidency, 1932–1936*. Lexington, Ky.: University of Kentucky Press, 1968.

Gleason, Philip. *The Conservative Reformers: German-American Catholics and the Social Order*. Notre Dame, Ind.: University of Notre Dame Press, 1968.

Koenker, Ernest B. *The Liturgical Renaissance in the Roman Catholic Church*. Chicago: University of Chicago Press, 1954.

McAvoy, Thomas T. *The Formation of the American Catholic Minority*. Philadelphia: Fortress Press, 1967.

———. *The Great Crisis in American Catholic History, 1895–1900*. Chicago: Henry Regnery Co., 1957.

———, ed. *Roman Catholicism and the American Way of Life*. Notre Dame, Ind.: University of Notre Dame Press, 1960.

Marx, Paul B. *Virgil Michel and the Liturgical Movement*. Collegeville, Minn.: Liturgical Press, 1957.

Moynihan, James H. *The Life of Archbishop John Ireland*. New York: Harper & Row, 1953.

O'Brien, David J. *American Catholics and Social Reform: The New Deal Years*. New York: Oxford University Press, 1968.

Ong, Walter J. *American Catholic Crossroads*. New York: Macmillan Co., 1959.

———. *Frontiers in American Catholicism: Essays on Ideology and Culture*. New York: Macmillan Co., 1957.

Phillips, Charles S. *The Church in France, 1848–1907*. New York: Macmillan Co., 1936.

Sheean, Arthur. *Peter Maurin, Gay Believer*. New York: Hanover House, 1959.

Shields, Currin. *Democracy and Catholicism in America.* New York: McGraw-Hill Book Co., 1958.

Shuster, George N. *The Catholic Spirit in America.* New York: Dial Press, 1927.

Vidler, Alec R. *The Modernist Movement in the Roman Church.* Cambridge: At the University Press, 1934.

Ward, Leo R., ed. *The American Apostolate.* Westminster, Md.: Newman Press, 1952.

Weber, Ralph E. *Notre Dame's John Zahm.* Notre Dame, Ind.: University of Notre Dame Press, 1961.

25. PROTESTANTISM SINCE THE CIVIL WAR

Abell, Aaron I. *The Urban Impact on American Protestantism, 1865–1900.* Cambridge, Mass.: Harvard University Press, 1943.

Barnes, William Wright. *The Southern Baptist Convention, 1845–1953.* Nashville, Tenn.: Broadman Press, 1954.

Bass, Clarence B. *Backgrounds to Dispensationalism: Its Historical Genesis and Ecclesiastical Implications.* Grand Rapids, Mich.: William B. Eerdmans Co., 1960.

Buck, Paul H. *The Road to Reunion.* Boston: Little, Brown and Co., 1947.

Cochran, Thomas C. *The Inner Revolution.* New York: Harper & Row, 1967.

Cross, Robert D. *The Church and the City, 1865–1910.* Indianapolis: Bobbs-Merrill Co., 1967.

DeGroot, Alfred Thomas. *New Possibilities for Disciples and Independents, with a History of the Independents, Church of Christ Number Two.* Saint Louis: Bethany Press, 1963.

Dombrowski, James. *The Early Days of Christian Socialism in America.* New York: Columbia University Press, 1936.

Farish, Hunter D. *The Circuit Rider Dismounts.* Richmond, Va.: Dietz Press, 1938.

Findlay, James F., Jr. *Dwight L. Moody: American Evangelist, 1837–1899.* Chicago: University of Chicago Press, 1969.

Handy, Robert T., ed. *The Social Gospel in America, 1870–1920: Gladden, Ely, Rauschenbusch.* Library of Protestant Thought. New York: Oxford University Press, 1966.

Higham, John. *Strangers in the Land: Patterns of American Nativism, 1860–1925.* New Brunswick, N.J.: Rutgers University Press, 1955.

Hopkins, Charles H. *A History of the YMCA in North America.* New York: Association Press, 1951.

———. *The Rise of the Social Gospel in American Protestantism, 1865–1915.* New Haven: Yale University Press, 1940.

Kraus, C. Norman. *Dispensationalism in America: Its Rise and Development.* Richmond, Va.: John Knox Press, 1958.

MacKenzie, Kenneth M. *The Robe and the Sword: The Methodist Church and the Rise of American Imperialism.* Washington, D.C.: Public Affairs Press, 1961.

Mann, Arthur. *Yankee Reformers in the Urban Age: Social Reform in Boston, 1880–1900.* Cambridge, Mass.: Harvard University Press, Belknap Press, 1954.

May, Henry F. *Protestant Churches and Industrial America.* New York: Harper & Brothers, 1949.

Sandeen, Ernest R. *The Roots of Fundamentalism, British and American.* Chicago: University of Chicago Press, 1970.

Sinclair, Andrew. *Prohibition: The Era of Excess.* Boston: Little, Brown and Co., 1962.

Spain, Rufus. *At Ease in Zion: Social History of Southern Baptists.* Nashville, Tenn.: Vanderbilt University Press, 1967.

Thompson, Ernest Trice. *The Spirituality of the Church: A Distinctive Doctrine of the Presbyterian Church in the United States.* Richmond, Va.: John Knox Press, 1961.

Weisenburger, Francis P. *Ordeal of Faith: The Crisis of Churchgoing America, 1865–1900.* New York: Philosophical Library, 1959.

Woodward, C. Vann. *The Burden of Southern History.* Baton Rouge: Louisiana State University Press, 1960.

26. LIBERAL TRENDS IN NINETEENTH-CENTURY RELIGIOUS THOUGHT

Bixler, J. Seelye. *Religion in the Philosophy of William James.* Boston: Marshall Jones Co., 1926.

Bowden, Henry W. *Church History in the Age of Science.* Chapel Hill: University of North Carolina Press, 1971.

Brown, Ira. *Lyman Abbott.* Cambridge, Mass.: Harvard University Press, 1953.

Buckham, John Wright, *Progressive Religious Thought in*

America: A Survey of the Enlarging Pilgrim Faith. Boston: Houghton Mifflin Co., 1919.

Carter, Paul A. *The Spiritual Crisis of the Gilded Age.* DeKalb, Ill.: Northern Illinois University Press, 1972.

Cauthen, Kenneth. *The Impact of American Religious Liberalism.* New York: Harper & Row, 1962.

Foster, Frank H., *The Modern Movement in American Theology.* New York: Fleming H. Revell Co., 1939.

Greene, John C. *Darwin and the Modern World View.* Baton Rouge: Louisiana State University Press, 1961.

———. *The Death of Adam: Evolution and Its Impact on Western Thought.* Ames, Iowa; Iowa State University Press, 1959.

Hofstadter, Richard. *Social Darwinism in the United States, 1860–1915.* Philadelphia: University of Pennsylvania Press, 1945.

Hutchison, William R., ed. *American Protestant Thought: The Liberal Era.* New York: Harper & Row, 1968.

McGiffert, Arthur C., *The Rise of Modern Religious Ideas.* New York: Macmillan Co., 1915.

Moore, Edward C. *An Outline of the History of Christian Thought since Kant.* New York: Charles Scribner's Sons, 1912.

Persons, Stow, ed. *Evolutionary Thought in America.* New Haven: Yale University Press, 1950.

———. *Free Religion: An American Faith.* New Haven: Yale University Press, 1947.

Post, Albert. *Popular Free Thought in America, 1825–1850.* New York: Columbia University Press, 1943.

Radest, Howard B. *Toward Common Ground: The Story of the Ethical Societies in the United States.* New York: Frederick Ungar Co., 1969.

Roth, Robert J. *American Religious Philosophy.* New York: Harcourt, Brace & World, 1967.

Smith, John E. *The Spirit of American Philosophy.* New York: Oxford University Press, 1963.

White, Edward A. *Science and Religion in American Thought: The Impact of Naturalism.* Stanford, Calif.: Stanford University Press, 1952.

Wiener, Philip P. *Evolution and the Founders of Pragmatism.* Cambridge, Mass.: Harvard University Press, 1949.

Williams, Daniel Day. *The Andover Liberals: A Study in American Theology.* New York: King's Crown Press, 1941.

Young, Frederic H. *The Philosophy of Henry James, Sr.* New York: Bookman Associates, 1951.

27. ECUMENICAL AND INTER-FAITH DEVELOPMENTS

Bell, George K. A. *The Kingship of Christ: The Story of the World Council of Churches.* Baltimore: Penguin Books, 1954.

Brown, Robert McAfee, and Scott, David H., comps. and eds. *The Challenge to Reunion.* New York: McGraw-Hill Book Co., 1963.

——, and Weigle, Gustave. *An American Dialogue.* Garden City, N.Y.: Doubleday & Co., 1960.

Cavert, Samuel McCrea. *The American Churches in the Ecumenical Movement, 1900–1968.* New York: Association Press, 1968.

Douglass, H. Paul. *Church Unity Movements in the United States.* New York: Institute of Social and Religious Research, 1934.

Eckardt, A. Roy. *Elder and Younger Brothers: The Encounter of Jews and Christians.* New York: Charles Scribner's Sons, 1967.

Gilbert, Arthur. *A Jew in Christian America.* New York: Sheed & Ward, 1966.

Handy, Robert T. *We Witness Together: A History of Cooperative Home Missions.* New York: Friendship Press, 1956.

Hutchison, John A. *We Are Not Divided: A Critical and Historical Study of the Federal Council of the Churches of Christ in America.* New York: Round Table Press, 1941.

Lee, Robert. *The Social Sources of Church Unity.* Nashville, Tenn.: Abingdon Press, 1960.

Macfarland, Charles S. *Christian Unity in the Making: The First Twenty-Five Years of the Federal Council of the Churches of Christ in America, 1905–1930.* New York: Federal Council of Churches of Christ in America, 1948.

Murch, James D. *Cooperation without Compromise: A History of the National Association of Evangelicals.* Grand Rapids, Mich.: William B. Eerdmans Co., 1956.

Rosenzweig, Franz. *Judaism Despite Christianity: The "Letters on Christianity and Judaism" between Eugen Rosenstock-Huessy and Franz Rosenzweig.* Edited by Eugen

Rosenstock-Huessy. University, Ala.: University of Alabama Press, 1969.

Rouse, Ruth, and Neill, Stephen C. *A History of the Ecumenical Movement, 1517–1948.* Philadelphia: Westminster Press, 1954.

Schoeps, Hans J. *The Jewish-Christian Argument.* New York: Holt, Rinehart & Winston. 1963.

Visser 't Hooft, Willem Adolph, ed. *The First Assembly of the World Council of Churches.* New York: Harper & Brothers, 1949.

28. RELIGIOUS HISTORY FROM WORLD WAR I TO THE VIETNAM WAR

Abrams, Ray H. *Preachers Present Arms.* New York: Round Table Press, 1933.

Allen, Frederick L. *Only Yesterday: An Informal History of the 1920s.* New York: Harper & Brothers, 1931.

———. *Since Yesterday.* New York: Harper & Brothers, 1940.

Atkins, Gaius Glenn. *Religion in Our Times.* New York: Round Table Press, 1932.

Bailey, Kenneth K. *Southern White Protestantism in the Twentieth Century.* New York: Harper & Row, 1964.

Bennett, David H. *Demagogues in the Depression: American Radicals and the Union Party, 1932–1936.* New Brunswick, N.J.: Rutgers University Press, 1969.

Braeman, John, et al., eds. *The 1920s.* Columbus: Ohio State University Press, 1968.

Brown, William A. *The Church in America: A Study of the Present Condition and Future Prospects of American Protestantism.* New York: Macmillan Co., 1922.

Carter, Paul A. *The Decline and Revival of Social Gospel, 1920–1940.* Ithaca: Cornell University Press, 1956.

Clark, Walter Huston. *The Oxford Group: Its History and Significance.* New York: Bookman Associates, 1951.

Dabney, Virginius. *Dry Messiah: The Life of Bishop Cannon.* New York: Alfred A. Knopf, 1949.

Eckardt, A. Roy. *The Surge of Piety in America: An Appraisal.* New York: Association Press, 1958.

Furniss, Norman K. *The Fundamentalist Controversy, 1918–1931.* New Haven: Yale University Press, 1954.

Gasper, Louis. *The Fundamentalist Movement*. The Hague: Mouton & Co., 1963.

Gatewood, William B., Jr., ed. *Controversy in the Twenties: Fundamentalism, Modernism, and Evolution*. Nashville, Tenn.: Vanderbilt University Press, 1969.

Ginger, Ray. *Six Days or Forever? Tennessee v. John Thomas Scopes*. Boston: Beacon Press, 1958.

Gusfield, Joseph R. *Symbolic Crusade: Status Politics and the American Temperance Movement*. Urbana, Ill.: University of Illinois Press, 1966.

Herberg, Will. *Protestant, Catholic, Jew: An Essay in American Religious Sociology*. Garden City, N.Y.: Doubleday & Co., 1955.

Hocking, William Ernest, ed. *Rethinking Missions: A Laymen's Inquiry after One Hundred Years, by the Commission of Appraisal*. New York: Harper & Brothers, 1932.

Howlett, Duncan. *The Fourth American Faith*. New York: Harper & Row, 1964.

Landis, Benson Y. *The Third American Revolution*. New York: Association Press, 1933.

Lenski, Gerhard. *The Religious Factor: A Sociological Study of Religion's Impact on Politics, Economics, and Family Life*. Garden City, N.Y.: Doubleday & Co., 1961.

Machen, J. Gresham. *Christianity and Liberalism*. New York: Macmillan Co., 1923.

McLoughlin, William G., ed. *Religion in America*. Boston: Houghton Mifflin Co., 1968.

Marty, Martin E. *The New Shape of American Religion*. New York: Harper & Brothers, 1959.

Mecklin, John Moffatt. *The Ku Klux Klan: A Study of the American Mind*. New York: Harcourt, Brace & Co., 1924.

Merz, Charles. *The Dry Decade*. Garden City, N.Y.: Doubleday, Doran & Co., 1931.

Meyer, Donald B. *The Protestant Search for Political Realism, 1919–1941*. Berkeley and Los Angeles: University of California Press, 1960.

Miller, Robert M. *American Protestantism and Social Issues, 1919–1939*. Chapel Hill: University of North Carolina Press, 1958.

Nash, Ronald H. *The New Evangelicalism*. Grand Rapids, Mich.: Zondervan Publishing House, 1963.

Riesman, David, with Glazer, Nathan, and Denney, Reuel.

The Lonely Crowd: A Study of the Changing American Character. New Haven: Yale University Press, 1950.

29. TWENTIETH-CENTURY THEOLOGICAL CURRENTS

Bridges, Hal. *American Mysticism from William James to Zen*. New York: Harper & Row, 1970.

Ferm, Vergilius, ed. *Contemporary American Theology*. New York: Round Table Press, 1932.

Hammar, George. *Christian Realism in American Theology: A Study of Reinhold Niebuhr, W. M. Horton, and H. P. Van Dusen*. Uppsala: Appelberg, 1940.

Henry, Carl F. H. *Fifty Years of Protestant Theology*. Boston: W. A. Wilde Co., 1950.

Hoedemaker, Libertus A. *The Theology of H. Richard Niebuhr*. Boston: Pilgrim Press, 1970.

Kegley, Charles W., and Bretall, Robert W., eds. *Reinhold Niebuhr: His Religious, Social, and Political Thought*. New York: Macmillan Co., 1956.

———. *The Theology of Paul Tillich*. New York: Macmillan Co., 1952.

Nash, Arnold S., ed. *Protestant Thought in the Twentieth Century*. New York: Macmillan Co., 1951.

Soper, David W. *Major Voices in American Theology*. Philadelphia: Westminster Press, 1953.

Wieman, Henry N., et al. *Religious Liberals Reply*. Boston: Beacon Press, 1947.

30. BLACK MOVEMENTS AND VOICES IN THE TWENTIETH CENTURY

Breitman, George. *The Last Year of Malcolm X: The Evolution of a Revolutionary*. New York: Merit Publishers, 1967.

Brink, William, and Harris, Louis. *The Negro Revolution in America*. New York: Simon & Schuster, 1964.

Cleage, Albert B., Jr. *The Black Messiah*. New York: Sheed & Ward, 1968.

Cone, James H. *Black Theology and Black Power*. New York: Seabury Press, 1969.

Cronon, E. David. *Black Moses: The Story of Marcus Garvey*

and the Universal Negro Improvement Association. Madison: University of Wisconsin Press, 1955.

Drake, St. Clair, and Cayton, Horace R. *Black Metropolis: A Study of Negro Life in a Northern City*. New York: Harcourt, Brace & Co., 1945.

Essien-Udom, E. U. *Black Nationalism: The Search for an Identity*. Chicago: University of Chicago Press, 1962.

Fauset, Arthur H. *Black Gods of the Metropolis: Negro Cults in the Urban North*. Philadelphia: University of Pennsylvania Press, 1944.

Fullinwider, S. P. *The Mind and Mood of Black America*. Homewood, Ill.: Dorsey Press, 1969.

Harris, Sara, and Crittenden, Harriet. *Father Divine, Holy Husband*. Garden City, N.Y.: Doubleday & Co., 1953.

Katz, Schlomo, ed. *Negro and Jew*. New York: Macmillan Co., 1966.

Lincoln, C. Eric. *The Black Muslims in America*. Boston: Beacon Press, 1961.

Little, Malcolm. *The Autobiography of Malcolm X*. New York: Grove Press, 1965.

———. *Malcolm X Speaks*. Edited by George Breitman. New York: Grove Press, 1966.

Lomax, Louis E. *The Negro Revolt*. New York: Harper & Row, 1962.

Meier, August, Rudwick, Elliott, and Broderick, Francis L., eds. *Black Protest Thought in the Twentieth Century*. 2d ed. Indianapolis: Bobbs-Merrill Co., 1971.

Powell, Adam Clayton, Jr. *Marching Blacks: An Interpretive History of the Rise of the Black Common Man*. New York: Dial Press, 1945.

Wright, Nathan, Jr. *Black Power and Urban Unrest*. New York: Hawthorne Books, 1967.

31. SPANISH-SPEAKING AMERICANS

Grebler, Leo, et al. *The Mexican American People: The Nation's Second Largest Minority*. New York: Free Press-Macmillan, 1970.

Lewis, Oscar. *A Study of Slum Culture: Backgrounds for La Vida*. New York: Random House, 1968.

Moore, Joan W. *Mexican Americans*. Englewood Cliffs, N.J.: Prentice-Hall, 1970.

Rand, Christopher. *The Puerto Ricans*. New York: Oxford University Press, 1958.

Scotford, John R. *Within These Borders: Spanish-Speaking Peoples in the U.S.A.* New York: Friendship Press, 1953.

Sexton, Patricia Cayo. *Spanish Harlem*. New York: Harper & Row, 1965.

Steiner, Stan. *La Raza: The Mexican-Americans*. New York: Harper & Row, 1968.

32. RELIGION IN THE 1960S AND 1970S

Altizer, Thomas J. J., and Hamilton, William. *Radical Theology and the Death of God*. Indianapolis: Bobbs-Merrill Co., 1966.

Beardslee, William A., ed. *America and the Future of Theology*. Philadelphia: Westminster Press, 1967.

Bjornstad, James. *Twentieth-Century Prophecy: Jeane Dixon and Edgar Cayce*. Minneapolis: Bethany Fellowship, 1969.

Braden, William. *The Private Sea: LSD and the Search for God*. Chicago: Quadrangle Books, 1967.

Callahan, Daniel. *The New Church: Essays in Catholic Reform*. New York: Charles Scribner's Sons, 1966.

———, ed. *The Secular City Debate*. New York, Macmillan Co., 1966.

Childs, Brevard S. *Biblical Theology in Crisis*. Philadelphia: Westminster Press, 1970.

Christ, Frank L., and Sherry, Gerard E., eds. *American Catholicism and the Intellectual Ideal*. New York: Appleton-Century-Crofts, 1961.

Cooper, John Charles. *Radical Christianity and Its Sources*. Philadelphia: Westminster press, 1968.

———. *The Roots of the Radical Theology*. Philadelphia: Westminster Press, 1967.

Cox, Harvey, ed. *The Situation Ethics Debate*. Philadelphia: Westminster Press, 1968.

Cutler, Donald R., ed. *The Religious Situation: 1969*. Boston: Beacon Press, 1969.

Farley, Edward. *Requiem for a Lost Piety*. Philadelphia: Westminster Press, 1966.

Glazer, Nathan, and Moynihan, Daniel P. *Beyond the Melting Pot: The Negroes, Puerto Ricans, Jews, Italians, and Irish of New York City*. Cambridge, Mass.: MIT Press, 1963.

Gleason, Philip, ed. *Contemporary Catholicism in the United States*. Notre Dame, Ind.: University of Notre Dame Press, 1969.

Graham, Aelred. *Conversations: Christian and Buddhist*. New York: Harcourt, Brace & World, 1968.

———. *The End of Religion: Autobiographical Explorations*. New York: Harcourt Brace Jovanovich, 1971.

Greeley, Andrew M. *Religion in the Year 2000*. New York: Sheed & Ward, 1969.

———, et al. *What Do We Believe? The Stance of Religion in America*. New York: Meredith Press, 1968.

Gustafson, James M., ed. *The Sixties: Radical Change in American Religion. Annals of the American Academy of Political and Social Science* 387 (1970)

Hales, Edward E. Y. *Pope John and His Revolution*. Garden City, N.Y.: Doubleday & Co., 1965.

Hamilton, Kenneth. *God Is Dead: The Anatomy of a Slogan*. Grand Rapids, Mich.: William B. Eerdman's Co., 1966.

Hill, Samuel S., Jr. *Southern Churches in Crisis*. New York: Holt, Rinehart & Winston, 1967.

Lambert, Richard D., ed. *Religion in American Society. Annals of the American Academy of Political and Social Science* 332 (1960).

Marty, Martin E., and Peerman, Dean G. *New Theology*. 9 vols. New York: Macmillan Co., 1964–72.

Marty, Martin E. *Second Chance for American Protestants*. New York: Harper & Row, 1963.

Merton, Thomas. *Mystics and Zen Masters*. New York: Farrar, Straus, and Giroux, 1967.

Montgomery, Ruth. *The Gift of Prophecy: The Phenomenal Jeane Dixon*. New York: Bantam Books, 1966.

Needleman, Jacob. *The New Religions*. New York: Doubleday & Co., 1970.

Neusner, Jacob. *Judaism in America: Adventure in Modernity*. Englewood Cliffs, N.J.: Prentice-Hall, 1972.

Niebuhr, H. Richard. *Radical Monotheism and Western Culture, with Supplementary Essays*. New York: Harper & Brothers, 1960.

Noonan, John T., Jr. *Contraception: A History of Its Treatment by Catholic Theologians and Canonists*. Cambridge, Mass.: Harvard University Press, 1965.

O'Connor, John. *The People versus Rome: Radical Split in the American Church*. New York: Random House, 1969.

O'Dea, Thomas F. *American Catholic Dilemma: An Inquiry into the Intellectual Life.* New York: Sheed & Ward, 1958.
———. *The Catholic Crisis.* Boston: Beacon Press, 1968.
Ogletree, Thomas W. *The Death of God Controversy.* Nashville, Tenn.: Abingdon Press, 1966.
Reich, Charles. *The Greening of America.* New York: Random House, 1970.
Revel, Jean François. *Without Marx or Jesus: The New American Revolution.* Garden City, N.Y.: Doubleday & Co., 1970.
Roszak, Theodore. *The Making of a Counter-Culture: Reflections on the Technocratic Society and Its Youthful Opposition.* Garden City, N.Y.: Doubleday & Co., 1969.
Suzuki, Daisetz T. *An Introduction to Zen Buddhism.* Foreword by C. G. June. New York: Grove Press, 1964.
Vahanian, Gabriel. *The Death of God: The Culture of Our Post-Christian Era.* New York: George Braziller, 1961.
Wakin, Edward, and Scheuer, Joseph F. *The De-Romanization of the American Catholic Church.* New York: Macmillan Co., 1966.

33. BIOGRAPHIES AND AUTOBIOGRAPHIES

Allen, Alexander V. G. *The Life and Letters of Phillips Brooks.* 2 vols. New York: E. P. Dutton & Co., 1900.
Anderson, Courtney. *To the Golden Shore: The Life of Adoniram Judson.* Boston: Little, Brown and Co., 1956.
Beecher, Lyman. *Autobiography of Lyman Beecher.* Edited by Barbara Cross. 2 vols. Cambridge, Mass.: Harvard University Press, 1961.
Cahan, Abraham. *The Rise of David Levinsky.* 1917. Reprint. Introduction by John Higham. New York: Harper & Row, Torchbooks, 1960.
Cartwright, Peter. *Autobiography of Peter Cartwright.* Edited by Charles L. Wallis. Nashville, Tenn.: Abingdon Press, 1956.
Channing, William Henry. *The Life of William Ellery Channing.* Boston, 1880.
Cheney, Mary Bushnell. *Life and Letters of Horace Bushnell.* New York, 1880.
Day, Dorothy. *The Long Loneliness.* New York: Harper & Row, 1952. [An autobiography.]

DuBois, W. E. B. *Dusk of Dawn: An Essay toward an Autobiography of a Race Concept.* New York: Harcourt, Brace & World, 1940.

Dupree, Hunter. *Asa Gray.* Cambridge, Mass.: Harvard University Press, 1959.

Earhart, Mary. *Frances Willard: From Prayers to Politics.* Chicago: University of Chicago Press, 1944.

Ellis, John Tracy. *The Life of James Cardinal Gibbons, Archbishop of Baltimore, 1834–1921.* Milwaukee: Bruce Publishing Co., 1952.

Forbush, Bliss. *Elias Hicks: Quaker Liberal.* New York: Columbia University Press, 1956.

Fosdick, Harry Emerson. *The Living of These Days: An Autobiography.* New York: Harper & Brothers, 1956.

Fox, George. *The Journal of George Fox.* Edited by John L. Nickalls. Cambridge: At the University Press, 1952.

Frothingham, Octavius B. *Boston Unitarianism, 1820–1850: A Study of the Life and Work of Nathaniel Langdon Frothingham.* New York, 1890.

Gannett, William C. *Ezra Stiles Gannett: Unitarian Minister in Boston, 1824–1871.* Boston, 1875.

Guilday, Peter. *The Life and Times of John Carroll, Archbishop of Baltimore, 1735–1815.* New York: Encyclopedia Press, 1922.

Holden, Vincent F. *The Yankee Paul: Isaac Thomas Hecker.* Milwaukee: Bruce Publishing Co., 1958.

Lurie, Edward. *Louis Agassiz: A Life in Science.* Chicago: Chicago University Press, 1960.

Mathews, Basil J. *John R. Mott: World Citizen.* New York: Harper & Brothers, 1934.

Merton, Thomas. *The Seven Storey Mountain: An Autobiography.* New York: Harcourt, Brace & Co., 1948.

Middlekauf, Robert. *The Mathers: Three Generations of Puritan Intellectuals, 1596–1728.* New York: Oxford University Press, 1971.

Morgan, Edmund S. *The Gentle Puritan: A Life of Ezra Stiles, 1727–1795.* New Haven: Yale University Press, 1962.

Murdock, Kenneth B. *Increase Mather: The Foremost American Puritan.* Cambridge, Mass.: Harvard University Press, 1925.

Nethercot, Arthur H. *The First Five Lives of Annie Besant.* Chicago: University of Chicago Press, 1960.

––––. *The Last Four Lives of Annie Besant*. Chicago: University of Chicago Press, 1963.

Noyes, George W., ed. *The Religious Experience of John Humphrey Noyes*. New York: Macmillan Co., 1923.

Omer, Englebert. *The Last of the Conquistadors: Junípero Serra, 1713–1784*. New York: Harcourt, Brace & Co., 1956.

Perry, Ralph Barton. *The Thought and Character of William James*. 2 vols. Boston: Little, Brown and Co., 1935.

Philipson, David. *Max Lilienthal*. New York: Bloch Publishing Co., 1915.

Repplier, Agner. *Mère Marie of the Ursulines: A Study in Adventure*. Garden City, N.Y.: Literary Guild of America, 1931.

Rusk, Ralph L. *The Life of Ralph Waldo Emerson*. New York: Charles Scribner's Sons, 1949.

Stevenson, Dwight E. *Walter Scott: Voice of the Golden Oracle*. Saint Louis: Christian Board of Publication, 1946.

Stonehouse, Ned B. *J. Gresham Machen: A Biographical Memoir*. Grand Rapids, Mich.: William B. Eerdmans Co., 1954.

Thomas, Benjamin. *Abraham Lincoln*. New York: Alfred A. Knopf, 1952.

Weiss, John. *Life and Correspondence of Theodore Parker*. New York, 1864.

Wise, Isaac Mayer. *Reminiscences*. Translated and edited by David Philipson. 2d ed. New York: Central Synagogue of New York, 1945.

Woolman, John. *The Journal and Major Essays of John Woolman*. Edited by Phillips P. Moulton. New York: Oxford University Press, 1971.

Ziff, Larzer. *The Career of John Cotton: Puritanism and the American Experience*. Princeton, N.J.: Princeton University Press, 1962.

Zwierlein, F. J. *Life and Letters of Bishop McQuaid, Prefaced with the History of Catholic Rochester before His Episcopate*. 3 vols. Rome and Louvain, 1925.

INDEX